Implementing SAP®
ERP Sales & Distribution

Glynn C. Williams

New York   Chicago   San Francisco
Lisbon   London   Madrid   Mexico City
Milan   New Delhi   San Juan
Seoul   Singapore   Sydney   Toronto

The McGraw·Hill Companies

Library of Congress Cataloging-in-Publication Data

Williams, Glynn C.
 Implementing SAP ERP sales & distribution / Glynn C. Williams.
   p. cm.
 ISBN 978-0-07-149705-3 (alk. paper)
 1. SAP R/3. 2. Sales management—Computer programs. 3. Physical
distribution of goods—Management—Computer programs. I. Title.
 HF5548.4.R2W56 2008
 658.850285'53—dc22

2008008060

McGraw-Hill books are available at special quantity discounts to use as premiums and sales promotions, or for use in corporate training programs. To contact a representative, please visit the Contact Us pages at www.mhprofessional.com.

Implementing SAP® ERP Sales & Distribution

1234567890   DOC DOC   0198

ISBN   978-0-07-149705-3
MHID   0-07-149705-6

Sponsoring Editor Lisa McClain	**Technical Editors** Dustin Ainsworth Keenan Jones	**Composition** International Typesetting and Composition
Editorial Supervisor Janet Walden	**Proofreader** Divya Kapoor	**Illustration** International Typesetting and Composition
Project Manager Vastavikta Sharma, International Typesetting and Composition	**Indexer** Claire Splan	**Art Director, Cover** Jeff Weeks
Acquisitions Coordinator Mandy Canales	**Production Supervisor** George Anderson	**Cover Designer** Pattie Lee

Contents at a Glance

About the Author

Glynn Christopher Williams is an SAP ERP systems and business analyst, born in England and educated in South Africa. He currently resides on the outskirts of London, England. Over the last decade, he has consulted and implemented SAP SD in over 34 countries, having been on location in more than 17. He has consulted to some of the world's largest companies, including Hewlett-Packard, Honeywell, and Schneider Electric. His international experience, coupled with extensive knowledge of the SD module, integrated modules (such as FI, PS, WM, and MM), and diverse business processes, allows him to share fantastic time-saving tips, as well as provide easy-to-understand assistance in implementing SAP ERP Sales and Distribution module.

About the Technical Reviewers

Dustin Ainsworth is an SAP Sales & Distribution Systems and Business Analyst. He is a post-graduate of the University of Kwazulu-Natal (BA-LLB). He is SAP SD Certified. He specializes in Sales & Distribution as well as Materials Management (MM) and Demand Planning (APO-DP). He has implemented SAP SD versions 4.0B, 4.6C, 4.7 Enterprise, EEC5, as well as specific industry solutions such as IS-DIMP (Manufacturing & Mining) and Gas. He has had the privilege of dealing with some of the largest blue-chip companies in South Africa, namely SABMiller, Daimler Chrysler, Barlow World, Consol Glass, and the Linde Group, among others. Any queries can be sent to da@sapww.com.

Keenan Jones is an SAP Sales & Distribution systems consultant and business analyst. He has over a decade of worldwide experience in consulting in the Sales and Distribution module of SAP and has worked on releases from R3 3.0 to ECC6. His thorough knowledge of the SD module permits him to integrate SD seamlessly with other modules and the new functionalities recently released by SAP. Keenan's knowledge of the technical capabilities and capacities of SAP accompanied by his extensive ABAP programming skills permit him to easily integrate businesses' functionality into a standard system, for example, by writing customized front-ends for the SAP SD functionality. Any queries can be sent to kj@sapww.com.

This book is dedicated to my darling wife, Wendy, and my little angel girl, Breeze.
You both light up my life.

Contents

Preface

This book is designed to help you in implementing the mySAP ERP Sales and Distribution (SD) module. It is a compilation of notes, tips, and tricks I have learned in various implementations while on assignment in over 17 countries.

After completing these projects I found myself with a whole spectrum of knowledge, gleaned from day-to-day investigations and tasks as well as from the wonderful individuals I have had the pleasure of working with. This, coupled with the new functionalities released by SAP since the first publication in 2000, as well as the numerous requests by associates friends and colleagues forced me to compile this new version of how to implement the Sales and Distribution module of SAP.

I hope you will find this book to be a valuable source of trustworthy advice given in an easy-to-access format with direct answers. Instead of having to read ten pages to obtain one point, my desire is that you find ten points in one page.

This book is not only directed at the consultant implementing the SAP SD module, but is also intended as a valuable tool for the IT/IS department left to maintain the system post-implementation. If one has a thirst for knowledge, one should be able to use the tools, tips, and techniques in this book to expand one's capability within SAP generally, not only within SD.

This book is not a remake nor a copy of the help files SAP offers, nor is it in any way directed or controlled by SAP. Nor does it intend to replace SAP training.

Instead it is intended to enhance your knowledge of the SD module in SAP. By providing easily accessible implementation guides, fantastic time-saving tips, as well as direct easily accessible information on the do's and don'ts of implementing and maintaining the sales and distribution module of SAP.

In this book we have developed a few guidelines that will offer instant understanding and promote ease of use.

- First, all transaction codes will be shown with square brackets—for example, [SPRO]. The actual transaction code to be used in this case is SPRO without the brackets. (I have only identified them in brackets to quickly identify them as transaction codes and to differentiate them from tables.)

- Where you see this sign next to a paragraph it denotes a tip or trick. These tips and tricks are fantastic time savers, and have been gathered the hard way. Be sure to make the most of them.

- Where you see this sign next to a paragraph it denotes a piece of advice or an area for you to notice.

Acknowledgments

A book of this proportion would not have been possible without the support of family, friends, and colleagues. A big thank you to my family for their encouragement. A big thank you too, to Wendy and Breeze for permitting me to work long hours and to sacrifice some of our together time to complete this work. A special thank you to Keenan Jones and Dustin Ainsworth, for a wonderful job on the technical review and editing. You both went the extra mile! Thank you to the superb team at McGraw-Hill: to Lisa McClain, the senior editor, and her associates, Mandy Canales, Janet Walden, and Claire Splan. Wow, you guys are amazing—thank you for all your hard work. Thank you to Vastavikta Sharma, for your great attention to detail and enormous effort, and to the production supervisor George Anderson, the cover designer Pattie Lee, and art director Jeff Weeks. Thank you to my colleagues at Schneider Electric for all their assistance and support. Thank you to all the wonderful people I have had the pleasure of working with and meeting over the years. Thank you for your tips, tricks, advice, and enthusiasm when I was preparing to write this book. And finally, to my Lord Jesus, thank you ... for everything.

Introduction and Master Data

In this chapter you will start your road map with SAP. We will introduce the new SAP terminologies and how the products are related. We then begin with basic data, such as how SAP functions and where it accesses the information in the system. We will go through the different versions and structures of master data—material, customer, organizational, and all related data, followed by covering the Enterprise Structure, resulting in a clear picture of how the data is inter-related.

Introduction to SAP

SAP was founded in 1972 in Walldorf, Germany. The name is an acronym for "Systeme, Anwendungen, Produkte in der Datenverarbeitung," meaning "systems, applications, and products in data processing." SAP is in a consistent state of change with over 9,000 developers and researchers adapting it to the market and striving to offer consistently better business solutions. As a result, the company is the world's leading enterprise resource planning software provider.

With over 30 years of experience and being utilized in over 25 industries and approximately 34,600 companies, it is estimated that SAP has approximately 120 million users in more than 120 countries around the world. With such an impressive history it is not surprising that today SAP offers a wide range of solutions, products, and applications.

This book is focused on the mySAP ERP application, which is the follow-up product to SAP R/3 software. mySAP ERP is one of the applications within the mySAP Business Suite, which includes

- mySAP ERP
- mySAP Supply Chain Management (SCM)
- mySAP Customer Relationship Management (CRM)
- mySAP Supplier Relationship Management (SRM)
- mySAP Product Lifestyle Management (PLM)

At the time of writing this book, the latest release of mySAP ERP is SAP ERP Central Component (ECC6). Within mySAP ERP there are a number of applications, such as Financials and Manufacturing. Of these applications we are focusing on the Sales and Distribution application.

mySAP ERP is an application that is designed for mid-size to large customers, as opposed to SAP Business One, which is the application SAP designed for smaller organizations.

mySAP ERP is built on the SAP Netweaver platform, which is an open source business process platform that permits customers to create, among other things, tailor-made business solutions. These customized applications can be used in conjunction with powerful, already existing applications of Netweaver to integrate with mySAP ERP, creating solutions ranging, for example, from seamless integration with Microsoft Office to customer- or supplier-facing web portals.

This book is not a general list of functionalities found in the mySAP Business Suite, nor does it focus on all applications within mySAP ERP, nor is it a list of release notes listing the differences between R/3 and ECC. It is instead a compilation of over a decade of consultants' hands-on SAP Sales and Distribution implementation advice, all based upon the latest release of mySAP ERP.

SAP Application Integration

SAP is an ERP software product that seamlessly integrates the different functions in a business (such as sales, procurement, and production). SAP provides rich functionality in each of these business areas without sacrificing the convenience of an integrated system.

These applications update and process transactions in real time, allowing seemingly effortless integration and communication between areas of a business. For example, you can create a billing document and release it to Accounting and observe the updated billing values in a customer analysis immediately, without having to wait for day-end or month-end processing.

The SAPGUI

The SAP graphical user interface, or SAPGUI, runs on all well-known operating systems. The appearance of the screens and the menus displayed on them are configurable.

In ECC there are numerous SAPGUIs. For example, the basic SAP screen looks similar to Figure 1-1. This screen will be referred to as the SAP menu. It is often obtainable by using transaction code [S000].

There's also a GUI available for SAP processes, for users without direct access to their desktop computer. This is possible through the use of a web portal as seen in Figure 1-2.

Customizing Tools

The cornerstone to SAP is the ability to configure the system to meet the needs of your business. This is done by customizing or adapting the system and application to respond like your business.

This is the process of mapping SAP to your business processes. An example of a business process would be capturing a customer sales order.

This process of configuring SAP is generally time consuming and costly, as one needs to fully understand the business processes and then find a solution in SAP to meet these requirements and customize it in the system while at the same time taking into account best business practices, international standards, and possibly a bit of business re-engineering.

The objective of this book is to teach you how to develop and enhance the Sales and Distribution module of mySAP ERP to its fullest potential, using time-saving tips and techniques, in order for you to effectively meet your business objectives.

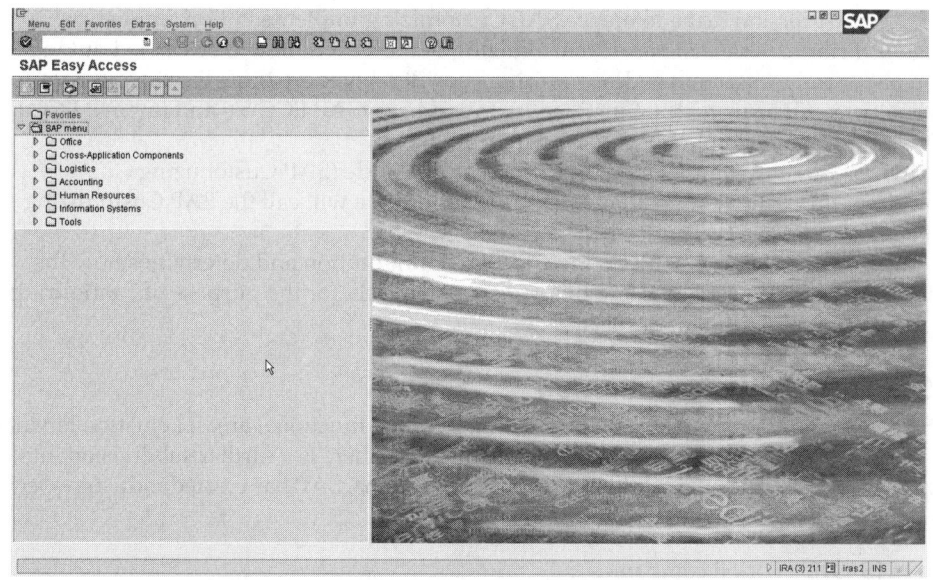

FIGURE 1-1   The standard SAPGUI

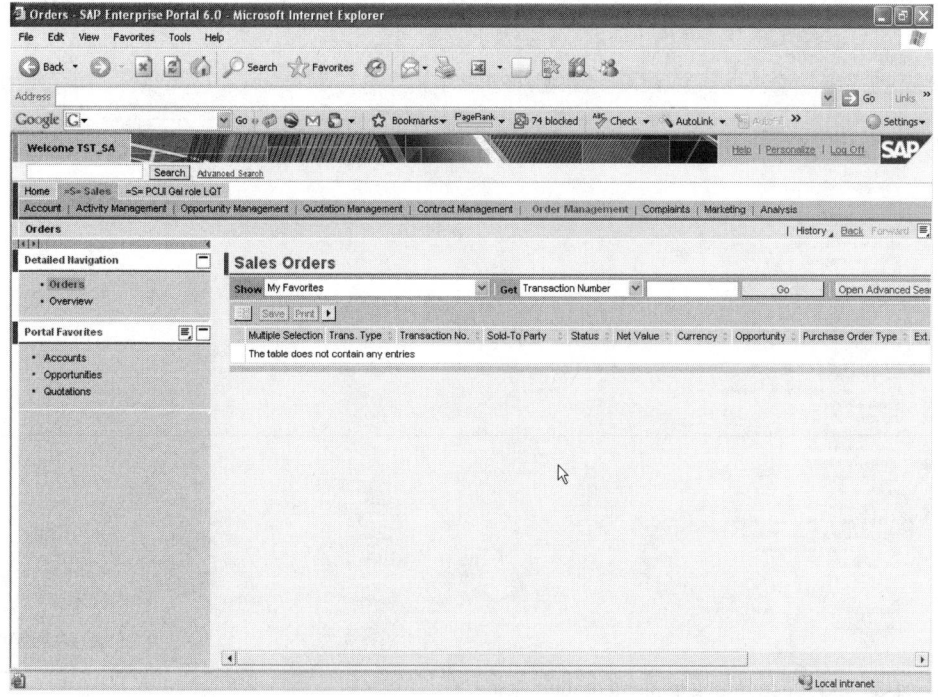

FIGURE 1-2   The portal SAPGUI

From SAP version 3, the reference SAP Customizing Implementation Guide was available. Prior to version 3 of SAP, customizing of the system had to be carried out via menu paths and transaction codes, requiring considerably more time. For the purposes of this book we will be using the functionality found in mySAP ECC 5.0 and mySAP ECC 6.0 (ECC - ERP Central Component) as a reference.

Figure 1-3 is an example of the Implementation Guide (SAP Customizing Implementation Guide) or customizing screen, which we will call the SAP Customizing Implementation Guide.

This screen is the backbone for mySAP ERP configuration and determines how the system functions. We will be using this screen extensively for the purpose of configuring the Sales and Distribution module.

mySAP ERP Applications Overview

mySAP ERP applications are categorized into three core functional areas: Logistics, Financial, and Human Resources. Of these three functional areas, there is a further subdivision into applications or modules. In addition to these applications, SAP has created industry-specific solutions (ISs). A few examples of these are

- **IS-OIL**   For oil companies
- **IS-T**   For the telecommunications sector

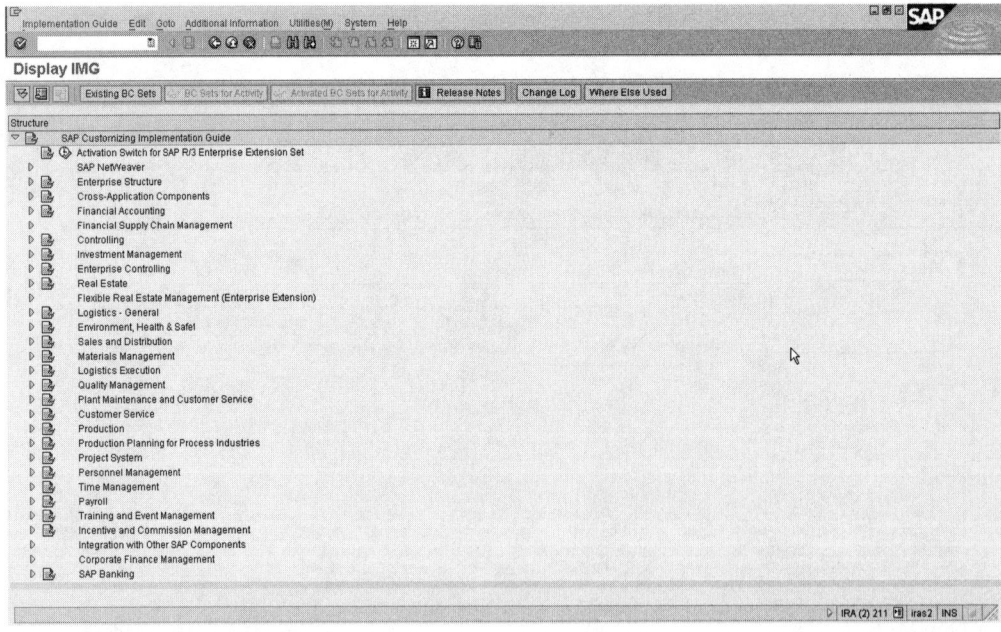

Copyright by SAP AG

FIGURE 1-3   SAP Customizing Implementation Guide

- **IS-B**   For banks
- **IS-Retail**   For retail

In addition to these industry solutions there are standard cross-application components. These tools are not dedicated to one unique application or module; they are used throughout the system to integrate and automate SAP processes.

The following is a brief description and overview of a few of the major functional areas in SAP.

Financial Applications

This application component contains, among others, the following modules:

- **FI**   Financial Accounting
- **CO**   Controlling
- **EC**   Enterprise Controlling
- **IM**   Investment Management
- **PS**   Project System

Human Resources Applications

The Human Resources module includes support for salary and payroll administration, as well as areas such as work schedule models. This core functional area is country-specific, due to country-related taxes, employee benefits, and employment laws.

This functional area contains, among others, the following modules:

- **PA**   Personnel Administration
- **PT**   Personnel time Management
- **PY**   Payroll

Logistics Applications

Logistics (referring to the supply chain) is the largest of the three functional areas. It includes, among others, the following modules:

- **SD**   Sales and Distribution
- **MM**   Materials Management
- **PP**   Production Planning and Control
- **LE**   Logistics Execution
- **QM**   Quality Management
- **CS**   Customer Service

We will be focusing on the Sales and Distribution (SD) module of mySAP. Refer to www.sapww.com for more tips and tricks relating to these and other modules.

Sales and Distribution Module (SD)

The Sales and Distribution module remains one of the key modules in mySAP ERP. It has always been one of the largest and most complex modules in SAP.

The SD module is made up of the following multiple components:

- Basic Functions and Master Data in SD Processing (SD-BF)
- Pricing and Conditions (SD-BF-PR)
- Extra Charge (SD-BF-EC)
- Availability Check and Requirements in Sales and Distribution
- Credit and Risk Management (SD-BF-CM)
- Material Sorting (SD-BF-AS)
- Output Determination (SD-BF-OC)
- Sales (SD-SLS)
- Scheduling Agreements for Component Suppliers (SD-SLS-OA)
- Customer Service Processing (SD-SLS-OA)
- Foreign Trade/Customs (SD-FT)
- Billing (SD-BIL)
- Payment Card Processing (SD-BIL-IV)
- Sales Support: Computer-Aided Selling (CAS)
- Electronic Data Interchange/IDoc Interface (SD-EDI)
- Shipping (LE-SHP)
- Transportation (LE-TRA)
- Reports and Analyses (SD-IS-REP)
- Business Package for Internal Sales Representative (mySAP ERP)

In this book we will explain how to configure the majority of these components in the system.

SAP Basics

This section is a guide to navigation and usability of an SAP system from transaction codes to user settings and the matrix copy.

Basic Transaction Codes

Transaction codes are the short path to a specific screen in SAP. For example, the transaction code [VA22] brings you to the Change Quotation screen, as shown in Figure 1-4. To view the transaction code from within the screen you are accessing, select System | Status.

In this book the standard menu path is always described from the SAP Easy Access Screen (unless specifically stated from the SAP Customizing Implementation Guide). This "Easy Access Menu" is generally the first screen that users will face in the system. Because it is the

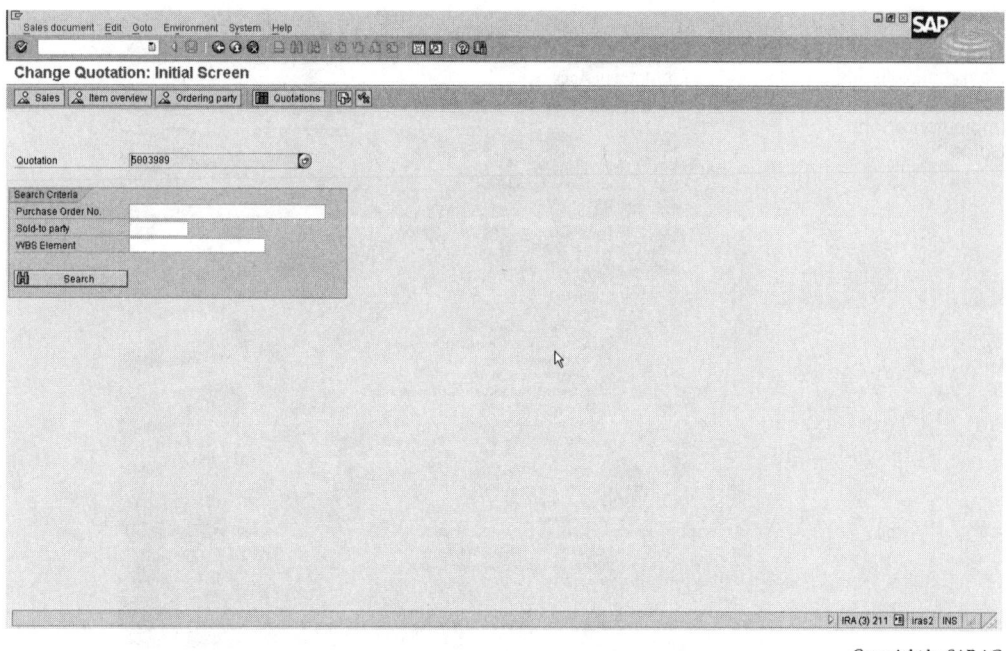

FIGURE 1-4   Here the transaction code is [VA22], which is the Change Quotation transaction code.

first screen users will face, it may be highly configured using area menus to restrict the transactions the user will be using. To revert back to the original user menu from this screen, simply select the menu path Menu I SAP menu [transaction code S000].

An example of using the menu path to get to the SAP Customizing Implementation Guide from the SAP Easy Access Screen is

SAP menu I Tools I Customizing I IMG I SPRO - Execute Project

as seen in Figure 1-5.

The [SPRO] transaction code is the shortcut for the SAP Customizing Implementation Guide.

Please refer to Chapter 5 to read about creating your own transaction codes.

Here are a number of simple transaction codes you will get accustomed to using:

Code	Description
VA01	Create sales document
VL01N	Create outbound delivery with reference
VF01	Create billing document
SPRO	Enterprise SAP Customizing Implementation Guide

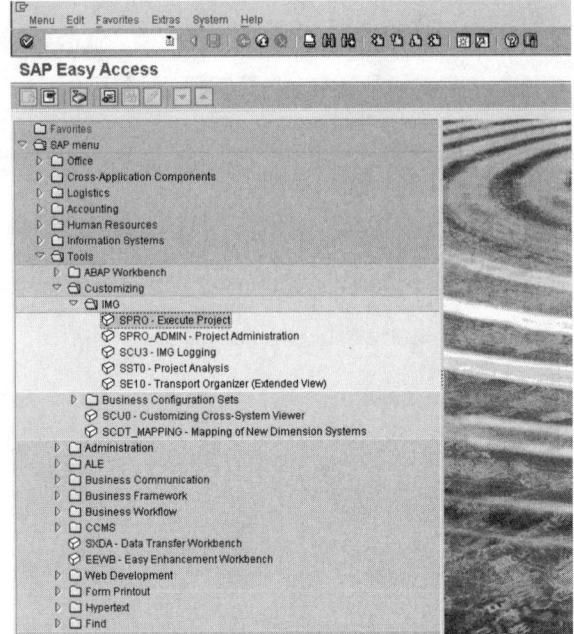

Copyright by SAP AG

A fantastic navigation tip is to use the central "Easy Access" menus, which provide a menu tailored to the function you are processing. For example, all transactions related to sales master data may be found by using [VS00]. Refer to the following list for transaction codes to further menus.

Code	Description
VS00	Sales master data
VC00	Sales support
VA00	Sales
VL00	Shipping
VT00	Transportation
VF00	Billing
VX00	Foreign trade

An example of the Easy Access Menu for sales master data is shown in Figure 1-6. Naturally, there are thousands of such codes and it would be irrelevant to list them all. However, if anyone is looking for a specific transaction code, a time-saving tip is to use [SE16n] with table TSTC. (See Chapter 2 for information on [SE16] and [SE16n] (the data browser) and tables.)

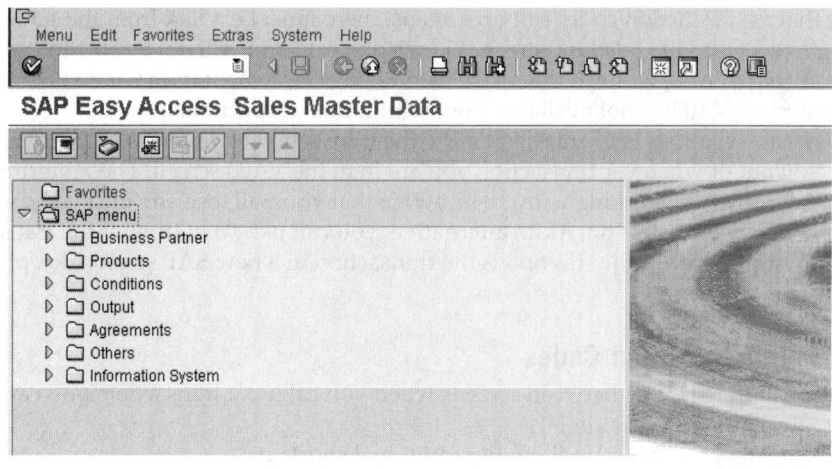

Copyright by SAP AG

FIGURE 1-6 Easy Access Menu for sales master data

To get a list of transactions including a particular text string, use the table TSTCT. You can also use asterisks as wildcards. For example, entering *change mas* in the text field will give you the following list of transactions.

Language	Transaction Code	Text
E	BGM2	Change Master Warranty
E	C202	Change Master Recipe
E	CC01	Create Change Master
E	CC02	Change Master
E	CC03	Display Change Master
E	FO62U	Change Master Settlement Unit
E	FS02	Change Master Record
E	FSP2	Change Master Record in Chart/Accts
E	FSS2	Change Master Record in Company Code
E	MFS0	LFP: Change Master Plan
E	OS51	Change Master Statuses
E	OS52	Change Master Matchcode
E	OS53	Number Ranges for Change Master
E	OS54	Change Master Control Data

Note that as transaction codes call up screens, there must be a link from the screen you are trying to access to the relevant screen you wish to call. You will not be able to use the transaction code [VA00] while in the SAP Customizing Implementation Guide because the screen related to [VA00] is not available from within this transaction.

A tip in cases like this is to enter /n before the transaction code. For example, [/nVA00] will take you out of whatever transaction you are in to the VA00 screen. The /n terminates the transaction you are working with, so be aware that you will lose any unsaved data in the screen you are currently on. As an alternative, you can use /o in front of the transaction code (for example, [/oVA00]. This opens the transaction in a new SAP session, keeping your existing screen in place.

Shortcuts in Transaction Codes

To save time in transferring between screens when you call up a transaction, you can utilize the shortcut commands in Table 1-1.

The following function keys allow for additional shortcuts:

F1	Help
F3	Back
F4	Lists possible entries or matchcode (see next section) for the field you are accessing
F8	Executes a transaction or report

These function codes are to be used from a specific field—for example, from the customer group field.

Pressing F1 gives you the Help screen, as shown in Figure 1-7.

The Help dialog box may be displayed differently based upon the user settings. To change the display options of the Help screen, select the menu from the SAP easy access screen [S000] Help | Settings as seen in Figure 1-8.

Shortcut	Description
/n	Ends the current transaction.
/nxxxx	Moves you from anywhere into transaction xxxx. Note, however, that you are terminating the current screen and will lose any unsaved data.
/nVA00	Moves you from anywhere into the sales screen [VA00].
/i	Deletes the current session.
/nend	Logs off from the system.
/nex	Logs off from the system without a confirmation prompt.
/o	Generates a session list. (A session is a window into SAP, similar to having multiple documents/windows open in an application on a pc.)
/oXXXX	Opens transaction xxxx in a new session.
/oVA00	Opens transaction VA00 in a new session.

TABLE 1-1   Shortcut Commands

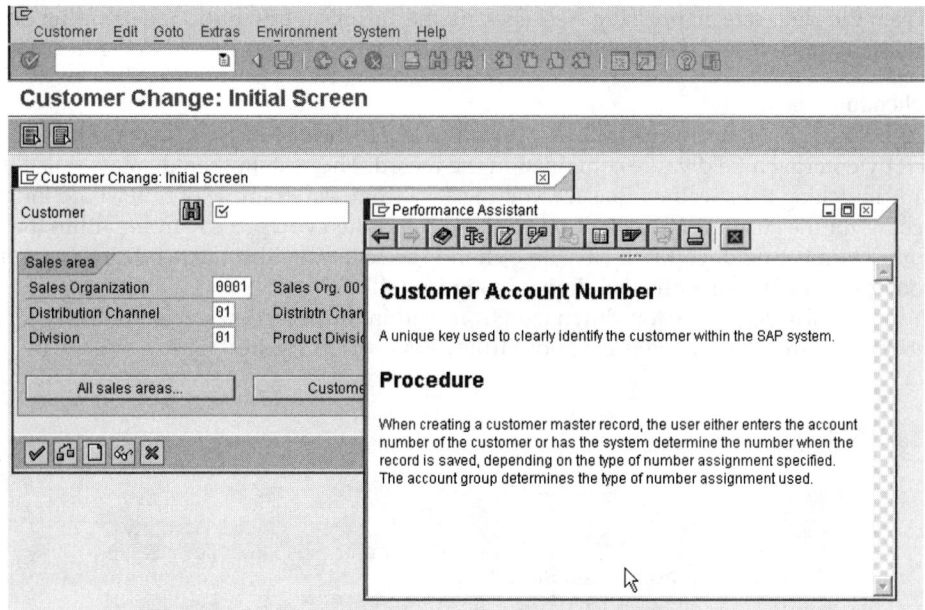

FIGURE 1-7   Help screen called from function key F1.

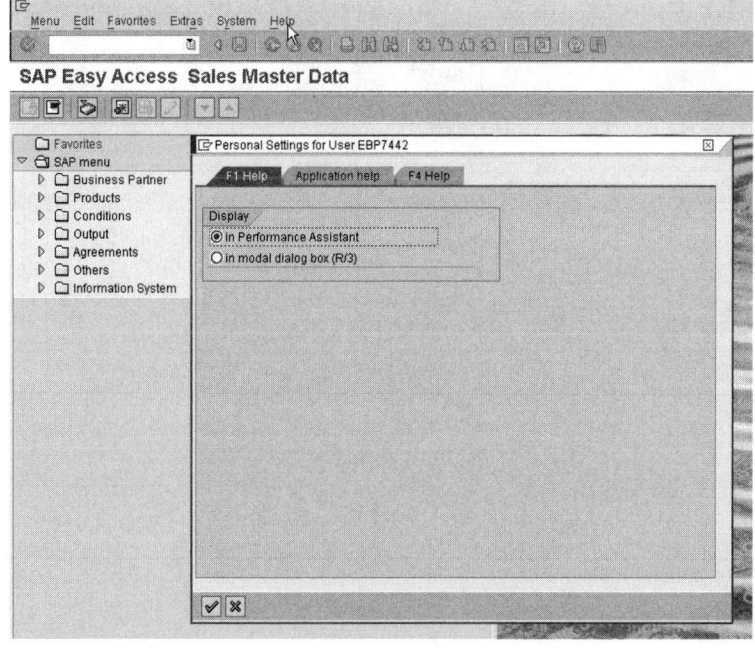

FIGURE 1-8   Changing the Help screen display options.

From the Help screen, pressing F9 or clicking the Technical Info button, depending on your display option, will give you the technical information screen shown in Figure 1-9.

Matchcode

A matchcode is a comparison key. It allows you to locate the key of a particular database record by entering a field value contained in the record. The system then displays a list of records matching the specifications for you to select from. An example of this would be searching for the customer number in the sales order. When you press F4 from within the customer number field, you will have an option to select a suitable matchcode to obtain the customer number you are after, as shown in Figure 1-10.

You may also click the drop-down icon from within this selection screen to display a number of different matchcodes to choose from, as shown in Figure 1-11.

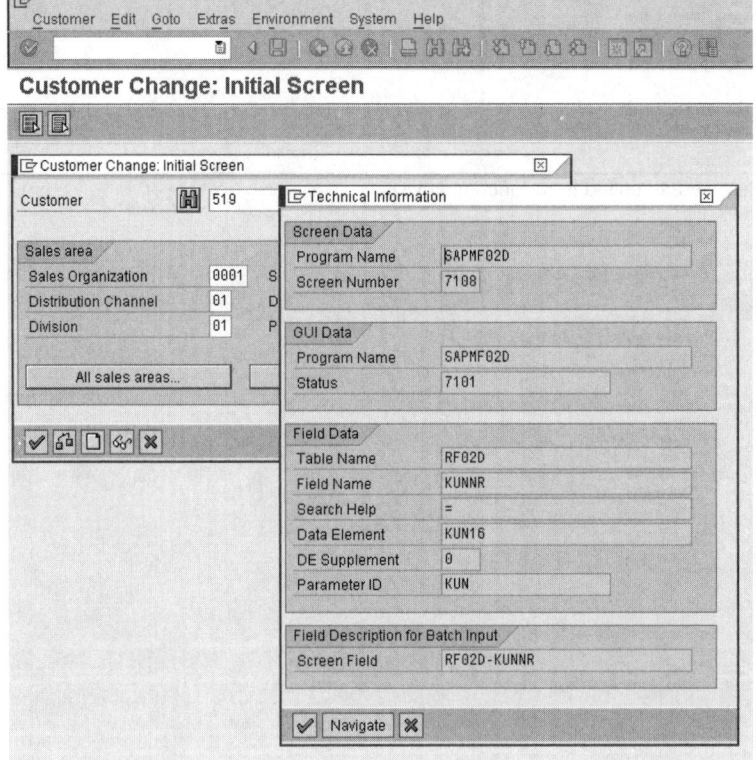

FIGURE 1-9   Technical information screen

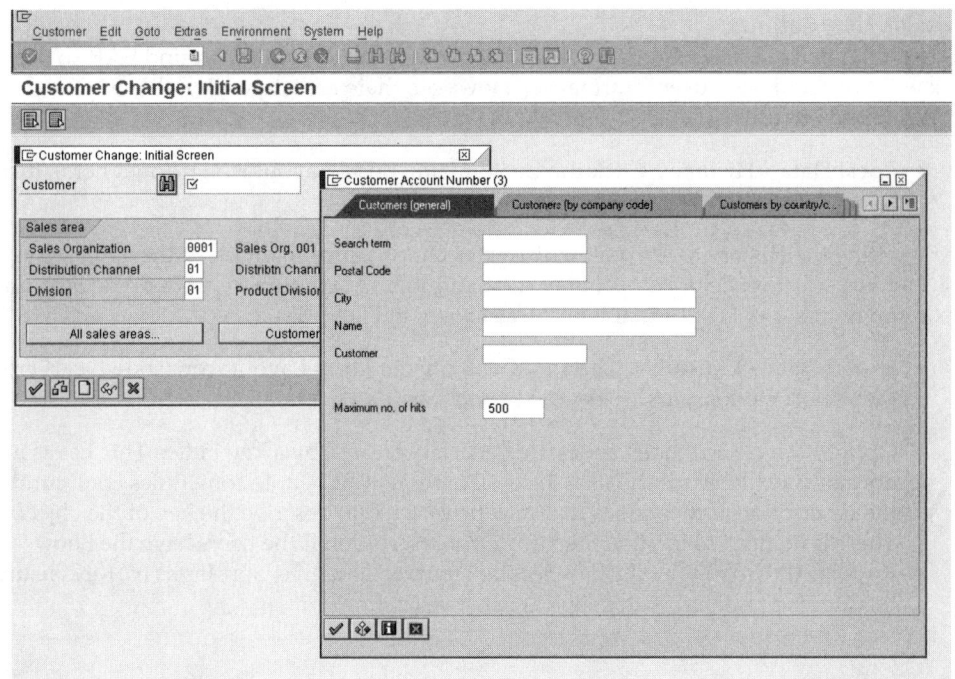

Figure 1-10   Using a matchcode to select a customer

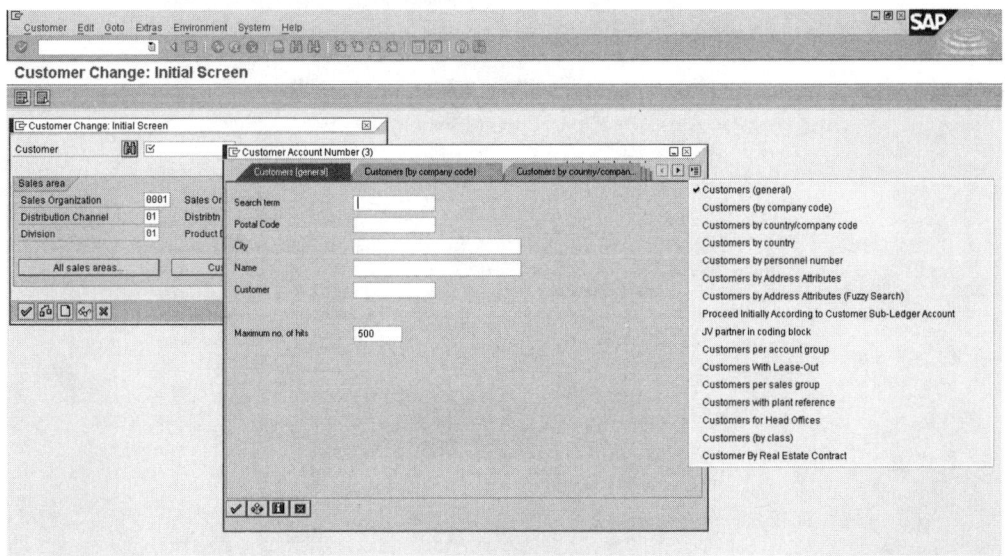

Figure 1-11   Selection of different matchcodes

Advisable User Settings

It is expected that you already have a sound knowledge of navigation around SAP, so this book will not detail basic user information. However, there are a few advisable SAP user settings for you to utilize:

- **Local Data – History**   Click the Customizing Local Layout icon (shown here), then select Options, and select Local Data tab.

By setting the History to On, you will always have a drop-down list of the values you last used in a selection field, according to the Expiration, Maximum Permitted File Size, and Maximum Number of Entries that you set, as shown in Figure 1-12.

- **Expert Data – Controls**   Click the Customizing Local Layout icon (shown earlier), then select Options, and select the Expert tab.

Options selected in matchcodes are generally created by a key index. This key is not normally available for the user to see. Consequently, people sometimes configure the description of the values that may be selected to describe the key of the object. There is no need to include the key in the description if the users have the Show Keys in All Drop Down Lists" checkbox marked as active. Sort Items by Key ensures the user is presented with a logical list to select from.

FIGURE 1-12
Local Data -
History settings

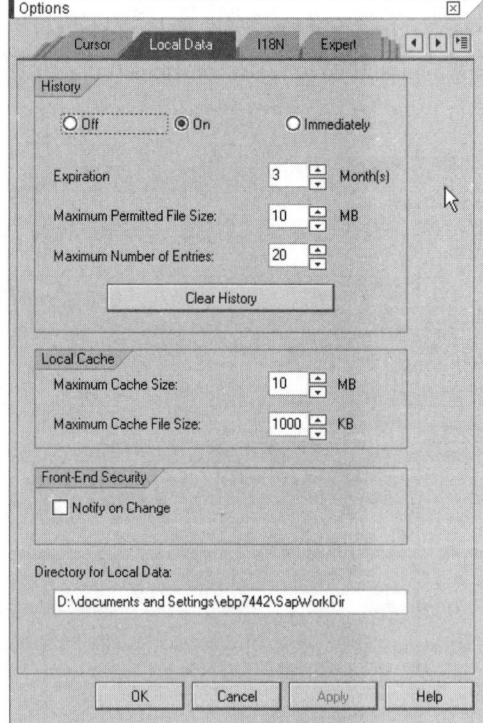

The Matrix Copy

The copy and paste function in SAP is called the Matrix Copy. Use the Matrix Copy to copy more than one line of text by clicking on the dialog box or screen one wishes to copy from and pressing the commands as described:

1. Press CTRL-Y, then select the text by dragging the mouse from the top left to the bottom right of the selection.

2. Once the text is highlighted, press CTRL-C.

3. Insert the text by moving to the new location and pressing CTRL-V.

Introduction to SD Customer Master Data

Master data forms the basis of all transactional processing. This is especially true for Sales and Distribution processing. Master data creation, ownership, and maintenance are the responsibility of all modules. The structure and data within a company's master data govern how the system is to respond to future transactions or analysis.

Customer Master Data

Customer master data in SD is divided into three main areas.

- **Basic Data**   This data remains the same for the customer regardless of which organization he buys from your company. Examples of this type of data are the customer address and contact details.

- **Organizational Data**   This is customer data related to your organizational structure—for example, the customer may prefer stock to be delivered from plant YX01 when an order is placed in a specific sales area. (Sales area is explained later.) The customer may then wish stock to be delivered from a plant closer to his location YX02 when a sales order is placed in another sales area. A customer master record may exist for many sales areas. You can then have different data for the different sales areas, even though you are taking the order from the same customer and using the same customer number.

- **Company Code Data**   A customer master record must also have company-related data. This data is used for financial accounting purposes. An example of company code data is the reconciliation account. A customer master record may exist for more than one company code—for example, when you have more than one company in your organization and the customer can buy from any one of them.

A *sales area* is a specific combination of a sales organization, a distribution channel, and a division. The *sales organization* is the legal entity responsible for the sale. You usually have a sales organization for each company code. The *distribution channel* is the way you send your product to the market—for example, you may have a retail distribution channel and a wholesale distribution channel. A *division* is a product division—for example, original equipment or spare parts. The combination of these represents the sales area. So when a customer places an order with sales organization ABC in the retail distribution channel for spare parts, you have identified the sales area. The processes may differ when a customer purchases from the same sales organization and the same division, but is purchasing wholesale, so the sales area would then be different as well. (Due to the distribution channel being different, that is wholesale.)

The customer master sales area data allows you to specify different master data (for example different payment terms) based on the sales areas.

There are additional forms of customer master data—for example, the customer credit master record, which is related to the customer master record, shown in Figure 1-13. However, these additional forms of master data are not mandatory and are covered in their own chapters in this book.

 We describe how to maintain the customizing, insert, and remove fields, as well as partner functions, of the customer master record later in this chapter.

Enterprise Structure

You must set the Enterprise Structure of your company (commonly referred to as the "organizational data" in SAP) before you can process SD transactions. For example, without a sales area it is not possible to create a sales order in SAP.

This organizational data reflects the structure of your business. Every transaction occurs within this structure. The organizational data is like the steel girders in a building, so setting it up correctly is essential. Once it is set, changing the Enterprise Structure of the business will be time consuming.

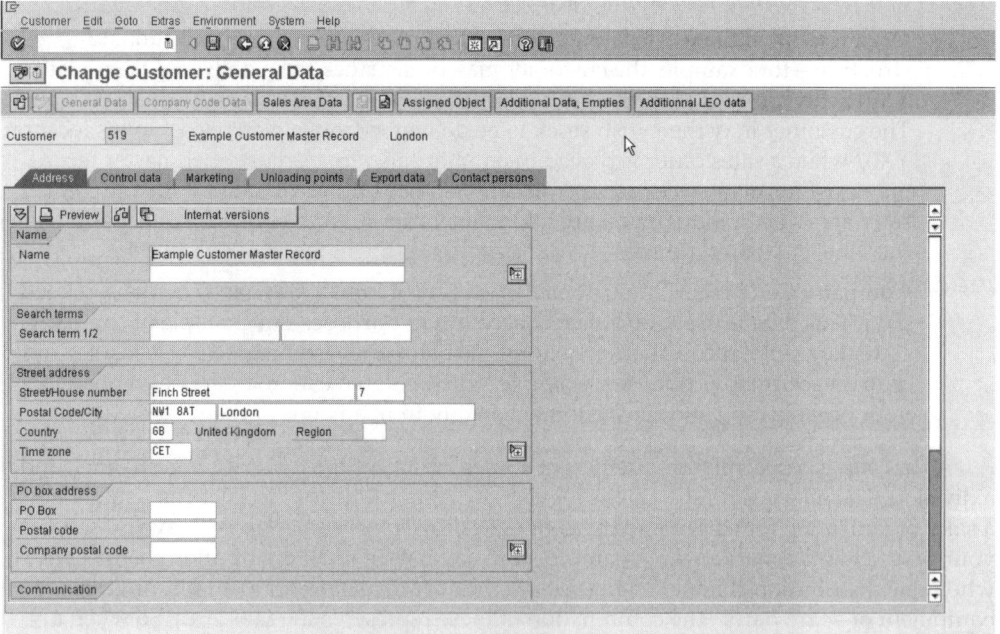

Figure 1-13   Customer master record

The more thought you give to the organizational structure, the easier mySAP ERP SD will be to configure and use. You must understand how the business functions and have exhaustive knowledge of the impact of using specific elements to map the companies organizational structure into mySAP ERP.

Organizational data is comprised of:

- **A Sales Organization**   An organizational unit that sells and distributes products, negotiates terms of sale, and is responsible for these transactions.

- **A Distribution Channel**   The channel through which materials or services reach customers. Typical distribution channels include Internet sales, wholesale, retail, and direct sales. You can assign a distribution channel to one or more sales organizations. A customer can be delivered from multiple distribution channels. A material master record can be maintained with different sales organization and distribution channel views, allowing different data to be accessed—for example, the delivering plant.

- **A Division**   Product groups can be defined for a wide-ranging spectrum of products. For every division you can make customer-specific agreements on, for example, partial deliveries, pricing, and terms of payment. Within a division you can carry out statistical analyses or set up separate marketing.

Figure 1-14 shows a basic organizational structure. In sales organization 1000, SD business transactions can be carried out for distribution channel 10 and 20 and division 01 and 02. In sales organization 2000 transactions can only be proccessed through distribution channel 10 and division 01 and 02. Likewise, transactions in sales organization 3000 can only be done through distribution channel 10 division 01.

Sales organizations should be kept to a minimum; try to have only one per company code. You should have a very good business reason to have more than one sales organization per company code. For example, only have another sales organization if the company sells completely differently in an area—for example, if sales processed in Los Angeles are handled differently to sales processed in San Francisco.

A rule of thumb is that if the material can be sold in both sales organizations and there is one company code, then there should only be one sales organization.

FIGURE 1-14
Organizational data
in SAP

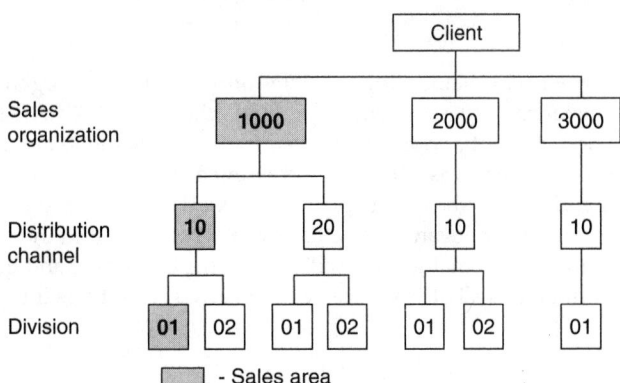

Master data records are multiplied by each additional organizational element you have. Thus, 10 customer master records with 2 sales organizations, 2 distribution channels, and 2 divisions would have a total of 80 customer master record views. Add another sales organization and you have 120 customer master record views.

Adding divisions does not multiply the material master views; however, it does multiply the customer master views. For example, add a division to our 80 customer master views and we suddenly have 120 customer master views. However, add the division to the material master views, and we still end up with 80.

TIP   *To reduce the master data you require, you can combine sales areas for customer master data purposes—see the Implementation Guide (IMG | Sales and Distribution | Master Data | Define Common Distribution Channels (and Division)).*

We know a sales area is compiled of a sales organization, a distribution channel, and a division. A sales area is used for reporting purposes; all data relevant for sales can be defined per sales area. For example, you can define pricing per sales area, or do your sales information analyses per sales area. You can also control configuration based on the sales area—for example, you can allow some sales processes for one sales area (for example, product samples), but not for another.

SAP Customizing Implementation Guide

The Implementation Guide is used to collectively group the areas that must be customized, as well as to form a structure for documentation.

Additional information may be added to the guide to make navigation more simple. Figure 1-15 shows the standard mySAP Implementation Guide.

If you select the menu path (Additional Information | Application Components) you can see the application to which the SAP Customizing Implementation Guide node is assigned, as shown in Figure 1-16. One is also able to see the Release Notes icons (shown here) attached to the area of the SAP Customizing Implementation Guide where SAP standard documentation exists for the latest release of SAP.

Copyright by SAP AG

We start with implementing the Sales and Distribution organizational elements.

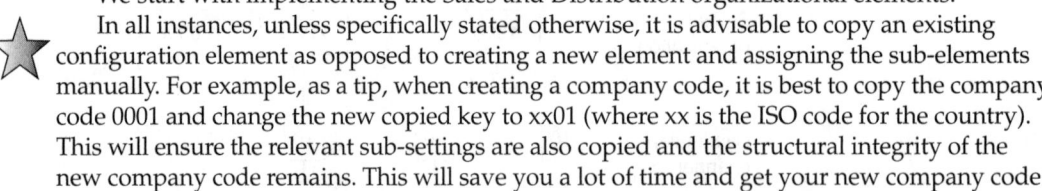

In all instances, unless specifically stated otherwise, it is advisable to copy an existing configuration element as opposed to creating a new element and assigning the sub-elements manually. For example, as a tip, when creating a company code, it is best to copy the company code 0001 and change the new copied key to xx01 (where xx is the ISO code for the country). This will ensure the relevant sub-settings are also copied and the structural integrity of the new company code remains. This will save you a lot of time and get your new company code working immediately. Later, you can change any sub-settings if you wish.

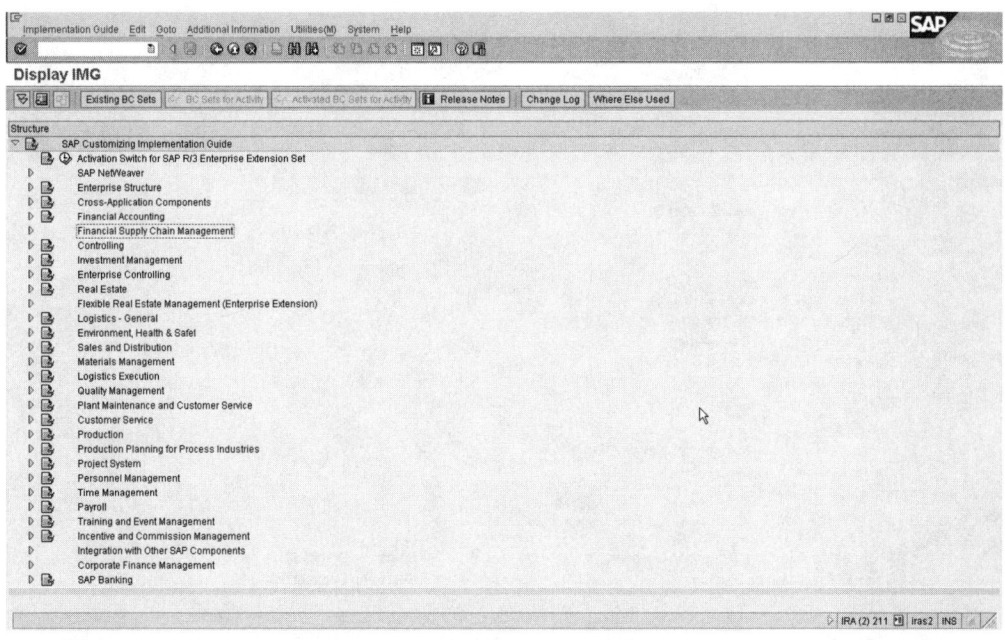

Copyright by SAP AG

FIGURE 1-15   Standard mySAP Implementation Guide

Defining a Sales Organization

Here is how you define your sales organizations.

Menu Path   SAP Customizing Implementation Guide | Enterprise Structure | Definition | Sales and Distribution | Define, Copy, Delete, Check Sales Organization

One is able to see the menu path in the SAP Customizing Implementation Guide in Figure 1-17.

NOTE   *A sales organization can belong to only one company code. You can also define your own sales document types to be limited to within a sales organization. Later we will assign sales offices to a sales organization.*

Defining a Distribution Channel

Here is how you define your distribution channel.

Menu Path   SAP Customizing Implementation Guide | Enterprise Structure | Definition | Sales and Distribution | Define, Copy, Delete, Check Distribution Channel

---

NOTE   *A distribution channel may belong to more than one sales organization.*

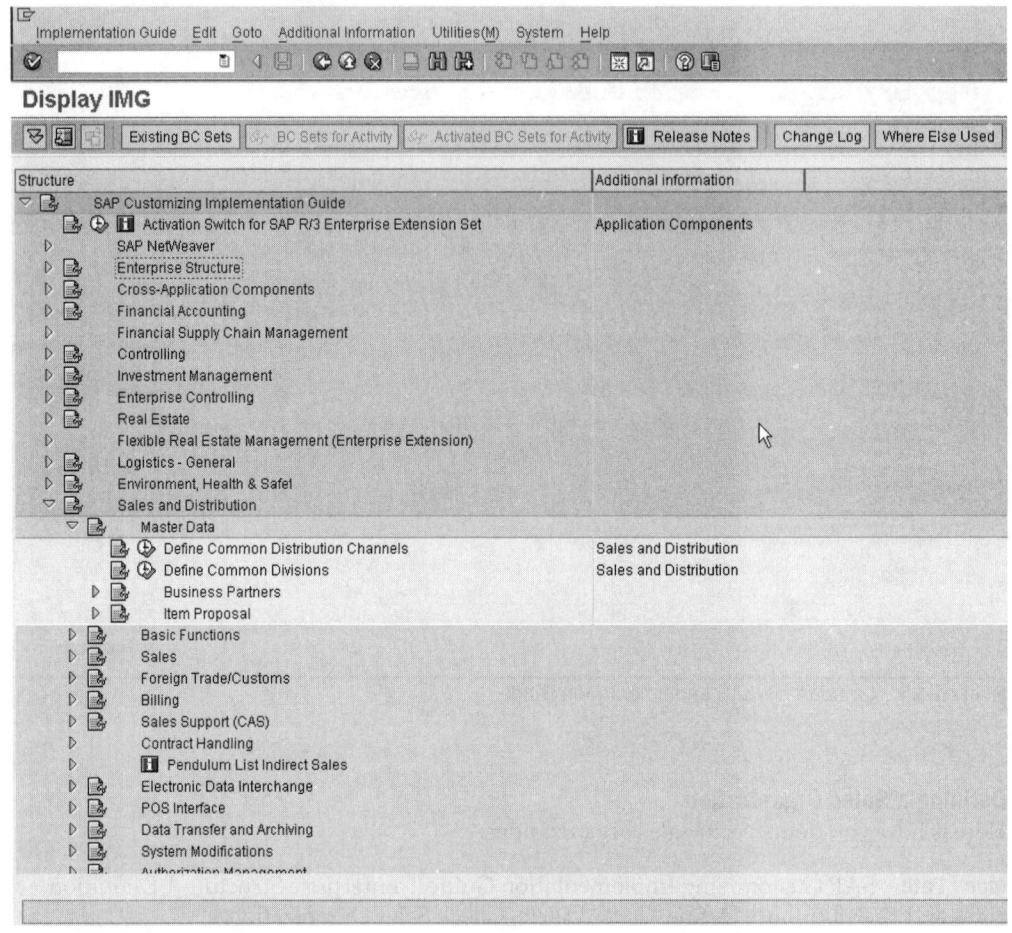

FIGURE 1-16   Standard mySAP Implementation Guide with Additional Information

Sales Offices and Sales Groups

Inside every organization is a team responsible for the sales. This team can be complex, allowing its own structure to be determined in order to optimize their functions and reporting based on their actions. This internal organizational structure has the following elements:

- **Sales Office**   Your organization may require your sales teams to be structured along geographical aspects of the organization. These geographical groups are easily created using the term *sales office*. A sales office is in turn assigned to a sales area. A sales office may be assigned to more than one sales area. For example, when you create a sales order for a sales office, that sales office must be assigned to the same sales area the sales order is assigned to.

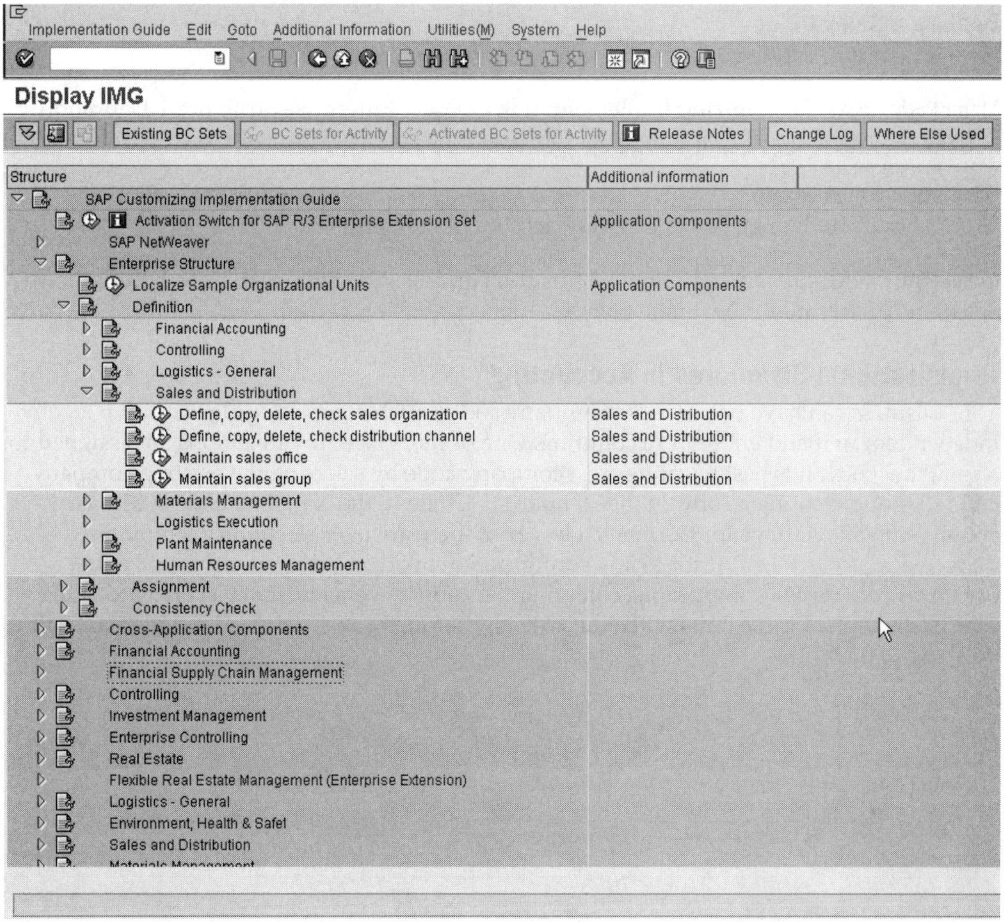

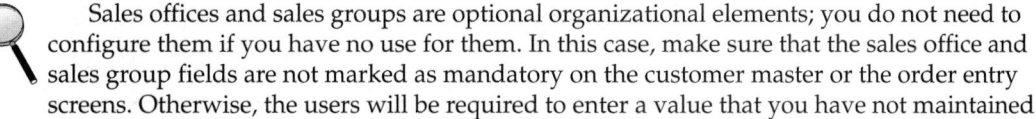

Implementation Guide   Edit   Goto   Additional Information   Utilities(M)   System   Help

Display IMG

| | Existing BC Sets | BC Sets for Activity | Activated BC Sets for Activity | Release Notes | Change Log | Where Else Used |

Structure	Additional information	
SAP Customizing Implementation Guide		
Activation Switch for SAP R/3 Enterprise Extension Set	Application Components	
SAP NetWeaver		
Enterprise Structure		
Localize Sample Organizational Units	Application Components	
Definition		
Financial Accounting		
Controlling		
Logistics - General		
Sales and Distribution		
Define, copy, delete, check sales organization	Sales and Distribution	
Define, copy, delete, check distribution channel	Sales and Distribution	
Maintain sales office	Sales and Distribution	
Maintain sales group	Sales and Distribution	
Materials Management		
Logistics Execution		
Plant Maintenance		
Human Resources Management		
Assignment		
Consistency Check		
Cross-Application Components		
Financial Accounting		
Financial Supply Chain Management		
Controlling		
Investment Management		
Enterprise Controlling		
Real Estate		
Flexible Real Estate Management (Enterprise Extension)		
Logistics - General		
Environment, Health & Safet		
Sales and Distribution		
Materials Management		

FIGURE 1-17   Menu path within the SAP Customizing Implementation Guide to create sales organizations

- **Sales Group**   The staff of a sales office may be subdivided into sales groups. For example, sales groups can be defined for individual divisions within the sales team.

- **Salespersons**   Individual personnel master records are used to manage data about salespersons. You can assign a salesperson to a sales group in the personnel master record.

Sales offices and sales groups are optional organizational elements; you do not need to configure them if you have no use for them. In this case, make sure that the sales office and sales group fields are not marked as mandatory on the customer master or the order entry screens. Otherwise, the users will be required to enter a value that you have not maintained.

Defining a Sales Office
Here is how you define your sales offices, as shown in Figure 1-18.

Menu Path   SAP Customizing Implementation Guide | Enterprise Structure | Definition | Sales and Distribution | Maintain Sales Office

Defining a Sales Group
Here is how you define your sales group, as shown in Figure 1-19.

Menu Path   SAP Customizing Implementation Guide | Enterprise Structure | Definition | Sales and Distribution | Maintain Sales Group

Organizational Structures in Accounting
Your business can have one or more company codes. Each company code is its own legally independent unit and entity in Accounting. One or more sales organizations are assigned to a company code. It is best to configure a company code by selecting the existing company code 0001 and creating a copy. In the standard SAP client, the company code 0001 has country-specific settings for Germany. However, there are over 40 country templates delivered in mySAP ERP. Prior to any configuration taking place, you can localize the organizational units—for example, changing the country version from Germany to USA. The localization of these units will overwrite any settings already carried out in these units.

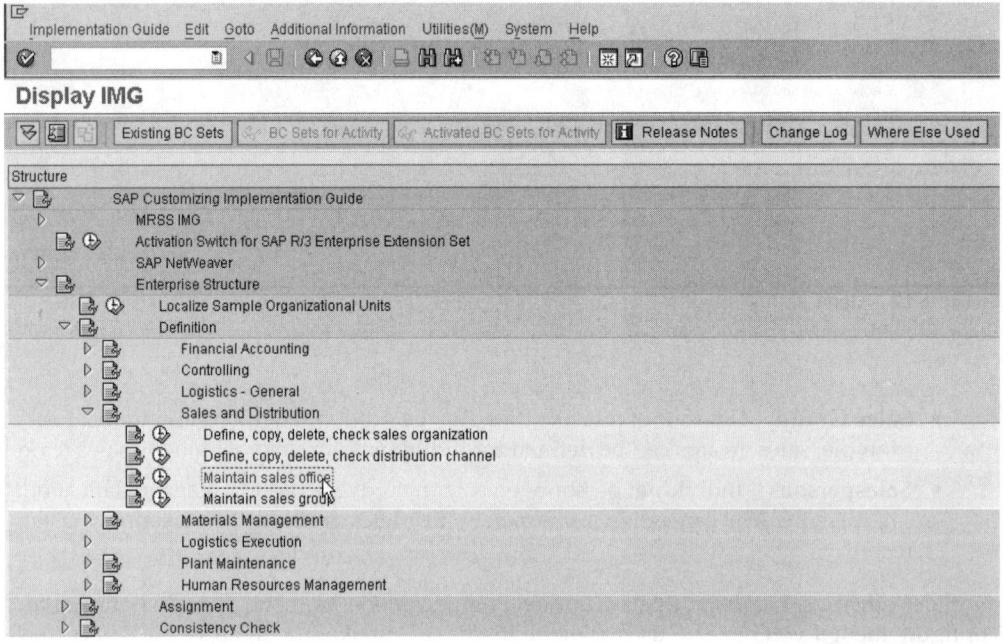

Copyright by SAP AG

FIGURE 1-18   Defining a sales office

FIGURE 1-19
Defining a sales
group

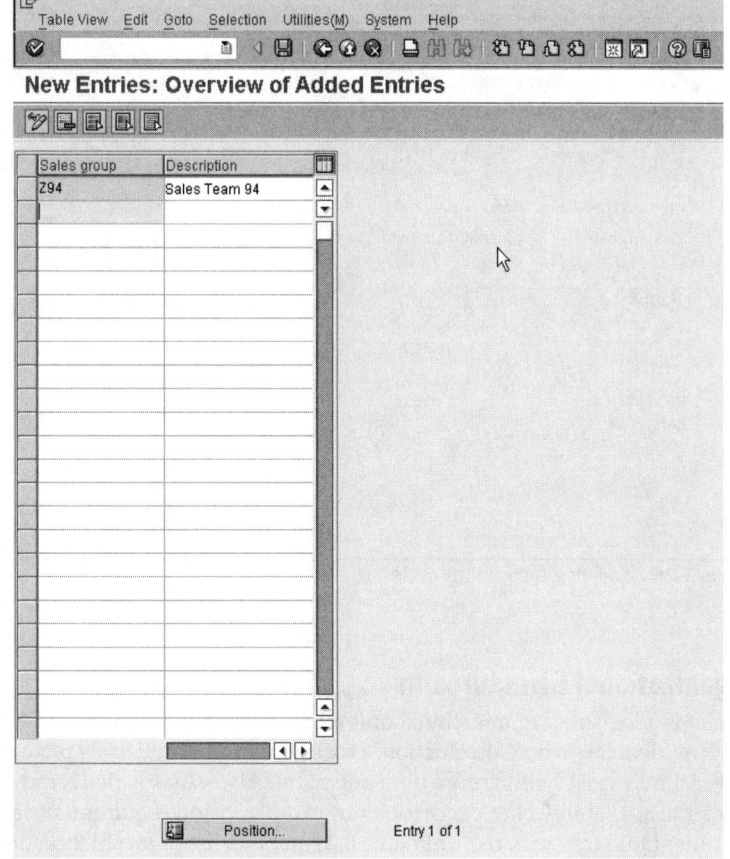

Copyright by SAP AG

This localization of the organizational unit is vitally important for countries that have complicated business processes, such as Brazil. It is advisable to install the country version as well as refer to the country template. (The country template is a range of customizing settings for a country that are generally required by all businesses that operate within the country.)

Defining a Company Code

Here is how you define a company code, as shown in Figure 1-20.

NOTE *The SAP Customizing Implementation Guide does not refer to creating a company code. As mentioned previously, the company code should be created by copying an existing company code.*

Menu Path   SAP Customizing Implementation Guide | Enterprise Structure | Definition | Financial Accounting | Edit, Copy, Delete, Check Company Code

There are other organizational units in Accounting that we are interested in, such as the credit control area, which we will cover in Chapter 10.

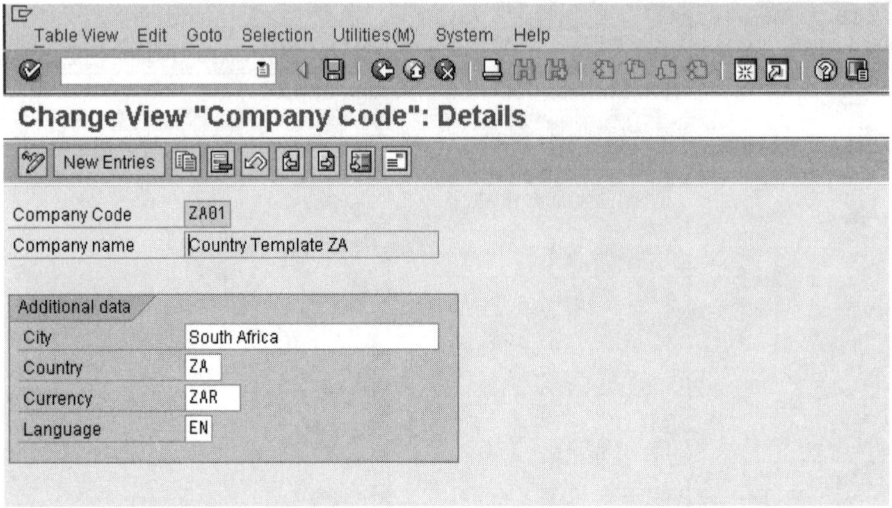

Copyright by SAP AG

FIGURE 1-20   Defining a company code

Organizational Structures in Logistics

A *plant* is a logistics organizational unit where materials are produced or goods and services are provided. It is where production, procurement, and materials planning are executed. A material may exist within more than one plant. Also, stock is delivered to a customer from a plant, the availability check is carried out in a plant, and requirements are passed from the sales document into the stock requirements list (that is, a list of production or procurement requirements) of a plant.

A *storage location* defines a storage area for the stock in a plant. One or more plants are assigned to a company code. And one or more storage locations are assigned to a plant.

- A plant can only exist within one company code. The plant, its buildings, equipment, and stock all belong to the legal entity represented by the company code.

- A plant may be assigned to more than one combination of sales organization and distribution channel. So you may sell stock from the same plant into different sales areas.

- A plant may have more than one shipping point. (A shipping point may also be assigned to more than one plant.) A *shipping point* is a place where deliveries are processed within the plant.

The assignment of plants to company codes is depicted in Figure 1-21.

Shipping points are defined in the Sales and Distribution application component. They are configured in the SAP Customizing Implementation Guide under Logistics Execution, as described in the next section.

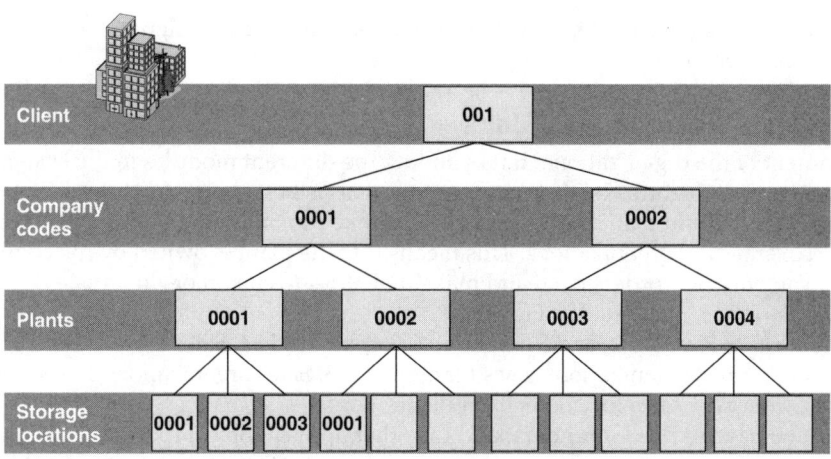

FIGURE 1-21   Plant assignment to company code

Defining a Shipping Point

A shipping point is assigned to one or more plants and can be divided into several loading points. However, deliveries are created for shipping points.

Generally, companies create deliveries using a background job, running the delivery due list. The shipping point is used as a criterion for delivery creation, so if you have express shipping and want the background job to run more frequently for these deliveries, it is advisable to have an express shipping point. This shipping point may be used for the scheduled background job and may be executed more frequently (for example, every 15 minutes) than the other shipping points.

You can configure the shipping point to be defaulted automatically in the sales order or delivery based upon the plant (used in the sales document), loading group (of the material), and shipping condition (of the customer master). For example, for a plant in Southern California, if the loading group is air transport and the shipping condition is express, use the Express Air Transport Shipping Point. The person responsible for processing these deliveries will see the delivery in their delivery due list when the sales order is saved.

If the plant is in Northern California and the shipping condition is express and the loading group is road transport, another shipping point will be proposed. So the delivery will appear in another delivery due list.

Here is how you define your Shipping point.

Menu Path   SAP Customizing Implementation Guide | Enterprise Structure | Definition | Logistics Execution | Define, Copy, Delete, Check Shipping Point

A shipping point is the top level of organization in shipping. Deliveries are always initiated from exactly one shipping point. A shipping point can be subdivided into several loading points. A *loading point* is a voluntary entry, merely a subdivision of a shipping point. It is manually entered into the header data of the delivery. For example, if a shipping point has five loading bays, you may create five loading points in SAP to represent each one.

Now that the organizational units have been defined, we can assign the units into an organizational structure.

Assignment of Organizational Units

In assignment of the organizational data you link the different modules in the system by defining how the structures relate to one another. This is best shown by the association of sales organizations and plants. A plant is always linked to one company code, and can be linked to several sales organizations. This means that the plant is owned by the company code and can only take orders from and make deliveries to customers in its sales organization. This is illustrated in Figure 1-22.

In Figure 1-22 Plants 1, 2, and 3 belong to Company code 1. Sales organization 1 uses Plants 1 and 2. Sales organization 2 uses Plants 2 and 3. Sales organizations 1 and 2 can make cross-company sales for goods from Plants 4 or 5.

After you have defined your data, and the other application components have defined theirs (such as the company codes having been defined by FI and the plants by MM), it is time to assign the SD organizational data.

The assignments are extremely easy settings to make once you understand how the structures should be built up (as explained previously). They are assigned in the following structure paths in the SAP Customizing Implementation Guide:

- SAP Customizing Implementation Guide | Enterprise Structure | Assignment | Sales and Distribution:
    - Assign sales organization to company code.
    - Assign distribution channel to sales organization.

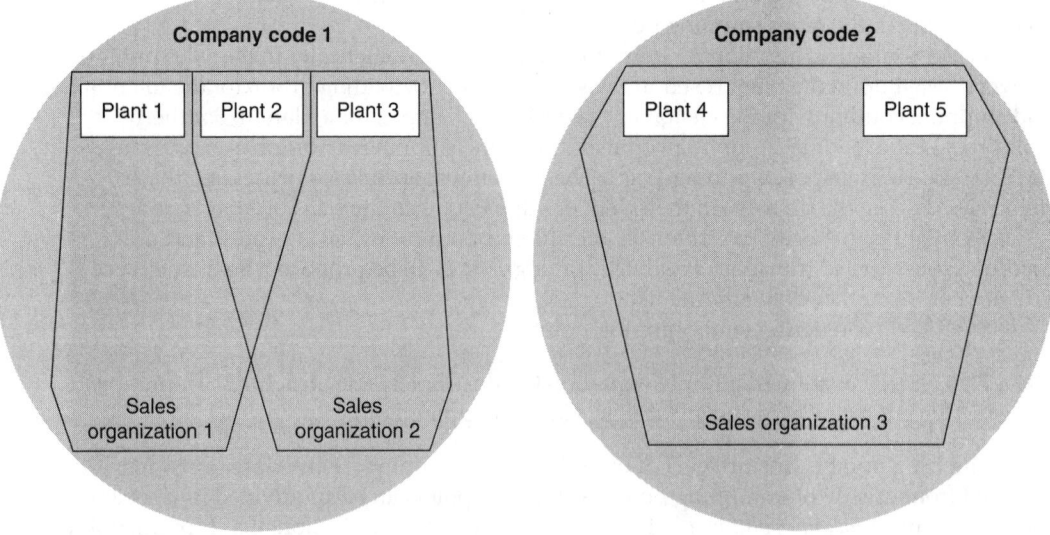

Figure 1-22   Plant association with sales organizations

- Assign division to sales organization.
- Set up sales area.
- Assign sales office to sales area.
- Assign sales group to sales office.
- Assign sales organization, distribution channel, and plant.
- Assign sales area to credit control area. (We will cover the credit control area assignment in detail in Chapter 10.)
- SAP Customizing Implementation Guide | Enterprise Structure | Assignment | Logistics Execution:
  - Assign shipping point to plant.

Shipping points are assigned to the plant here, but their determination is not defined here. Please refer to Chapter 6 for information about shipping point determination.

After the assignment you should have a business organizational structure similar to the following:

Company Codes	
Great Britain	GB10
Ireland	IE10

Sales Organizations	
Great Britain	GB01
Ireland	IE01

Distribution Channels	
Internet	10
Retail	20

Division	
Default	01

Sales Office	
Dublin	000001
London	000001

Sales Group	
Default	001

Plants	
North GB	GB01
South GB	GB02

Shipping Points	
Standard	GBST
Express	GBEX

Loading Point	
Standard	0001

Business Area

A business area is a subdivision of a company code for accounting purposes. You can draw financial reports based on the business area. If the FI (Finance) team decides to use business areas, every transaction in SAP is assigned to a business area in the same way it is assigned to a company code.

For example, Company Acme produces and sells widgets from two different plants. They want to draw financial reports for each plant. You would define two business areas and then make the assignment based on the plant. Whenever a sale happens out of one of the plants, the transactions are assigned to its sales area. You can review the financial reports for each of the plants separately, or together for the company.

Business areas can be assigned based on the plant and division, or based on the sales area. You need to choose one way of assigning the business area. Then you can assign the business area created in the FI module to either the plant and division, or to the sales area. Business areas are assigned from the following menu path:

Menu Path   IMG | Enterprise Structure | Assignment | Sales and Distribution | Business Area Account Assignment

Master Data Configuration

This chapter deals with master data related to the sales and distribution module. It also introduces one to the ABAP dictionary and the data browser, including tables relevant to master and transactional data for SD.

Customer Master Records

The customer master record is the basis for all sales transactions as well as deliveries and payments. Customer master records can represent different entities based on the role they play in the transaction. We'll be using and discussing the following customer master records:

- **Sold to Party**   The partner or customer that places the sales order request.
- **Ship to Party**   The partner or customer that receives the delivery of the goods or services.
- **Bill to Party**   The partner or customer that receives the invoice.
- **Payer Party**   The partner or customer that is responsible for the payment of the invoice.

Other important customer master records are created, such as *inter-company customers*, which represent the company that is behaving like a customer because they are placing orders with another company in the same client.

Another important customer master record is a *one-time customer,* which is a customer master record that represents a general customer. This may be used for customers that buy infrequently or who only transact with the business once. Instead of creating individual customer master records for each of these individuals, you can use the general customer master record.

To create a customer master record in mySAP ECC, follow this menu path.

Menu Path   SAP Easy Access | SAP menu | Logistics | Sales and Distribution | Master Data | Business Partner | Customer | Create

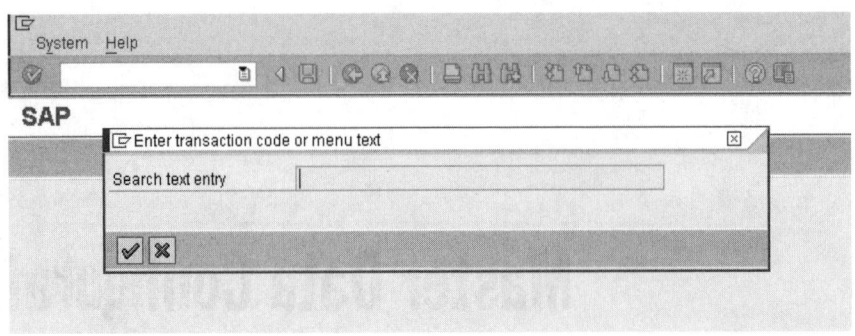

FIGURE 2-1   Dialog box to search the menu

As this is our first navigation within the Easy Access Menu, it is time for a great tip. If you know of an object in the menu, but don't know of the navigation menu path to find the object, you can use the transaction code [SEARCH_SAP_MENU] to search for a specific object. This will call up the dialog box shown in Figure 2-1. This even works when searching for a transaction code—for example, [SPRO]. The result, shown in Figure 2-2, allows you to follow the navigation within the menu to locate the object.

Search for a Transaction Code or Menu Title

Node	Transaction code	Text
Nodes		[Hilfsprogramme]
Preceding node		[Lohnsteuerdaten für den Mitarbeiter]
Preceding node		Tax
Preceding node		Reporting
Preceding node		Annual
Preceding node		Subsequent Activities
Preceding node		Germany
Preceding node		Europe
Preceding node		Payroll
Preceding node		Human Resources
Nodes	SPRO	Customizing
Preceding node		Settings
Preceding node		Administration
Preceding node		Business Information Warehouse
Preceding node		Information Systems
Nodes	SPRO	Execute Project
Preceding node		IMG
Preceding node		Customizing
Preceding node		Tools

FIGURE 2-2   Response from the menu search

Another tip is to include the technical names of the menu path. You can activate this setting by using the Extras I Settings menu path from the SAP Easy Access Menu, then checking the Display Technical Names checkbox. This will then show the resultant menu path with the technical name (transaction code), as shown in Figure 2-3.

Customer Master Record Transaction Codes

One creates the different views of customer master records, using the menu path outlined next.

Menu Path   SAP menu I Logistics I Sales and Distribution I Master Data I Business Partner I Customer I VD01 – Sales and Distribution (or XD01 – Complete)

- **[VD01]**   Create general and sales and distribution views of the customer master record, as shown in the example in Figure 2-4.

- **[XD01]**   Create general and central customer master views or company code data.

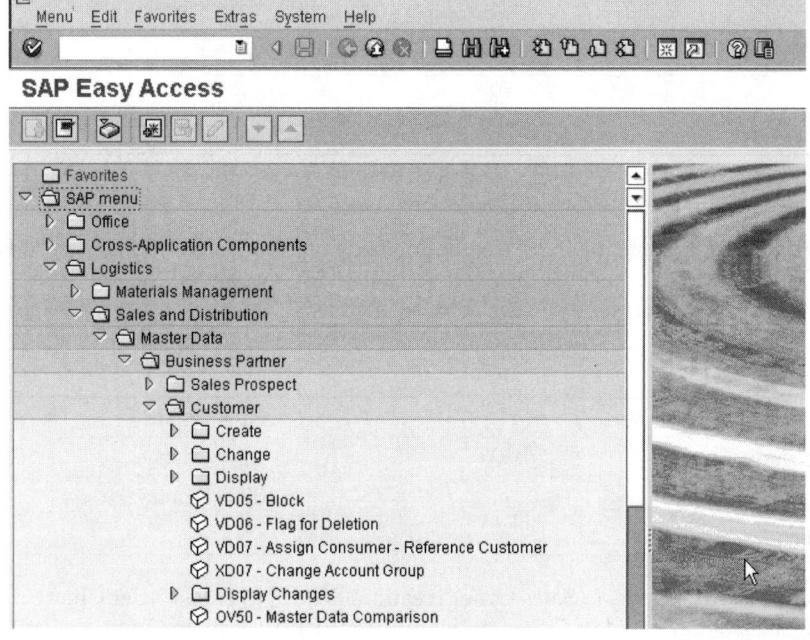

FIGURE 2-3   Transaction codes are displayed in the menu.

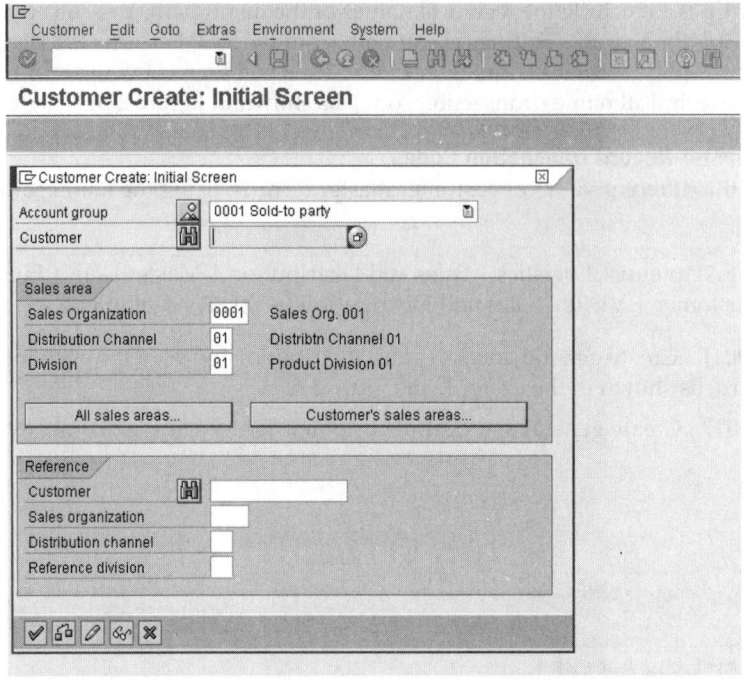

Copyright by SAP AG

FIGURE 2-4   Create customer master record sales organization and basic data.

   Very generally, the original SAP transaction code naming conventions used to work as follows. The first two characters of the transaction code represented the application, while the last two characters represented the activity, such as:

Prefixes	Suffixes
VA = Sales Order	01 = Create
VL = Delivery	02 = Change
VT = Shipment	03 = Display
VF = Billing	

Therefore [VA01] refers to Sales Order creation, [VA02] to Sales Order Change, and [VA03] to Sales Order Display. Once you learn the structure of the naming convention of the transaction code, remembering navigation will be easier.

Preparations for Creating Customer Master Data

When you create a customer master record, the system knows which fields are relevant (and so which fields to turn "on" and "off" in the screens) by using the assigned account group. You generally do not need all of the fields provided by SAP and you can use the account group to switch off irrelevant fields. For example, the Ship to Party account group does not need the Payment Terms field, so you can switch off this field for the Ship to Party account group (0002 in SAP standard).

The account groups are defined in Finance, but they can be accessed with the following menu path.

Menu Path   SAP Customizing Implementation Guide | Financial Accounting | Accounts Receivable and Accounts Payable | Customer Accounts | Master Records | Preparations for Creating Customer Master Records | Define Account Groups with Screen Layout (Customers) [OBD2]

To configure your own account group, first, always copy an initial SAP standard account group. By always copying the standard component, the system copies all underlying assignments and the existing field status settings. Follow these steps:

1. Highlight the account group you wish to copy—for example, 0001.

2. Select the copy button, shown here.

3. Change the account group number to start with the letter Z—for example, changing 0001 to Z001.

Copyright by SAP AG

SAP uses the prefixes Z and Y to denote customer-specific configuration. SAP promises not to overwrite these entries during upgrades in order to ensure it does not overwrite client-specific values/entries. (There are approximately 78 SAP standard entries that have the prefix Z and Y. These can all be found in table TDKZ.)

Select the data of the customer master account group that you wish to change:

- General data
- Company Code data
- Sales data

Let's say you are editing the Sold to Party account group 0001, thus creating a new version of the Sold to Party account group Z001, which must have a required entry for statistical data:

1. Double-click on Sales data.

2. Double-click on Sales.

You now have a screen where you can cause certain fields to be Displayed Only, Suppressed Only (not visible for input), Optional Entry, or, for the purpose of this example, Required Entry. After you have selected your changes, click the save button, shown here.

Copyright by SAP AG

Do not forget to allocate this new account group into the list of allowed account numbers for partner determination; otherwise, you will not be able to create any customer master records using this new account group. (Partner determination will be covered later in this chapter.)

The structure of master data in the customer master record is comprised of these three areas:

- **General Data**   This includes information such as address, telephone number, etc., and is maintained for every customer. This data is only identified by the customer number, and is not specific to the company code or sales area. Maintaining the data is possible from both the company code view ([XD02]) and the sales and distribution view ([VD02]).

- **Company Code Data**   This data is mostly of interest to the accounting department. It includes, for example, information on the reconciliation account and dunning procedures and withholding tax. This data applies to only one company code. Transaction code [XD01] is used to create customer master data, with company code relevant data.

- **Sales and Distribution Data**   This data is only of interest for the sales and distribution area. It includes, for example, data on pricing or shipping. This data only applies to one sales area, and therefore is dependent on the sales structure (sales organization, distribution channel, division).

When changing a customer master record from transaction code [VD02], you can click the button Customer/Sales Areas. This will give a list of combinations of sales organizations, distribution channels, and divisions for which the customer has already been created.

You need not have different customer numbers if your customer was serviced by more than one company code. In other words, you don't need separate account numbers to refer to the same customer just because they buy from different companies within your organization. Nor would you have different customer numbers if your customer was serviced by more than one sales organization.

It is possible to have different data for the same customer for different sales areas. You define the customer once in the general data view. And then you define the company code or sales area–specific data for that customer in the company code or sales area views.

Credit management is linked to the customer master but will be covered in Chapter 10. A short summary of customer master data relevance is:

- Company Code **Data** applies to one company code.
- Sales and Distribution **Data** applies to one sales area.
- Basic **Data** remains the same regardless of the company code or sales area selected.

Therefore if you edit the customer master record you must specify the customer number and company code, using transaction code [XD02], in order to access the screens containing company code data.

Control over the customer master records is vitally important to ensure consistency in reporting and usage of the system. If you do not intend to use all the address fields of the customer basic data view, it is advisable to suppress the fields. Often, companies leave all the fields open and maintainable, resulting in non-uniformity of address field usage. This leads to messy layouts for output and inconsistent reporting.

Material Master Data

The material master data is used by the system to represent the product or service your company is selling or producing. It is compiled in much the same way as the customer master record using multiple views to represent the same material within the different areas of the business. For example, the plant view contains all the plant-specific material and can be different for each plant in the organization.

To create material master data records, use the following menu path.

Menu Path   SAP Menu I Logistics I Sales and Distribution I Master Data I Products I Material I Other Material I Create (or by using the transaction code [MM01])

You are presented with the following screen as shown in Figure 2-5.

You will notice that one mandatory field is the material type. Material type is similar to the customer account group in the way that it governs what fields are relevant for data input. It also controls how the material behaves.

A few common material types are

- **HAWA-**   Trading good
- **NLAG-**   Non-stock material
- **FERT-**   Finished product
- **VERP-**   Packaging material
- **DIEN-**   Service

It is possible to create your own versions of these material types; however, this is done in the Materials Management module.

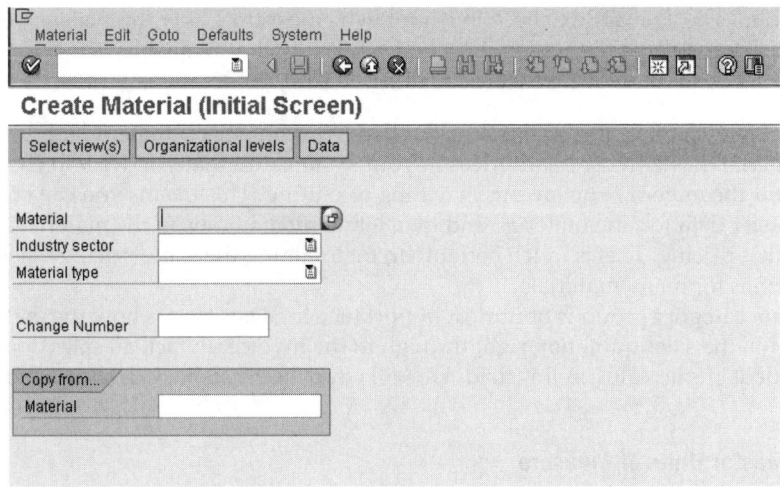

Copyright by SAP AG

FIGURE 2-5   Creating material master data.

The Material Type field is mandatory on the [MM01] screen as this screen is used to create all types of materials. Should you follow the standard menu path and create, for example, a "trading good," the system does not need a material type entered as it is defaulted by the system based on the menu selection.

As you can see, you have the option to create with reference to an existing material. This is a popular way to quickly create a new material from one that exists already and is very similar.

There are a number of views you may select from. As with the customer master record, you have sales views as well as accounting views. A few relevant material master views are as follows:

- **Accounting 1, 2**   Valuation and costing information. Examples of fields would be standard price, past and future price, and moving average cost price.

- **Material Requirements Planning (MRP) 1, 2, 3, 4**   Information for material requirements planning (MRP) and consumption-based planning/inventory control/ availability check. Examples of fields include safety stock level, planned delivery time, and reorder level for a material. A crucial field value for MM, PP, and SD is the MRP type, which will be covered with the schedule line categories in Chapter 3.

- **Purchasing**   Data provided by Purchasing for a material. Examples of fields include purchasing group responsible for a material, over- and under-delivery tolerances, and the order unit.

- **General Plant Data Storage 1, 2**   Information relating to the storage/warehousing of a material. Examples of fields include unit of issue, batch management, and storage conditions.

- **Sales Org Data 1, 2 and Sales—General/Plant data**   Information pertinent to sales orders and pricing. These views are most relevant for the SD team. Examples of fields include delivering plant, taxes, pricing reference material, and item category group. The availability check indicator, which controls how the system determines if stock is available for a sales order and when it will be available, is included here as well. These subjects are covered in detail in Chapter 3.

The pricing reference material is a field where you can enter a material for which you have a material master record and prices in your system and that you wish to use as a reference for the material you are busy creating or editing. This means you can create the pricing master data for one material, and then let many materials in the material master reference that pricing. This is much better than maintaining the same pricing master data multiple times for many materials.

The item category group is of utmost importance to SD. It covers how the material behaves from the sales quotation right through to the invoice. In fact, all sales documents are dependent on the value in this field. We will cover item category determination in Chapter 3.

Material Master Units of Measure

A material can be stored, transported, and sold in various units of measure. In mySAP ERP, you can define various units of measure that are maintained in the sales and distribution screens of the material master record.

However, you only need to maintain the fields of the units of measure if they deviate from the base unit of measure. You can enter the following units of measure in the Sales and Distribution screens:

- **Base Unit of Measure** This is the unit of measure used as a basis for all transactions. All quantity movements in other units of measure, should any exist, are converted automatically by the system into the base unit of measure. For instance, the base unit of measure may be pieces—as an example, stock of widgets is managed in pieces.

- **Alternative Unit of Measure** If a product is managed in the base unit of measure "piece" but is sold in the sales unit "box," you must define the conversion factor. The alternative unit of measure can define, for example, that one box of this material contains five pieces.

- **Sales Unit** The unit of measure in which materials are sold is referred to as a sales unit (for example, piece, box, or bottle). The value you define in the material master record is proposed during business transactions relevant for sales. You can replace them with other alternative units of measure in the sales order. For example, if you sell widgets in boxes, then you would use the box unit of measure as the sales unit.

- **Delivery Unit** The delivery unit refers to the unit in which materials can be delivered. Only exact multiples of the delivery unit can be delivered. For example, with a delivery unit of 30 bottles, 30, 60, or 90 bottles can be delivered, but not 100 bottles.

Quantity Specifications

SAP uses two different quantity specifications for the material master record:

- **Minimum Order Quantity** The minimum order quantity refers to the minimum quantity the customer must order. A warning message appears if the minimum order quantity is not reached during order entry.

- **Minimum Delivery Quantity** The minimum delivery quantity refers to the minimum quantity you must deliver to the customer. The minimum delivery quantity is automatically checked during delivery processing. A warning message appears during delivery processing if you enter a delivery quantity lower than the minimum delivery quantity.

 As unusual as it may seem, should you wish to restrict the quantity a customer may order, you should use a quantity contract as explained in Chapter 4.

Customer-Material Info Records

Customer-material information is information on a material that applies to a specific customer when they buy a specific material. For example, the customer may have its own description for your material. You can record this customer-specific information for a material in a customer-material info record.

The data in the customer-material info record has priority when master data is copied into an SAP transaction. When you create a sales order, for example, the default material data will be copied from the customer-material info record. If that does not exist, SAP will use the material data for the sales area.

You can create customer-material info records by using the following menu path.

Menu Path   SAP menu | Logistics | Sales and Distribution | Master Data | Agreements | Customer Material Information | [VD51] – Create

 It may also be accessed from the relevant customer master record. From within the customer master record (that is, inside [VD02]), select Environment | Customer Material Information.

This data is dependent on the sales area, so data created for sales organization 1000 will be different than data created for sales organization 2000.

Figure 2-6 shows the screen you are faced with when creating a customer material information record.

Enter the material that you store in your plant or sell. Enter the customer's product name or description. Select the entry and select details.

You now have the information relevant to the sale and shipment of this particular material, as shown in Figure 2-7. Of special importance is the plant for determination in the sales order. The main attribute of the customer-material info record is the Customer Material, where the customer could give his description of his material CONNECTOR_001 and we would automatically determine our product of BVL10.

 The system defaults the plant data in the sales order from the relevant entries in the master records based upon the following priority:

1. Customer-material info master record

2. Customer master record

3. Material master record

The default entries will apply to the order item unless manually overwritten in the sales document.

Another important entry is the Delivery Priority. This field is used as a selection parameter when creating the delivery—for example, in the Delivery Due List (which is covered in Chapter 6). It is also used for rescheduling. As the rescheduling process in SAP is a complex one, it is advised you do not alter the process or use this field for any purpose other than what it was created for.

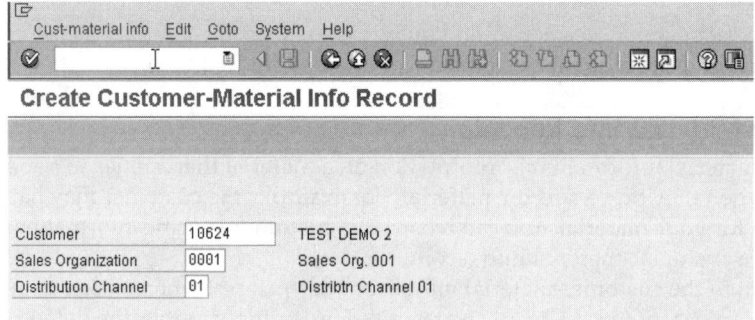

Figure 2-6   Creating a customer-material info record.

Change Customer Material Info Record : Item Screen

Material	BVL10 HBVL100
Sales Organization	X101 X101 Sales Org. 1
Distribution Channel	06 Outside Group
Customer	10624 TEST DEMO 2

Customer material

Customer Material	CONNECTOR_001
Customer description	
Search term	

Shipping

Plant	X101 CORE DC GB profile 0
Delivery Priority	2 Normal item
Minimum delivery qty	C3S

Partial delivery

Part.dlv./item		Underdel. tolerance	%
Max.Part.Deliveries	9	Overdeliv. tolerance	%
		☐ Unlimited tolerance	

Control data

Item usage	

FIGURE 2-7   Item details of the customer-material info record.

Make sure the relevant indicator is set on the sales document type so that the system will read the customer-material info record. See Chapter 3, "Sales Document Types."

Master Data Specifics

In this section we will cover elements that affect master data as well as introduce master data in tables.

Master Data Sharing, Common Distribution Channels, and Common Divisions

You are able to define common distribution channels and divisions. This is possible for two master data areas of mySAP ERP: For all master-relevant data and for all condition-relevant data. This negates the requirement for having multiple copies of master data, with the only differing parameter being the distribution channel or division.

You would use this option when you do not want to differentiate the master data based on the sales organization. For example, if you define many sales divisions for reporting purposes, you will have to create customer master sales screens for every combination of sales organization, distribution channel, and division. But if you make the division common, then you only have to maintain the customer master sales screens for the various sales organizations, distribution channels, and the common division.

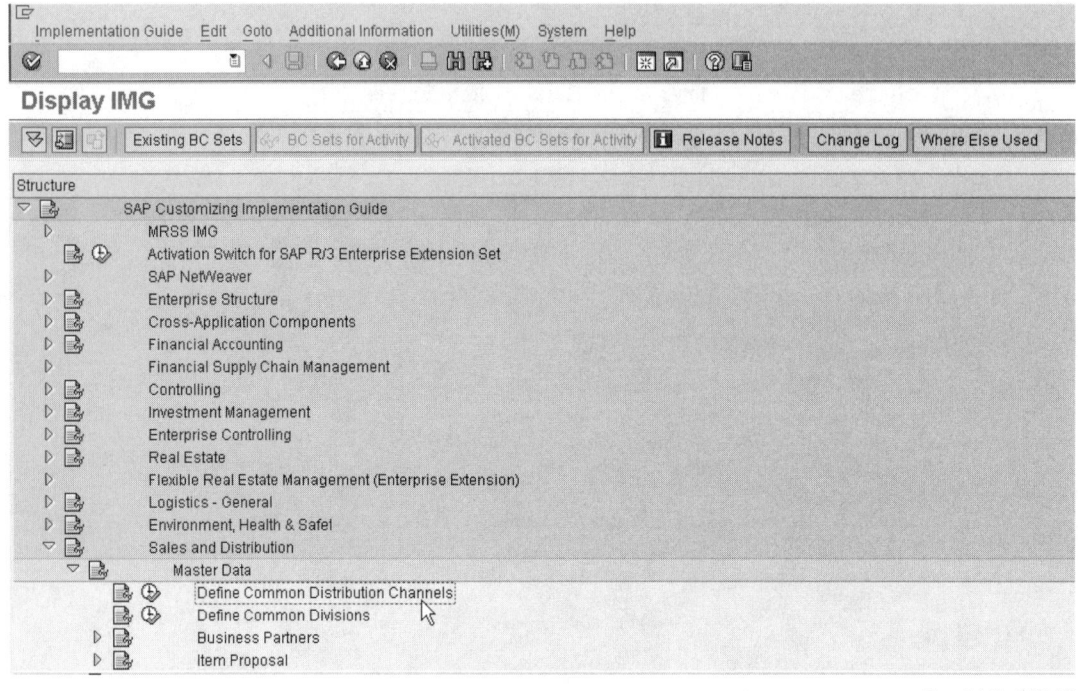

Figure 2-8   SAP Customizing Implementation Guide menu path for common distribution channels.

You can define common distribution channels and divisions using the following menu paths, as shown in Figure 2-8.

Menu Path   SAP Customizing Implementation Guide | Sales and Distribution | Master Data | Define Common Distribution Channels [VOR1]

You can group the distribution channel and division separately for either the master data (which combines customer master and material master records), or group the distribution channel and division separately for condition records, or both the master data and condition records.

For example: You have a product range that is not different for the four different distribution channels you have. (The four distribution channels could be telesales, retail, industry, and wholesale.) Neither is there a difference in the customers details when they purchase through one channel or the other. Thus, you do not wish to create four views of customer master and material master records, based upon the four sales areas. Select one distribution channel and division to use as the master or common one—for example, retail. Create the customer master records and material master records in the common distribution channel (retail). Then assign the other distribution channels you created in the organizational structure setup to this one.

Whenever SAP sees a distribution channel linked to the common distribution channel, it will use the master data for the common distribution channel.

Don't forget, this means you can only create or change master data in the distribution
channel that is being referenced. In the previous scenario that would mean you can only
change data for the retail distribution channel. Even if you should access a customer or
material master in change mode and press F4 (matchcode search help for possible entries)
and select telesales, industry, or wholesale, you will receive a message stating "Sales area is
not defined......"

The same is true for the sharing of conditions. If conditions are shared, you need only
create a condition in the distribution channel or division you are using as the reference.
Obviously, this only pertains to conditions that are specific to the distribution channel and
or division (that is, these fields are in the condition key).

Customer Groups

The customer group is a grouping of customers that is configured under master data in the
SAP Customizing Implementation Guide. After defining the group and allocating it a two-
digit alphanumeric key, you may assign the group to the customer master record.

The customer group is a wonderful field that is copied into the header and item level of
the sales document. This is very useful for reporting and pricing purposes.

You can define the customer group using the following menu path.

Menu Path   SAP Customizing Implementation Guide I Sales and Distribution I Master
Data I Business Partners I Customers I Sales I Define Customer Groups [OVS9]

Simply assign a two-digit alphanumeric key to the text description you would best use
to define your customer grouping.

Now proceed to the customer master record [VD02] sales screen and enter the appropriate
customer group. Should you want this field to be a mandatory field, so that no customer
master record may be created without this entry, you may define it as mandatory using the
account group as we saw earlier in this chapter.

The customer group is a field that can be used to generate statistics as well as to create
condition records such as pricing—for example, should you wish to offer discounts per
wholesale customer group, but not per retail customer group. It is especially useful as it is
on the sales tab of the customer master record and therefore it is on the customer related
table of the customer master record that is table KNVV.

Sales Districts, Sales Offices, and Sales Groups

Sales districts, sales offices, and sales groups can refer to differing geographical areas or
regions, or merely used as a grouping term on the customer master record. In their truest
use, a sales district refers to a region where the customer is located. The sales office refers to
a sub-group of the sales district, and the sales group is a sub-group of the sales office. Often,
the sales group is used to represent a sales team or even a sales person.

These data fields are copied into the header and item data of the sales order. They can be
used for statistical purposes as well as for pricing.

The company implementing SAP may have specific requirements pertaining to the
sales group—for example, by giving individual sales people's names to each value in the
list. If you use sales group in this sense, it is advisable to use a generic term—for example,
Employee A.

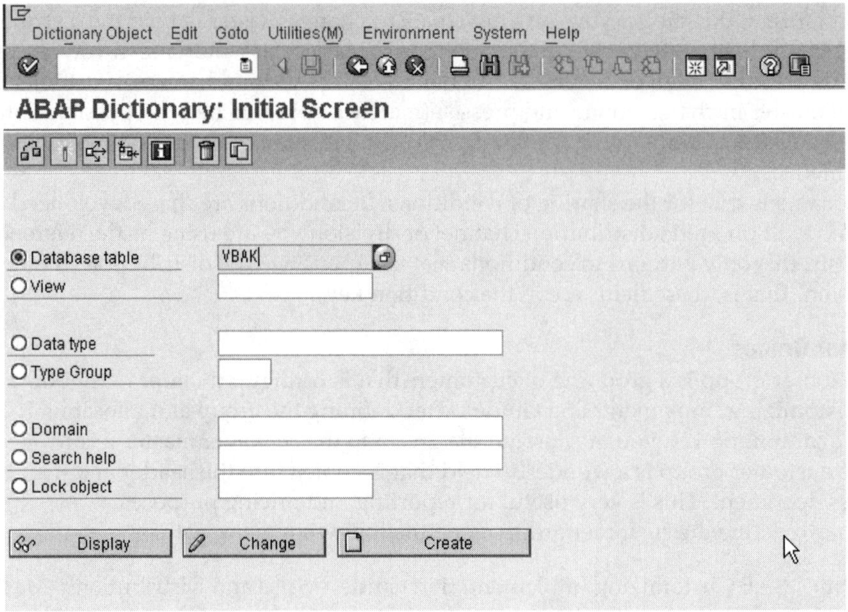

FIGURE 2-9   ABAP Dictionary

If you use sales district, sales office, and sales group for other purposes, you may change the *data element*, which describes the field in the GUI. To change the data element, proceed to the ABAP Dictionary [SE11], seen in Figure 2-9, and place the ABAP field name in the Data Type field, then select Change. Select the Field Label tab, where you will be able to maintain the short, medium, and long texts related to the field.

To configure the sales districts, use the following menu path.

Menu Path   SAP Customizing Implementation Guide | Sales and Distribution | Master Data | Business Partners | Customers | Sales | Define Sales Districts [OVR0]

Create a new entry that is an alphanumeric key of up to six characters. Enter a description that is easily identifiable in order to prevent confusion in the assignments of the sales districts in the customer master record.

The sales office and sales group are defined in the organizational structure. To configure the sales offices, use the following menu path.

Menu Path   SAP Customizing Implementation Guide | Enterprise Structure | Definition | Sales and Distribution | Maintain Sales Office

To configure the sales groups, use the following menu path.

Menu Path   SAP Customizing Implementation Guide | Enterprise Structure | Definition | Sales and Distribution | Maintain Sales Group

KNA1	General data in customer master
KNVV	Sales data in customer master
KNB1	Customer master (company code) data
KNKK	Credit management customer master: Control area data
KNKA	Customer master credit management: Central data
KNVP	Customer partner functions

TABLE 2-1   Customer Master Tables

After the definition of the sales office and sales group, you must assign them to their location in the organizational structure. The sales office is assigned to a sales area using the following menu path.

Menu Path   SAP Customizing Implementation Guide | Enterprise Structure | Assignment | Sales and Distribution | Assign Sales Office to Sales Area [OVXM]

The sales group is assigned to the sales office using the following menu path.

Menu Path   SAP Customizing Implementation Guide | Enterprise Structure | Assignment | Sales and Distribution | Assign Sales Group to Sales Office [OVXJ]

Master Data Tables

Master data is stored in the database in tables and fields. This master data is copied into the transaction data whenever a new transaction is created. For example, the customer master data is copied into the sales order when a sales order is created.

These tables may be grouped into a logical database. You can locate the logical databases used in SAP using transaction code [SE36]. There are many logical databases in SAP but I cannot show them all in this book; however, they are listed on a useful website: www.sapww.com. A few SAP tables related to customer and material master records are listed in Tables 2-1 and 2-2.

The ABAP Dictionary: An Introduction

To view the fields used in the structure of these tables, use the ABAP Dictionary, which you can access with the following menu path.

MARA	Material master: General data
MBEW	Material valuation
MARC	Plant data for material
MARD	Material master: Storage location/batch segment
MVKE	Material master: Sales data

TABLE 2-2   Material Master Tables

Menu Path   SAP Menu I Tools I ABAP Workbench I Development I SE11 – ABAP Dictionary [SE11]

As this book is not intended to be on ABAP, we will not be discussing areas that are not relevant to SD. However, take note of the ABAP Dictionary initial screen, seen in Figure 2-9, as we will be referring to it often.

Once you are in the ABAP Dictionary view you are presented with the display shown in Figure 2-10. This is an example of the table KNVV showing the field names and their characteristics. This view is also accessible in display mode using the transaction code [SE12].

On the left side in Figure 2-10, you will find the fields that exist in the table you selected. A field has the following characteristics:

- A field name
- An identifier to indicate the field is part of a key of the table definition
- An identifier to indicate the field has initial values when defined
- The data element, which holds the description (see earlier on in this chapter) that the system uses in the user interface
- A data type—for example, currency only
- The field length – number of characters
- A decimal allocation

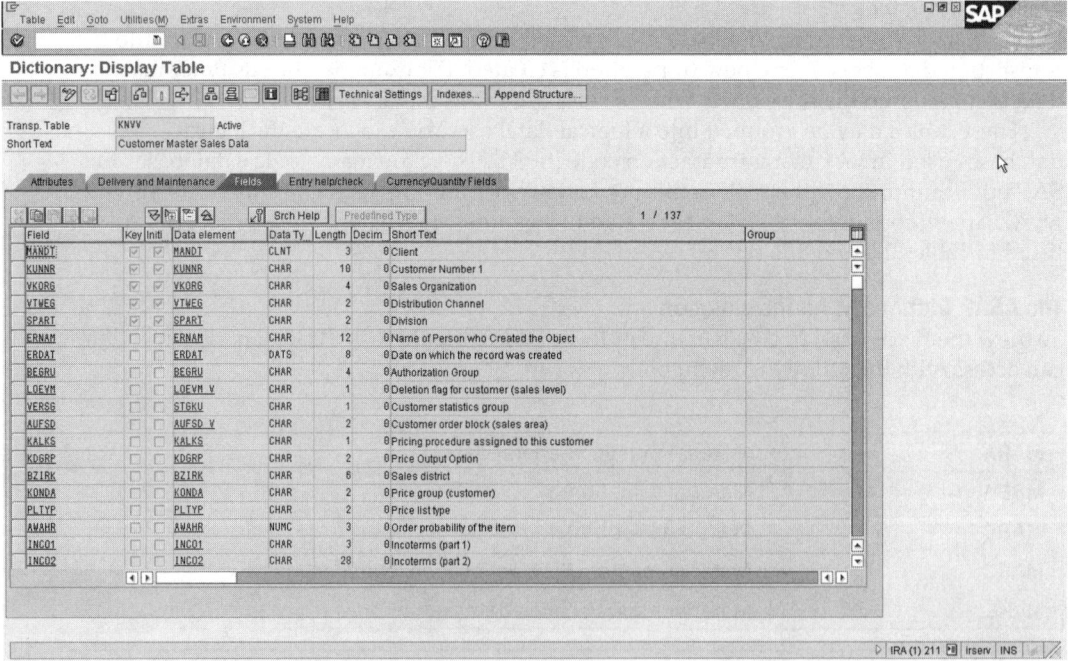

Copyright by SAP AG

FIGURE 2-10   The ABAP Dictionary view of table KNVV.

VBAK	Order header
VBAP	Order item
VBEP	Order schedule line
VBPA	Partner functions
VBKD	Business data
LIKP	Delivery header
LIPS	Delivery item
VBRK	Billing header
VBRP	Billing item
VBPA	Partners
VBUK	Status header
VBUP	Status items
VBFA	Document flow

TABLE 2-3   Commonly Used Tables in SD

In Sales and Distribution the tables listed in Table 2-3 are often referred to, so it is worthwhile knowing these tables by heart. Information access is easy when we use these tables in conjunction with the Data Browser in SAP. These tables are transactional relevant tables, data is populated into these tables after a transaction has been saved.

Should you wish to see the entries of the tables, use the Data Browser transaction code [SE16] or the new version [SE16N].

The Data Browser: An Introduction
The data browser is a tool used to display all the contents of a table in SAP. It is accessed with the following menu path.

Menu Path   SAP Menu | Tools | ABAP Workbench | Overview | SE16 – Data Browser [SE16]

Insert a table name and press ENTER to see the Data Browser selection screen shown in Figure 2-11.

Select Settings | User Parameters to see the settings shown in Figure 2-12. There you can select field name or field label. Field label will show you the field description, which is easily understandable but may not offer you the reliability you are looking for. (It is easy to mistakenly confuse two fields using text descriptions.) On the other hand the field name is the actual field in the database and the ABAP programs.

The Data Browser [SE16] has been updated with a newer version, called from transaction code [SE16N], which is referred to as the "General Table Display." This new version has similar functionality as the previous version and is described in detail at the end of Chapter 4.

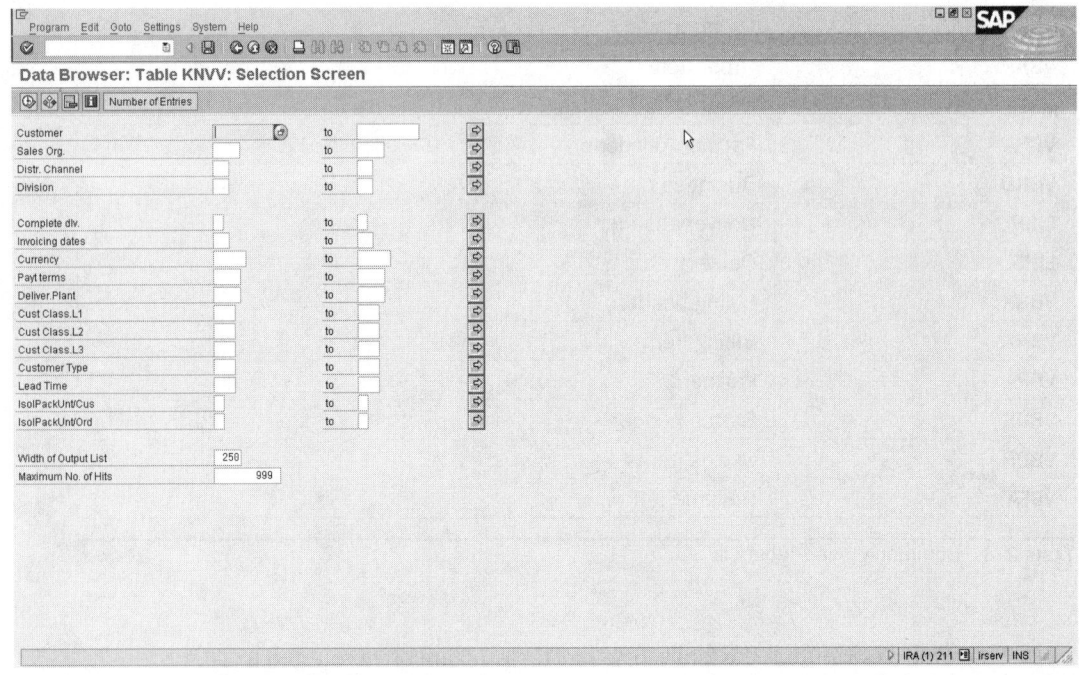

FIGURE 2-11 Data Browser selection screen

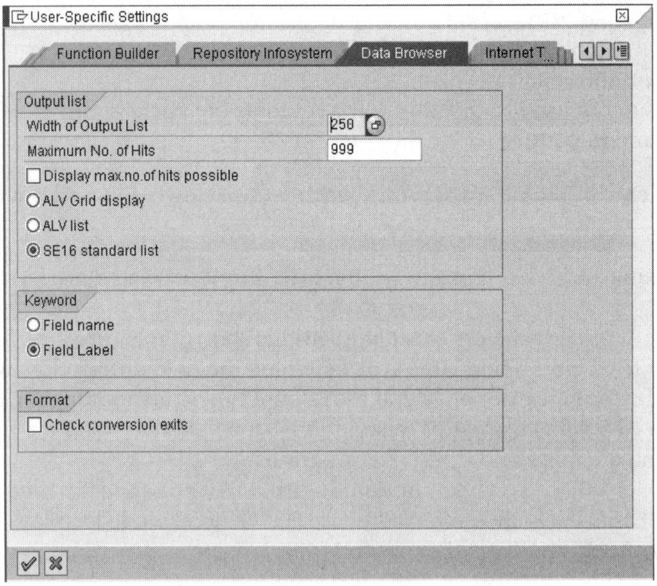

FIGURE 2-12 Data Browser user settings

You may also change the display option to use an ABAP List Viewer (ALV), as opposed to a standard list. You may increase the width of the output list and the maximum number of hits as a default. If you use the ALV grid, you can easily display the data in a spreadsheet that you can save, so you can effectively download the data to a spreadsheet via the ALV grid.

Should you not have the required data (field names) in the selection screen, from the Data Browser [SE16] select Settings | Fields for Selection to get the screen shown in Figure 2-13.

Prior to executing the selection, it is advisable to restrict your entries by setting a maximum number of hits (SAP version 3 onwards) and using a restrictive search depending on your selection requirement—for example, all sales documents from sales organization 0001 only, and created in the last month. Otherwise, you may end up reading every entry in the database, which can cause slow system performance.

Should you wish to only know the total quantity of values, click the Number of Entries button. It is amazing how many times people forget to do this. This will produce the answer much faster than the time it takes for the system to read every record in a large table. The number of entries button is located at the top of the selection parameters screen.

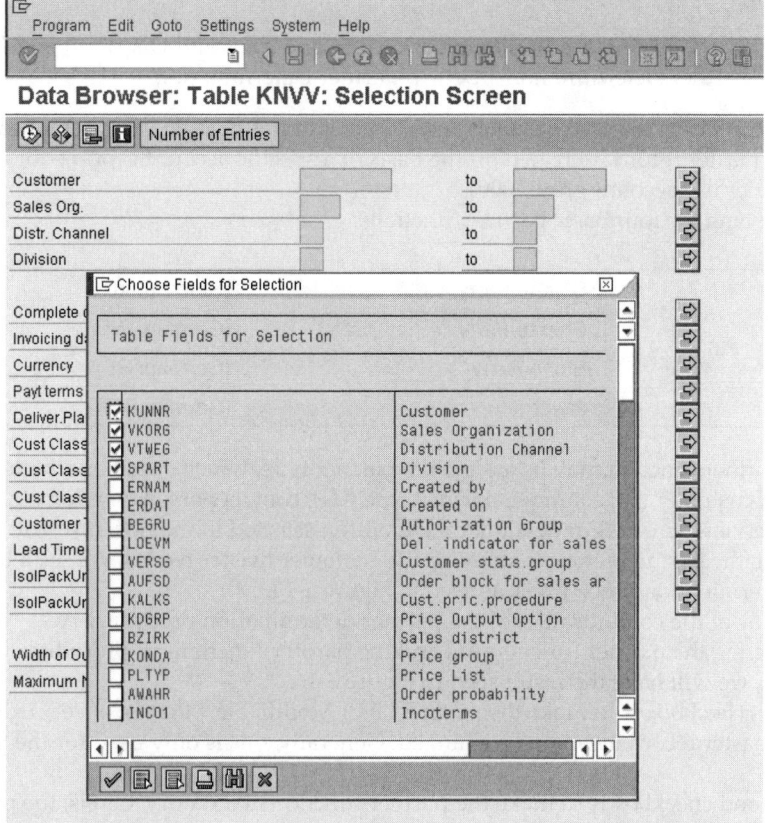

Figure 2-13   Data Browser selection settings

To discover the field and table name of a specific field, place your cursor on the desired field and press F4 (Help), followed by F9 (Technical Information).

Partner Determination

Business transactions may have one or more partners involved in the transaction. For example, when an order is placed, you have the Sold-to Party placing the order. You may have a different Ship-to Party (entity receiving the delivery) for the order. The invoice may go to another entity called the Bill-to Party and still another entity may make the payment (the Payer).

Automatic partner determination happens in the sales document, delivery, billing documents, sales activities, and customer master record. This automatic partner determination is configurable. In this section, we'll cover how to set up the partner determination, including what partners are possible in a business transaction, what partners are required, and what types of customers from the customer master can fulfill the partner roles. For example, you must have a Sold-to Party in the sales order. But the Sold-to Party cannot be a customer who is created as account group 0002 (the Ship-to Party).

To configure partner determination, use the following menu path.

Menu Path   SAP Customizing Implementation Guide ǀ Sales and Distribution ǀ Basic Functions ǀ Partner Determination ǀ Set Up Partner Determination

By referring back to master data, covered earlier in this chapter, we see that each partner (customer) master record is created on the basis of a specific account group—for example, Sold-to parties use account group 0001.

We also note the four basic partner functions:

SP	Sold-to Party	(German -AG)
SH	Ship-to Party	(German -WE)
BP	Bill-to Party	(German -RE)
PY	Payer	(German -RG)

Each partner function may be assigned a partner type, which specifies whether this partner is a customer (for example, partner type KU), contact person, vendor, etc.

The overview screen is dependent on the option selected in the IMG. We will look at maintaining the partner determination for the customer master record. We see a list of all partner determination procedures, as seen in Figure 2-14.

Let's look at the configuration of the partner determination procedure AG.

By selecting the partner function AG and the partner functions in procedure, as seen in Figure 2-15, we will have the result seen in Figure 2-16.

The first checkbox is to make the partner "Not Modifiable," that is, once it is in the customer master record it cannot be changed. Generally, this is only used for the Sold-to Party.

The second checkbox is to make the partner function mandatory, that is, the partner must be determined or manually entered in the customer master record.

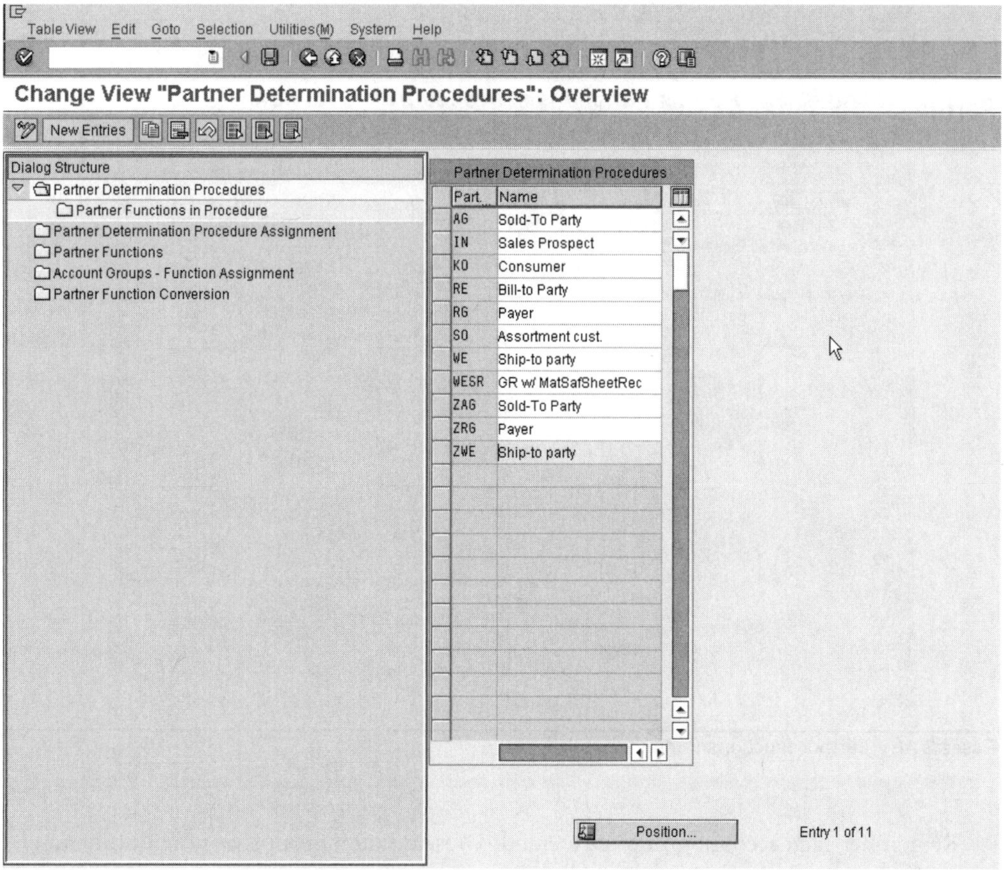

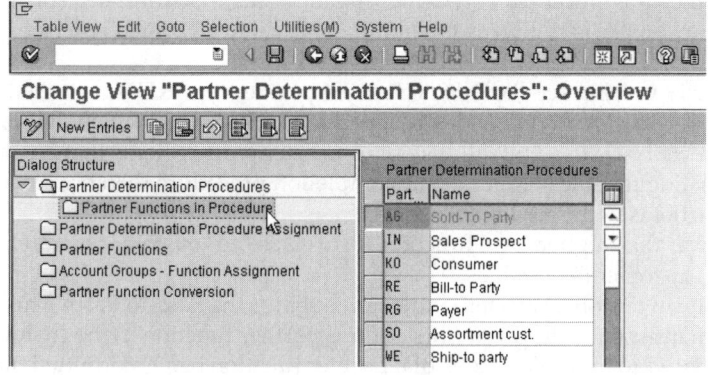

Copyright by SAP AG

FIGURE 2-14   Partner determination procedures

Copyright by SAP AG

FIGURE 2-15   Partner determination procedure navigation

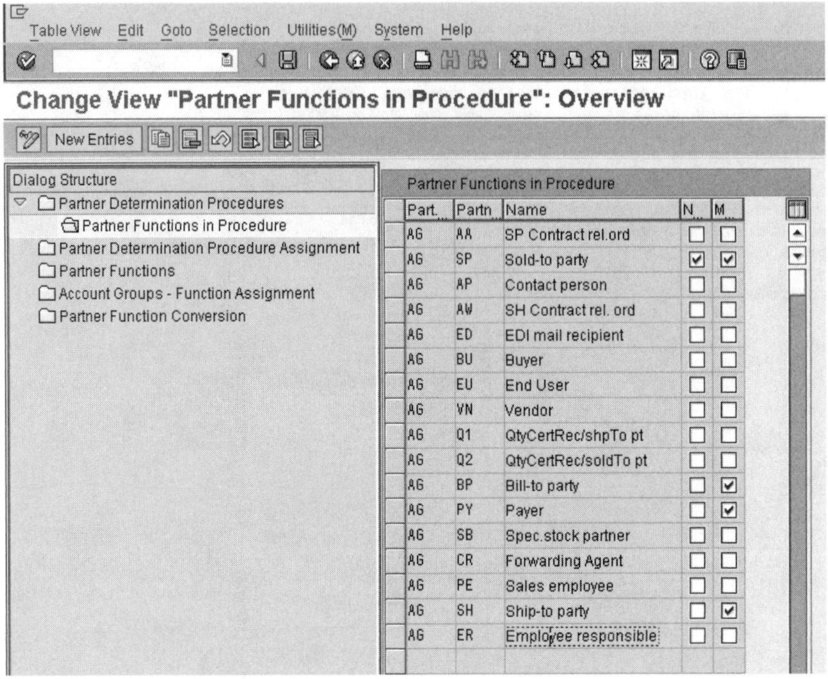

FIGURE 2-16   Partner functions in procedure

Remember each account group we created. Those account groups would not function without a partner determination procedure being assigned to them. In Figure 2-17, we see the partner procedure AG assigned to the account group 0001.

Below partner determination procedure assignment, partner functions are defined. For example, the partner determination procedure AG has the mandatory partner function AG. Let us look at the "definition" of the partner function AG in Figure 2-18. The definition of the partner function AG is shown as the highlighted value SP, which will be explained a little later.

In Figure 2-18 you can see the Sold-to Party is partner type KU – customer.

While the in-completion procedure assigned to the SP partner function is 07, this in-completion procedure is used by the system to register partner fields that are not filled at the time of creating the sales order. The in-completion procedure then prompts the user to complete these fields with missing values.

We will cover the "higher-level function" as well as the "customer hierarchy type" in Chapter 9 in "Customer Hierarchies."

The "unique in customer master" indicator is set for the Sold-to Party. This indicates that the system must only allow one entry of this partner function in the customer master record. As opposed to multiple entries of a partner function being permitted, for example Ship-to Party.

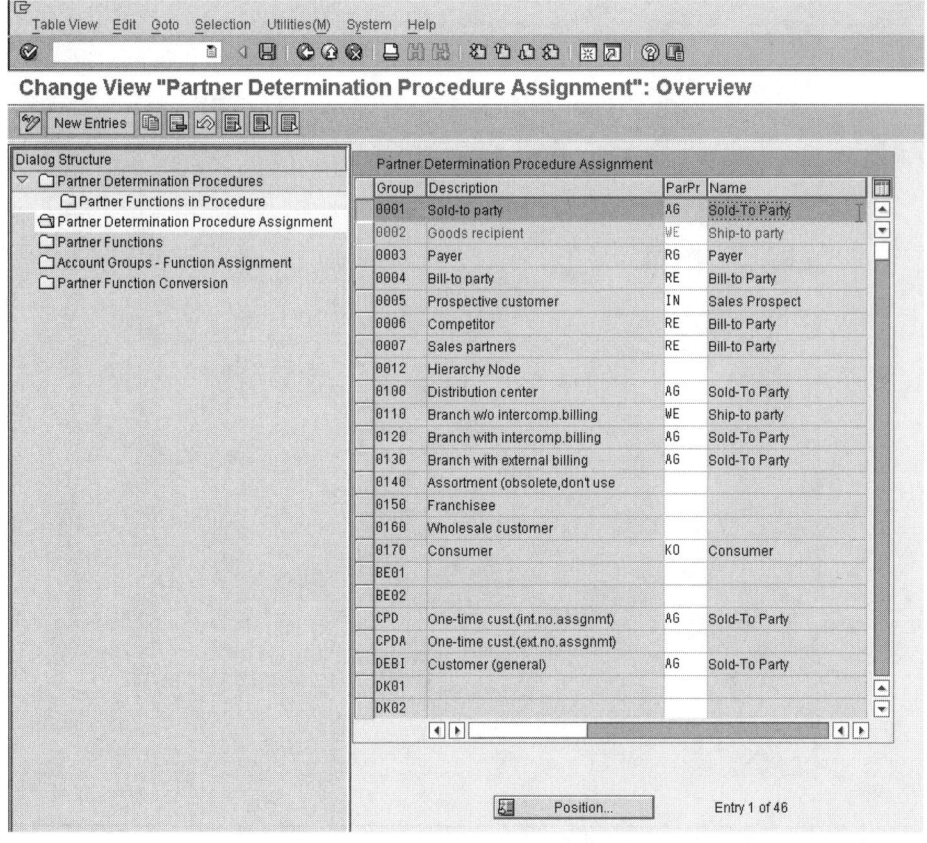

FIGURE 2-17   Partner determination procedure assignment

The next step is to assign the valid account groups to the partner functions as seen in Figure 2-19. Only account groups in this list can play this role. For example, the Sold-to Party can be a sold-to party (account group 0001) or a prospective customer (account group 005), etc.

Should you create a new customer account group—for example, a copy of 0001—do not forget to assign the new account group to the list of allowed account groups for partner determination.

Finally, it may seem confusing that the partner function AG is referred to as SP. The reason for this is that the German definition for the partner function was initially AG for "Auftraggeber." You are now able to change the partner function's value according to the language the translation is created for and the language with which the user logs onto the system, as seen in Figure 2-20.

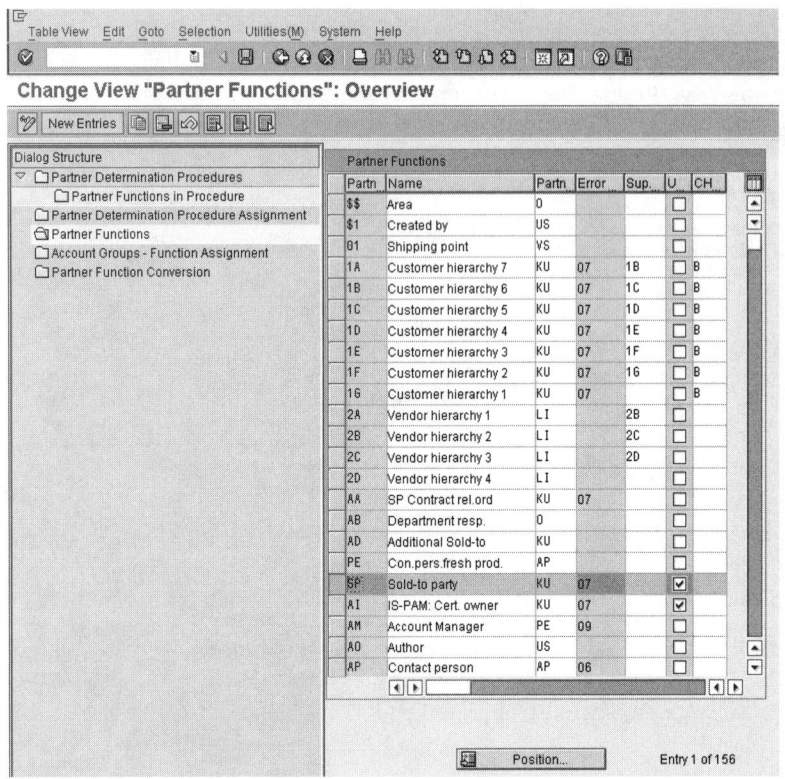

FIGURE 2-18 Partner function AG is defined as SP.

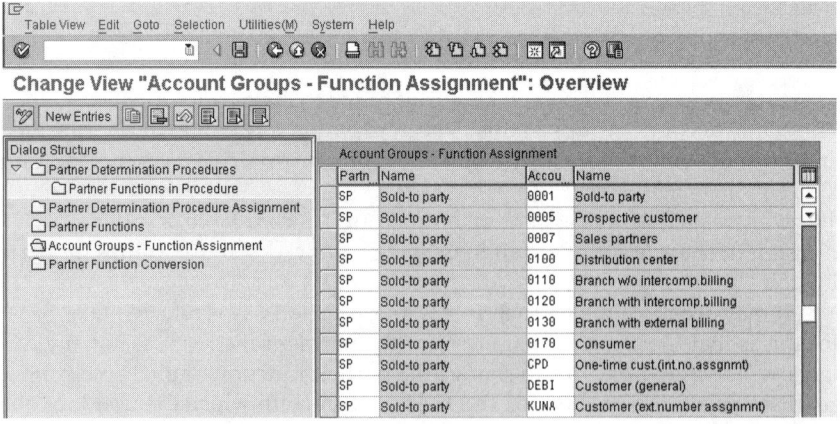

FIGURE 2-19 Account group assignment to partner function

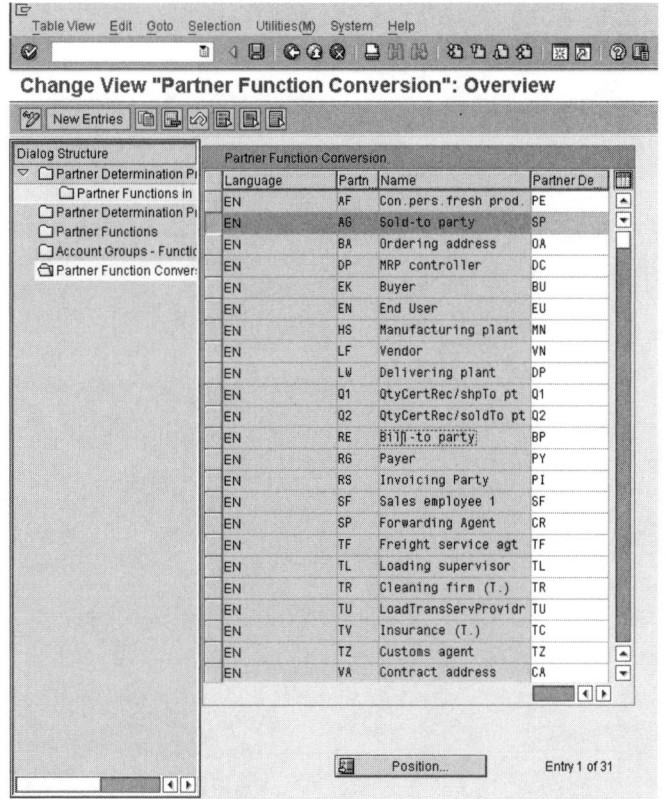

FIGURE 2-20   Translation of partner function from AG to SP for language EN.

Sales Documents

S ales documents are a core part in the Sales and Distribution module of mySAP ERP. In this section we focus on the components of a sales document and how they are configured.

Overview of a Sales Document

Many processes start with a sales document, usually a sales order. A delivery document is created based on the data in the sales order, and finally the billing document is created from the delivery data.

Each sales document is divided into three levels:

- **Header Level (Table VBAK)** This level of the sales document is responsible for master data such as customer material master as well as sales area and organization data. The settings at document type control in the SAP Customizing Implementation Guide, which we will define later, determine how this sales document functions.

- **Item Level (Table VBAP)** This level of the sales document is responsible for material item data such as order quantity and material master data. This is controlled by the item category settings of the SAP Customizing Implementation Guide.

- **Schedule Line (Table VBEP)** This level of the sales document is responsible for delivery dates and delivery quantity. This is controlled by the schedule line item category settings of the SAP Customizing Implementation Guide.

In addition, you have business data (table VBKD), which can exist at header or item level. An example of business data is the incoterms for the sales order, which are copied from the ship to party master data into the sales order header business data. By default, this header business data applies to all the items on the sales order. You can change the incoterms at header level and the change will apply to all the items.

You can also change the incoterms for one of the order items. This change applies only to that item. So we have item business data. The header business data no longer applies to that item. Future changes to the header incoterms do not apply to the order item incoterms.

Basic Sales Order Process

A *sales order* is a contractual agreement between a sales organization and a customer (Sold-to Party) for the supply of services or products over a specific period of time and in certain quantities.

A sales order gets the master data from the customer master record and the material master record for a specific sales area. This data is manipulated into context according to the sales document type, item category, and schedule line category.

The sales order can be created with a reference to a preceding document (for example, a quotation), in which case the data from the preceding document is copied into the new document. Thus, the information of a quotation will be copied from the quotation into the sales order.

When the delivery document is created, the sales order data is transferred into it, using additional delivery or shipping information for the delivery note.

Following the goods issue, the information is passed on to billing, if billing is necessary.

NOTE *Integration with other modules can happen throughout the process. For example, an interface with warehouse management could happen during the delivery processing.*

The number of variables in the sales order process is vast; at the highest level, one could have a quotation followed by a contract followed by a call off sales order. We will not define and configure every possible flow. Instead, we will configure the main building blocks used by most organizations for the Sales and Distribution business processes.

As stated earlier, each document (quotation, order, delivery, or invoice) is represented by a document type. For example, a standard quotation is AG, a standard sales order is TA (German), a standard delivery is LF, and a standard invoice is F2. Sales document types can have a translation into other languages, thus a sales order may be TA (German) or it may be OR (English).

SAP has a language translation table, where you may determine whether a user should enter, for example, TA or OR as a sales document type representing order; when logged on in English, the system will propose OR automatically for order. To access the language translation table, choose SAP Customizing Implementation Guide | Sales and Distribution | Sales | Sales Documents | Sales Document Header | Convert Language For Each Sales Document Type

We will use the unconverted German version of sales document types unless otherwise specified. Thus, the above document flow would look like the following representation of sales document types:

> AG → TA → LF → F2

We will map out the sales document flows valid for each section during the description of the section.

Number Ranges

Each document is numbered. A number range is assigned to a document type. Number ranges are also used for master data objects, such as customer master records. (You assign the number range to the customer's account group.)

Number ranges are assigned throughout the system. However, for the purposes of this example we will look at assigning number ranges to a sales item proposal. Since the logic is the same, you will be able to assign number ranges to any document or object based on this example.

Menu Path   SAP Customizing Implementation Guide | Sales and Distribution | Master Data | Item Proposal | Define Number Ranges for Item Proposals [OVZA] or [VN01] etc.

There are two forms of number ranges:

- **Internal**   The system automatically proposes the number range and the next available number to be used.

- **External**   The system allows the user to specify a number that has not already been used and is within the number range for the object.

On the overview screen, as seen in Figure 3-1, select the Intervals button.

FIGURE 3-1   The number range overview

You are then presented with the number range interval key. As we will see in the product proposal defined later in this chapter, we use item number range 11 for internal and 12 for external. You can see the relevant sequence in Figure 3-2.

To create a new number range, first find the exact requirements of the business. They may want the number range to be shared by numerous document types, so it will have to have a large interval because it will number many transactions. You need to consider how many transactions will be processed so you can define a large enough number range.

Find an interval that is not yet used and select the Interval button.

Next, enter your alphanumeric key (for example, Y1) followed by the From and To numbers for the range. Then indicate if the number range is internal or external.

For most document types you may only want to use an internal number assignment.

Should you be doing any data conversion of old documents—for example, sales documents into new mySAP ECC6 documents—ensure your number range matches the permitted range of the country/legal entity. For example, in Brazil the number ranges are unique and one is not permitted to have gaps in sequence.

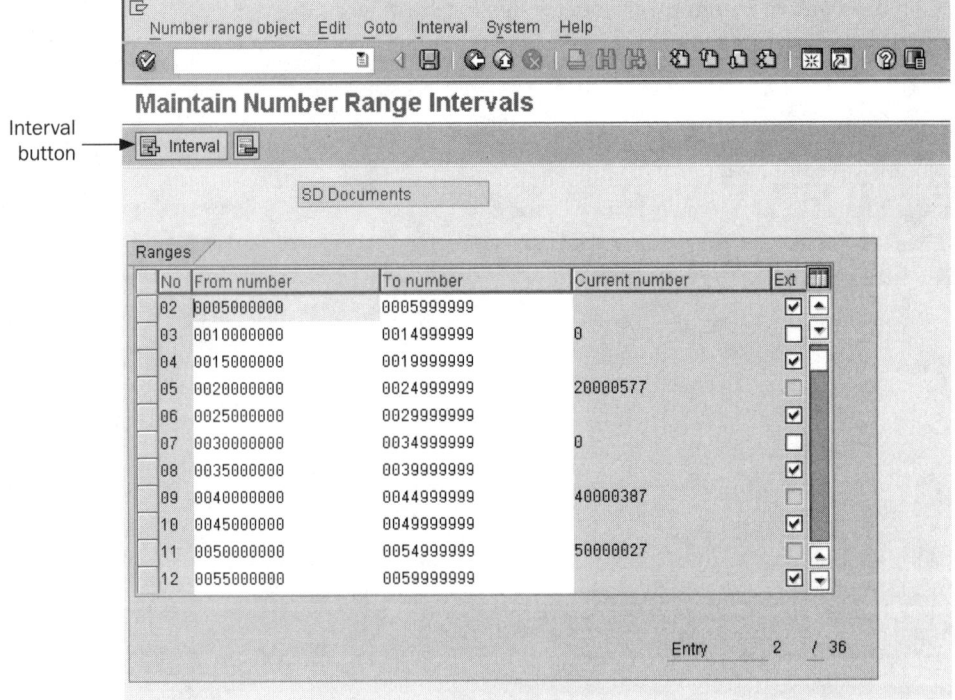

FIGURE 3-2   Number range intervals

Number ranges are manually transported through clients. A client is the environment you are working in. Generally, companies have a system with a client for each environment—for example, a development environment or the quality or production environment.

When transporting the number range interval, the intervals you have in the client you are exporting into will be deleted first, then the number range and assigned status will be created in the new client. Also note that the number range assignments to document types or other objects are not transported with this manual transport. I recommend that you create the number ranges individually in each client rather than transport them. This is because if you transport the number ranges, you could cause a problem with duplicate entries in the database. If this situation happens, the SAP program will abort and the data will not be saved.

For example: In client 001 you have a number range from 0000001 to 9999999. The current number is 000084. In client 002, you have the same number range, but the current number is 0003429. These represent records in the database. Now you transport from 001 to 002. Your new starting number is 0000084 in client 002. When you try and save the record, the system assigns 0000085 to the document. But document 0000085 already exists in the database. The transaction terminates with an error and the data is not saved.

In this case you need to check the last number in the table using transaction code [SE16] or [SE16n] and then change the number range status to reflect the last number used. Then the next number assigned will be unique.

Item Proposals (Product Proposal)

An *item proposal* is a list of materials and order quantities that are regularly ordered together by a customer. They are sales-area–specific and can be referenced when creating the sales order. Each time a sales order is created and the item proposal referenced, the system automatically copies the item proposal from which to select materials and quantities. This can greatly speed up order entry time by the sales people.

Menu Path SAP Customizing Implementation Guide | Sales and Distribution | Master Data | Item Proposal | Define Item Proposal Types [VOV8]

Using item proposals in the sales order is different than using bills of material in the sales order. A *bill of material (BOM)* is a record linked to a material that details the individual components that make up the material. For example, a computer may have a BOM that consists of screen, keyboard, and processor. When you enter the computer material in the order, SAP will explode the BOM and enter the individual items instead. See Chapter 5 for more information.

Item proposals may be related or unrelated items. For example, if the customer is a hardware store and they regularly order nails, screws, and hammers, you can create an item proposal with the nail, screw, and hammer materials.

The list of document types seen in Figure 3-3 shows all the sales document types in the system. We will look at them in detail later. To start your introduction to sales documents we will go through the configuration settings in this item proposal first.

Select document type PV – Item Proposal and click the Details button as shown here.

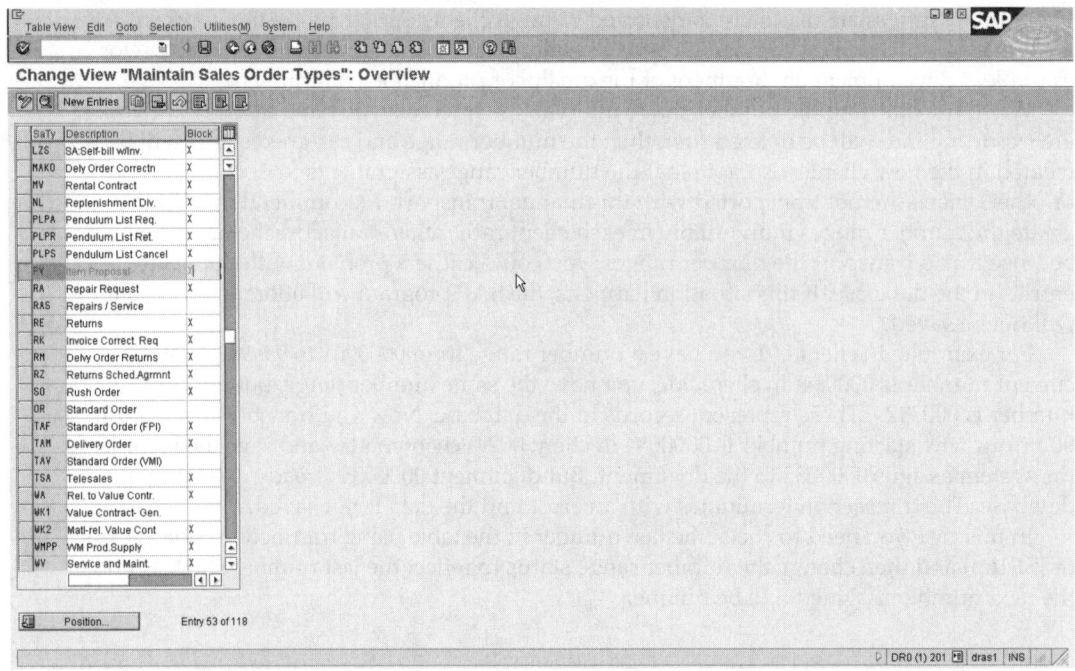

FIGURE 3-3 Item proposal

You are then presented with the screen shown in Figure 3-4.
What this tells us is the following:

NOTE *For the purpose of this example we will only refer to the filled-in entries.*

- The document category is "D." The document category controls how the system behaves. It is pre-determined in SAP and cannot be added to.

- The document type is blocked.

- It has an internal and external number range key, which we referred to earlier on.

- The item and sub-item increment on the sales order (that is, the sequence in which items in the order are numbered) is 10.

- Document probability is 100 percent. (It is best to leave this field as 100 percent for sales documents unless you wish to plan your material requirements based upon this setting and the respective setting in the customer master record. It is not possible to change the value of this field for item proposals though, as an item proposal is merely a tool and is not valid for deliveries or invoicing.)

Table View   Edit   Goto   Selection   Utilities(M)   System   Help

Change View "Maintain Sales Order Types": Details

New Entries

Sales Document Type	PV	Item Proposal	
SD document categ.	D	Sales document block	X
Indicator			

Number systems

No.range int.assgt.	11	Item no.increment	10
No. range ext. assg.	12	Sub-item increment	10

General control

Reference mandatory		Material entry type
Check division		☐ Item division
Probability	100	☐ Read info record
Check credit limit		Check purch.order no
Credit group		☐ Enter PO number
Output application	V1	Commitment date

Transaction flow

Screen sequence grp.	MA	Product Proposal	Display Range	UALL
Incompl. proced.	16	Item proposal	FCode for overv.scr.	UER1
Transaction group	5	Item proposal	Quotation messages	
Doc. pric. procedure	C		Outline agrmt mess.	
Status profile			Message: Mast.contr.	
Alt.sales doc. type1			ProdAttr.messages	
Alt.sales doc. type2			☐ Incomplet.messages	
Variant				

Scheduling agreement

Corr.delivery type		Delivery block
Use		
MRP for DlvSchType		

Shipping

Delivery type		Immediate delivery
Delivery block		
Shipping conditions		
ShipCostInfoProfile		

Billing

Dlv-rel.billing type		CndType line items
Order-rel.bill.type		Billing plan type
Intercomp.bill.type		Paymt guarant. proc.
Billing block		Paymt card plan type
		Checking group

Requested delivery date/pricing date/purchase order date

Lead time in days		☑ Propose deliv.date
Date type		☐ Propose PO date
Prop.f.pricing date		
Prop.valid-from date		

FIGURE 3-4   Sales document type – Settings for an Item proposal document type (*Continued*)

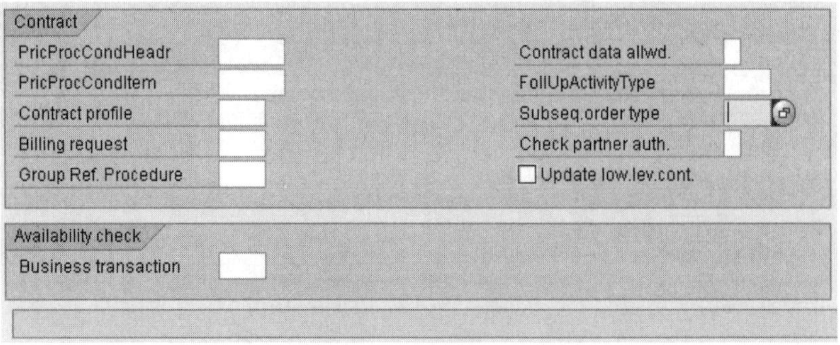

Contract

PricProcCondHeadr		
PricProcCondItem		
Contract profile		
Billing request		
Group Ref. Procedure		

Contract data allwd.		
FollUpActivityType		
Subseq.order type		
Check partner auth.		
☐ Update low.lev.cont.		

Availability check

Business transaction

FIGURE 3-4 Sales document type – Settings for an Item proposal document type (*Continued*)

Document probability is mainly used for quotations and orders. Customers who place quotations may place a fixed order 80 percent of the time. This means that the quote document probability is 80 percent. You can look at all the quotes in the system and be reasonably sure that you will have to deliver 80 percent of the quantity. So you can plan your MRP based on this value.

- Output application is used in output determination, which we'll cover in Chapter 9. Output determination sets what outputs, such as printouts and e-mail messages, are created.

- Screen sequence, display range, and function code for overview screens are all values that can be manipulated. They control how the interface is represented in the sales document—that is, should you wish the system to propose a different screen for quotations than for orders, you can change these entries. Generally, you need a skilled ABAP resource to create specialist screen overviews. The function code for overview screen determines which overview (or item list) screen users will see when they create a sales document of this type. For example, if a customer material is always used, you could default the overview screen to a screen that includes this field.

- The incompletion procedure identifies which fields are considered incomplete if the values are null. This is covered in Chapter 4.

- Transaction group controls the data to be updated in the respective tables for each transaction of the respective document type.

- Document pricing procedure is an indicator that determines what pricing procedure the system will use in this sales order. For the purpose of product proposals, it is indicating "C." Which is used in pricing procedure determination, please refer to pricing procedures in Chapter 8 for further data.

Once you are satisfied with the settings, select the Copy button, as shown here, then enter a key with the customer name range permitted by SAP starting with a Y or a Z, followed by a description.

Now that the document type is created, we need to ensure the correct number range is assigned.

Proceed to the next level in the SAP Customizing Implementation Guide: "Define Number Ranges for Item Proposals." Refer to the "Number Ranges" section earlier in this chapter.

To use the item proposal:

1. Go to transaction code [VA51] and create the proposal.

2. Go to transaction code [VA01] and create your sales order, then select Edit | Propose Items.

You can select Propose Default, With Quantity, Without Quantity and Offer a Selection List.

Sales Document Types

Sales document types control how the sales document must function. For example, a returns order to receive goods back from a customer will function differently than a sales order or a quotation.

The sales document is comprised of three general levels of data and control:

- The *sales document header*, which is controlled by the sales document type
- The *sales document item*, which is controlled by the sales item category
- The *sales document schedule line*, which is controlled by the schedule line category

The sales document type controls the central header details of the sales order—for example, the pricing procedure to be assigned to the sales document, or what type of document the sales document is. For now, we will focus on the configuration of the standard basic sales order process for the document flow: TA (order) → LF (delivery) → F2 (billing).

Menu Path SAP Customizing Implementation Guide | Sales and Distribution | Sales | Sales Documents | Sales Document Header | Define Sales Document Types [VOV8]

When dealing with the configuration of sales document types, generally one of two functions are performed. One either creates a new document type or alters an existing document type. It is recommended you follow these few basic guidelines:

- When creating a new document type, one should always reference the document type that is the closest match to the one you are aiming to create. For example, should you need a new sales order document type, you should copy document type TA (OR in English). Once you have copied the document type, the system copies all assigned data such as item category, schedule line category determination, and copying rules. You can then make the changes from this copy.

- When you want to change an SAP document type, it is better for you to copy the document type and assign it a new name in the customer name range (Y or Z). For example, if you wish to change the pricing procedure determination indicator for document type TA, it would be better to copy TA to ZTA and then make the changes. This leaves the SAP standard settings in place.

We will next look at the configuration settings necessary for a sales order document type.

When copying or creating a new document type you must be sure the name range selected begins with the letter Z or Y. SAP allows the use of objects beginning with the letter Z or Y. SAP will not overwrite any of these document types during upgrades.

To copy a sales document type, select the document you wish to copy and click the Copy button we used earlier in this chapter. The document type is OR and its description is "Standard order." If copied, change the name to ZOR or something similar.

When you click Copy the system will prompt with a dialog box asking if you would like the entry to be valid for copy control rules. Select Yes to ensure the copy control rules are automatically created, as seen here:

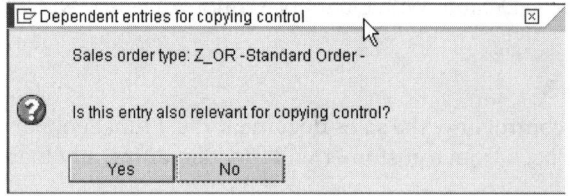

NOTE *When you create a delivery from a sales order, SAP copies the data from the sales order into the delivery. You can define the copy control rules that determine the data that is copied and the order types that may be copied into corresponding delivery types.*

When you save the sales document the system will automatically display the tables that will be updated with control values as seen in Figure 3-5.

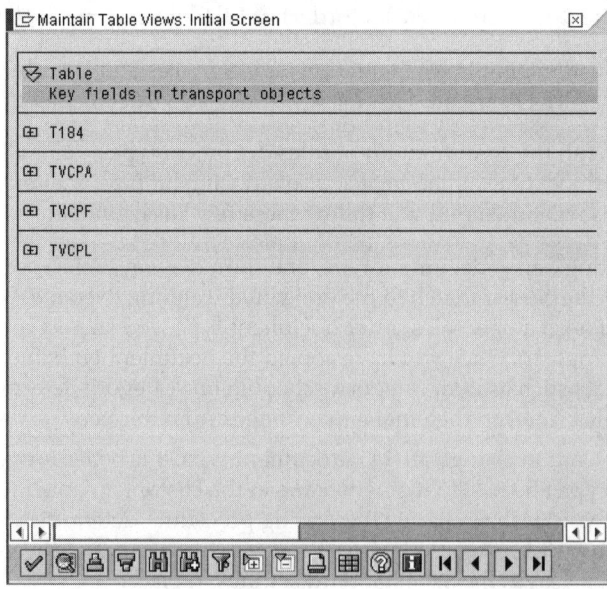

FIGURE 3-5 Control tables automatically updated on sales document type creation with reference

```
                                                                    ⌐
      Table View   Edit   Goto   Selection   Utilities(M)   System   Help

   ⊘  [                    ] ▤   ◁ 🖫 | 😊 😊 😊 | 📄 🗏 🗏 | 🗐 🗐 🗐 🗐 | 🗷 🗷 | 🗗 🗗

   Change View "Maintain Sales Order Types": Details

   🖉  New Entries  🗐 🗐 🗐 🗐 🗐 🗐

   Sales Document Type   [Z_OR]  [Standard Order      ]
   SD document categ.    [C]                              Sales document block    [ ]
   Indicator             [ ]
   ┌ Number systems ─────────────────────────────────────────────────────────────
   │  No.range int.assgt.   [01]                 Item no.increment    [10 ]
   │  No. range ext. assg.  [02]                 Sub-item increment   [10 ]
   └──────────────────────────────────────────────────────────────────────────────

   ┌ General control ────────────────────────────────────────────────────────────
   │  Reference mandatory   [ ]                  Material entry type       [ ]
   │  Check division        [2]                  ☑ Item division
   │  Probability           [100]                ☑ Read info record
   │  Check credit limit    [ ]                  Check purch.order no      [ ]
   │  Credit group          [ ]                  ☐ Enter PO number
   │  Output application    [V1]                 Commitment  date          [ ]
   └──────────────────────────────────────────────────────────────────────────────

   ┌ Transaction flow ───────────────────────────────────────────────────────────
   │  Screen sequence grp.  [AU]  Sales Order    Display Range        [UALL]
   │  Incompl.proced.       [11]  Standard Order  FCode for overv.scr. [UER1]
   │  Transaction group     [0]   Sales order     Quotation messages   [ ]
   │  Doc. pric. procedure  [A]                   Outline agrmt mess.  [ ] [ ]
   │  Status profile        [        ]            Message: Mast.contr. [ ]
   │  Alt.sales doc. type1  [    ]                ProdAttr.messages    [A]
   │  Alt.sales doc. type2  [    ]                ☐ Incomplet.messages
   │  Variant               [           ]
   └──────────────────────────────────────────────────────────────────────────────
```

FIGURE 3-6   Header, number systems, general control, and transaction flow of a sales document type

To ensure we understand the sales document configuration settings, I have listed the values and interpretation below per section of document type as shown in Figure 3-6.

- The document category is C, meaning a sales order document type, rather than a quote, etc.

- The sales document is not blocked for processing but can be used by the business.

- Internal number range interval is 01.

- External number range interval is 02.

- The items in the sales order increase in increments of 10; the sub-items increase in intervals of 10.

- The document does not have a mandatory reference (such as a reference to a quotation) before an order may be created.

- The division of the material or item is copied into the sales order.

- There is a check with an error message to see if this division is equal to the header division.

- The probability of this order being completed and fulfilled is 100 percent.

- The system must read the customer material info record, should one exist.

- The credit limit check is blank, which means no check. See "credit management" in Chapter 10.

- The system must not check the purchase order number.

- The output application is assigned for sales. See "output determination" in Chapter 9.

- The commitment date is not checked. The commitment date will be recalculated if changes are made to the material, quantity, requested delivery date, or delivery time. See the discussion of availability check later in this chapter.

- The screen sequence group controls the way data is displayed, and in what sequence.

- The display range determines what items in the sales order are displayed—for example, all items or only header items for a BOM.

- The function code for overview screens is the function code that determines what data and layout you see in the sales order—for example, item overview or item detail.

- The incompletion procedure at sales document header is 11. See incompletion procedures in Chapter 4.

- The transaction group determines what indices must be updated with reference to this sales order.

- Quotation messages and contract messages are set with an indicator B. Quotations, contracts, and master contracts are the three preceding key document types. So when you create a sales order you may want the system to give you a warning if open quotations exist. This setting B checks to see if the item is available on any other quotations or contracts for this Sold-to Party. Perhaps the user would then create the order with reference to that quotation or contract.

- The document pricing procedure is this indicator plus the indicator on the customer master and the relevant sales area these determine which pricing procedure to use. See Chapter 8 on pricing.

- Status profile is used to assign a status profile to the particular document type. It is also assigned at item category level.

- Message master contract checks to determine if any master contracts exist while you are creating a document type "contract."

- With product attribute messages, the system can error or warn to check manually entered products for the attributes to see if the Ship To party accepts them. In the case of automatic material entry, such as material determination, this check is ignored.

- With the incomplete messages indicator blank, the system will inform you at the time of saving that the document is incomplete. However, you will still be able to save the document.

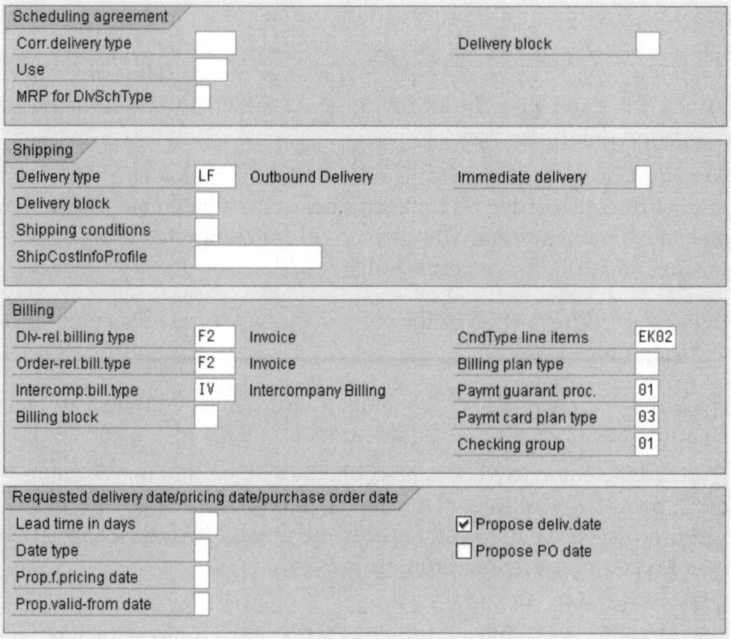

FIGURE 3-7 Scheduling agreement, shipping, billing, and requested delivery date details of a sales document type

The additional sales document type fields shown in Figure 3-7 are explained as follows:

- The scheduling agreement area is used by scheduling agreement document types. This will be covered in Chapter 4.
- The correction delivery type is used for scheduling agreements.
- The usage field is used to indicate on the sales order what the customer uses the material for. This entry will be copied into all items, or it may be placed into items individually in the sales order.
- MRP for delivery schedule type is used for scheduling agreements in order for them to set if the system should use just in time (JIT) processing or forward the demands on to material requirements planning (MRP).
- Delivery blocks can be automatically set for scheduling agreements. A blank entry indicates no delivery block.

By referring to the shipping section seen in Figure 3-7 we can see the following data:

- This is the standard shipping screen. It indicates that this document type is relevant for delivery, and the delivery type to be used for automatic processing is LF.
- There is no automatic delivery block entered in the sales order.

- The shipping conditions are proposed by the customer master record. Should an entry have existed in this field, this entry would have taken precedence and overwritten those found on the customer master record. The shipping condition value is used to determine the shipping point. See Chapter 6 for information on shipping point determination.

- The immediate delivery indicator is not set. This flag creates a delivery immediately after saving the sales order. So for each sales order you create, the delivery is created automatically by the system. The delivery is not completed and the picking, packing (if relevant), and goods issue must still be carried out.

By referring to the billing section of the sales document type as seen in Figure 3-7, we can see the following data:

- This document is relevant for invoicing and for delivery-related invoicing, the system automatically uses invoice document type F2.

- When an order-related invoice is possible the system will use document type F2 for automatic processing as well. (This makes sense if you wish your order and delivery relevant products to be invoiced at the same time.) The inter-company billing document type for automatic processing is IV.

- There is no automatic posting of a billing block on the sales order. It may be necessary, however, to have a billing block for credit notes, which we will look at later in this chapter.

  This means that the order cannot be billed until the billing block is removed. Using a billing block is a safety feature. For example, you may have a background job that creates invoices. When you save the order, this background job will see the order and then invoice it if it is for order-related billing. Using the billing block will prevent this from happening until the order has been checked and the billing block explicitly removed. The condition type for line items is used to determine the costing of the line item; it must be equal to the condition type allocated on your pricing procedure.

- The billing plan type is either periodic billing, where the entire value to be billed to date is billed in full on the billing plan date (for example, a rental agreement), or milestone billing, where the total value to be billed is distributed between the individual billing plan dates (for example, for a project based on project milestones, where the value billed on each date can be a fixed amount or a percentage).

- Payment guarantee procedure indicates to the system what form of guarantee procedure to use for this sales document. These are risk management. For more information, see credit management Chapter 10.

- Payment card plan type is an essential setting should you want your system to accept payment cards in the sales order process.

- Checking group is used to determine how the system carries out the checking of payment card data.

By referring to Figure 3-7 you may see the settings that affect the requested delivery date:

- Lead time in days is the requested delivery date in the sales order. It is recommended this be left as a zero in most instances.

- The propose delivery date checkbox is checked to propose the current date as the delivery date.

- Date type allows the user to set the format of the delivery schedule line date for internal system use—for example, date, week, month, etc.

- Proposal for pricing date allows you to specify the valid-from date for the pricing of the reference document, or the requested delivery date, or the current date.

- Propose valid-from date allows you to determine when the valid-from date for pricing should be. This is used, for example, in quotations.

- Propose PO date proposes the current date as purchase order date.

Figure 3-8 is the final portion of the configuration settings of the sales document. It refers to the contract and availability check:

- Pricing procedure conditions at header level refers to contract conditions. (Refer to contracts in Chapter 4.)

- Pricing procedure conditions at item level refers to contract conditions. (Refer to contracts in Chapter 4.)

- Contract profile is a default setting that will propose default data such as validity dates into the contract you are creating. (Refer to Contract profiles in Chapter 4.)

- Billing request is also associated with contracts. (Refer to contracts in Chapter 4.)

- Group reference procedure is used for master contracts to determine which data is to be copied or proposed into lower-level contracts. The referencing procedures are configured with master contracts later in this chapter.

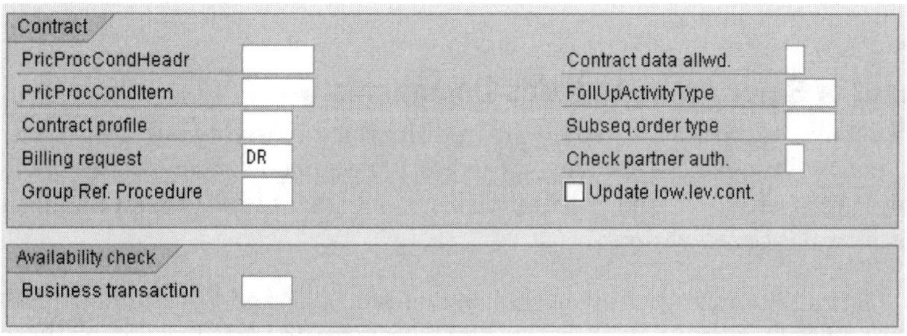

FIGURE 3-8   Contract and availability check details

- Contract data allowed controls what data is to be copied over contract item data from header contract data. If you do not want contract data for this sales document type, leave the field blank.

- Follow up activity type is used to initiate and assist in the speedy creation of a sales activity work list, such as a follow-up phone call or a follow-up sales letter.

- A subsequent order type is assigned here should you define a follow-up action for the contract. For example, if you wish your contract to create a quotation for a new contract one week before the contract end date, you would specify what type of quotation document type (e.g., AG) that would be.

- The check partner authority field is used by the system to check the partner type creating a release order against the contract. Only those partners with the partner function AG (Sold-to Party) or AA (Sold-to Party for release orders) as well as higher-level partners in a hierarchy are allowed to create release orders.

- The update lower-level contracts field is used by the system to update lower-level contracts, should the data you are changing be the master contract. These changes are then passed down to the lower-level contracts via workflow. Should this field not be checked, the system will only update the lower-level contract when it is re-processed.

- The business transaction for ATP field is used by the system to signal that communication must take place with the APO system to determine the ATP of this sales document type.

NOTE *ATP means "available to promise" and refers to when the business will be able to supply the goods being ordered—that is, when will procurement and production have the goods ready for shipping to the customer, preferably by the customer's requested delivery date.*

NOTE *APO is the Advanced Planner and Optimizer, an additional software component offered by SAP to allow a business to plan procurement and production.*

Assignment of Sales Areas to Sales Documents

If the sales document types you created are permitted to be used by all sales areas, there is no need to create settings here. However, there may be a need to assign sales documents to specific sales areas—for example, if a unique sales document type is used for all sales orders from a specific sales organization.

Menu Path   SAP Customizing Implementation Guide | Sales and Distribution | Sales | Sales Documents | Sales Document Header | Assign Sales Area To Sales Document Types [OVAZ]

You may assign reference sales organizations as well as reference distribution channels and divisions. Do not confuse this referencing with the assignment of common distribution channels and common divisions. The referencing done here is only used by the system to determine which sales documents are permitted for which sales areas. If all sales document types are allowed for use by all sales areas, leave the assignment fields blank.

Creating Order Reasons for Sales Documents

You can create order reasons as to why a customer is purchasing or using a sales document. This is helpful in determining the trigger which creates the sales order, which in turn may be useful for analysis on order entry. The order reason can be "sales call" or "good price" or while processing returns can be "poor quality" or "material damaged."

Menu Path   SAP Customizing Implementation Guide | Sales and Distribution | Sales | Sales Documents | Sales Document Header | Define Order Reasons [OVAU]

You create the order reasons for the business, for the standard sales order cycle as well as the returns cycle and any other sales processes. The order reason may be used for the logistics information system (LIS), thus you may report on or use this field in a matrix for sales information.

Should the order reason be a crucial field for your reporting, you can assign it to an incompletion log for the particular sales order to ensure no sales order may be saved or further processed until the order reason has been completed. For more information on incompletion logs see Chapter 4.

Defining Purchase Order Types for Sales Documents

This is particularly useful for sales analyses. One is able to create a default list of order reasons to enable order capturing to determine whether the sales document originated from a telephone call or mail shot, or even to indicate the sale originated from the Internet.

This is a useful grouping term, as seen in Figure 3-9.

Sales Order Item Categories and Determination

The sales item category is one of the most important fields in the SAP sales order. It controls the sales document flow and also impacts the schedule line category. The item category of the sales order affects the delivery and finally impacts the billing process as well. Keeping to our basic sales flow, we will look at the integration of the item category into the following document flow: TA (order) → LF (delivery) → F2 (billing).

Defining Item Categories

Unlike the sales document type, which is entered manually into the sales order at order creation, the item category is automatically determined by the system. It is then able to be changed manually in the sales document, if required.

Menu Path   SAP Customizing Implementation Guide | Sales and Distribution | Sales | Sales Documents | Sales Document Item | Define Item Categories

Unlike the sales document type, which is entered manually into the sales order at order creation, the item category is automatically determined by the system. It is then able to be changed manually in the sales document, if required.

To create a new item category, select the item category that closely resembles your requirement. Then click the Copy button, and change the key to begin with a Y or a Z. As in the sales document type creation, you will be prompted with a dialog box (as seen in the next illustration) asking if this item is valid for copy control. Select Yes to ensure the same

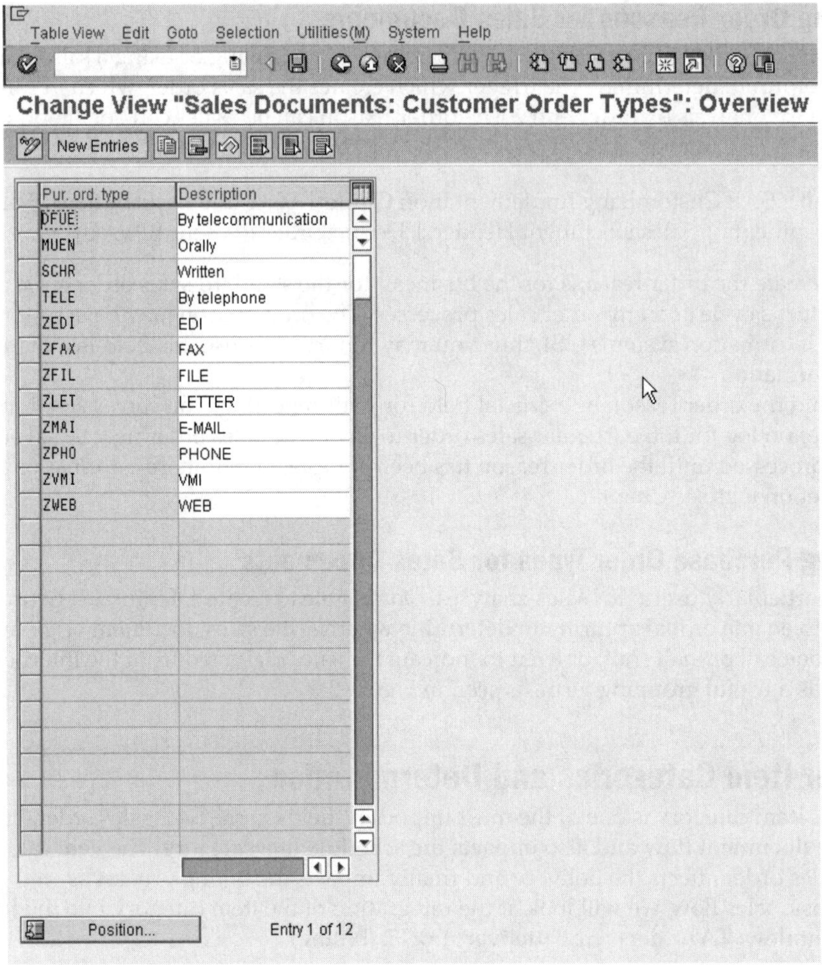

Table View Edit Goto Selection Utilities(M) System Help
Change View "Sales Documents: Customer Order Types": Overview
New Entries
Pur. ord. type
Description
DFUE By telecommunication
MUEN Orally
SCHR Written
TELE By telephone
ZEDI EDI
ZFAX FAX
ZFIL FILE
ZLET LETTER
ZMAI E-MAIL
ZPHO PHONE
ZVMI VMI
ZWEB WEB
Position...
Entry 1 of 12

FIGURE 3-9 Sales purchase order types

copy rules in existence for the item you used as a reference will be replicated for your new item category.

Dependent entries for copying control
Item category: Z_TN -Standard Item -
Is this entry also relevant for copying control?
Yes
No

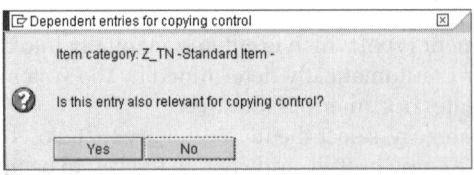

On saving your item category you will be prompted with a dialog box as seen in Figure 3-10, which shows the tables that have been automatically updated due to the creation of this item category, including those relevant for its copy control rules.

By using the standard item category TAN and by focusing on specific parts of the item category, we will highlight the impacts of the configuration for each field in the item category in mySAP ERP.

The business data of the item category, as seen in Figure 3-11, controls the following:

- The item type is the controlling indicator to the system; for standard items, leave the field blank.

- The completion rule is used to determine when the item is deemed to be complete. For standard processing this too can be left blank. However, should you wish to utilize these rules you must ensure you have set the update document flow indicator in copy control (see "Copy Control," later in this chapter). You may use the completion rule if you use call-off orders for contracts for example. If the contract is for 1000 units, each time you create an order, the open quantity is adjusted for the new order. So if you create an order for 150 units, the open quantity on the contract becomes 850. The contract is complete either with the first order reference, but usually when the full quantity has been referenced.

- The special stock indicator should be set for items that are processed as special stock. For example, should you use consignment stock at your customer's site this indicator should read W. For standard processing, it may be left blank.

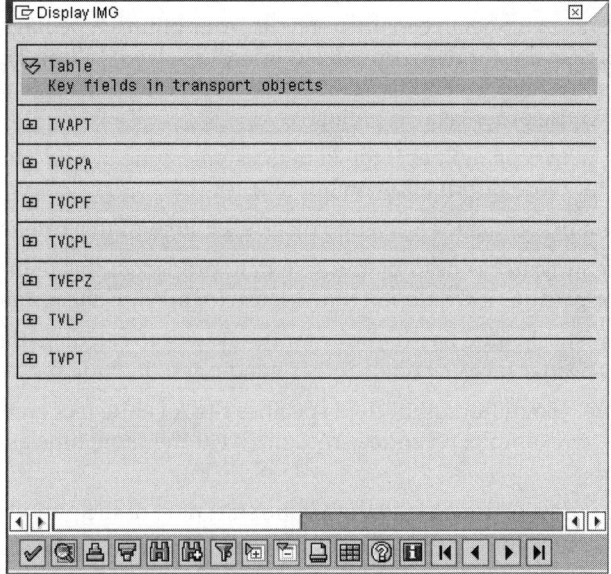

Copyright by SAP AG

FIGURE 3-10 Tables automatically updated from item category creation

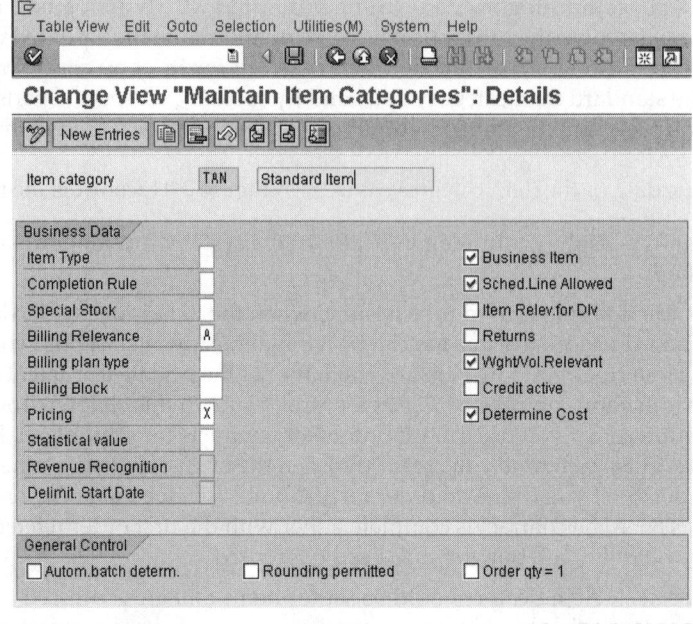

Figure 3-11   Business data and general control field settings in the configuration of an item category

- Billing relevance works in conjunction with your billing type flags to determine if this item is relevant for delivery-related or order-related billing. Thus, setting this as A indicates this item is valid for delivery-related billing. Items that don't have a delivery will use order-related billing.

- The billing plan type defines if the item does milestone or periodic billing. (See Chapter 7 for more information on billing.)

- The billing block indicator is used to block each item of this category for billing.

- The pricing indicator is used by the system to propose if this item category is relevant for pricing. It would not make sense to indicate a text item for pricing.

- Use the statistical value flag if you want the system to calculate the total values of all items at header level, or on the other hand not to include the value of the item.

- The revenue recognition input field specifies the revenue recognition category for this item—for example, revenue is recognized at the same time as the invoice was created.

- Delimit start date is used to determine the start date of the period in which revenues are to be recognized.

- Business item is used to flag if the system should allow the item business data to be different from the business data at the header level. (Business data is a group of sales details, shipping details, and billing details. It is found at both item and header level and stored in table VBKD.)

- Schedule line allowed is used to determine if this sales item category is allowed a schedule line. This is one of the most important item settings as it determines if the item is relevant for schedule lines and therefore delivering or not. Refer to schedule line categories later on in this chapter.

- Item relevant for delivery indicates to the system to copy the item from the sales order into the delivery note. This, however, should not be set for standard items, as a standard item would have a schedule line and thus be able to be determined as delivery-relevant. This flag should be used to indicate to the system to copy such items as text items into a delivery.

- Should the item be a returns item category—for example, REN—then the returns flag should be set.

- Weight/volume relevant is an indicator that tells the system if weight and volume are relevant and if the system should calculate these fields for these characteristics.

- Credit active indicates that this item is relevant for credit control updating and credit statistics. (For more information on credit management, see Chapter 10.)

- Determine cost is an indicator that tells the system to use the condition type VPRS on the pricing procedure to indicate the cost price of this item. (For more information on pricing, see Chapter 8.)

The general control area seen in Figure 3-11 includes the following settings:

- Automatic batch determination indicates to the system to carry out batch determination for this item at the time of the sales order. (Batch determination is the process whereby one allocates a material batch to an item. This can happen at the time of the order, at the time of the delivery, or even in the warehouse management module. A batch refers to a quantity of material that shares the same characteristics. For example, if you are making blue paint, the color might be slightly variable based on the production batch, so customers may want to order the blue paint from the same batch.)

- Rounding is set in the customer material information record or the material master record and allows the system to round up or down the order quantity to make, for example, a specific package size. A materials base unit of measure is one unit. However the sales order must create orders in layers, where one layer is equivalent to five units; thus, the system will round the order quantity from say two units up to five units in the sales order.

- Order quantity is equal to one. This is self-explanatory. Check this indicator should you wish your sales item to be limited to a quantity of one per line item.

Transaction flow data (shown in Figure 3-12) controls the following:

- The incompletion procedure at line item level. This is explained in Chapter 4.

- The partner and text determination procedures are in Chapter 4.

- The item category statistics group is used by the logistics information system to indicate which item categories are relevant for statistical updating—for example, for sales reporting. You can assign statistics groups to each of the following: Item category,

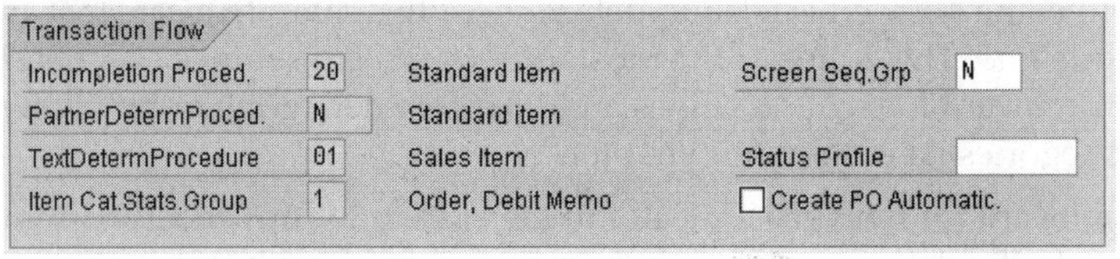

FIGURE 3-12   Transaction flow data in an item category

sales document type, customer material, shipment type, and transportation service agent. When you generate statistics in the logistics information system, the system uses the combination of specified statistics groups to determine the appropriate update sequence. This update sequence in turn determines for which fields the statistics are generated.

- Screen sequence group is used to control which screens you see when displaying a line item.

- The status profile is a key that indicates a staus profile as discussed in Chapter 4. A status profile may be assigned at header and item level.

- Create purchase order automatically is an indicator for Application Link Enabling to enable automatic creation of a purchase requisition and purchase order for third-party items.

Figure 3-13 shows the settings refering to a bill of materials or a configured item and it is best to leave this section until we cover bills of materials in this Chapter 5. Figure 3-13 also depicts configuration settings relevant for value contracts:

- The field for value contract material, may have a material number entered here. Should the user not enter a material at the line item level for a value contract, the system can then copy this material into the value contract item. This is useful for copying the material-relevant data such as tax determination into the value contract.

- Should the value contracts target quantity be exceeded, the system will respond according to the indicator set at the contract release control field.

- Service management has the repair procedure setting, which indicates the repair procedure that will be used for this item, which in turn determines which sub-items may be created in a sales order.

- Billing form determines how resource-related billing items are invoiced.

- Dip profile, the Dynamic Item Processor Profile, is used to calculate and summarize items to be billed for resource-related billing.

This completes the configuration settings of a sales item category. This sales item category is then used by the system to determine the schedule line category. It is also used by the system in conjunction with the MRP type of the material to determine the requirement type or requirements class, which primarily controls the excecution of the availability check and the transfer of requirements.

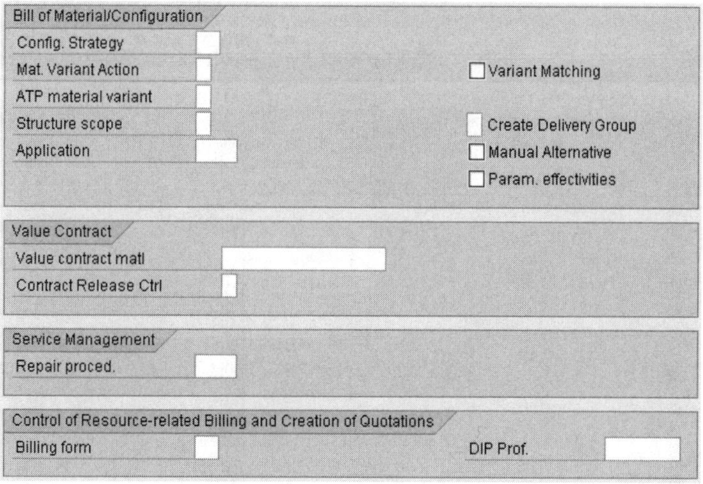

Bill of Material/Configuration	
Config. Strategy	
Mat. Variant Action	☐ Variant Matching
ATP material variant	
Structure scope	☐ Create Delivery Group
Application	☐ Manual Alternative
	☐ Param. effectivities

Value Contract
Value contract matl
Contract Release Ctrl

Service Management
Repair proced.

Control of Resource-related Billing and Creation of Quotations
Billing form   DIP Prof.

FIGURE 3-13 Sales item category BOM, value contract, service management, and resource-related billing settings

Item Category Determination

The system uses the item category group field of the material master record as the main indicator to determine the item category in the sales order. The system uses this field in combination with the sales document type, being processed, for example, as TA. It is these two indicators plus an indicator setting the usage of the item category (for example, is this item a text item), plus an indicator determining if another higher-level item exists that will determine the item category in the sales order document. This is shown in Figure 3-14.

Item categories are created first and then assigned. To assign the item categories, follow the menu path.

Menu Path   SAP Customizing Implementation Guide | Sales and Distribution | Sales | Sales Documents | Sales Document Item | Assign Item Categories

The item category determination may be changed manually. The allowed manual assignments shown on screen is three values, as seen in Figure 3-14. However, if you select the line and select details you will be able to define up to 11 manual values.

Item Category Groups

It is possible to create your own item category groups (the component of the material master that determines the item category in the sales order). To create an item category group, follow the menu path

Menu Path   SAP Customizing Implementation Guide | Sales and Distribution | Sales | Sales Documents | Sales Document Item | Define Item Category Groups

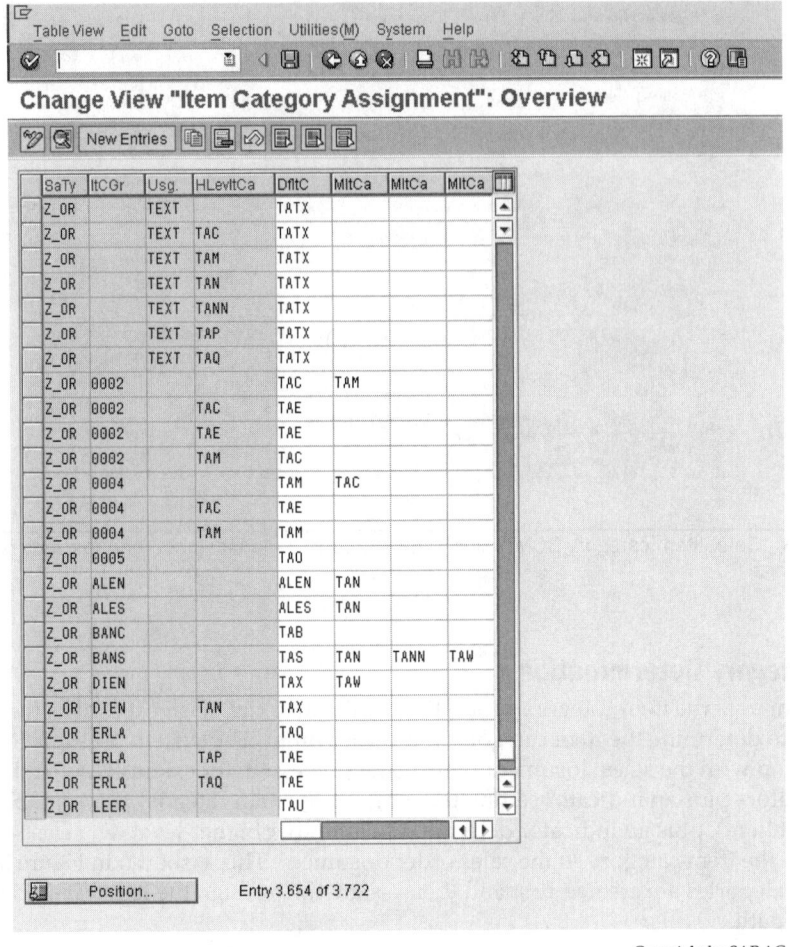

Table View Edit Goto Selection Utilities(M) System Help

Change View "Item Category Assignment": Overview

New Entries

SaTy	ItCGr	Usg.	HLevItCa	DfltC	MltCa	MltCa	MltCa
Z_OR		TEXT		TATX			
Z_OR		TEXT	TAC	TATX			
Z_OR		TEXT	TAM	TATX			
Z_OR		TEXT	TAN	TATX			
Z_OR		TEXT	TANN	TATX			
Z_OR		TEXT	TAP	TATX			
Z_OR		TEXT	TAQ	TATX			
Z_OR	0002			TAC	TAM		
Z_OR	0002		TAC	TAE			
Z_OR	0002		TAE	TAE			
Z_OR	0002		TAM	TAC			
Z_OR	0004			TAM	TAC		
Z_OR	0004		TAC	TAE			
Z_OR	0004		TAM	TAM			
Z_OR	0005			TAO			
Z_OR	ALEN			ALEN	TAN		
Z_OR	ALES			ALES	TAN		
Z_OR	BANC			TAB			
Z_OR	BANS			TAS	TAN	TANN	TAW
Z_OR	DIEN			TAX	TAW		
Z_OR	DIEN		TAN	TAX			
Z_OR	ERLA			TAQ			
Z_OR	ERLA		TAP	TAE			
Z_OR	ERLA		TAQ	TAE			
Z_OR	LEER			TAU			

Position...   Entry 3.654 of 3.722

Copyright by SAP AG

FIGURE 3-14   Item category determination

These may then be assigned to a material type as a default. Thus each material you create that is based on a particuler material type can have a defaulted item category, which can be manually changeable in the material master record. This may be allocated by following the next menu path.

Menu Path   SAP Customizing Implementation Guide | Sales and Distribution | Sales | Sales Documents | Sales Document Item | Define Default Values For Material Type

Item Category Usage

An item categories usage is defined by SAP when creating a sales order. The system determines, for example, that the usage refers to a text item as opposed to a deliverable item when you enter test in the order item rather than a material number. Based on this usage, the system will use the item category determination to propose an item category.

Higher-Level Item

The higher-level item is another determining factor in item category determination. The system finds a higher-level item category by looking at any linkage of items and then tracing back to the main item category.

For example: A bill of materials (BOM) is a material that is made up of many component materials. An example could be a computer, which could be sold as a computer but represented on the sales order as a monitor, a hard drive, a keyboard, and a mouse.

In a BOM you have a header item, usually an item category group LUMF. This would promote a standard item category of, for example, TAP (as seen in Figure 3-15). A sub-item is then proposed as an item category TAN (as seen in Figure 3-15, second line).

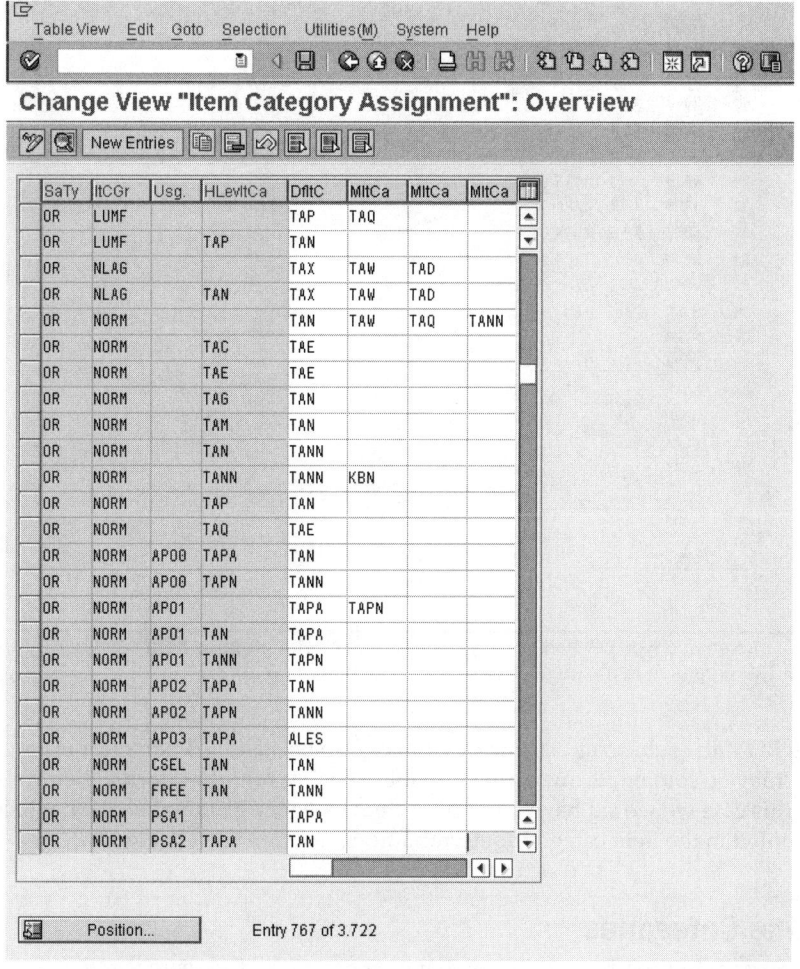

Change View "Item Category Assignment": Overview

SaTy	ItCGr	Usg.	HLevItCa	DfltC	MltCa	MltCa	MltCa
OR	LUMF			TAP	TAQ		
OR	LUMF		TAP	TAN			
OR	NLAG			TAX	TAW	TAD	
OR	NLAG		TAN	TAX	TAW	TAD	
OR	NORM			TAN	TAW	TAQ	TANN
OR	NORM		TAC	TAE			
OR	NORM		TAE	TAE			
OR	NORM		TAG	TAN			
OR	NORM		TAM	TAN			
OR	NORM		TAN	TANN			
OR	NORM		TANN	TANN	KBN		
OR	NORM		TAP	TAN			
OR	NORM		TAQ	TAE			
OR	NORM	APO0	TAPA	TAN			
OR	NORM	APO0	TAPN	TANN			
OR	NORM	APO1		TAPA	TAPN		
OR	NORM	APO1	TAN	TAPA			
OR	NORM	APO1	TANN	TAPN			
OR	NORM	APO2	TAPA	TAN			
OR	NORM	APO2	TAPN	TANN			
OR	NORM	APO3	TAPA	ALES			
OR	NORM	CSEL	TAN	TAN			
OR	NORM	FREE	TAN	TANN			
OR	NORM	PSA1		TAPA			
OR	NORM	PSA2	TAPA	TAN			

Position...   Entry 767 of 3.722

FIGURE 3-15   Sales doc type OR and item category group LUMF propose item category TAP. Sales doc type OR and item category group LUMF and higher item category of TAP propose item category TAN.

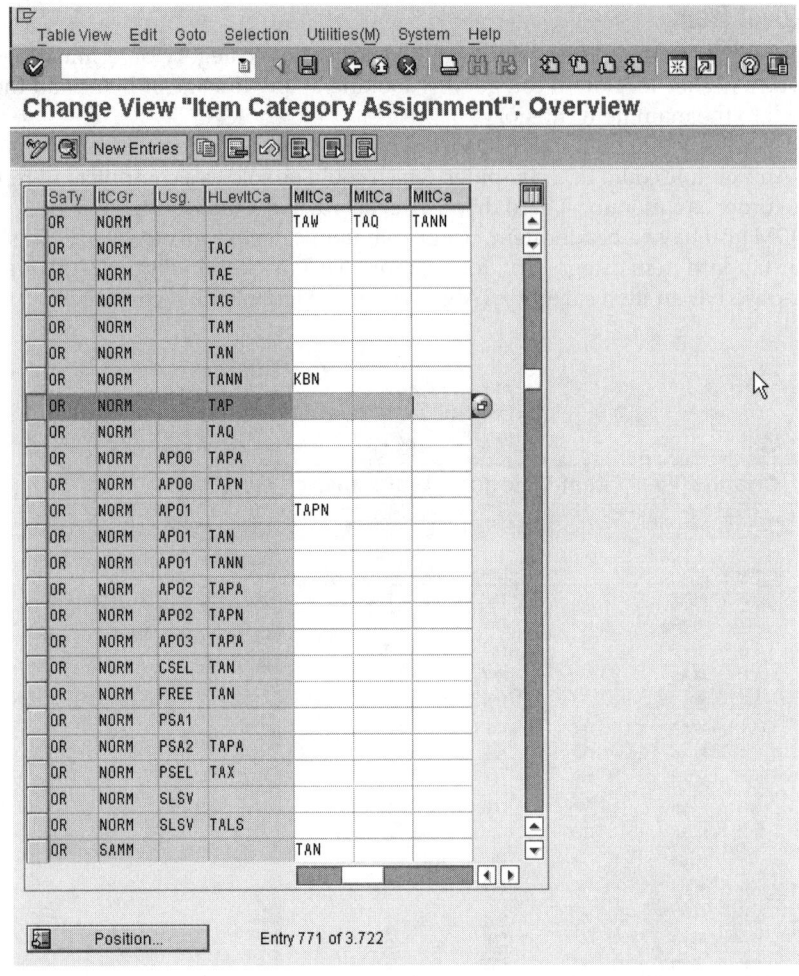

FIGURE 3-16 Sales doc type OR and item category group NORM propose item category TAN. Even higher level TAP proposes item category TAN (see highlighted line).

In the BOM the sub-items assigned to it may also be standard parts (for example, a keyboard may be sold on its own), thus capable of being resold as normal items if sold alone. In this case we would have a standard item category group of NORM, which would be represented in the item category determination structure seen in Figure 3-16.

Schedule Line Categories

An item category controls how the document item functions. each item is split into one or more schedule lines. These schedule lines represent when the item will be delivered. For example, an order for 100 units may be delivered over four different weeks—25 units each week.

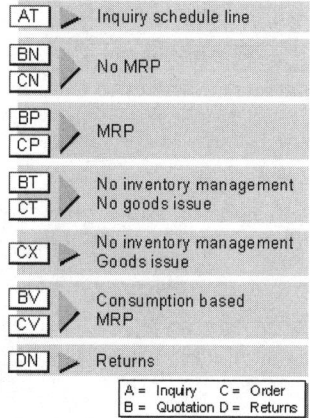

Copyright by SAP AG

FIGURE 3-17   Schedule line category behavior control

The schedule line category controls the materials requirements planning and the execution in shipping. The schedule line category is determined based upon the item category and the MRP (materials requirements planning) type on the material master record of the item. It is possible for items with a schedule line to not be relevant for a delivery. Figure 3-17 depicts a basic overview of the standard functions of a few schedule line categories.

Defining Schedule Line Category

Keeping to our basic sales flow, we will look at the integration of the schedule line category into the following document flow: TA (order) → LF (delivery) → F2 (billing).

Menu Path   SAP Customizing Implementation Guide ∣ Sales and Distribution ∣ Sales ∣ Sales Documents ∣ Schedule Lines ∣ Define Schedule Line Categories [VOV6]

Represented in the IMG (IMG-Implementation Guide) are only two assignments: First, to create or define the schedule line category, as seen in Figure 3-18, and second, to assign it. We will first look at the schedule line category control and its characteristics.

This schedule line category is the standard CP, which is relevant for MRP. It has an alphanumeric two-digit key as well as a short description.

As seen in Figure 3-18, the business data section of the schedule line category defines the following:

- Whether a delivery block is automatically created for this schedule line category, (remember a delivery block can be set as automatic for any of the following):
  - Sales document type
  - Schedule line category
  - Delivery type
  - Shipping activity, such as picking and goods issue

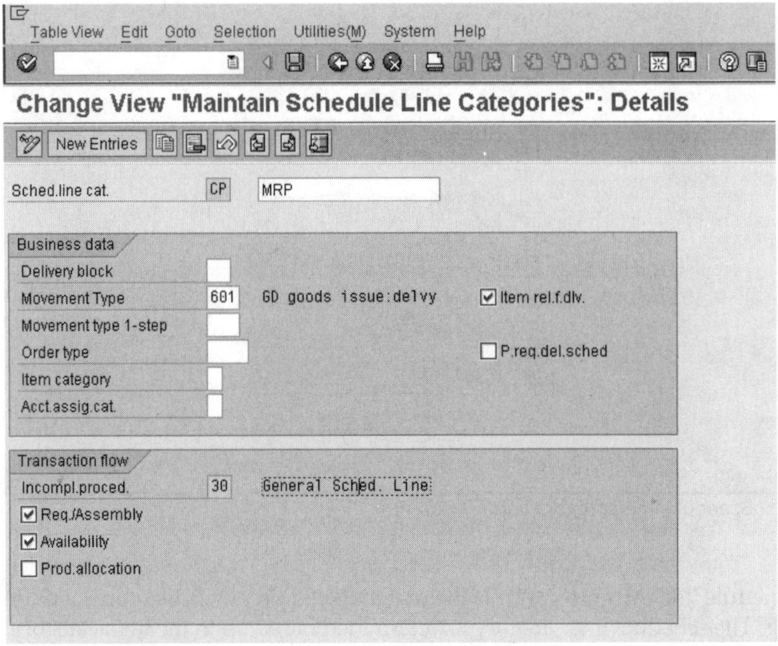

Copyright by SAP AG

FIGURE 3-18   Define schedule line category

- For every movement of stock in the SAP system there is a movement type, which represents the inventory movement. For example, a movement of stock between plants has a movement type which is different from the movement of stock for a customer sale, which in turn is different from the movement type for receipt of stock for a customer return. This field indicates which SAP inventory movement to use for schedule line category CP. CP is assigned to item category TAN, which is a standard item category representative of a material to be sold to a customer. The goods movement is a movement from our stock as a sale to our customer. It would be correct to leave this field blank for items for which no stock movement happens. Likewise, should this schedule line be assigned to a return item category, you should ensure the movement type here is relevant for returns, such as a goods receipt.

- The movement type 1-step is used when two goods movements need to happen for a schedule line category—for example, in a stock transfer (the issue of stock from one plant and another movement for the receipt of the stock into another plant).

- The order type is the assignment of the purchase requisition type to the schedule line, which allows the system to automatically create a purchase requisition for this schedule line category. This is used for third-party sales—for example, if the customer places the order with you, but you need to buy the material from your supplier for delivery to the customer. The system can automatically create the purchase requisition to purchase the material from the supplier.

- Item category is not to be confused with the sales document item category. This is the item category of the purchasing document or purchase requisition.
- The account assignment category is used to determine which account assignment is necessary for the item.
- The item relevant for delivery indicator must be set to indicate to the system that this schedule line category is delivery-relevant.
- The purchase requisition delivery scheduling is an indicator you must set, should you want the system to re-determine the delivery dates of the schedule line based on the expected receipt times generated from the purchase requisition.

The transaction flow data of the schedule line is depicted as follows:

- The incompletion procedure is used to assign the fields that render a schedule line incomplete; it is covered more in Chapter 4.
- The requirements/assembly indicator is used to transfer the requirements for the material to production (for materials produced in house, or to procurement for material purchased from a supplier). This demand will be shown in the stock requirements list, which we will cover in Chapter 5.
- The availability check indicator is used by the system to determine if this item is relevant for availability checking. This will be covered more in Chapter 5.
- Should product allocation be active for this schedule line category, set the product allocation indicator as active.

When creating the schedule line category, ensure you follow the SAP naming conventions; for customer objects, that requires the prefix Z or Y. In the standard SAP R/3 System, the naming conventions of the key of the schedule line categories are as follows:

First Character of the Key	Usage
A	Inquiry
B	Quotation
C	Sales order
D	Returns

Second Character of the Key	Usage
T	No inventory management, e.g., services
X	No inventory management with goods issue
N	No planning
P	MRP
V	Consumption-based planning

Thus our earlier example of CP stands for "sales order with MRP."

Schedule Line Category Determination

The schedule line category determination is carried out automatically by the system on the basis of the following: The item category of the sales order line item plus the MRP type found on the material master, MRP 1 screen, of the material master record. (See Figure 3-19.)

Menu Path SAP Customizing Implementation Guide | Sales and Distribution | Sales | Sales Documents | Schedule Lines | Assign Schedule Line Categories

The schedule line category may be changed manually to any of the manual options entered in this screen. The number of manual assignments shown on screen is four values, as seen in Figure 3-19. However, if you select the line and select details you will be able to define up to nine manual values.

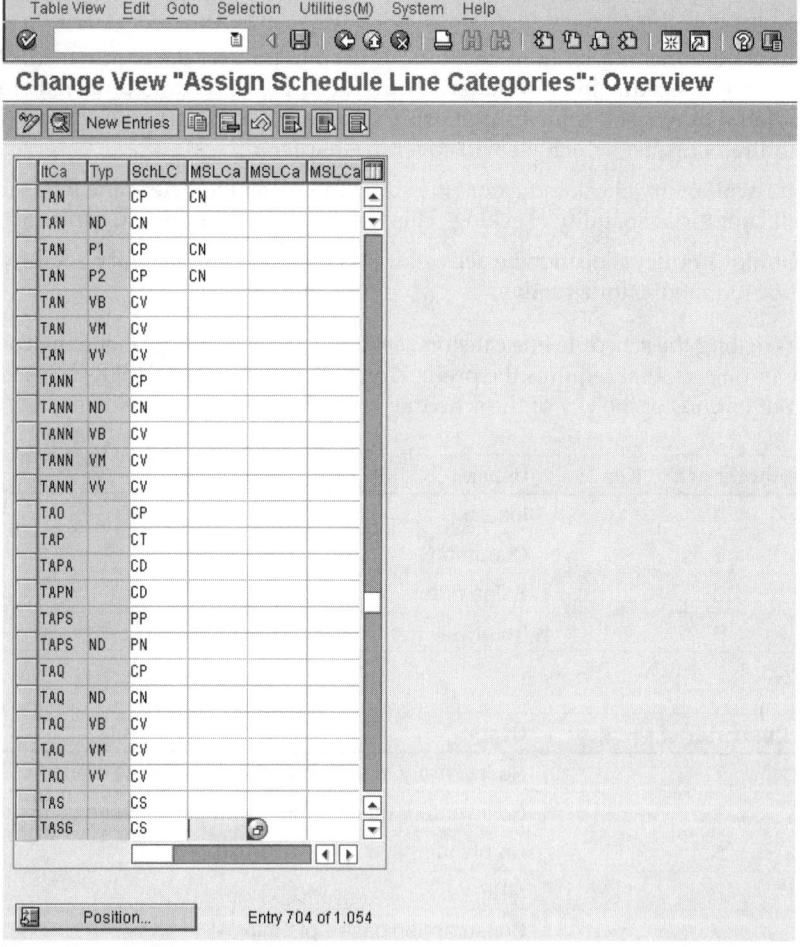

Copyright by SAP AG

FIGURE 3-19 Schedule line category determination

Summary Overview of a Sales Document

We have now been able to configure the basic backbone of the sales document. We have looked at the customer and material master data, the sales document types, and the determination rules for item categories and schedule lines. We have also seen what these various elements control. This is all based upon the standard sales transaction flow (TA (order) → LF (delivery) → F2 (billing)).

To create a sales order using the sales document you have just created, use the following menu path.

Menu Path   SAP Menu I Logistics I Sales and Distribution I Sales I Order I [VA01] - Create

Unfortunately, as this book is aimed at the SAP consultant and not the user, we will not go into detail about how to create a sales order.

There are many fields on the sales order and accessing them is not difficult. Use the ABAP Dictionary (transaction code [SE11]) with the table name to see the fields—for example, VBAK for the sales header.

Table 3-1 is a list of fields with a short explanation on how the field is updated in the sales document. This includes the most important table and field names as well as an indication of where the entry in the sales order would have originated from. This makes a valuable reference for analysis and control.

Organizational Data	Description	Origination
VBAK-VKORG	Sales organization	Chosen
VBAK-VTWEG	Distribution channel	Chosen
VBAK-SPART	Division	Chosen
VBAK-AUART	Sales document type	Chosen
VBAK-KALSM	Pricing procedure	Customer indicator plus document indicator plus sales area
Header Data	**Description**	**Origination**
KUAGV-KUNNR	Sold to party	Customer master record
VBAK-VKBUR	Sales office	Customer master record
VBAK-VKGRP	Sales group	Customer master record
VBKD-PRSDT	Pricing date	Entered, copied, or automatic
VBAK-AUDAT	Document date	System entry
VBAK-AUGRU	Order reason	Entered
VBAK-WAERK	Document currency	Customer master record
VBKD-KONDA	Price group	Customer master record
VBKD-BZIRK	Sales district	Customer master record
VBKD-KDGRP	Customer group	Customer master record
VBAK-VSBED	Shipping condition	Customer master record
VBKD-INCO1	Incoterms	Customer master record
VBKD-ZTERM	Payment terms	Customer master record

TABLE 3-1 Sales Order Table and Field Names (*Continued*)

VBAK-LANDTX	Departure country	Country of plant
VBAK-STCEG_I	Destination country	Country of ship to party
VBKD-PERFK	Billing schedule	Customer master record
VBKD-ABSSC	Payment guarantee procedure	Customer indicator plus document indicator
VBKD-BSTKD	Purchase order number	Entered
VBAK-KVGR1 through 5	Additional data	Customer master record
Item Data	**Description**	**Origination**
VBAP-PSTYV	Item category	Automatic
RV45A-KWMENG	Order quantity	Entered
VBAP-MATNR	Material	Entered
VBAP-MATWA	Material entered	Entered
VBAP-CHARG	Batch number	Automatic
VBAP-PMATN	Price reference material	Material master record
VBAP-PRODH	Product hierarchy	Material master record
VBAP-MATKL	Material group	Material master record
VBAP-WERKS	Plant	Cust. material info record or customer or material master
VBAP-VSTEL	Shipping point	Plant plus shipping conditions plus loading group
VBAP-ROUTE	Route	Automatic or manual
VBAP-LPRIO	Delivery priority	Customer material info record or customer master
VBAP-KDMAT	Customer material	Customer material info record
VBAP-MVGR1 through to 5	Additional data	Material master record
VBAP-POSNR	Item number	Automatic
Schedule Line	**Description**	**Origination**
VBEP-POSNR	Schedule line	Automatic
VBEP-ETENR	Schedule line number	Automatic
VBEP-ETTYP	Schedule line category	Automatic
RV45A-ETDAT	Delivery date	Automatic or manual
VBEP-WMENG	Order quantity	entered
VBEP-BMENG	Confirmed quantity	Automatic
VBEP-MBDAT	Material availability date	Automatic
VBEP-LDDAT	Loading date	Automatic
VBEP-WADAT	Proposed goods issue date	Automatic, can be changed in delivery
VBEP-TDDAT	Transportation date	Automatic
VBEP-VSTEl	Shipping point	Plant plus shipping point plus loading group
VBEP-BWART	Movement type	Schedule line category

TABLE 3-1 Sales Order Table and Field Names (*Continued*)

Copy Control

Copy control in sales order processing is used by the system to determine what document types, item categories, and schedule line categories (the three tiers of the sales order) may be copied into each other—for example, when you are copying from a quote to an order, from an order to a delivery, or from a delivery to an invoice. This permits all three tiers of data to be copied into sales, delivery and billing documents (including contracts, schedule agreements etc).

For Sales Documents
Use this option to control the copying between sales documents such as contracts, quotes, and orders.

Menu Paths   SAP Customizing Implementation Guide | Sales and Distribution | Sales | Maintain Copy Control for Sales Documents | Copying Control: Sales Document to Sales Document [VTAA]

SAP Customizing Implementation Guide | Sales and Distribution | Sales | Maintain Copy Control for Sales Documents | Copying Control: Billing Document to Sales Document [VTAF]

For Delivery Documents
Use this option to control copy from the sales order to the delivery.

Menu Path   SAP Customizing Implementation Guide | Logistics Execution | Shipping | Copying Control | Specify Copy Control for Deliveries [VTLA]

For Billing Documents
Use this option to control copy from the sales order (for sales order–related billing) or the delivery (for delivery-related billing) into the billing document.

Menu Paths   SAP Customizing Implementation Guide | Sales and Distribution | Billing | Billing Documents | Maintain Copying Control For Billing Documents | Copying control: Sales document to billing document [VTFA]

SAP Customizing Implementation Guide | Sales and Distribution | Billing | Billing Documents | Maintain Copying Control For Billing Documents| Copying control: Delivery document to billing document [VTFL]

SAP Customizing Implementation Guide | Sales and Distribution | Billing | Billing Documents | Maintain Copying Control For Billing Documents | Copying control: Billing document to billing document [VTFF]

Sales Process Overview

It cannot be stressed how important it is to take careful note of your copy control rules. The following common scenarios give examples of the copying control you will need. These are in no way the only process flow models you will have or need. However, they serve to highlight the basic principals of copying control.

Scenario A (Standard Sales Order Process)
Quotation (represented by a Sales Document type) → Sales Order (represented by a Sales Document type) → Delivery (represented by a Delivery Document type) → Invoice (represented by a Billing Document type)

This basic scenario will need the copying rules set up to allow a sales document type to be copied into another sales document type (Quotation → Sales Order); as well as a sales document type to be copied into a delivery document (Sales Order → Delivery); and finally a delivery document into a billing document (Delivery → Invoice).

Scenario B (Returns Process)

Invoice (represented by a Billing Document type)→ Returns Sales Order (represented by a Sales Document type)→ Returns Delivery (represented by a Delivery Document type)→ Credit for Returns (represented by a Billing Document type)

Please refer to "The Returns Process," later in this chapter, for further explanation.

Scenario C (Credit Memo Process)

Invoice (represented by a Billing Document type) → Credit Memo Request (represented by a Sales Document type)→ Credit Memo (represented by a Billing Document type)

Please refer to "The Credit Process," later in this chapter, for further explanation.

Copy Control for Sales Documents

At the header level you can see the document types that can be copied into one another (as shown in Figure 3-20)—for example, OR into OR or (TA) into (TA)(German). This is an SAP standard setting that is used in order to create a sales document with reference to another sales document—for example, when a customer wants to repeat an order.

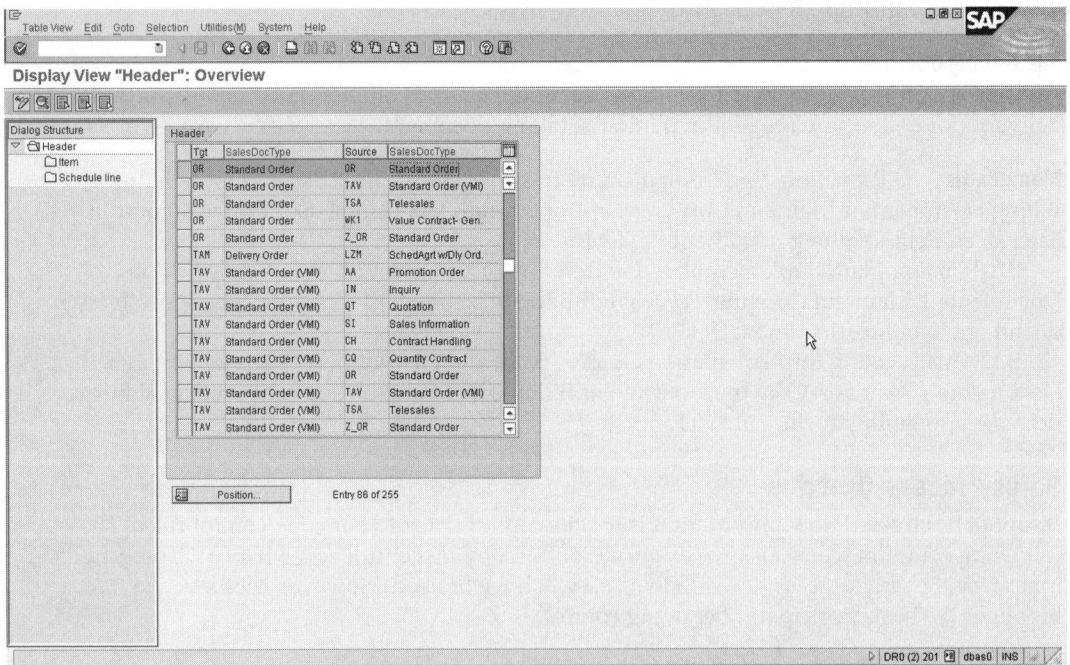

FIGURE 3-20   Sales document header copy control

Say, for example, you wish to create a sales order without having to re-create all the item lines. You can simply copy the data by creating the order with reference to another sales order. In the procedure where we defined a product proposal you set up the copying rules allowing a product proposal to be used as a reference when creating a sales order.

The header data as well as the item data and schedule line must be configured to be copied into or referenced from.

When you copy a sales document type to a new sales document type, the system automatically creates the copying control rule to be equivalent to the item you are copying. For example, if you create a new sales order document type ZZOR, made with reference from the standard document type OR, the system will automatically copy all item categories and schedule line categories that were previously assigned to OR and assign them as relevant to ZZOR. Similarly, when you copy item categories and schedule line categories, the system will copy the copy control rules at the same time (if you indicated that you want to copy them).

By selecting the document type we would like to configure or change, and then clicking the Details button, as shown here, we are able to view the configuration for the header transfer of data.

Copyright by SAP AG

Copying rules are set up at the header level for sales, delivery, and billing documents. They are set up at item level for sales, delivery, and billing documents. However, they are only set up at schedule line level for sales document types. This is because you don't have schedule lines in deliveries or invoices.

Sales Document to Sales Document

In Figure 3-21, we see the header copy control rules for sales document to sales document.

- We have the source document type OR and the target document type OR.

- The copying requirements are rules or certain criteria that must be met before the copy can take place. This example has the copying requirements 002 Header-diff. customer. (Refer to requirements and formulas in Chapter 8.)

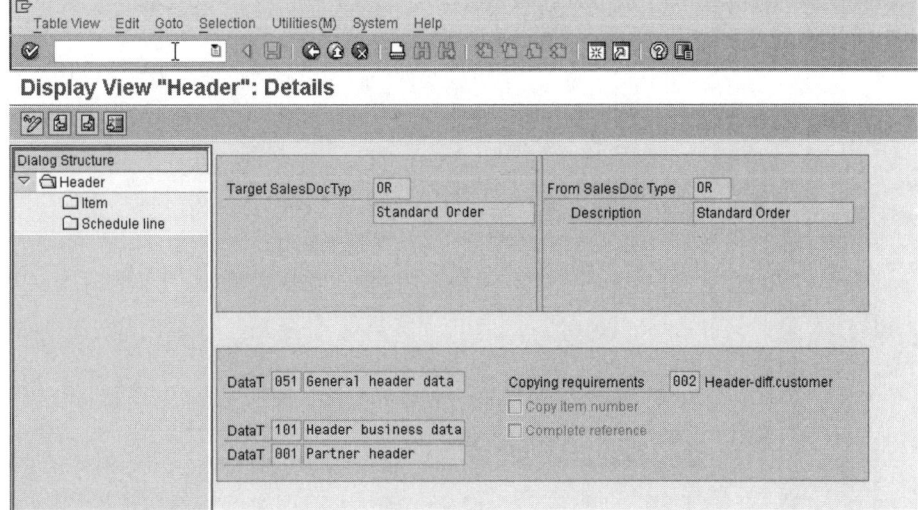

Copyright by SAP AG

FIGURE 3-21   Header copy control rules for sales document to sales document

- There are three data transfer routines:
  - The data transfer at header level "DataT" in this example has the setting "051" "General header data." This copies the general header data between sales documents.
  - The data transfer at header level "DataT" in this example has the setting "101" "Header business data." This copies the header business data between sales documents.
  - The data transfer at header level "DataT" in this example has the setting "001" "Partner header." This copies the header partners between sales documents.
- Copy item number is used when you copy the entire previous document into a new document; the same header and item numbers you had will be copied. If you don't use this option and you copy only some of the items from the reference document, the item numbers will be re-sequenced.
- Complete reference is useful in copying legally approved quotations into a sales document. It restricts the user into copying the entire document, as opposed to partially copying data.

If you double-click the Item folder under the dialog structure on the left, you will see the screen shown in Figure 3-22.

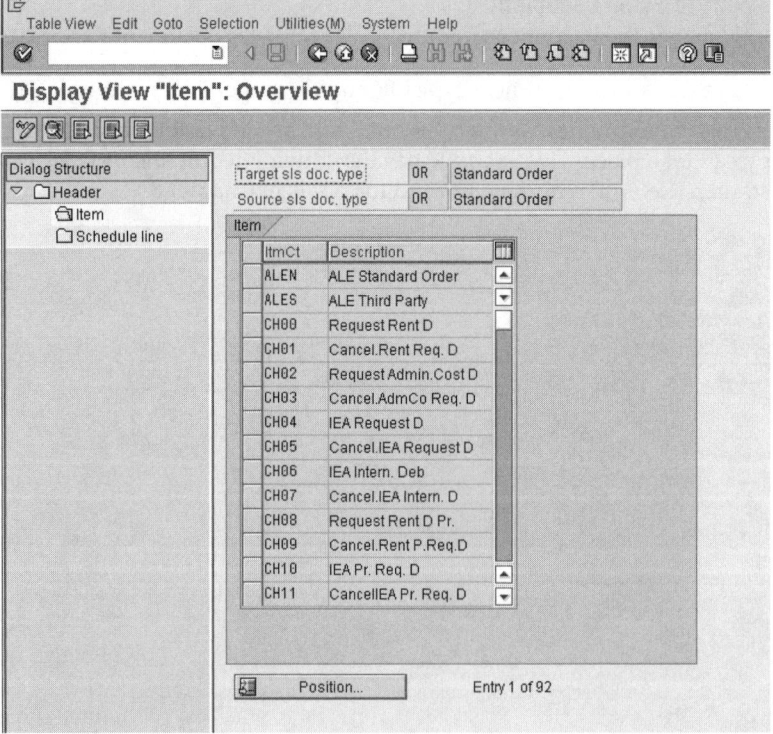

FIGURE 3-22   Item copy control for sales document OR to OR

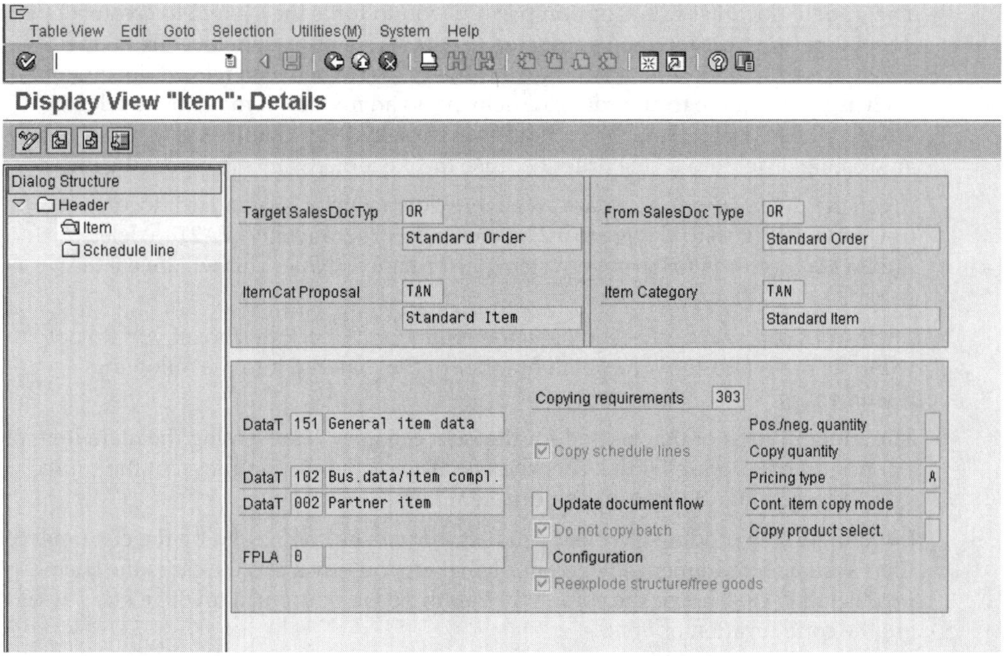

Copyright by SAP AG

FIGURE 3-23 Item category TAN copy control rules for sales document OR to OR

By selecting item category TAN and clicking the Details button, we can see the copy control rules pertaining to TAN in Figure 3-23.

- We have the source document type OR with item category TAN and the target document type OR with item category TAN.

- The copying requirements are rules or certain criteria that must be met before the copy can take place. This example has 303 for the copying requirements; if you select the match code you will see the description as "always an item." (Refer to requirements and formulas in Chapter 8.)

- There are three data transfer routines. Our example has the following:

  - DataT has the value "151" "General item data."

  - DataT has the value "102" "Bus.data/item compl."

  - DataT has the value "002" "Partner item."

- The FPLA field is a routine that checks that certain billing plan requirements have been met and then copies relevant billing plan data into the proceeding document.

- The copy schedule lines check box must be checked should you wish the data of this item's schedule line to be transferred to the new document. Be sure to also create the schedule line copy control rules in this case.

- The update document flow option permits you to force the system to create a document flow record when a transfer of data happens at item level from one document to another. Document flow is always useful between related documents—such as from a quote to an order to a delivery to an invoice. It may not be relevant when you use copying purely for data entry reasons—for example, when you copy an existing order into a new order because the customer wants to repeat the order.

If you previously used an update document flow value of X (standard document flow) and you wish to change to a 2, you can use program SDVBFA21 to delete unnecessary records to improve system performance. (Note: This will delete the records from VBFA as well.)

- The do not copy batch checkbox is self-explanatory. Check this box if you do not want the system to copy the batch number of the material into the following document.

- The configuration option is used for the item category representing the main item of a configurable product. If this checkbox is checked the configuration of the source item is copied into the new sales document item.

(A configurable product is a basic product that can be configured by the customer to their specific requirements. For example, when you buy a car, the car is the basic product. You can choose the color, whether there is a sunroof, a tow bar, etc. These are the configuration options.)

- The reexplode structure/free goods checkbox is used when you wish the system to redetermine the bill of materials in the sales document. The system does not copy the actual BOM from one sales document into another but copies the main material and then reexplodes the BOM into its components. The table entries for copying item category TAE to TAE are no longer required and are ignored if they exist.

- The positive/negative qty option is used for document flow if you have specified the completion indicator on the item category. You can leave this field blank when copying from a sales order to another sales order. But for copying from a quote or a contract to a sales order, you may want to reduce the open quantity on the quote or contract when an order is created.

- Copy quantity is best left blank. This forces the system to copy the quantity of the field best suited for the document type being referenced. You can force the target or order quantity to be used.

- The pricing type is an extremely important field. It is worthwhile keeping this entry in mind when creating your pricing condition types. As a rule of thumb, you should have all item categories for a particular sales document with the same settings. Generally, you may use pricing type B (carry out new pricing), G (copy pricing elements unchanged and redetermine taxes), or C (copy manual pricing elements and redetermine the others).

When using condition B all manual pricing condition types are lost.

If you want to copy the sales order to the invoice without changing the sales order conditions, use pricing rule G. This will copy the pricing conditions from the order into the invoice without changing them, but will redetermine the taxes.

When using copying rule pricing type G the following condition type categories are redetermined:

D	Taxes
C	Volume-based rebate
I	Inter-company billing conditions
R	Invoice list conditions
L	Condition types with condition category L
G	Cost conditions
E	Cash discount conditions

 When copying rules are being defined, you may refer to OSS note 24832 and 26115, which I have found to be useful. Also refer to Pricing in Chapter 8.

Back to the item category copy rules:

- The cont. item copy mode option governs the copy control for materials in value contracts.
- The copy product selection option should be left blank if you wish the system to carry out a new product selection in the target document you are creating.

If you double-click the Schedule Line folder on the left side in the dialog structure, you will see a screen similar to Figure 3-24.

Now select the schedule line category and select details as shown in Figure 3-25:

- We have the source document type OR with item category TAN and schedule line category of CP, and the target document type OR with item category TAN and schedule line category of CP.
- The copying requirements are rules or certain criteria that must be met before the copy can take place. This example has 501 for the copying requirements with the description "Scheduled qty > 0." (Refer to requirements and formulas in Chapter 8.)
- Data transfer has the value "201, Gen.sched.line data."

Billing Document to Sales Document

When copying from a billing document type into a sales document type, you again have the same layout of screens, however, *without* the following

- Copy quantity
- Contract item copy
- Copy product selection
- Reexplode structure free goods

There is also no requirement to copy schedule line categories.

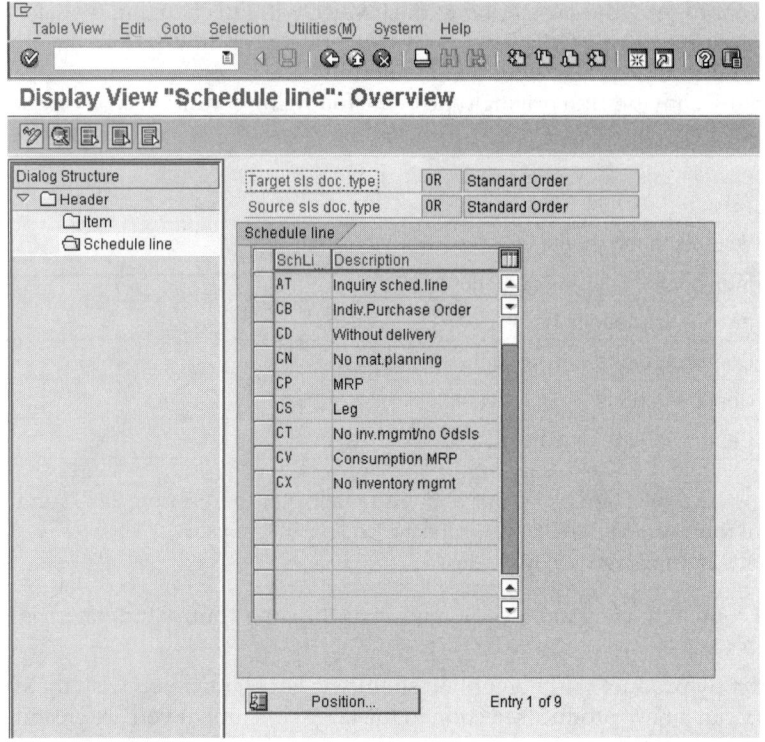

Copyright by SAP AG

FIGURE 3-24   The schedule line categories relevant for copy control between sales document OR to OR with item category TAN to TAN

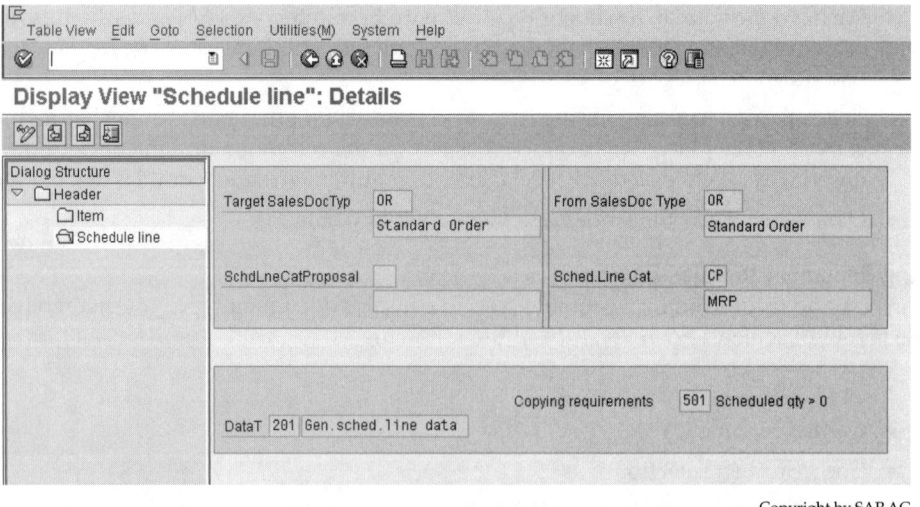

Copyright by SAP AG

FIGURE 3-25   The copy control rules for sales document type OR to sales document type OR with schedule line category CP

Sales Document to Delivery Document

When copying from a sales document into a delivery document type, you again have header data and item data but no schedule line data. The schedule line data is not copied into the delivery because the delivery item is a result of the schedule line and actually "replaces" the schedule line. For example, suppose you have an order item for 100 units and have two schedule lines—one this week for 20 items and one next week for 80 items. When you create the delivery this week, the delivery item is created for the 20 items. So the delivery item is a combination of the order item data and the schedule line dates and quantities.

Thus all the schedule line data has been used to create and form the basis of the delivery document.

Sales Document to Billing Document

The same data is required when copying from a sales document into a billing document or from a delivery document into a billing document. Using the delivery document to billing document as an example, as shown in Figure 3-26, we can see the following:

- We have the source document type LF and the target document type F2.

- The copying requirements are rules or certain criteria that must be met before the copy can take place. This example has the copying requirements set at 003 with the description "Header/dlv.-related." (Refer to requirements and formulas in Chapter 8.) That is, if the delivery is not relevant for delivery-related billing, you cannot do this copy.

- The determine export data option identifies if the export data must be redetermined in the billing document. This may be useful if there is a large time lag between the sales document, delivery document, and billing document creation.

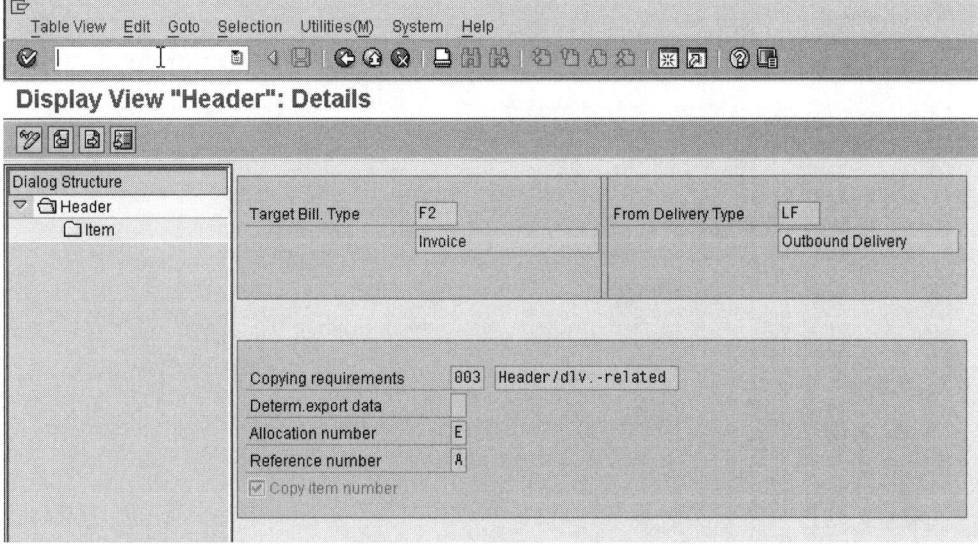

Copyright by SAP AG

FIGURE 3-26 Delivery document LF to billing document F2

- The allocation number is passed on to accounting. It makes clearing easier in Finance. In some instances you may wish the allocation number to always be the delivery number—for example, when using self-billing.

- The reference number is passed on to accounting. It makes clearing easier in Finance. In some instances you may wish the reference number to always be the delivery number—for example, when using self-billing. Or it may be the customer's purchase order number. When they get their statement, they will see this reference number next to the invoice. Since it is their own purchase order number, they know what the invoice is for.

- The copy item number checkbox is used when the source document item number is to be copied into the billing document.

In Figure 3-27 we see the item level copy control rules. The source and target document types are seen, as well as the source item category.

- The copying requirements field is set at 004, which determines if the preceding document has a valid status with which to create a billing document item.

- The data VBRK/VBRP field is used to split deliveries into more than one invoice, or to group deliveries into a single invoice. This is useful, for example, if one invoice should be created from a single delivery.

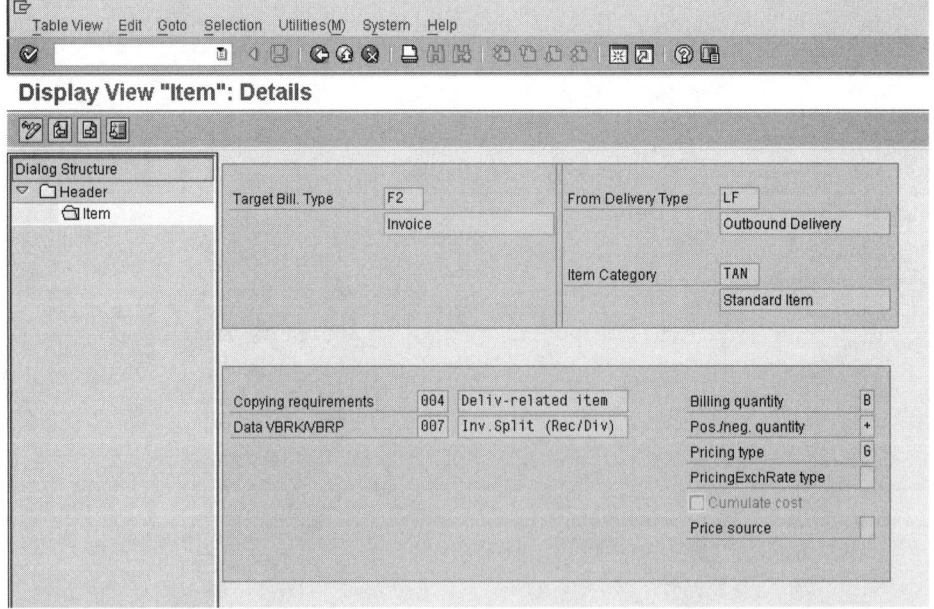

Copyright by SAP AG

FIGURE 3-27 Copy control delivery document LF to billing document F2 item detail

VBRK-ZUKRI is a field that is compiled from the values of the structure ZUK, which is used to determine if invoice items must be combined into one invoice. It is compiled by any field contents you choose, but has a limit of 40 characters (combination criteria in the billing document).

When the invoice is created by the system, it fills the ZUKRI field for each invoice item. Then it groups together all the items with the same ZUKRI field into one invoice.

For example, if you want to create one invoice per day per order, you would put the order number and billing date in the ZUKRI field. All deliveries for the same order on the same day will have the same data in field ZUKRI, so they will be combined into one invoice. If the order is different or the date is different, the ZUKRI field will be different and a new invoice will be created for that item.

When you create the invoice in transaction VF01, you enter all the documents you want to bill and press ENTER. The system shows you the invoices that will be created from these documents. You can select any two invoices and click on the show split criteria option. This will show you why SPA chose to create two invoices in this case instead of one.

- Billing quantity is equal to the quantity you wish to use for billing. In delivery-related billing from a sales order, it should usually be set as a B, indicating delivery quantity, less invoiced quantity.

- The positive/negative quantity value determines how the value taken from the source document will affect the billing documents, for example:

  - Delivery to invoice: Positive

  - Delivery to cancellation: Negative

  - Delivery to pro-forma invoice: No effect

- The pricing type is governed by the same rules as in the sales document.

- The pricing exchange rate type is used by the system to determine which date to use as the basis for the exchange rate.

- The cumulate cost checkbox is used to determine if the cost (usually condition type VPRS) is to be rounded up from the sub-items to a main item. This is used, for example, in bills of materials to determine if the costs are passed up to the header item. This is especially needed if the sub-item is not relevant for billing.

- The price source field is used to determine where the system obtains its pricing values. Leaving the field blank indicates the values are taken from the sales document.

In copying from one billing document into another billing document—for example, an invoice into an invoice cancellation—the same copy control rules must be maintained.

Do not forget to enter the delivery document type in the sales order document type when you configure the document type. Similarly, you must enter the invoice document type in the sales order document type configuration. These are both used in the default processing of the sales document. For example, if you have order-related billing you specify that billing type ZF2 must be used for this order type by entering ZF2 on the configuration of sales document type ZOR.

As you will see in billing, the invoice cancellation type for the billing type is assigned to the billing document type.

Special Sales Document Types

There are many sales document types and SAP allows you to create many more. However, the sales document types we will focus on are the standard process most commonly used in SAP Sales and Distribution. These documents encompass their own business process procedures. The document flows we will look at are the following: the quotation; special sales orders such as the cash sale process and rush order process; the credit and debit cycle; as well as the returns and invoice correction request process, which is a combination of the credit and debit document. We will also look at contracts and scheduling agreements.

Menu Path   SAP Customizing Implementation Guide | Sales and Distribution | Sales | Sales Documents | Sales Document Header | Define Sales Document Types [VOV8]

In the following document types, instead of repeating each field, I have simply listed the settings that should be allocated to that document and the reason why they should be chosen.

The Quotation

(Sales document type AG (QT in English))

The quotation is a sales document type that comes before the sales order and after an inquiry. It is used as a proposed agreement of a price and quantity for a particular material or service for a particular date. Most quotations have a validity date.

The quotation can have pricing and schedule lines. It can have output assigned and credit checks assigned.

The quotation is useful in business processes to determine if the material will be available at the right time for the customer at the right price. Should the quotation be satisfactory it may be copied into a sales order. Depending on the customizing entries, you can copy the pricing elements and the header data, as well as the item, material, and order quantities into the sales order.

Ensure your quotation has sales document category B for quotations. I recommend you set all document types relevant to read the customer material information record so set the indicator to "read info record." The screen sequence group can be set at AG, which is SAP standard for quotations. The transaction group should be set as 2.

It is also recommended you set a value for the quotation messages option. This will read the item level or header level to indicate to the user when he is creating a new quotation that an open quotation already exists for the customer if set at header level, or an open quotation already exists for the customer and material if set at item level.

Do not forget to set the item category determination and schedule line category determination as well as the copy control rules—for example, from a quotation to a sales order.

The standard item category used in quotations is AGN.

Order Probability   When a sales inquiry or quotation is created you may want to know what the probability is that the customer will follow through with a purchase.

The system uses an order probability percentage from the customer master record and combines it with the order probability percentage of the sales document type. The combination of the two percentages results in an order probability percentage and refers to the likelihood that the quote will become an order.

The Cash Sale Process

(Sales document type BV)

You will use the cash sale process when the customer places the sales order and picks up and pays for the goods at the same time—for example, when you walk into a store and purchase goods. The system automatically proposes the current date in the sales order as the date for the delivery and billing.

Once the sales order is saved, the system then creates a delivery automatically and prints out a cash sale invoice, which may be given to the Sold-to Party. This cash sale invoice is a paper form created via output determination (see Chapter 9).

The delivery can be relevant for picking. (See Chapter 6 for more information on the delivery and picking process.) Or if the goods are not to be picked (if, for example, the sold to party already has them), then the delivery can be marked not relevant for picking and the goods issue can happen automatically in the background so that the invoice can be created.

Note the billing can occur in the standard process. Also there is no accounts receivable postings from the billing document as the customer has already settled the invoice. Instead the invoice amount is posted directly to a cash account.

The Rush Order Process

(Sales document type SO)

For the rush order process the customer places the order and collects the items immediately, or the materials are shipped immediately. However, the customer is invoiced later.

The system automatically creates a delivery when the sales order is saved. However, no invoice is printed; instead the system follows the standard procedures for creating the billing document (that is, the invoice is created once the delivery has been goods issued).

Both the rush order process and the cash sale process utilize the shipping conditions passed on from the sales document. The shipping conditions in turn are used to determine the shipping point and the route.

The only difference between a rush order and a standard order is that the rush order has an immediate delivery creation. This delivery, however, may still need to progress through the logistics process of picking, packing, loading, and goods issue processing.

The Credit Process

(Sales document type G2)

There are two types of credit procedures. In the first the customer returns previously purchased products and requires a credit. This we will look at later in this chapter in "The Returns Process." The second general form of credit procedure is when the customer is credited without returning any goods. This would be used in the following examples:

The customer discovers the products that were sent him are defective and the costs to initiate a return delivery would exceed the costs obtained in rehabilitation or repair of the product. Thus, the customer is instructed to scrap the material and is subsequently issued a credit note. There is no return.

The second scenario is when the customer is overcharged for a product or service and is issued a credit for the difference. Again, there is no movement of material.

You can automatically set a billing block that may be released by an authorized person prior to the billing (credit) being carried out. It is the billing (the credit note) that credits the customer's account in accounts receivable.

You should consider setting a mandatory indicator that the credit memo request may only be created with reference to the invoice document that originated with the problem. That way you ensure traceability. You should also ensure the document flow checkbox is checked in the copy control rules to ensure you have a history.

It is also possible to make it mandatory to enter an order reason on the credit note, which can explain why the credit was given.

The standard item category used by credit memos is G2N.

You may not wish to credit the customer for everything on the invoice. For example, you may not wish to give a credit for the entire freight charge. In this case you can have a new returns pricing procedure that is similar to the standard pricing procedure you use but not have the freight condition type. The conditions are copied over, excluding freight. In this new pricing procedure you can also have an additional manual condition type. (Refer to pricing in Chapter 8.)

The Debit Process

(Sales document type L2)

The debit process is used when a customer is undercharged for a material or service. A debit memo request is created and invoiced using standard billing procedures. There is no movement of material.

You can automatically set a billing block that may be released by an authorized person prior to the billing being carried out. This is not too commonly used because we are increasing the customer's accounts receivable, so there is no fraud risk as there is with the credit process. The billing is the actual creation of the debit note from the debit memo request.

You may set a mandatory indicator that the debit memo request can only be created with reference to the invoice document that originated with the problem. Also, activate the document flow checkbox on the copy control rules in order to retain the document flow history.

It is also possible to select an order reason on the debit note, and make this field mandatory in the document type incompletion procedure.

Disputed amounts usually arise from incorrect pricing master data. So rather than debiting the customer for the disputed amount, it is recommended that you credit the customer for the disputed sales document in full, then correct the pricing and create another standard debit that will use the correct pricing with the correct amounts. This procedure can be followed for all disputed short priced orders (and the reverse can be used for overpriced orders).

Standard SAP will not allow the creation of inter-company invoices for order-related billing documents. Instead see OSS note 63459. The basic concept of this OSS note is that you need to assign an output type (ZZIV) to the external invoice (the customer's credit or debit) at the header level. This output type then needs to be activated via a run of the print program RSNAST00 and the inter-company credit or debit will be created. This process is well supported by SAP and you should not worry about its implementation.

The standard item category used by debits is L2N.

The Returns Process

(Sales document type RE)

The returns process is different from the standard credit process in that a return delivery is made. While we cannot assume to map all the functionality you may require in the physical process, such as goods receipt and warehouse management movement, we will look at the basic flow of the returns order procedure.

The returns order can be created with reference to an invoice to ensure traceability of the process. It may be worthwhile ensuring this is mandatory (settings on the sales document type) when creating the returns order type.

It may also be worthwhile ensuring the returns order reason was entered on the sales document, thus it may be necessary to add this in an incompletion procedure.

You may wish to copy the pricing unchanged from the invoice back into the sales order. (There is no need to indicate a negative value in the copying control rules; since the system sees the document type as a return it automatically posts the entries in the finance document as opposite entries on the ledger.) By using the same pricing values you ensure a complete reversal of the invoice.

Do not forget to activate the update document flow checkbox on the copy control rules, between billing (invoice) and sales document (return).

It is advisable to have a billing block assigned to the return order in the sales document header configuration to initiate a billing block automatically, in order to prevent a credit for returns being created until an authorized person releases the billing block.

Once the returns delivery is created and goods receipted, the material is receipted back into the plant. The material should use a goods movement that receives the stock into blocked stock. Once the blocked stock has been inspected, you can either scrap it or rework it if the stock is faulty; or, if the stock is saleable, you can put it into unrestricted use stock. The stock is then available for the next sales order.

It is advisable to indicate a shipping condition that is specifically used for returns; thus, all return deliveries or goods receipts may be done by a specific shipping point. (See shipping point determination in Chapter 6.) This is useful when running the delivery due list. You can select only to process the returns deliveries, as well as offer better visibility of stock movements.

The standard item category used by returns is REN.

After the creation and goods issue of the delivery, the billing block is removed from the sales order and the invoice is created, with reference to the sales order. This way you are able to create a credit for the return in the sales order, which in turn has the order quantity copied from the preceding invoice. The credit memo then automatically reduces the customer's accounts receivable balance.

SAP creates the billing document from the returns order rather than from the delivery so that the customer can receive the credit without waiting for the goods receipt to take place if, for example, it may take a while for the stock to be returned to the plant, but the customer wants the credit immediately.

Invoice Correction Request

(Sales document type RK)

This document proposes a new way of processing complaints and issuing credit and debit memos. The document allows you to correct the quantity and or the price for one or more faulty items on an invoice.

Each invoice correction request is made in reference to an (mandatory) invoice. (You cannot create one in reference to an order or quotation.) Each invoice correction request contains two items for each item in the invoice. The first item is the value and quantity copied from the invoice; this appears as the credit item. The second item is the debit item, which represents the correct quantity and or value. Should you change this second debit item due to new pricing, etc., the difference between the two would then be automatically passed on to billing as either a credit or debit memo.

It would be advisable to set an automatic billing block on the sales document type, as in the number of instances you may wish to credit the customer.

The billing document type assigned to the invoice correction request is order-related and is document type G2 (credit memo). It has the characteristic K, which indicates a credit memo.

The system creates a credit memo for a positive total value and a debit memo for a negative total value.

The title of the printout for the credit or debit memo depends on the characteristic that has been assigned to it (sales document category) and not the total value.

The copy control at item category level from the billing document to the invoice correction request must have the pricing type E (adopt pricing components and fix values).

Due to the classification type D of the sales document type RK, an additional two fields are generated in the copying control at item level. These are a second item category proposal and a second pricing type. Both of these fields relate to the debit memo item in the invoice correction request, as seen in Figure 3-28.

There are many business processes which differ in complexity according to the business model used, for example, repair or servicing of products, however one should be able to create ones' own document types including associated settings, for example item categories and assignments from the information in this chapter.

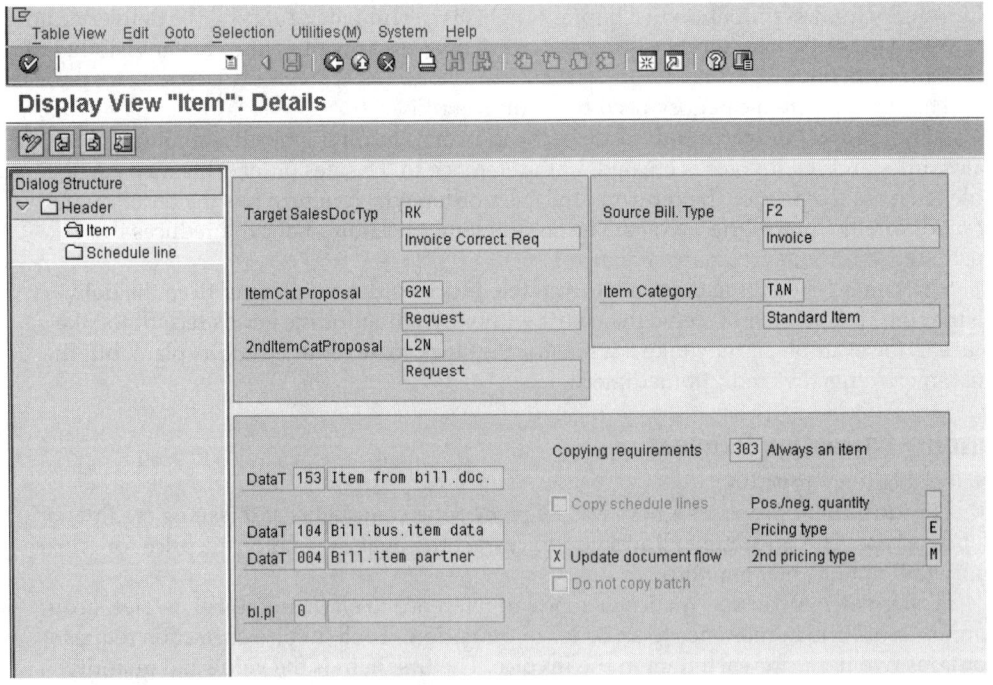

FIGURE 3-28 Invoice correction request copy control rules

Contracts and Special Processes

This chapter focuses on sales contracts and special processes, with specific tips on their use and configuration in mySAP ERP.

Numerous business relationships relate to contracts or agreements with customers and the represented business, based upon material, price, and quantity over a fixed period of time. Contracts facilitate planning on behalf of the business and guarantee a fixed price agreement with the customer.

In SAP the term "contracts" is represented as quantity contracts, value contracts, service contracts, and group master contracts.

It is advisable to use a different number range for contracts (see "Number Ranges" in Chapters 3 and 10) as this ensures an easier time searching for documents and referencing contracts later.

The area in the IMG for configuration of the contracts process is the same as the standard sales document types unless specifically stated. Thus, to configure the contract document type, use the following menu path.

Menu Path   SAP Customizing Implementation Guide I Sales and Distribution I Sales I Sales Documents I Sales Document Header I Define Sales Document Types [VOV8]

Quantity Contracts

The *quantity contract* is a contract that happens after the quotation but before an order. Quantity contracts are used mainly to limit the quantity the customer can buy and to offer special pricing. Generally, quantity contracts are used when the demand for a material is greater than the available supply, and the business has to implement measures to limit the supplied quantity evenly between its customer base.

The SAP standard sales document type for quantity contracts is KM or CQ (English).

The quantity contract does not transfer requirements. This means that:

- It does not create a requirement for stock within the plant and subsequently there is no confirmation of stock within the plant for the contract.
- It does not require production to make the stock to satisfy the contract.
- It does not require material management to purchase the stock to satisfy the contract (if it is a trading good).

The requirement is placed on the plant when the release order is created with reference to the quantity contract. The contract itself has no schedule lines. It does have a validity date.

The contract allows the customer to have a special price per material for a limited quantity. This quantity decreases each time an order is made by the stock ordered.

Once the contract validity date expires or the customer has purchased the full quota of stock, the contract expires, and a new one must be created.

Quantity contracts have no schedule lines or specific delivery dates, as they are not delivered. An order from a contract is called a *release order*; the delivery is done from the release order.

For example, a contract is made with a quantity of 1,000 items. Then each order the customer places with reference to this contract will decrease the available quantity of this contract. So if the customer places an order for 100 units, the open contract quantity becomes 900 units.

Note that this only applies if you have set the Update Document Flow checkbox as enabled on the item category in the copy control rules. If this is not set, the customer can order as much as he would like, without regard to the contract quantity being updated.

Quantity contracts can be used to limit the customer's purchasing; you can block the standard order type for a customer and so force him to use an order type that must be created with reference to a quantity contract. Thus, this customer is limited to only ordering 1,000 items.

A quantity contract has validity periods and can have cancellation rules.

To create a contract, use the following menu path.

Menu Path   SAP Menu | Logistics | Sales and Distribution | Sales | Contract | [VA41] - Create

To make a release order, simply create a standard sales document with reference to the contract. Use the following menu path.

Menu Path   SAP Menu | Logistics | Sales and Distribution | Sales | Order | [VA01] - Create

After a release order has been created it will automatically decrease the available quantity for the customer. This will be seen when viewing the contract and when creating new orders.

Set up the quantity contract by using the following menu path.

Menu Path   SAP Customizing Implementation Guide | Sales and Distribution | Sales | Sales Documents | Sales Document Header | Define Sales Document Types

Quantity contracts have their own pricing procedures, texts, partners, and so on, like any other document type. They also have their own item categories.

Don't forget to set up the copy control to other order document types you may be using as release orders.

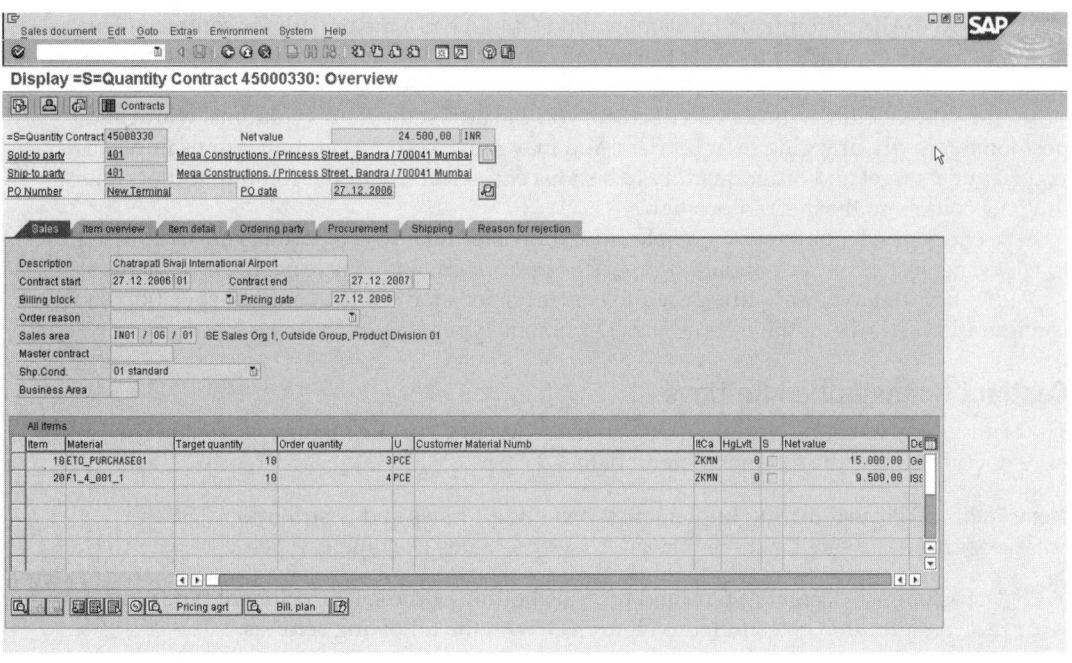

Copyright by SAP AG

FIGURE 4-1   Quantity contract showing target quantity of 10 pce and order quantity of 3 pce and 4 pce

In a quantity contract the quantity available in the contract is called the "Target Quantity." The quantity that has been consumed by call off orders is called the "Order Quantity." In Figure 4-1 we see a quantity contract with two line items with a target quantity of 10 pce for each line item, of which there are release orders of 3 and 4 pce.

As an example in the document flow for item 10 in this example, one can see the release order for 3 pce in Figure 4-2.

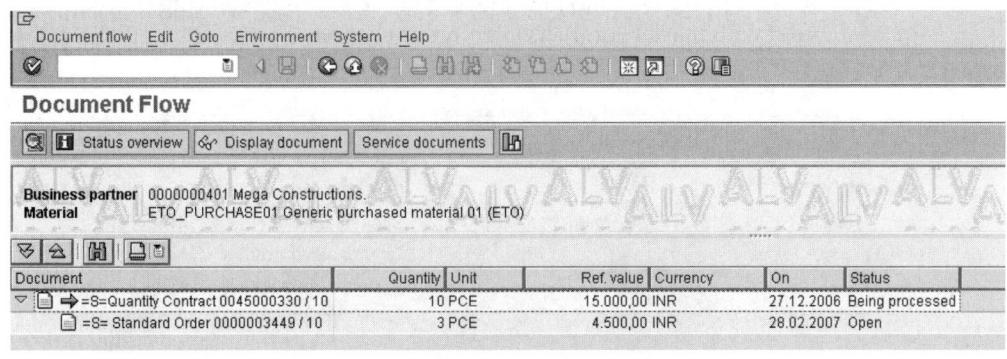

Copyright by SAP AG

FIGURE 4-2   Document flow from contract shows release order for item 10

The IMG (SAP Customizing Implementation Guide) has a menu path for contracts. This relates to master contracts, value contracts, and contract data that relates to contract profiles and cancellations.

In the sales document order entry screen, you can adjust the item's columns' width and position by simply dragging their borders. You may move columns around. For example, if you want the target and order quantity to be adjacent, select one of the column headers and drag the column to the desired position.

The check partner authorization field is used to determine which partners are authorized to release against a contract. Should no check be performed, you may leave the field blank.

Now that we have been introduced to contracts, let's look at the contract-specific configuration settings on the Define Sales Document Types screen.

Contract Configuration Settings

The contract has its configuration settings maintained in the same manner as a standard sales document. Use the following menu path.

Menu Path   SAP Customizing Implementation Guide I Sales and Distribution I Sales I Sales Documents I Sales Document Header I Define Sales Document Types

Select a contract document type and near the bottom of the sales document type you will see a configuration box similar to Figure 4-3, with the following settings:

- Price procedure condition header and item are pricing procedures, and configured as price procedures. However, they do not replace the price procedure used in the contract. The standard price procedure determination is used. Instead, the values in these fields are used for supplemental price agreements.

- The contract profile is discussed in detail in the next section.

- The billing request is used for service contracts, to bill the customer for a service that was not agreed to in the original service agreement. The standard SAP sales document type to perform this billing is LV, which is a debit memo request for service contracts.

- The group reference procedure is used for master contracts to determine which data is to be copied, or proposed, into lower level contracts. The referencing procedures are configured with master contracts later in this chapter.

Contract			
PricProcCondHeadr		Contract data allwd.	Y
PricProcCondItem		FollUpActivityType	
Contract profile	Z001 =S= Contract	Subseq.order type	ZOR
Billing request		Check partner auth.	A
Group Ref. Procedure		☐ Update low.lev.cont.	

FIGURE 4-3   Contract settings on Define Sales Document Types screen

- The contract data allowed field is a critical field used by the system in contracts. As contract data, for example, validity periods and cancellation data may be kept at the header level as well as at the item level of the contract. This field indicates to the system what to do when data differs between the header and item levels. With the setting as an X, the system will not copy any changes you make in the header level into the item levels. This is also true even if the data at header and line item were identical prior to the header data being changed. With the setting as Y, the system automatically copies all header data into the item in the contract (only if the header and item contract data were identical prior to the changes).

- The follow-up activity type is used to speed up the creation of follow-up activities. For example, the follow-up sales activity type 0002 (telephone call) is specified for sales document type WV (service contract). You create a follow-up activity work list for contracts in Sales Support (CAS) and maintain the selection criteria as required. This is maintained in the following menu path.

Menu Path   Sales Support (CAS) | SAP Customizing Implementation Guide | Sales and Distribution | Sales Support (CAS) | Sales Activities

- Should the follow up action have been "create quotation," you would need to enter a quotation document type, in the field subsequent order type. Then when you select from within the list of contracts when you select Sales Document | Create Subsequent Order, the system will propose the order type you entered in this field.

- The update lower level contracts field need not be initiated, as the contract in question is not a master contract. This field is used by the system to update lower-level contracts, should the data you are changing be the master contract. These changes are then passed down to the lower-level contracts via workflow. Should this field not be set, the system will only update the lower-level contract when it is re-processed.

- The check partner authorization field checks that the partner either is the Sold-to Party of the contract or has a partner function of AA (which indicates an authorized release partner). This is the standard checking rule A. Alternatively, in the standard checking rule B, the system then checks if the partner wishing to release from the contract is a lower level customer in the customer hierarchy, to the Sold-to Party in the contract.

You may also create multiple Ship-to Parties for the specific contract. The standard Ship-to Party partner function is WE (German translation). However, you may have more than one Ship-to Party; thus, you may assign Ship-to Parties with the partner function AW.

Assign both the release Sold-to Parties and the release Ship-to Parties to the Sold-to Party of the contract in the customer master record. When you create the individual contracts the system will propose these assigned partners.

Please also refer to "Partner Determination" in Chapter 9, where this configuration is explained.

Contract Profiles

To define contract profiles, use the following menu path.

Menu Path SAP Customizing Implementation Guide | Sales and Distribution | Sales | Sales Documents | Contracts | Contract Data | Define Contract Profiles

To define your own contract profile, select a standard contract profile and copy.

An example of a contract profile is seen in Figure 4-4. You have a contract start date and end date. For example, the start date is the acceptance date and the end date is the start date plus the validity period. This contract also has a validity date of one year. The profile also has a cancellation procedure, as well as an action date and action date rule.

The rules for determining dates are configured as follows.

Defining Rules for Determining Dates

To define contract profile dates, use the following menu path.

Menu Path SAP Customizing Implementation Guide | Sales and Distribution | Sales | Sales Documents | Contracts | Contract Data | Define Rules For Determining Dates

As seen in Figure 4-5, the rule is based upon a group of characteristics as follows. The baseline date is the start date for the calculation. In the previous example the baseline date is equal to the billing date. The time period is the value that will later be multiplied by the time unit; in this example the unit is 3, which is equal to "month." The calendar ID is the key for the factory calendar. The factory calendar takes into account non-working days and public holidays, so the resultant date may be later when calculated using a factory calendar, the importance of which is often undervalued. See "Factory Calendars" in Chapter 6.

Set the contract data checkbox to force the system to always use header contract data to determine the baseline date, as opposed to the item or header data dependent on the usage of the date rule.

Defining Validity Period Categories

To define validity period categories, use the following menu path.

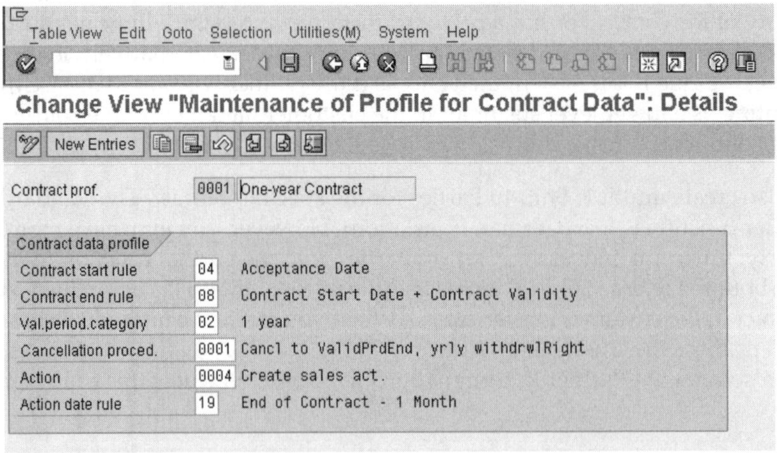

Copyright by SAP AG

Figure 4-4 Contract profile

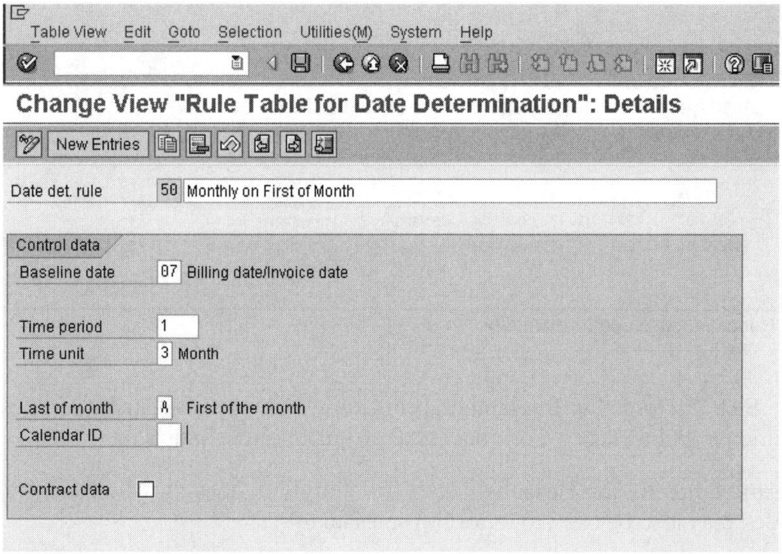

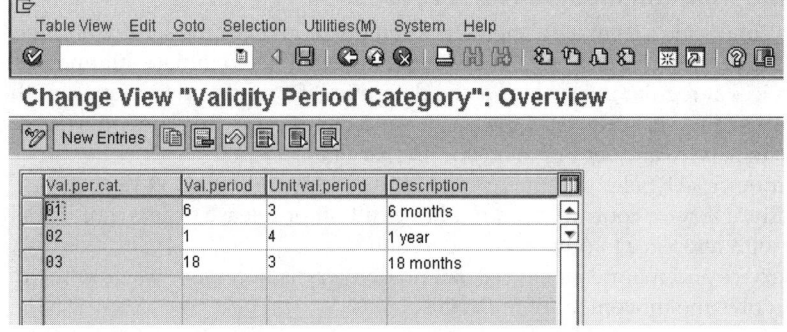

Copyright by SAP AG

FIGURE 4-5   Rules for determining dates

Menu Path   SAP Customizing Implementation Guide | Sales and Distribution | Sales | Sales Documents | Contracts | Contract Data | Define Validity Period Categories

As seen in Figure 4-6 the rule is used to simply make a category of date that is used often. The category 03 in this example uses the value of 18 and the unit of 3, which represents months, therefore defining the validity period as 18 months.

Contract Cancellation

To define the contract cancellation period, use the following menu path

Copyright by SAP AG

FIGURE 4-6   Defining validity period categories

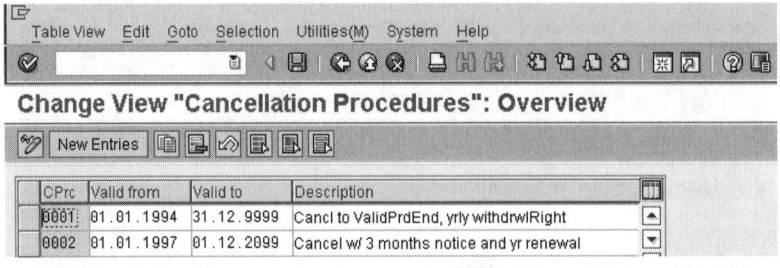

FIGURE 4-7   Cancellation procedure validity

Menu Path   SAP Customizing Implementation Guide | Sales and Distribution | Sales | Sales Documents | Contracts | Contract Data | Control Cancellation

- **Define Cancellation Reasons**   Here one simply defines the cancellation reason, which may also be used to report on sales analyses.

- **Define Cancellation Procedures**   This description of configuration task in the IMG relates to the Figure 4-7, which shows the cancellation procedure validity.

- **Define Cancellation Rules**   Here the rules of the cancellation procedure are defined. For example, in Figure 4-8, the rule 0001 takes the contract cancellation baseline date as the start date of the contract. It then set the rule valid to 12, which is a date rule meaning one week. Within that period of one week, the contract may then be cancelled on any day up to the last day of the one-week period. (The notice value is 1 and the unit is day, therefore the contract may be cancelled up to one day before the end of the week.)

The system uses these settings to automatically enter the validity period and date determination in the contract. This is done by assigning the contract profile to the sales document type representing the contract, for example, WV.

Service and Maintenance Contract Process

The service contract is a legal agreement between the receiver of the service and the business supplying the service. It is used by the business, for example, to initiate automatic billing of routine services at regular intervals and can determine if a cancellation request of the contract is valid. It is used by the receiver of the service as a contract he can claim on, with easy access to requests for service and set prices on specific services.

The standard SAP Sales document type for a service contract is WV.

Generally, a service contract need not have call off or release orders, nor does it need to be created with reference to other sales documents.

For a service and maintenance contract no delivery is necessary because the transaction does not involve the movement of materials.

The service contract may have periodic or milestone billing (see Chapter 7) and bill the customer according to a schedule of billing dates.

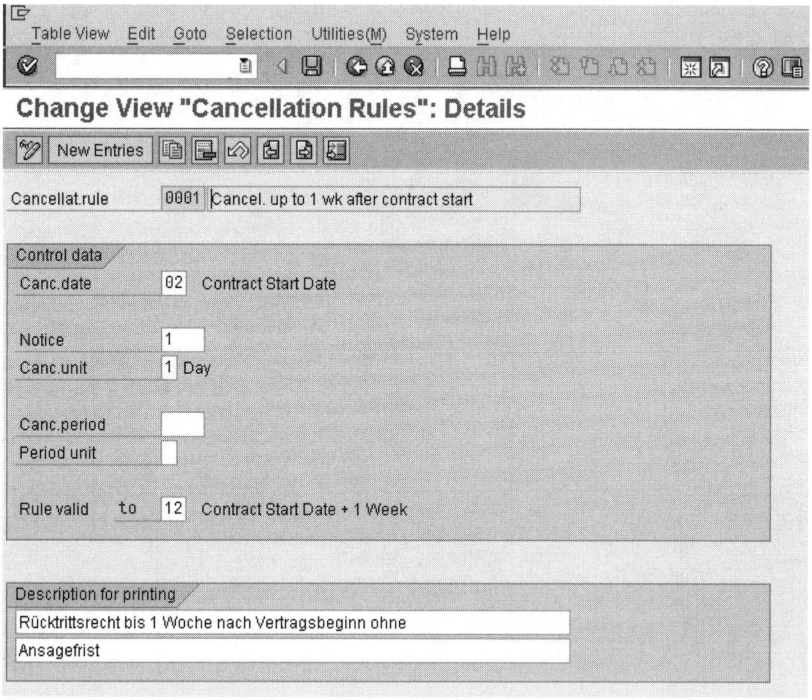

Copyright by SAP AG

FIGURE 4-8   Defining cancellation rules

A service contract integrates with the CS (Customer Service) module in ECC. This permits the CS module to arrange the technicians for the service in accordance with the service contract. Should a service that was not initially part of the original service agreement be completed, it may be billed with a billing request. (Sales Document type LV may be copied.)

The item category used by service contracts is very important. It is best to understand the business before you try and customize it. The service item can be any one of the following:

- A service task, once off

- A material used in the service

- Time charged for a technician's hourly rate

The standard item category for a service is WVN. You may need additional item categories because of the different types of items available on a service contract. Remember to copy this standard and change the necessary fields.

The standard item category has been created to represent a service that is carried out and billed periodically, as seen in Figure 4-9 with billing plan I.

The standard item category has a completion rule C, which determines the item to be fully referenced when target quantity is fully reached. This particular item category is relevant for order-related billing according to a billing plan, as well as utilizing a billing plan type 02, which indicates periodic billing.

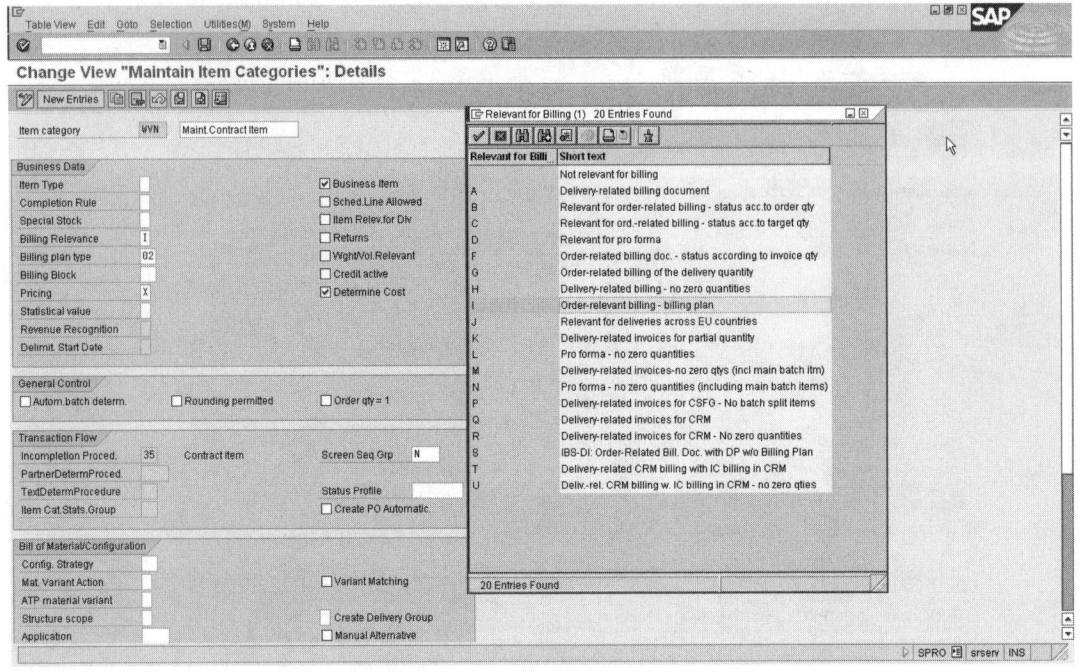

FIGURE 4-9 Item category WVN billing plan

This item category does not have any schedule lines allowed.

SAP provides standard material types for service items. DIEN is the material type generally used for standard services and KMAT for configurable services (or products).

After setting up the relevant document type and item categories, you can map the copy control rules.

To create a service contract, use the following menu path.

Menu Path SAP Menu I Logistics I Sales and Distribution I Sales I Contract I VA41 - Create

Enter the relevant details, including the material and target quantity.

Value Contract Process

The value contract is similar to the quantity contract in that it limits the material or services to a customer. However, instead of limiting due to quantity of stock, the contract and its ceiling is based upon total value.

The value contract is created and maintained the same way as the other standard contracts and document types. However, SAP has created its own configuration menu path in the IMG. The only reason I can see for this is to assist in the implementation of online documentation, making the documentation readily available by merely double-clicking on the function related to contracts in the IMG.

To configure a value contract, use the following menu path.

Menu Path   SAP Customizing Implementation Guide | Sales and Distribution | Sales |
Sales Documents | Contracts | Value Contract | Maintain Value Contract Type And
Contract Release Type

An Assortment Module

An assortment module is an order entry tool that displays a list of materials and services that
can be released from a value contract. It has a validity date and a restriction in that only the
materials and services that belong in the same sales organization and distribution channel for
which your release order is being made will be displayed.

To create an assortment module, as shown in Figure 4-10, use the following menu path.

Menu Path   SAP Menu | Logistics | Sales and Distribution | Master Data | Products |
Assortments | Assortment | Module | WSO1 - Create

Press ENTER and you see the screen shown in Figure 4-11, where you may enter the
materials in the assortment and their respective validity dates.

Now that the background is done, you can create a value contract. You do not need to
utilize an assortment module—you can create a value contract per a product hierarchy
range or you can create a value contract per material.

There are two types of value contracts in SAP: The standard value contract and the
material-related value contract.

Standard Value Contract WK1   This value contract is sufficient for the majority of cases where
you need a contract based upon total value for an assortment of materials per customer. You
can specify a product hierarchy or an assortment module for value contracts of this type.

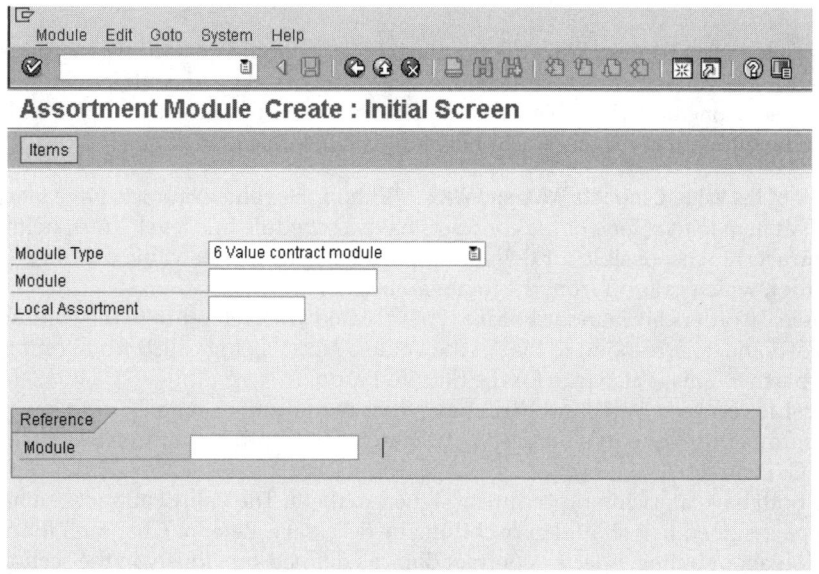

Copyright by SAP AG

FIGURE 4-10   Creating an assortment module

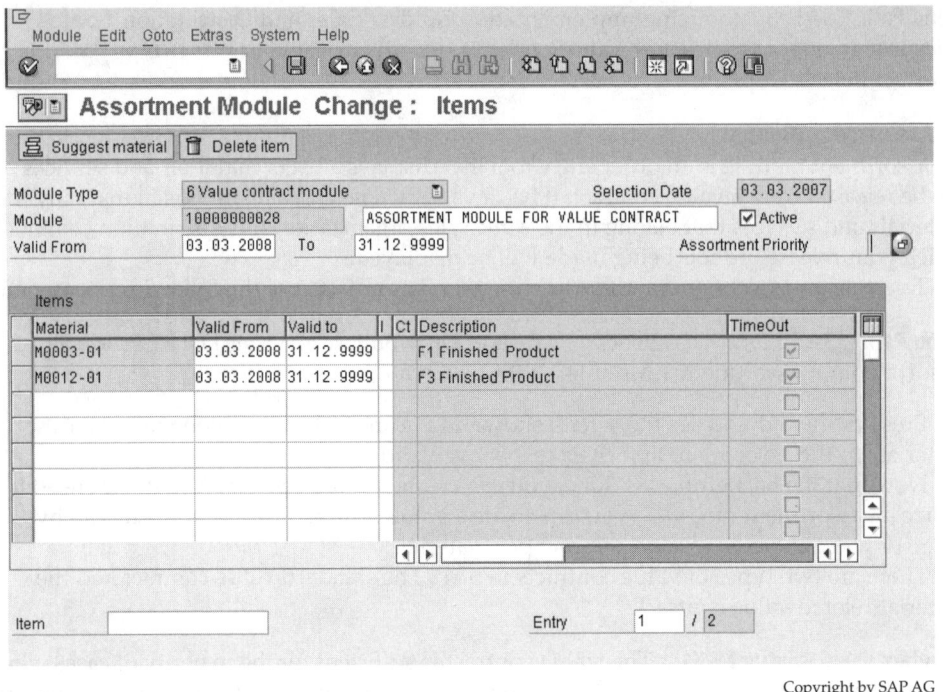

FIGURE 4-11   Add materials to an assortment module

Material-Related Value Contract WK2   This value contract should be used when you need the functionality of a value contract. However, when using this type of contract you generally restrict its use to one material. This value contract also uses a contract start and end date, which can be different in this contract at item level than at header level.

Similarities of the Value Contracts WK1 and WK2   Both of the value contracts have a header level and an item level. None of the contracts have a schedule line level. Thus, neither of these contracts are responsible for delivering products. Each of the value contracts has a release order, which calls off from the total value.

The release orders are standard order types created with reference to the contract. The Sold-to Party must correspond to that of the value contract being called from, or it must be a release partner. This is also true for the Ship-to Party.

The value contracts WK1 and WK2 have their own number range. Try to keep all contract number ranges equal for ease of use later. They both have the sales document category G (contract).

They both have a pricing procedure assigned to them. The value contract can have a billing type assigned to it should order billing be necessary. Refer to Chapter 3 for more information about billing. Specific contract data, as defined previously in the section on quantity contracts, may be selected and assigned.

Do not forget the copy control rules from WK1 or WK2 to TA and from item categories WKN or WKC to TAN (standard item category) or WAN (release order item category). (WKN is the standard item category for WK1 contracts. WKC is the standard item category for WK2 contracts. This will let you create release orders for the value contract.)

Regarding the necessary configuration for the item categories, it is proposed you select the completion rule E for the contract item category, indicating the item is deemed to be complete when total target value is reached.

Should the item be relevant for billing, you must enter the billing indicator n. (Refer to Chapter 7.)

Due to there being no schedule lines permitted, be sure not to select the schedule lines allowed field.

The value contract material setting at item category level, for example, in item category WKN, will automatically default in the sales document should you not enter a material. Be sure that the material you enter here has the correct item category determination. Item category group on material master plus the sales document type will propose the item category.

The contract release control, which is set at the item category level, defines if the item must give an error or a warning or no response when a contract that is complete is being used as a reference to create a release order. A setting of - D is recommended. (This will propose a warning if the total value has been reached.)

The release order can be created in any currency. The system automatically converts the currency of the release order to that of the currency in the value contract on the pricing date of the release order.

The value contract is deemed as complete once the total value is reached, or the validity period has been met, or a reason for rejection has been entered for the line items.

You can control how the system must respond to complete value contract items by changing the settings in the item category WKN. Here you may define a warning message, an error message, or no reaction required from the system if the item is complete and the user is trying to create a release order. No reaction means that the system will accept the contract and allow the release order even though the item is complete.

To create a value contract, use the following menu path.

Menu Path   SAP Menu I Logistics I Sales and Distribution I Sales I Contract I [VA41] - Create

Select the contract you wish to create—for example, WK1.

After creation of the contract you may call off from it using a release order. To do this, use the following menu path.

Menu Path   SAP Menu I Logistics I Sales and Distribution I Sales I Contract I Subsequent Functions I [V-01] - Order

Then select the Create with Reference button shown here.

Enter the contract number followed by the call off party. If no call off party is entered, it will be proposed automatically.

Create with Reference

Copyright by SAP AG

After selection of the materials and creation and saving of the release order, the system will update the value contract by adjusting for the value that was called off.

The release order value is calculated automatically and updated into the value contract. The remaining value in the contract is the original value less the total open order and delivery values as well as the total of invoiced value items.

Should there be any negative process flows—for example, returns or rejected line items of the release order—the system also takes this into account when updating the open contract value with the automatic update.

Master Contracts

A master contract is a contract in which you group other contracts as lower-level contracts. Thus the master contract has the general data that is relevant for all lower-level contracts over a specified period.

Contracts are grouped in order to ensure all data in the lower-level contracts remains consistent as well as ensuring terms granted in the master contract are copied into all lower-level contracts.

The documents that can be grouped under a master contract are

- Quantity contracts
- Value contracts
- Service contracts

A master contract contains header data only: The billing plan data, the partners data, business data, and contract data.

To understand and configure a master contract, it is important to understand what the business wants from contract grouping. *Contract grouping* is the process whereby several lower-level contracts are linked to one master contract to ensure data consistency. When you link a lower-level contract to a master contract the header data of the master contract is passed down into the lower-level contract.

For this to happen the lower-level contract and the higher-level contract must be assigned to the same sales area. Note that you may not assign a hierarchy of contracts together. You may only have one master contract with many lower-level contracts assigned to it.

To group contracts, you must first determine the referencing requirements. Use the following menu path, as seen in Figure 4-12.

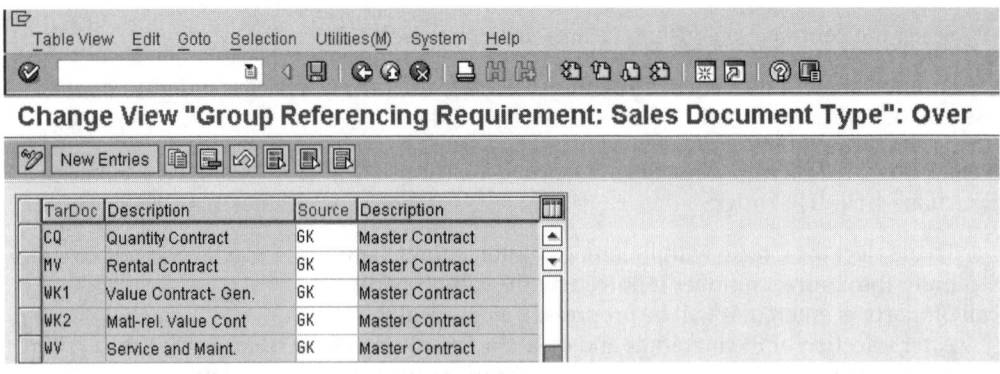

FIGURE 4-12   Grouping reference contracts sales document types

Menu Path SAP Customizing Implementation Guide | Sales and Distribution | Sales | Sales Documents | Master Contract | Define Referencing Requirements | Define Reference Sales Document Types

In this activity you assign the contracts that can be referenced by the main master contract. Note that you are able to create other master contract document types in the same way you are able to create other sales document types. (We will cover the data required in the master contract document type a little later.)

The process of assigning reference document types is useful if you want to force quantity contracts to be assigned to a particular master contract.

The screen in Figure 4-12 shows on the left the contract types that reference the GK contract as the source.

Now that the document assignments are done, the most crucial procedure is defining the referencing. To do this, use the following menu path.

Menu Path SAP Customizing Implementation Guide | Sales and Distribution | Sales | Contracts | Master Contract | Define Referencing Requirements | Define Referencing Procedures

There should be no need for you to create a new reference procedure as displayed in Figure 4-13. However, should you require one, select the sample procedure as delivered in the standard system group procedure SDGK. Copy the procedure and rename it. Select Copy All, from the pop-up dialog box to copy all subsequent entries. It is always recommended to copy all subsequent entries and to delete the entries not required afterwards.

As you are familiar with tables and field names from Chapter 1, you can use the transaction code [SE12] to read the short text of the field entries of a certain table, or [SE11] to read the table and all its fields with descriptions. Feel free to remove fields you do not require from your newly created copy.

The data represented here is divided into five columns. Column 1 and 2 are the table and field names. Column 3 is a partner function column—for example, the Ship-to Party. (Refer to "Partner Determination" in Chapter 2.) Column 5 indicates if the system is to give a message to a lower-level contract each time it wants to update this lower-level contract with data from a master contract.

Column 4 has the copy rules assigned to it. These copy rules are as follows:

A	Indicates the contract must have the same value in the field for the higher- and lower-level contract. Should these fields not match, that is, if you change the value in the field of the lower-level contract, the reference will no longer be carried out. Thus the contracts will not be allowed to be linked.
B	Indicates the value in the field is to be copied from the master contract and cannot be changed in the lower-level contract. Thus, fields deviating in the lower-level contract are not allowed.
C	Indicates proposal fields. This occurs when the master contract copies or proposes the data into the lower-level contract. However, the value of these fields are allowed to be overwritten in the lower-level contract.

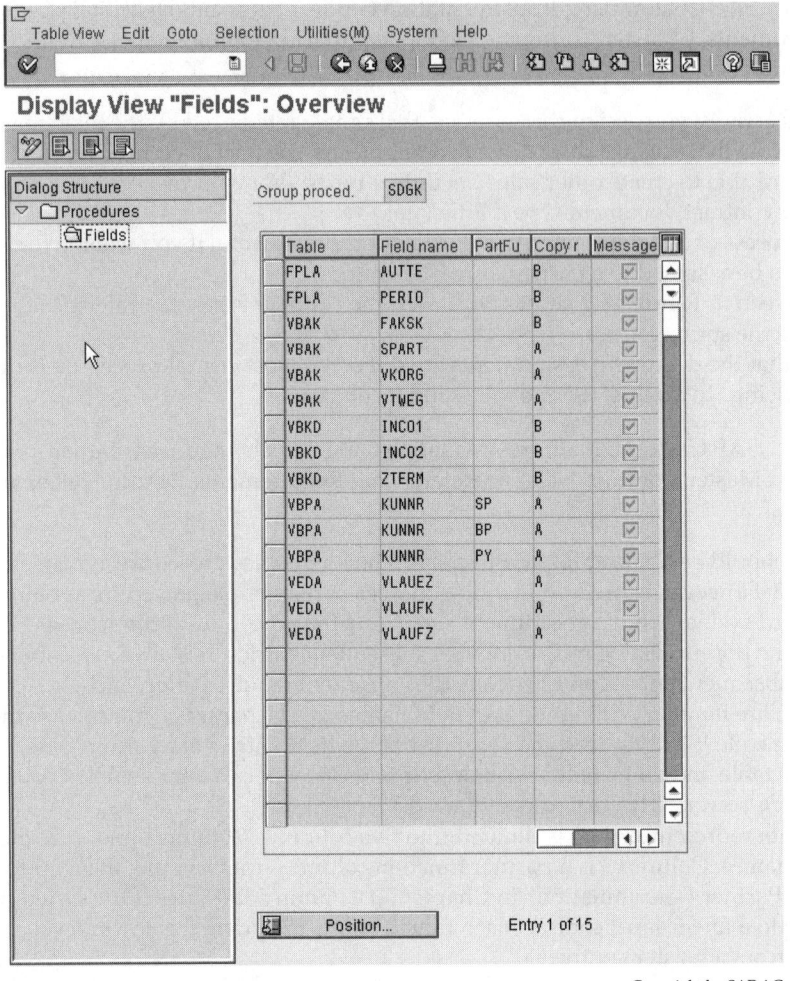

FIGURE 4-13 Defining referencing procedures

If you change one of these fields in a master contract the system will only copy the proposal fields into the lower-level contract if the values of both the master and lower-level contract were equal before the master contract was changed. This is referred to as *standard application logic*.

Now that we have defined the background of the master contracts, we need to define the document type and associated process.

Defining Master Contracts

To define a master contract, proceed as you would to define any sales document type in the IMG. The standard sales document type for a master contract is GK.

To create or change this document, remember to select, copy, rename, and save. Ensure the document type has the following configuration entries: The SD document category must be a 0- for master contract. The screen sequence group must be GK or a copy of GK. The transaction group must be 4 to represent a contract.

You may wish to select the contract messages field and enter a value of A. The system will propose a list of master contracts with the same header data for you to select from, should one already have been created.

The contract profile should represent the date procedures you wish to have defaulted. The reference procedure is the same one that was defined in the previous section on master contract reference tables and fields earlier with the copy rules A, B, and C.

The update lower-level contract field is crucial. If selected, this field will cause the associated lower-level contracts to be updated immediately after a change has occurred in a higher-level contract according to the rules specified in the referencing procedures. This is carried out via workflow, which will be explained in the next section. Should this field not be indicated, the system will only update a lower-level contract once that contract is called for processing.

In the automatic updating via workflow when the field's value is set, should the system find an error in the updating, the user who changed the master contract will receive a workflow item enabling him to make the changes in the lower-level contract manually.

Do not forget about the message indicator set in the referencing procedure in the fifth column, discussed in the previous section, use this message to indicate to the user what data is to be changed in the lower-level contract.

No delivery type or billing type is necessary, as the master contract is not relevant for deliveries or billing documents.

Do not forget to set up the copy control rules. This is necessary at header level only because there are no items or schedule lines.

To link a contract to a master contract, use the following menu path.

Menu Path   SAP Menu | Logistics | Sales and Distribution | Sales | Contract | [VA41] - Create

Here you create a master contract. It is recommended that you create a master contract first and then proceed with creating the other individual lower-level contracts. You are then able to assign the lower-level contracts to the higher-level contract.

The master contract has the overview screen shown in Figure 4-14. You can see it does not have any item details. And you can also see the reference procedure. Once a lower-level contract has been assigned to a master contract you can no longer assign another reference procedure to the master contract.

After assigning the lower-level contracts to the master contract, you are nearly finished with the master contract process. The only remaining data to configure is the workflow, which is issued once a contract is to be updated.

Master Contracts Workflow

A *workflow* is a sequence of steps that are processed manually by people or automatically by the system.

Generally, workflow is handled by a specialist workflow resource, so we will not be looking into the configuration of workflow objects in detail in this book. We will, however,

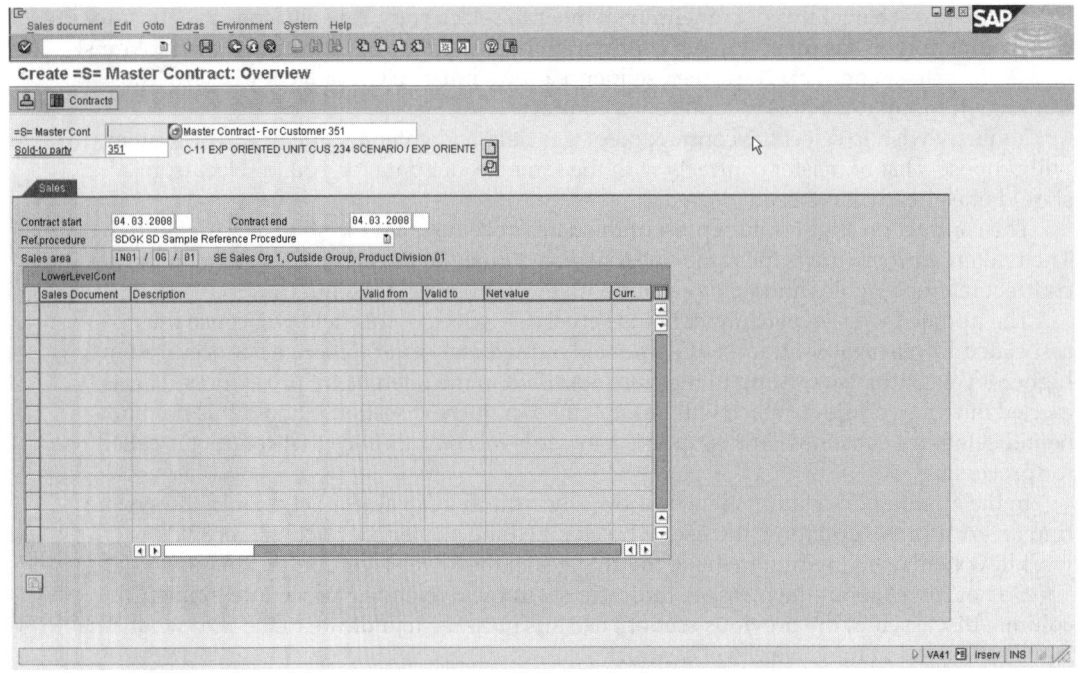

FIGURE 4-14   Master contract

look into the simple task of assigning agents to the workflow task for the master contract requirements. Use the following menu path.

Menu Path   SAP Customizing Implementation Guide | Sales and Distribution | Sales | Contracts | Master Contract | Activate Workflow for Master Contracts | Activate Event Linkage

Page down until you reach the workflow object type for master contracts, which is BUS2095, as seen in Figure 4-15.

Select the object and select Display. You are presented with the screen shown in Figure 4-16. Select Linkage Activated and save.

Then select SAP Customizing Implementation Guide | Sales and Distribution | Sales | Contracts | Master Contract | Activate Workflow for Master Contracts | Maintain Assignment of Agents.

You need to determine which task you require the workflow to maintain and for which you need to assign agents. Presuming we use Task 20000141, as seen in Figure 4-16, you are presented with the screen shown in Figure 4-17. Select Task | Display | Additional Data | Agent Assignment | Maintain. Then click the Create Agent Assignment button or press F5.

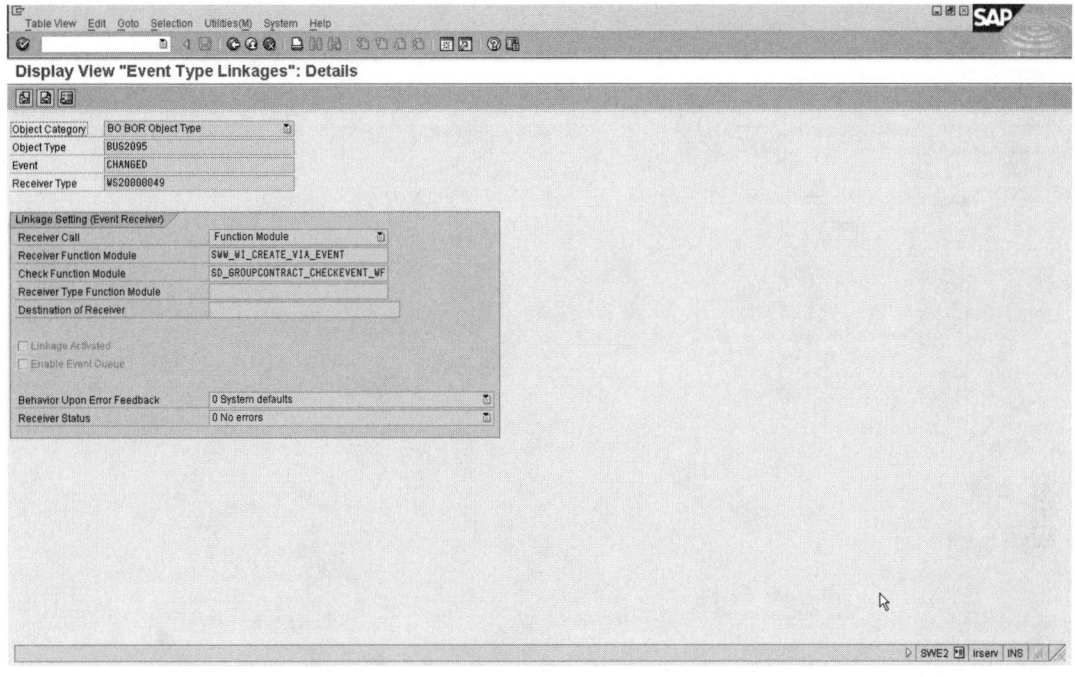

Copyright by SAP AG

FIGURE 4-15 Object type BUS2095 for master contract workflow

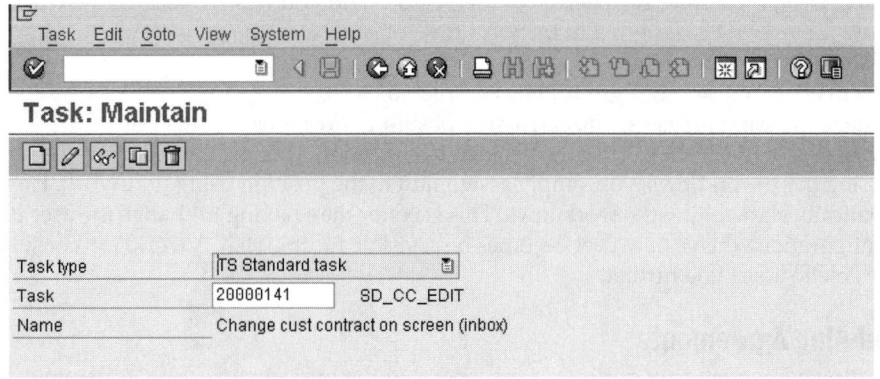

Copyright by SAP AG

FIGURE 4-16 Display object type BUS2095

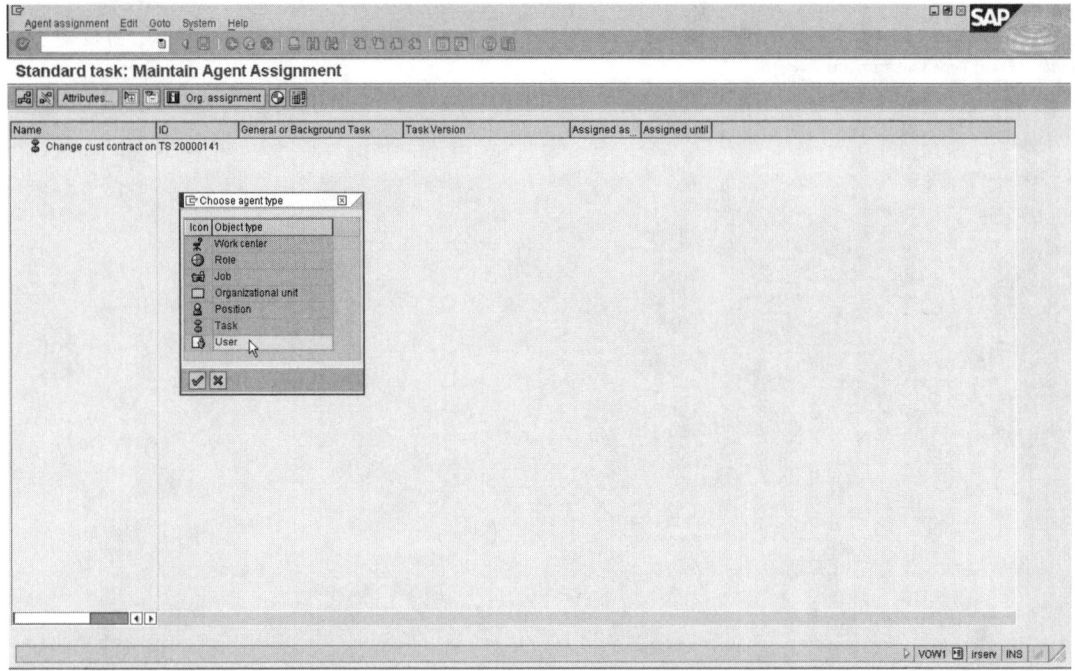

Copyright by SAP AG

FIGURE 4-17   Maintaining a task

You are presented with the following screen as shown in Figure 4-18.

Select User, then enter the user ID of the person who you wish to receive the workflow.

Now the user ID is assigned to the workflow object. Now click the Generate button, shown here.

The master contract configuration is completed.

Copyright by SAP AG

Instead of assigning users, you can assign positions. Positions are set up in transaction code [PPOMW]. A user is assigned to a position. When a new user has the task of processing these workflows, you simply assign him to the position using [PPOMW]. He will automatically start getting the workflows. This is better than having to change the user ID in the configuration when a new user becomes responsible for this task. A workflow consultant will be able to assist you further.

Scheduling Agreements

Scheduling agreements are outline agreements that the business has with a customer. They contain delivery dates and quantities to be delivered. These dates are then entered as schedule lines in the delivery schedule of the agreement.

The scheduling agreement is processed by delivering the schedule lines as they become due.

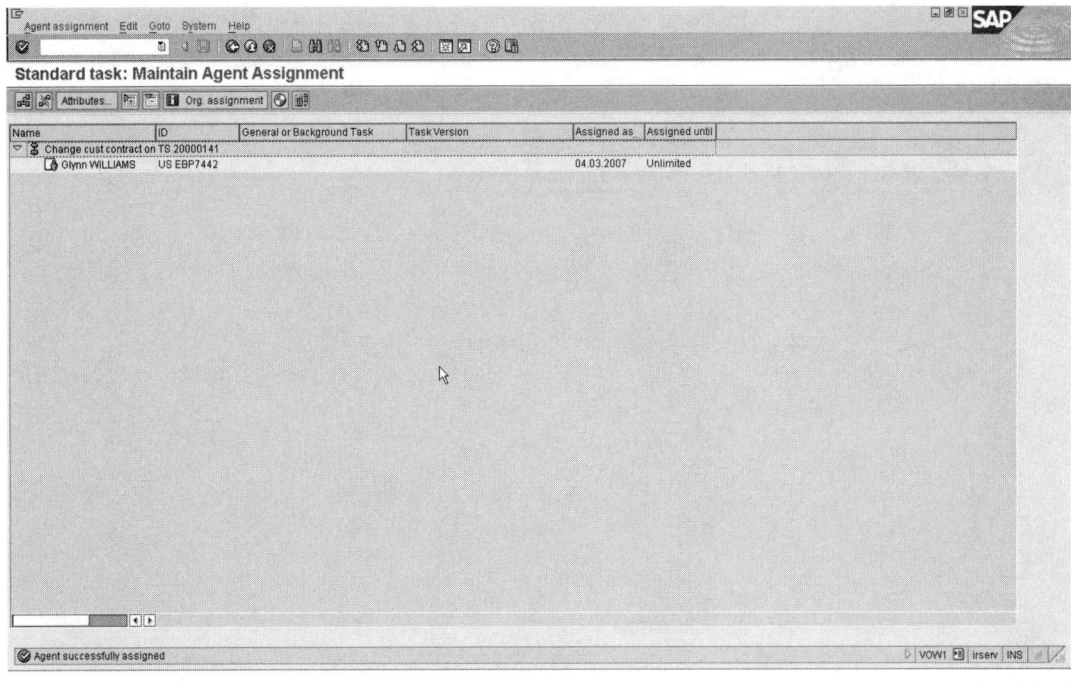

Copyright by SAP AG

FIGURE 4-18 Assigning a user to workflow task

The Background Configuration

To configure scheduling agreements, use the following menu path.

Menu Path   SAP Customizing Implementation Guide | Sales and Distribution | Sales | Sales Documents | Scheduling Agreements with Delivery Schedules | Define Schedule Line Types

Schedule line types are not schedule line categories. Schedule line types are used for information purposes only. Should you need to create one, follow the standard process of copying and changing an SAP standard. We will be focusing on 9 – JIT (Just in Time) delivery scheduling. Use the following menu path.

Menu Path   SAP Customizing Implementation Guide | Sales and Distribution | Sales | Sales Documents | Scheduling Agreements with Delivery Schedules | Maintain Planning Delivery Sched. Instruct./Splitting Rules

The planning delivery schedule is an internal delivery schedule used to plan requirements more efficiently. It is subdivided into three sections:

- **Maintain Delivery Schedule Splitting Rules**   These instructions, shown in Figure 4-19, determine the characteristics of the planning delivery schedule.

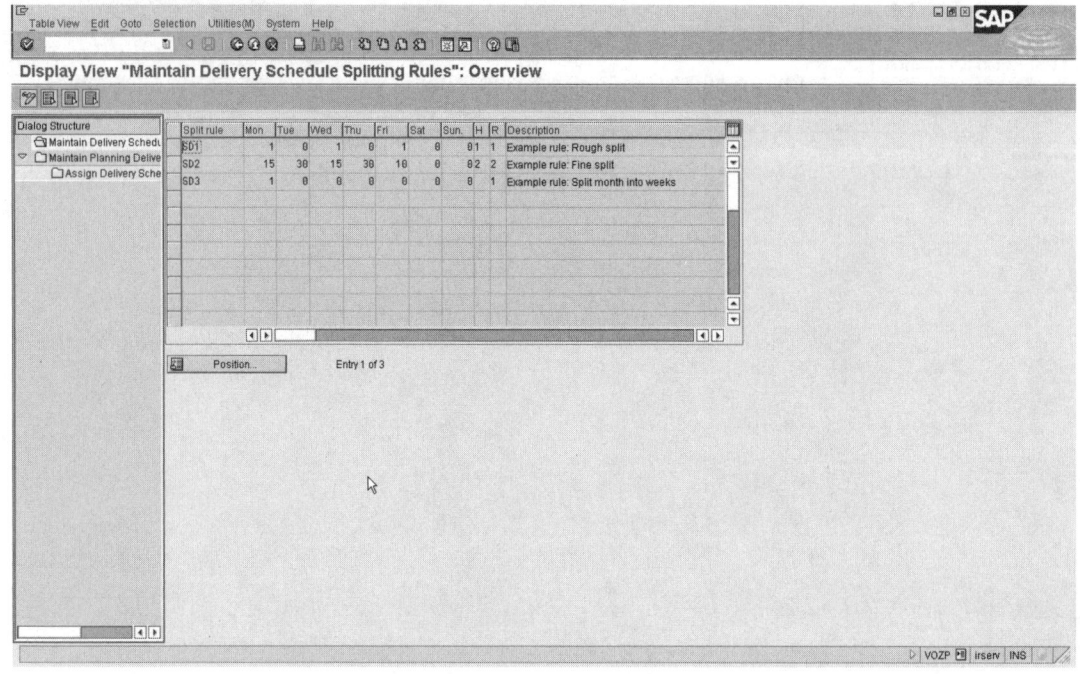

FIGURE 4-19 Maintain delivery schedule splitting rules

- **Maintain Planning Delivery Schedule Instructions** These instructions, shown in Figure 4-20, define the split of schedule line quantities between the different days in the planning delivery schedule and the forecast delivery schedule.

- **Assign Delivery Schedule Splitting Rules** These instructions, shown in Figure 4-21, assign the splitting rules to the planning delivery schedule.

(You may have more than one splitting rule for each instruction. You may thus assign a date type and a splitting rule range to each splitting rule, which will allow the system to carry out the splitting rules in sequence.)

Proceed by setting up the planning delivery schedule instructions first. This determines if schedule line categories are relevant for deliveries and how the planning delivery schedules are to be generated.

Note schedule lines in the planning delivery schedule replace those in the forecast delivery schedule with regards to planning relevance, and if required, delivery relevance.

The two examples of SAP1 and SAP2, shown in Figure 4-20, are useful in explaining the overview of this functionality.

SAP1 indicates that the schedule lines in the planning delivery schedule are relevant for delivery and should replace the schedule lines in the forecast delivery schedule, should their dates lie outside the dates of the JIT delivery schedule. This is indicated by a check in the checkbox in column D.

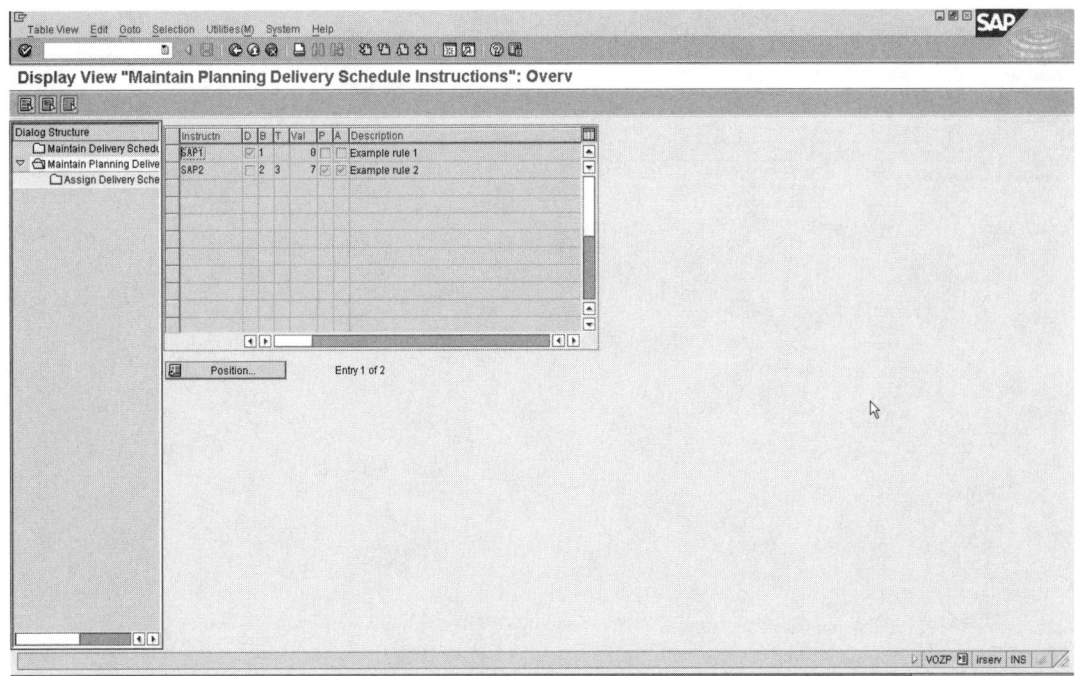

FIGURE 4-20   Maintain planning delivery schedule instructions

Column B is crucial—it indicates the baseline date used by the system for the planning of delivery schedules. Should no date be entered here, the system will not generate any schedule lines in the planning delivery schedule. You may select date type 1, which sets the delivery schedule date as the base date, or date type 2, which selects the planning delivery schedule generation as the base date.

Column T represents the date type, for the validity period, of the delivery schedule split. It is used to indicate if the validity period is measured in weeks or months. The validity period is the period of time in weeks or months that the delivery schedule split is valid. The system does not take into account the schedule lines in the forecast delivery schedule, whose date lies after the validity end date. The associated column Val represents the value in units to determine the end date of the validity period. Thus, example SAP2 has a date type of 3, which is months, and a value of 7—that is, 7 months after the baseline date of column B.

Column P indicates whether the system should adopt schedule lines from a previous planning delivery schedule when generating a new planning delivery schedule. This would only be valid for those schedule lines occurring after the validity end date of the delivery schedule split.

Column A indicates if the system should automatically generate a planning delivery schedule when a forecast delivery schedule is created.

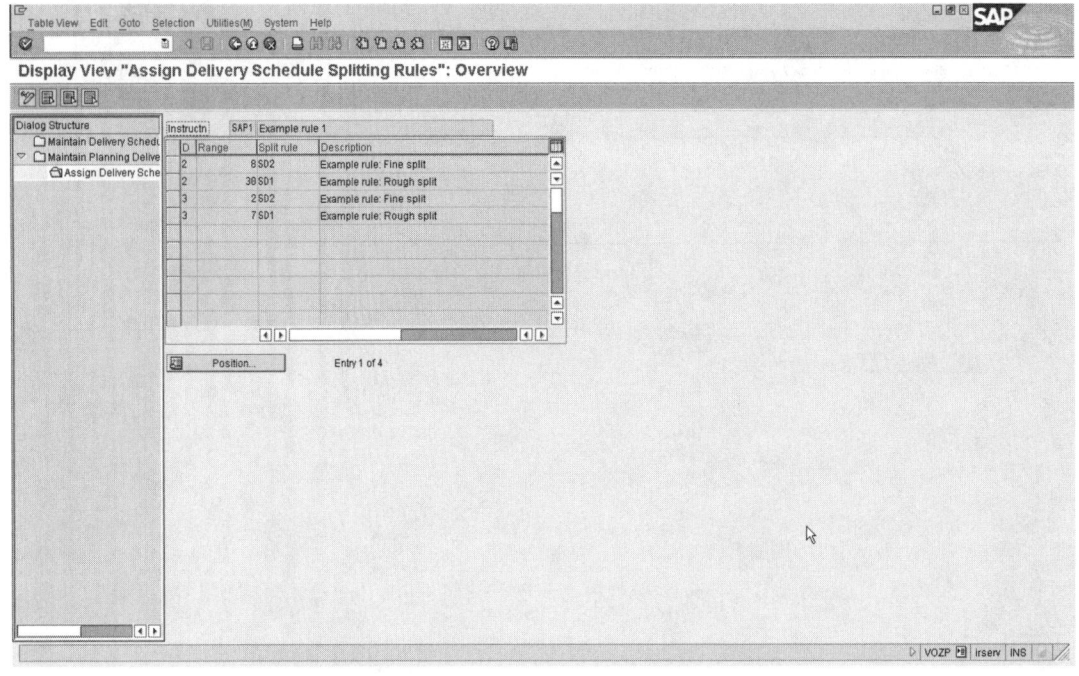

Copyright by SAP AG

FIGURE 4-21   Assign delivery schedule splitting rules

Proceed to maintaining the delivery schedule splitting rules. Highlight the instruction for example SAP2 and double-click on Maintain Delivery Schedule Splitting Rules.

Here you define the split share sum into daily periods, as shown in Figure 4-21. Should you have an initial schedule line quantity of 600 pieces, using split rule SD1, that schedule line will be divided up into three equal schedule lines of 200 pieces each (600 ÷ 3 = 200). Each 200 pieces are to be delivered on Monday, Wednesday. and Friday.

 It is easier to make the splits add up to 100 so you can work with a percentage of the total schedule line quantity. For example, the split rule SD2 adds up to 100, causing 15 percent of the schedule line quantity to be delivered on Mondays, 30 percent on Tuesdays, and so on.

Column H defines the holiday rule for the delivery schedule split. You can select to treat the holidays as workdays or you can choose to have the schedule line quantity move to the last preceding workday, or choose to have the system split the quantity via the remaining days according to the delivery split.

The calendar of the Ship-to Party is used to control the goods receipt of the Ship-to Party, this calendar is assigned to the schedule agreement items, unloading point. This calendar may be changed using the assigned user exit C_CALENDAR. Refer to "User Exits" in Chapter 10.

Column R represents the rounding rule for schedule line quantities. You may select to round up to three decimal places, or to three decimal places according to the sales unit. Or you may round up to a multiple of the delivery rounding quantity.

After you have defined your delivery schedule splitting rules, assign them a brief description for ease of use later.

When you have completed the task and saved, go back to Maintain Planning Delivery Schedule Instructions. Select the instruction again—for example, SAP2—and then select Assign Delivery Schedule Splitting Rules.

The split rules we have defined (for example, SD1, etc.) are now assigned to a date range using weeks and months as the date type followed by the range of this date type. Thus, in the example in Figure 4-21, the date range is eight weeks (from the start of the baseline date) for using split rule SD2.

Although the split rule range and the delivery schedule split influence schedule line splits, the split validity period overrides the splitting rule range in every case.

One is now able to proceed with the sales document type configuration. Proceed as with any other sales document type configuration process.

A scheduling agreement does not need to have release orders. You can create the delivery directly from the scheduling agreement. This is the benefit of having a scheduling agreement.

The pricing procedure can be the same as that of the standard sales orders. Thus you can leave the document pricing procedure indicator blank or set it the same as for standard sales orders.

The transaction group must be 3, indicating this sales document transaction is a scheduling agreement.

Figure 4-22 shows the scheduling agreements section of the sales document type configuration. The correction delivery type is LFKO. (A correction delivery is used when the customer returns goods before accepting them and processing goods receipt. The correction delivery will update the cumulative quantity in the scheduling agreement, to indicate that the original delivery quantity is still available to be called off in the scheduling agreement.) The usage indicator can be any indicator you set. The value set here will default into all scheduling agreements at header level and thus be copied into all items. This is the default usage as found on the line item of the sales document. (This is often a field used in analysis of sales transactions.)

The MRP for delivery schedule type defines how the schedule lines are to be controlled. This value is proposed when creating a scheduling agreement.

Standard deliveries are created for the scheduling agreements, thus the delivery type used is LF.

The standard billing type is used as well. However, just as you may copy and change the sales document types, you may also copy and change the delivery and billing documents should this be necessary. (Refer to Chapter 6 for information on deliveries and Chapter 7 for information on billing.)

Scheduling agreement		
Corr.delivery type	LFKO	Delivery block
Use	S	
MRP for DlvSchType	A	

Copyright by SAP AG

FIGURE 4-22 Scheduling agreement settings on sales document type

In item category configuration for schedule line agreements, the standard item category is LZN. LZN behaves like a standard item category. It is relevant for delivery-related billing as well as pricing and it does allow schedule lines.

The schedule line categories used are:

- **CP**   MRP (materials requirements planning). CP is the standard schedule line category posting requirements through to materials planning and doing the availability check.

- **CV**   Consumption MRP. CV is also a standard schedule line category that does do an availability check. However, CV does not post the demand through to MRP.

- **CN**   No materials planning. CN does no availability check and no MRP.

Proceed with creating the scheduling agreement by using the following menu path.

Menu Path   SAP Menu | Logistics | Sales and Distribution | Sales | Scheduling Agreement | [VA31] - Create

Use the standard sales document type LZ. Enter the relevant data such as customer number and material number, as well as the order quantities for the materials.

To enter the delivery dates for the item, select the items and select Item | Schedule Lines.

Deliveries are automatically created from the schedule lines of the scheduling agreement. These deliveries happen when the delivery due list is run on the same date as the schedule line is relevant for deliveries. You are also able to create the delivery manually using transaction code [VL01] or following the procedures in Chapter 6.

Consignment Stock Process

With consignment the business allows stock or materials to sit at the customer's site or allows stock to sit at its own site reserved for the customer. This is done on an agreement that the customer will sell or consume as many of these materials as he can. Only after he has consumed any or sold any and informed the business will the business transfer the stock to the customer's ownership and issue an invoice. Should the customer not wish to sell or consume any more material, he informs the business and they take the stock back.

All requirements transferred from consignment sales orders to materials planning are transferred as individual requirements. This occurs regardless of what the availability checking group setting is on the respective material master record.

Consignment stock is monitored in the system by customer and material and the consignment quantity is controlled separately from the available stock for standard sales orders. This type of stock is referred to as *special stock*. Another form of special stock is returnable packaging.

The Consignment Fill-Up

When the business delivers stock to a customer on consignment, it is called *consignment fill-up*. The consignment fill-up uses a standard sales order document type KB. This KB order type is then followed by a standard delivery LF.

The consignment fill-up sales document type KB, as well as all other consignment-related sales document types, should have the sales document category setting C (sales order).

It is also advisable to use a different number range as you will want consignment sales process to be highlighted as a different sales procedure than the standard sales cycle.

It is also advisable not to report on these fill-ups as bookings for statistical purposes, as these fill-ups in no way indicate a sale. They are just a way to move stock from unrestricted use to the customer's consignment. To report on bookings and billings, you should use the consignment issue process.

The delivery type used is the standard LF. (Refer to Chapter 3.)

The big changes to the standard sales order process are due to the customer not being billed for any of these items. So no invoice is relevant. Thus the sales document type setting for order-related billing and delivery-related billing should be configured as not relevant for billing documents.

The item category used as standard for consignment fill-ups, KBN, should be set as not relevant for billing as well as for no pricing. Thus the business data of the item category should look similar to Figure 4-23.

The item does allow schedule lines. This is a fundamental element in the consignment process. The schedule line category determines how deliveries are to perform and what types of goods movements are carried out. The standard schedule line categories to be used are E0 and E1.

Schedule line category E1, as shown in Figure 4-24, is to be used with MRP. It uses availability checking.

The schedule line states the item is relevant for deliveries and when the delivery happens the item must use movement type 631, which, at the time of goods issue, posts the stock into a special consignment category in the delivering plant's stock for that customer and material. (Refer to Chapter 6 for more information on the delivery process.)

Do not forget to set up the sales document copying control for sales document, item category, and schedule line category.

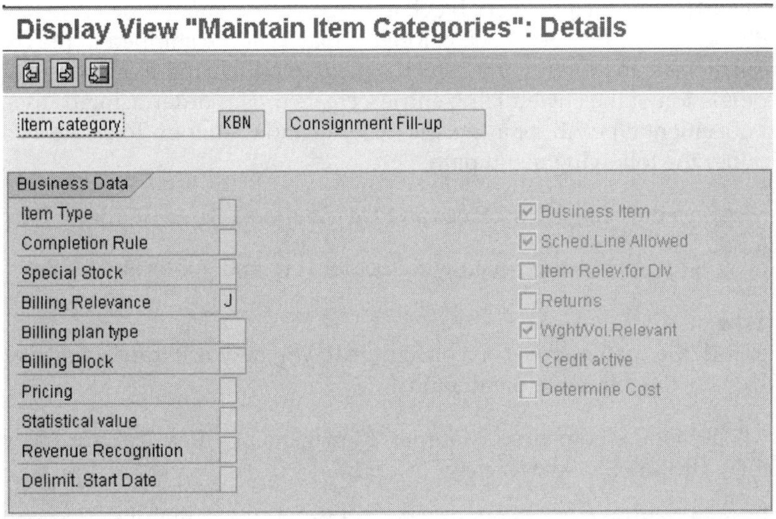

Copyright by SAP AG

FIGURE 4-23   Business data of KBN item category

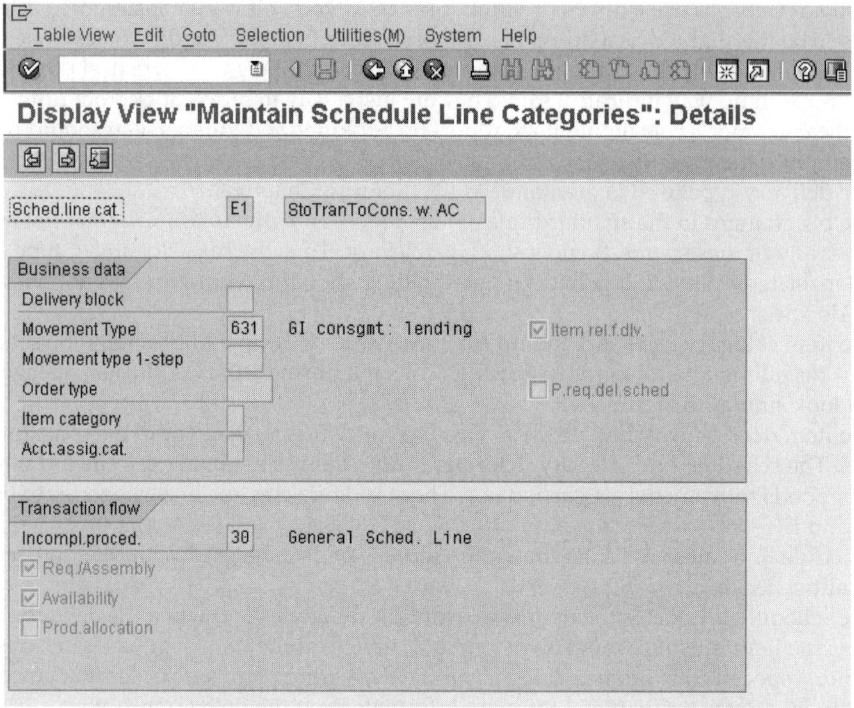

Copyright by SAP AG

FIGURE 4-24 Schedule line category E1

You may wish to assign a delivery block to the sales document type KB, as this will automatically propose a delivery block before the materials are shipped to the consignee. That way you are able to monitor what stock you are sending, and if it is authorized.

After completion of the customizing entries, create a sales order using transaction code [VA01] and document type KB for a specific material and customer. To create a consignment fill-up order, use the following menu path.

Menu Path   SAP Menu I Logistics I Sales and Distribution I Sales I Order I [VA01] - Create

Enter the order type. Next, proceed with the delivery and goods issue.

Stock Overview
To view the stock the customer has on consignment, you may use transaction code [MB58] or [MMBE], or use the following menu path.

Menu Path   SAP Menu I Logistics I Materials Management I Physical Inventory I Environment I MMBE - Stock Overview

Enter the material and the plant that delivered the material. Select Execute. You will see a list of stock for that material in that plant. Should you not select a plant but merely enter the material and select Execute, the system will propose material in all the plants within a company code.

If you double-click on one of the line values—for example, on the plant—you will see a breakdown of the stock in that plant according to its stock type.

You are presented with the stock overview screen shown in Figure 4-25. Should stock be available and be on consignment at the customer's site, you will see an entry that appears as special stock. In Figure 4-25 this appears in the hierarchy as follows: Client / Company Code / Plant / Storage Location/ Batch / Special Stock.

Thus you are able to view the consignment stock total represented at a customer as well as the batches that make up that total.

When a consignment fill-up is carried out, the system checks the available quantity of stock in the delivering plant to see if this quantity can be met. When the system proceeds with a consignment issue or consignment pick-up, the system checks the customer consignment stock (as seen here) to see if there is an available quantity.

Now that we have completed the consignment fill-up, the stock exists under the consignee's control. The consignee may consume or sell the material. On a regular basis the customer will inform the business of his stock usage.

As the business is usually only informed after the consumption happens, it is not sensible to have any checking in the consignment issue cycle. For example, there is no need to have a billing block or delivery block.

It is possible to have an automatic credit check on consignment issues as you may determine open items that are unpaid.

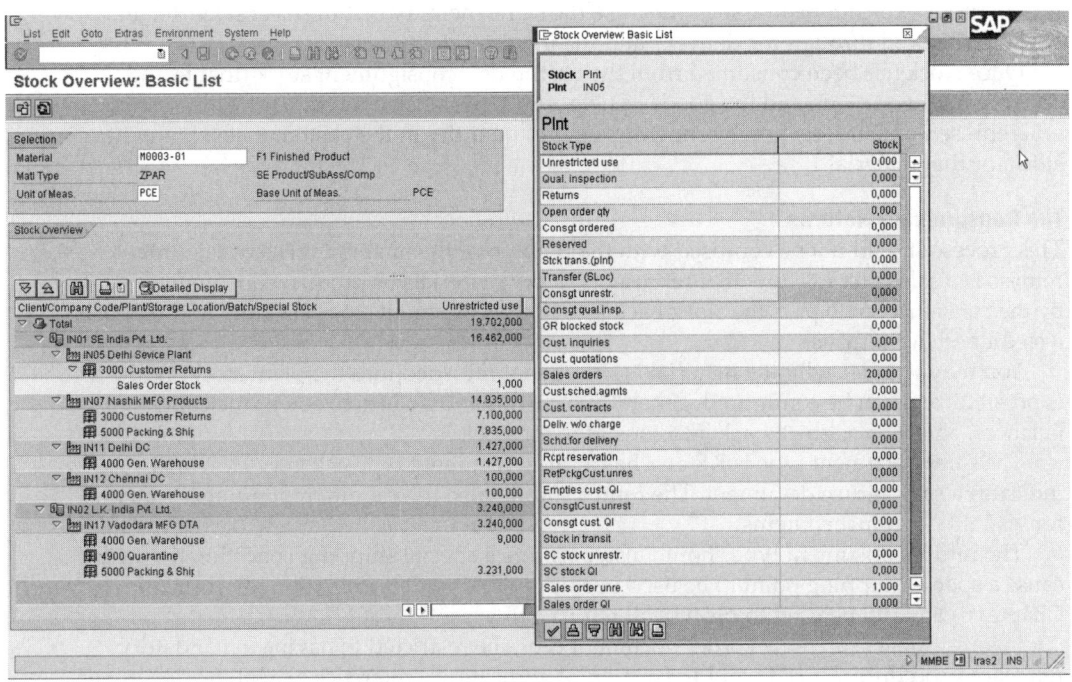

Copyright by SAP AG

FIGURE 4-25   Stock overview showing stock type

However, a manual credit check should be done on the consignee *before* every consignment fill-up is done, because once the stock is under the consignee's control it is not physically possible to stop the consignee from consuming stock even though he is over his credit limit. Also, as he usually only informs the business after the stock has been consumed, the business has to process the transaction to record the consumption.

The Consignment Issue

The customer only pays when and if he sells or consumes the materials. The business records the sale to the consignee via order type KE. A standard delivery LF is then completed, followed by the invoice.

The consignment issue document type is KE and has a sales document with category C. It has a standard delivery type LF. This document type is relevant for billing. It should be relevant for delivery-related billing using a standard delivery type F2.

The standard item category used is KEN. Item category KEN is relevant for billing as well as pricing. It has schedule lines and should determine the cost of the item.

The item category has a special stock indicator that is used to indicate that the material being controlled must be controlled as special stock. For consignment, the special stock indicator used is a W.

The standard schedule line categories used are C0 and C1. Schedule line category C1 does an availability check and materials requirements planning. The movement type associated with the transaction checks for available consignment stock at the consignee's site. The schedule line is relevant for deliveries.

To create a consignment issue order, use the same menu path, but select sales document type KE. Proceed through the delivery and the invoice.

Once stock has been consumed from the customer's consignment stock (that is, the delivery has been made and the goods issue posted), the stock overview [MMBE] screen will represent this transaction by showing a lower quantity in the customer consignment stock for that material.

The Consignment Returns

This process should not be confused with the pick-up of the materials. The consignment returns is a sales process flow that represents faulty materials or product consumed or sold by the consignee, who puts the stock back into his consignment stock as faulty and requests a credit note for returns.

 You may wonder why the material is simply not returned into the plant stock. While it is possible, and can be configured, generally, a customer manages his own stock and balances, and returns stock back into consignment stock.

The sales document type is KR and has a sales document type category H, which indicates a sales return document. The return should also have a different number range for visibility of returned items.

The returns document type should also promote a special shipping condition that will cause a special shipping point to be used in shipping point determination (discussed in Chapter 6) and can be used to process all return deliveries.

I would suggest all return order document types be restricted to having a mandatory reference procedure. Thus, I would assign an M, indicating a reference to a billing document. Do not forget to assign the reference document in the copying control rules and make sure you select update document flow in the copying control rules. This will ensure visibility of the path through consumption of the stock to return of the stock.

It is recommended you utilize the same return pricing procedure as that of the standard sales documents. This will ensure that your pricing and subsequent credit for returns as well as costs are kept constant.

The assigned delivery type is LR.

The delivery-related or order-related billing type should be RE.

It is valid to automatically propose a billing block in order to check if the credit is authorized and valid. Thus assign the standard billing block 08.

The item category in the sales document that is passed through to the invoice is KRN. Item category KRN also has the special stock indicator W to indicate the consignment process. The item is relevant for delivery-related billing. It is valid for pricing.

The standard schedule line category used in the system for consignment returns is D0.

The movement type used is the receipt of customer's consignment. The item is relevant for delivery. However, no transfer of requirements should be carried out and no availability check should be done. This is due to the fact that the business is receiving the goods back into its plant. They cannot do an availability check, as the articles are at the customer's site. Nor does it make sense to transfer requirements to its materials management.

The stock is moved back into the customer's consignment stock (not the business' plant). The logic is that the customer will call to pick up the unused goods and simply consume other material that is not faulty. Thus, the customer's consignment stock will increase by the quantity he returned.

To create a consignment returns order, proceed as you have for a fill-up and consignment issue; however, use sales document type KR

The Consignment Pick-Up

The consignment pick-up process is the last and final process linked to the consignment procedure. It is responsible for the picking up of faulty materials, as well as the picking up of excess materials not yet consumed by a consignment issue.

The sales document type KA should have the SD document category C, this being sales order.

Depending on your business it may be beneficial to have a reference mandatory. This will restrict all consignment pick-ups from being made unless they make reference to a fill-up order type. You can restrict the reference to being mandatory to an order type, thus setting C, and then further control the referencing procedure by using the copying control rules. Again, ensure in the copying control rules that you indicate to report a document flow.

As the stock is coming back into the warehouse or plant, you will want a specific returns shipping point to be automatically determined, so assign the special shipping conditions you use to determine this. Refer to "Shipping Point Determination" in Chapter 6.

No invoice is necessary, as the goods are not changing ownership. The materials are still in the possession of the business, and remain in possession of the business until the act of goods issue in the consignment issue process. Goods issue is the trigger that transfers ownership from the business to the consignment consumer.

The standard item category for consignment pick-ups is KAN.

The standard schedule line categories of the consignment pick-up process are F0 and F1. Schedule line category F1 is relevant for delivery as well as transfer of requirements and availability check.

Do not forget the availability check is done against the consignment stock on the customer's site. To create a consignment pick-up, proceed as you have with all other sales document types using transaction code [VA01] followed by creating the delivery.

Display Consignment and Returnable Packaging at Customer

As previously discussed SAP has a standard overview for consignment and returnable packaging. (For more information on returnable packaging, refer to Chapter 6.) This overview lists all the consignment for all materials in all plants for all customers. It is an invaluable tool for a comprehensive overview of goods on consignment. You may access it by using the following menu path.

Menu Path SAP Menu | Logistics | Materials Management | Inventory Management | Environment | Consignment | MB58 - Consignment at Customer

You will see an overview screen as follows in Figure 4-26.

This overview shows the material and respective quantity as well as the respective customer.

We can now see an example of this in the stock overview[MMBE], as shown in Figure 4-27.

The consignment stock process can work across borders and company codes (see "Intercompany Billing" in Chapter 7). However, you may experience difficulties when trying to accommodate certain legal regulations, such as Intrastat and Exstrastat requirements in Europe.

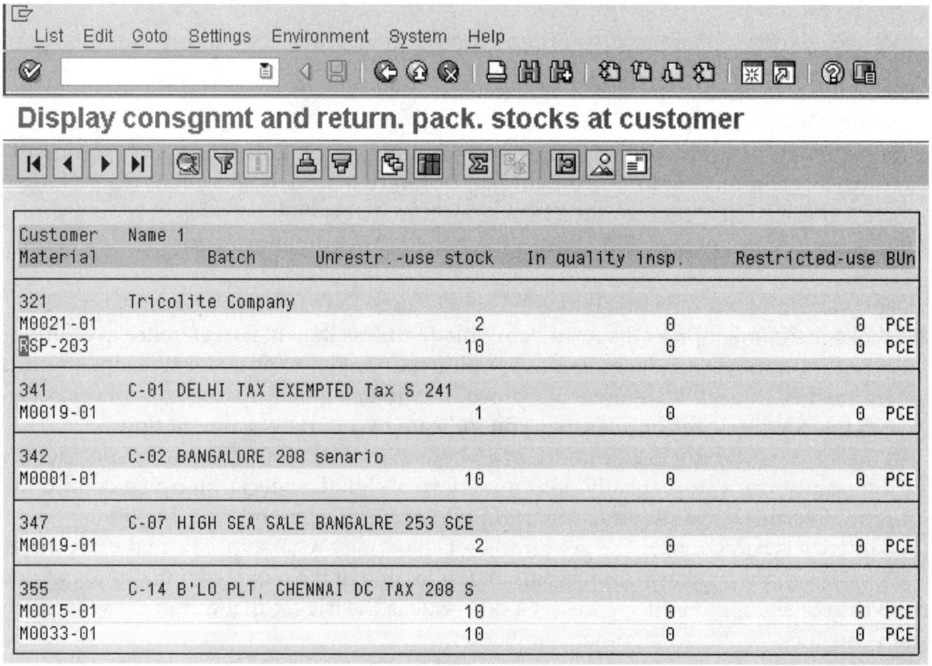

Copyright by SAP AG

FIGURE 4-26 Consignment stock at customer

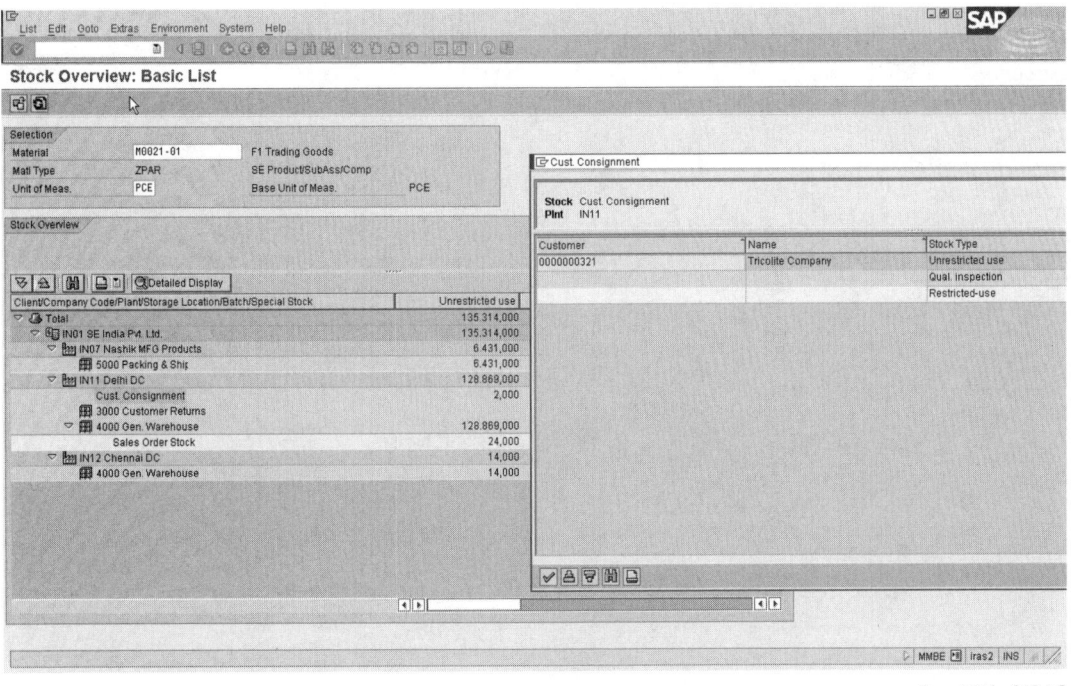

FIGURE 4-27   Stock overview showing customer consignment

For this process SAP has developed an invoice named WIA. It is relevant for cross-EU border invoicing only with plants abroad. It is called via the billing indicator J on the item category calling up this WIA invoice. This will only be necessary for goods movements across borders where there is no invoice to show values. It would be relevant for KAN and KBN item categories.

Sales Document Lists

Lists are used throughout the system to generate an overview of documents displayed in a certain style and totaled by a certain parameter. You will use lists in all document processes, from inquiries to invoices. As the procedure is standard throughout, I will concentrate on the configuration of one example—sales order lists.

There are many sales document lists that are used, the most common in Sales and Distribution being the sales document list [VA05].

If you proceed to the bottom of the screen and select the small matchcode shown in Figure 4-28, you will see the program being used for sales document list in [VA05] is SAPMV75A.

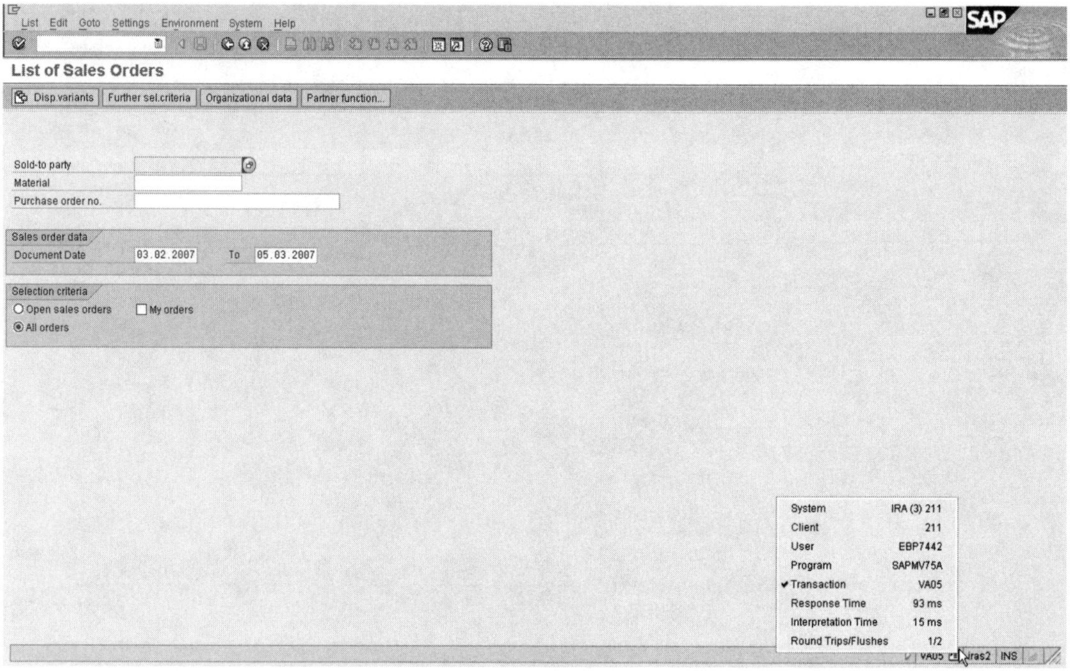

Copyright by SAP AG

FIGURE 4-28 SAPMV75A used in VA05 transaction

The selection parameter screen you see when you execute this program is now changed according to configuration as seen in the next section.

Sales Document List Configuration

To configure sales document lists, use the following menu path.

Menu Path SAP Customizing Implementation Guide | Sales and Distribution | Sales | Lists | Define Selection Criteria

This sets up additional fields we would like to use as selection criteria, as shown in Figure 4-29.

The first column is the program name. The second column is the transaction group—for example, the transaction group for sales orders is 0. The third column is the display group, which changes the fields you have in the list. The fourth column is the display variant that sequences the list fields, once it has been executed. The fifth column controls whether the field may be summed up (totaled) or not. The sixth column displays the sequence on the selection screen the field will occupy. The seventh column is the field name.

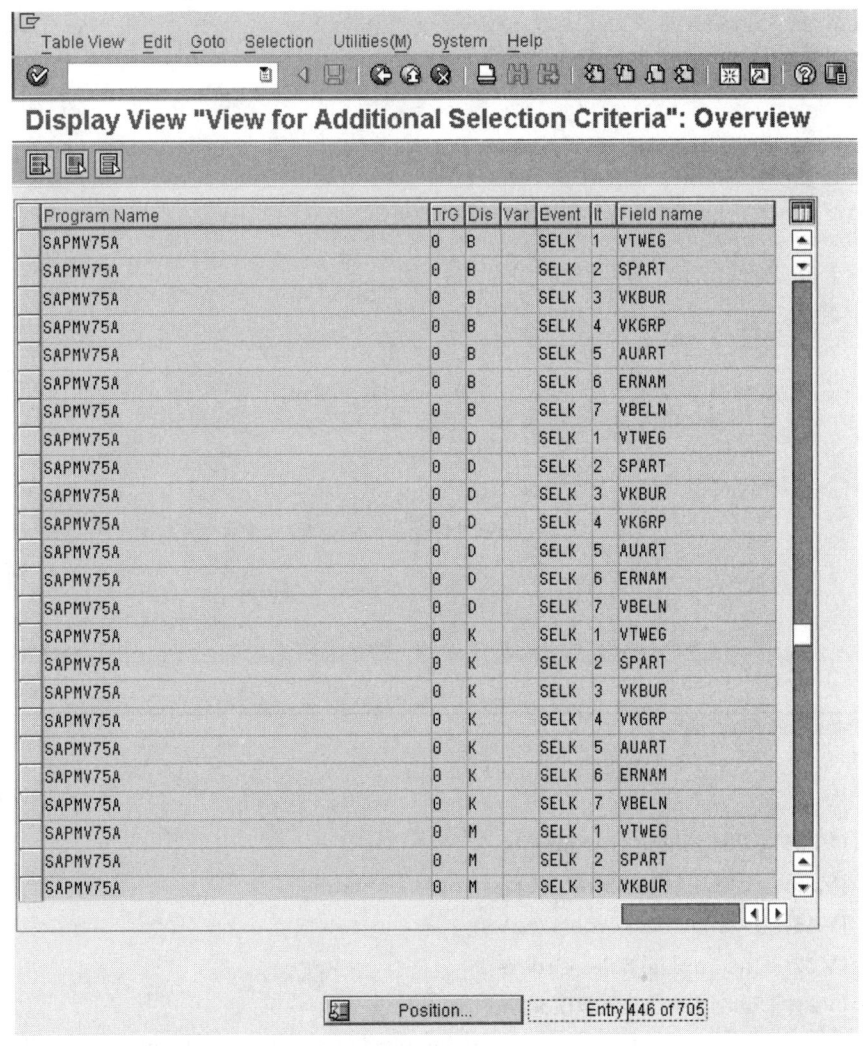

Copyright by SAP AG

Figure 4-29   Settings for SAPMV75A

Should you execute [VA05] you are presented with the screen shown in Figure 4-30.

Should you click the Further Selection Criteria button, you will have the selection options shown in Figure 4-31.

Lists in Sales and Distribution Processing

There are many sales document lists and work lists. The most common of them are listed here:

- **[VA05]**   List of Sales Orders
- **[VL06O]**   Outbound Delivery Monitor - Picking, Goods Issue, List Deliveries

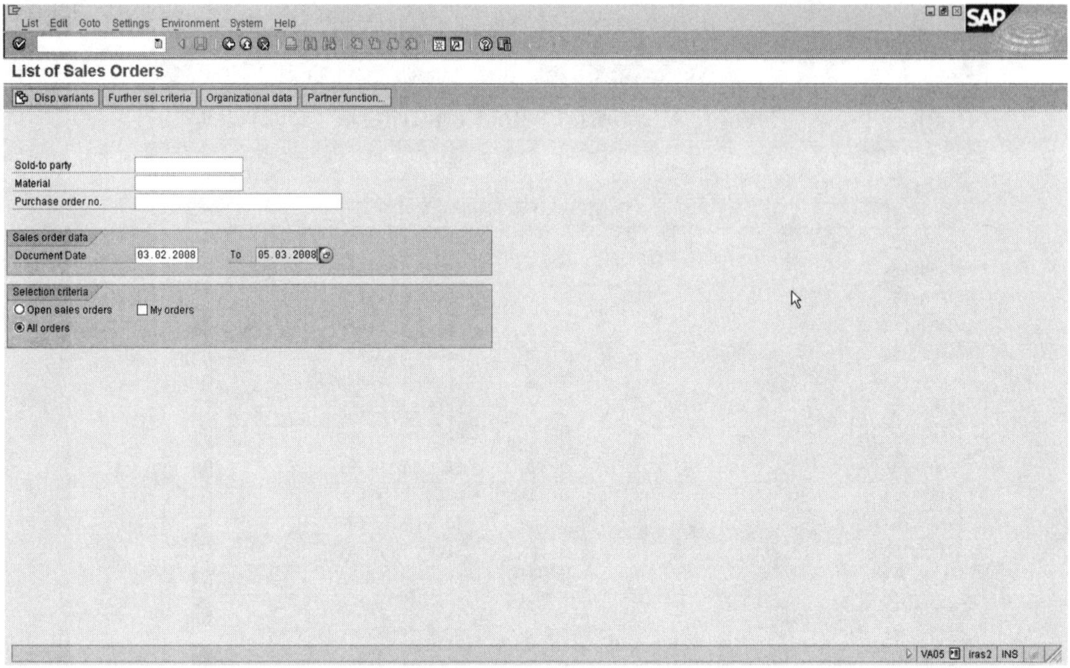

Copyright by SAP AG

FIGURE 4-30 Sales document list

- **[VF05]** List Billing Documents
- **[V.26]** Sales Documents by Object or User Status
- **[V.15]** Display Backorders (Sales)
- **[V.02]** Incomplete Sales Orders
- **[V23]** Sales Documents Blocked for Billing
- **[V_UC]** Incomplete Sales Documents (use SD document category J for deliveries)
- **[VL06O]** Outbound Delivery Monitor - Picking, Goods Issue, List Deliveries
- **[VT11]** Transp. Planning List (Shipment)
- **[VFX3]** Blocked Billing Docs

Sales Document Status Profiles Management

In a sales document you have statuses at header and item level. These are used to control the stage/status the sales document is in. In Figure 4-32 we see the status tab, at item level of a sales document. The bottom part of the tab, Completeness, indicates how complete the

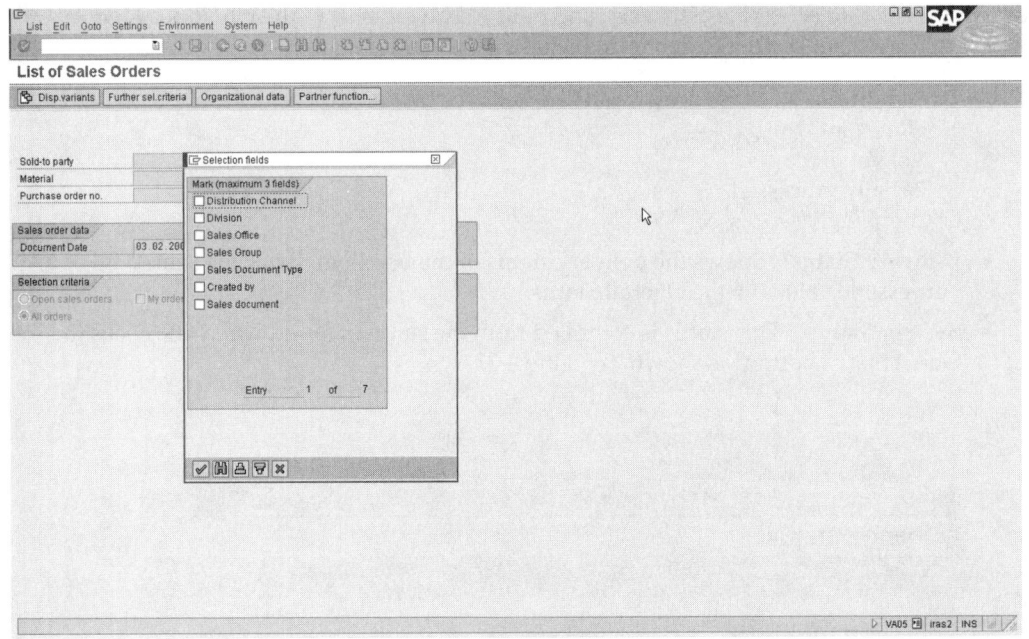

FIGURE 4-31   Sales document list with additional selection options

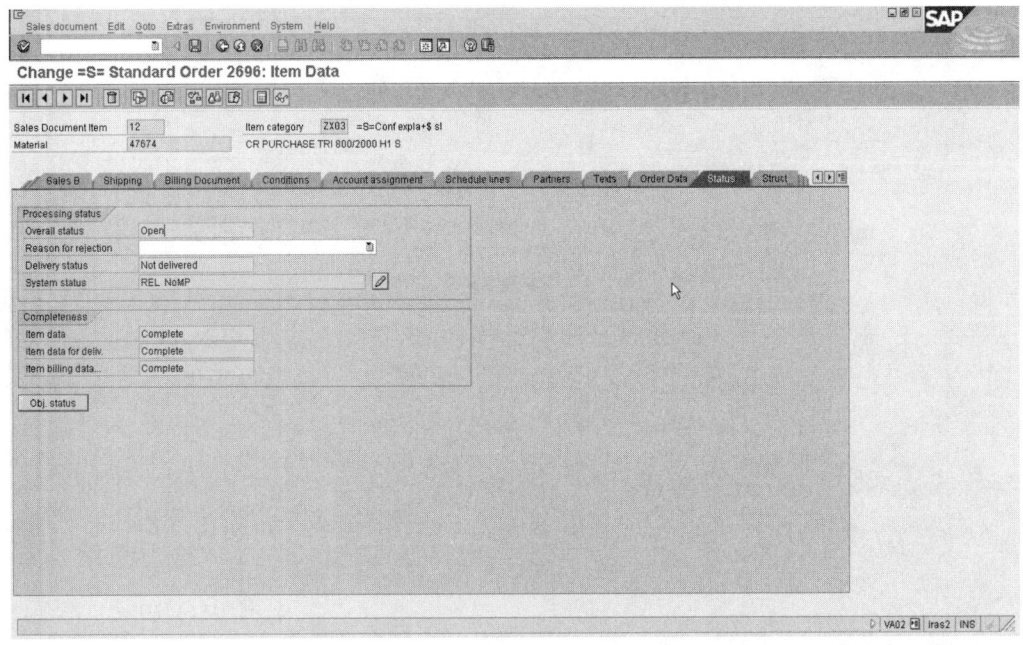

FIGURE 4-32   Status tab at item level

sales document data is for sales, delivery, and billing. The top part of the tab, Processing Status, indicates what stage the item is in, including the following fields:

- **Overall Status**   Shows the overall line item status. Possible values are
  Not Relevant
  A: Not yet processed
  B: Partially processed
  C: Completely processed

- **Delivery Status**   Shows the delivery status of the line item. It has the same permissible values as the Overall Status.

- **System Status**   This status is compiled from the statuses found when one clicks the Object Status button, as shown in Figure 4-33.

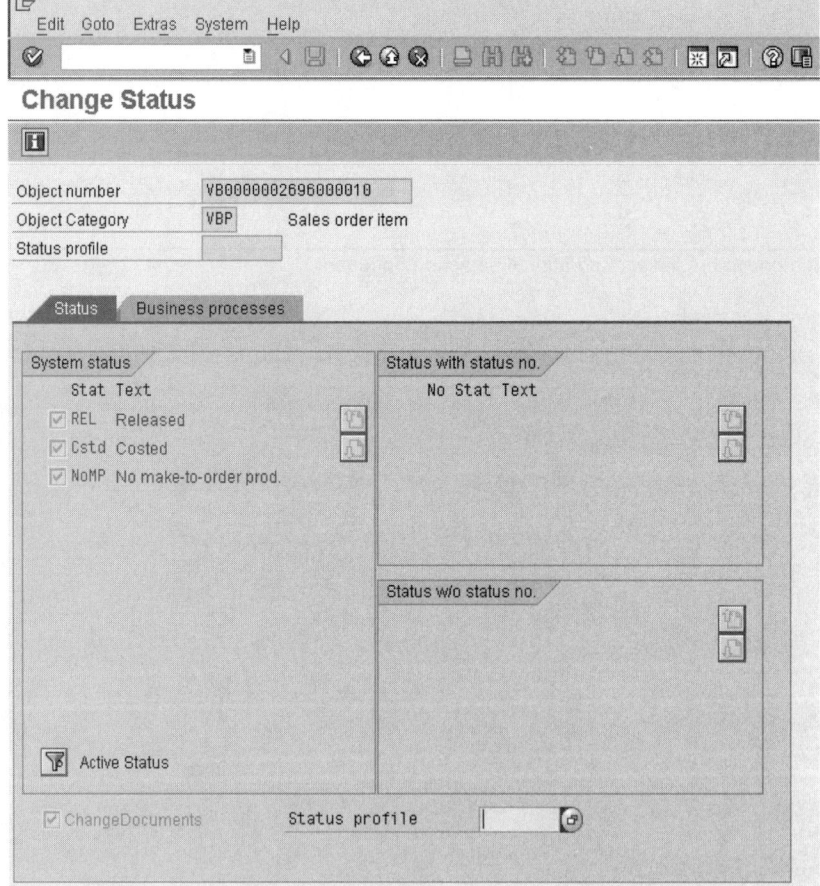

Copyright by SAP AG

FIGURE 4-33   Line item object status

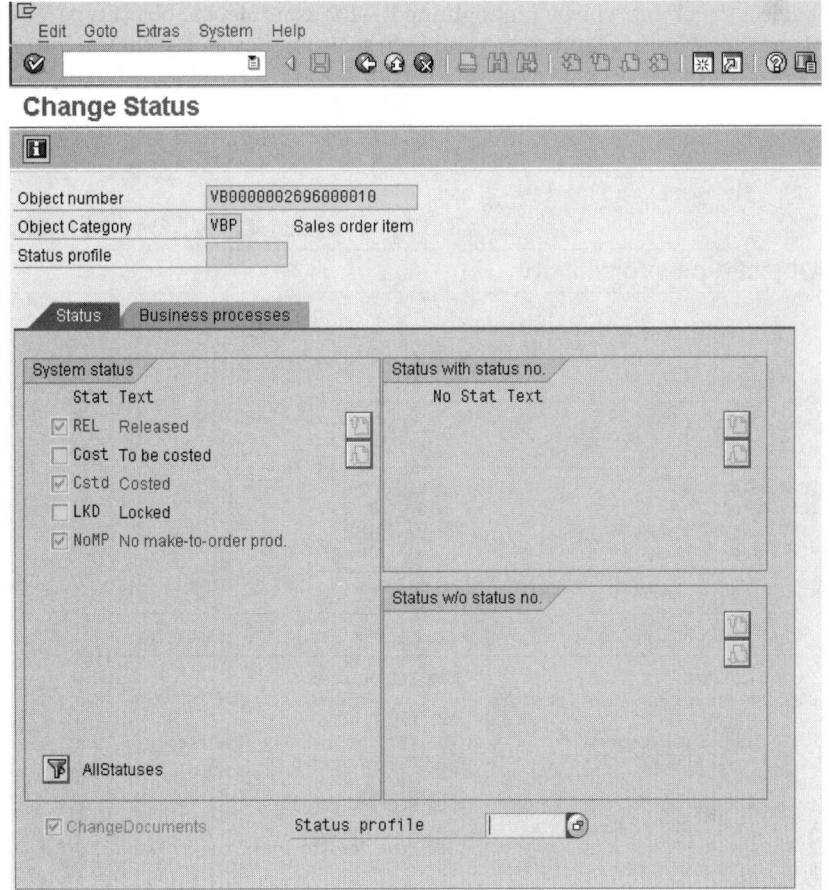

Copyright by SAP AG

FIGURE 4-34   All statuses at line item level

If you click the Filter button, shown here, you will see the inactive statuses, as shown in Figure 4-34. Active statuses are always highlighted in blue.

Copyright by SAP AG

Statuses are configured and their schema may be changed as long as there are no objects that have already referenced the status procedure.

If you select the object type by highlighting it—for example, the object type VBP in this document shown earlier in Figure 4-33—and then selecting Extras | Technical Information | Object Type, you will see a screen similar to Figure 4-35.

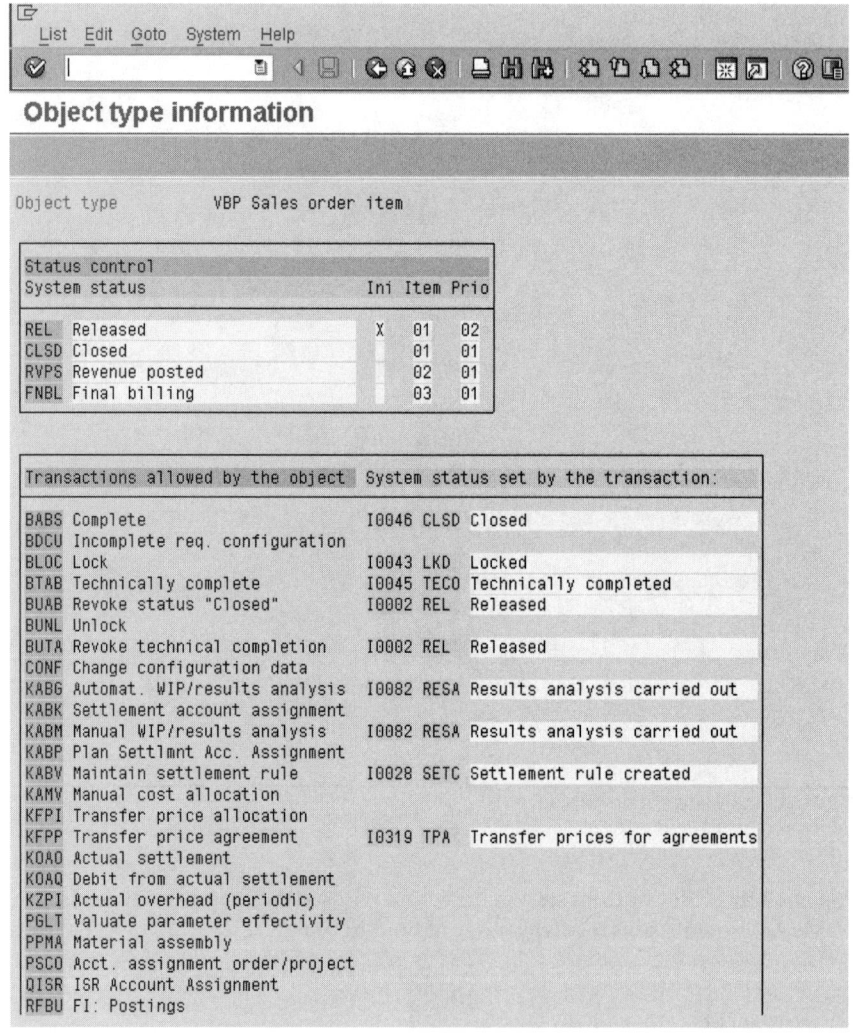

Object type information

| Object type | VBP Sales order item |

Status control
System status		Ini	Item	Prio
REL	Released	X	01	02
CLSD	Closed		01	01
RVPS	Revenue posted		02	01
FNBL	Final billing		03	01

Transactions allowed by the object	System status set by the transaction:
BABS Complete	I0046 CLSD Closed
BDCU Incomplete req. configuration	
BLOC Lock	I0043 LKD Locked
BTAB Technically complete	I0045 TECO Technically completed
BUAB Revoke status "Closed"	I0002 REL Released
BUNL Unlock	
BUTA Revoke technical completion	I0002 REL Released
CONF Change configuration data	
KABG Automat. WIP/results analysis	I0082 RESA Results analysis carried out
KABK Settlement account assignment	
KABM Manual WIP/results analysis	I0082 RESA Results analysis carried out
KABP Plan Settlmnt Acc. Assignment	
KABV Maintain settlement rule	I0028 SETC Settlement rule created
KAMV Manual cost allocation	
KFPI Transfer price allocation	
KFPP Transfer price agreement	I0319 TPA Transfer prices for agreements
KOAO Actual settlement	
KOAQ Debit from actual settlement	
KZPI Actual overhead (periodic)	
PGLT Valuate parameter effectivity	
PPMA Material assembly	
PSCO Acct. assignment order/project	
QISR ISR Account Assignment	
RFBU FI: Postings	

FIGURE 4-35   Object VBP status

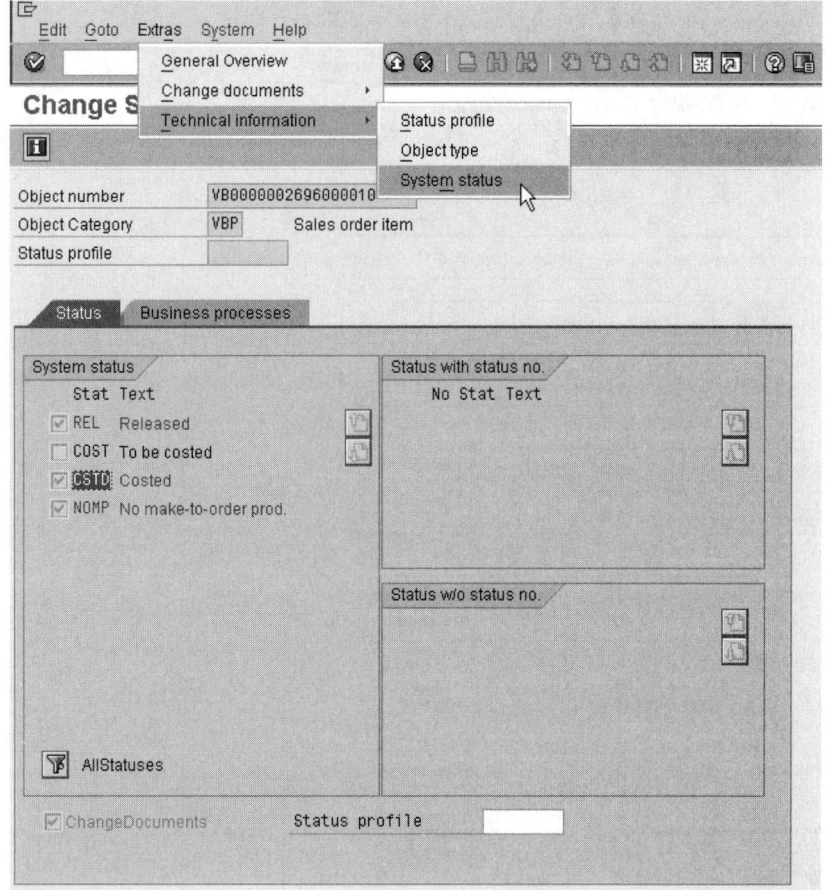

Copyright by SAP AG

Figure 4-36   Select a status, then the menu path

You can select each status individually, as shown in Figure 4-36, then select the menu path to see a screen like the one shown in Figure 4-37. You can now see that the system status I0165 - CSTD is in the object category VBP, and see which processes set and release the status.

It is possible to create your own statuses by creating a status profile. This can be seen in our sales document header example in Figure 4-38.

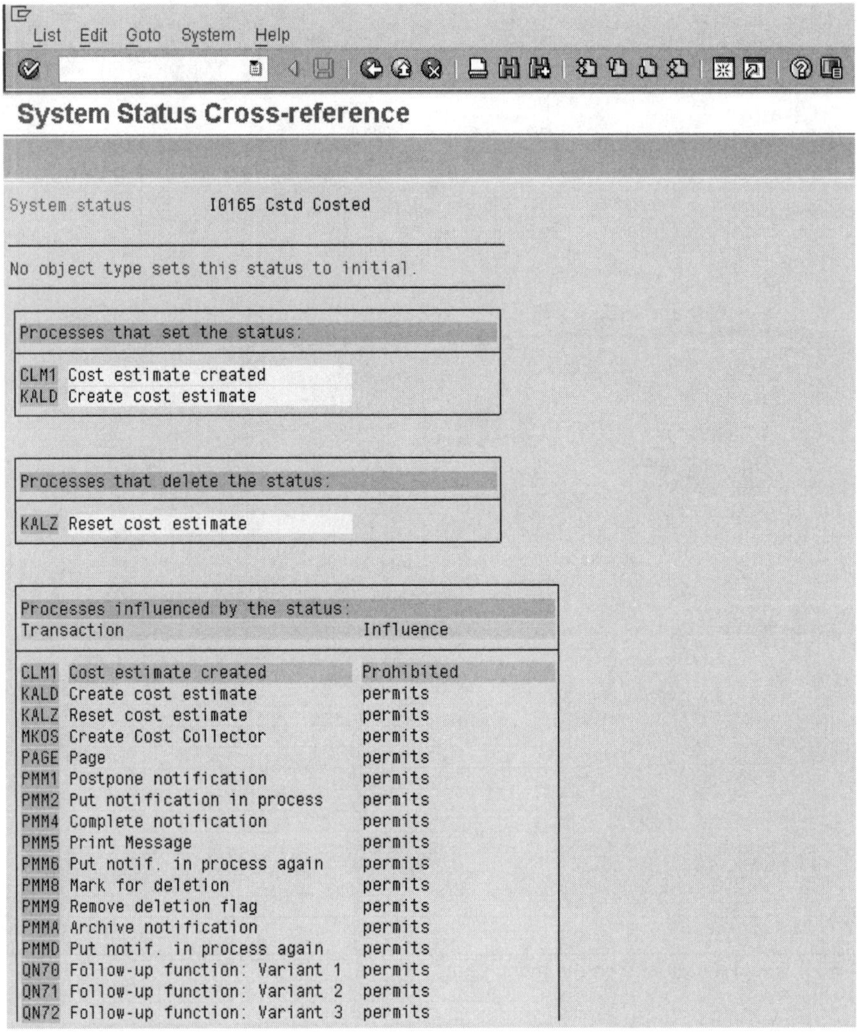

List   Edit   Goto   System   Help

System Status Cross-reference

System status   I0165 Cstd Costed

No object type sets this status to initial.

Processes that set the status:

CLM1 Cost estimate created
KALD Create cost estimate

Processes that delete the status:

KALZ Reset cost estimate

Processes influenced by the status: Transaction	Influence
CLM1 Cost estimate created	Prohibited
KALD Create cost estimate	permits
KALZ Reset cost estimate	permits
MKOS Create Cost Collector	permits
PAGE Page	permits
PMM1 Postpone notification	permits
PMM2 Put notification in process	permits
PMM4 Complete notification	permits
PMM5 Print Message	permits
PMM6 Put notif. in process again	permits
PMM8 Mark for deletion	permits
PMM9 Remove deletion flag	permits
PMMA Archive notification	permits
PMMD Put notif. in process again	permits
QN70 Follow-up function: Variant 1	permits
QN71 Follow-up function: Variant 2	permits
QN72 Follow-up function: Variant 3	permits

FIGURE 4-37   Processes that set and release the status

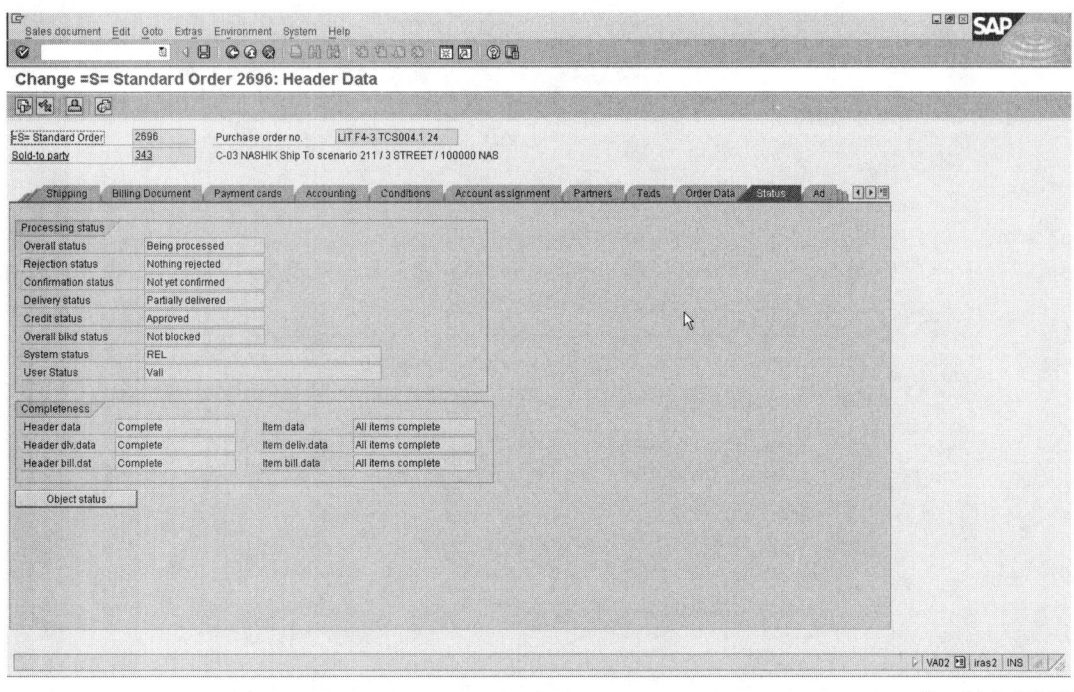

Copyright by SAP AG

FIGURE 4-38   Sales document header status tab

Click the Object Status button. This will present you with a screen similar to what you see in Figure 4-39 but not identical, due to the fact that Figure 4-39 is an example of a configured status profile called ZORDER.

Configuring Status Profile

To configure a status profile, use the following menu path.

Menu Path   SAP Customizing Implementation Guide | Sales and Distribution | Sales | Sales Documents | Define And Assign Status Profile | Define Status Profiles

You can create a copy of an existing profile using the prefix "Z," as shown in Figure 4-40.

Enter a two-digit number representing the status step. (It is best to leave a gap of at least ten per step so the profile is easy to change later should you need to.)

Enter a four-character key representing the status step. (These do not need to begin with a "Z.")

Enter a description of the status that the users will be able to understand.

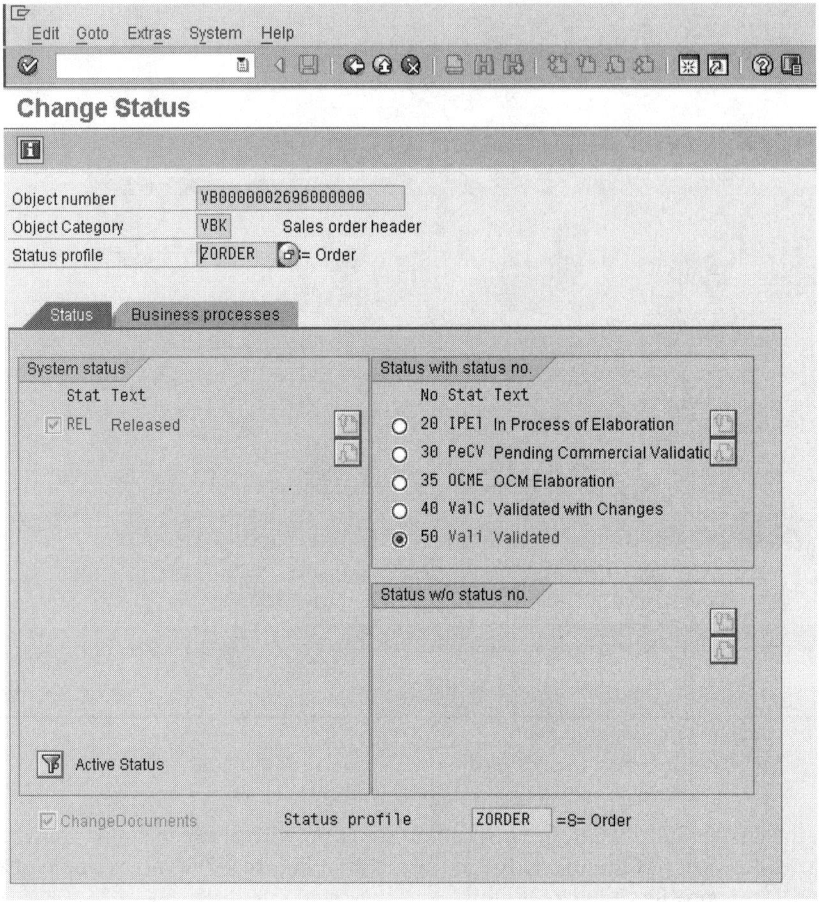

Copyright by SAP AG

FIGURE 4-39 Statuses called from status profile

When an object, such as a sales order, is created, the status that the profile is automatically set to must be active in the Initial Status column.

The lowest and highest number controls the milestone the object has reached, and allows for it to go back to an initial status or increase to the next status. An object may have more than one status at the same time. However, only one of the statuses may have a status number. If another status with a status number is activated, the old status with a status number is deactivated.

The authorization code is the user authorization object the user must possess in order to make changes relating to that status. In this example the authorization object the user must have is ZCOMVAL. The system checks the authorization object B_USERSTAT.

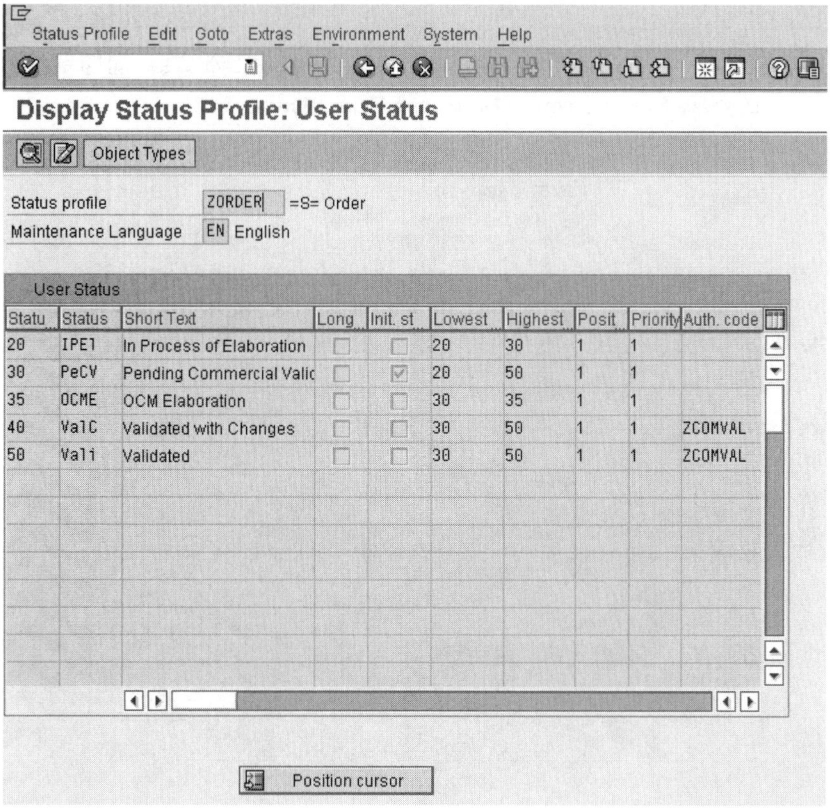

FIGURE 4-40 Defining a status profile

If you double-click on the status you will proceed to a screen similar to Figure 4-41, which controls whether a transaction has any control over the sales status. This is used in workflow management. (Workflow is out of the scope of this book.)

In Figure 4-41 we see that Create Billing Document and Create Delivery are forbidden with the status PECV.

Object types are not changeable in SAP. The two most common sales object types are

- **VBK** Sales order header
- **VBP** Sales order item

If you create a status profile and wish to test this profile, simply highlight any line in your status profile and select Extras | Status Simulation, for example, as shown in Figure 4-42.

After clicking the Status Maintenance button, you will see the screen the users will see when they use the status.

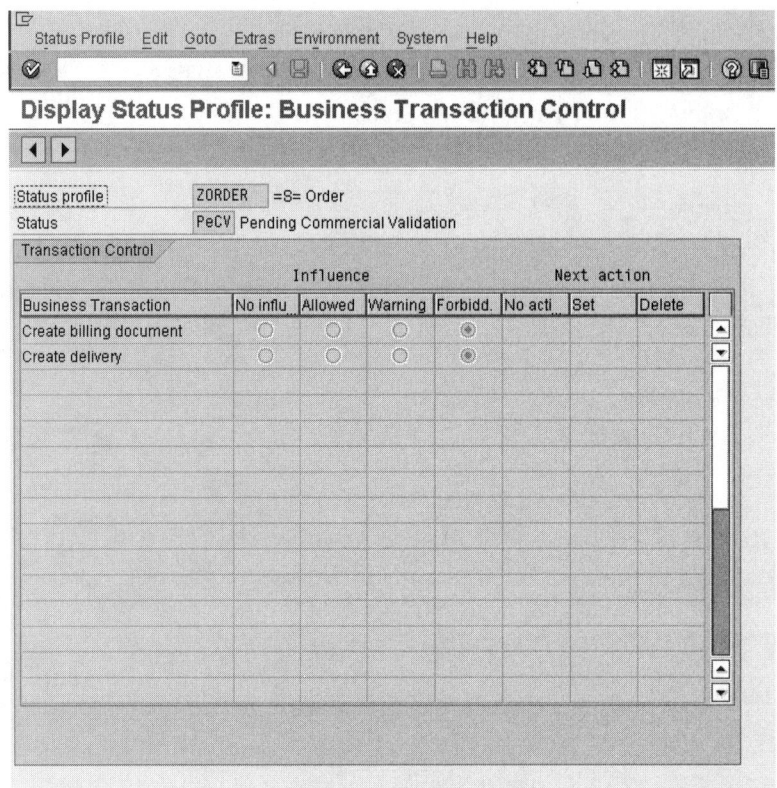

Copyright by SAP AG

FIGURE 4-41   Transaction control

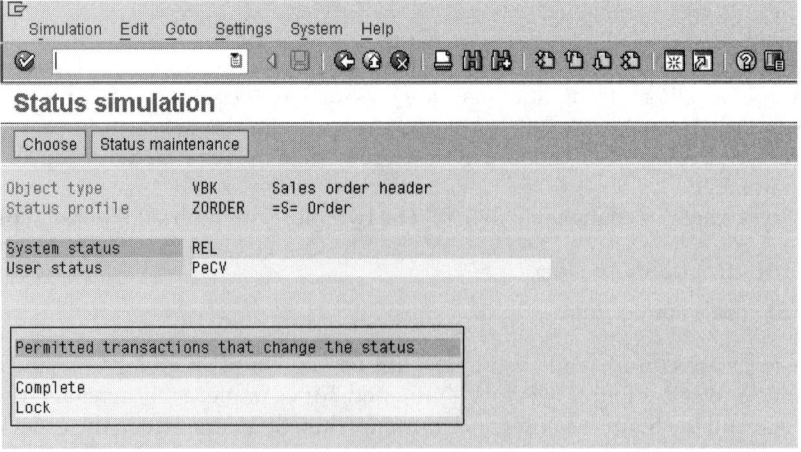

Copyright by SAP AG

FIGURE 4-42   Status simulation

Don't forget to assign the status profile to your sales document type using the following menu path.

Menu Path   SAP Customizing Implementation Guide | Sales and Distribution | Sales | Sales Documents | Define and Assign Status Profile | Assign Order Types/Status Profiles

You can also assign a status profile to item categories using the following menu path.

Menu Path   SAP Customizing Implementation Guide | Sales and Distribution | Sales | Sales Documents | Define and Assign Status Profile | Allocate Status Profile to Item Categories

It is wise to have a different profile at item level than that at header level (if profiles must exist at both levels) in order to avoid user confusion.

Going back to the sales document header status tab we looked at in Figure 4-38, we see the following:

- The completeness section identifies if the document header is complete regarding sales, delivery, and billing.
- The user status is the active status of the document status profile.
- The system status is released.
- Blocked status is self-explanatory.
- Credit status is approved. (This will be covered in detail in Chapter 9.)
- The delivery status is partially delivered.
- The confirmation status is not yet confirmed.
- The rejection status is not rejected and overall status is being processed.

Tables used to display statuses of a sales document are

- **VBUK**   Sales Document: Header Status and Administrative Data
- **VBUP**   Sales Document: Item Status

   A useful database views to display statuses of a sales document is

- **VBAKUK**   Sales Document Header and Status Data

Sales Incompletion Procedures

To see a list of incomplete sales documents, use the transaction code [V.00]. To configure a sales incompletion list, use the following menu path.

Menu Path   SAP Customizing Implementation Guide | Sales and Distribution | Basic Functions | Log of Incomplete Items | Define Incompleteness Procedures

Here you define the fields that, if incomplete, will render the sales document as incomplete. You set the fields to be relevant for incompletion checking at header item and schedule line level, as seen in Figure 4-43.

Now select the header, for example, and click Procedures. You are now able to select and copy an incompletion procedure—for example, 11, Standard Order, You can create a copy and name it Z1.

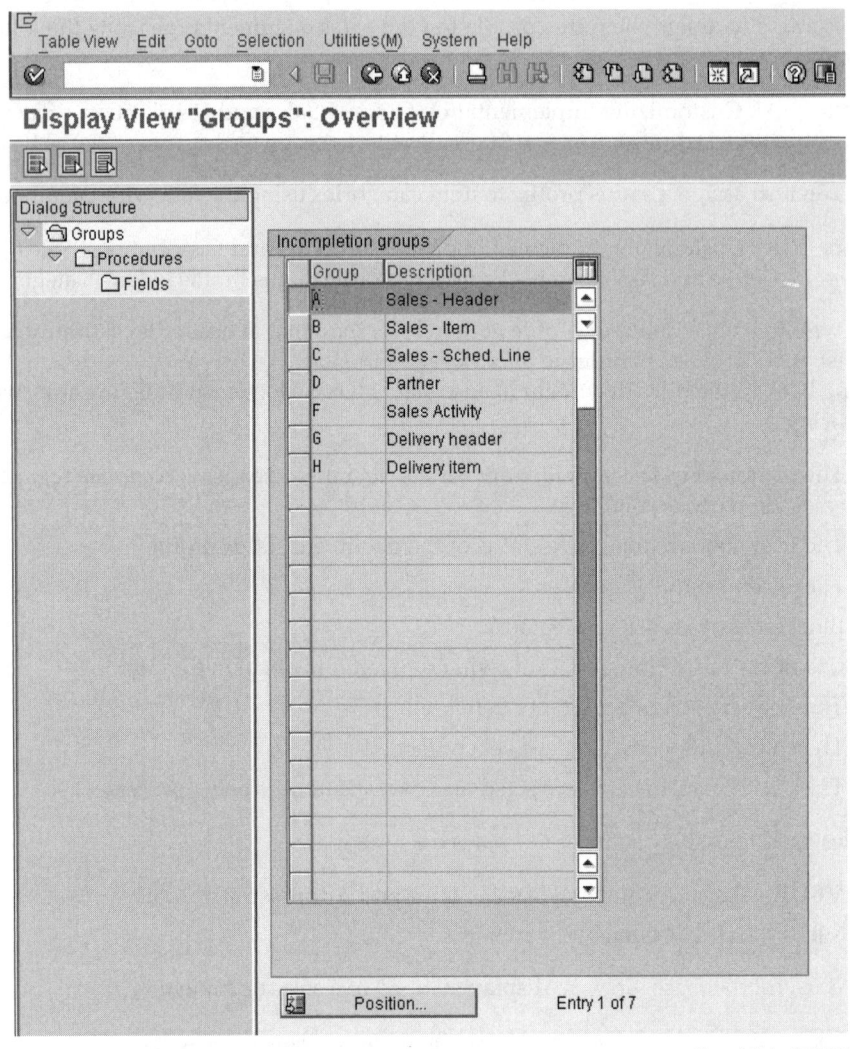

FIGURE 4-43   Defining incompletion procedures

You can see the fields used in the incompletion procedure 11 at header level in Figure 4-44.
The fields are self-explanatory. Take special note of screen assignment field (the Scr
column). This is the function code for the overview screen used when the user double-clicks
on a value in the incompletion procedure that needs fixing/completing. Also, the status
indicator is used to determine which future processes the incompleteness of the field will
block. For example, if the INCO terms are missing, you cannot create the delivery. These
status groups are configurable by selecting SAP Customizing Implementation Guide | Sales
and Distribution | Basic Functions | Log of Incomplete Items | Define Status Groups.

The warning message will give the user a warning if the field is incomplete.

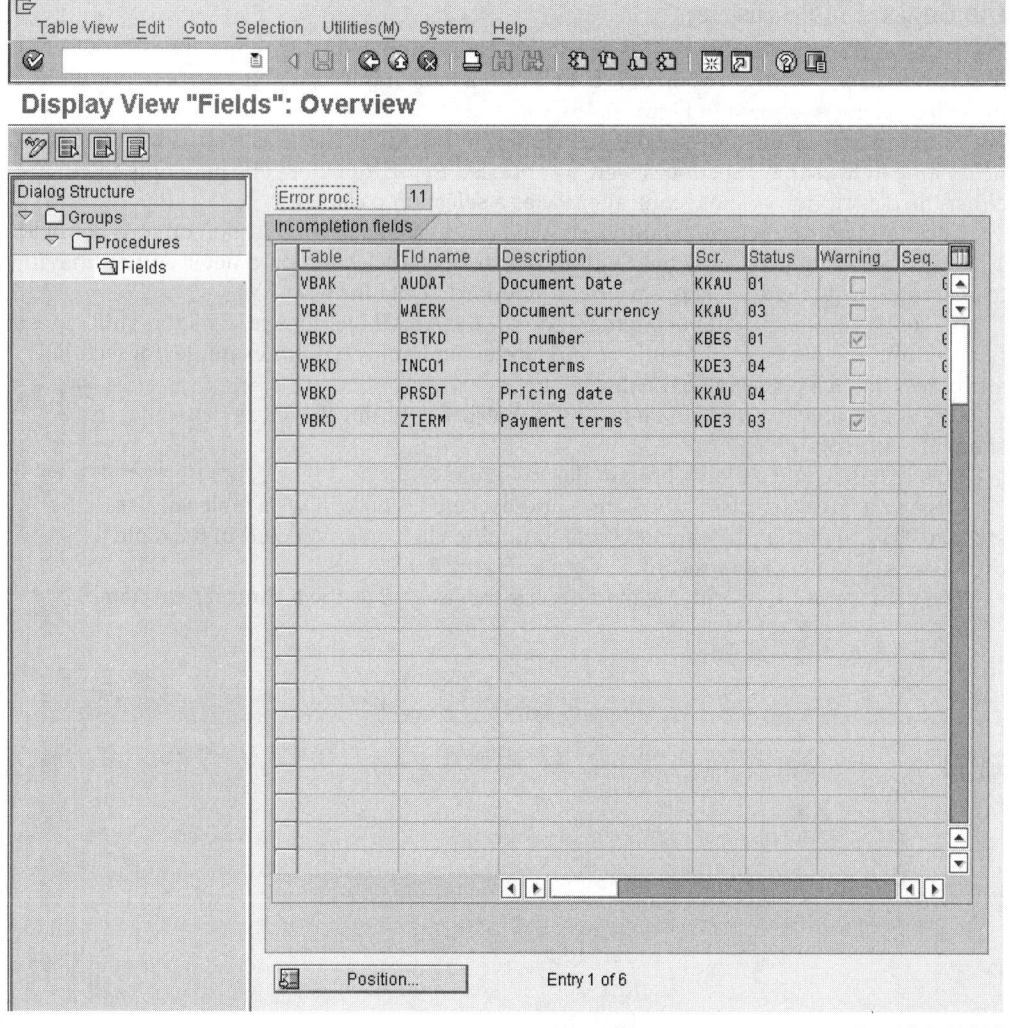

Table View   Edit   Goto   Selection   Utilities(M)   System   Help

Display View "Fields": Overview

Table	Fld name	Description	Scr.	Status	Warning	Seq.
VBAK	AUDAT	Document Date	KKAU	01	☐	6
VBAK	WAERK	Document currency	KKAU	03	☐	6
VBKD	BSTKD	PO number	KBES	01	☑	6
VBKD	INCO1	Incoterms	KDE3	04	☐	6
VBKD	PRSDT	Pricing date	KKAU	04	☐	6
VBKD	ZTERM	Payment terms	KDE3	03	☑	6

Error proc. 11

Incompletion fields

Dialog Structure
▽ ☐ Groups
  ▽ ☐ Procedures
      ☐ Fields

Position...   Entry 1 of 6

FIGURE 4-44   Incompletion procedure 11 sales document header fields

Now all that is left is to assign the incompletion procedure to the sales document header, sales document item, or sales document schedule line you require.

Take careful note that should you create an incompletion procedure and use it in processing, then subsequently change the incompletion procedure or delete it, any sales document you have that is incomplete with the old procedure will stay incomplete and you will not be able to process it.

The General Table Display

The general table display [SE16N] is similar to transaction code [SE16] the "Data Browser." It is a more user friendly version of [SE16]. Enter a table name and press ENTER to populate the fields names as shown in Figure 4-45.

With this screen one may see the description of the ABAP name as well as the technical field name in the same selection screen, as opposed to [SE16] where one may only view either the description or the technical name as a selection parameter.

Click the Multiple Selection button, shown here, to give a list of selection options per field.

One is also able to use any field within the table as a selection parameter without having to be limited to 40 field selections as in the standard "Data Browser."

[SE16N] outputs the data using the " ALV" - the ABAP List Viewer, which permits most fields within the data search results, to be selected and analyzed, for example, for technical attributes or to list possible field values.

One is also able to place a total on any numerical column, as well as place subtotals on a column value.

This will give you a dialog box similar to Figure 4-46.

Once you have completed the values and executed, you will see a table similar to the standard [SE16] output. You are also able to double-click on any record in the table to display the contents of that record, as seen in Figure 4-47.

The data is now seen with the field description as well as the technical field name.

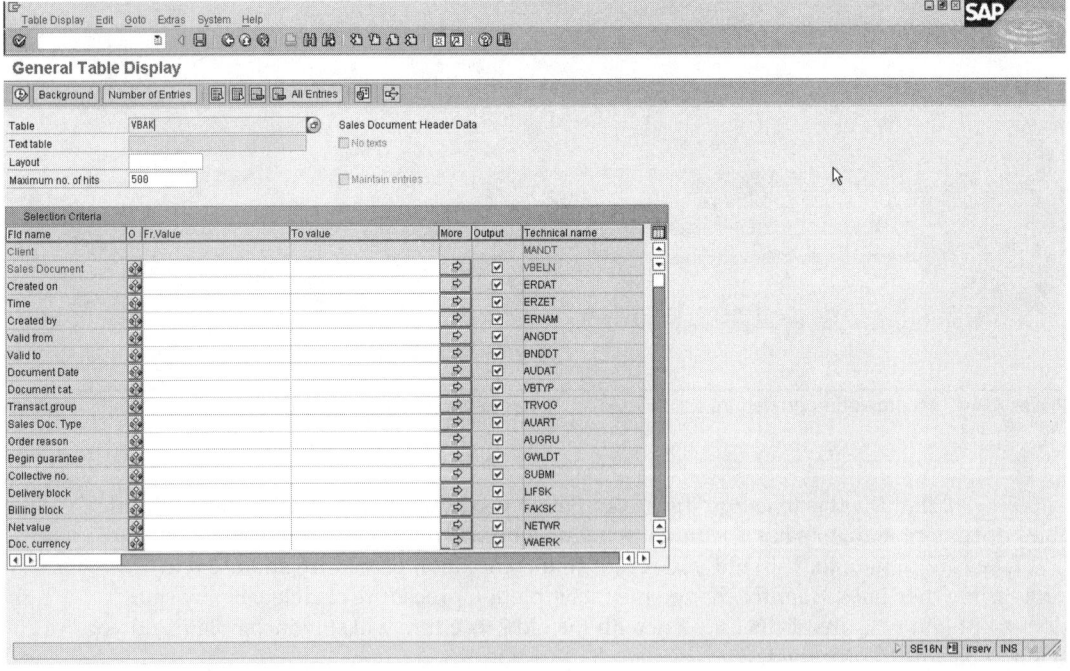

FIGURE 4-45   Initial screen of [SE16N]

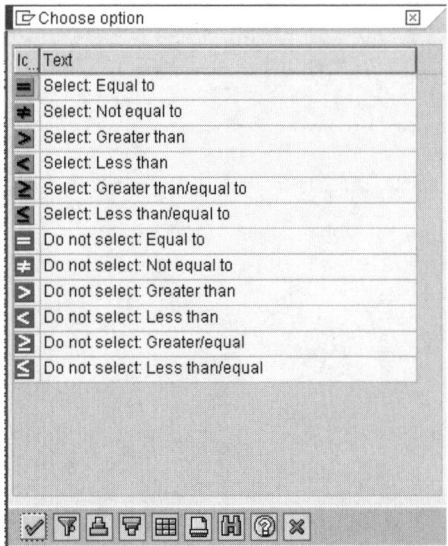

FIGURE **4-46**   Multiple selection option dialog box

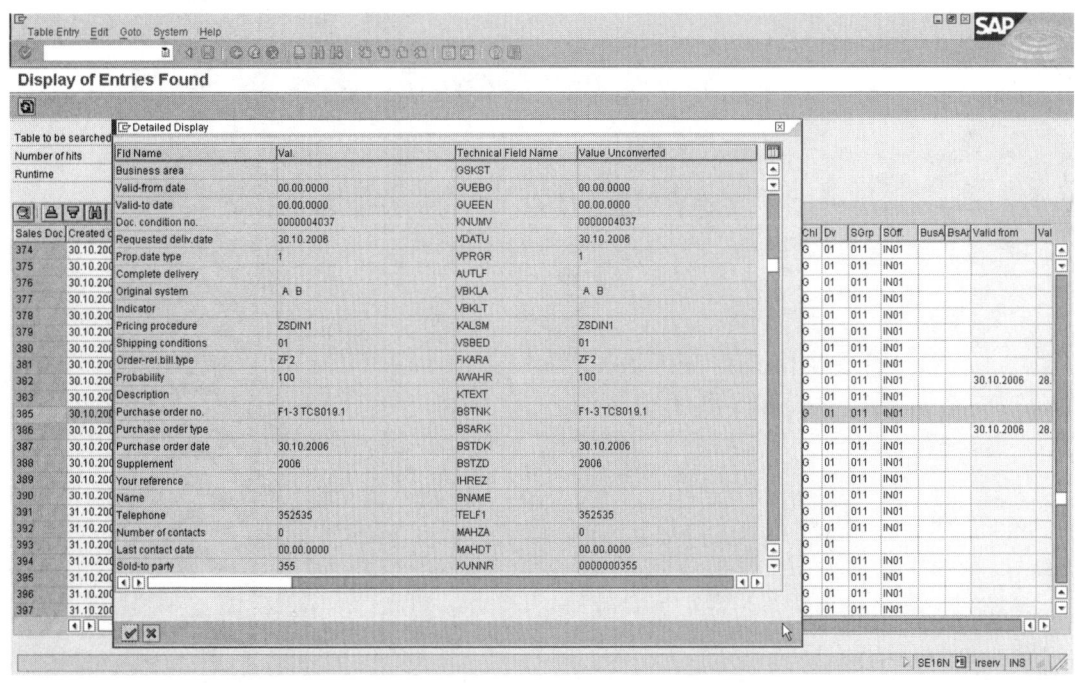

FIGURE **4-47**   A record in the table

Available to Promise and Transfer of Requirements

This chapter details material determination, listing, and exclusion, as well as important interactions with the supply chain, specifically in the transfer of requirements from sales and the configuration of the available to promise (ATP) check.

Material Determination

Material determination is a method in SAP SD to determine the material to be used in the sales order. Material determination uses the condition technique to substitute one material in the sales order for another when certain conditions are met.

Material determination is triggered by the material entered in the line item of the sales order. This material may be used to automatically exchange one of the business' products for another during certain periods—for example, Christmas time—using a specially wrapped product. Or it may be used to exchange a customer-specific part number for one of the businesses part numbers. Material determination may also use a dialog box with a number of products that the user may select from.

An Introduction to the Condition Technique

Material determination is also useful for substituting an old product that is to become obsolete or a new product that is to be released by your company at a specific date. Material determination can automatically swap the old product for the newer product at the time of the sales order creation, based on a validity date.

Material determination is sometimes referred to as *product selection* and can be automatic or manual. This is useful, for example, when the customer may not want the specially wrapped product at Christmas, but would prefer the standard product.

The configuration options available for material determination are

- **Blank value**   Automatic substitution – Item will be replaced
- **A**   Substitute products are displayed for selection
- **B**   General material determination with selection, without ATP

For example option "blank." Maybe the swapping of an obsolete product.

Material determination uses the condition technique to automatically propose a new value. The condition technique is used extensively and is described in great detail in "Pricing" in Chapter 8. However, its basic elements are described in the configuration of this process.

Maintaining Prerequisites for Material Determination

To configure material determination, use the following menu path.

Menu Path   SAP Customizing Implementation Guide | Sales and Distribution | Basic Functions | Material Determination | Maintain Prerequisites for Material Determination

You'll see a dialog box similar to Figure 5-1.

Defining Condition Type

Begin the configuration of material determination by defining the "condition type," which is actually the same as defining the type of material determination as illustrated in Figure 5-2.

Menu Path   SAP Customizing Implementation Guide | Sales and Distribution | Basic Functions | Material Determination | Maintain Prerequisites for Material Determination | Define condition types [OV12]

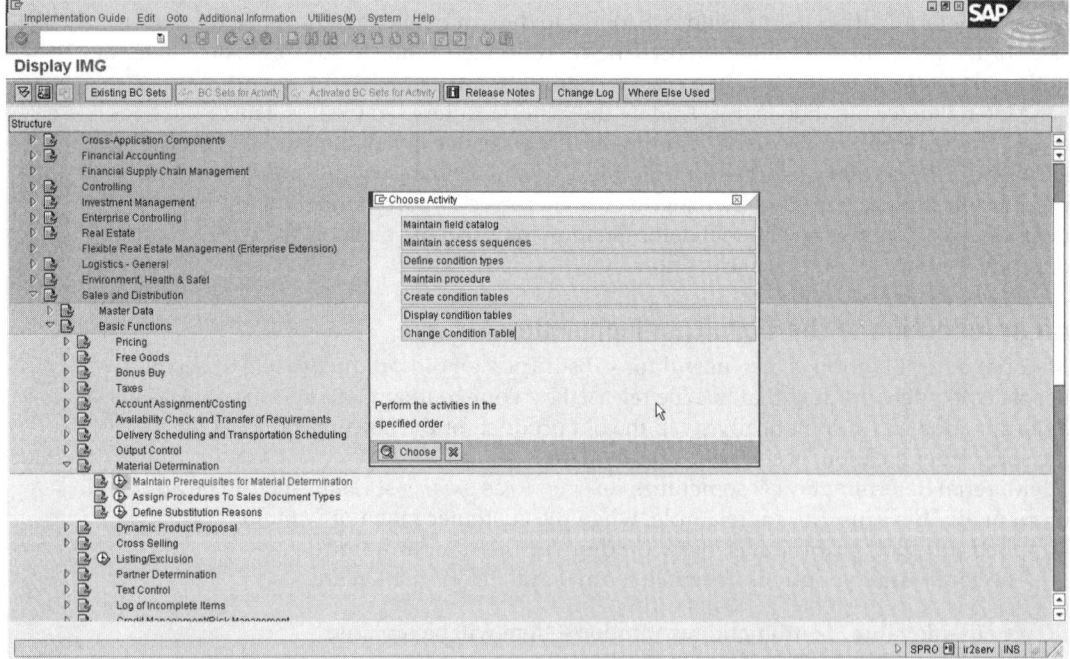

Copyright by SAP AG

FIGURE 5-1   Condition technique options for material determination

FIGURE 5-2
Defining condition
type (material
determination type)

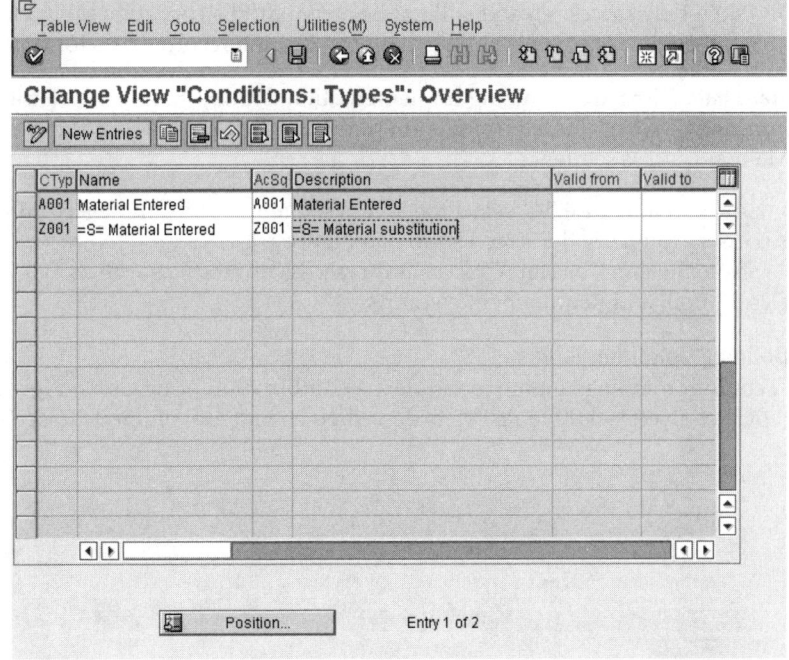

Copyright by SAP AG

Should you wish to have a new material determination condition type, remember to copy the standard and change its name to Z*xxx*. For the purpose of this example we will copy the standard condition type A001.

You need not have a validity date here, as it is better to constrict your entries with validity dates when you create your condition records later.

The access sequence is assigned to the condition type.

Defining Access Sequence

The access sequence must exist before you can assign it to a condition type. In this example access sequence A001 is assigned to condition type A001.

An access sequence is a sequence of steps that the system follows in sequential order to obtain a condition record. The condition record has a value that is assigned to it.

The access number is the order in which the system will read the access sequence. The system will run through each step of the access sequence in sequential order until it finds an exact match for the defined table. If a record exists for that table, the system will come back with the data; if no record exists or no match is found, the result will be that no condition record exists for this condition type.

For example, if we had access numbers 10, 20, 30, and 40, the system will start with the lowest entry, which is 10. It will then try and process everything assigned to the step 10. Should it not be able to process the line, it will then proceed to access 20, and so on.

Should it reach access 40 and still not be able to find a condition record for the table in the access sequence, the result will be that no condition record exists for this condition type.

Menu Path   SAP Customizing Implementation Guide | Sales and Distribution | Basic Functions | Material Determination | Maintain Prerequisites for Material Determination | Maintain access sequences

As seen in Figure 5-3, select the access sequence for example A001 and double-click Accesses. You'll see the screen shown in Figure 5-4.

Note the entry has an AcNo column (access number) as well as Tab (table key), Description, and Requirement columns.

Defining Condition Tables

A condition table is merely a tabulated combination of fields. In Figure 5-4 the first table key used is 001. Table 001 is described as material entered. To see the fields used in

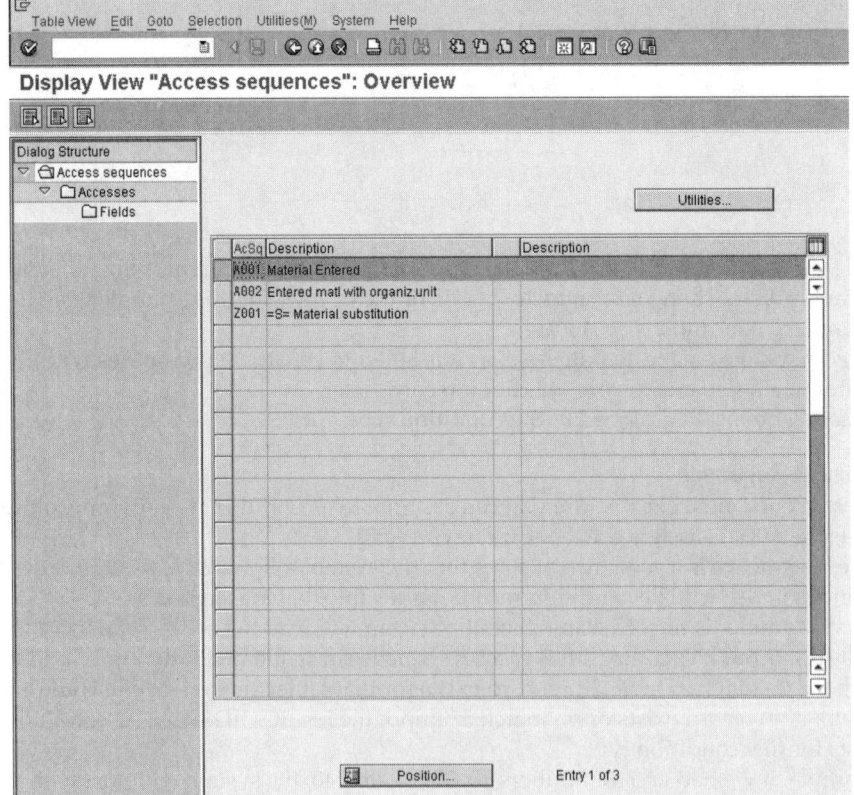

Copyright by SAP AG

FIGURE 5-3   Maintain access sequences

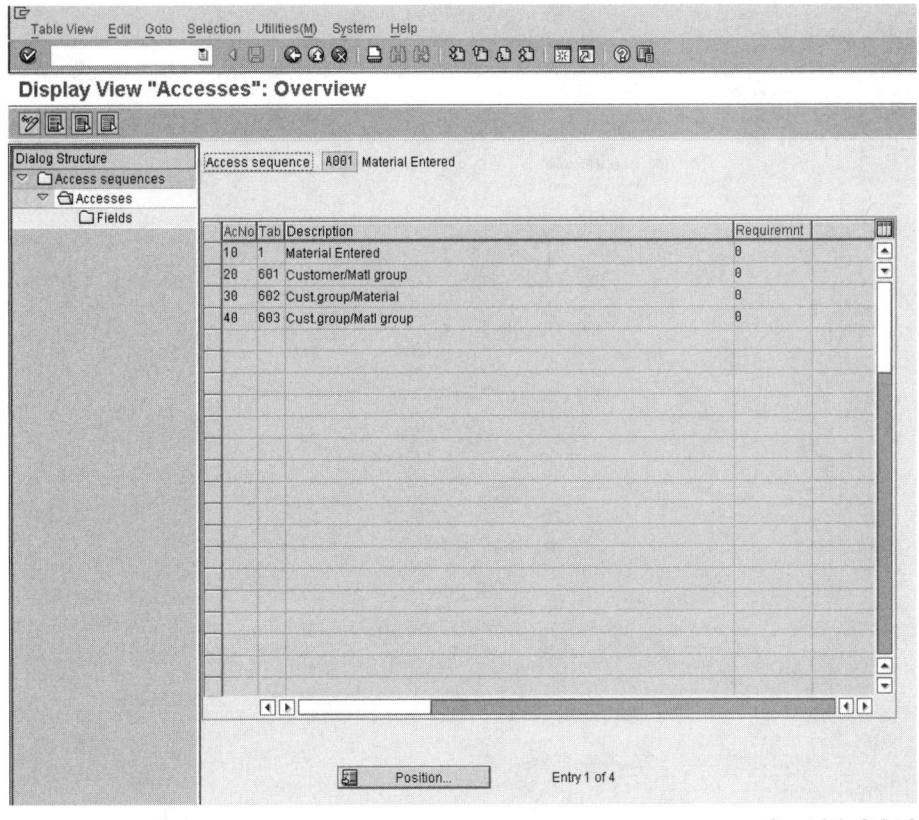

Copyright by SAP AG

FIGURE 5-4   Access sequence structure of access sequence A001

this table, highlight the table and select Fields on the left side. You will see a screen similar to Figure 5-5.

To see these condition tables, use the following menu path.

Menu Path   SAP Customizing Implementation Guide I Sales and Distribution I Basic Functions I Material Determination I Maintain Prerequisites for Material Determination I Display Condition Tables

Enter 001 in the table selection and press ENTER.

You are now presented with condition table 001 as shown in Figure 5-6, which consists of the field "Material entered." This field has been selected from a list of fields in the field catalog. (The *field catalog* is a list of allowed fields for material determination. It is maintainable—that is, you are able to add more fields to it for you to select from. However, we will cover that in "Pricing" in Chapter 8.)

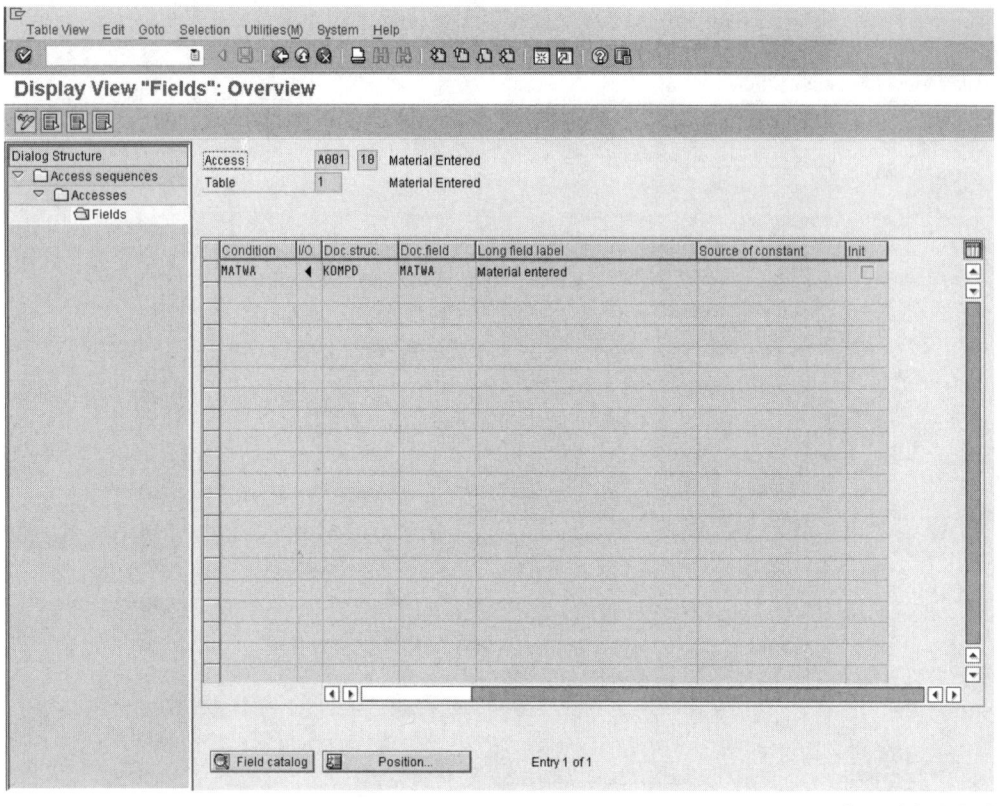

Copyright by SAP AG

FIGURE 5-5 Fields relating to condition table 001

Should you click the Technical View button, you will see the actual SAP field name being selected as shown in Figure 5-7.

Now return to the Maintain Access Sequence screen shown in Figure 5-4.

On the right side of the description you have a Requirement column. This requirement is similar in theory to those you used in copying control. That is, it restricts entries being accessed. The system will look at the access line, read the requirement, and if the scenario fails the requirement, it will proceed to check the next access number.

Determination Procedure

When a sales order is created and the determination procedure is accessed, the procedure then calls the condition types in sequence. The condition types then each individually calls the access sequence and subsequently calls the condition tables, which the system then checks to see if a valid condition record exists.

FIGURE 5-6
Selected field
for table 001

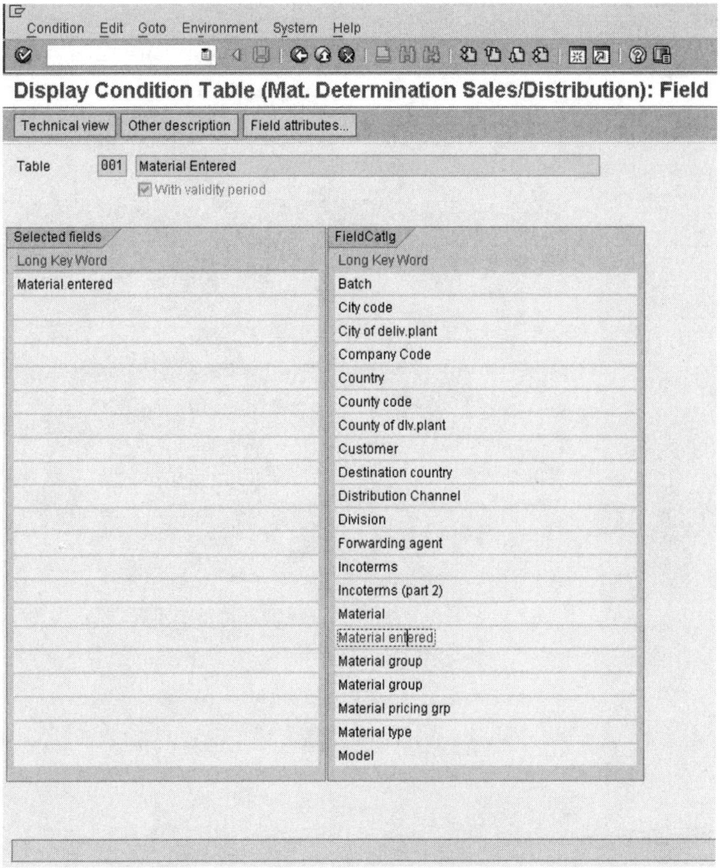

Display Condition Table (Mat. Determination Sales/Distribution): Field

| Technical view | Other description | Field attributes... |

Table   001   Material Entered
☑ With validity period

Selected fields	FieldCatlg
Long Key Word	Long Key Word
Material entered	Batch
	City code
	City of deliv.plant
	Company Code
	Country
	County code
	County of dlv.plant
	Customer
	Destination country
	Distribution Channel
	Division
	Forwarding agent
	Incoterms
	Incoterms (part 2)
	Material
	Material entered
	Material group
	Material group
	Material pricing grp
	Material type
	Model

Copyright by SAP AG

Menu Path   SAP Customizing Implementation Guide | Sales and Distribution | Basic Functions | Material Determination | Maintain Prerequisites for Material Determination | Maintain procedure (to access the material determination procedure)

Select the procedure A00001 and double-click Control Data on the left. You will see a determination screen, which, as shown in Figure 5-8, is the same basic layout that is used in pricing (just enhanced a bit further) as well as many other areas.

This procedure again has steps that can range from 01 up to 999, although in Figure 5-8 you only see step 10. The step has a further breakdown into a counter, which is like a mini-step in a step. For example, the system could have step 10 counter 1, step 10 counter 2, and step 10 counter 3. It would then execute these steps in that sequence.

FIGURE 5-7
Technical view
of field selected
in table

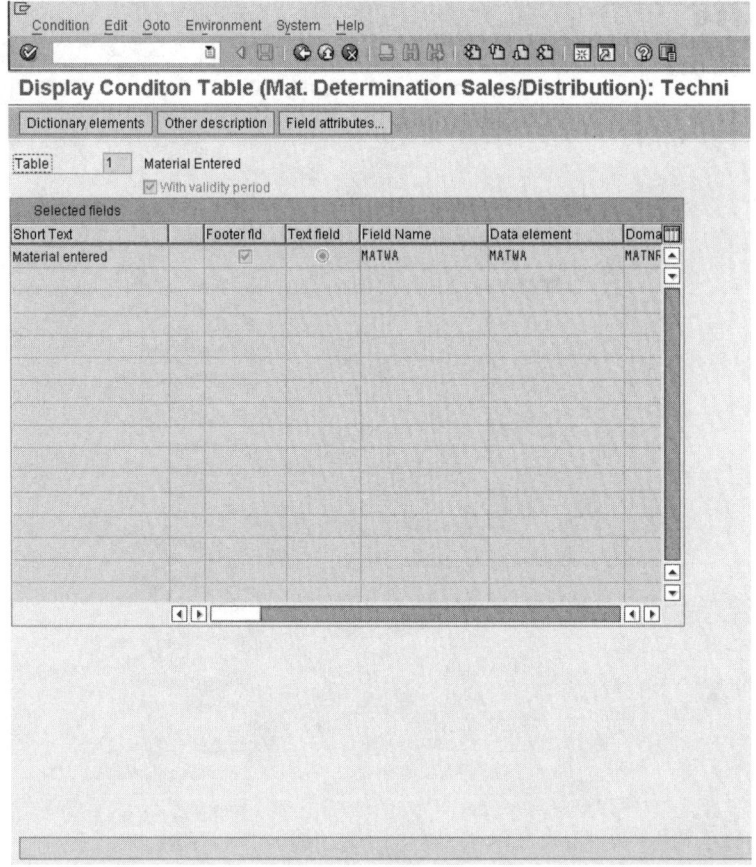

A condition type is assigned to the determination procedure. A requirement can also be entered for the condition type, again as a check to see if it must be accessed. In this example there is no limitation in the form of a requirement.

Now that the determination procedure has been done you need to assign it to a sales document type for which you would like to see material determination to be carried out. To assign it to a sales document type, use the following menu path.

Menu Path   SAP Customizing Implementation Guide | Sales and Distribution | Basic Functions | Material Determination | Assign Procedures to Sales Document Types [OV14]

By assigning the material determination procedure to the sales document type, you are activating material determination. Whenever that sales document type is used, the system will execute material determination. Generally, I find you may want all the document types to

FIGURE 5-8
Determination
procedure

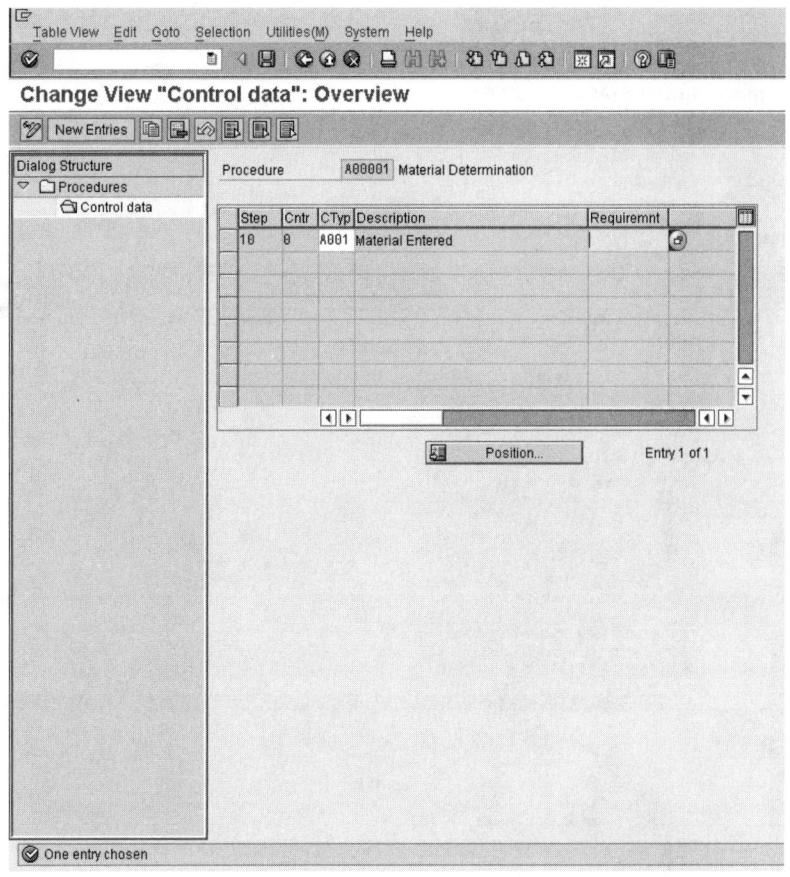

Copyright by SAP AG

be active for a single material determination procedure as it would cause the user community to be confused if they get different results using different sales orders (comparing a quotation to an order, for example).

Now all that is left is for you to create a condition record for the condition type A001. To create condition records for a condition type, use the following menu path.

Menu Path   SAP Menu | Logistics | Sales and Distribution | Master Data | Products | Material Determination | [VB11] - Create

1. Enter the material determination type—for example, A001.

2. If you select Key Combination, you will see the condition tables in the access sequence. For this example, select Material Entered.

3. You are now able to create your condition record as seen in Figure 5-9.

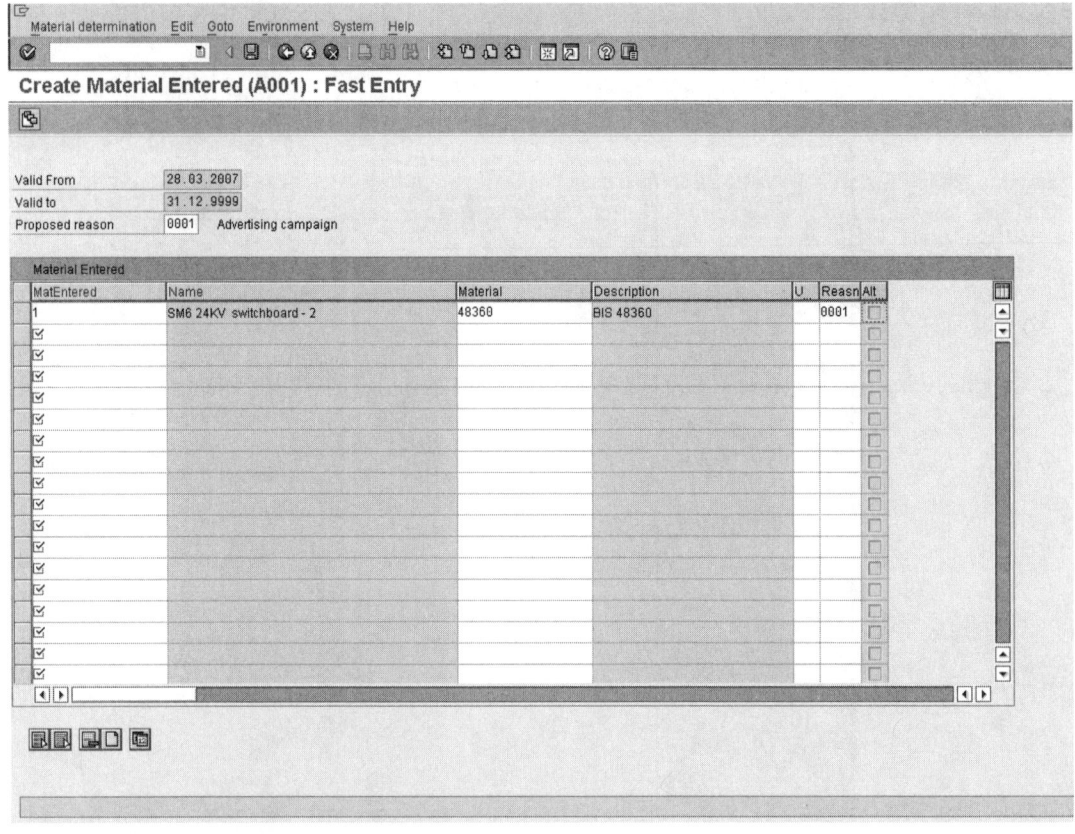

FIGURE 5-9   Condition record for condition type A001

This completes the introduction to the condition technique. I have explained it in a way that is easy to follow, however, it is not the simplest of methods to implement. After you have become confident with the condition technique, the best procedure I find to follow is this:

1. Put the fields you will need into the field catalog.

2. Create the condition tables you will need.

3. Create the access sequence you will need.

4. Assign the condition tables to the access sequence.

5. Create the condition types.

6. Assign the access sequence to the condition types.

7. Create the determination procedure (if necessary) and assign the condition types to it.

8. Assign the determination procedure.

9. Lastly create your condition records.

Defining Substitution Reason

As mentioned, this completes the introduction to the condition technique. However, for material determination you need a substitution reason. A *substitution reason* is a rule that controls the material determination's execution.

To define substitution reasons, use the following menu path.

Menu Path   SAP Customizing Implementation Guide | Sales and Distribution | Basic Functions | Material Determination | Define Substitution Reasons [OVRQ]

As seen in Figure 5-10, the substitution reason has a four-digit key and description that is used as a reference in the condition record. Attached to this key is a set of rules.

The first column is Entry, which controls whether you would like the system to print the name or number of the original material or the substituted materials name or number on the order confirmations.

The next column is the Warning indicator. If checked, it will indicate a warning message to the user that material determination is about to take place.

The Strategy column is used to indicate if the substitution should be automatic or if the proposed material determination items should be displayed via a dialog box for selection. The alternatives are

- **Blank Value**   Automatic – The item will be replaced
- **A**   Substitute products are displayed for selection
- **B**   General material determination with selection, without ATP

FIGURE 5-10
Defining
substitution
reasons

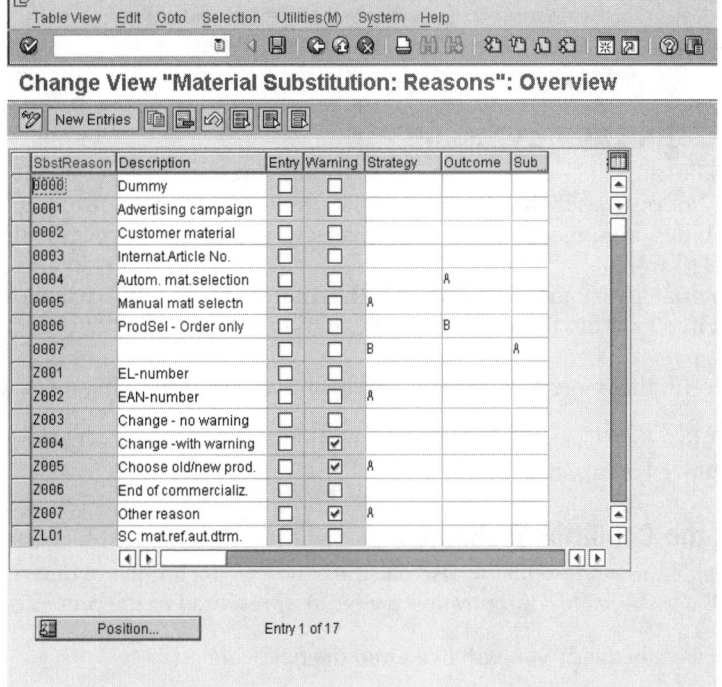

When using material determination you may enter the material to be swapped in the standard Material Entered column of the sales order. However, when using the customer - material information record you may only enter the customer's material in the Customer Material field of the sales order. Should you be using material determination to indicate automatic swapping of the customer number automatically one to one, be careful not to use the customer material information record, as this may confuse the user as to where he should enter the data.

The automatic substitution that happens in the background *only* occurs according to the availability check (if you select as a sub-item). Suppose you have four products for the system to do an automatic substitution on, and you have stock of one of them but not the other three. The system will propose and consume that one for which you have stock. This can cause problems, because if this one material is procured correctly, due to there being a demand for it, it may automatically fill up, causing a continual cycle where only this material is ever used and the other three are not consumed.

The Outcome column allows you to select whether the proposed item from material determination should automatically replace the existing material or if it should be displayed as a sub-item in the sales order.

Remember, if you use the outcome sub-items be sure to configure your item category determination correctly. That is, the main item that is being substituted should have the usage indicator PSHP (product selection higher level item) and the sub-item material that is being displayed as a sub-item should have the usage indicator PSEL.

Only one schedule line is proposed by the system for the line item for which automatic substitution occurs when the item is a represented as a sub-item.

Lastly, when using a one-to-one automatic swapping of materials, the material entered does not need to be created in the system. However, should you use the outcome displayed as sub-items, *both* materials need to be configured in the system.

Material Listing and Exclusion

Material listing and exclusion is used to list the products or services specific customers may or may not purchase. That is, you may list products a specific customer may not buy or that are excluded from the customer. Or conversely, you may list products the customer may only select from.

Material listing and exclusion uses the condition technique to determine its values and procedure. It applies to two partner functions in Sales and Distribution: the Sold-to Party and the payer.

To configure material listing and exclusion, use the following menu path.

Menu Path   SAP Customizing Implementation Guide I Sales and Distribution I Basic Functions I Listing/Exclusion

Using the Condition Technique

Material listing and exclusion also use the condition technique to determine valid records. We will use the same configuration procedure presented in the previous section:

1. Put the fields you will need into the field catalog.
2. Create the condition tables you will need.

3. Create the access sequence you will need.

4. Assign the condition tables to the access sequence.

5. Create the condition types.

6. Assign the access sequence to the condition types.

7. Create the determination procedure (if necessary) and assign the condition types to it.

8. Assign the determination procedure.

9. Lastly, create your condition records.

Step 1: Put the Fields You Will Need into the Field Catalog

Menu Path SAP Customizing Implementation Guide I Sales and Distribution I Basic Functions I Listing/Exclusion I Maintain Allowed Fields for Listing/Exclusion

Add any additional fields you will need for the condition tables you are planning to create. You can do this by clicking the New Entries button. Then press F4 and you will see a list of fields per table from which you may select and add to the field catalog, as shown in Figure 5-11. Double-click on the entry you wish to add to the list of available fields.

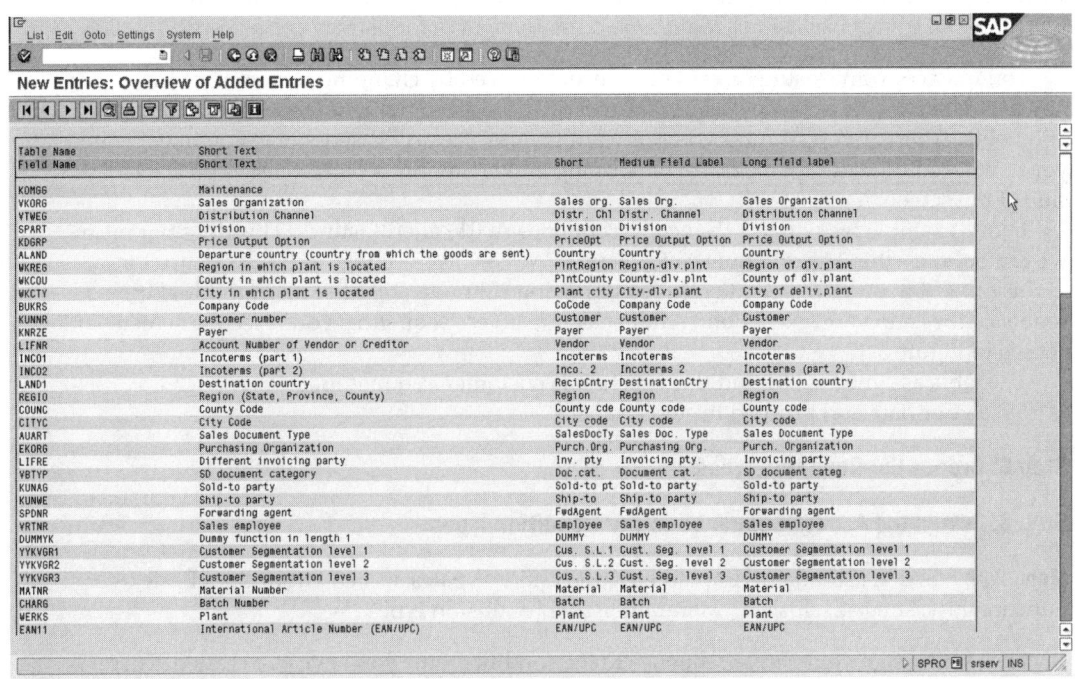

Copyright by SAP AG

FIGURE 5-11 Select fields to add to the field catalog

Step 2: Create the Condition Tables You Will Need

Menu Path   SAP Customizing Implementation Guide | Sales and Distribution | Basic Functions | Listing/Exclusion | Maintain condition tables for listing/exclusion

Create the condition table you will be using in the access sequence—for example, condition table 901.

Condition table 001 is the SAP standard table and consists of the customer and material fields. New entries should follow the suggested SAP naming convention, for example, 900 onwards. Be sure never to change the standard SAP condition tables.

Select entries to add to your table by double-clicking the fields on the right.

By clicking Other Description four or so times you will see the long text version of the fields name controlled by the data element. (Data elements are covered in Chapter 11.) Be sure to check the technical name of the field as well by accessing the table where the field exists (for example, VBAP) and compare the entry with the technical view of the field in the field catalog.

After you have created your table, proceed to steps 3 and 4.

Step 3: Create the Access Sequence You Will Need

Step 4: Assign the Condition Tables to the Access Sequence.

Menu Path   SAP Customizing Implementation Guide | Sales and Distribution | Basic Functions | Listing/Exclusion | Maintain access sequences for listing/exclusion

You may copy an existing access sequence, followed by changing the name of the newly created access sequence. This will also copy all subsequent entries such as tables and fields. Alternatively, should you not want to copy the access sequence, you may create your own. Either way, after creating or copying and changing, select Accesses on the left side of the screen.

In our example we will use the access sequence A001 called Listing. (This does not mean we can only use this access sequence for listing. We can also use this access sequence for exclusion. But in order to keep to clear customizing rules we will have an individual access sequence for listing and exclusion.) After selecting access sequences you'll see the screen shown in Figure 5-12.

The table assigned is 001 and the selection is customer and material.

Save your data and proceed to steps 5 and 6.

Step 5: Create the Condition Types

Step 6: Assign the Access Sequence to the Condition Types

Menu Path   SAP Customizing Implementation Guide | Sales and Distribution | Basic Functions | Listing/Exclusion | Maintain listing/exclusion types

Here you assign your access sequence to the condition type you have just created. There should be no need to create more condition types than those offered in the standard system for material listing and exclusion. However, should there be a need to create one, merely copy a SAP standard condition type and assign your access sequence to it as shown in Figure 5-13.

After saving proceed to step 7.

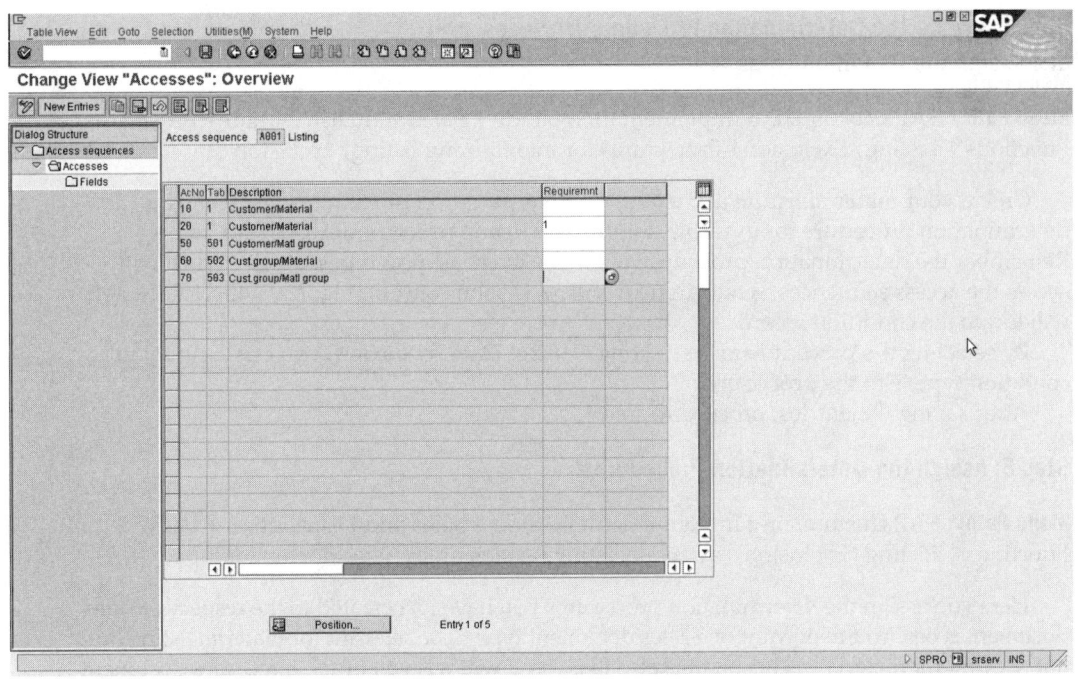

Copyright by SAP AG

FIGURE 5-12   Access within access sequence A001

FIGURE 5-13
Assigning an
access sequence
to a condition type

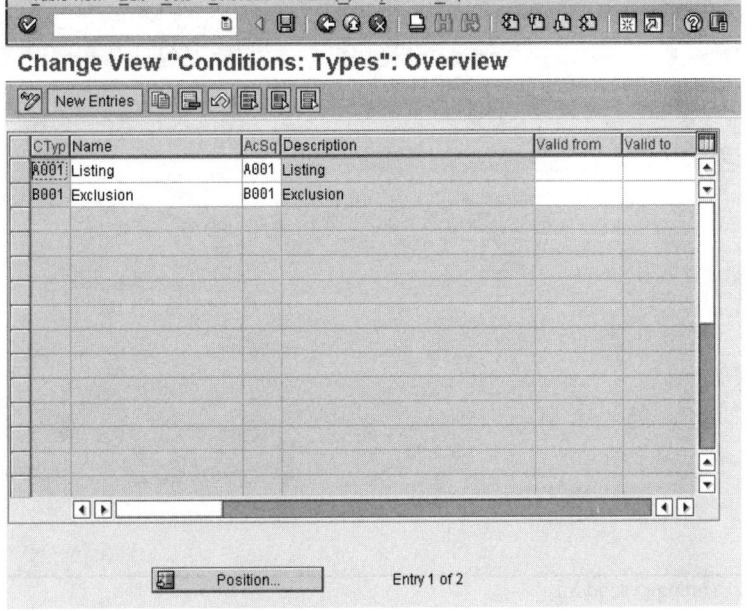

Copyright by SAP AG

Step 7: Create The Determination Procedure (If Necessary) and Assign the Condition Types to It

Menu Path   SAP Customizing Implementation Guide | Sales and Distribution | Basic Functions | Listing/Exclusion | Procedures for maintaining listing/exclusion

Create your material listing and exclusion determination procedures by creating a determination procedure for example, Figure 5-14, using procedure A00001 for listing. Remember the determination procedure will hold the condition types which in turn will access the access sequences, which in turn will access the condition tables, which ultimately will locate the condition records.

By selecting the procedure and selecting Control Data on the left, you can assign your condition type/s to the procedure.

After saving the entries, proceed to step 8.

Step 8: Assign the Determination Procedures

Menu Path   SAP Customizing Implementation Guide | Sales and Distribution | Basic Functions | Listing/Exclusion | Activate listing/exclusion by sales document type

Here you assign the determination procedures you have just created to the respective sales document types. You may want one sales document type to be relevant for material listing but not relevant for material exclusion. It is also likely you will wish all order entry sales document types, as opposed to some and not others, to use listing or exclusion procedures.

An example of the assignment is shown in Figure 5-15.

After saving the entries, proceed to step 9.

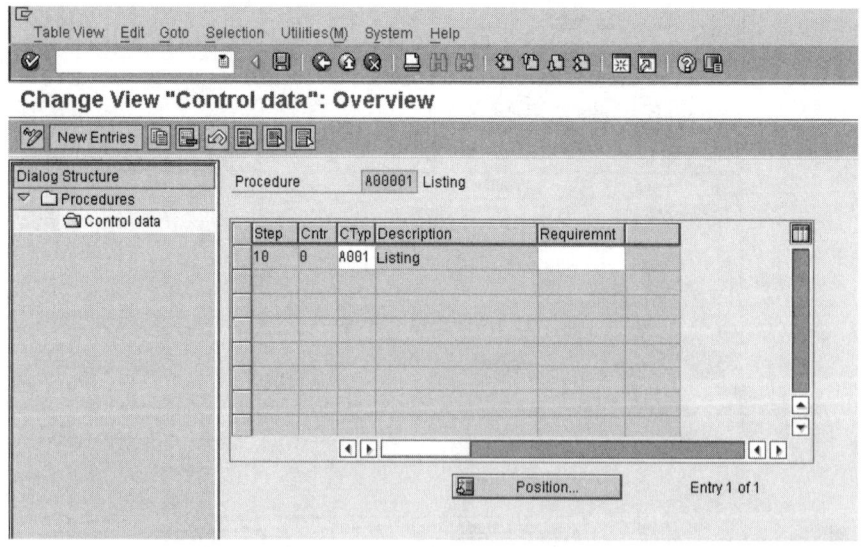

FIGURE 5-14   Listing procedure

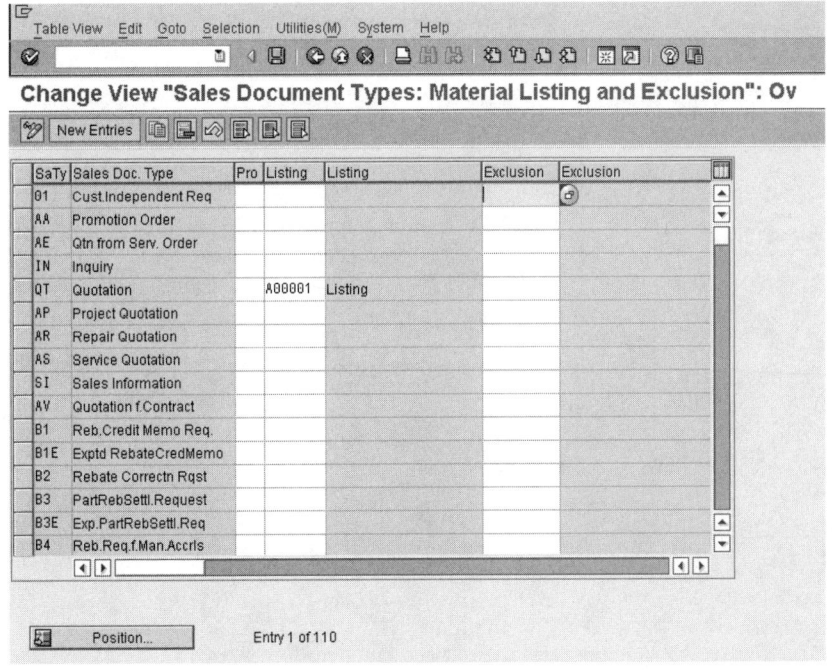

Copyright by SAP AG

FIGURE 5-15   Assign a determination procedure to a sales document type

Step 9: Create the Condition Records

The majority of condition records are created in the SAP easy access menu screen, not in the SAP Customizing Implementation Guide (with a few exceptions, such as account assignments in revenue account determination.). To create the condition records, use the following menu path.

Menu Path   SAP Menu I Logistics I Sales and Distribution I Master Data I Products I Listing/Exclusion I [VB01] - Create

1. Enter the listing or exclusion condition type. We will use listing condition type A001.

2. From the key combination, select the table, from the key combination, for which you are entering a record, if you have more than one table in the condition's access sequence.

3. Press ENTER.

4. Enter the values for your customer and all valid materials that he is allowed to order, as shown in Figure 5-16.

5. Save your data.

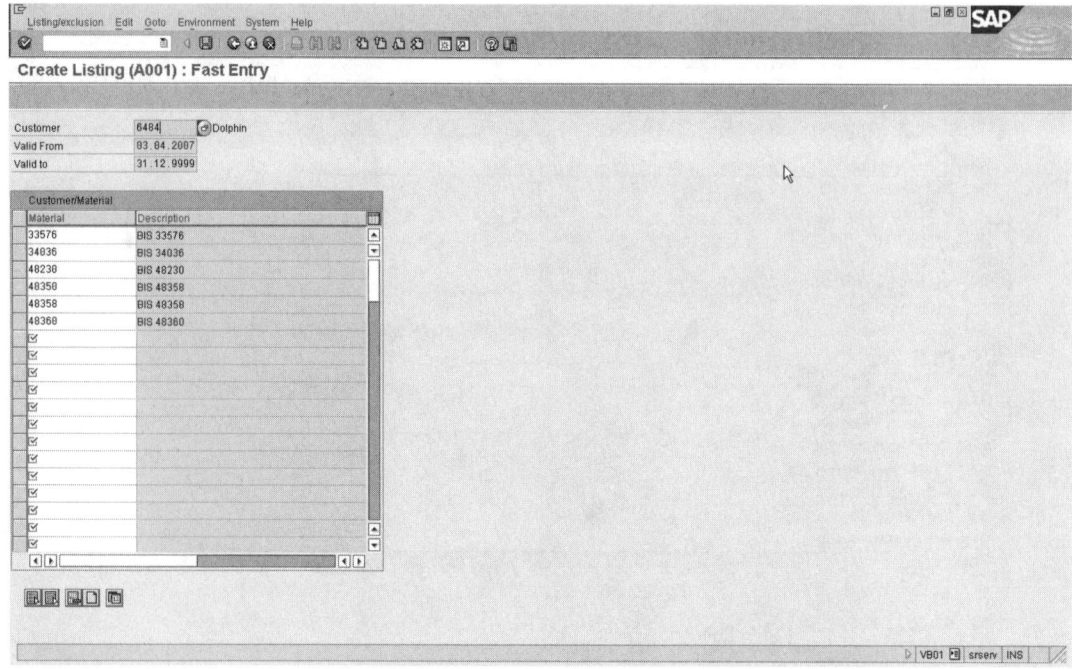

FIGURE 5-16 Create a condition record for A001.

 When creating the sales order the system will first check to see if the material the customer is ordering is allowed for the sales area the order is placed in. Then it checks to see if the material is excluded for that customer and lastly it checks to see if the material is on a list of allowed materials for the respective customer.

 The system will check the listing and exclusion of the Sold-to Party first. If it does find a listing or exclusion for the sold to party, it does not check further; however, should it not find an entry for the Sold-to Party, it then proceeds to check if a listing or exclusion is created for the payer. Should no entry exist for either the Sold-to Party or the payer partner roles of the customer master record, the customer may order any product that is created in the sales area for which the order is being created.

Materials Requirements Planning and Transfer of Requirements

During sales order creation, a line item in the sales order may create a schedule line. The schedule line represents the customer's requested delivery date and quantity to be delivered. This information is transferred (transfer of requirements) to materials requirements planning (MRP). MRP is then able to determine if there is enough quantity of stock available for the scheduled delivery date. The transfer of requirements aims to ensure that the materials ordered are ready for the requested delivery date.

The transfer of requirements is closely integrated with the Materials Management (MM) and Production Planning (PP) modules, which are both part of Logistics within the SAP ERP Central Component of SAP. Thus transfer of requirements must be closely configured in association with the respective logistics teams.

To configure transfer of requirements, use the following menu path.

Menu Path   SAP Customizing Implementation Guide | Sales and Distribution | Basic Functions | Availability Check and Transfer of Requirements | Transfer of Requirements

As described earlier, the schedule lines in the sales order transfer the requirements through to MRP. You are able to select for which documents you would like the transfer of requirements to happen. For example, you may not wish any transfer of requirements to happen for quotations. However, you may want the transfer of requirements to happen for standard sales orders.

Individual or Collective Requirements

The transfer of requirements can either be a transfer of requirements with an individual requirement or a transfer of requirements with collective requirements. This is set in the Availability check field on the material master record in the Sales: General/Plant view. Use transaction code [MM01] - to create a material and transaction code [MM02] - to change a material master record.. Not only does this control how the availability check is processed, but also how the requirements are transferred to MRP.

Individual requirements are, as the name implies, an individual transference of demand to MRP for each schedule line. An advantage of this is that the availability overview (transaction code [CO09]) will show the order quantity, the sales document number, the item number, and requirements class (see requirements class later in this section) for each schedule line for which a demand has been created. Often one may refer to the stock requirements list (transaction [MD04]) and view a requirement from a sales document, however with this view it is difficult to see if a requirement has been confirmed, that is stock has been allocated to the requirement. By using the availability overview transaction [CO09] one is able to see the confirmed "allocated" quantity for a requirement. The view of the availability overview is configured using a checking group, please refer to availability control and checking groups, later in this chapter.

Collective requirements are a collective grouping of requirements created either daily or weekly and transferred to MRP. The documents created in collective requirement processing cannot be individually identified from the availability overview. Collective requirements are useful to a business that deals with a large volume of sales orders per day, as it allows the business to have a clearer view of the availability overview as well as speeding up response time within the system.

To access the availability overview screen, shown in Figure 5-17, use the following menu path.

Menu Path   SAP Menu | Logistics | Materials Management | Inventory Management | Environment | Stock | Availability Overview

One may also use the transaction code [CO09].

By clicking on the Total Records button, the overview will display all the documents that have requirements.

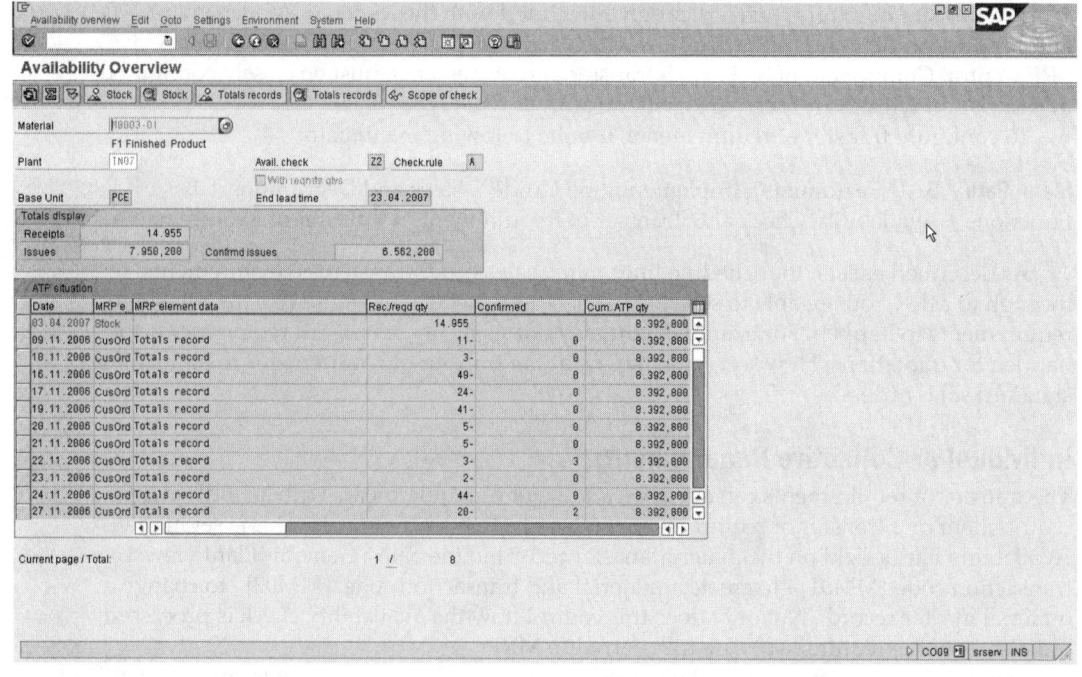

FIGURE 5-17 Availability overview

There are a number of key transactions relating to integration between logistics in MM and SD in this menu path. They include

- [MMBE] - Stock Overview
- [MD04] - Stock/Requirements List
- [MB53] - Plant Stock Availability
- [CO09] - Availability Overview
- [MB52] - Warehouse Stock
- [MB5M] - Expiration Date List
- [MB5B] - Stock for Posting Date
- [MB5T] - Stock in Transit
- [MBBS] - Valuated Special Stock
- [MBLB] - Stock with Subcontractor

The system will automatically create individual requirements for materials with collective requirements indicated on the material master for transactions that create special stock—for example, consignment, returnable packaging, or make-to-order stock.

Transfer of Requirements

Essentially, the same control elements are used for the transfer of requirements as are used for the availability check.

The transfer of requirements is dependent on the following data:

- The requirements type
- The requirements class
- The checking group
- The schedule line category

The requirements class is the key factor in the transfer of requirements. It is based on the requirements type for the sales document.

These requirements classes are also used in Production Planning (PP), so be sure to integrate with PP and Materials Management (MM) in any changes you envision in the SD module. The requirements type and, eventually, requirements class are determined in the strategy group so all changes made there should also be coordinated through PP.

The strategy group may be found on the material master (transaction code [MM02]) MRP 3 view under planning.

For the transfer of requirements to be carried out, you need to ensure a few criteria are met:

- A plant must be assigned to the sales document line item level.
- The schedule line category must be switched on for transfer of requirements.
- The transfer of requirements must be switched on at the requirements class level.
- A checking group must be defined and allocated to the material master record in the Sales: General/Plant view in the availability check field.

When the transfer of requirements is switched on at requirements class level, it can be switched off at schedule line level. However, you cannot switch on the transfer of requirements at schedule line level if it is switched off at requirements class level.

Settings for the transfer of requirements specific to schedule lines are only relevant for sales documents—for example, the sales order. In the shipping documents, however, the settings for the requirements class apply.

The requirements class is determined from the requirements type of the material.

An example of how the transfer of requirements is carried out is seen in Figure 5-18.

The customer orders 100 pc for the requested delivery date of 06/01/08. Block A represents the **availability check**, which shows the confirmed quantities at schedule line level. Block B represents the **passing on of requirements**, which shows the passing on of the demand for 100 pce for 06/01/08.

The result would be the quantities as confirmed in the schedule lines, with an open order quantity of 10 pce, which would be confirmed once stock has been re-entered into the plant, for example. (And MRP (Material Requirements Planning) had been run to re-allocate stock to open order quantities.)

Consumption Modes

The consumption mode defines whether, and in which direction on the time axis from the requirements date the consumption of customer requirements with planned independent requirements should occur. The requirements date corresponds to the date the sales order items were created.

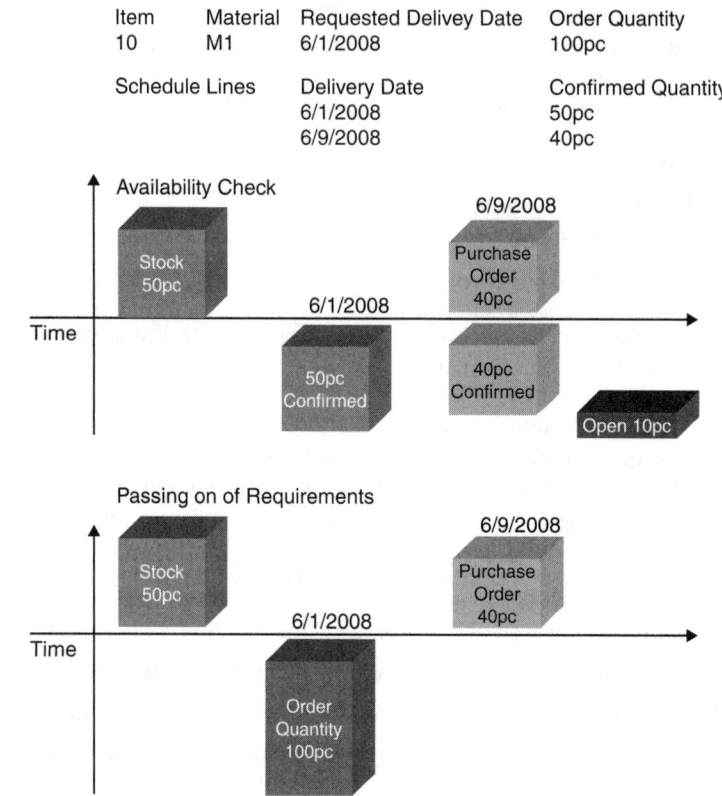

Figure 5-18
Transfer of requirements in Sales and Distribution

Item	Material	Requested Delivey Date	Order Quantity
10	M1	6/1/2008	100pc
Schedule Lines		Delivery Date	Confirmed Quantity
		6/1/2008	50pc
		6/9/2008	40pc

One has the following options:

- **No planning consumption**

- **Backwards consumption only**   Starting from the requirements date, backwards consumption is carried out within the relevant consumption period.

- **Forwards consumption only**   Starting from the requirements date, forward consumption is carried out within the relevant consumption period.

- **Backwards/forwards consumption**   Starting from the requirements date, backwards consumption is performed first of all. Then, if no planned independent requirements can be allocated before the requirements date, forward consumption is performed. Both procedures are carried out for the relevant consumption period.

- **Forwards/backwards consumption**   Starting from the requirements date, forward consumption is performed first of all. Then, if no independent requirements can be allocated after the requirements date, backwards consumption is performed. Both procedures are carried out for the relevant consumption period.

Planning Materials

It is possible to create a common planning material and assign similar materials to it. Independent requirements are created for the planning material to cover the requirements that are expected for the materials assigned to the planning material. Thus, customer requirements for these materials are consumed by the independent requirements of the planning material. This means that you do not have to create independent requirements for each material.

You assign the planning material to the materials on the MRP 3 screen. You must also enter the appropriate strategy group for planning using planning materials on the MRP 3 screen.

You are not able to perform a transfer of requirements from the sales or delivery documents when using a planning material. Rather, the actual requirement from the order or delivery consumes the independent requirement of the planning material. The independent requirement is thus reduced. Then when MRP is run, requirements are created for the order or delivery, and for the balance of the independent requirement. For example, with an independent requirement of 100 tons and an order of 20 tons, the order becomes a requirement of 20 tons, and the independent requirement is reduced to 80 tons. The total requirement is still 100 tons.

The Stock Requirements List

The stock requirements list is the central table to planning and stock control. It is accessed via various menu paths, but the simplest menu path is as follows.

Menu Path SAP Menu | Logistics | Materials Management | Material Requirements Planning (MRP) | MRP | Evaluations | [MD04] - Stock/Reqmts List

Figure 5-19 is an example of the stock requirements list for a material with individual requirements.

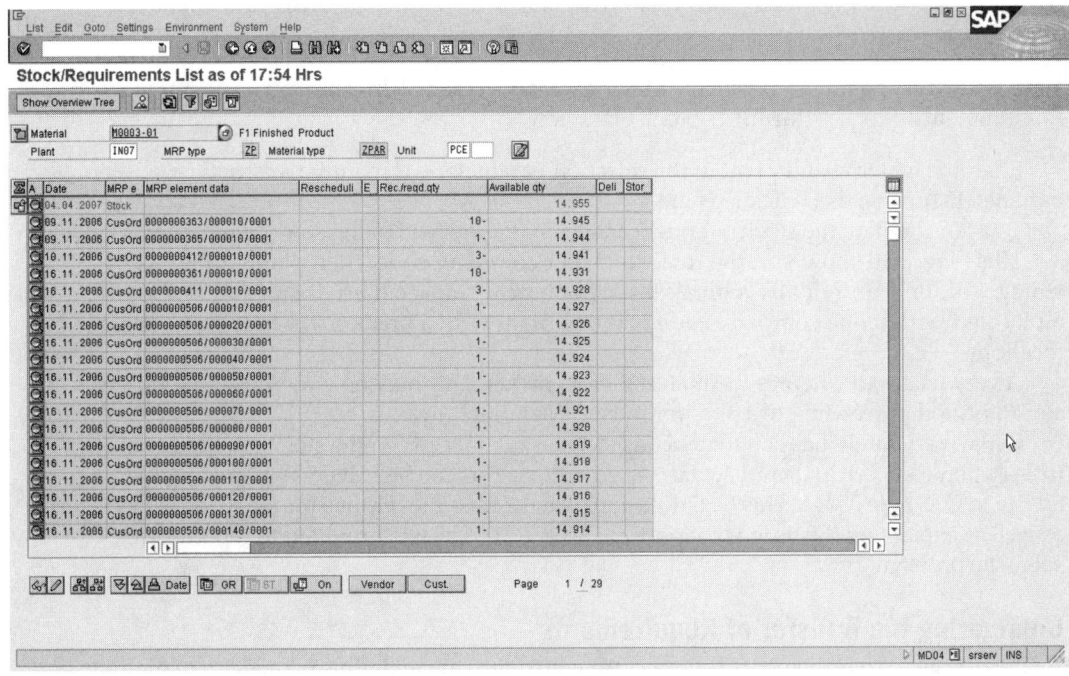

Copyright by SAP AG

FIGURE 5-19 Stock requirements list

You can clearly see the order number as well as the line item and schedule line placing the demand on plant IN07. For example, 0000000363/000010/0001 refers to:

0000000363/000010/0001	Sales document number
0000000363/**000010**/0001	Item number
0000000363/000010/**0001**	Schedule line number

The first line displays the available stock in the plant as 14,955 pce. The next line shows a customer order, which is the result of transfer of requirements from a sales order for a quantity of 10 pce. reducing the available quantity to 14,945 pce.

One may select additional data for the data element by selecting the magnifying glass adjacent to the line. One is then able to display or change the original element—for example, a sales document or purchase order.

You are also able to switch to total records by clicking the Sum button, shown here.

Copyright by SAP AG

There is a lot of functionality behind this stock requirements list. It is advisable to explore all the options and menu paths.

The Stock Overview

Another view of stock that is invaluable to the interpretation of the available stock and the situation of stock levels in a plant is the stock overview (previously used in consignment stock). There are many menu paths to this display; however, the following menu path is simple to use.

Menu Path   SAP Menu | Logistics | Materials Management | Inventory Management | Environment | Stock | [MMBE] - Stock Overview

Enter the material and plant in the selection parameters. If required, restrict the selection parameters further, then click Execute.

You can compare the stock overview as seen in Figure 5-20 to the stock requirements list.

This view will show you the total stock per company code, then plant, followed by storage location, and finally a breakdown per batch. You see there is stock of 14,955 pce, all located within one company code and one plant with a breakdown in two storage locations.

A very useful tool here is the material movements. This may be viewed by selecting the stock line and proceeding to | Environment | Material Movements.

It may very rarely happen that inconsistencies occur between the stock requirements list (transaction code [MD04]) and actual placed orders. This can be solved by following the advice in OSS note 25444. This OSS note explains the possible reasons for the inconsistencies, as well as explaining the usage of report ZSDRQCR21, which is provided to report on and solve the problem.

Configuring the Transfer of Requirements

As the transfer of requirements is very closely linked to the materials management module, we will be focusing on the SD configuration areas only.

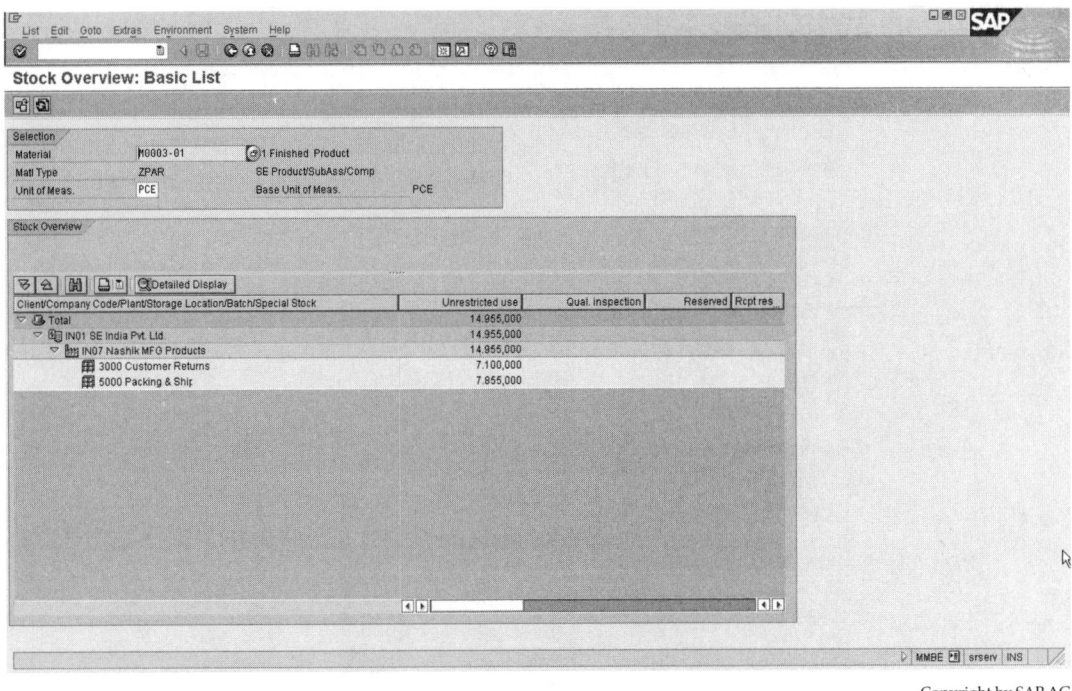

Copyright by SAP AG

FIGURE 5-20   Stock overview

Defining Requirements Classes

To define requirements classes, use the following menu path.

Menu Path   SAP Customizing Implementation Guide I Sales and Distribution I Basic Functions I Availability Check and Transfer of Requirements I Transfer of Requirements I Define Requirements Classes

The requirements class is the controlling factor for the availability check and transfer of requirements for all sales documents types. The system uses the entries at requirements class level as a default and brings the data into the sales order. The schedule line category is used to fine-tune the settings at requirements class level.

Generally, SD will not need to create a new requirements class for standard business processes. However, should a new requirements class be necessary, simply copy and rename the class that most closely resembles the requirements class you need. Ensure you rename the class using the SAP standard allowed naming convention that begins with a Z.

A useful tip is to select the requirements class you wish to configure and then click the Display button (the magnifying glass). This will produce an easily configurable overview of the indicators you may set at the requirements class level. The requirements class 030 is displayed in Figure 5-21.

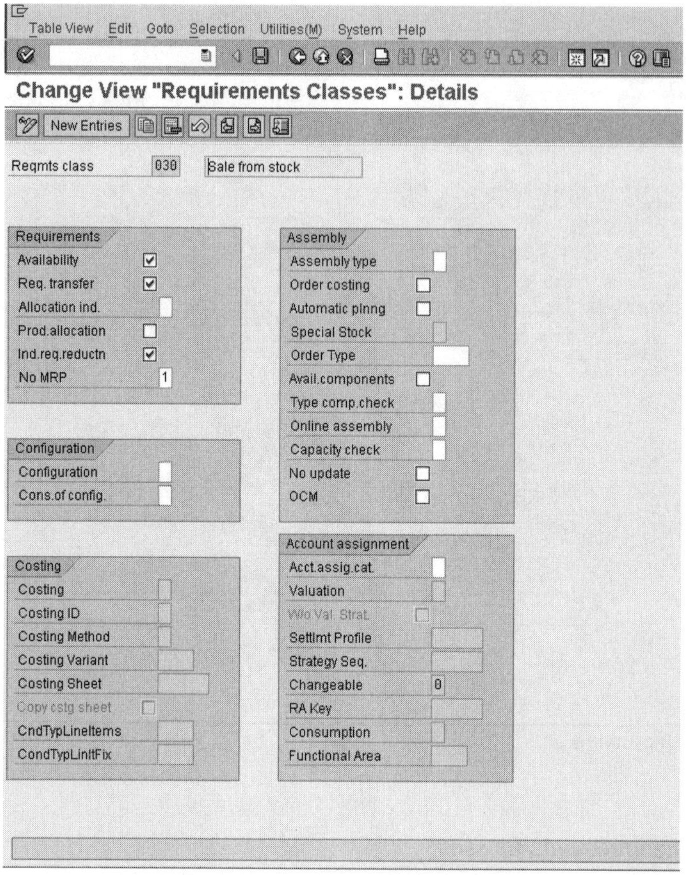

FIGURE 5-21
Requirements
class

Use the indicators to select if this requirements class must carry out an availability check and/or transfer of requirements.

Defining Requirements Types

Once the requirements class has been created, you need to define requirements types.

A requirements type is allocated to a single requirements class; however, a requirements class may be allocated to more than one requirements type. The requirements type is displayed in the sales order. It is based on the item category and the MRP type of the material. It is possible to change the requirements type at the time of creating the sales order.

Assign the requirements class you created to a requirements type. It is possible to create your own requirements types too, by selecting and copying the current value, followed by using a naming convention beginning with Z.

Determination of Requirement Types Using Transaction

Once this assignment has been made proceed to - determination of requirement types using transaction.

Menu Path   SAP Customizing Implementation Guide | Sales and Distribution | Basic Functions | Availability Check and Transfer of Requirements | Transfer of Requirements | Determination of requirement types using transaction

Here you assign the requirements type to the relevant item category in the sales order and MRP type found on the material master record. The MRP type is used in the material master to determine how a material is planned—for example, automatic reorder point planning, manual reorder point planning, forecast-based planning, no planning, etc.

There is a pre-defined search strategy that the system uses to determine the requirements type as follows:

1. First, an attempt is made to find a requirements type using the strategy group in the material master.

2. Then if the strategy group has not been maintained, the system will determine it using the MRP group.

3. If, however, the MRP group has not been defined, the system uses the material type instead of the MRP group when accessing the corresponding control tables.

4. If no requirements type is found, the system assumes a special rule and attempts to find a requirements type by the item category and the MRP type.

5. If this is not possible, a final attempt is made to find a requirements type with the item category only.

6. If the final attempt fails, the system declares the transaction as not relevant for the availability check or transfer of requirements.

Should you not want this strategy to be used to search for a requirements type, but instead you would like the system to immediately determine the requirements type based on the item category and MRP type as you assigned them, you may select an alternative search strategy in the column next to the one where you assign the requirements type, as shown in Figure 5-22. For this particular example you would select 1, which determines that the source is used as the item type and MRP type strategy.

Defining Procedure for Each Schedule Line Category

Once this assignment has been made proceed to the menu path for - Define Procedure For Each Schedule Line Category.

Menu Path   SAP Customizing Implementation Guide | Sales and Distribution | Basic Functions | Availability Check and Transfer of Requirements | Transfer of Requirements | Define Procedure For Each Schedule Line Category

As discussed previously, the transfer of requirements and the availability check can be fine-tuned at the schedule line category level. Note that this allows you to deactivate a setting at the schedule line level *only* if already set at the requirements class level.

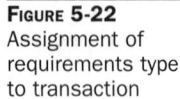

Figure 5-22
Assignment of
requirements type
to transaction

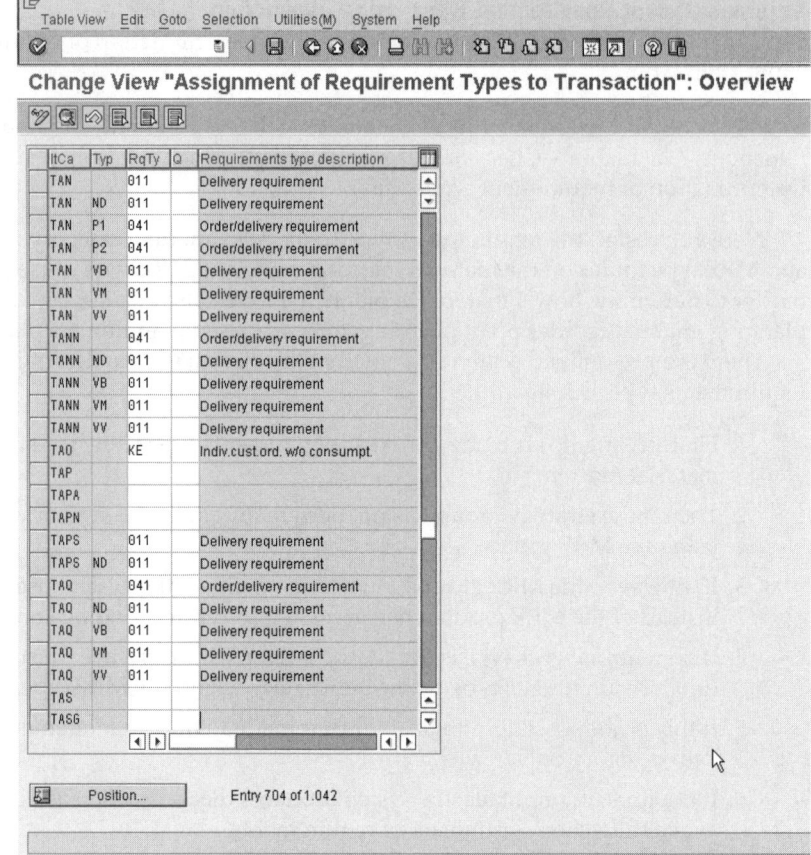

Copyright by SAP AG

Thus, you may select that a particular requirements class is active for the availability check or transfer of requirements, and then decide that at the schedule line level you do not wish the schedule line to transfer requirements.

However, it is not possible to not have selected the requirements class as relevant for transfer of requirements and then to try and activate it at the schedule line level.

Proceed with indicating which schedule line category will be available for transfer of requirements and availability check (and/or product allocation, which is also controlled in the requirements class). This is seen in Figure 5-23.

Block Quantity Confirmation in Delivery Blocks

After completing this, proceed to the section on Block Quantity Confirmation In Delivery Blocks.

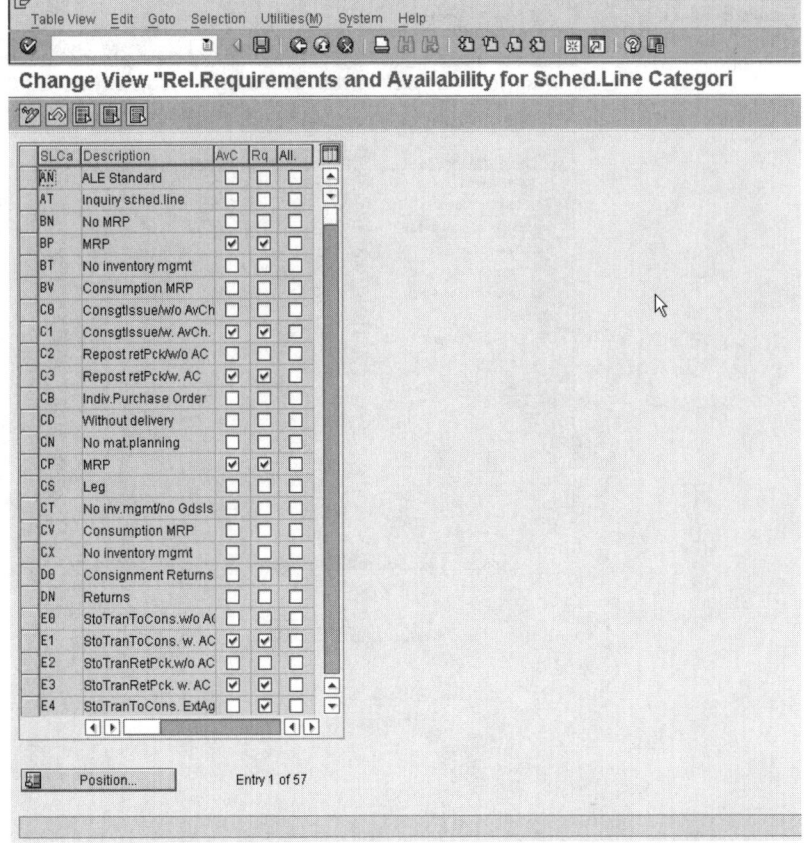

Copyright by SAP AG

FIGURE 5-23
Schedule line
level activation

Menu Path   SAP Customizing Implementation Guide | Sales and Distribution | Basic Functions | Availability Check and Transfer of Requirements | Transfer of Requirements | Block quantity confirmation in delivery blocks | Deliveries: Blocking Reasons/Criteria, as seen in Figure 5-24.

This blocking indicator is used to control many functions:

- **Order**   Blocking of the sales document for delivery.
- **Confirmation**   Blocking of the confirmation from availability check; thus, the stock will not be confirmed in the schedule line level and the stock will be available for other sales documents.
- **DDueList**   Blocking of sales document for automatic creation by the delivery due list. With this block in place, only manually created deliveries via VL01N will be possible.
- **Picki**   Blocking of picking.
- **Goods**   Blocking of goods issue.

FIGURE 5-24
Delivery block
control

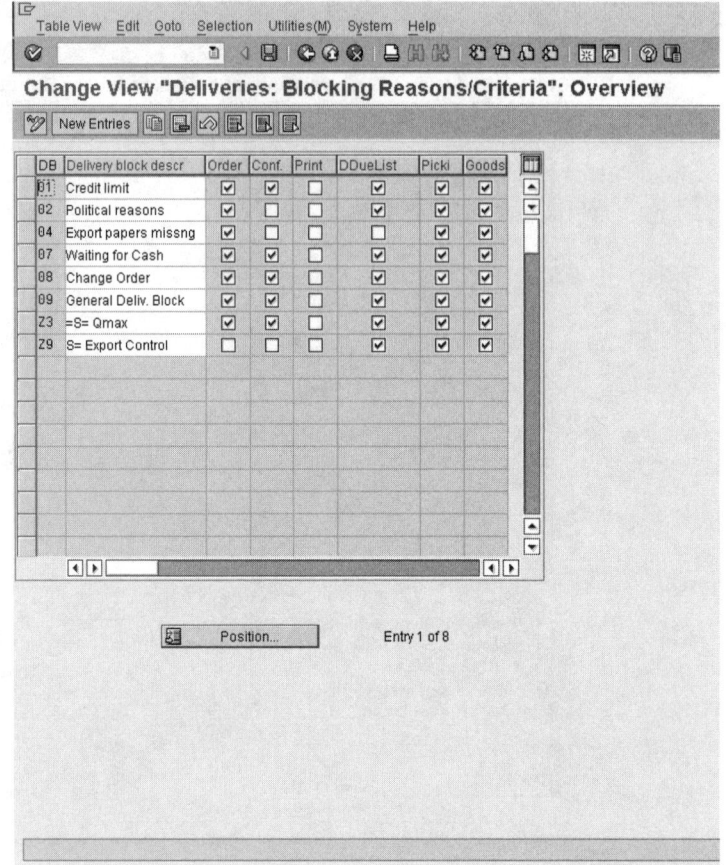

Change View "Deliveries: Blocking Reasons/Criteria": Overview

DB	Delivery block descr	Order	Conf.	Print	DDueList	Picki	Goods
01	Credit limit	☑	☑	☐	☑	☑	☑
02	Political reasons	☑	☐	☐	☑	☑	☑
04	Export papers missng	☑	☐	☐	☐	☑	☑
07	Waiting for Cash	☑	☑	☐	☑	☑	☑
08	Change Order	☑	☑	☐	☑	☑	☑
09	General Deliv. Block	☑	☑	☐	☑	☑	☑
Z3	=S= Qmax	☑	☑	☐	☑	☑	☑
Z9	S= Export Control	☐	☐	☐	☑	☑	☑

Position...   Entry 1 of 8

To set a deferment period for the block of the confirmation of the reservation of the transfer of requirements from MRP, as shown in Figure 5-25, proceed with the menu path

Menu Path   SAP Customizing Implementation Guide I Sales and Distribution I Basic Functions I Availability Check and Transfer of Requirements I Transfer of Requirements I Reasons for and Scope of Deliv.Blocks: Transfer of Req.Block

In standard sales order processing the system transfers the requirements to MRP. However, in some cases you may need to block a transaction—for example, due to a bad result of the credit check. In cases where the transaction is blocked, the requirement still sits in MRP and still reserves a quantity. This often is unfavorable, thus you may indicate here that the system does not reserve the stock. It will still transfer the requirement to MRP, however, it will not reserve the quantity.

You are able to set a limit to the number of days you would want the system to postpone this block on confirmation of requirements. This may be carried out by setting a number of days to the block, in the Def Period column.

FIGURE 5-25
Transfer of
requirements
block deferment
setting

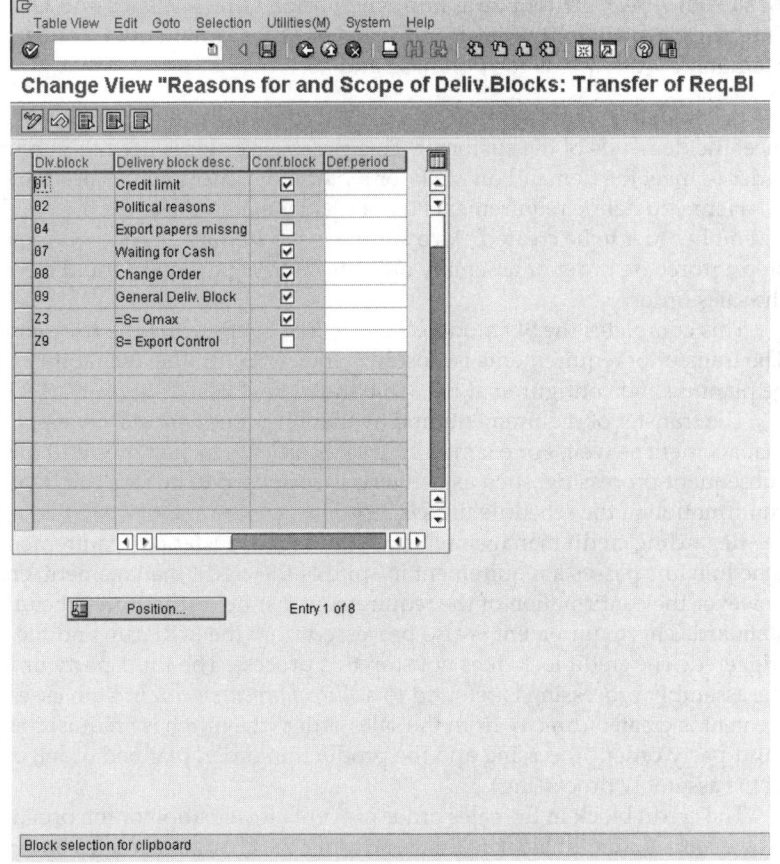

Change View "Reasons for and Scope of Deliv.Blocks: Transfer of Req.Bl

Dlv.block	Delivery block desc.	Conf.block	Def.period
01	Credit limit	☑	
02	Political reasons	☐	
04	Export papers missng	☐	
07	Waiting for Cash	☑	
08	Change Order	☑	
09	General Deliv. Block	☑	
Z3	=S= Qmax	☑	
Z9	S= Export Control	☐	

Position...   Entry 1 of 8

Block selection for clipboard

Copyright by SAP AG

This postponement period will only affect the order confirmation if the postponement falls within the confirmation period. For example, should a material be ordered on 10/01 and confirmed for 10/02 and the period for the block is 10 days, the resulting confirmed date would be 10/11. On the other hand, however, should the original schedule line be confirmed in 20 days, thus 10/21, the block would have no affect on the sales order.

Maintaining Requirements for Transfer of Requirements

Menu Path   SAP Customizing Implementation Guide | Sales and Distribution | Basic Functions | Availability Check and Transfer of Requirements | Transfer of Requirements | Maintain Requirements For Transfer Of Requirements

In the same way that requirements are used in access sequences—that is, a number of preconditions must exist for the transaction to be carried out—requirements may also be used to determine that the transfer of requirements to MRP is not carried out unless a number of conditions are met.

You are also able to set requirements on the implementation guide menu path.

Menu Path   SAP Customizing Implementation Guide | Sales and Distribution | Basic Functions | Availability Check and Transfer of Requirements | Transfer of Requirements | Maintain requirements for purchase and assembly orders

In standard sales order processing a purchase order may need to be created in order to meet the demands of the customer. This purchase order is used to purchase new stock in order to meet the demand on MRP for a particular customer's sales order.

Here you define requirements that must be met in order for the purchase order or assembly order to be created. An example is the standard SAP requirement 101, which will stop a purchase order or assembly order from being created should a credit block exist on the sales order.

This completes the SD module's aspects of configuring the transfer of requirements. The transfer of requirements is closely associated with the availability check. They should be planned and configured at the same time.

 The transfer of requirements and availability check are closely associated with credit management as well. For example, if a sales order is locked by credit management, all subsequent processing, such as delivery, is supposed to be stopped. For this purpose, the confirmation in the schedule lines is reset.

Regarding credit management and standard Transfer of Requirements - the requested schedule line passes a requirement in spite of the credit management, credit control block, however the confirmation of the requirement can be configured to be unconfirmed as in standard. This requirement is also processed from the MRP run and the procurement is triggered. The credit lock does not stop this process. The third-party order processing and the assembly processing is referred to as *direct procurement*. In both cases, the procurement element is created directly from the sales order (the purchase requisition in the case of the third-party order processing and the production order, planned order, or the like in the case of the assembly processing).

The credit block in the sales order prevents the creation of the procurement element. However if the credit block is first set during the change of a sales order, the procurement element is deleted again. As long as the credit block is set in the sales order, no procurement or production occurs for this sales order.

If a sales order is released from the credit block, an availability check is carried out again for this order. The availability check tries to confirm the requested quantities.

In case of the direct procurement, a purchase requisition or a production order is created again in the background.

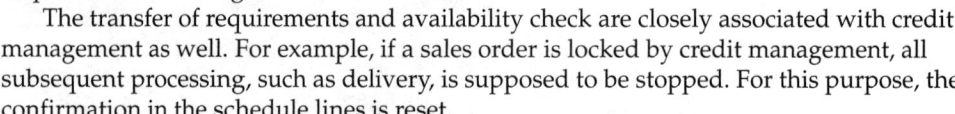 It is possible in some instances that the subsequent operations and purchase requisitions that have been used may not have been deleted. For example, in a service order, they may have simply been locked, as all processes should be on hold due to the credit block.

When the document is released, a new document (for example, a new service order) may be created to continue the process. The first service order and the new service order now relate to a single sales document. (If you are interested, service documents would be obtainable from transaction code [IW39] - List of All Service Orders.)

Availability Check

The availability check forms an integral part of the business sales process. It determines if the requested delivery quantity can be available for shipping in order to meet the customer's requested delivery date.

The availability check is carried out at a Plant level. It results in a material availability date. This represents the date the system has determined the requested material will be available. Added to this date is the pick pack time, the loading time, and the transportation scheduling time, which may or may not be added, depending on how long it is. All of these dates result in a planned goods issue date, which is the planned date the goods are transferred from the business' ownership and control, possibly to a shipping agent. The shipping dates are then added to the goods issue date, resulting in a delivery date. This automatically determined delivery date is then communicated to the customer when the sales order is placed.

Terminology Used in the Availability Check

Backorder processing is the processing of a backorder, which in itself is a sales order that has not been confirmed in full or not confirmed at a certain delivery date.

Rescheduling is a proposal of how confirmed quantities already assigned to sales orders may be reassigned to other orders that have a higher priority—for example, an earlier requested delivery date.

ATP is an acronym for "availability to promise," which is the basis of the availability check. The system is able to automatically calculate the available quantity to promise or commit to a sales document based upon a number of rules that we shall define later.

ATP takes into account all movements into and out of the warehouse.

The stock examined for ATP may be safety stock, stock in transfer, stock in quality inspection, and blocked stock. The planned receipts and planned issues of the stock associated with ATP may be purchase orders, purchase requisitions, planned orders, production orders, reservations, dependent reservations, dependent requirements, sales requirements, and delivery requirements.

If the business produces *special stock,* such as made-to-order goods or consignment stock, the ATP check may be carried out against the special stock.

Replenishment lead time is the time needed to produce the requested stock. It can comprise the time taken by the business to produce a material or the time taken to externally procure the material from a vendor. This includes the goods receipting time. Thus the replenishment lead time is the time taken for the material to become available. Replenishment lead time is only used when doing an ATP check.

The value of the replenishment lead time for a material is specified on the material master record. It may be determined in one of two ways:

- The replenishment lead time for an *externally procured material* is determined based on the total of the processing time for purchasing, the planned delivery time, and the goods receipt processing time. These settings may be made on the Purchasing and MRP 2 views of the material master record.

- The replenishment lead time for an *internally procured material* is based on the in-house production time, seen on the MRP 2 view as well as the goods receipt processing time, or alternatively if set, from the total replenishment lead time, which is found in the material master record on the MRP 3 view.

If a sales order is created and there is no available stock and the ATP check is set to include replenishment lead time, the system will automatically confirm the desired quantity for the end of replenishment lead time based on whether the material is externally or internally procured. Thus should you have an order for 100,000 pieces of material xyz and the system has no available stock, it will still give a confirmed date according to the end of the lead time. Should there be partial stock available, the system will confirm this partial quantity and move the remaining quantity to the end of replenishment lead time. It does not do an availability check outside of the replenishment lead time. If replenishment lead time is three days for a specific material, it will not do an availability check outside of those three days as it automatically thinks it will definitely have stock on the fourth day.

To examine stock on hand you may use the availability overview, proceed with the menu path.

Menu Path   SAP Menu | Logistics | Sales and Distribution | Sales | Environment | Availability Overview

Transaction code [CO09]

To examine stock on hand from a created order, proceed in order change mode [VA02] to the schedule line, then select the menu path Environment | Availability.

There are three types of availability checks:

- The availability check on the *basis of the ATP quantities* as previously described.

- The availability *check against product allocation*, with which one is able to do an availability check against product allocation, allowing a predefined distribution quantity of products to customers.

- The third availability check takes place in the stand-alone APO (Advanced Planner and Optimizer) planning system from SAP.

Basic Elements of the Availability Check
We now have enough background into the availability process to configure the logic behind ATP.

Checking Groups
The checking group defines what type of requirements we will pass on. Do we record summarized requirements—that is, daily or weekly summed up requirements in the stock requirements list? Or do we record individual requirements—that is, a line for each sales order and line item and schedule line in the stock requirement list?

The advantages of individual requirements over summarized requirements are as follows:

- Backorder processing is possible for individual processing.

- We can access the order and line items and schedule lines in the stock requirements list [MD04]. This gives one greater control over the available stock and the requirements placed on the stock.

The disadvantages are

- There may be slightly more impact on system performance as each demand is placed immediately into the stock requirements list.

Do not forget the system automatically uses individual requirements for special stock movements such as consignment stock, returnable packaging, etc., even if summarized requirements have been selected.

The checking groups are configurable. However, SAP standard uses the following checking groups:

- 01 to represent daily requirements
- 02 to represent individual requirements

The checking group plus the checking rule determine how the availability check is to be performed. The availability check (field - MARC-MTVFP) used to be called the checking group for example in SAP R/3 4.0 and is now called "Availability check" in mySAP ERP ECC is found on the material master record on the MRP 3 view.

Checking Rule
The *checking rule* is used to control the scope of the availability check for each transaction in sales and distribution. The control of the availability check is defined by the checking group on the material master record and the checking rule representing the transaction.

Schedule Line Category
The availability check may be fine-tuned at the schedule line level, in the same way as the transfer of requirements was carried out at the schedule line level. Those schedule lines that are not relevant for availability check may be switched off at schedule line level by ensuring the availability check indicator is not flagged.

Delivery Item Category
The delivery item category can be used to control whether an availability check takes place in deliveries. This setting in the availability check is used to switch the availability check off in deliveries.

Requirements Class
The requirements class as used in the transfer of requirements controls the relevance for planning, requirements planning strategy, and requirements consumption strategy. It is also responsible to determine if an availability check is to be performed for the material on the basis of the ATP quantity and whether the transfer of requirements is passed on.

Requirements Type
The requirements type refers to the requirements class and its features. The requirements class is assigned to the requirements type in the transfer of requirements.

Required Data for the Availability Check to Be Utilized
In order for the availability check to be carried out, the following data, in addition to the configuration entries, described later, must be defined in the system:

- The availability check must be switched on at requirements class level. Refer to the transfer of requirements configuration process (transaction code [OVZG]). See Figure 5-26.
- For the availability check in the sales documents, the indicator must be set at the schedule line category level (transaction code [OVZ8]). See Figure 5-27.

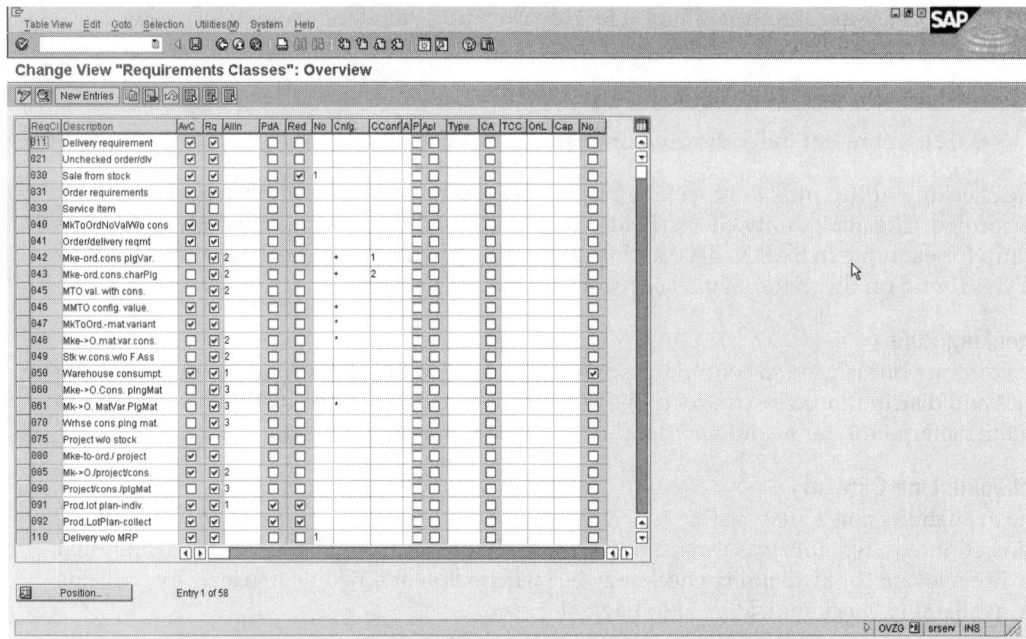

FIGURE 5-26   Requirements class view—availability check activation

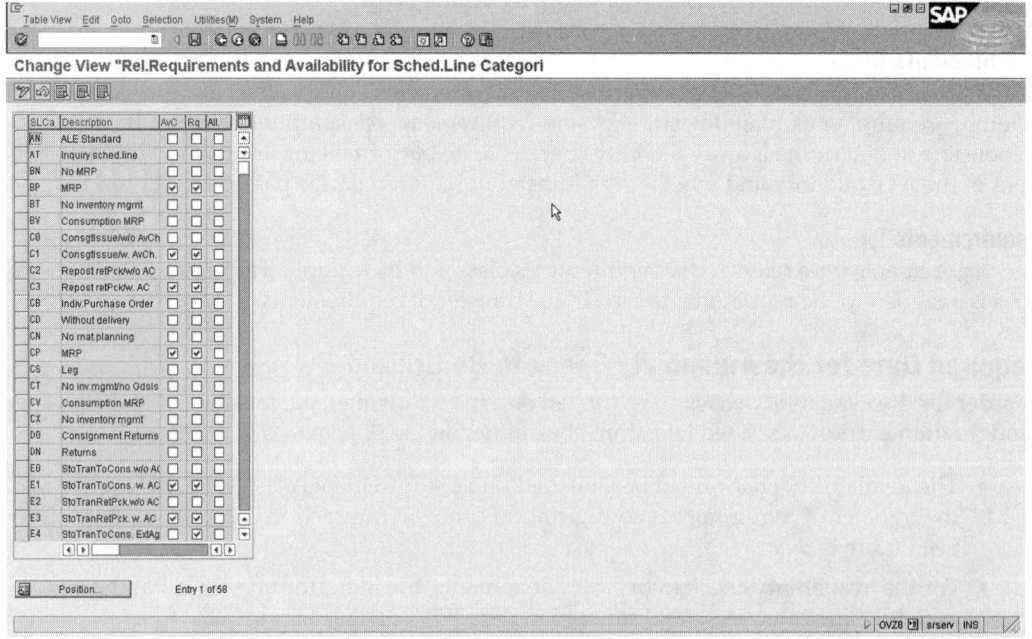

FIGURE 5-27   Schedule line category—availability check activation

- A requirements type must exist by which the requirements class can be found. Again, refer to the transfer of requirements (transaction code [OVZH]). See Figure 5-28.
- A plant must be defined in the sales order for the line item. It can either be automatically proposed by the system from the customer, determined from the customer material information record or the material master record, or can be entered manually in the document.
- A checking group must be defined in the material master record, this is field "MARC-MTVFP" (Availability check) on the MRP 3 view of the material master record, that is the Availability check field.

Configuring the Availability Check with ATP Logic

We can now progress to the configuration of the availability check.

Defining Checking Groups

To define checking groups, use the following menu path.

Menu Path   SAP Customizing Implementation Guide | Sales and Distribution | Basic Functions | Availability Check and Transfer of Requirements | Availability Check | Availability Check with ATP Logic or Against Planning | Define Checking Groups

You may use the standard SAP checking groups of 01 for summarized requirements and 02 for daily requirements, or you may create your own entries. Should you create your own, do not forget to copy and name them using the SAP allocated range beginning with a Z.

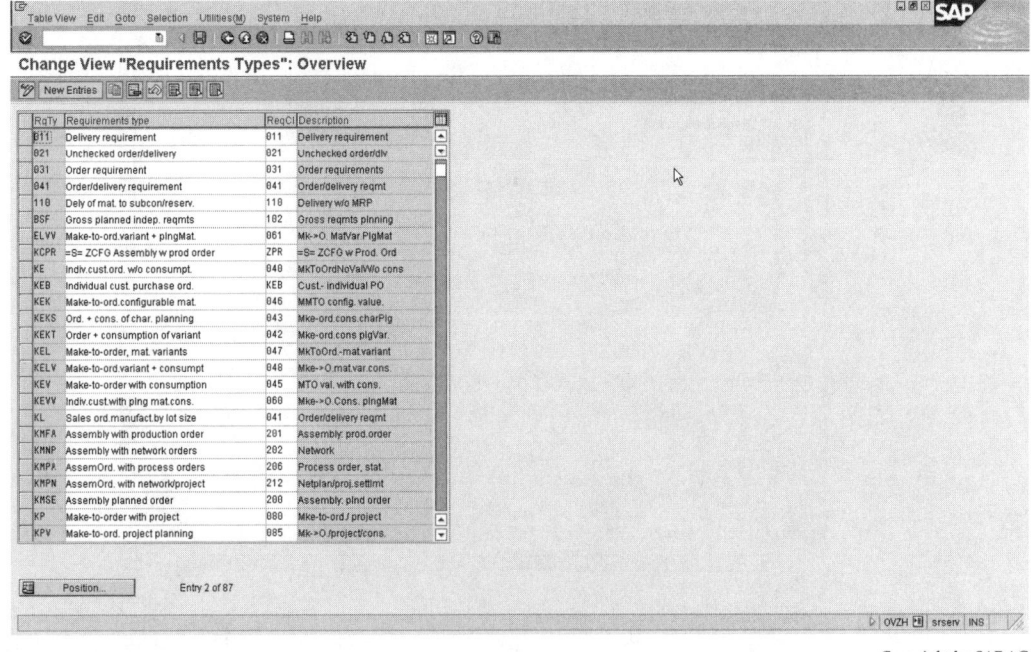

Copyright by SAP AG

FIGURE 5-28   Requirements class to requirements type assignment

The columns Total Sales and Total Deliveries, as seen in Figure 5-29, are selection options whereby you may configure a checking rule to sum up requirements to post to MRP either individually or by day or week.

Do not forget that by selecting to use the summarized requirements you will lose out on the connection to the individual sales order and associated line item in the stock requirements list (transaction code [MD04]).

Note column 5: Block QtRq. Check this setting if you want several users to be able to process the material simultaneously in different transactions without blocking each other.

The No Check setting is used when you want a material not to be relevant for an ATP check, thus no check is carried out for the material with a checking rule indicating "no check." This would be set, for example, for materials for which there is such a high quantity of stock it would be impossible and unnecessary to validate the available quantity.

Defining Material Block for Other Users

To define a material block for other users, use the following menu path.

FIGURE 5-29
Define checking groups

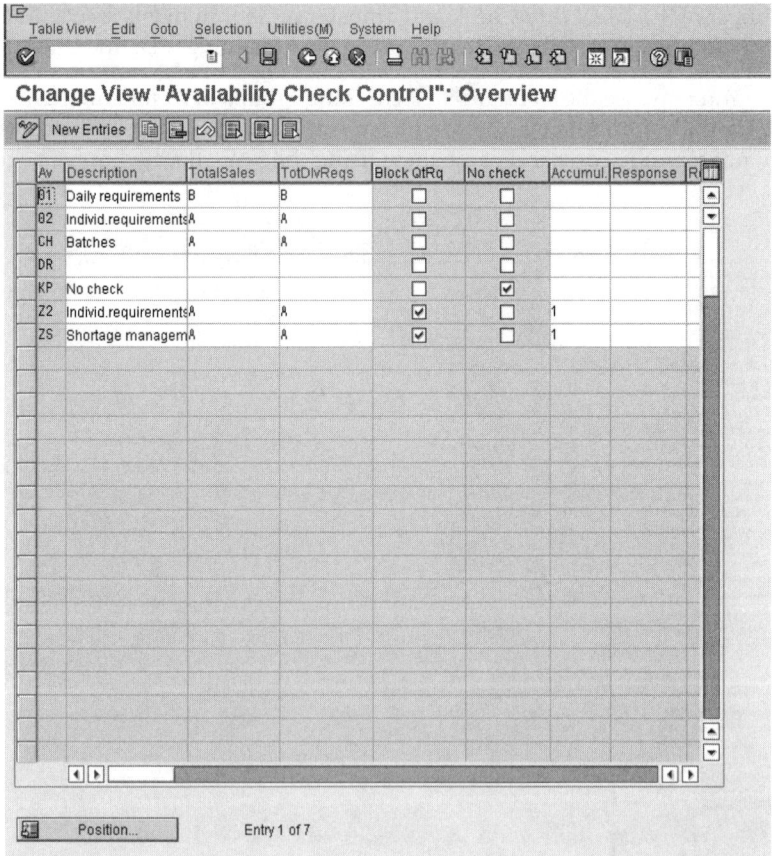

Menu Path   SAP Customizing Implementation Guide | Sales and Distribution | Basic Functions | Availability Check and Transfer of Requirements | Availability Check | Availability Check with ATP Logic or Against Planning | Define Material Block For Other Users

As seen in Figure 5-30, this is an indicator that allows you to block the particular material from being checked for availability if it is already being checked for availability at the same time by another user. This block serves a valuable purpose. Should the block not be set, two users may confirm the same quantity for the same material at the same time. It is defined at of the level of the process that initiates the availability check process.

Defining Default Value for Checking Groups
To define the default value for checking groups, use the following menu path.

Menu Path   SAP Customizing Implementation Guide | Sales and Distribution | Basic Functions | Availability Check and Transfer of Requirements | Availability Check | Availability Check with ATP Logic or Against Planning | Define Checking Groups Default Value

FIGURE 5-30
Blocking criteria
specification

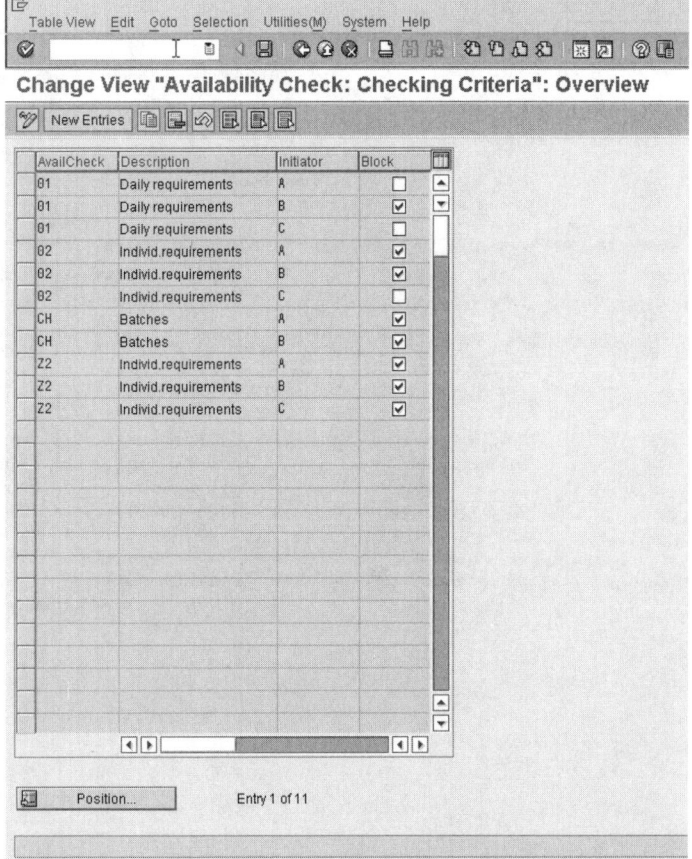

We have defined the checking groups. These checking groups are introduced into the sales order based on the setting in the material master record. However, should no entry exist in the material master record, one is able to set a default value per material type and plant. This default value will be used by the system based upon the material type of the material master record and the plant in the sales order, unless an entry exists in the material master record, whereby it will be overwritten by the material master checking group.

Carry Out Control of the Availability Check

Here you finally define what values must be checked in order for the system to determine the available quantity. Use the following menu path.

Menu Path   SAP Customizing Implementation Guide I Sales and Distribution I Basic Functions I Availability Check and Transfer of Requirements I Availability Check I Availability Check with ATP Logic or Against Planning I Carry Out Control For Availability Check

Select the line item and click the Display button. You will see a screen similar to Figure 5-31.

In this section you tell the system what stock is on hand and what inward and outward movements of stock it must take into account when performing the availability check.

FIGURE 5-31
Carry out control of the availability check (SD Order)

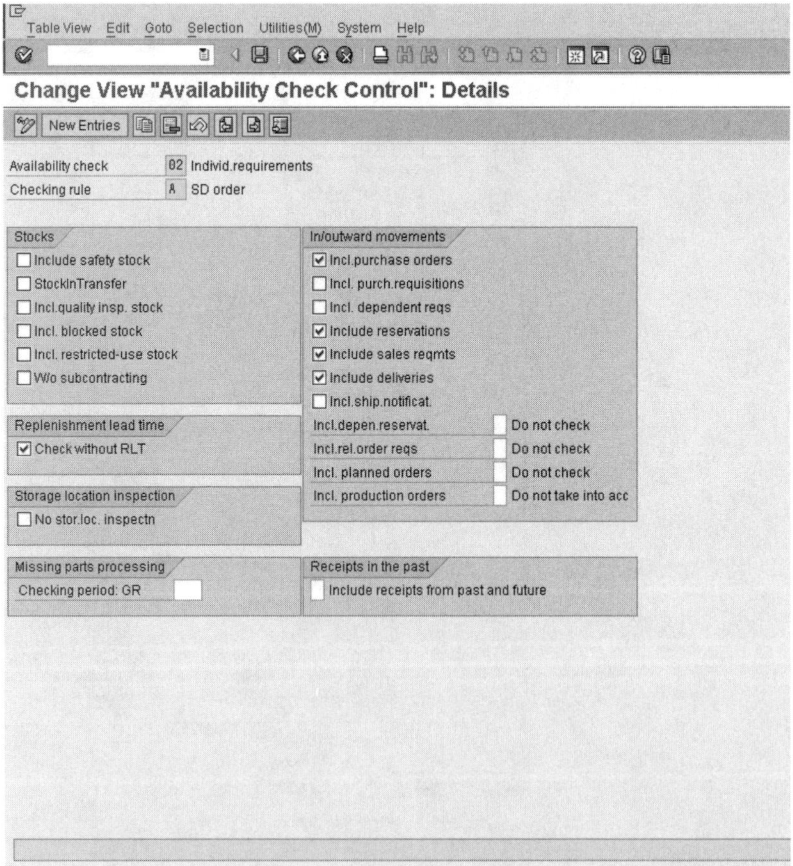

These settings are based on the checking group that is assigned to the material master record, and the checking rule that is predefined and assigned to the sales and distribution transaction.

The carry out control for availability check must be maintained for both the sales order and delivery as seen in Figure 5-32.

For example, you may want to include specific stock or incoming stock for the sales order, but at the time of the delivery only include physical stock on hand that is prepared to be shipped.

Select which type of stock you wish to take into account when carrying out the availability check. Some of the options include

- Safety stock

- Stock in transfer

- Quality inspection stock

- Restricted use stock (batch stock)

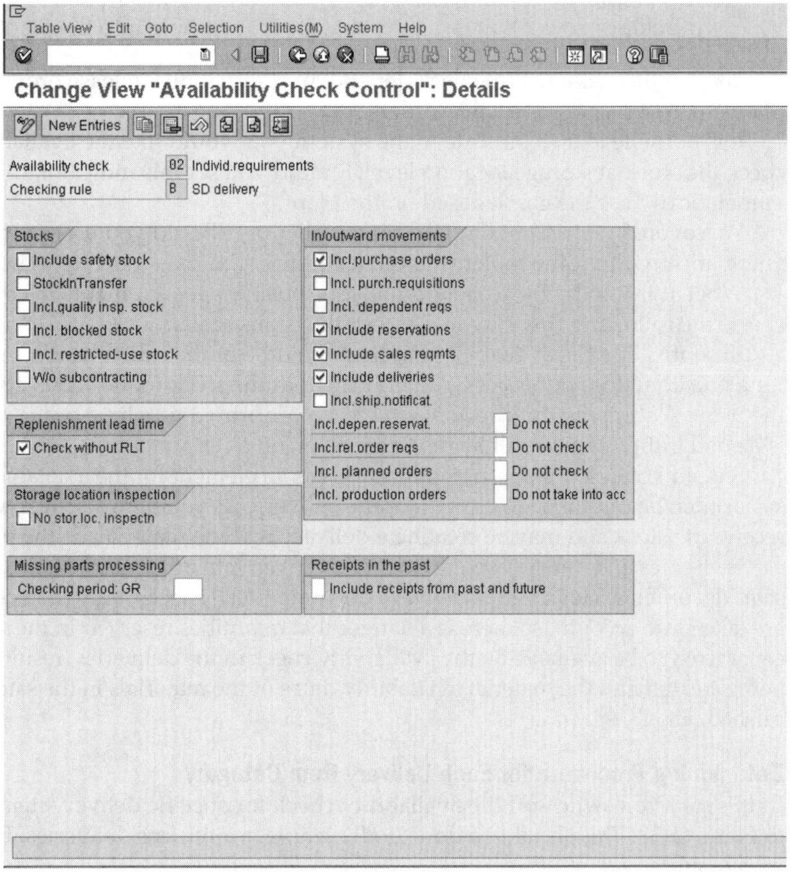

FIGURE 5-32
Carry out control of the availability check (SD Delivery)

Now select the planned inward and outward movements of stock you would like to take into account when doing an availability check:

- **Include purchase orders**   This is slightly better than purchase requisitions as it tells the system to include actual orders placed for more stock.

- **Include purchase requisitions**   This is used by the system to determine if it should use the requisition for purchasing to obtain more stock in the availability check.

- **Include dependent requirements**   This is used by the system to indicate if dependent requirements such as components of a production order are taken into account.

- **Include reservations**   This is used to determine if the system should take into account the reservations of stock for this material.

- **Include sales requirements**   This is used to include the requirement based on a sales transaction such as previous orders placed for the material or even quotations.

- **Include deliveries**   This is used by the system to include requirements passed on from a delivery document for this material.

- **Include shipping notifications**   This is used by the system to include confirmed purchase orders, that is, surety that stock is coming into the plant or warehouse.

You are then able to also check dependent reservations, release order requirements, planned orders, and production orders.

It is possible to also indicate to the system you would like the availability check not to check the stock at storage location level. Should you set this indicator, the system will automatically use the check based on the plant.

We covered replenishment lead time earlier on. Should you *not* want the system to automatically check the replenishment lead time, you may indicate so here.

While it is impossible to determine your business requirements in configuring the ATP check, the following tips may make your decisions easier.

In controlling the availability check at the time of the sales order, a purchase requisition for a line item does not necessarily indicate that the stock requested is going to come into the plant. A shipping notification, which is a confirmed purchase order, on the other hand, is a good indicator you will be receiving stock on a certain date.

Should you select shipping notifications as an element for the availability check in the sales order, be careful if selecting it for the delivery. As you may discover, you actually did not receive the stock and may be creating a delivery with no materials in the plant or warehouse.

Both sales and delivery requirements are taken into account in the availability check in sales documents. However, in delivery document ATP checks, only the delivery requirements are taken into account, so there is a danger that quantities reserved in the sales documents are considered to be available by the availability check in the deliveries, resulting in the deliveries being created and the material availability dates of the materials in the sales documents being pushed out.

Determining Procedure for Each Delivery Item Category

In this step you switch off the availability check for specific delivery item categories, as seen in Figure 5-33. This should be done, for example, for returns deliveries. Use the following menu path.

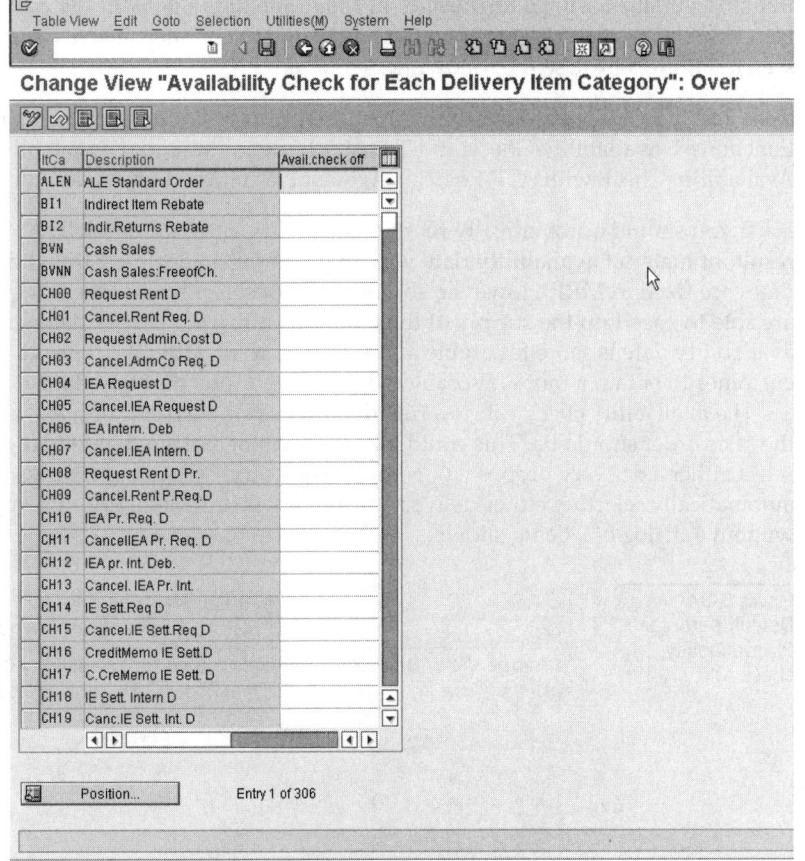

FIGURE 5-33
Delivery item
category
deactivation

Menu Path SAP Customizing Implementation Guide | Sales and Distribution | Basic Functions | Availability Check and Transfer of Requirements | Availability Check | Availability Check with ATP Logic or Against Planning | Determine Procedure For Each Delivery Item Category

Checking Rule for Updating Backorders

The checking rule used here is the same checking rule as is configured in the carry out control of the availability check. This checking rule is used in the availability overview (transaction code [CO09]) and during backorder processing (transaction code [CO06]).

Use the following menu path.

Menu Path SAP Customizing Implementation Guide | Sales and Distribution | Basic Functions | Availability Check and Transfer of Requirements | Availability Check | Availability Check with ATP Logic or Against Planning | Checking Rule For Updating Backorders

Defining Default Settings for Results of the Availability Check in the Sales Order

Here you define per sales organization, distribution channel, and division (sales area), as seen in Figure 5-34. Use the following menu path.

Menu Path SAP Customizing Implementation Guide | Sales and Distribution | Basic Functions | Availability Check and Transfer of Requirements | Availability Check | Availability Check with ATP Logic or Against Planning | Define Default Settings

If you should automatically fix the date and quantity of the delivery date, then the resultant material availability date will be set. Should you select this indicator, the delivery dates are fixed in MRP. However, should you not select fixed date and quantity and you are able to speed up the supply of the materials into your plant, the resultant material availability date is more favorable and you may reschedule the dates in order for the customer to obtain a more favorable ATP date and thus delivery date.

The availability check rule is a rule defining what the result of the availability check in the sales order should be. This could take the form of a dialog box where the user is able to select either a delivery proposal or complete delivery. Or it could take the form of the system automatically selecting either delivery proposal, one time delivery, or complete delivery, without a dialog box being shown.

FIGURE 5-34
Default settings for availability check rule

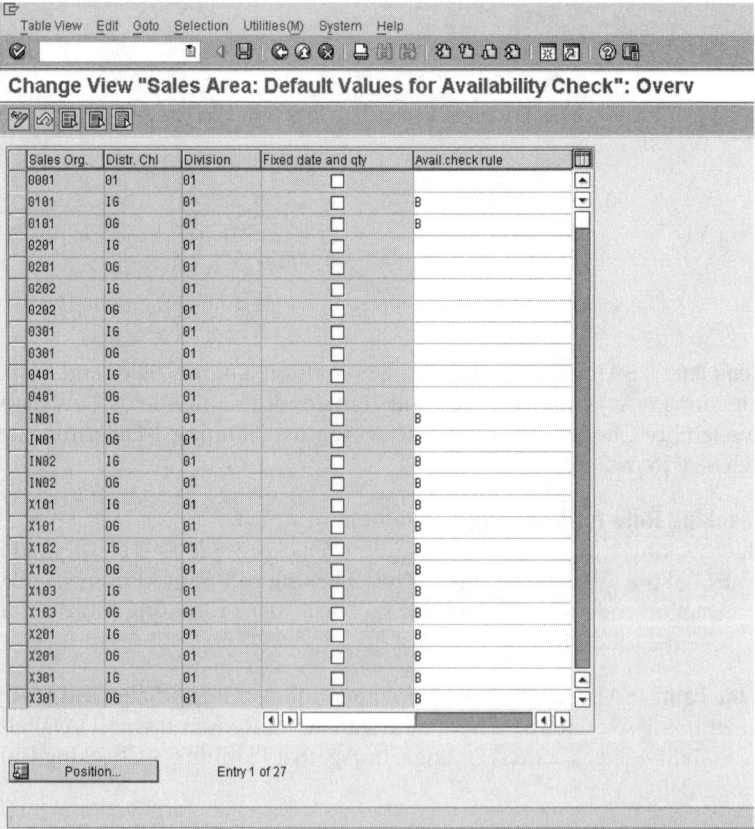

Change View "Sales Area: Default Values for Availability Check": Overv

Sales Org.	Distr. Chl	Division	Fixed date and qty	Avail. check rule
0001	01	01	☐	
0101	I6	01	☐	B
0101	06	01	☐	B
0201	I6	01	☐	
0201	06	01	☐	
0202	I6	01	☐	
0202	06	01	☐	
0301	I6	01	☐	
0301	06	01	☐	
0401	I6	01	☐	
0401	06	01	☐	
IN01	I6	01	☐	B
IN01	06	01	☐	B
IN02	I6	01	☐	B
IN02	06	01	☐	B
X101	I6	01	☐	B
X101	06	01	☐	B
X102	I6	01	☐	B
X102	06	01	☐	B
X103	I6	01	☐	B
X103	06	01	☐	B
X201	I6	01	☐	B
X201	06	01	☐	B
X301	I6	01	☐	B
X301	06	01	☐	B

Position...   Entry 1 of 27

The availability checking rule set here does not only determine what the user sees when carrying out an availability check online. It also determines the result of the availability check in background mode. In Figure 5-35, the entry in brackets defines how the system behaves in background mode. For example, option E will always use a delivery proposal in background mode. The other options include the following:

One-Time Delivery   The system will try to confirm the material for the requested delivery date. Should it not be able to confirm stock for the requested delivery date, it will confirm a value of zero.

Complete Delivery   The system will only confirm a delivery date on a date when the entire scheduled ordered quantity for that line in the sales order is available. For example, should the quantity ordered be 100 pce for an order on January 1st with a requested delivery date of January 1st and you have 90 pce available, the system will wait until 100 pce may be confirmed, which may be at the end of lead time for the material. If the lead time is one month the complete delivery will only be made on the 1st of February.

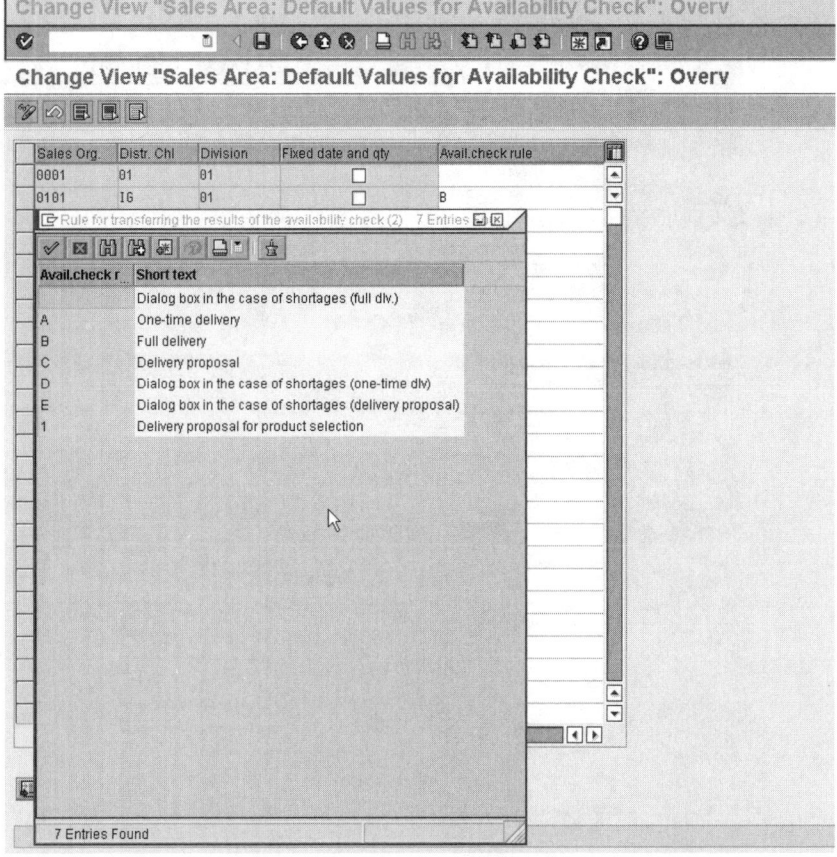

Copyright by SAP AG

Figure 5-35   Background mode where dialog box is used in front office processing

Delivery Proposal   The system will confirm the quantity it has available for the requested delivery date. It will then create another confirmation on the resulting outstanding material for the end of lead time, or for when new stock is due to be available. Using the previous example, the system will confirm the 90 pce immediately and use forward scheduling to propose the delivery date (for example, plus six days), and then it will confirm a second delivery date for the remaining 10 pce at the end of lead time, that is, February 1st.

Sales Document Processing   From within the sales document you may select an availability check across plants. From the availability control screen, select from within the availability control in the sales document line item. Select Goto | Other Plants, as seen in Figure 5-36.

This will display a list of plants that the user can select from to check for ATP quantity. Only those plants in which the material is maintained will be diplayed.

In the availability control screen select Goto | Scope of Check. The system will display the automatic control of the availability check—that is, the selections that are considered in the availability of the stock.

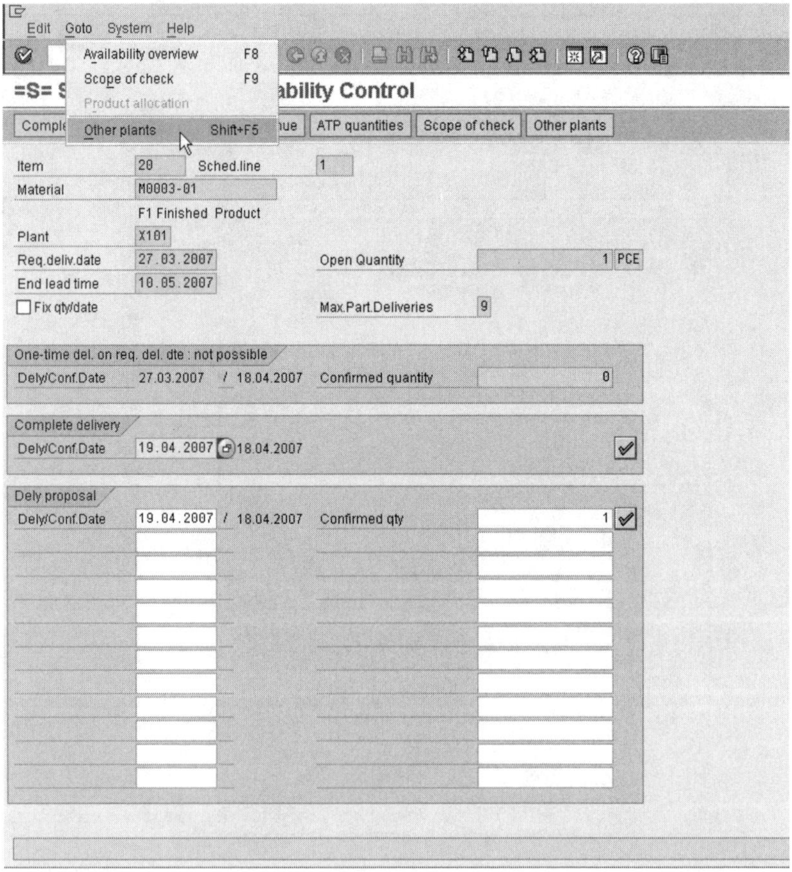

FIGURE 5-36
Other plant
check for
ATP quantity

| Edit | Goto | System | Help |

| Availability overview | F8 |
| Scope of check | F9 |
| Product allocation |
| Other plants | Shift+F5 |

=S= S...ability Control

| Comple | Other plants | ...ue | ATP quantities | Scope of check | Other plants |

Item   20   Sched.line   1
Material   M0003-01
              F1 Finished Product
Plant   X101
Req.deliv.date 27.03.2007   Open Quantity   1 PCE
End lead time   10.05.2007
☐ Fix qty/date   Max.Part.Deliveries   9

One-time del. on req. del. dte : not possible
Dely/Conf.Date   27.03.2007   / 18.04.2007   Confirmed quantity   0

Complete delivery
Dely/Conf.Date   19.04.2007 ⊙18.04.2007   ✔

Dely proposal
Dely/Conf.Date   19.04.2007 / 18.04.2007   Confirmed qty   1 ✔

One may receive two specific messages related to product allocations and ATP, when carrying out an availability check on a line item:

- **"Product allocation found changes to the confirmation"**   This means that the customer purchasing the stock has exceeded his allowed quantity and the product allocation has limited the quantity he may consume for this material, for this particular line item. It is possible to see his allocated quantity by selecting Goto | Product Allocation from the availability control screen. This will also show the consumed quantity and the quantity the customer still has available to consume.

- **"No feature combination exists…"**   This message is also linked to product allocation. However, this message will mean that no availability check will be carried out as the system has tried to do an availability check according to product allocation but has found that there are errors in the setup of the process. One possible error could be that the customer is absent from a planning hierarchy (used in product allocation). It could also be that an incorrect schedule line category is being used, which is trying to allocate according to product allocation, but neither the customer nor the transaction are relevant for product allocation.

This concludes the section on material listing and exclusion, material determination and the transfer of requirements and ATP check, from the view of the sales and distribution module.

CHAPTER

Logistics Execution Process

Here we configure deliveries, transportation, routes, and determination as well as packaging. This chapter deals with copy control, picking, simple warehouse management processes, and special stock.

Delivery Process

The delivery process is a continuation from the sales process. It is generally used in outbound processing to move goods from the plant to the shipping vendor to the customer. However, the returns process of inbound deliveries is also included as a standard SAP delivery process, where instead of "posting goods issue" for outbound deliveries, we "post goods receipt" for an inbound flow of products back into our plant.

A delivery document can be created with reference to a sales document such as an order or a scheduling agreement (which was discussed in Chapter 4). Or it may be created, for example, with reference to an inbound return sales document.

In mySAP ERP, the shipping functions have been removed from the Sales and Distribution section of the SAP Customizing Implementation Guide. Instead, they have been placed in the Logistics Execution section. However, it is critical that the people responsible for the SD module understand this topic.

Delivery Document Configuration

A delivery document type is similar to the sales order document type. Whereas in the sales process the sales document structure and control were defined largely by the sales document type, in the delivery process the delivery document type controls how the delivery is to function. The structure of the delivery document is very similar to a sales document type in that a delivery document has a header and item structure. The output of an SAP delivery is a goods movement.

Defining Delivery Types
The SAP delivery document is usually the step subsequent to a sales document type and preceding a billing document. However, a delivery is not restricted to being created from a sales document type. Use the following menu path.

Menu Path   SAP Customizing Implementation Guide | Logistics Execution | Shipping | Deliveries | Define Delivery Types [0VLK]

The delivery document type, shown in Figure 6-1, has fewer control settings than the sales document type.

The associated settings of the delivery document type are as follows:

- **Document Category**   This is a critical field that identifies to the system what document type is being used. It is used in internal table controls, for example, to determine system responses and messages.

- **Number Systems**   Here you assign the particular number range that your delivery will follow, as well as the item increment in the delivery document type.

  You may create the number ranges relevant for delivery documents by selecting SAP Customizing Implementation Guide | Logistics Execution | Shipping | Deliveries | Define Number Ranges for Deliveries [VN01]

  After creating the interval, you may assign your delivery document number range to the document type. (See Chapter 3 for more information on number ranges.)

- **Order Reference**   With this setting enabled, you can create this delivery without reference to a sales document type. You must specify a "pseudo" sales documents type in the Default Order Type field. This will cause the system to use the control data set for this referenced pseudo document type.

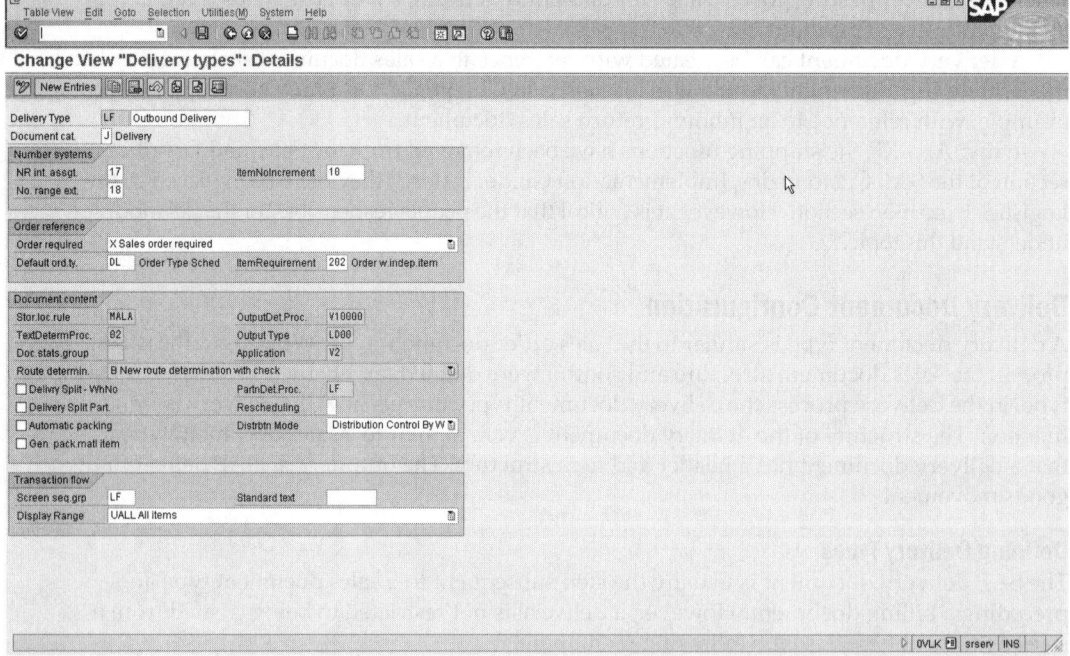

Copyright by SAP AG

FIGURE 6-1   Define delivery document type

When it is necessary to have a specific goods movement assigned to a delivery that has no sales document type used as a reference, your pseudo sales document type must have an item category followed by an assigned schedule line category. It is this schedule line category that must have the assigned goods movement.

Here's an example of a pseudo sales document: The warehouse asks for a specific delivery, which must not be created from a sales order but is to use a special goods movement type. This goods movement type—for example, 901—is used to show the return of stock to a supplier.

1. You would configure this by copying a standard delivery type such as LF, and naming it ZLF.

2. Then you would copy a sales document type such as TA and name it ZTA.

3. Next you would copy an item category TAN and name it ZTAN.

4. Finally you would copy a schedule line category such as CP and name it ZCP. Assigned to this schedule line category would be the movement type 901.

5. You would then assign the sales document type ZTA to the delivery type ZLF as the default order type.

6. Do not forget your individual settings in the relevant document types and item categories, as well as the copy controls settings. The specific control of the item categories in the delivery will be covered a little later.

The item requirement must be fulfilled before an item can be processed in a delivery created without reference to a sales document type.

- **Document Content** Most of the fields in the document content screen are not configurable from this view. They are mostly determined in individual settings that then allocate the settings to the delivery document type. They are shown in the delivery document type for ease of understanding and control.

   Only the delivery split according to warehouse number, the delivery split according to additional partners, the rescheduling, the automatic packing indicators, the general packing material item, and the distribution mode are controllable from this section.

- In this section the storage location rule specifies how the system determines the picking/storage location when you create a delivery without entering a picking/storage location for the item.

   The storage location is determined by a combination of shipping point + plant + storage condition. However, this only applies if the storage location rule on the delivery document type is MALA. (Storage location rules are defined in materials management and warehouse management, and are not covered in this book.)

- The output determination procedure and output type are used by the system in allocating output to the delivery document type. (Output is described in Chapter 9.)

- The text determination procedure is used by the system to determine where texts are allocated from in the delivery. (Text determination is described in Chapter 9.)

- The document statistics group is the determining field that updates the logistics information structures (LIS). It is not possible to assign a value to this field here. You are able to assign a value to the delivery document type in the control settings for LIS. Note that it is only advisable to assign a statistics group value to those deliveries and delivery items that do not contain a reference to an order.

- You are able to assign a delivery split per warehouse number, that is, items belonging to different warehouse numbers will be split into different deliveries. You can also force a delivery split by partners by setting the delivery split part checkbox.

- The assignment and control of route determination will be covered later in this chapter.

- The settings for the application are internally used by the system to allocate output—for example, whether the output is used for sales orders or for delivery documents, etc.

- The partner determination is also not available to set in the delivery document type. it is set in the assignment of document types to the partner determination procedure. Partner determination procedures will be covered in Chapter 9.

- The rescheduling indicator is used to control the rescheduling of backlog deliveries.

- The automatic packing indicator controls if the packing proposal should be adhered to and the items in the delivery automatically packed or not. If you permit the delivery document type to automatically create packing items based on the configuration for packing (see packing later in this chapter), then check the generate packing material item checkbox.

- If you use a decentralized warehouse management system, you will wish to update the system automatically. This is defined by the setting in distribution mode.

- **Transaction Flow**   In the definition of the delivery document type, in the transaction flow you may define the following:

- Screen sequence group is used to determine the screens and the sequence in which the SAP system should display them for a certain delivery type.

- The display range controls the data display for the delivery items. For example, you can limit the display to only the main items and to suppress all items dependent on main items.

- The standard text field is not used in ERP ECC6.

An example of the standard delivery document types in ERP ECC are

Standard delivery	LF
Delivery without reference	LO
Returns delivery	LR
Returns delivery from a purchase order	RL
Replenishment delivery	NL

The standard SAP version of a delivery that may be made without reference to a sales order is delivery document type LO.

Delivery Item Categories and Determination

A delivery item category is similar to the sales document item category in that it controls how the item is to behave in the document type. Generally, the delivery item category has the same naming convention as the sales document item category from which it is determined; however, it has its own control features.

Defining the Delivery Item Category

To define delivery item categories, use the following menu path.

Menu Path SAP Customizing Implementation Guide | Logistics Execution | Shipping | Deliveries | Define Item Categories for Deliveries [0VLP]

We will configure these a little later.

Defining Delivery Item Category Determination

First, we need to discover from where the delivery item category is determined. If an order item or a schedule line is copied into a delivery, the item category used in the sales order is also copied. For example, if a TAN item category is used in the sales document type, the system will propose a TAN in the delivery document as well.

For items independent of orders in the delivery (for example, packaging material that is entered in the delivery) or for deliveries that have no reference to a sales document, the item category is determined by the delivery item category determination table.

This item category is determined, as seen in Figure 6-2, by the delivery type plus the item category group of the material plus the usage of the item plus the item category of the higher level item, similar to the item category determination procedure in the sales order.

To configure delivery item category determination, use the following menu path.

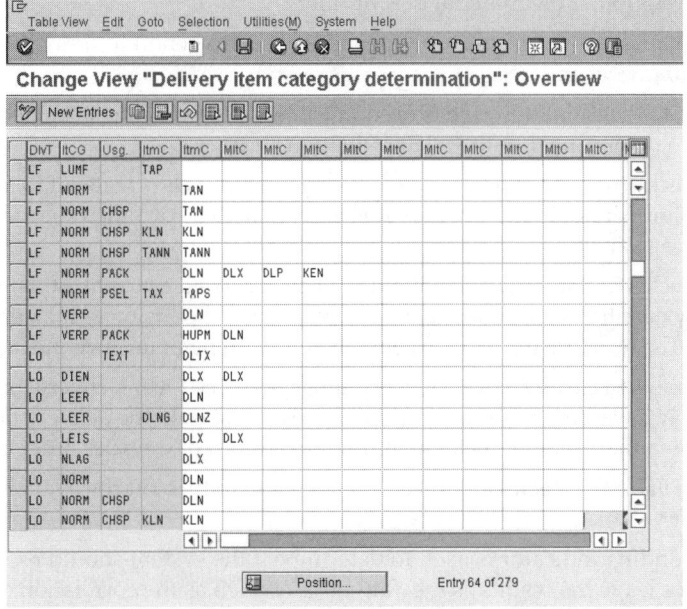

DlvT	ItCG	Usg.	ItmC	ItmC	MItC	MItC	MItC	MItC	MItC	MItC	MItC	MItC	MItC	MItC
LF	LUMF		TAP											
LF	NORM			TAN										
LF	NORM	CHSP		TAN										
LF	NORM	CHSP	KLN	KLN										
LF	NORM	CHSP	TANN	TANN										
LF	NORM	PACK		DLN	DLX	DLP	KEN							
LF	NORM	PSEL	TAX	TAPS										
LF	VERP			DLN										
LF	VERP	PACK		HUPM	DLN									
LO		TEXT		DLTX										
LO	DIEN			DLX	DLX									
LO	LEER			DLN										
LO	LEER		DLNG	DLNZ										
LO	LEIS			DLX	DLX									
LO	NLAG			DLX										
LO	NORM			DLN										
LO	NORM	CHSP		DLN										
LO	NORM	CHSP	KLN	KLN										

Change View "Delivery item category determination": Overview

Position... Entry 64 of 279

FIGURE 6-2 Delivery item category determination

Menu Path   SAP Customizing Implementation Guide | Logistics Execution | Shipping | Deliveries | Define Item Category Determination in Deliveries

The SAP system will still need an underlying schedule line category, thus, should a delivery item category be able to copy an item category from a sales order, a schedule line category must still be maintained in order for the system to propose the correct goods movement type and subsequent financial postings for the goods movement.

The availability check in the delivery is still carried out and controlled by the delivery item category regardless of whether the delivery item category has the same name as the item it is referenced from in the sales order, or if it is determined in the delivery.

The delivery item category determination is especially useful for assigning batch items to standard delivery items. For example, should you carry out batch determination in the delivery, you are able to assign a delivery item category to an item that has a usage defined as CHSP- batch split. (This will create a delivery line item for each batch, even if the product on the delivery is the same and was represented by a single sales document line item.)

Don't forget you can view the usages of the item category in table TVVWT, which may be easier than looking at each in configuration individually.

Defining a Delivery Item Category Continued

The delivery item category is represented by the following settings as seen in Figure 6-3.

The item category is assigned to a document category; in this case the document category is for deliveries, represented as a "J."

- The Material Number 0 Allowed field is used to permit the item to be created without having a reference to a material reference. This is used in examples for text items, where one creates a line item with a special item category and types text in the description of the material description.

- The statistics group for the item category is used to generate statistics in the logistics information system.

- The stock determination rule is used in conjunction with the stock determination group to determine the stock determination strategy.

- The Check Quantity of 0 field specifies whether you can create an item that has a zero quantity and, if you do, how it is to react with a warning or error message or no message at all.

- The Check Minimum Quantity field is a check carried out against the minimum delivery quantity on the material master record and the customer material information record. The response from the system can be a warning or an error message.

- It is possible to create an over-delivery, thus the Check Over Delivery indicator is used to display a warning message or an error message should the delivery quantity exceed the limit in the customer material information record or the sales order quantity.

- The Availability Check Off indicator allows you to turn off the availability check for a delivery item.

- The Rounding indicator is used to determine if the system should round up, round down, or leave the results as they are in cases such as the correlation of multi-level bills of material in the delivery if the non-availability of a particular BOM in another partial BOM were to cause decimal positions. This would only impact you if you were using large numbers with indivisible partial quantities in a BOM.

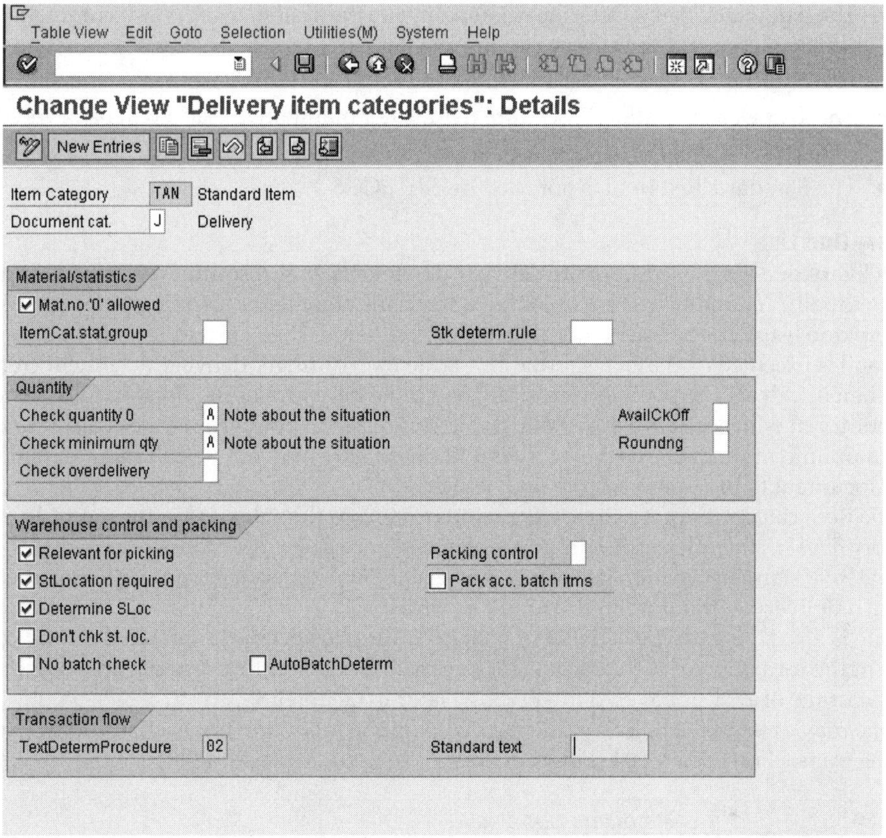

FIGURE 6-3   Delivery item category control

- The Relevant for Picking indicator is used to switch on picking relevance for a particular item. This item is then available in the picking list and to be transferred to warehouse management. It would not be advisable to make all items relevant for picking; for example, you would not pick service items such as a technicians hours. Generally, unless you do physical picking from the warehouse, you do not need picking. Picking is therefore not required for non-stock, value, and service items.

- The Storage Location Required field indicates a storage location must be entered for this item before the delivery can be completely processed. Likewise, the Determine Storage Location field is an indicator used by the system to indicate automatic determination of the storage location for the delivery item. The Don't Check Storage Location field is used to stop the system from checking that the material exists in the storage location that was determined.

- The No Batch Check field ensures the system does not check to determine if the batch entered in the delivery line item exists in the system or not. Thus, should you enter a batch in the line item when the batch is not in the system, the system will accept it anyway.

- The Automatic Batch Determination field tells the system to carry out automatic batch determination in the delivery for this line item. (Automatic batch determination can happen at the line item level in the sales order or the delivery.)

- The Text Determination Procedure field is not maintainable and will be covered in "Text Determination" in Chapter 9.

- The Standard Text field is not used in ERP ECC6.

Delivery Due List

The delivery due list is used to create delivery documents en masse automatically as opposed to individually. A number of companies have a specific emergency shipping point for their delivery due list to create emergency deliveries. A variant is then created for this shipping point and is executed on a much shorter time scale than ordinary delivery document creation.

When one deals with delivery creation, one must be aware of the fiscal requirements of the country in which you are operating. Some countries do not permit a sales order to be broken up into more than one delivery, and likewise they may not permit more than one sales document to be combined into one delivery.

The item categories of a delivery are referenced from the sales order; for example, item category TAN in the sales order proposes item category TAN in the delivery.

The SAP standard version uses DLN as the standard item category used to represent an item in a delivery without reference to a sales order.

One is also able to define a delivery split according to specific criteria in the copy control rules. In the formation of the data transfer one may set up splitting criteria. Splitting criteria and the usage of ZUK is covered in "Pricing" later in Chapter 8.

One may execute the delivery due list by using the following transaction codes. (Note that the transaction code VL04 should no longer be used after SAP 4.0b.)

[VL10A]	Sales orders fast display
[VL10B]	Purchase orders fast display
[VL10C]	Sales orders items
[VL10D]	Purchase orders items
[VL10E]	Sales orders schedule lines
[VL10F]	Purchase orders item schedule line
[VL10G]	Sales and purchase orders fast display
[VL10H]	Sales and purchase orders items fast display
[VL10I]	Sales and purchase orders item schedule line

Although the processing program is the same for all transaction codes, the control is determined by the role defined in [VL10CUA] and scenario defined in [VL10CUV] as found on the User Role tab.

An example of an executed delivery due list is seen in Figure 6-4; note the column headings. You may add additional columns to the layout by pressing CTRL-F8 or clicking the Change Layout button. This will present you with a screen similar to Figure 6-5, where you can simply select fields on the right side and click the arrow button.

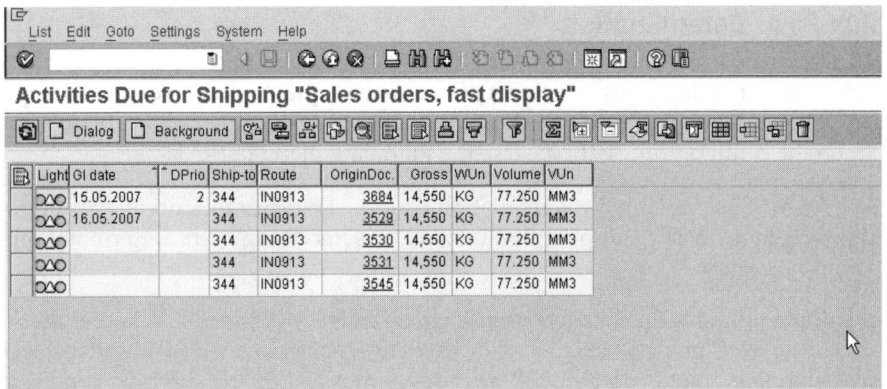

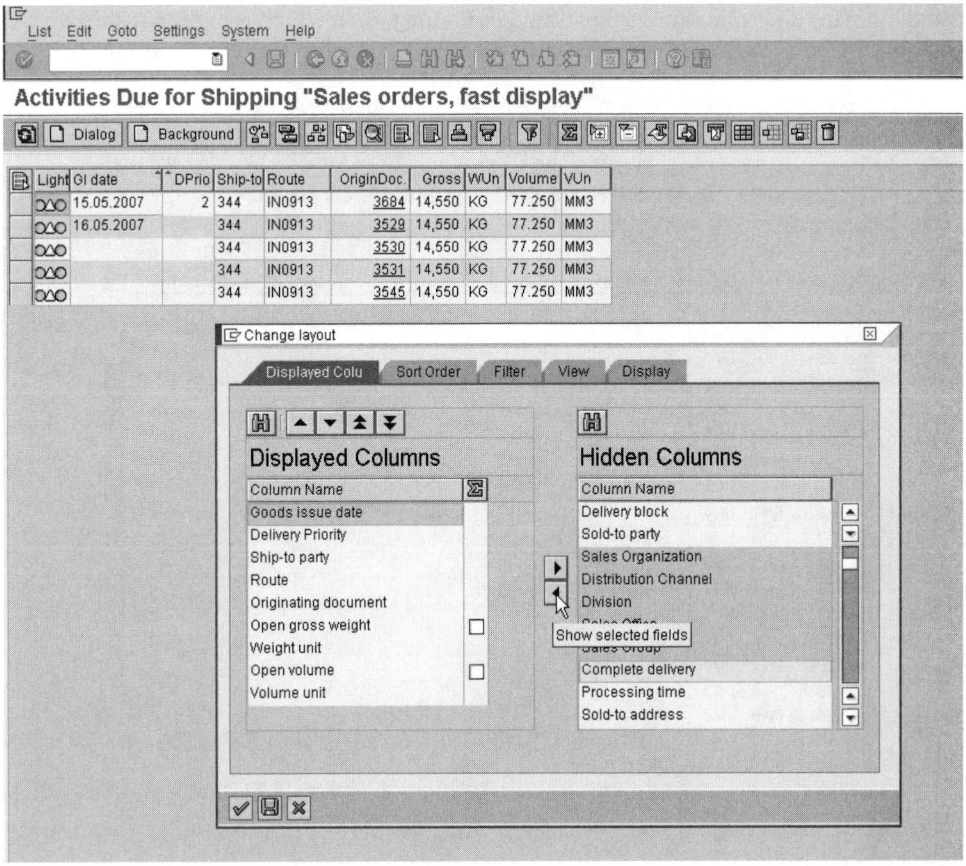

Copyright by SAP AG

FIGURE 6-4   Delivery due list

FIGURE 6-5   Copying new columns to the layout

Shipping Point Determination

Shipping points are independent organizational units that are linked to a plant and represent the point of departure or receipt of materials. A plant may have many shipping points. A delivery is created from one shipping point only. Shipping points are determined based upon the configuration settings. Use the following menu path.

Menu Path   SAP Customizing Implementation Guide I Logistics Execution I Shipping I Basic Shipping Functions I Shipping Point and Goods Receiving Point Determination I Assign Shipping Points

The shipping point is the location from which a delivery originates. Whether that location be a physical or a systemic location, no delivery may be made without a shipping point. The shipping point is determined by the system based on the shipping conditions, which are either entered manually in the sales order or copied from the customer master record. (Shipping conditions may also be copied from the sales document type if not maintained on the customer master.) The loading group, which is copied from the material master record, and the delivering plant of the line item in the sales order are also shipping conditions. This determination is illustrated in Figure 6-6, in which we see that shipping conditions 01 plus loading group Z001 plus plant IN03 propose shipping point IN01.

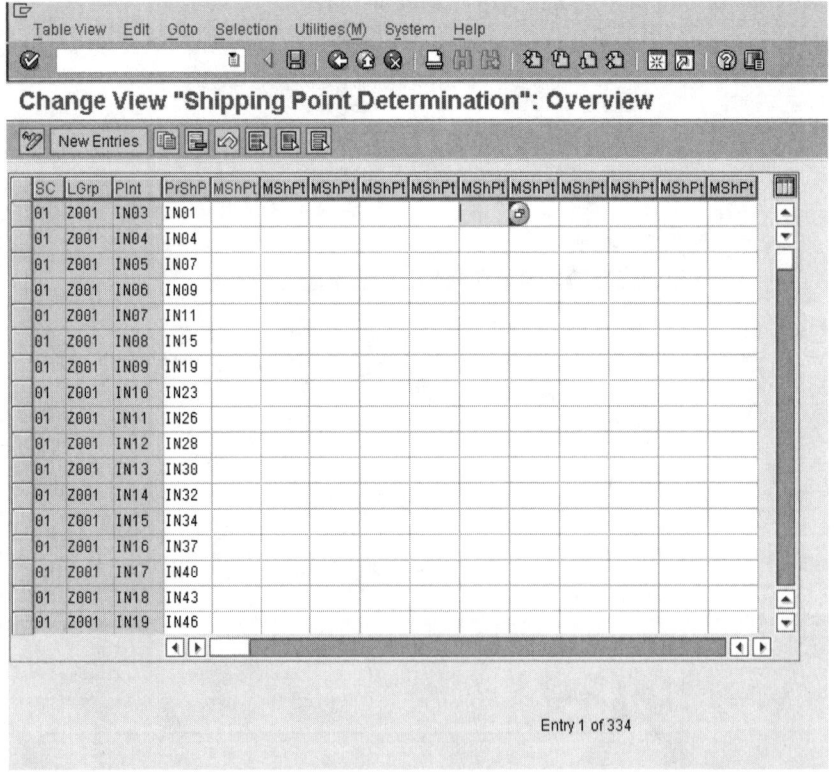

FIGURE 6-6   Shipping point determination

Should a customer ask for a complete delivery, it makes sense that you should not have multiple shipping points manually entered for each line item in the sales order, or else the customer will receive multiple deliveries.

As each delivery is created via a shipping point, and each run of the delivery due list is made with reference to a particular shipping point, you may want to have an express shipping point. This way, you are able to run the due list every half hour for one shipping point only to create deliveries for that particular plant. Likewise, in the sales order the user knows that if he manually enters a specific express shipping point, he will have the delivery created within half an hour. The remainder of the deliveries may be created via the delivery due list in the normal processing run.

Configuring the Shipping Point Determination

To configure the shipping point determination, use the following steps:

Define Shipping Conditions

Menu Path   SAP Customizing Implementation Guide | Logistics Execution | Shipping | Basic Shipping Functions | Shipping Point and Goods Receiving Point Determination | Define Shipping Conditions

The shipping conditions are entered in the customer master record in the shipping screen and in the sales document type. These settings are then copied into the sales document during order creation and are used to determine the shipping point. The shipping conditions may be manually changed in the sales order, or they may be defaulted to a particular sales document type. Should they be defaulted to a particular sales document type, the system will ignore the setting on the customer master record.

Proceed with copying a shipping condition and changing the name to represent your requirements, using the prefix Z. The shipping condition is a two-character alphanumeric key, as seen in Figure 6-7.

Menu Path   SAP Customizing Implementation Guide | Logistics Execution | Shipping | Basic Shipping Functions | Shipping Point and Goods Receiving Point Determination | Define Shipping Conditions by Sales Document Type

As discussed earlier, the shipping conditions defined by sales document type override the shipping conditions automatically proposed by the system from the customer master record. This is useful, for example, in returns.

In returns processing a returns delivery must be made with a shipping point that represents the incoming goods. It would not be recommended to use the same shipping point for returns or receiving goods as you do for outgoing deliveries. Thus you may assign all returns sales document types their own returns shipping condition and thus promote a returns shipping point.

Having a returns shipping point allows greater visibility of material movements in the system and in the plant, as well as allowing the processing of the delivery due list for returns orders only.

Defining Loading Groups

Menu Path   SAP Customizing Implementation Guide | Logistics Execution | Shipping | Basic Shipping Functions | Shipping Point and Goods Receiving Point Determination | Define Loading Groups

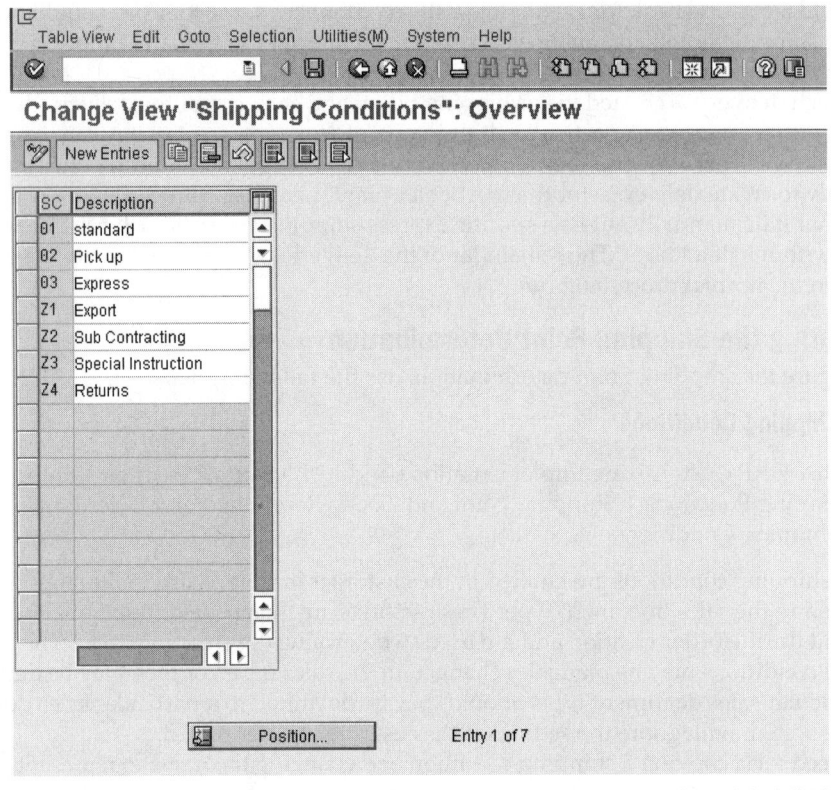

Copyright by SAP AG

Figure 6-7   Shipping conditions

The loading group is used in the determination of the shipping point and is copied from the material master record.

As a delivery is not possible without a loading group, it is recommended you ensure that the field loading group of the material master record is a mandatory field. This way, no material master record may be created without a respective loading group.

The loading group, as seen in Figure 6-8, is a four-character alphanumeric key, which you may copy and rename with a prefix of Z.

Assigning Shipping Points

Menu Path   SAP Customizing Implementation Guide | Logistics Execution | Shipping | Basic Shipping Functions | Shipping Point and Goods Receiving Point Determination | Assign Shipping Points

First, it is worthwhile to do a background check on your organizational data. Ensure your correct delivering plants have been maintained in the system as well as the correct shipping points. Use the following menu path.

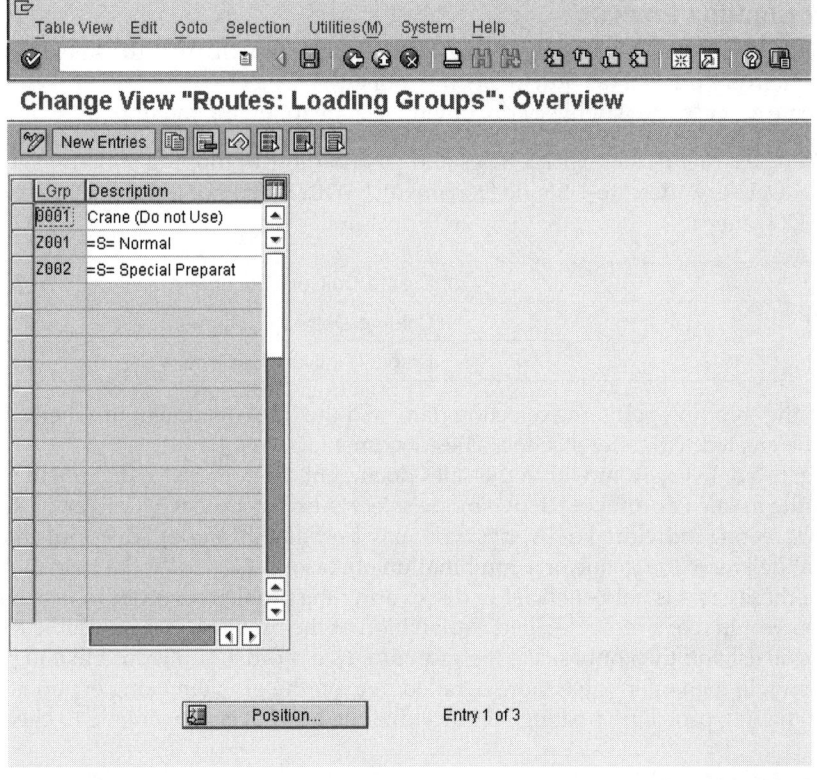

Figure 6-8   Loading group

Menu Path   SAP Customizing Implementation Guide | Enterprise Structure | Definition | Logistics Execution | Define, Copy, Delete, Check Shipping Point | Define Shipping Point

Also ensure you have allocated your shipping points to the respective plants, using the following menu path.

Menu Path   SAP Customizing Implementation Guide | Enterprise Structure | Assignment | Logistics Execution | Assign Shipping Point to Plant

Now, to assign the shipping points, use the following menu path.

Menu Path   SAP Customizing Implementation Guide | Logistics Execution | Shipping | Basic Shipping Functions | Shipping Point and Goods Receiving Point Determination | Assign Shipping Points

Assign the proposed shipping point and the allowed manual shipping points to the combination of shipping condition, loading group, and plant, as illustrated earlier in Figure 6-6.

Delivery Creation Process

It is possible to create a delivery individually via the menu path, from the sales document, or via the delivery due list (as previously mentioned).

To create an individual delivery document, use the following menu path.

Menu Path   SAP Menu | Logistics | Sales and Distribution | Shipping and Transportation | Outbound Delivery | Create | Single Document | With Reference to Sales Order (Create Delivery Document)

[VL01N]	Create Delivery Document
[VL02N]	Change Delivery Document
[VL03N]	Display Delivery Document

Enter the shipping point, the selection date, and the sales document number, should the delivery be created with reference to a sales document.

To create a delivery from within the sales document, from the sales document overview screen while in sales document change mode select Sales Document | Deliver.

When creating individual deliveries, you may find that the system does not create an individual delivery, due to one or a combination of reasons. Generally, the help message offered in these cases is not beneficial in discovering the problem in order to fix it. In cases where you would like a more detailed explanation of the problem, it is advisable to use the delivery due list and then only select the individual sales order you would like to process. The system will then offer you a more detailed note on the problem being experienced.

When having problems creating an individual delivery, it is worthwhile to check the following:

- Is the sales document number correct?
- Is the shipping point selected equal to the one on the line item in the sales order?
- Has the line item in the sales order already been fully delivered?
- Does the schedule line have a confirmed quantity and date?
- Is the selection date correct? The selection date should be equal to or later than the confirmed delivery date at schedule line level in the sales order.
- Is there a delivery block on the line item in the sales order?
- Is there a delivery block on the schedule line in the sales order?
- What is the status of the sales order and the line item in question? This can be seen from the sales order by selecting Goto | Header | Status and Goto | Item | Status.

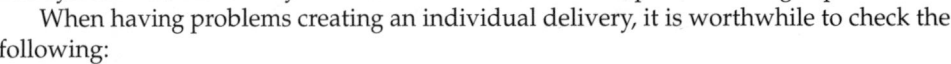

Using the transaction code [SE16] or [SE16n] one may use the "table" VBAKUK, which is actually a combined view of selected fields from the VBAK and VBUK tables. However, it allows you to access the statuses of the sales documents, as well as being useful in generating queries of data at header and item level.

Picking and Interfacing with Warehouse Management

Picking is the process in which the stock is selected from the storage facility to fulfill a delivery. One needs to pick the correct quantity of the right items for the delivery.

First, not all items are relevant for picking. You may have items such as text items or return items that are not picking-relevant. Picking is always carried out from a particular storage location, so for a delivery to be picking-relevant, a storage location must always be entered. If interfacing with warehouse management, the storage location in the delivery determines which storage location to use in the warehouse.

Picking is configured using the following menu path.

Menu Path   SAP Customizing Implementation Guide | Logistics Execution | Shipping | Picking

Defining Relevant Item Categories

SAP Customizing Implementation Guide | Logistics Execution | Shipping | Picking | Define Relevant Item Categories

Here you indicate to the system which item categories are relevant for picking. This indicator may either be set here, or when defining the delivery item category. Should the item not be relevant for picking, it is not necessary to have a storage location determined for the item either. Thus when creating the delivery item category, you would not need to indicate "determine storage location" or "storage location required."

Interface with Warehouse Management

If you have defined a warehouse in SAP and assigned it to a storage location, and you use this storage location in a delivery, then you must use Warehouse Management to do the picking for that delivery.

Warehouse Management is a module in its own right. In this section I'll introduce you to simple warehouse management processes.

The process for placing goods in the warehouse is as follows: The goods are received into the interim storage area for goods receipts (for example, from production). A transfer order is then created in WM to move the goods into the warehouse. This tells the warehouse staff where to put the stock. When the stock is put into the warehouse in the correct place, the transfer order is confirmed, which tells SAP that the goods have been moved out of the interim storage area (i.e., the loading and unloading area) into the warehouse.

The process for extracting the goods from the warehouse is as follows: You can create a transfer order [LT03] from the delivery, and SAP will choose stock from the warehouse to be delivered. This choice is based on a number of inventory methods, such as LIFO (last in, first out) and FIFO (first in, first out). The transfer order will instruct the warehouse staff where to get the stock from, and to deliver it to the interim storage area for goods issues.

Once all the stock has been picked, the transfer order is confirmed [LT12], which informs the system that the stock has been taken out of the warehouse and made available for loading in a loading bay or other such place.

If you created the transfer order from a sales delivery, SAP will confirm that the delivery has been picked when you confirm that you have fulfilled the stock quantity in the transfer order.

During confirmation of the transfer order [LT12], select Pick Quantity 2. This will result in the system automatically picking and post goods issuing the delivery document.

The order can now be loaded onto the truck, and the goods issued.

Should picking be done using Warehouse Management, once the delivery is created, you need to create a transfer order. To create a transfer order from the delivery from within the delivery select, select Subsequent Functions | Create Transfer Order.

It is also possible to create a transfer order for a delivery by using the following menu path.

Menu Path   SAP Menu | Logistics | Sales and Distribution | Shipping and Transportation | Picking | Create Transfer Order | [LT03] - Single Document

After the transfer order number has been created, it is necessary to confirm the transfer order by selecting Shipping and Transportation | Picking | Confirm Transfer Order [LT12].

Determining Storage/Picking Locations

The picking location is an area in which all picking is carried out in the same manner. The storage condition refers to the storage of the material in the plant or warehouse. It is found on the Plant Data/Warehouse 1 tab of the material master record.

Defining Rules for Picking Location

To define rules for the picking location, use the following menu path.

Menu Path   SAP Customizing Implementation Guide | Logistics Execution | Shipping | Picking | Determine Picking Location | Define Rules for Picking Location Determination

The entry maintained here is copied into the delivery header data. This entry here allows the system to determine the storage location automatically, should the storage location not have been maintained in the delivery manually.

Proceed in assigning a storage location rule—for example, MALA—to the delivery document type. (As previously discussed storage location rules, for example MALA are covered by materials and warehouse management modules and are not in scope for this book.)

Defining Storage Conditions

Menu Path   SAP Customizing Implementation Guide | Logistics Execution | Shipping | Picking | Determine Picking Locations | Define Storage Conditions

The storage condition is a two-character alphanumeric key that is used by the system to indicate the storage conditions for a material. This field is then used in combination with the plant and shipping point to determine the storage location.

Assigning Picking Locations

Menu Path   SAP Customizing Implementation Guide | Logistics Execution | Shipping | Picking | Determine Picking Locations | Assign Picking Locations

The picking location must be carried out from a storage location. The system bases the automatic determination of the storage location on the combination of the determination rule MALA assigned to the delivery document type with the shipping point and the delivering plant plus the storage condition on the material master record, as seen in Figure 6-9.

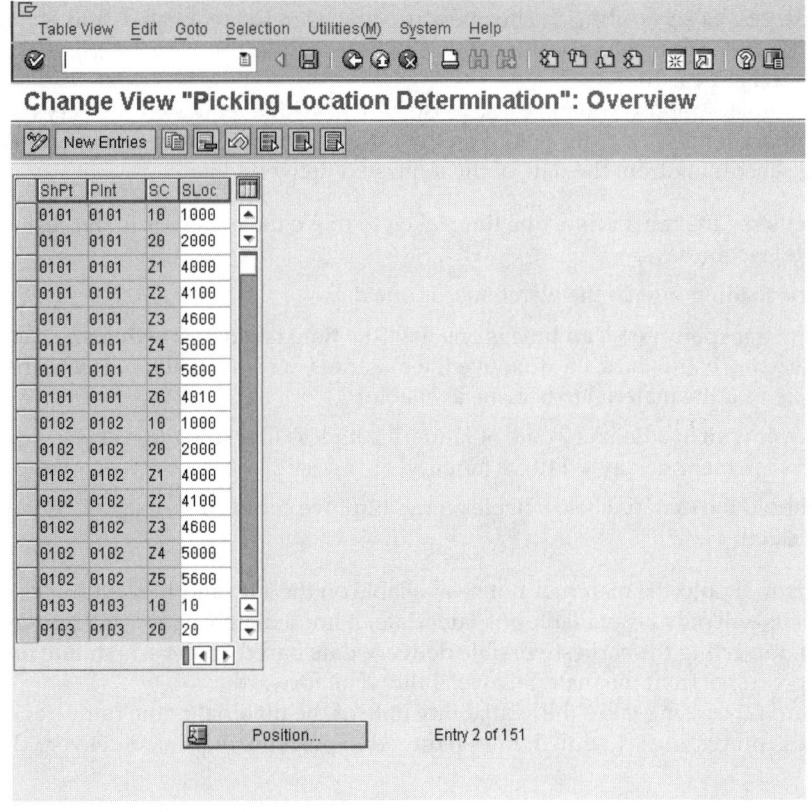

FIGURE 6-9 Storage location determination

Backward and Forward Scheduling

The customer specifies a requested delivery date that is placed into the schedule line of the sales order. The business must determine if it is able to carry out the associated functions in procuring the requested quantity and delivering it to the customer by the requested delivery date in the sales order.

The business functions required to be performed before a delivery date may be met are the following:

- Time taken to procure materials, such as obtaining materials from a supplier
- Time taken to plan the transportation, such as obtaining space on a ship
- Time taken to pick the items
- Time taken to pack the items
- Time taken to load the materials
- Time taken to transport the materials to the customer

This process of scheduling the business process from the requested delivery date backward in order to meet a specified delivery date is called *backward scheduling* and is illustrated in Figure 6-10.

For example, suppose you have a sales document with a requested delivery date on the 20th of January for a sales order placed on the 14th of January. The system carries out backward scheduling from the date of the requested delivery date:

- Let's say the transit time (the time taken to move the materials to the customer's site) is four days.

- The loading time in the warehouse is one day.

- The transportation lead time is one day (the time taken to schedule the containers, shipping companies, etc. to move the materials, which usually falls into the time taken for the material to become available).

- We now sit at a delivery date of January 20th less four days, less another one day, less another one day = 14th of January.

- Should the material be available on the 14th, we could confirm a delivery date of the 20th.

However, should the materials not be available on the 14th and indeed the system finds the materials will only be available at a later date, it immediately carries out *forward scheduling*, projecting the earliest possible delivery date based on the scheduling of the business processes from the material availability date forward.

Forward scheduling takes the availability date of the material in the future, and adds the business processing scheduled times required to meet the requested delivery date.

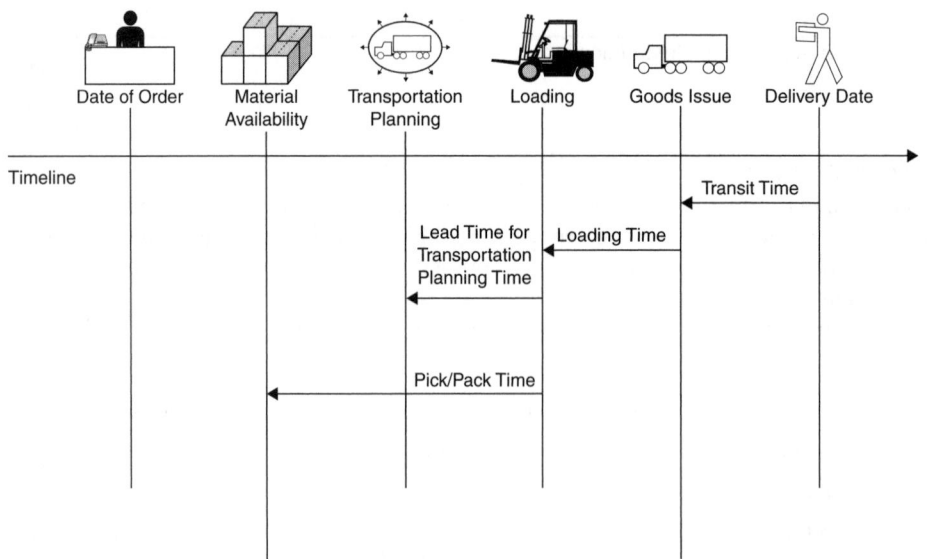

FIGURE 6-10 Backward scheduling

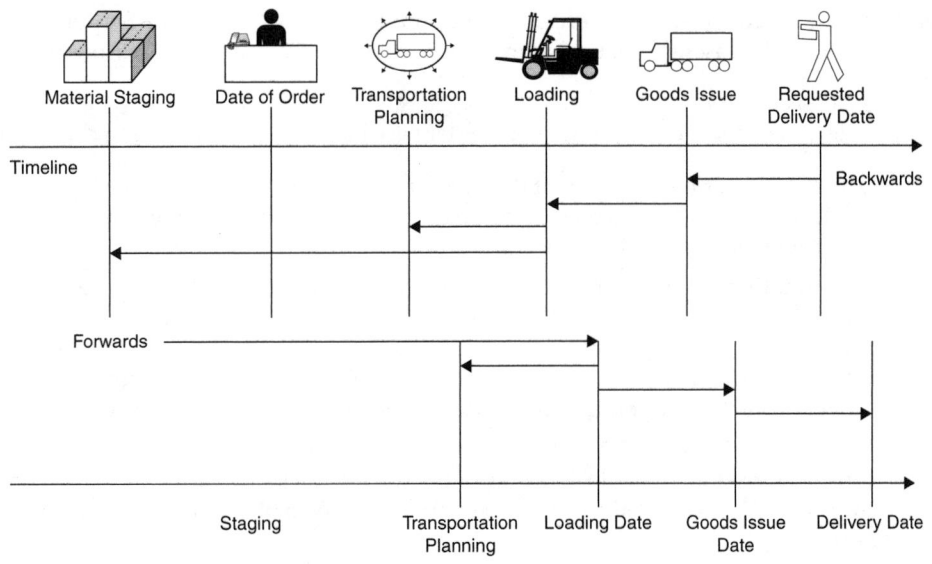

FIGURE 6-11   Backward then forward scheduling

Thus, should the stock be available on the 18th in the above example, the materials will arrive at the customer's site on the 18th plus six days $(4 + 1 + 1) = $ the 24th (less the time taken for transportation lead time, one day, as this step could have been carried out during the period waiting for the materials availability). Therefore, the delivery date based on forward scheduling would be the 23rd of January. An illustration of forward scheduling is shown in Figure 6-11.

If the route is not used when the pick/pack time or loading time is determined, the shipping point and the weight are the only factors used in determining the pick/pack time.

The shipping point and the loading group are used for determining the loading time.

The route is used to determine the transportation lead time and the transit time for transportation scheduling.

Delivery Blocks

Delivery blocks are very powerful in that they have the ability to not only block the delivery from being created but they may also block available stock from being assigned to a sales document that is blocked.

Blocking Reasons

There are many areas available in the Sales and Distribution module for blocking. Shipping or delivery blocks are commonly used and may be manually entered or automatically proposed in the sales order and the delivery documents.

One may configure these delivery blocks using the following menu path.

Menu Path   SAP Customizing Implementation Guide | Logistics Execution | Shipping |
Deliveries | Define Reasons for Blocking in Shipping | Deliveries: Blocking Reasons/Criteria

Transaction code [OVLS]

Figure 6-12 shows the configuration of the delivery block with the following checkboxes:

- **Order**   This setting will permit this block to be used to block a sales order for
  delivery processing. This block may be defaulted from the customer master record
  or placed manually in the sales order.

- **Confirmation**   This setting will block the confirmation of stock after an availability
  check. This means the schedule line of the sales order will have a confirmed
  quantity of 0. The requirement will still be passed to the MRP list but will not
  consume stock, which ensures the stock is available to be confirmed for other sales
  orders. Note that the confirmed schedule lines will be set to 0 only once the block is
  set and the document is saved.

- **Print**   This setting will block the output of the document. For example, if you have
  a document with a failed credit check, you may wish to block the order confirmation
  output.

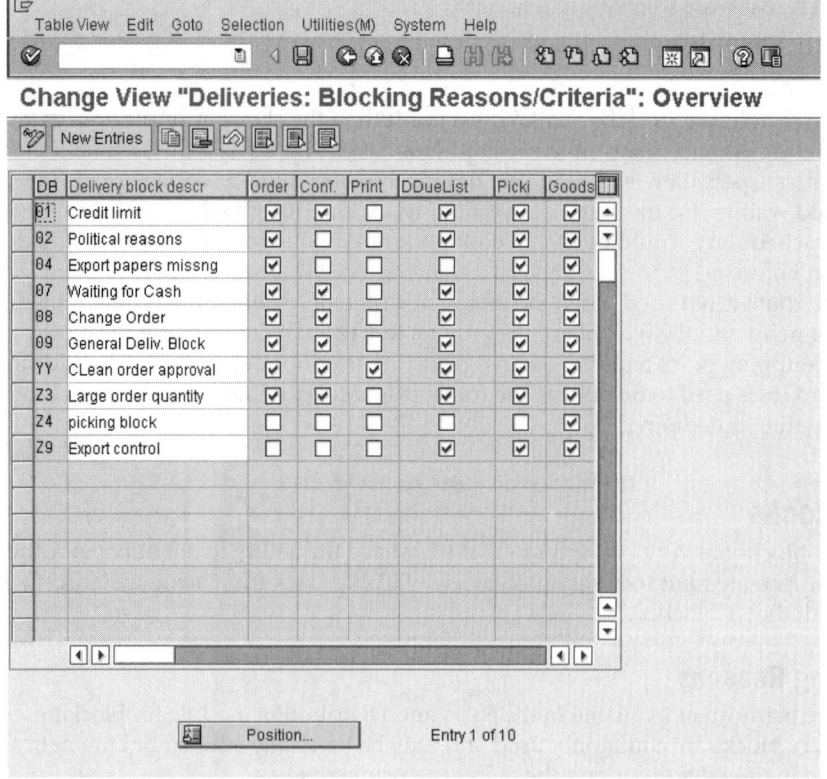

Copyright by SAP AG

FIGURE 6-12   Delivery block reasons/criteria

- **Delivery Due List**   This setting will block the sales document from being processed automatically by the delivery due list. It seems confusing to some people that a delivery block set manually in the sales document may block the delivery from being created individually, but does not block the delivery from being created with the delivery due list. If you wish to block both, then check this checkbox as well as the Order checkbox.

- **Picking**   This setting will block the picking. (This block is always effective, regardless of the assignment of the delivery block to the delivery document type seen in Figure 6-13.)

- **Goods Issue**   This setting will block the goods issue for the delivery document. (This block is always effective, regardless of the assignment of the delivery block to the delivery document type seen in Figure 6-13.)

After you have defined the delivery blocks, you must assign them to the delivery types for which they function, using the following menu path.

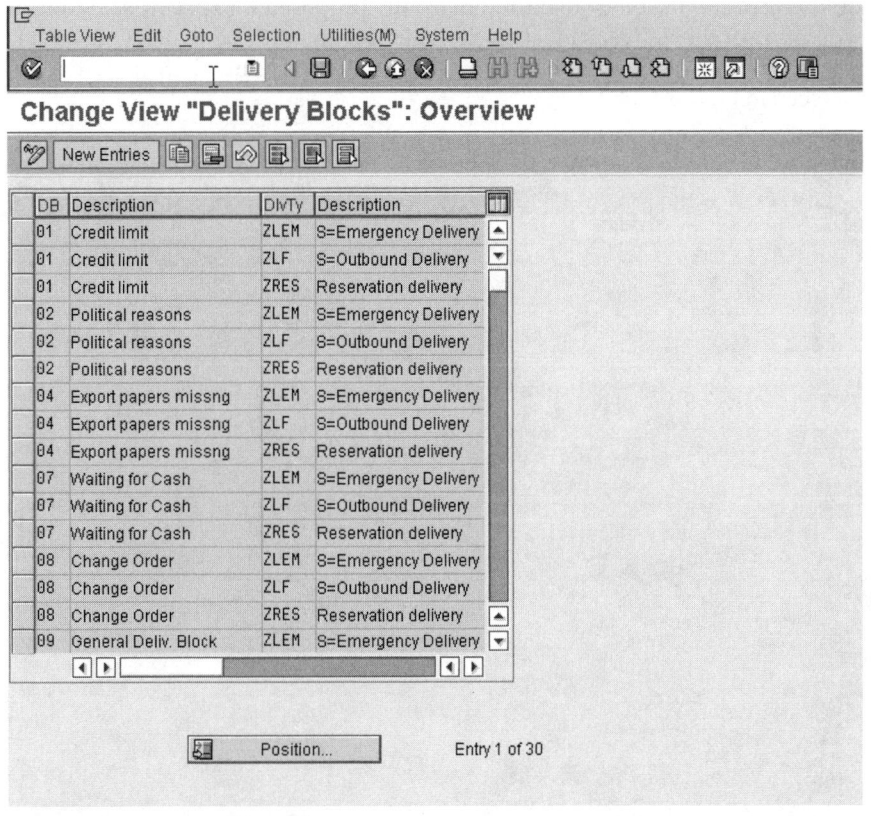

Copyright by SAP AG

FIGURE 6-13   Delivery block to delivery type assignment

Menu Path   SAP Customizing Implementation Guide | Logistics Execution | Shipping | Deliveries | Define Reasons for Blocking in Shipping | Delivery Blocks

Once set, delivery blocks must be removed manually from the sales order.

A delivery block set at header level in the sales document blocks the confirmation and sets it to 0. If you look in [MD04] the requirement is there, however, it does not consume ATP quantities. If you look in [CO09] the requirement does not reduce ATP quantities.

A delivery block set at schedule line level in the sales document does not block the confirmation. If you look in [MD04] the requirement is there. If you look in [CO09] the requirement does reduce ATP quantities.

Delivery Blocking at Header Level

Delivery blocks may be assigned manually in the sales order by entering the desired block in the header, using the following path.

Menu Path   From within the sales document | Goto | Header | Shipping | Then enter the delivery block

Should you desire the block to be automatically proposed for specific sales document types, you may set the delivery block in the sales document type which you wish to automatically block. This is done in the shipping area of the Maintain Sales Order Types screen, as seen in Figure 6-14.

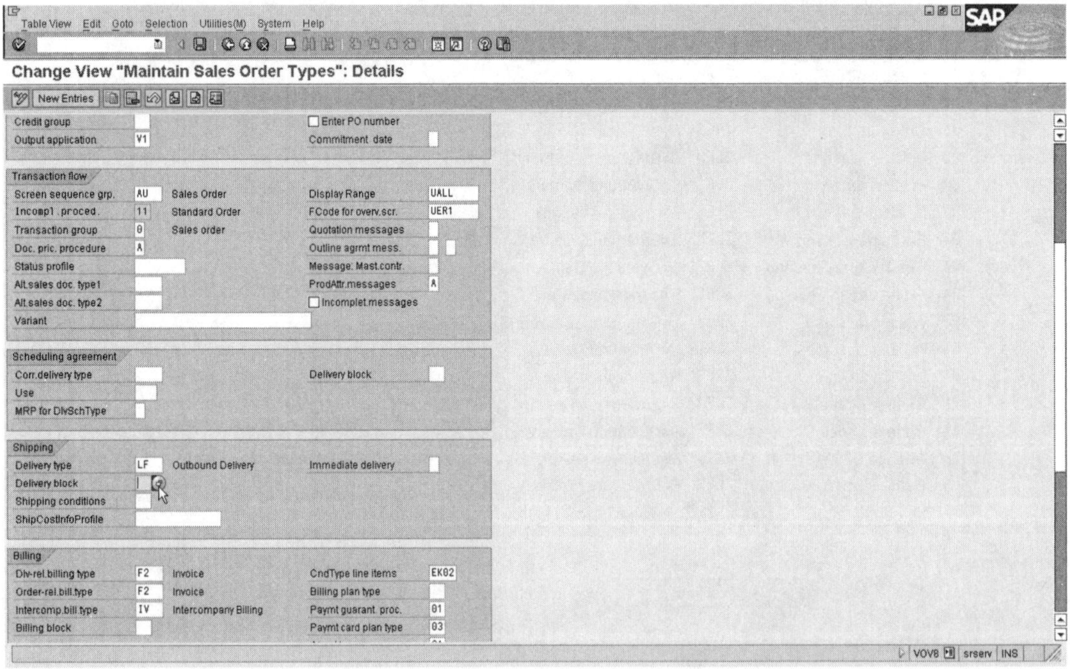

Copyright by SAP AG

Figure 6-14   Maintain Sales Document Type (Order Type)- set delivery block

However, this delivery block is only effective if it has been assigned in the respective delivery document type, as seen earlier in Figure 6-13.

Delivery Blocking at Schedule Line Level

Delivery blocks are also available at the schedule line level. These are simply delivery blocks that are manually entered in the sales document at the schedule line level.

It is possible to have the system automatically propose a delivery block in the sales document for particular schedule lines. This may be done by allocating the delivery block to the Schedule Line Categories screen, as seen in Figure 6-15.

This delivery block at schedule line level is always effective, regardless of whether the delivery block is assigned to the respective delivery document type or not.

The schedule line category block is very useful, as it is not copied in to the sales document item level but is effective only at the schedule line level. This allows you, for example, to create a sales order item and manually set the delivery block for some schedule

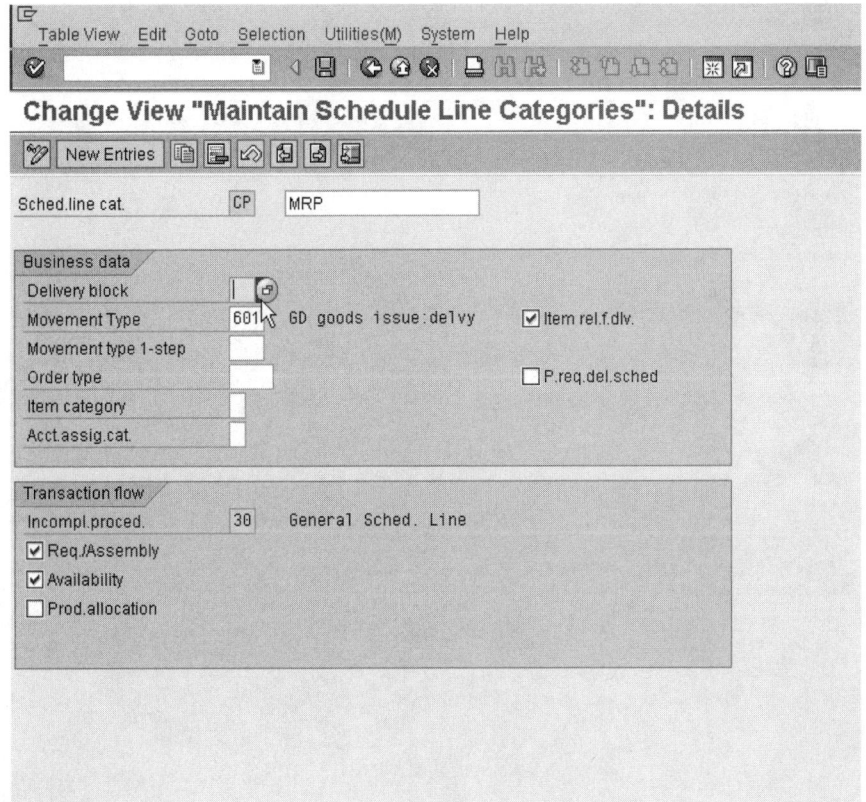

FIGURE 6-15 Assigning a delivery block to the Schedule Line Category

lines due for delivery with a delivery date of over one month, while still allowing deliveries for unblocked schedule lines to be created within the month and both sets of schedule lines originate from the same line item.

Delivery Blocks at the Customer/Header Level

You may also block a customer master record for a particular sales area, or for all sales areas as far as deliveries are concerned. This is done in transaction code [VD05], as seen in Figure 6-16. To set this block, use the following menu path.

Menu Path   SAP Menu | Logistics | Sales and Distribution | Master Data | Business Partner | Customer | [VD05] - Block

You can block the customer for a particular sales area or for all the sales areas for which the customer belongs. This block is then copied into the sales document.

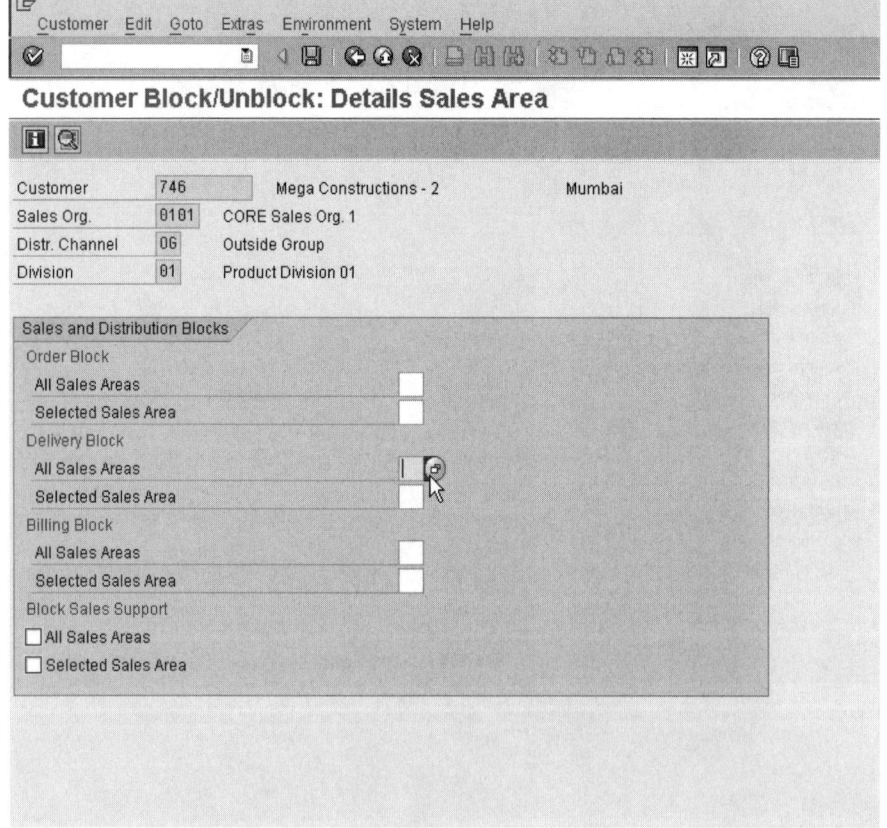

Copyright by SAP AG

FIGURE 6-16   Blocking on the customer master

Packing

Packing is carried out at the item level. One is able to determine that it is mandatory for a specific item to be packed or that it is only packed when necessary. This packed item then in turn may be packed again into a handling unit, which in turn may be packed into another handling unit, thus having the ability of creating a multiple level procedure.

Packing by Item Category

Packing is carried out at the item level. Thus, some items may be relevant to be packed, and other items may be forbidden to be packed. Each item category for which packing is to be carried out must have its corresponding setting at the item category level.

Menu Path   SAP Customizing Implementation Guide | Logistics Execution | Shipping | Packing | Packing Control By Item Category

- For those item categories for which packing must be carried out, set the indicator to A.

- For those item categories that cannot be carried out, set the indicator to B.

- For those item categories that do not have to be packed but for which packing may be carried out, leave the assignment blank, as shown in Figure 6-17.

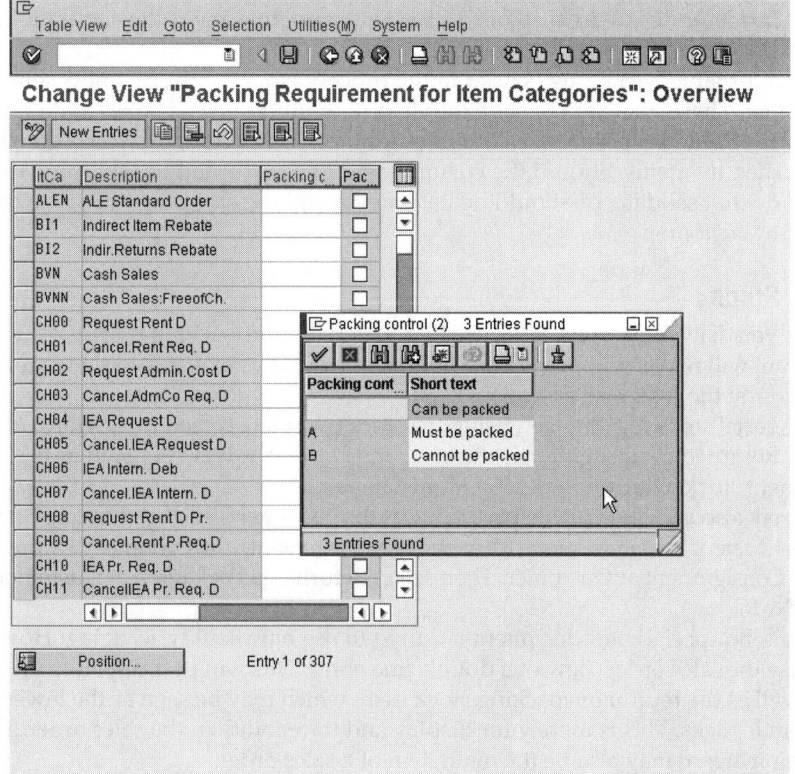

Copyright by SAP AG

Figure 6-17   Packing control by item category

You may select that should there be a batch split in the delivery, the system is to pack the main item with the accumulated batch quantity or the batch split items only. Should you wish the main item to be packed, leave the Pack Accumulated Batch field blank.

If handling unit inventory management is in use for a storage location, then the Pack Accumulated Batch setting has no impact.

Packing Requirements

Menu Path   SAP Customizing Implementation Guide | Logistics Execution | Shipping | Packing | Define Requirements for Packing in the Delivery

You may wish to create a requirement for packing. This requirement performs in the same way as all other requirements in the Sales and Distribution module, in that the criteria stipulated must be met in order for packing to be carried out. An example of a requirement here could be that no packing is to be carried out for items that have a credit block.

Returnable Packaging

Not all packaging materials are inexpensive enough for the cost of the sale to include the cost of the packaging as well. One may have packaging materials that are valuable, and should a customer decide to keep or destroy the packaging items, he should reimburse the business.

Thus returnable packaging is used in the process whereby the business sells items to the customer. These items are packed into handling units such as boxes and crates. The customer may then keep the boxes or crates for a certain period, by which time he must have returned the items. Should the customer not have returned the shipping units specified by that set date, or should he have destroyed the shipping units, the business may bill the customer.

Special Stock

The stock you deliver incorporates packaging materials. This packing is kept at the customer's location, but will remain the property of your company. The stock is recorded automatically as special stock at the customer's location.

This special stock may be seen using the stock overview screen using transaction code [MMBE]. Returnable packaging has the stock indicator of V. It is very similar to consignment stock, which was dealt with in Chapter 4.

You may also view returnable packaging at the customer's site by selecting SAP Menu | Logistics | Materials Management | Inventory Management | Environment | Consignment | [MB58] - Consignment at Customer. Then select Returnable Packaging at Customer, as seen in Figure 6-18.

There is no special sales document required to use returnable packaging. However, you should use the sales order view of a double line entry. This will permit you to view the main item as well as the returnable packing stock item, which may be seen as the lower level item to the item it packs. This is merely for display and traceability in the sales order. The packaging material may also be the main item of a sales order.

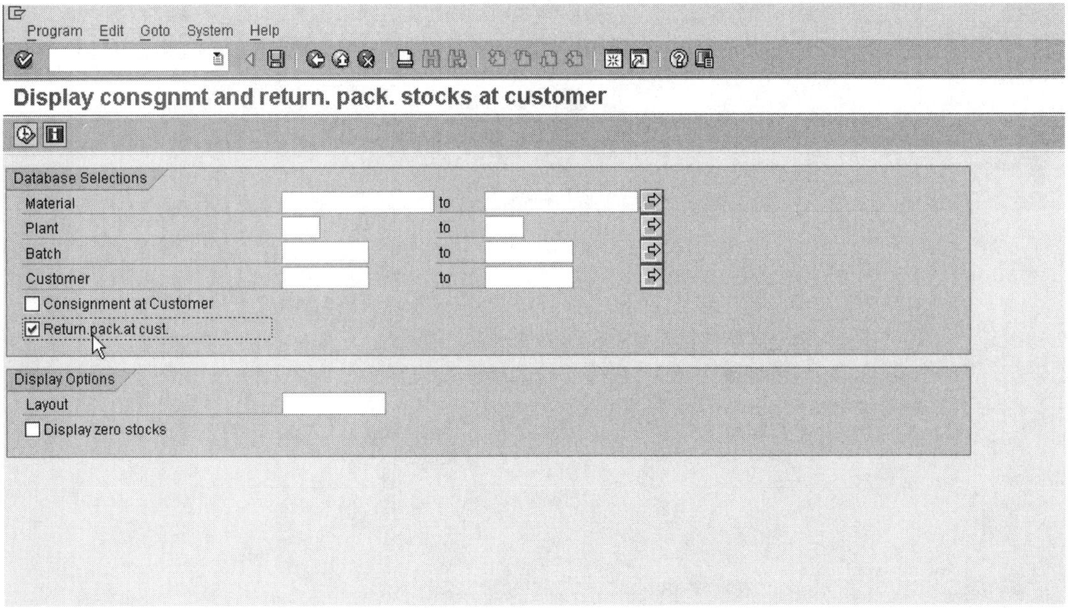

Copyright by SAP AG

FIGURE 6-18 Returnable packaging at customer's location

The packaging's material master record should use the material type VERP for packaging and the item category group LEIH. The item category group LEIH is the SAP standard for returnable packaging.

If you enter a packing proposal in the order (by selecting Extras I Packing Proposal from within the order document), it is copied into the delivery if the packing materials are inventory managed and are relevant for a delivery, which must be the case for returnable packaging.

You may see details relating to the handling unit and packing materials by selecting the handling unit from within the packing proposal. Then select Goto I Detailed HU I General Details, as seen in Figure 6-19.

The returnable packaging material follows the same rules as a standard material in that you must define an item category for it as well as the necessary copy control rules. SAP standard uses item category TAL.

Should you wish to create your own sales document item categories, you may copy and change the SAP standard that uses the item category LAN for the returnable packaging pick up and use the item category LNN for the returnable packaging issue. Do not forget to give your returnable packaging material a price. This price may be used when you create a returnable packaging issue, similar to a consignment issue where you invoice the end customer for the stock of returnable packaging.

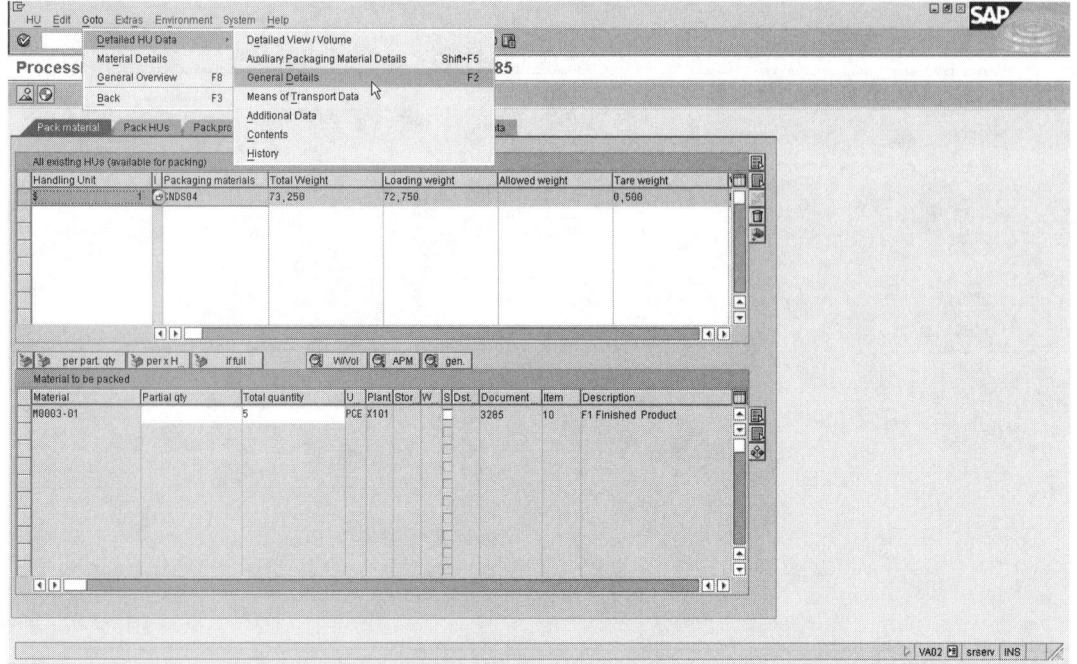

Copyright by SAP AG

FIGURE 6-19   View header details for the handling unit

The standard ECC ERP returnable packaging item categories are

TAL	Ret. Packag. Shipment
LAN	Ret. Packaging Pickup
LNN	Ret. Packaging Issue

Special Stock Partners

A special stock partner is a partner who is assigned to the customer master record in the sales order. You can have special stock partners for both returnable packaging and consignment stock. You may create a new customer for them by using the same account group as if you were creating a sold to party.

This partner need not be the sold to (SP), ship to (SH), bill to (BP), or payer (PY) partner. This partner instead may be the partner who actually "consumes" the materials.

For example, should a large organization have a central depot where all consignment stock goes to, then the consignment stock is shipped directly to each customer's plant as needed. The central depot would be registered in the system as a partner. One must then assign these special stock partners to the relevant Sold-to Party's customer master records. The special stock partners have the partner function key SB.

When materials are "consumed" by the special stock partner, should there be any consignment stock or returnable packing, the system automatically picks up the special stock partner and records the stock in the system as being stored at their site. You may view these allocations of stocks in the same ways as previously discussed using transaction code [MMBE] or [MB58].

Routes

Some companies use the same regular routes to ship goods to their customer. If you use the same routes for your shipping, it would be beneficial to use automatic route determination to control your logistics execution transportation.

Defining Routes

Route determination is automatically proposed for each sales document item in the sales order. It is a process whereby one is able to assign a specific route with transportation legs using different shipment types and carriers.

Route determination may also be redetermined in the delivery. This will use the weight group of the item, which may, if configured, propose a different route to be used.

Before one can assign the route determination to be used by the sales or delivery document, one needs to define the data that is used in the route determination. The configuration is carried out using the following steps.

Defining Routes

Menu Path SAP Customizing Implementation Guide | Sales and Distribution | Basic Functions | Routes | Define Routes | Define Modes of Transport

The modes of transport are self-explanatory. They may be, for example, road or plane. Define the mode of transport used in the business, and assign a two-character alphanumeric key with a meaningful description, as seen in Figure 6-20. This mode of transport has a mode of transport category assigned to it (seen in column SType).

In the SAP Customizing Implementation Guide, proceed to define shipping types.

Menu Path SAP Customizing Implementation Guide | Sales and Distribution | Basic Functions | Routes | Define Routes | Define Shipping Types

In this assignment, as seen in Figure 6-21, you assign the shipping types (column PT) along with the previously defined modes of transport (column MdTr) and a shipping type procedure group (STPG).

The shipping types are the actual "vehicles" used to transport the materials, and may be defined as a train, mail, etc.

The modes of transport are the types of transportation used to transport the materials, and may be defined as a road, etc.

The shipping type procedure group is used to calculate the costs relating to the transportation.

In the SAP Customizing Implementation Guide, use the following menu path.

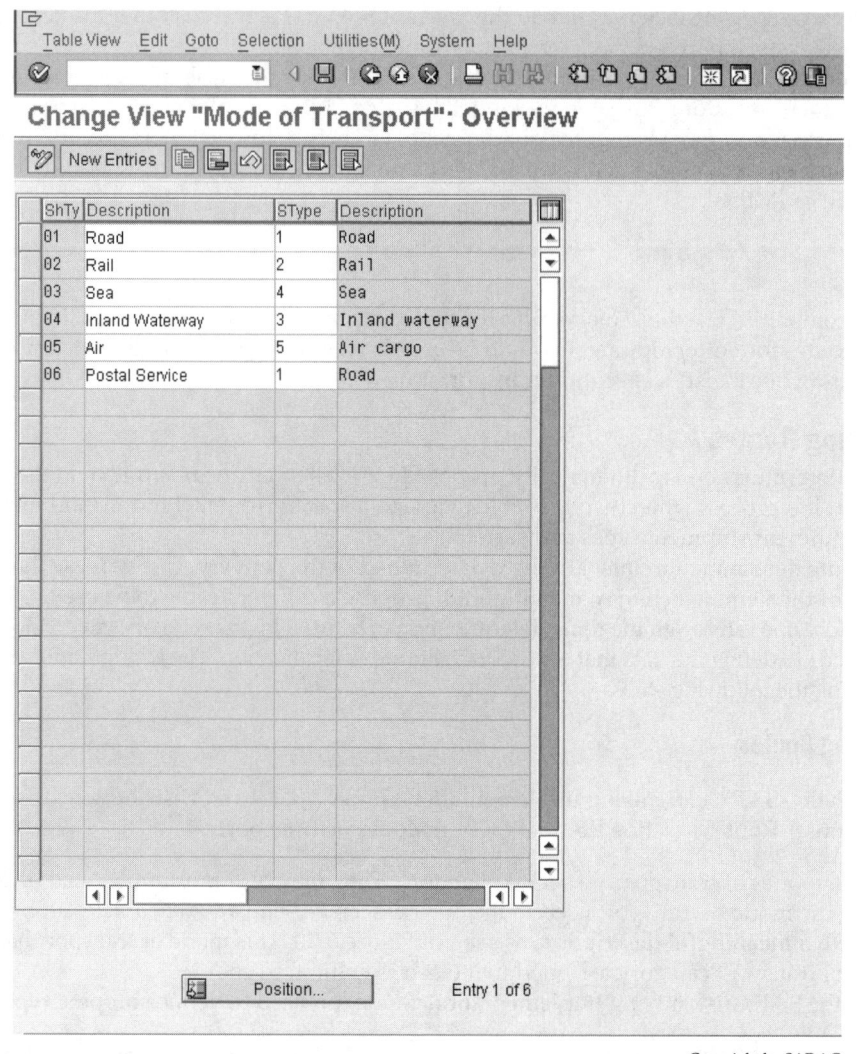

FIGURE 6-20 Mode of transport

Menu Path SAP Customizing Implementation Guide | Sales and Distribution | Basic Functions | Routes | Define Routes | Define Transportation Connection Points

Transportation connection points, as seen in Figure 6-22, may be airports, railway stations, border crossings, etc. They define points where transportation types connect, or where a transportation type crosses a border.

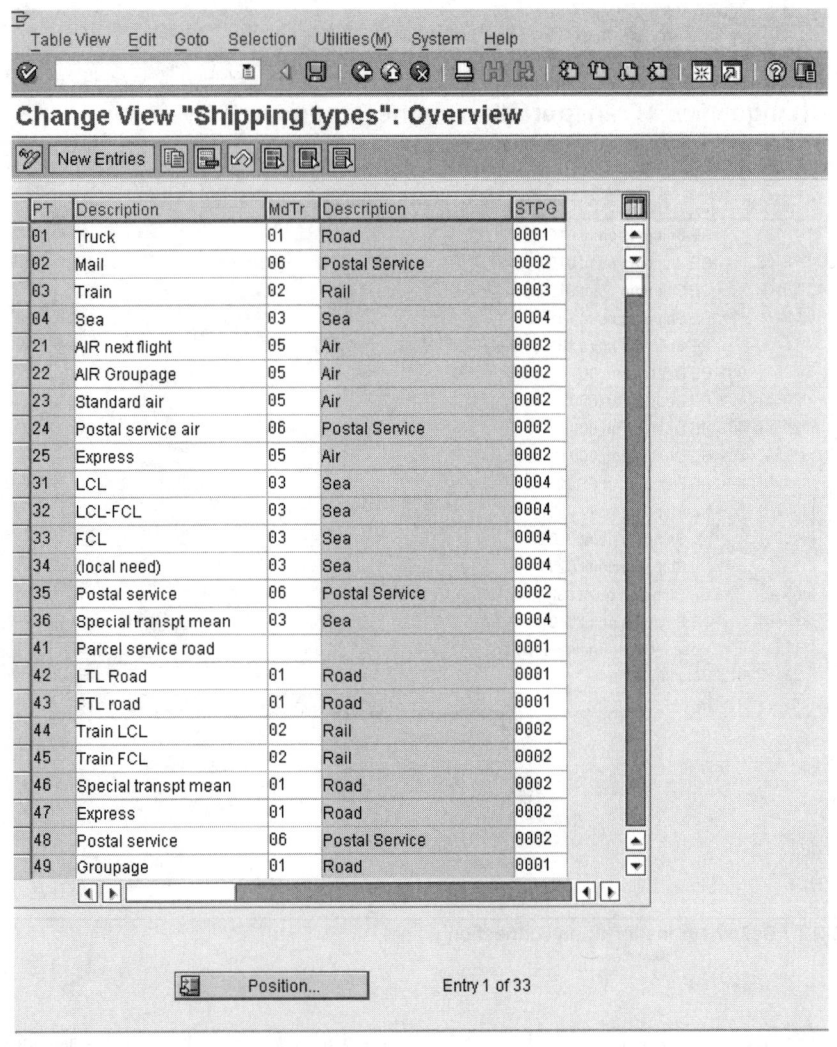

Copyright by SAP AG

FIGURE 6-21   Defining shipping types

After completing the transportation connection points, proceed with Define Routes and Stages.

Menu Path   SAP Customizing Implementation Guide I Sales and Distribution I Basic Functions I Routes I Define Routes I Define Routes and Stages

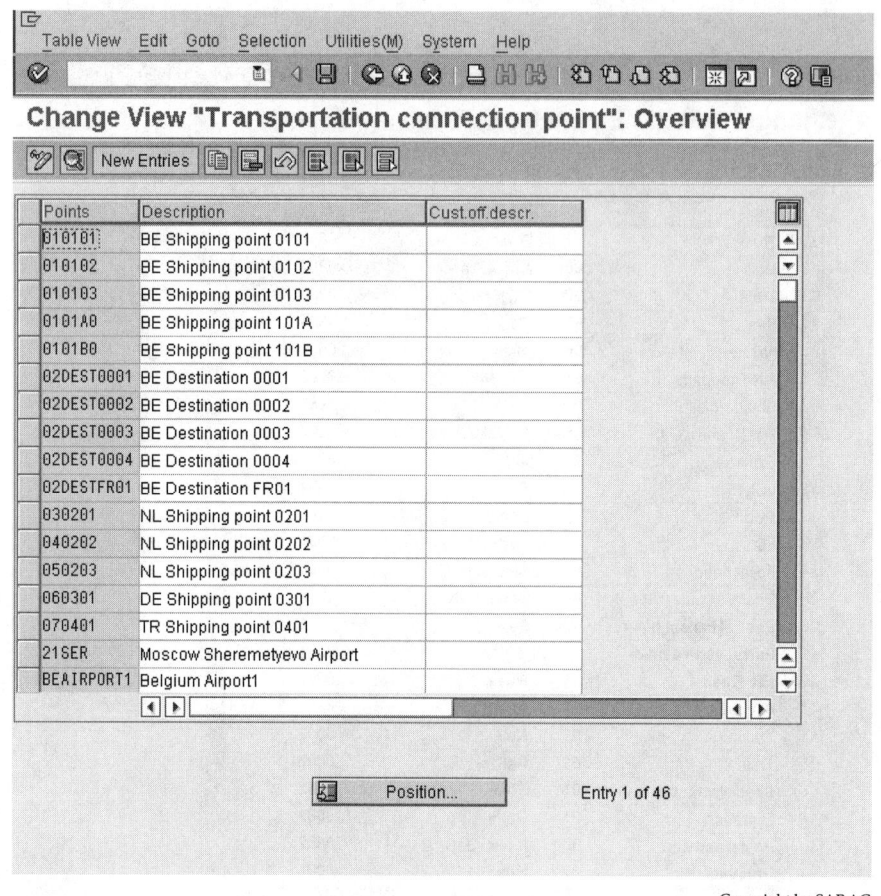

FIGURE 6-22 Defining transportation connection points

In this activity, as displayed in Figure 6-23, one defines the route with its associated route stages and transportation connection points.

Define a route with a six-character alphanumeric key with a description.

For the defined route you are able to set a forwarding agent or carrier (column ServcAgent), as well as define the transit times and the transit lead time, which is the number of days (column TransLdTm) or hours and minutes (column Tr.lead tim.) required for organizing a shipment for an item that is to be delivered via a certain route. One is also able to specify the distance to be traveled and the total transit duration.

After defining the route proceed with defining the route stages by selecting the route and the Route Stages folder in the file structure on the left side of the screen.

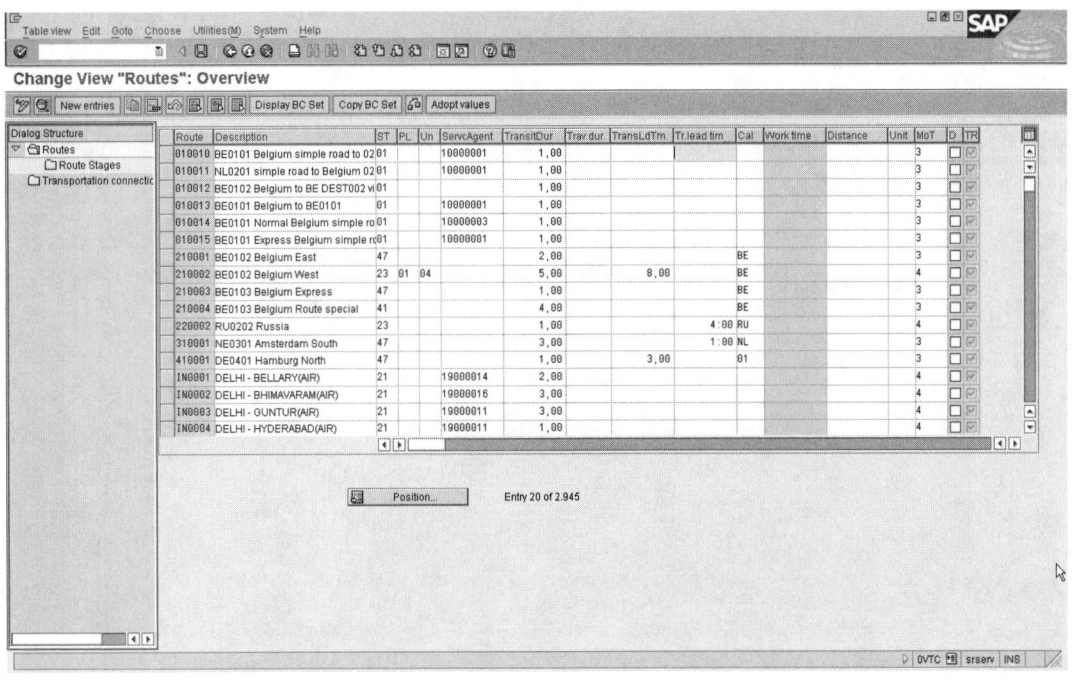

FIGURE 6-23   Defining routes and stages

Select your departure point from the list of transport connection points previously defined. Then select your destination point—for example, an airfield—which is also a connection point as previously defined. Proceed with a new entry and continue with the assignments.

Now that the route has been defined, you are able to proceed with an optional step of maintaining the stages for the routes. This would have been carried out for each individual leg. However, once you have many routes in the system and you need to define some "global" changes, you may proceed to the Maintain Stages for All Routes screen. This can be done by using the following menu path:

Menu Path   SAP Customizing Implementation Guide | Sales and Distribution | Basic Functions | Routes | Define Routes | Maintain Stages For All Routes

In the selection screen enter the data you wish to change. For this example, I have entered all stages defined as transport legs for route 000001, WHICH offers me the transport legs seen in Figure 6-24.

One is now able to expand these legs and select all of them. You will notice a red traffic light. After selecting them all, click on the Change button (shown with the pencil icon).

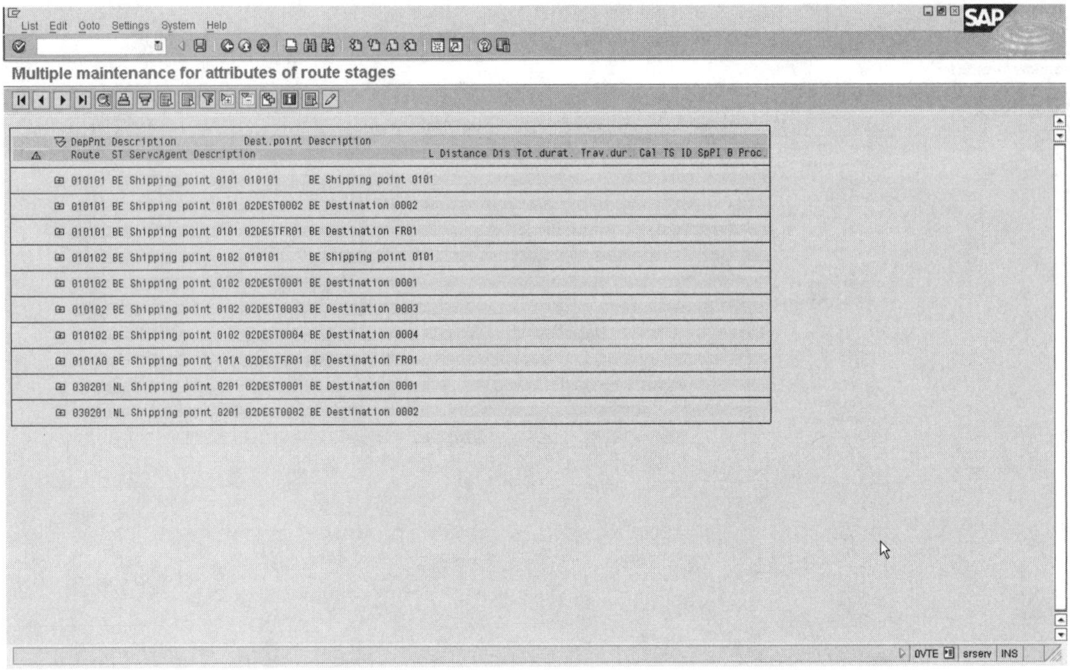

FIGURE 6-24   Multiple route maintenance

This will offer you a number of attributes, which you may now select and change. These changes will be assigned to all the originally selected legs. For example, one can set the shipping type to truck. Click the Execute button.

You will notice the traffic signal is displayed as yellow. After again selecting all of the items and clicking Save, you will notice the traffic signal indicates green. This signaling is merely there for one to use as an indicator of which items have been processed and which are still to be processed when working with a very large number of entries.

Now that the routes have been maintained, you are able to proceed with defining the route determination.

Route Determination

We have defined the route. Now one needs to define how the route is determined in the system.

Route determination occurs in the SAP system based on the following items:

- The country and departure zone (taken from the shipping point)
- The country and receiving zone of the Ship-to Party
- The shipping conditions as in the sales order
- The transportation group of the material master record
- The weight group (optional and only relevant in the delivery)

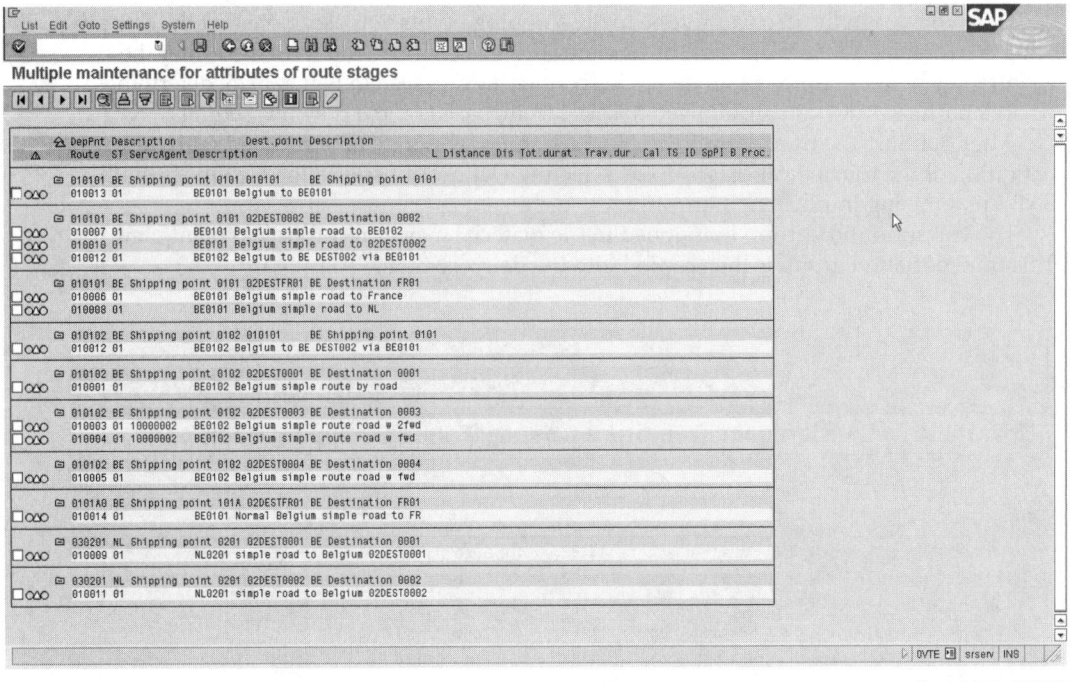

FIGURE 6-25   Changed routes

The system then copies the route as proposed in the sales order into the delivery document header.

The route already determined in the sales order and copied into the delivery may be redetermined in the delivery document. This redetermination may use the weight of the materials and must be indicated for each relevant delivery document types in customizing.

Proceed to the Define Transportation Zones screen.

Menu Path   SAP Customizing Implementation Guide | Sales and Distribution | Basic Functions | Routes | Route Determination | Define Transportation Zones

For route determination, you divide a country up into transport zones. A customer exists in a transport zone, and so does a shipping point. SAP determines the route for moving from a shipping point in the one zone, to the customer in the other zone (also taking into account other conditions like the weight of the materials and the shipping conditions of the customer).

Here you assign all the zones you require to use in route determination. Each zone has a description and an assignment to a country key. This country key is later used to detrmine what zones are relevant for what shipping points.

Now select Maintain Country And Transportation Zone For Shipping Point from the SAP Customizing Implementation Guide.

Here you assign the departure zone to the shipping points you use. Note that the shipping point is maintained for a plant and the plant resides in a country. You must also enter the country key of the shipping point here. This country key, as seen in Figure 6-26, determines what departure zones you are allowed to select from, based on the previous settings.

After defining the transportation departure zones, you may now proceed with the definition of the transportation group by selecting Define Transportation Groups from the SAP Customizing Implementation Guide.

The transportation group is assigned to the material master record sales/plant view. This transportation group is then copied into the delivery item.

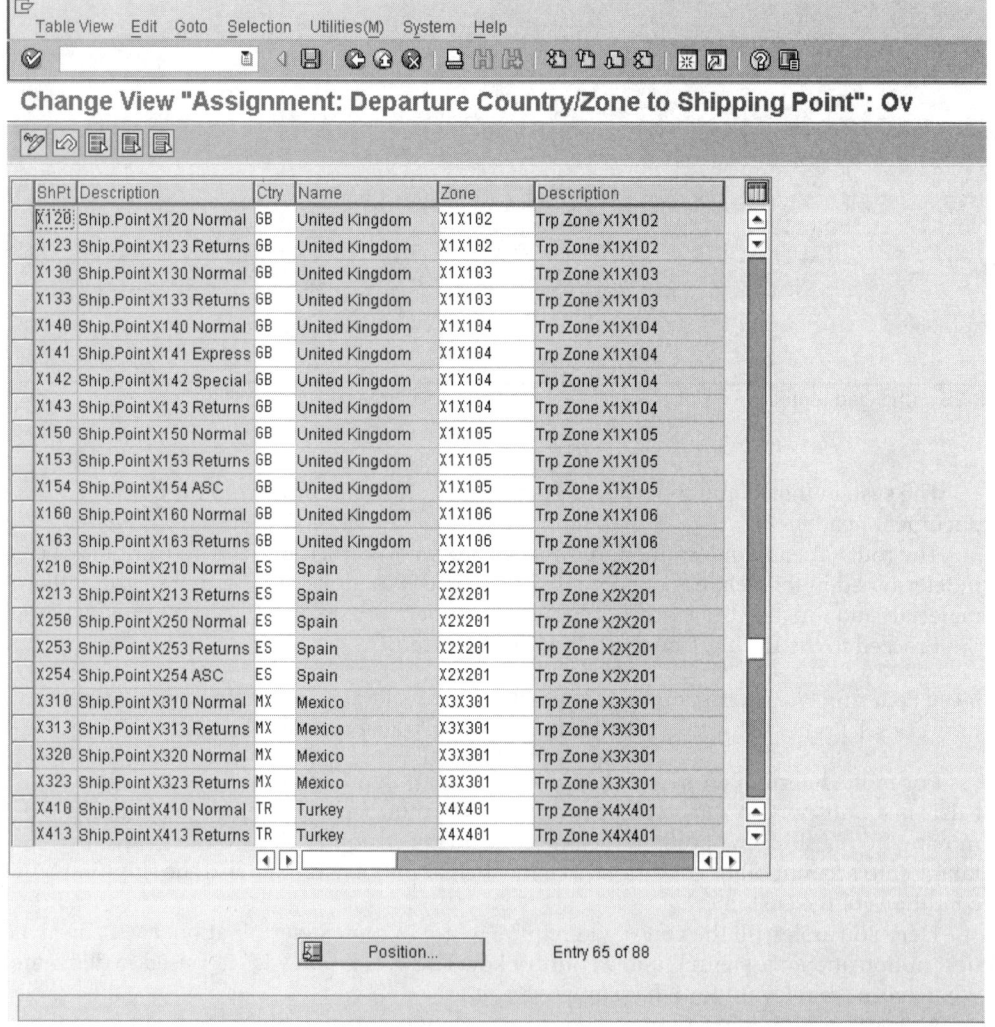

FIGURE 6-26   Maintain country and transportation zone for shipping point

As the transportation group is a prerequisite for the determination of the route, it is advisable to include it as a mandatory field for the material master record to ensure during the maintenance of the material that the field is never left empty.

Defining Shipping Conditions

The shipping conditions, are held on the customer master record. They are used to define the route determination as well as used in determining the shipping point. One is able to assign a shipping condition to a sales document. If this has been maintained the system will not copy the shipping condition from the customer master record.

Use the following menu path.

Menu Path   SAP Customizing Implementation Guide | Logistics Execution | Shipping | Basic Shipping Functions | Shipping Point and Goods Receiving Point Determination | Define Shipping Conditions

(We used shipping conditions to determine the shipping point earlier in this chapter.)

Shipping Weight Groups and Routes

You can use the weight group to further refine the route determination in the delivery.

This is configured by selecting SAP Customizing Implementation Guide | Sales and Distribution | Basic Functions | Routes | Route Determination | Define Weight Groups.

For example, let's say the customer shipping condition is "As soon as possible." It makes sense to send the stock by air. But this might be too expensive if the weight is more than 50KG.

So you can say for the customer that the shipping condition is: Up to 50KG, use the route that has a transportation type by air; over 50KG, use a road or sea route.

The weight group can therefore be used to determine the route, taking into consideration the weight of the delivery. This is very important when sending stock by rail or truck, for example.

It is generally cheaper to send the stock by truck rather than rail if the quantity is small, but for very large quantities, it is usually cheaper to use rail. For the smaller quantities, determine a route that is defined for road shipments; for large quantities, determine a route that is defined for rail shipments.

Define weight groups with a short meaningful description. We will see their use in the route determination.

 Always use the weight group as defined in "up to…" as this offers greater ease of use later. Now that we have all the components, we can now derive the route determination

Maintaining Route Determination

Proceed back to the SAP Customizing Implementation Guide path.

Menu Path   SAP Customizing Implementation Guide | Logistics Execution | Shipping | Basic Shipping Functions | Routes | Route Determination | Maintain Route Determination

Note that you are also able to locate this configuration area in the following path.

Menu Path   SAP Customizing Implementation Guide | Sales and Distribution | Basic Functions | Routes | Route Determination | Maintain Route Determination

By referring to Figure 6-27 we can see that the key to the routes is the country of departure plus the departure zone, plus the destination country, plus the receiving zone—for example, in the figure Austria and Region East is shipping to Austria and Region East.

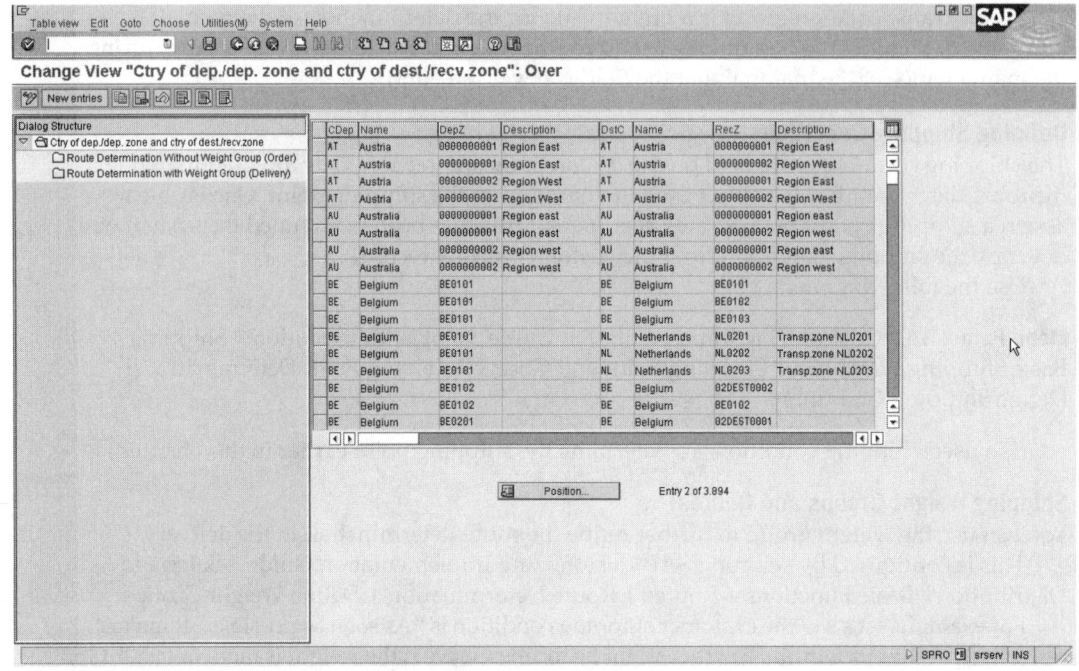

FIGURE 6-27   Route determination by country key

Select the entry and then select the Route Determination with Weight Group (Delivery) folder. In the file structure on the left side, you are able to see the configuration shown in Figure 6-28.

This assignment may now have all the proposed routes for further combination of shipping condition, weight group, and transportation group. We are now able to assign the route we previously maintained to this determination.

Should you wish the route in the delivery to be redetermined, proceed with the menu path:

Menu Path   SAP Customizing Implementation Guide | Sales and Distribution | Basic Functions | Routes | Route Determination | Define New Route Determination By Delivery Type

You are now able to assign an indicator of:

- **Blank**   Indicates no new check
- **A**   Indicates new route determination without check
- **B**   Indicates new route determination with check

The check performed is the comparison of the proposed route with the actual routes allowed in.

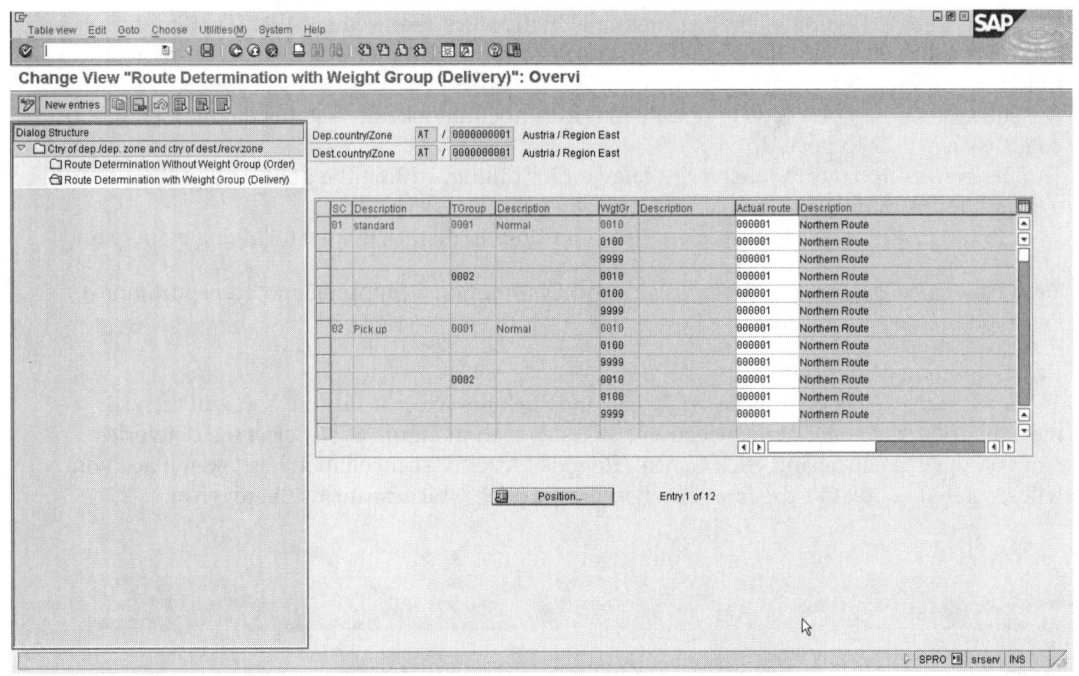

FIGURE 6-28   Route determination with weight group

Menu Path   SAP Customizing Implementation Guide | Sales and Distribution | Basic Functions | Routes | Route Determination | Define Allowed Actual Route By Proposed Route

In this assignment you merely assign additional routes to the proposed route that the system determines automatically. These additional routes may be entered manually or they may be used to determine if they are valid in the redetermination of the route in the delivery.

Posting Goods Issue in the Delivery

Goods issue is posted for a delivery causing the goods to be transferred into the hands of the carrier. In other words, the ownership of the goods leaves the business and transfers to the carrier. The carrier then relieves himself of ownership of the goods once the customer signs for the articles. Once goods issue is posted in a delivery, the system updates numerous records.

The posting of goods issue causes the system to update the stock quantities—that is, the warehouse or plant stock is decreased by the quantity of goods that have left the warehouse.

The system also automatically updates the posting to the general ledger accounts. Based on the account determination for the inventory posting, the system decreases the value of the stock on hand and increases the cost of goods sold. Later, when the invoice is created, SAP will update the revenue accounts and the amount to be received from the customer. This completes the sales transaction from an accounting perspective.

The system also updates the requirements in the stock requirements list. That is, once goods issue has occurred, there is no longer a need for a customer's delivery requirement to sit in the stock requirements list [MD04].

The system then proceeds to update previous documents with a status displaying that goods issue has been posted.

The system updates the deliveries relevant for billing, adding the delivery, if billing-relevant, to the billing due list.

You can reverse a goods movement/issue posting. To do this, use the following menu path.

Menu Path   SAP Menu | Logistics | Sales and Distribution | Shipping and Transportation | Post Goods Issue | Cancellation/Reversal

Transaction code [VL09]

Enter in the selection criteria you wish, and click the Execute button. You will then see the deliveries that match your selection criteria as seen in Figure 6-29. Select the deliveries that you wish to cancel and click Cancel/Reverse. After the cancellation has taken place you will see a dialog box like the one shown in Figure 6-29, which confirms the reversal.

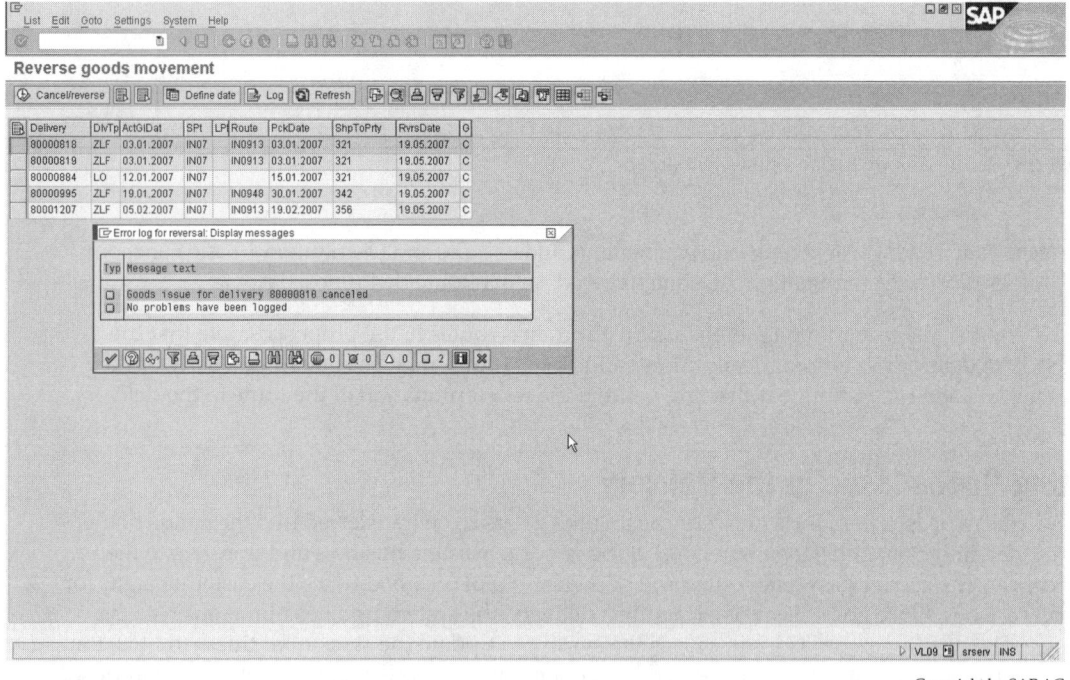

FIGURE 6-29   Cancel/reverse goods issue

Billing

In this chapter we progress to the implementation of and interfacing with billing documents, and continue the contract process of different billing plans. We also introduce resource billing related to customer service.

Billing Process

The business is able to invoice the customer for materials or services rendered. Generally, this takes place after the delivery process has been completed, whether this is a delivery of a physical item or a service. The billing process could be order- or delivery-related, and may include billing of standard deliveries as well as the creation of debit and credit memos. The billing process may even include invoicing for financial deposits for large projects prior to construction and inception of the project.

Defining Billing Document Types

The billing document is similar to the delivery document in that it has a header and item level, but no schedule line level, as in the sales documents. Thus one must configure the header document type and the relevant item categories.

To define the billing document type, use the following menu path.

Menu Path   SAP Customizing Implementation Guide | Sales and Distribution | Billing | Billing Documents | Define Billing Types | Define Billing Types

You may maintain a billing document type or create your own by copying and changing the billing type key. Remember when creating your own document types to use the name range beginning with the prefix of Z.

The header data of a billing document defines how the document is to behave. It has the standard number range assignments. However, note that the billing document only uses internal assignments. It is not possible to have an external number range for a billing document. The billing document is split up into control sections, which I'll cover next.

The General Control Data

The general control data, shown in Figure 7-1, includes the sales document category, which defines what type of document the system is using. The SAP standard for invoice is M. (You will remember the standard for a delivery is J, etc.)

The posting block stops automatic release of the billing document to accounting. This means the billing document must be manually released to accounting by selecting Billing | Change | Release to Accounting from the billing document.

The statistics checkbox indicates if this billing document is relevant for updating the information systems such as the sales information systems (SIS).

One must also assign a transaction group 7 for billing documents and 8 for pro forma invoices.

The billing category is a further sub-division of billing document type and transaction group. This category is used for selection of screen variants and classifications.

The document type is used when the accounting document is created.

The negative posting is only effective if the company code for which the posting is carried out permits negative postings. (In reality it is rarely used.)

The branch/head office is important as it determines which customer master record is used to update the accounting documents. Generally, if the payer is different than the Sold-to Party, the payer is transferred to Financial Accounting as the customer.

The credit memo with value data checkbox is used for credit memos, to set the baseline date as the date from the original billing document.

The invoice list type represents the document type that may be used to create invoice lists for this billing document. You may also state that such a billing document is related to the rebate process by indicating what rebate type of document it is in the rebate settlement field.

If the document is relevant for rebate accruals, you need to indicate it by checking the relevant for rebate checkbox.

The standard text field is currently not used.

The Cancellation Data

The cancellation data, as seen in Figure 7-2, is used by the system when a document type of the type you are defining is cancelled. The system will automatically use the cancellation billing type as well as any copying requirements you maintain here. Cancellation of sales documents seldom occurs, in standard business practice, instead, a credit or debit note is generally given. The Credit or Debit note may be issued for the discrepancy or alternatively a Credit note may be issued for the entire invoice, followed by a recreation of the billing document for the correct amount.

The SAP standard invoice cancellation type for F2 billing documents is S1. Cancellation of a cash sale uses SV; a cash sale has sales document type BV followed by a billing document type BV.

The reference number is passed to accounting. The allocation number is similar to the reference number.

Account Assignment/Pricing Data

The account assignment and pricing control area, as seen in Figure 7-3 is, used for both the account determination and pricing determination.

The account determination procedure is used by the system to propose to which general ledger accounts entries must be posted. The document pricing procedure indicator is used to determine the pricing procedure to be used, in conjunction with the sales area and the customer pricing procedure indicator. Both of these determination procedures will be covered in Chapter 8.

The account determination reconciliation account field is used to determine the reconciliation account to be used. This value is then used as opposed to the reconciliation account on the company code (KNB1-AKONT).

The account determination cash settlement field is used to determine if the value should be posted to a different account, as opposed to the standard increase in accounts receivables. In a cash sale there would be no need to increase the customer's open items. However, you may wish to post the value somewhere.

The account determination payment cards field is used to determine which general ledger accounts must be posted to for payment cards.

Output/Partners/Text Control Data

The billing document has a header and item level. However, the billing document does not have an item level that may be configured as in "define sales document item."

Cancellation		
Cancell.billing type	S1	Cancel. Invoice (S1)
Copying requirements		
Reference number		
Allocation number		

FIGURE 7-2 Billing document type cancellation control

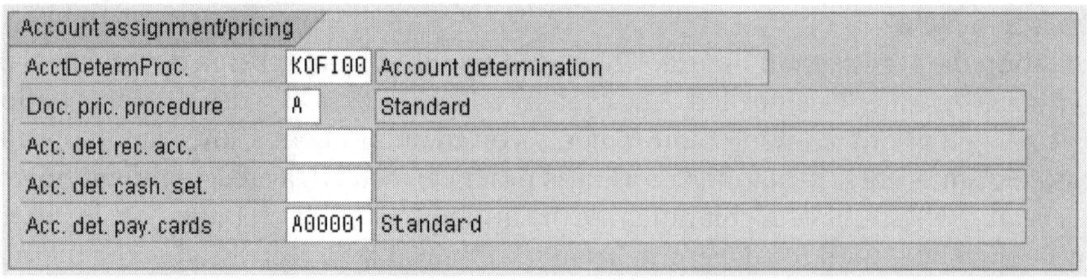

Account assignment/pricing		
AcctDetermProc.	KOFI00	Account determination
Doc. pric. procedure	A	Standard
Acc. det. rec. acc.		
Acc. det. cash. set.		
Acc. det. pay. cards	A00001	Standard

FIGURE 7-3   Billing document type account assignment and pricing control data

Rather, the data entered in the header document type here is used by the system in determining the output, partner, and text determination of the item level.

Referring to Figure 7-4, we can see that the output determination procedure, which is assigned to billing document types, is assigned here. In addition, the application of the output is assigned as V3, indicating billing. This combination will determine the billing document outputs.

The header and item partner determination key is the key that specifies the group of partner functions the system proposes automatically for a billing document of this type. These header partners may be mandatory, for example, for the Sold-to Party as well as the Bill-to Party and payer partner. The Ship-to Party, however, may be an optional entry. The text determination procedure for the header and item levels are also assigned to the billing document header. The output and text determinations are covered in Chapter 9.

General Billing Document Data

You can use the report SDCHECKVOFA to check your customizing settings for the billing types. Only some of the settings are checked.

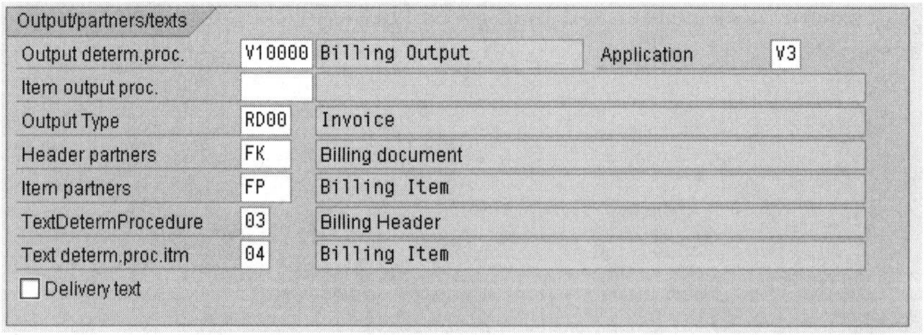

Output/partners/texts				
Output determ.proc.	V10000	Billing Output	Application	V3
Item output proc.				
Output Type	RD00	Invoice		
Header partners	FK	Billing document		
Item partners	FP	Billing Item		
TextDetermProcedure	03	Billing Header		
Text determ.proc.itm	04	Billing Item		
☐ Delivery text				

FIGURE 7-4   Billing document type output/partners text data

The SAP standard uses, among others, the following billing types:

F1	Order-related invoice
F2	Delivery-related invoice
F5	Pro forma invoice for sales orders
F8	Pro forma invoice for deliveries
G2	Credit memo
L2	Debit memo
RE	Credit for returns
S1	Cancellation invoice
S2	Cancellation credit memo
IV	Inter-company billing

For all billing documents like standard document types, it is necessary to maintain the copy control rules.

The item categories found in the billing document are copied from the preceding document. Thus item category TAN in the delivery document will be copied as item category TAN in the billing document. There are no settings to make for the item category in the billing document. However, the copy control rules must be defined at header and item level. The copy control for billing documents will be dealt with in detail a little later in this chapter. As you know, it is possible to have order-related billing as well delivery-related billing. Examples of commonly used sales documents that result in order-related billing are

- **CR** Credit memos
- **DR** Debit memos
- **RK** Invoice correction request

Special Billing Document Types

It is not possible to list all business scenarios, processes, and billing document types. However, there are a few that are very common that need to be mentioned, as they will not be discussed individually.

Pro Forma Invoice

The pro forma invoice uses the billing type F8. It is an invoice that does not post any financial amounts into any general ledger. It is used for information purposes only—for example, to accompany the shipment of products across a border post, thus being used to represent the actual value of the articles. The actual invoice may be sent to the customer via post.

Another example of the use of a pro forma invoice would be the invoice representing the value a customer must claim from a superior authority before the business sends him the actual payable invoice.

Cancellation Invoice

A standard cancellation invoice is billing type S1. The cancellation invoice is used when a billing document is found to have errors in it, and the original billing document needs to be cancelled and recreated.

Note that it is illegal in a number of countries to permit this capability in a system, so be careful copying the standard billing document type F2, as you may wish to exclude this functionality.

Inter-company Invoice

This billing document type, which will be discussed in more detail later, represents the internal invoice used between two company codes belonging to the same business. It is an internal invoice in the sense that it is not passed on to any external Sold-to Party or partner.

An inter-company sale refers to a sales transaction where more than one company code belonging to the business is used in the process. An intra-company sale refers to a transaction within one company code, such as intra-company stock transfers, where stock is moved between two plants within a single company code.

Collective Billing and Copy Control for Billing Documents

A billing document may be created individually or collectively. We'll examine how to control billing document creation, keeping in mind the copy control rules and the master data.

Introduction to Collective Billing

Billing documents may be created individually. That is, you may create an invoice for each sales order or billing document. Billing documents may also be created as collective billing documents. Invoices can be accumulated and created collectively—for example, on one day of the week, when all relevant data is equal, the system may combine multiple deliveries or sales document into one invoice.

This is done by using a combination of the factory calendar assigned to the payer master record and the billing copying rules.

To create collective invoicing for a customer, you must first define the billing factory calendar the payer is using. (Refer to "Factory Calendars" in Chapter 9.) This factory calendar is then assigned to the billing view of the customer master record for the payer. The billing calendar may indicate one day of the week as a working day, thus the system will only propose to create billing documents for this party once a week.

However, this does not mean that the deliveries and sales orders will be consolidated into one billing document. The copy control may require the invoices to be split (for example, if the payment terms are different). But it does mean that the billing documents will be created on that day. We will look at the splitting criteria a little later in this section.

Introduction to Copy Control for Billing Documents

The copy control for billing documents is split into three overall copy control rules. They define copy rules for header and item levels between sales documents.

- **Sales document to billing document**   This is used, for example, for credit memos and debit memos that have no delivery document.

- **Billing document to billing document**   This is used by the system to determine copying control, for example, between an invoice and an inter-company invoice.

- **Delivery document to billing document**   This is the most widely used copying rule, which covers the standard sales process.

As the copy control definition and maintenance is equal for all three types, we will only use the delivery document to billing document copy control rule as an example.

Billing Document Copy Control Rules: Delivery Document to Billing Document
Use the following menu path.

Menu Path   SAP Customizing Implementation Guide | Sales and Distribution | Billing | Billing Documents | Maintain Copying Control for Billing Documents | Copying Control: Delivery Document to Billing Document

We'll use the following scenario to create the billing document: We have created five sales orders for a single payer/customer. Of these five sales orders, we have created two deliveries due to the fact that the shipping point on one of the sales orders was different. (Three sales orders could be on one delivery document and two on the other, or four on one delivery document and one on the other.) Now we have the scenario whereby two deliveries of delivery type LF are to be billed.

Looking at the copy control rules from delivery type LF to billing document type F2, as seen in Figure 7-5, we may select the relevant copy control rules.

Select the document types, then click the Details button (the small magnify glass) in the taskbar. You will see a screen similar to Figure 7-6.

The target and source document types are self-explanatory. The copying requirements assign a number, which in turn is the key to a routine. The routine may be found in transaction code [VOFM] (Menu path: Copying Requirements | Billing Documents). We'll discuss more about VOFM later. The routine 003, which actually includes LV60A003, is used to check specific blocks and statuses to determine if the billing document may be created. The blocks and statuses it checks are as follows:

- Billing block
- Billing status
- Goods movement status
- Incompletion status for billing header
- Overall incompletion status for billing document
- POD (proof of delivery) status

The determine export data field is used to redetermine the export control (foreign trade data) automatically in the billing document. The reference number is passed to accounting. The allocation number is similar to the reference number. Both of these numbers may have defaults assigned to them on the billing document type.

For self-billing, the value of this field must be equal to a "C," meaning the delivery number is used as a reference. However, this also means that the delivery number will be passed to accounting as the reference field. The system therefore cannot combine deliveries like in a collective invoice as it does not know what number to use as a reference.

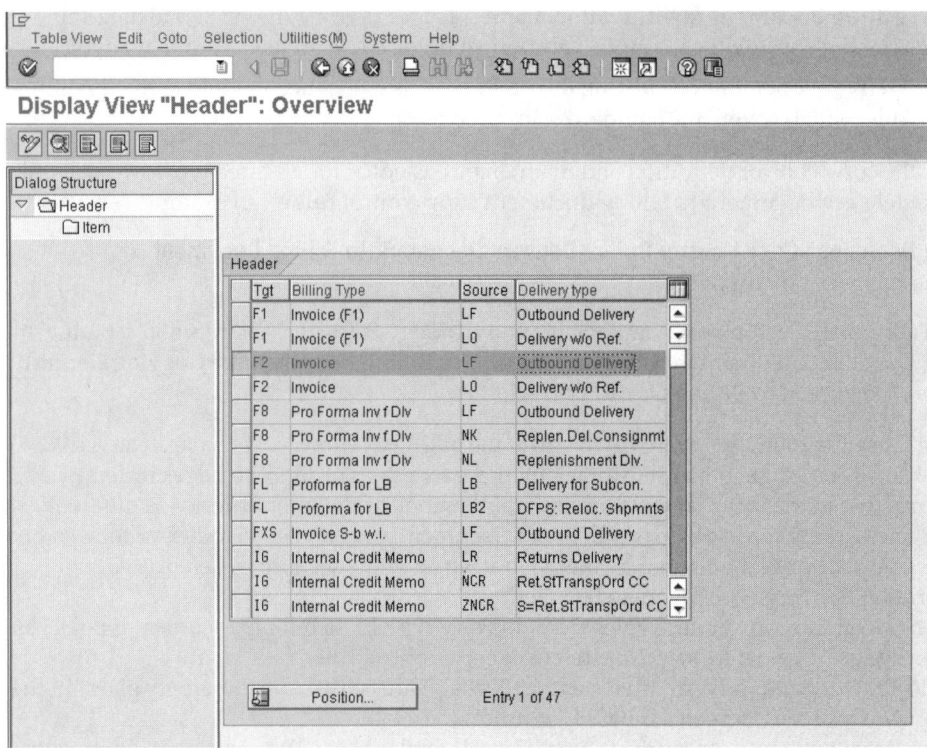

Copyright by SAP AG

FIGURE 7-5 Header target and source copy control

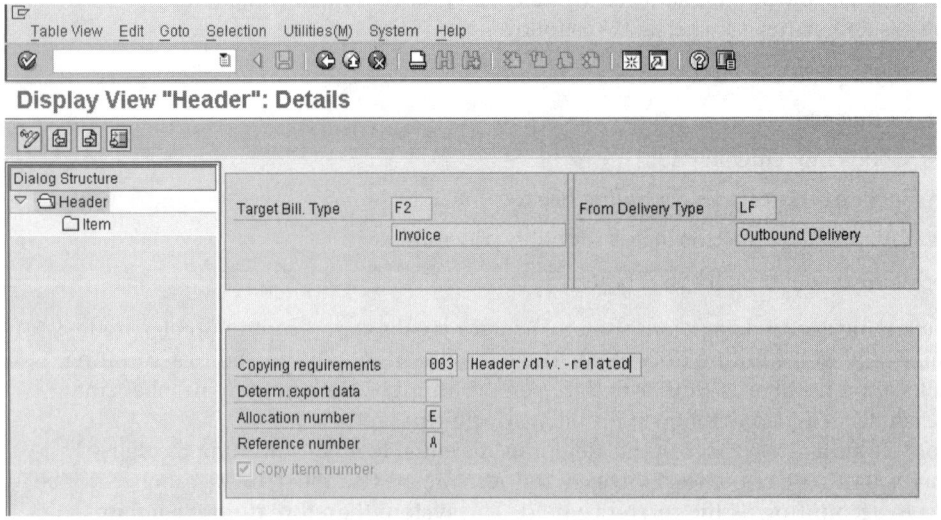

Copyright by SAP AG

FIGURE 7-6 Billing header copy control

The assignment number on table VBRK (VBRK-ZUONR) is actually the allocation number in the copy control at header level. If you set this field to check, for example, your sales document or delivery document, you will not be able to collectively bill documents as the value of this VBRK field will be different.

Billing Document Copy Control Item

Select the Item folder in the file structure on the left. You will then see a screen similar to Figure 7-7.

Select item category TAN, as shown in Figure 7-7, then click the Details button and you'll see a screen similar to Figure 7-8.

Using the example of TAN, as seen in Figure 7-8, we have a similar view to the copy control rules as seen in the sales documents.

The billing quantity is used to determine the quantity of items to be invoiced—for example, setting B indicates to invoice the delivery quantity less the already invoiced quantity.

The positive/negative quantity field is used to update the open/remaining quantity or value in the source document.

The pricing type determines what type of pricing the system is to automatically use. It is advisable to always use the pricing type of G (copy pricing elements unchanged and re-determine taxes). (Refer to "Pricing" in Chapter 8 for details on the use of these pricing types.)

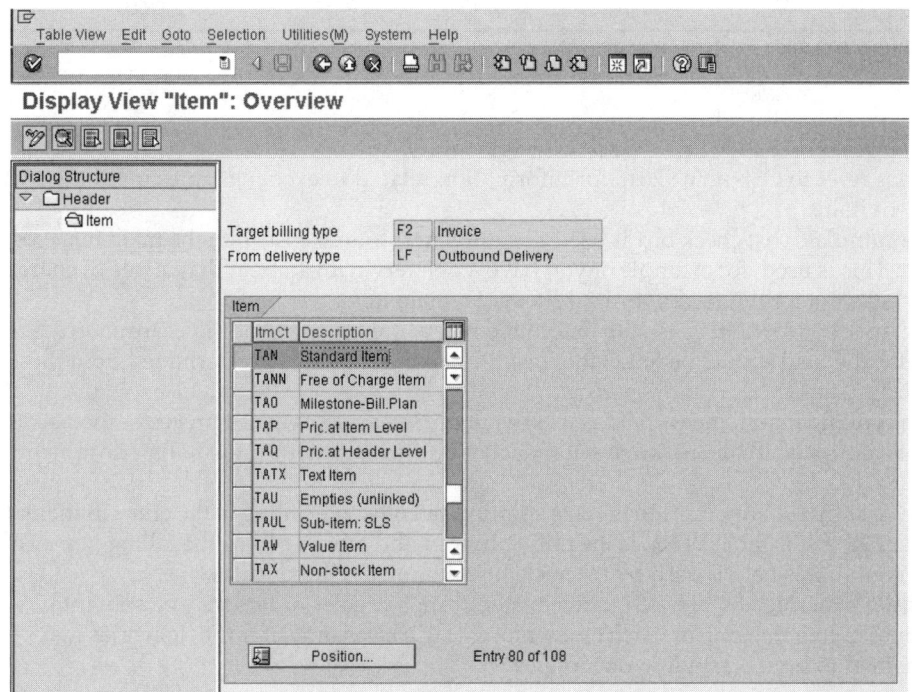

Copyright by SAP AG

Figure 7-7 Billing copy control - select item

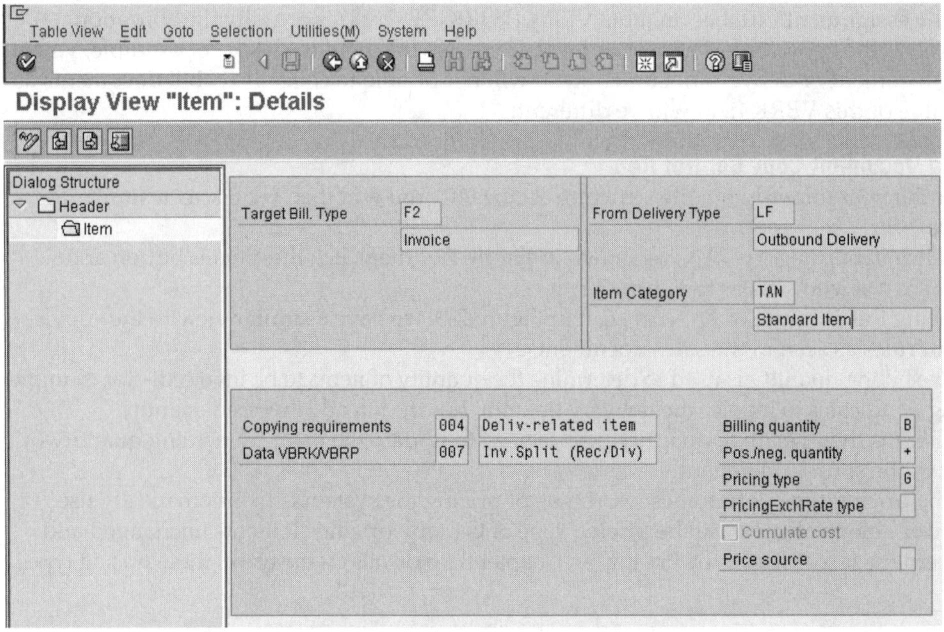

Copyright by SAP AG

FIGURE 7-8   Copy control rules for item category TAN

The pricing exchange rate type is self-explanatory.

Please refer to OSS note 92613 for information related to exchange rates in billing document items.

The cumulate cost check box is used to cumulate sub-item costs into the main item cost amount. This is used, for example, if you have a delivery with an item that is free of charge and not relevant for billing, but is a sub-item of a main item.

The price source field is used to determine where the pricing conditions are sourced. Generally, the field should be left blank, resulting in the copy being determined from the sales document.

The copying requirements field is used as in the sales and delivery process—that is, all elements requested by the requirement must be fulfilled in order for the billing document to be created.

The data that is important to invoice splitting or collective billing is the entry in the data VBRK/VBRP field. Table VBRK is the billing header and table VBRP is the billing item. The key entered in this field is used by the system to defining splitting rules.

For our example, the two deliveries created from five sales orders may be split into individual billing documents, each one representing a sales order. Or the deliveries may be combined to form one billing document.

The billing split uses a field in table VBRK called ZUKRI. This is a field with the ability to hold 40 characters. Generally, the routine allocated to this field uses an internal table in its calculation called ZUK. A value of a reference field to check is passed in the routine to a portion of the 40-character field. The contents of this 40-character value in field ZUKRI is then compared to the next record to be combined in the billing document. If these two values of VBRK-ZUKRI are not equal, the document will not be combined.

ZUK is a string of 40 characters that is stored on the billing header table (VBRK). Therefore, you cannot check a combination of field values in excess of 40 characters.

To create a splitting rule, proceed to transaction code [VOFM] and select Data Transfer | Billing Documents. Copy the standard **001 – Inv. Split (sample)**. This is done by merely overwriting the number—for example, type **900** over 001 and press ENTER. Note that you will need an access key to do development.

An example of a collective billing splitting criteria check is as follows:

```
FORM DATEN_KOPIEREN_003.
  DATA: BEGIN OF ZUK,
          MODUL(3) VALUE '003',
          VTWEG LIKE VBAK-VTWEG,
          SPART LIKE VBAK-SPART,
          VGBEL LIKE VBRP-VGBEL,
        END OF ZUK.
  ZUK-VTWEG = VBAK-VTWEG.
  ZUK-SPART = VBAK-SPART.
  IF KURGV-PERFK = SPACE.
    ZUK-VGBEL = VBRP-VGBEL.
  ENDIF.
  VBRK-ZUKRI = ZUK.
ENDFORM.
```

In the this example, table ZUK is comparing

- **VTWEG**   Distribution channel
- **SPART**   Division
- **VGBEL**   Document number of the reference document

Thus those deliveries that do not have the same entry in these fields will be assigned an individual invoice. (They will be split.)

Should a customer wish to have consolidated invoicing, his billing schedule date must resemble the dates he wishes to be billed on, and he must realize he will have his invoice split according to the splitting requirements set globally, not according to his individual requirements. The invoice split is defined per combination of document type and is not relevant to be configured per customer master or partner.

Use of Billing Splits in Billing Document Creation
One can see the reasons for an invoice split by selecting the documents one wishes to bill collectively, either from transaction code [VF04] or [VF01], as shown in Figure 7-9.

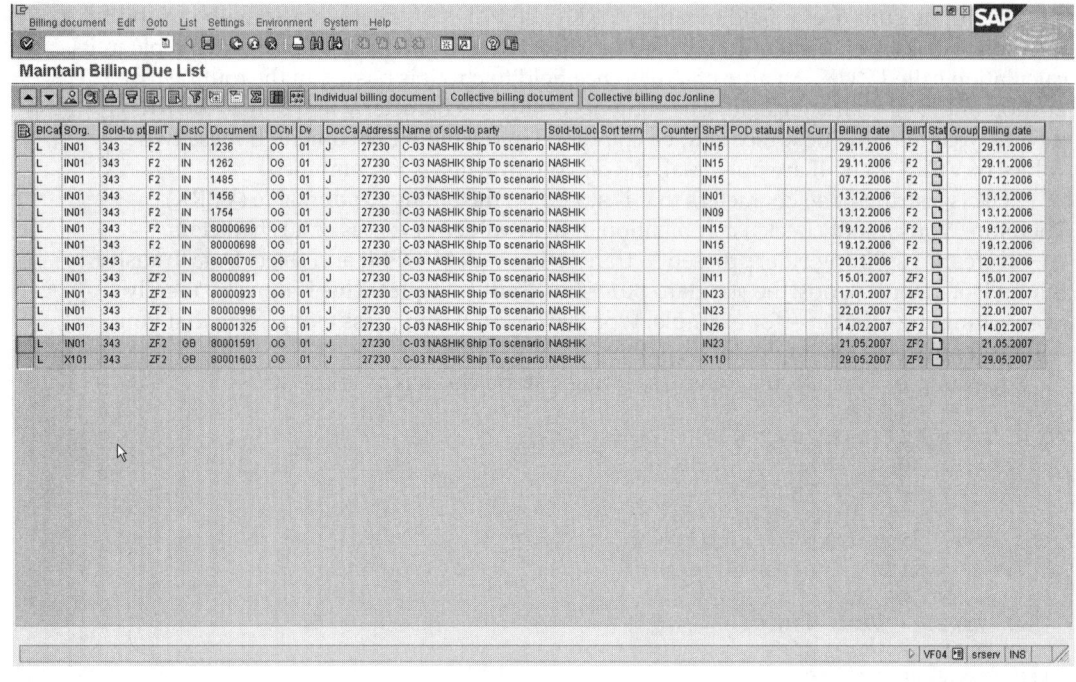

Copyright by SAP AG

FIGURE 7-9 Maintain billing due list

Remember too that you are telling SAP to combine documents by using a formula or special code; instead, whatever documents you select to be billed on a day will be collectively billed if you select the collective billing option. The system will then automatically split according to the criteria we have listed. This is true for delivery- and order-related billing—for example, it is possible to combine credit memo requests into a single credit memo.

In Figure 7-9 the last two delivery documents have been selected to be billed collectively. Should you click the Simulation icon (which looks like an abacus with 3 blue dots and 2 red dots) or alternatively press SHIFT-F5, you will see a screen similar to Figure 7-10.

Select both lines, then click the Split Analysis button and you will see the reasons why the split occurred.

Note in combination to the values in the VBRK-ZUKRI field, the system also checks the fields in VBRK, for example:

- SD document currency
- Sales organization
- Sales and distribution: pricing procedure
- Billing date for billing index
- Sales district
- Export indicator

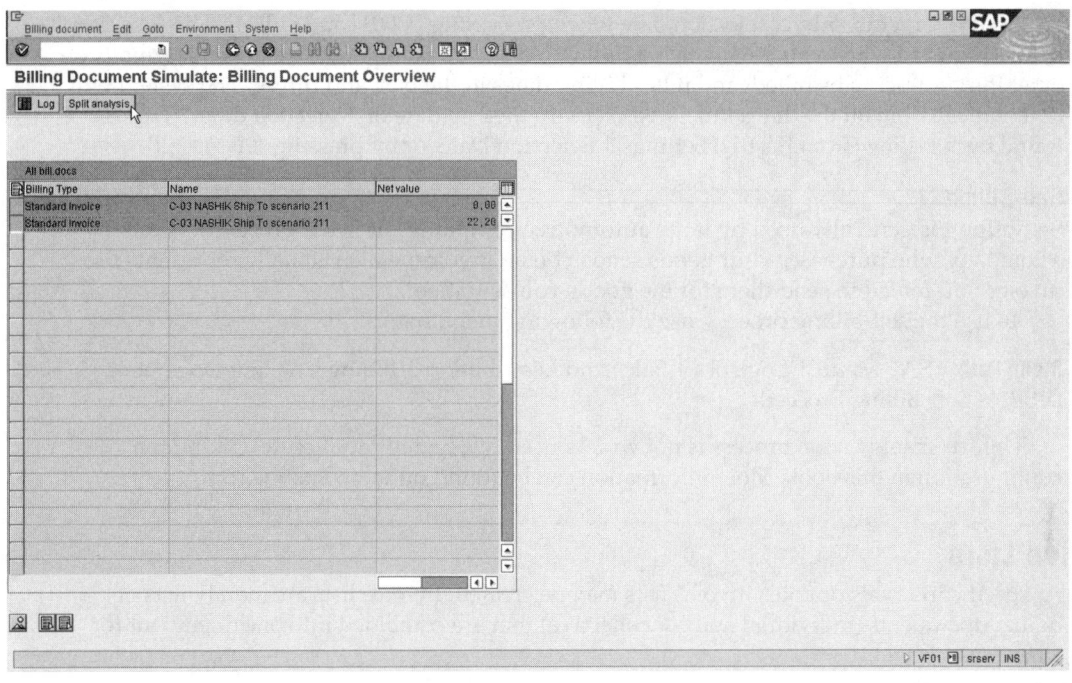

FIGURE 7-10   Selection for split analyses

- Company code
- Statistics currency
- Credit control area
- Tax departure country

Billing Document Creation and Usage

The aim of this book is the configuration and implementation of Sales and Distribution, not the system usage. However, these are the key transaction codes you may use in the system:

Menu Path   SAP menu | Logistics | Sales and Distribution | Billing | Billing Document |

- VF01 - Create
- VF02 - Change
- VF03 - Display
- VF11 - Cancel
- VF04 - Process Billing Due List
- VF06 - Background Processing - Create variant for background jobs for billing
- VFX3 - Blocked Billing Docs

Do not forget to enter a selection date when processing [VF01] and [VF04]. The selection date is required when you are invoicing billing plans. For example, let's say you manually enter the contract to be billed, and it has billing dates in the past and future. The system will automatically bill all the dates unless you specify the end date or "selection date." This is found by selecting (from [VF01]) Settings | Selection Date. or by pressing SHIFT-F7.

Self-Billing

Self-billing is generally used by large automotive companies. It is the process whereby a company who purchases your goods sends you an invoice, which actually represents the invoice you intend to send them for the goods you sent them.

To use the self-billing process, use the following menu path.

Menu Path   SAP Menu | Logistics | Sales and Distribution | Billing | Billing Document | [VSB1] - Self-Billing Proceed

Unfortunately, as the process is not widely used, we had to sacrifice describing the configuration in this book. More information can be found on www.sapww.com.

Invoice Lists

At specific intervals or dates invoice lists may be created. Invoice lists are merely lists of billing documents (individual and/or collective) that are combined into one document for a particular payer.

Creating Invoice List Types

To create an invoice list, use the following menu path.

Menu Path   SAP Customizing Implementation Guide | Sales and Distribution | Billing | Billing Documents | Invoice Lists

There are two types of invoice lists available in the SAP standard system:

For invoices and debit memos	**LR**
For credit memos	**LG**

An invoice list has header and item data. You cannot change the details of the invoices once they are in the invoice list.

For invoice lists to be used, the following prerequisites must be maintained:

- An invoice list type must be assigned to each billing type that you want to use to process invoice lists. The two invoice lists that may be used are LR and LG. Should you need an additional billing document type for invoice lists, copy the original and rename it beginning with a Z.

  Select Assign Invoice List Type to Each Billing Type. Here you assign the invoice list type to be used by the associated billing document types, as seen in Figure 7-11.

- Copying control requirements must be maintained between the billing document and the invoice list document. The system does not carry out copying at item level for billing documents. The Standard copying control requirement used in invoice lists is 016.

FIGURE 7-11
Assign an invoice list to a billing document

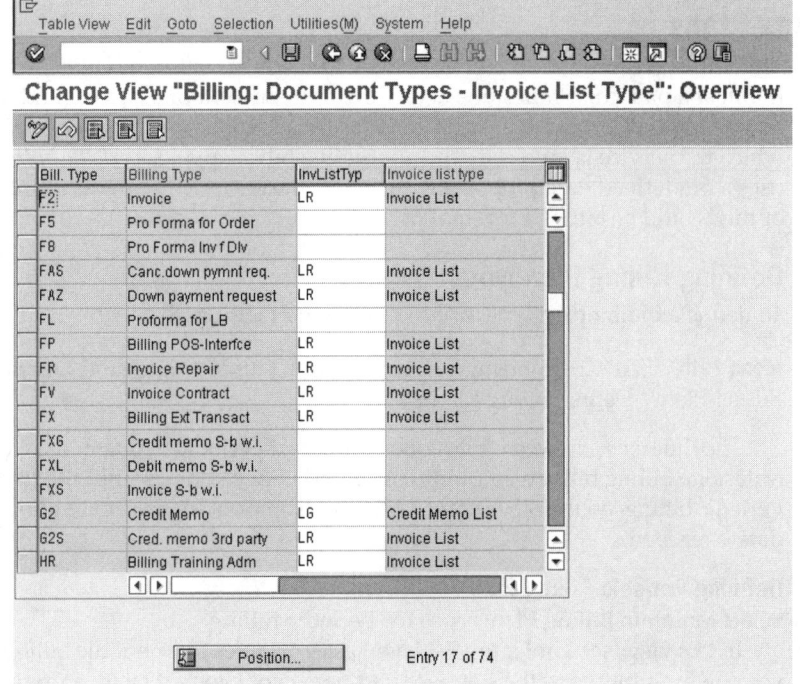

Copyright by SAP AG

- Should a factoring discount be used, use condition type RL00 or a Z copy [if created] and the factoring discount tax condition type MW15 [if required] must be maintained and placed in the pricing procedure.

  The condition type RL00 has a condition category value of R, which defines this condition type as used for invoice lists.

  For invoice lists to function, the following master data must be maintained:

- A customer calendar must be defined specifying dates on which invoice lists are to be processed—for example, once every two weeks. This is assigned to the customer's billing view in the customer master record.

- Output condition records for condition types LR00 and RD01.

We will leave the output assignments and condition type assignments in their respective determination procedures until we cover these determination sections in Chapter 9.

To create an invoice list, use the following menu path.

Menu Path SAP Menu | Logistics | Sales and Distribution | Billing | Invoice List | [VF21] - Create

Proceed with entering each billing document separately.

From within the billing document, select Header | Pricing. One is able to see the factoring discount as well as the factoring discount tax assigned to this invoice list.

Billing Plans

The SAP system uses two billing plans. One is called *milestone billing*, which is a final billing in full at a particular milestone according to items sold or services rendered. An example of this would be a project milestone, such as the completion of an architect's blueprint, for which the service is invoiced. The alternative billing plan is *periodic billing*. Periodic billing uses a predefined date proposal, which bills the customer at periodic intervals. An example of this would be billing for rental of an object.

Defining Billing Plan Types

To define a billing plan type, use the following menu path.

Menu Path   SAP Customizing Implementation Guide | Sales and Distribution | Billing | Billing Plan | Define Billing Plan Types

The difference between milestone billing and periodic billing may be described as follows. Milestone billing bills an amount distributed between dates until the total value is billed. Periodic billing, on the other hand, bills a total amount for each date until a predefined end date is reached.

Defining Periodic Billing Plan

Select Maintain Billing Plan Types for Periodic Billing.

In this view, seen in Figure 7-12, you assign values to a periodic billing plan type. To create your own, simply copy the standard and name your copy ID with a prefix of Z.

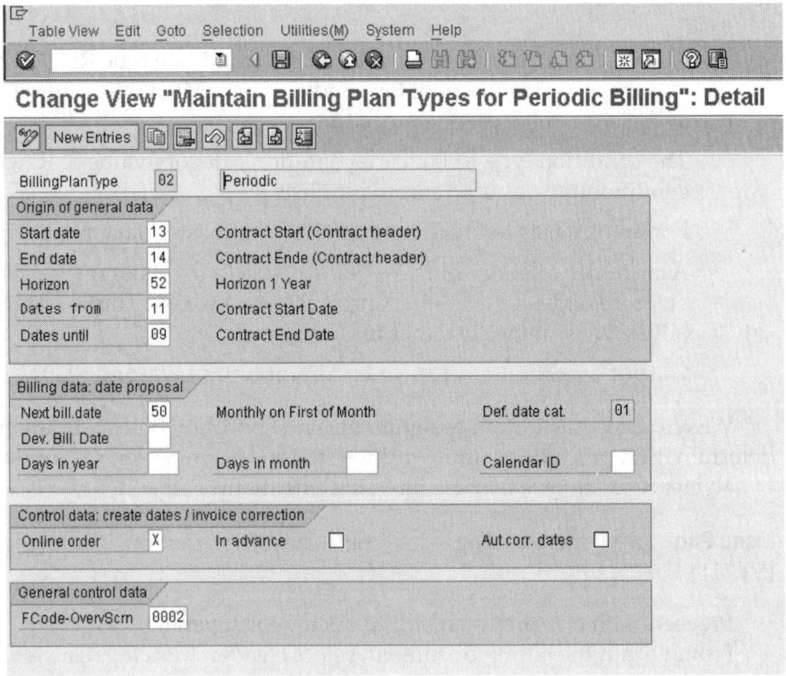

FIGURE 7-12
Maintain billing plan types for periodic billing

Note all date settings you use are not actual dates, but rather date rules. Therefore the start date is a date rule representing the contract start date.

In the origin of general data section, you assign a start date rule, which may be the start date of the rental contract, as well as an end date rule, which may be the contract's end date. The horizon is set as one year. Note that the horizon is not the end date of the billing plan; it is instead the last day that the billing plan will use to bill. The dates from and dates to rules are used to further restrict the start and end dates of the billing plan dates.

The period of the billing dates determines the frequency with which the billing dates are created in the billing plan and, in addition, whether a billing date is processed for billing on the first or last day of the month.

In the billing date: date proposal section, you define the next billing date for periodic billing. Figure 7-12 refers to "Monthly on First of Month." You may assign a deviation billing date, which is a rule that may be set to determine if the customer is billed, for example, two days prior to the billing date as determined by the system.

In the control data section, the online order field is used to set the deadlines to be created automatically in the sales order. The in advance field indicates whether the system should bill in advance. Should this indicator not be set, the system will automatically bill in arrears. The automatic correction dates field is used to automatically create a credit memo should the end date of the bill plan move closer to the start date, and for which a billing date has already been or is about to be executed.

One is then able to define which screen the system uses to display as its overview screen for a billing plan by setting the default FCODE.

Defining Milestone Billing Plan

Select Maintain Billing Plan Types for Milestone Billing.

This view, as seen in Figure 7-13, is similar to Figure 7-12. However, due to there being less data relevant for milestone billing, the only settings required here are the start date,

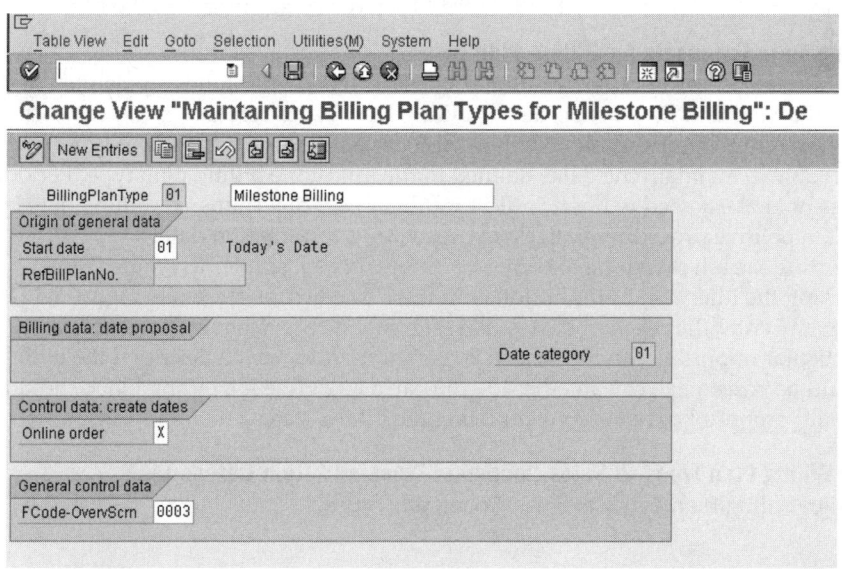

FIGURE 7-13   Maintain billing plan types for milestone billing

usually set as "Today's date" (the date of the document) and the reference bill plan number, which refers to the standard billing plan or invoice plan as configured in the PS (project systems) module.

The value of 01 in date category refers to "milestone billing" to determine the date proposals. The online order indicator determines if the system automatically creates the billing deadlines. Again, one is then able to define which screen the system displays as its overview screen by setting the default FCODE for overview screen of billing plan.

Defining Date Descriptions

Select Define Date Descriptions.

These date descriptions are merely used for informational purposes. Create a four-character alphanumeric key with a meaningful description.

Defining and Assigning Date Categories

Select Define and Assign Date Categories | Maintain Date Category for Billing Plan Type.

In this screen, as shown in Figure 7-14, assign a created date category with description to the billing plan type. In create mode you may assign a date description as previously defined, then assign the billing rules to the date category, as seen in Figure 7-15.

A value billing rule is used by the system in taking the full billing amount, such as $10,000, and dividing it up into partial amounts, such as $3,000, $2,000, $4,000, and $1,000. Alternatively, the milestone billing based as a percentage would determine percentages of the total billing amount to be billed—for example, 30 percent, 20 percent, 40 percent, and 10 percent.

The fixed date field is used to inherit the dates from the settings of the billing plan in PS (Project Systems). If, however, you wish to use a fixed date that does not fluctuate with the project milestones, then use a value of "0" here.

The billing block is used to set a billing block against all dates. This block is then removed automatically when PS confirms that a milestones has been reached. The billing type is the proposed billing type to be used for order-related billing relevant to this billing plan.

Maintaining Date Proposals for Billing Plan Types

Milestone billing has an allocation for date proposals. These milestones are defined in the settings on the Maintain Date Proposals for Billing Plan Types screen.

As seen previously, the milestone billing plan has a reference billing plan type. In this view one is able to maintain the dates defined in the milestone billing plan type. Periodic billing does not have a need to define milestone dates as it determines its billing date by following a repetitive procedure until finally reaching a termination date.

By selecting the bill plan type to copy, you'll see a screen similar to Figure 7-16.

By clicking the Maintain Dates button, you'll see a screen, as shown in Figure 7-17, in which you may enter the relevant dates and assignments in percentages or total value.

Of particular importance in this screen is the billing rule, which defines if the billing dates should be percentage or value-based. You can also define if a billing block should be automatically proposed or not after completing the billing dates.

Assigning Billing Plan Types to Sales Document Types and Item Categories

Select Assign Billing Plan Types to Sales Document Types.

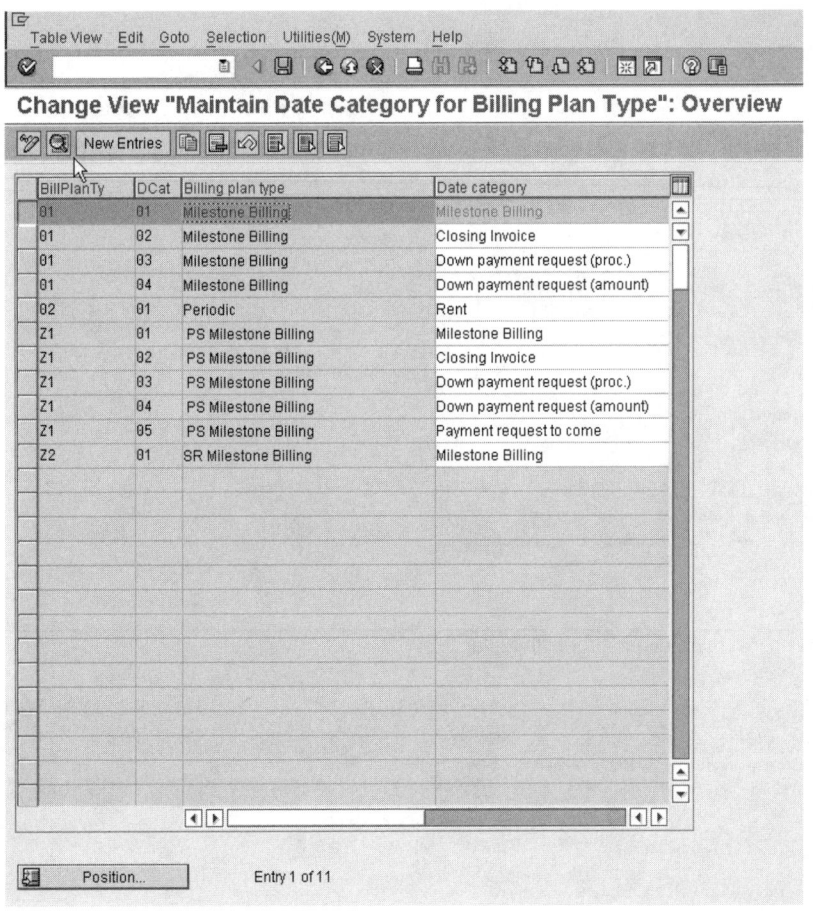

Copyright by SAP AG

FIGURE 7-14   Define and assign date categories

FIGURE 7-15
Maintain date
category

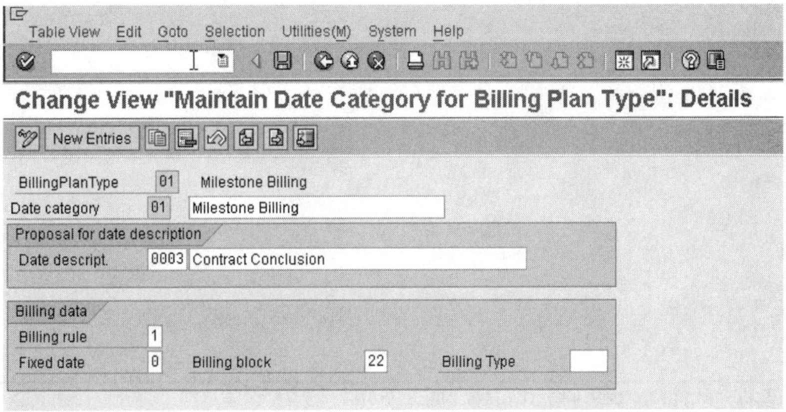

Copyright by SAP AG

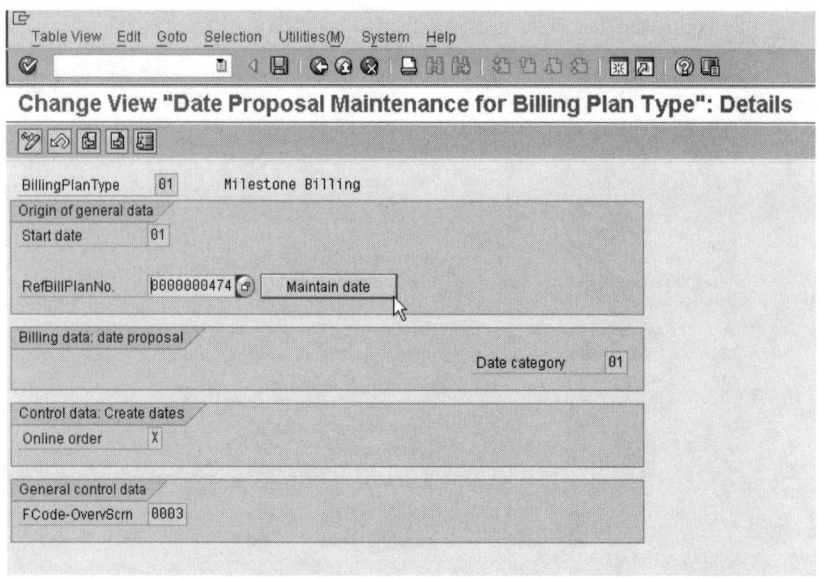

FIGURE 7-16 Date proposal maintenance for billing plan

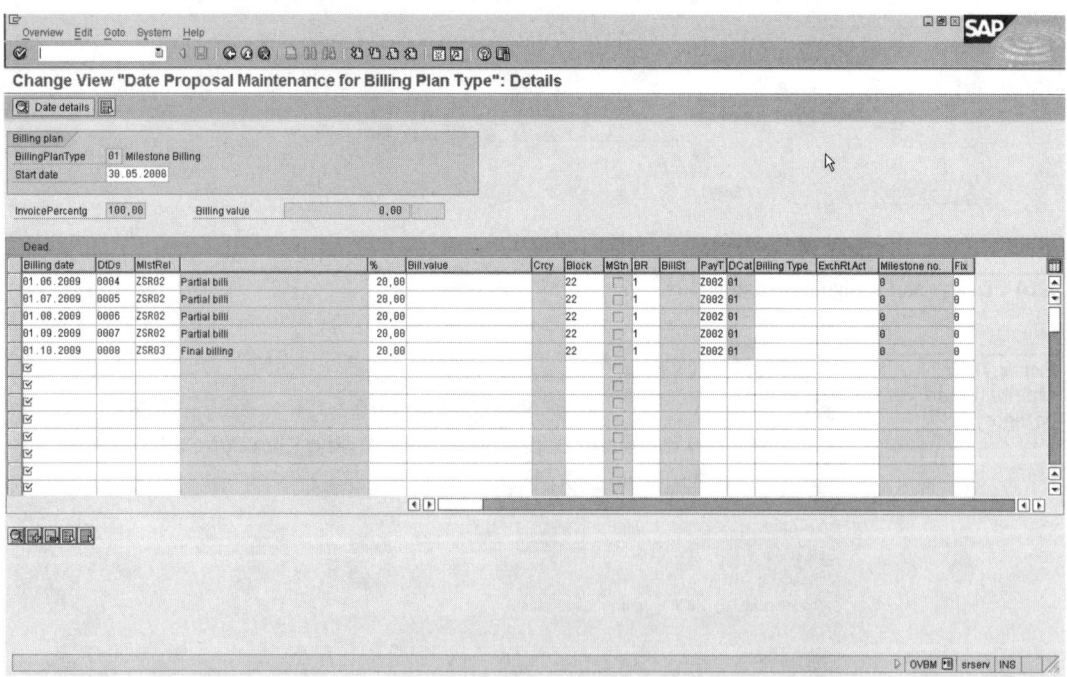

FIGURE 7-17 Maintain date proposal for billing plan

This section again is self-explanatory. One merely assigns the relevant billing plan type, be it milestone or periodic billing, to the necessary sales document types.

After assignment of the billing plan type to the sales document, select Assign Billing Plan Types to Item Categories.

As billing is carried out per item category, you can assign the relevance for billing to the sales document item. For example, the standard item category TAN would in most systems use "A," which is relevant for delivery-related billing. Other examples include item category MVN, which is a standard lease item category used for periodic billing, and item category TAO, which is created as a reference for milestone billing.

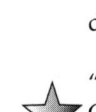

Each item category that is relevant for either of the billing plan types must be assigned a billing relevance of "I," which indicates that it's relevant for order-related billing. Assigned to the billing relevance would be the billing plan type—for example, milestone or periodic billing.

You can define the rules used in the system to define dates used in the billing plans. To define these dates, select Define Rules for Determining Dates.

The data maintained here is the same as previously defined in Chapter 4 in the section "Rules for Determining Dates." You may create these rules in either section; please refer to Chapter 4 for details.

A great OSS note on date usage and determination in billing plans is Note 537779.

It is possible to configure a periodic billing plan to not end when a contract ends. This can cause confusion when looking at reports.

Rebate Agreements

A rebate agreement, is an agreement between the business and a customer. This agreement takes the form of a special discount paid retroactively to the customer. This discount is based on the sales volume for the customer over a specific time period. The rebate is only relevant if the customer purchases the required sales volume.

The rebate agreement has separate condition records for each product the customer buys. These condition records specify the rebate amount or percentage due to the customer for each product. One is also able to specify a pricing scale so that the customer can earn a better rebate by ordering more products.

Because rebates are always paid retroactively, the system keeps track of all billing documents that are relevant for rebate processing. This includes standard invoices, as well as credit and debit memos related to the rebate.

The system may also post accruals automatically so that the accumulated value of a rebate is recorded for accounting purposes. A rebate agreement is finally settled when a credit memo is issued to the customer for the accumulated rebate total.

Defining Rebate Agreement Types

To define rebate agreement types, use the following menu path.

Menu Path SAP Customizing Implementation Guide | Sales and Distribution | Billing | Rebate Processing | Rebate Agreements | Define Agreement Types

The rebate agreement type determines which data the system is to automatically propose for the rebate agreement. The SAP standard has the following agreement types:

Agreement	Description
0001	Group Rebate
0002	Material Rebate
0003	Customer Rebate
0004	Hierarchy Rebate
0005	Independent of Sales Vol.
00E1	Exp. Group Rebate
00E2	Exp. Material Rebate
00E3	Exp. Customer Rebate
00E4	Exp. Hierarchy Rebate
00E5	Exp. Revenue Independent

We will use the example seen in Figure 7-18 of a material rebate that is rebate agreement type 0002.

By now you should be able to understand the different screen fields available for input. You may always refer to the SAP help by placing the cursor in the field and pressing F1 for further information. I will only explain a field if it has an unusual use or if there is some additional value to add.

To start, the default data for the validity period and payment method are self-explanatory.

The control data of a rebate includes the condition type group assigned to the rebate type. In our example, we are using the condition type group 0002.

The condition type group is not to be confused with the condition type used in pricing. A condition type group is not a condition type. The condition type group generally has more than one condition type assigned to it; however, it is possible to assign only one condition type to the condition type group. We will cover the assignment a little later. (Condition type groups are also described extensively in Chapter 8.)

The verification level is a key indicator that determines the level of detail one sees when displaying totals for a rebate agreement.

The manual accruals order type is actually a sales document type, which is assigned to the rebate agreement and is used in the manual accruals in a rebate agreement. Note that the sales document type assigned here should have an order-relevant billing type assigned to it. The SAP standard uses the billing type B4 for the sales document type R4.

Should you wish to make manual payments of the rebate to the recipient, you may indicate this in the payment procedure. When a manual payment is carried out, the system automatically creates a credit memo request of the type specified in the partial settlement field for the specified amounts. Thus, when the system carries out the final settlement, all partial payments are taken into account and the remaining balance is paid.

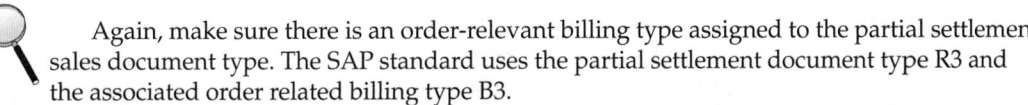

FIGURE 7-18
Rebate
agreement
types

Again, make sure there is an order-relevant billing type assigned to the partial settlement sales document type. The SAP standard uses the partial settlement document type R3 and the associated order related billing type B3.

Be sure to indicate that the system must reverse the accruals. This will ensure the system will reverse the accruals up to the amount specified in the manual payment. Should the accruals not be as high as the payment to be made, the system will reverse whatever accruals it has.

In the final settlement area, you must ensure the credit memo request for final settlement is assigned to the final settlement field. (Again, be sure that this credit memo request has the associated order-relevant billing type assigned to it in the sales document type.) The SAP standard uses the credit memo request B1 with billing type B1. One may also assign a minimum status, which is the status the rebate agreement must reach before the final settlement may be carried out.

You can't enter the following statuses as a minimum status for final settlement:

- **C**   Credit memo request already created for settlement
- **D**   Final settlement of agreement already carried out

Now that the rebate agreement type has been defined, you may proceed to the definition of condition type groups.

Condition Type Groups

To define condition type groups, use the following menu path.

Menu Path   SAP Customizing Implementation Guide | Sales and Distribution | Billing | Rebate Processing | Rebate Agreements | Condition Type Groups

In this activity you define the condition type group that is to be assigned to the rebate agreement. Should you need to create your own condition type group, you may copy and change the name using the prefix Z.

Condition type groups are also used, for example, in sales deals.

If you create a condition type group by copying one, the system does not copy the associated assignments of condition types. Thus you will need to make all the necessary assignments manually.

Assigning Condition Type/Table to Condition Type Groups

Select Assign Condition Types/Tables to Condition Type Groups.

In this activity, as seen in Figure 7-19, you can assign the condition types as found on the pricing procedure to the condition type group as found on the rebate agreement type. The Cntr, or counter number column, represents the access steps or the sequence in which the condition types will be determined. The No. column is actually equal to the pricing condition table number. (Please refer to "Pricing" in Chapter 8 for further details.) The condition type group 0004 in Figure 7-19 will use pricing condition types B004 and B005, therefore both condition types must be found in the pricing procedure.

Assigning Condition Type Groups and Agreement Types

Select Assign Condition Type Groups to Rebate Agreement Types.

As shown in Figure 7-20, you are presented with a list of agreement types as created in the system. These could be rebate agreements or sales deals or promotions and you are now able to assign the relevant condition type group.

You can now proceed with creating and maintaining the condition types and pricing procedures. Select Condition Technique for Rebate Processing.

However, we will not be dealing with the actual configuration necessary here. This is due to the fact that pricing procedures, the determination thereof, conditions types, tables, and access sequences are all dealt with in detail in Chapter 8. There are not many differences, other than what is described in the following paragraphs, between the determination and maintenance of those conditions used by rebates and those of standard conditions.

What is important to note here is that on the pricing procedure used with rebates, the condition subtotal (SubTo field), which is to be used as the basis for the rebate, should contain the value 7. This will ensure the value held in this line of the pricing procedure is passed to the field KOMP-BONBA, which will be used as the basis for the rebate in further processing.

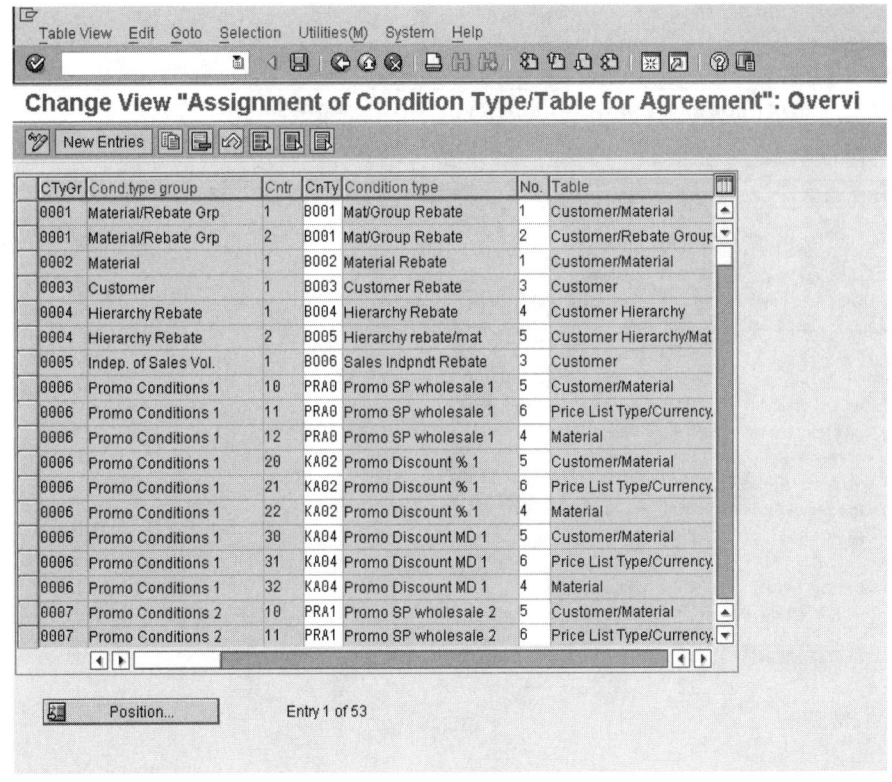

Figure 7-19 Assigning condition types/tables to condition type groups

Generally, the same value as used for the net value or net price for the item is also used for this rebate basis. You may want to have two lines in the pricing procedure, one for the basis of the rebate with sub-total 7, and another for the net value with sub-total 2.

The requirement 024 may be assigned to the condition type in the pricing procedure, which determines the condition is only accessed in the billing document.

Also note when defining the condition types used in rebate processing that our example, B002, must use condition class C (expense reimbursement).

As seen in Figure 7-21, the condition types used in rebate processing are slightly different from the standard condition types used, for example, for pricing or discounts, in that there is less data to maintain, while also including two additional rebate settings.

The two rebate settings used as follows:

- The rebate procedure indicates if the condition is dependent or independent of sales volume.

- The Provision Con field, which is actually the accruals correction procedure, indicates if accruals must be corrected when a partial rebate payment has been made.

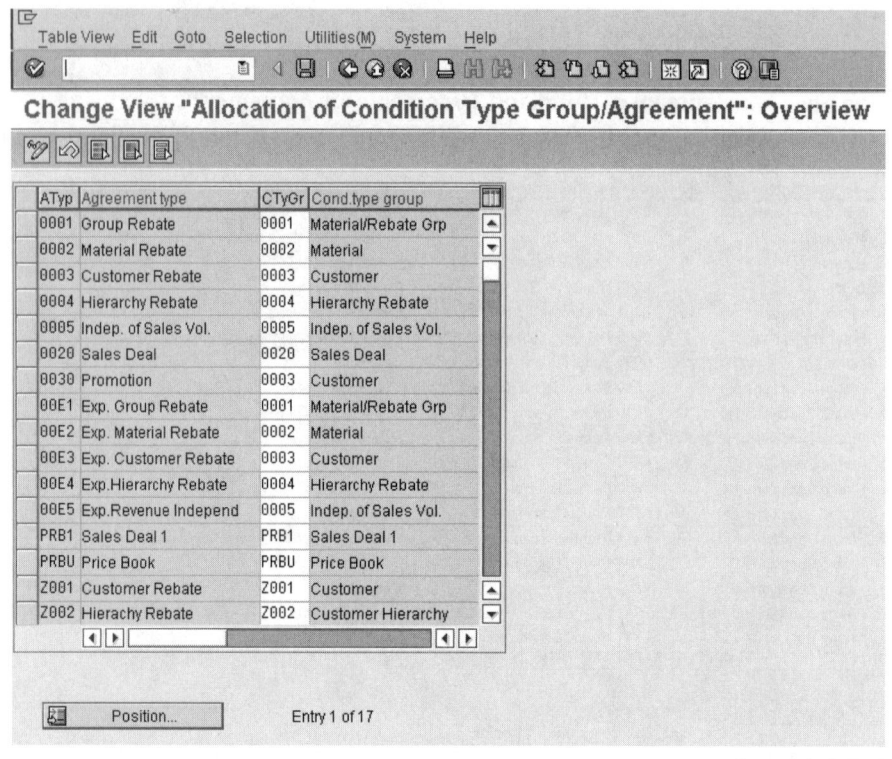

FIGURE 7-20   Assigning condition type groups to rebate agreement types

Account Determination for Rebates

Select Account Determination for Rebates.

Account determination and assignment will be dealt with in detail in Chapter 8. There are no significant differences between standard account determination rules and assignments for standard condition types and rebates other than the following.

Rebate condition types must have an account key assigned to them in the pricing procedure used by the sales document type for orders and billings. One account key is assigned for revenues and the opposite account key is assigned for accruals. These account keys are assigned individual general ledger accounts.

The SAP system uses the revenue account key ERB and the accrual account key ERU, as shown in Figure 7-22.

Selecting Billing Documents for Rebate Processing

Select Activate Rebate Processing | Select Billing Documents for Rebate Processing.

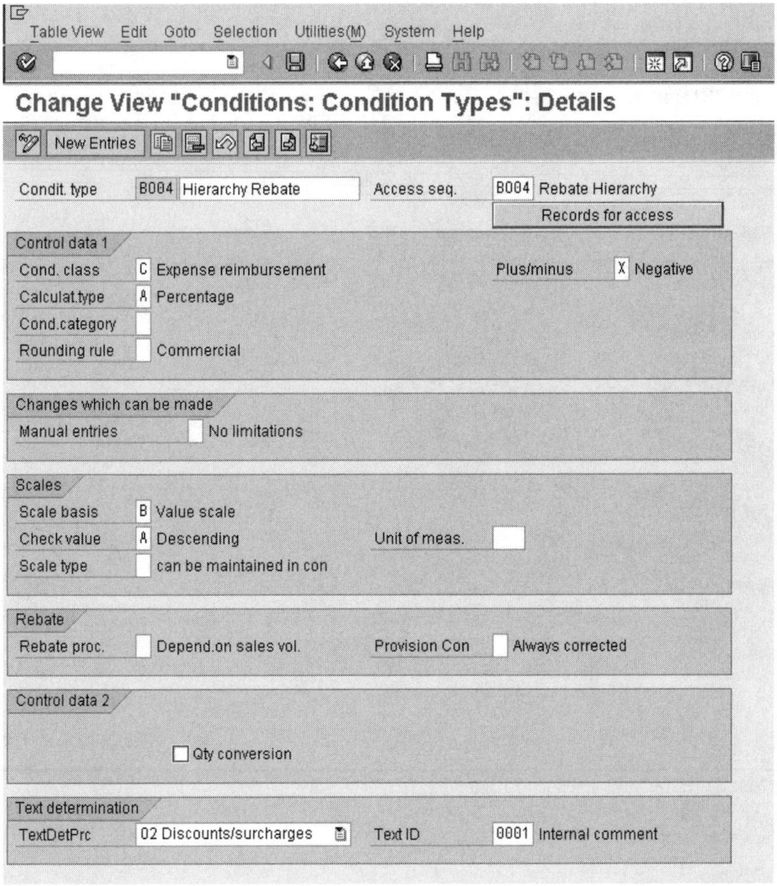

Copyright by SAP AG

FIGURE 7-21 Defining condition types (rebate)

Not all billing documents should be relevant for rebate processing. For example, it would not make sense to indicate a pro forma invoice as relevant for rebates.

However, it would make sense to indicate the standard billing document types F2 and BV, for example, as well as the associated credit memos—for example, G2.

You may not want the system to use debit notes for rebate processing. Or on the other hand, should you wish a debit note to increase the revenue for certain transactions, you may create your own new debit note request, as relevant for rebates, as well as create a new debit note billing type. And you can ensure this billing type is indicated as rebate relevant.

Activating Rebate Processing

Select Activate Rebate Processing | Activate Rebate Processing for Sales Organizations.

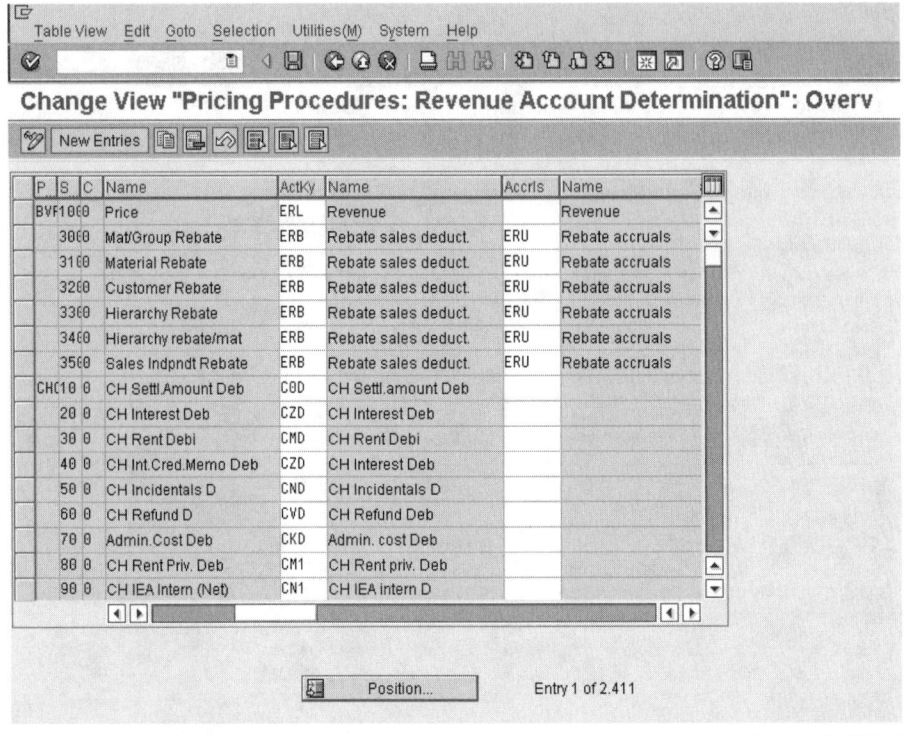

FIGURE 7-22   Account assignment keys ERB and ERU

One now activates the relevant sales organizations for rebate agreements, as shown in Figure 7-23.

Material Rebate Groups

Select Define Material Rebate Group.

These material rebate groups are merely an additional field that SAP offers in order for you to group together certain materials. This grouping of certain materials allows you to use this field and its value in a condition record as opposed to listing materials individually. Therefore, one may create a low rebate amount (condition record) for materials with a rebate group "Z1," followed by a medium amount "Z2," followed by a high amount "Z3."

The value of this MVKE-BONUS field should be maintained in the Sales Organization Data 2 view in the material master record.

Rebate processing is now configured. You must proceed to the SAP Easy Access Menu and maintain the necessary data relevant to rebate agreements.

Creating Rebate Agreements

To create rebate agreements, use the following menu path.

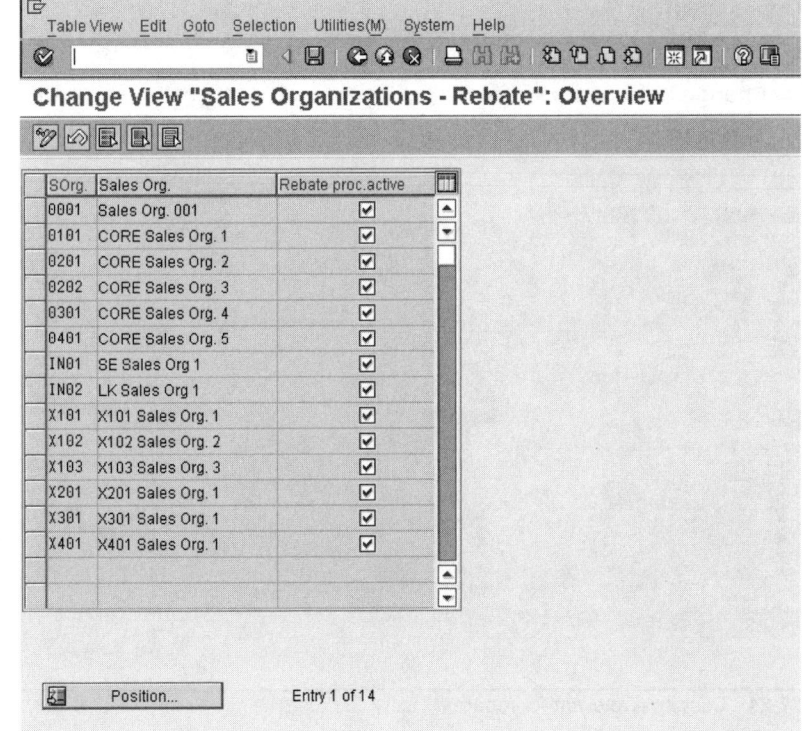

FIGURE 7-23
Activating rebate
agreements by
sales organization

Menu Path SAP Menu I Logistics I Sales and Distribution I Master Data I Agreements I Rebate Agreement I

The transactions codes related to Rebate Agreement processing are:

- [VBO1] - Create
- [VBO2] - Change
- [VBO3] - Display
- [VB(D] - Extend

In Create [VB02] enter the agreement type—for example, 0002.

In the overview screen, enter the necessary details including the rebate recipient. The system is able to use the Sold-to Party or Ship-to Party as well as the payer as the rebate recipient.

Be sure to indicate on the customer master record that the payer/customer is relevant for rebates. This is done on the billing document tab of the customer master record as shown in Figure 7-24.

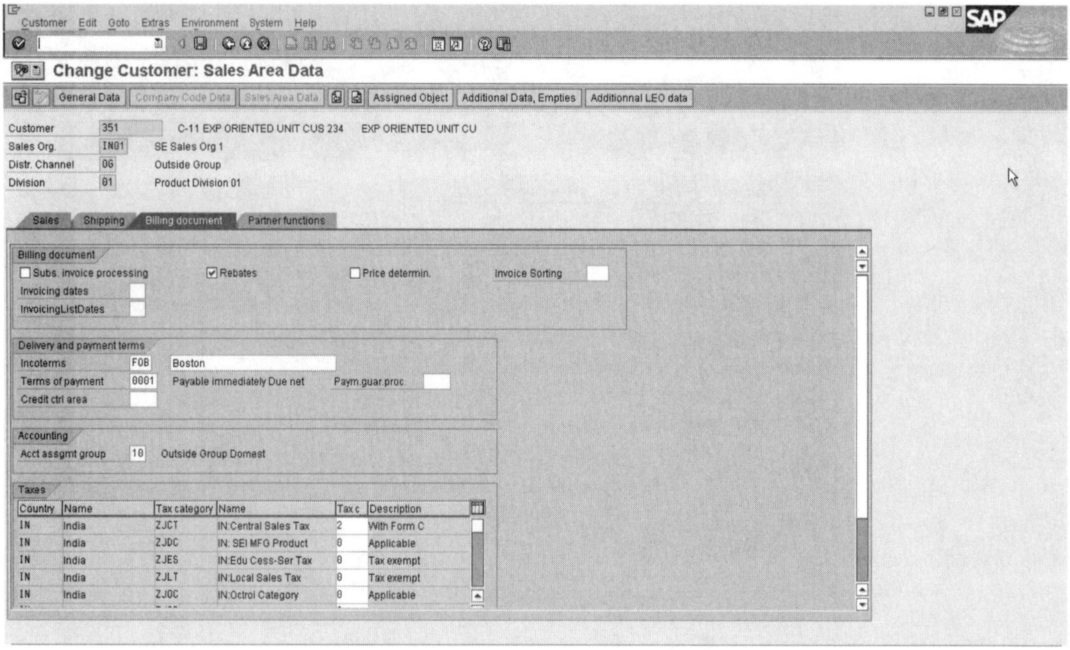

FIGURE 7-24 Customer relevant for rebates

Then click on the conditions button in the creation of the rebate agreement. This will take you through to an overview screen, seen in Figure 7-25, where you may enter details of the material, the rate, and accruals.

You can see an overview of the materials rebate data by selecting the condition record line and clicking Display. In this overview screen you'll find the material for settlement field, as seen in Figure 7-26. This field is important, specifically for rebates for which a material group rather than a material is used.

Should you use a rebate agreement that does not use materials as the basis for the rebate but instead uses, for example, a customer and material group, you would need to define a material the system may use in order to process the relevant credit memo requests. The system would then take all necessary data from this material for settlement field to create the credit memo requests and subsequent credit memo. So you should ensure the material for settlement field has the correct master data maintained—for example, account assignment, tax determination sales details, etc.

You can then save the agreement and create the sales documents for the sold to party for which rebates are relevant.

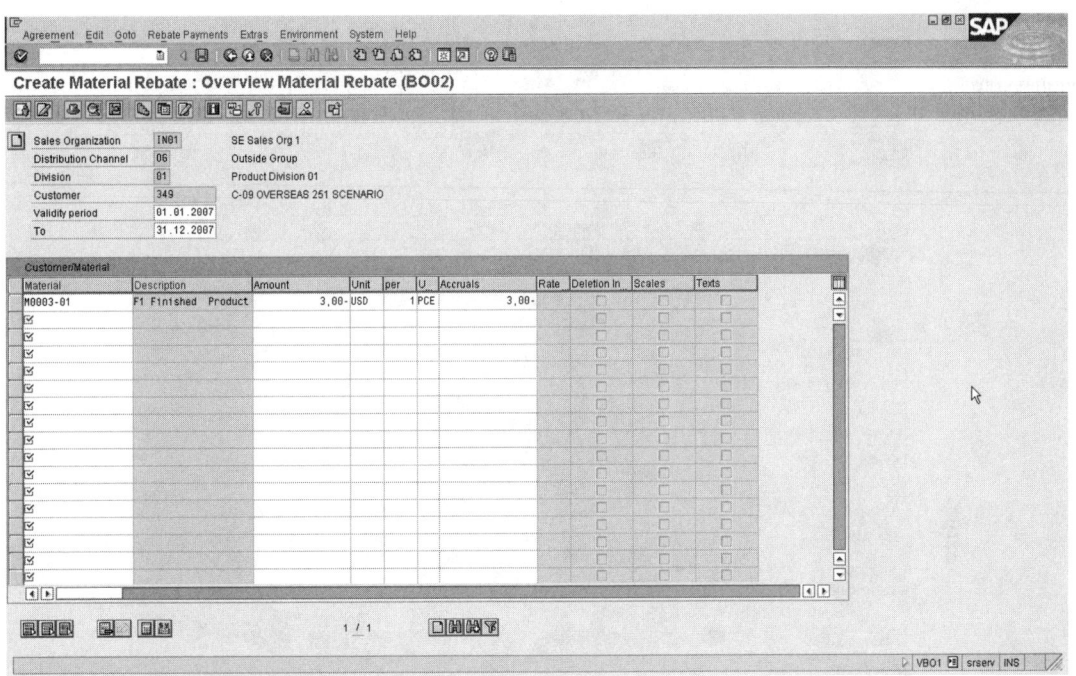

Copyright by SAP AG

FIGURE 7-25   Create rebate conditions

After creating and billing the sales documents, you may proceed back to the rebate agreement [VB02] and click the Sum button to display business volume. This will then display all sales orders created for the associated rebate and all relevant rebate basis figures. The setting in verification level determines what level of data you see. Click the Verification Level button, then click the Scope button. You are then able to select your data view, as seen in Figure 7-27.

By ensuring the agreement status indicator is set to the minimum status required for settlement, as seen in Figure 7-28, and by clicking the Execute Settlement button, one is able to automatically create a credit memo request for rebate settlement.

You can then proceed in creating the credit memo to settle the rebate amount.

Retroactive Rebate Processing

You can create a rebate agreement with a validity period starting in the past. Note when maintaining a retroactive agreement that the system does not post accruals for billing documents created in the past.

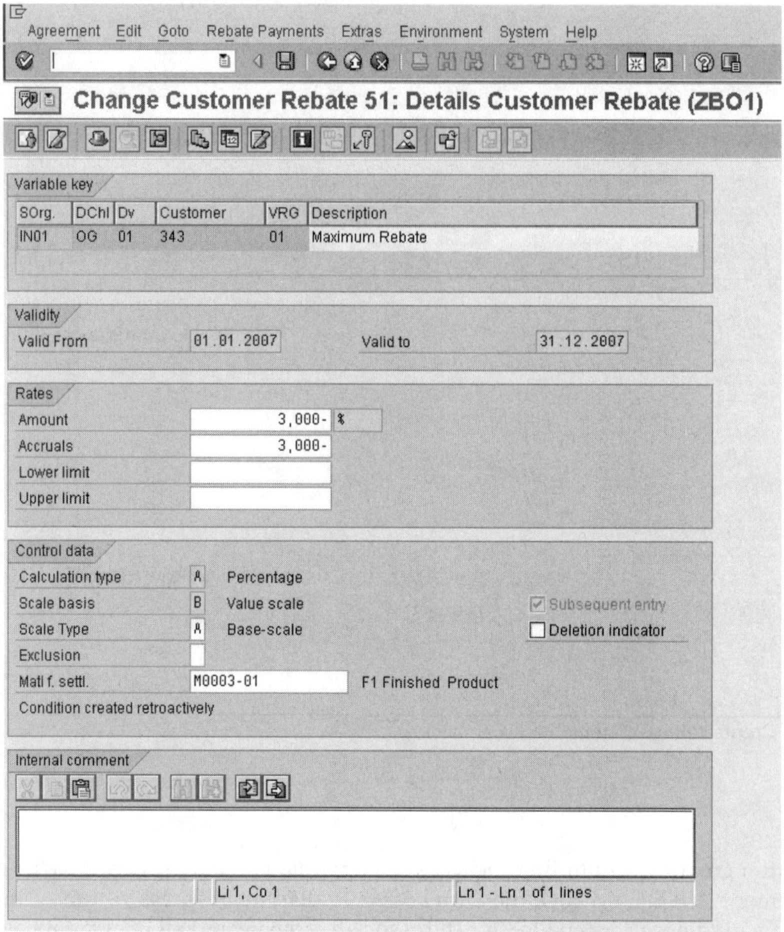

FIGURE 7-26 Details of condition record (note Matl. f. settl field)

Select Compare Rebate Basis And Correct Accruals in the IMG. With report RV15B002 you can check a specific rebate agreement with regards to the amount due for rebate to the accrual amount posted. These values may differ if you implement rebate processing retrospectively and thus wishes to take into account old billing documents. You may post a rebate correction request to correct the accruals.

Should you reset rebate processing or alter the pricing procedures, the subtotals used to calculate the rebate in the billing documents may not be available. If this is the case, you may select Recalculate Subtotals for Rebate Processing in the IMG.

This is merely a program RV15B003, which is executed with the selection criteria as the desired billing document number range.

Following this execution of the program, one will need to restructure the billing rebate index. The rebate index is used to settle retroactive rebate agreements. Should you change one of the following determining factors you will need to restructure the index:

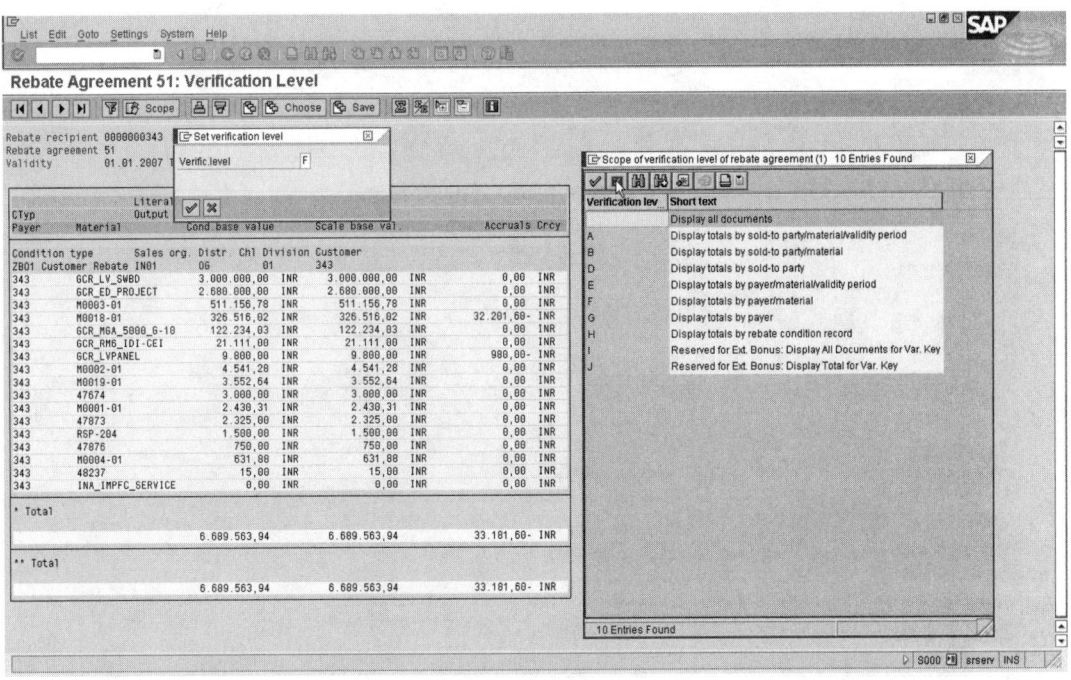

Copyright by SAP AG

FIGURE 7-27 View rebate agreement details

- New rebate relevance of sales organizations
- New rebate relevance of billing types
- New rebate relevance of payers
- Creation or inclusion of new accesses for rebate processing

To re-create the rebate index, select Create Billing Index.

Enter the parameters for the desired update, that is, the billing document number range as well as the scheduled run dates. Note that this updates the index of table VBOX—SD Document: Billing Document: Rebate Index. The system uses this index, which is updated once the billing document is released to accounting, to determine *any* documents that may be relevant for rebates. The document need not have a rebate condition at the time of the update.

One is also able to re-create the setup of statistical data. This is useful if there was an error in the statistical indicator assignments to the customer or material and/or the sales area. Standard SAP uses the information structure S060 for rebates. Select Simulate and Execute Setup of Statistical Data.

 You may wish to refer to the following SAP notes on rebates: SAP Note 75778 is a great note on rebate processing configuration and SAP Note 410579 is the rebate processing FAQ.

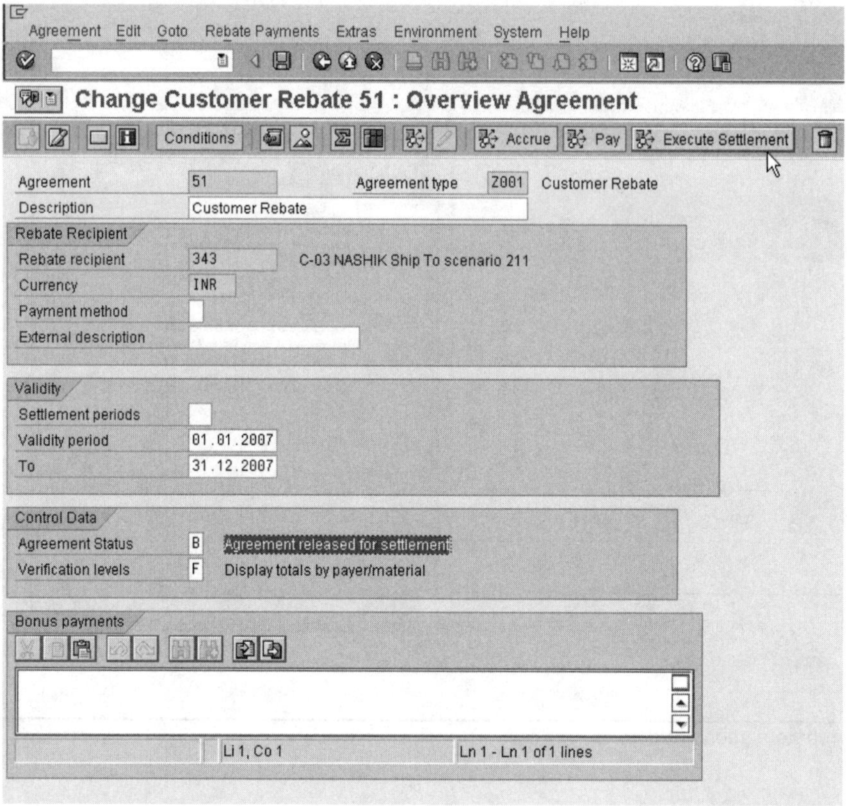

Copyright by SAP AG

FIGURE 7-28   Change rebate agreement

Inter-company Business Processing

By assigning sales organizations and plants, you create a link between sales organizations and company codes. This means that it is possible to sell goods from a plant linked to a different company code than the company code to which the sales organization is linked.

Inter-company Sales Transaction

An inter-company sale transaction occurs when a sale occurs and the sales organization belongs to a different company code than that of the delivering plant. To create inter-company sales transactions, use the following menu path.

Menu Path   SAP Customizing Implementation Guide | Sales and Distribution | Billing | Inter-company Billing

An inter-company sale may be described with the following example. The customer orders stock from the sales organization (for example 3001). The sales organization (3001) belongs to a company code, for example, 3000. The sales organization (3001) then creates the sales order and indicates the delivering plant as a plant that belongs to a different company code, for example, company code 1000.

The sales organization (3001) then invoices the customer for materials purchased. The system automatically creates an inter-company billing document at the same time as the customer's billing document is created. This inter-company invoice is sent from the delivering plant to the selling sales organization.

This is defined as an inter-company sales transaction.

The result of an inter-company sales transaction is that the system will create two billing documents. The first is the standard customer billing document that is sent from the sales organization to the customer who receives the goods. The second is the inter-company billing document that is sent from the delivering plant to the sales organization.

Inter-company Stock Transfer

When dealing with different company codes, you may find a need to transfer stock between company codes. Should the stock be transferred within the same company code, there is no need for an inter-company transaction. However, should the stock be transferred between different company codes, then there is a transference of value and cost and thus an inter-company sale.

For example, company code 3000, which has plant 3000, creates a purchase order to purchase stock from plant 1000 based in company code 1000. The stock is then delivered to plant 3000. Company code 1000 then creates an inter-company invoice and bills company code 3000 for the stock.

This process is defined as an *inter-company stock transfer.*

Defining Order Types for Inter-company Sales Transaction Billing

To define order types, use the following menu path.

Menu Path   SAP Customizing Implementation Guide | Sales and Distribution | Billing | Inter-company Billing | Define Order Types for Inter-company Billing

In order for an inter-company sales transaction to be carried out, you need to define which sales document types may be used in conjunction with inter-company sales. The SAP standard for an inter-company sale billing document type is IV. Thus, should inter-company sales be permitted for sales document type OR, you must assign an inter-company billing type for example IV to this sales document.

Assigning Organizational Units by Plant

Select Assign Organizational Units by Plant.

In this process one assigns a sales area to the delivering plant, as seen in Figure 7-29. A sales area is the combination of sales organization, distribution channel and division. The delivering plant then uses this assignment to process the inter-company billing.

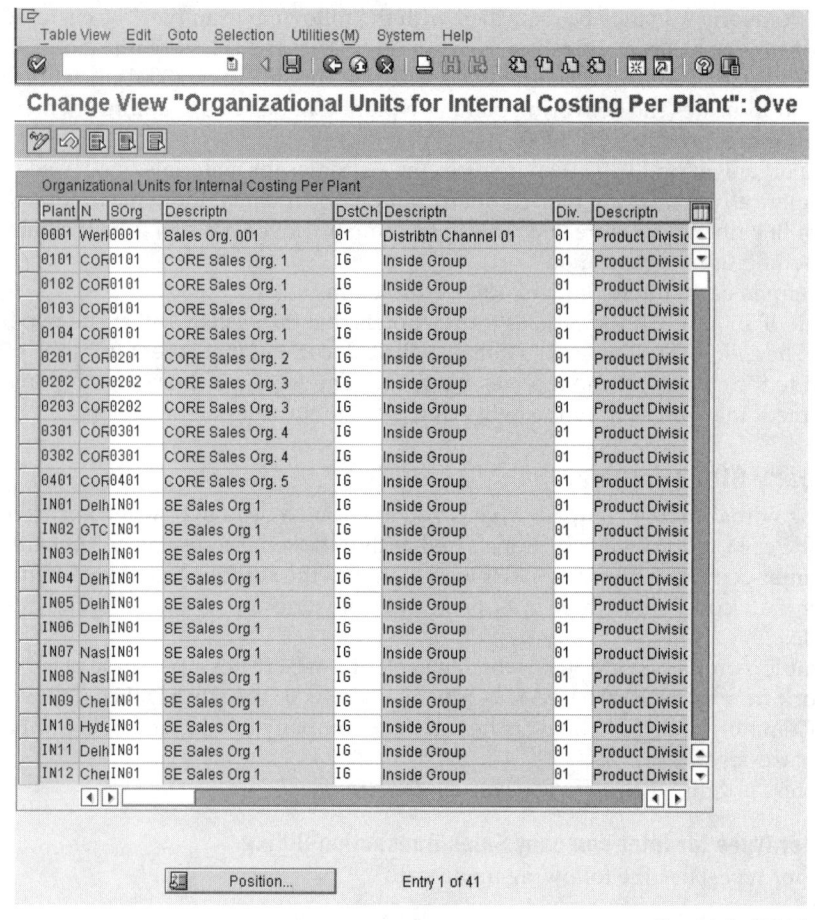

FIGURE 7-29   Assigning organizational units by plant

Defining Internal Customer Number by Sales Organization

Select Define Internal Customer Number by Sales Organization.

In this step you can define the internal customer number, which represents the sales organization that is to be invoiced in inter-company sales processing, as seen in Figure 7-30.

This customer number must be created in the system for the sales area specified.

For inter-company sales processing to be functional there remains a number of master data maintenance tasks that must be done.

Following is a checklist for inter-company sales processing:

- The enterprise structure must be maintained correctly—that is, the plants must be assigned to the correct company codes, as well as to the correct combination of sales organization and distribution channel.

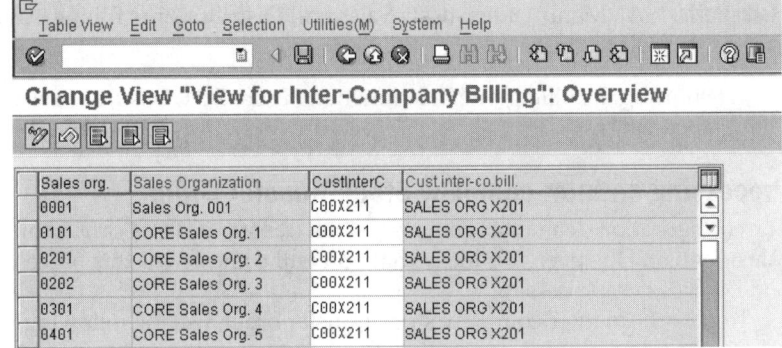

- The inter-company customer numbers must be assigned to the relevant sales organizations
- The delivering plant must be assigned the sales organization.
- The material to be sold must exist in the original and delivering plant.
- The sales order must be relevant for inter-company sales and have an assigned billing document type.
- The copy control rules must be defined between the standard invoice—for example, F2—and the inter-company invoice—for example, IV.
- The pricing procedure may have a special condition type assigned to it. This special condition type may represent the price to the inter-company sales organization. Or it may represent a special discount offered to the inter-company sales organization for the materials sold. The SAP standard system has the following condition types:
  - **PI01**   To represent inter-company price as quantity dependant
  - **PI02**   To represent inter-company condition as a percentage

Processing an Inter-company Sales Transaction

To create an inter-company sales transaction, proceed with creating the standard sales order. On the sales order, change the delivering plant at line item level. Create a delivery for the new shipping point represented for the delivering plant. Proceed with the delivery functions of picking, packing, and posting goods issue. Create an external invoice, this invoice is the invoice as sent to the customer. Then create an inter-company invoice. This invoice will represent the billing document between the delivering plant and the selling sales organisation.

An internal inter-company invoice may be created by entering the delivery number again for processing when using transaction code [VF01] or using the following menu path.

Menu Path   SAP Menu I Logistics I Sales and Distribution I Billing I Billing Document I Create

You can select documents due for inter-company billing by using the billing due list (transaction code [VF04]) or by using the following menu path.

Menu Path   SAP Menu I Logistics I Sales and Distribution I Billing I Billing Document I Process Billing Due List

When using the billing due list, shown in Figure 7-31, be sure to select the inter-company billing documents.

Processing an Inter-company Stock Transfer Order

The configuration of an inter-company stock transfer order is carried out in Materials Management. However, it is likely that you will come across this process in standard Sales and Distribution processing.

To process an inter-company stock transfer order, use the following menu path.

Menu Path   SAP Menu I Logistics I Materials Management I Purchasing I Purchase Order I Create I Vendor/Supplying Plant Known [ME21N]

Enter in the details of the supplying plant and the organizational data and press ENTER. You will now be able to enter the materials and the plant which is to receive the items.

After completion of the stock transfer order, the system will process a delivery followed by an inter-company invoice. Do not forget that the material must be created in both sales areas and both plants.

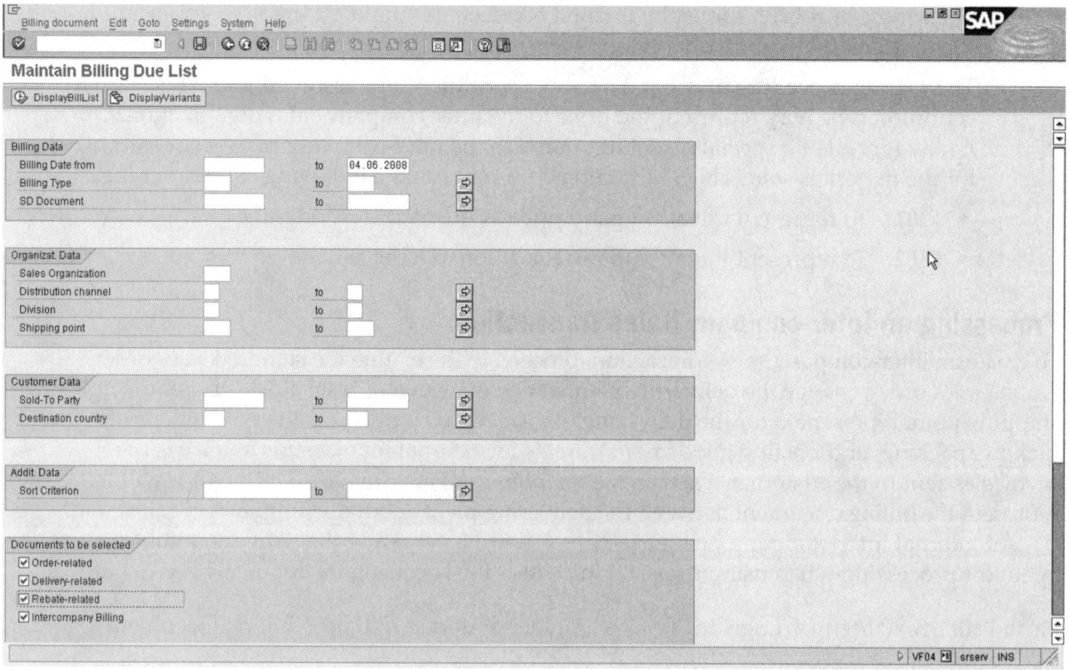

Copyright by SAP AG

FIGURE 7-31   Maintaining the billing due list

Payment Terms

Payment terms are the terms of payment the company offers the customer. Based upon the payment term a discount may be given for prompt payment. If the customer does not pay, it is possible to institute dunning, whereby the customer is "dunned," that is, sent letters in a level of severity in accordance with the time period that he has not responded or paid. Although this topic belongs in the finance module, you will deal with payment terms a lot and need to know where to access the data within them.

Configuring Payment Terms

To configure the terms of payment, use the following menu path.

Menu Path   SAP Customizing Implementation Guide I Financial Accounting I Accounts Receivable and Accounts Payable I Business Transactions I Incoming Invoices/Credit Memos I Maintain Terms of Payment [OBB8]

If you select an item, then click the Details button, you will see a screen similar to Figure 7-32.

It is possible to have an installment payment with a payment term too. Use the following menu path to get to a screen similar to Figure 7-33.

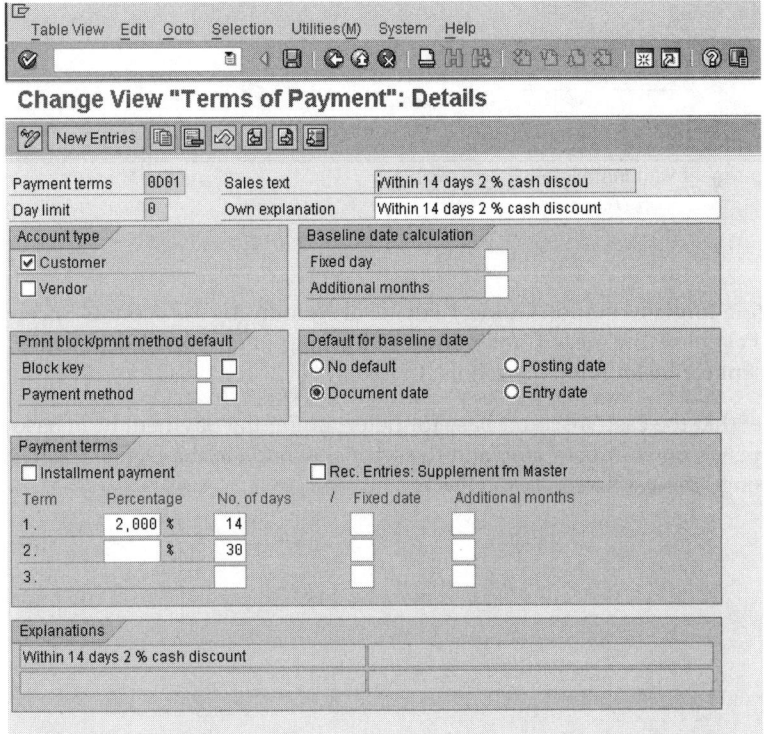

Copyright by SAP AG

FIGURE 7-32   Terms of payment

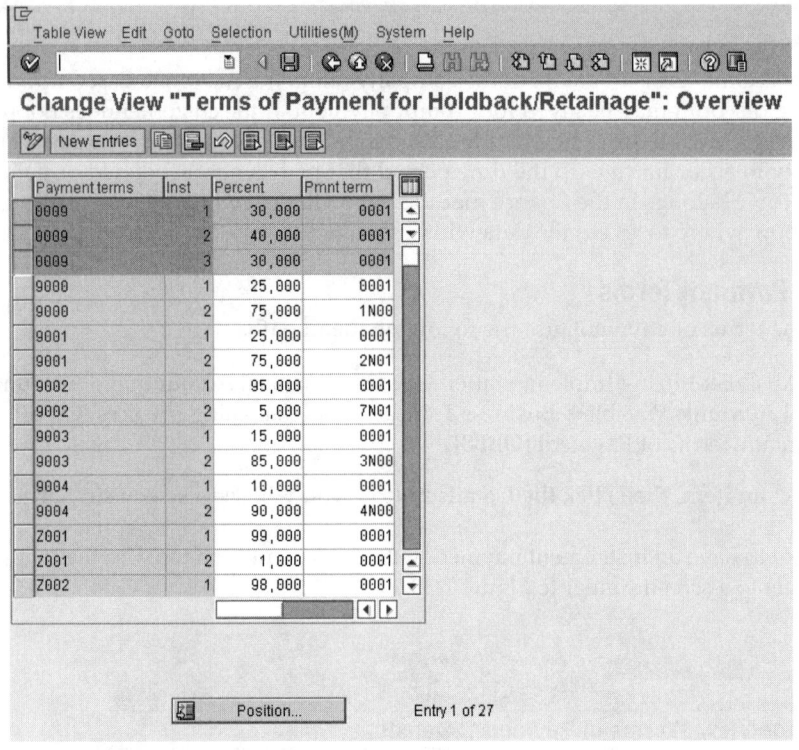

FIGURE 7-33   Terms of payment with installment

Menu Path
SAP Customizing Implementation Guide I Financial Accounting I Accounts Receivable
and Accounts Payable I Business Transactions I Incoming Invoices/Credit Memos I Define
Terms of Payment for Installment Payments [OBB9]

Don't forget that the cash discount base for determining the payment term base should
be set. This depends on your company and the setting is made in the Define Cash Discount
Base for Incoming Invoices screen in the IMG.

8

CHAPTER

Pricing and Taxes

This chapter covers the condition technique in detail, as well as pricing structure. We look at formulas and routines as well as requirements. We implement tax determination and account assignment.

The Condition Technique

The condition technique is the single largest configuration technique used in the Sales and Distribution module. Understanding how the condition technique operates will allow you to understand how the system reacts in different scenarios.

The condition technique is used in pricing, text determination, output determination, and material determination—basically anywhere you have a condition record. The condition technique is the technique that SAP uses to find a choice from among a number of alternatives. SAP makes the choice based on conditions, hence the name "condition technique."

For example, let's say SAP must find a price for a product, but a number of prices can exist for the product. There could be the list price that applies to that group of products, a special price for that customer, or a specific price for that product.

What product is being sold, who it is being sold to, and the product group the product belongs to are all called *conditions*. They are specific situations that apply to that sale. Different conditions (for example, different products) will have different prices.

The different conditions and the prices associated with each are stored in SAP in condition records.

So, for example, SAP can first look for a price for a customer and product. If one is not found, it can continue looking at the other conditions—for example, for a product price. If a price is still not found, it can look for a product group price. These condition records are all grouped in a condition table. You may have many tables; each table is accessed by the system in a specific sequence called an access sequence.

An access sequence of condition tables is assigned to a condition type. You can therefore have condition types for prices (which contain, for example, the conditions customer and product price, product price, and product group price), discounts, and so on.

Condition types are grouped together in a determination procedure. A determination procedure is simply "a process to determine a value using the condition technique."

The result of the search is a value for the condition, or a *condition value*.

These examples show the condition technique used in pricing, but you will see it is used in many other areas of SAP. For example, it is also used in account determination. Whenever a transaction is posted to accounting, SAP must find (or determine) which account to post the revenues and discounts to.

There is, therefore, a determination procedure to find the accounts, called the *account determination procedure*. This procedure contains a condition type to find which account to post to, based on the conditions of the sale. The condition type searches all the records that contain accounts for conditions that match the sale in the order of the access sequence. As soon as it finds a record that matches the conditions, it returns a condition value—in this case, the general ledger account.

The condition technique is used because you may wish to post to different accounts under different conditions. For example, sales of a certain material can go to one revenue account and sales of other materials to a different account; or export sales can go to one account, local sales to another account.

Depending on all these conditions (the material, types of sale, etc.), SAP can find a different account. The condition technique is used to find the right account under the right conditions.

The Condition Technique as Used in Pricing

The condition technique is the single largest configuration technique used in the Sales and Distribution module. It is used throughout the pricing section. (Please refer to the thorough introduction to the condition technique in the beginning of Chapter 5.)

In pricing a number of alternatives are available on which to base a price of a product. These alternatives are variable according to specific conditions at the time of the sale.

For example, a customer wishes to purchase a product such as a television. This television has a standard sales price of $500.00 to all customers. However should the customer be part of a large corporation, a different pricing structure is used, offering a lower sales price of $450.00. This is governed by the condition technique.

The condition technique says if a pricing condition record such as "large corporate customers" is found for a particular customer, then he is offered the cheaper sales price. However, if no condition record is found, proceed to the next condition, which is merely a standard material price.

We know from previous introductions on the condition technique that a condition record that is the actual record found on the basis of specific values in fields is placed in a condition table.

A *condition table* is a table of fields used to find that condition record, and it is placed into an access sequence. An *access sequence* is the sequential placing of condition tables in a logical order to obtain a condition record.

An access sequence is assigned to a condition type, and this condition type is placed into a determination procedure such as the pricing procedure.

In the simple example used earlier, we would have the following structure:

- A standard pricing procedure—for example, RVAA01.
- Inside this structure we would have a pricing condition type PR00 (standard price).
- This condition type would use the access sequence PR00 (standard access sequence for pricing).

- The access sequence could have two steps and two condition tables in logical order from the most specific condition to the most general condition. Thus the first access could be sales organization plus distribution channel plus customer and material, which is the standard condition table 005. And the second condition could be sales organization plus distribution channel and material, which uses the standard condition table 004. (The exclusive indicator would be used to ensure no duplicate pricing is carried out. This will be covered later.)

- At least two condition records could be created, one for each table. One condition record would be for the material only and one condition record would be for the material and customer.

The purpose of this section is to investigate different uses and ensure optimal performance in the use of the condition technique in pricing.

Defining Condition Types

To define a condition type, use the following menu path.

Menu Path SAP Customizing Implementation Guide | Sales and Distribution | Basic Functions | Pricing | Pricing Control | Define Condition Types | Maintain Condition Types [V/06]

Condition types are used to define pricing elements such as prices, discounts, surcharges, or taxes.

Should you wish to make any alteration to the condition type or assign a new access sequence to an existing condition type, copy the condition type that represents the nearest outcome you are after and change its key to begin with the letter Z. Then proceed to change the condition type to suit your needs.

Following are a number of useful SAP standard condition types one may use to copy from:

B001	Group Rebate	Expense reimbursement	Percentage
B002	Material Rebate	Expense reimbursement	Quantity dependent
B003	Customer Rebate	Expense reimbursement	Percentage
B004	Hierarchy Rebate	Expense reimbursement	Percentage
HA00	Percentage Discount	Discount or surcharge	Percentage
HB00	Discount (Value)	Discount or surcharge	Fixed amount
K005	Customer/Material	Discount or surcharge	Quantity dependent
K007	Customer Discount	Discount or surcharge	Percentage
KF00	Freight	Discount or surcharge	Gross weight dependent
PR00	Price	Prices	Quantity dependent
R100	100% Discount	Discount or surcharge	Percentage
RA00	% Discount from Net	Discount or surcharge	Percentage
RA01	% Discount from Gross	Discount or surcharge	Percentage
RB00	Discount (Value)	Discount or surcharge	Fixed amount

Other condition types are always used, however, there is not often a need to copy and alter them. Condition types that would fall into this category would be

EDI1	Cust. expected price	Prices	Quantity dependent
EDI2	Cust. expected value	Prices	Fixed amount
EK01	Actual costs	Prices	Quantity dependent
EK02	Calculated costs	Prices	Quantity dependent
PI01	Intercompany price	Prices	Quantity dependent
PI02	Intercompany %	Prices	Percentage
VPRS	Cost	Prices	Quantity dependent
KUMU	Cumulation Condition	Discount or surcharge	Formula

The condition types used to determine taxes are country-specific, thus I have not selected any in the previous table.

To use as an example, we will create a condition type representing a percentage discount from the sales price of a product, based on the conditions of sales organization, customer price group, and material (this information comes from the sales order). Our access sequence will have a second step of searching for a condition record to offer the discount based on the material only.

We'll begin by selecting the closest resemblance to the condition type we are after in the list of standard condition types. This would be the standard condition type K007. In Figures 8-1 and 8-2 you will see the details that define how the condition type is to perform. Here we are copying the standard condition type K007 and creating condition type Z007.

In Figure 8-1 we see the condition type is automatic—that is, a condition record will be found, if one exists, automatically. This is seen by the assignment of an access sequence, K007. Should there be no access sequence, the condition type can then either be assigned a value manually or via a routine/formula.

The condition class is A, which determines that the condition type is a discount or surcharge.

This condition class is used by the system to determine what conditions it must re-determine and when. For example, a copying rule may indicate to copy pricing conditions unchanged and re-determine taxes; the system would then use this indicator to determine what condition types are taxes, etc.

Specific rules are applied to the pricing type, in copy control, the pricing type G means "Copy pricing elements unchanged and redetermine taxes."

The system will then re-determine the following condition types:

- Taxes (condition class D)
- Rebate (condition class C)
- Intercompany billing conditions (condition category I)
- Invoice list conditions (condition category R)
- Condition types with condition category L
- Cost conditions (condition category G)
- Cash discount conditions (condition category E)

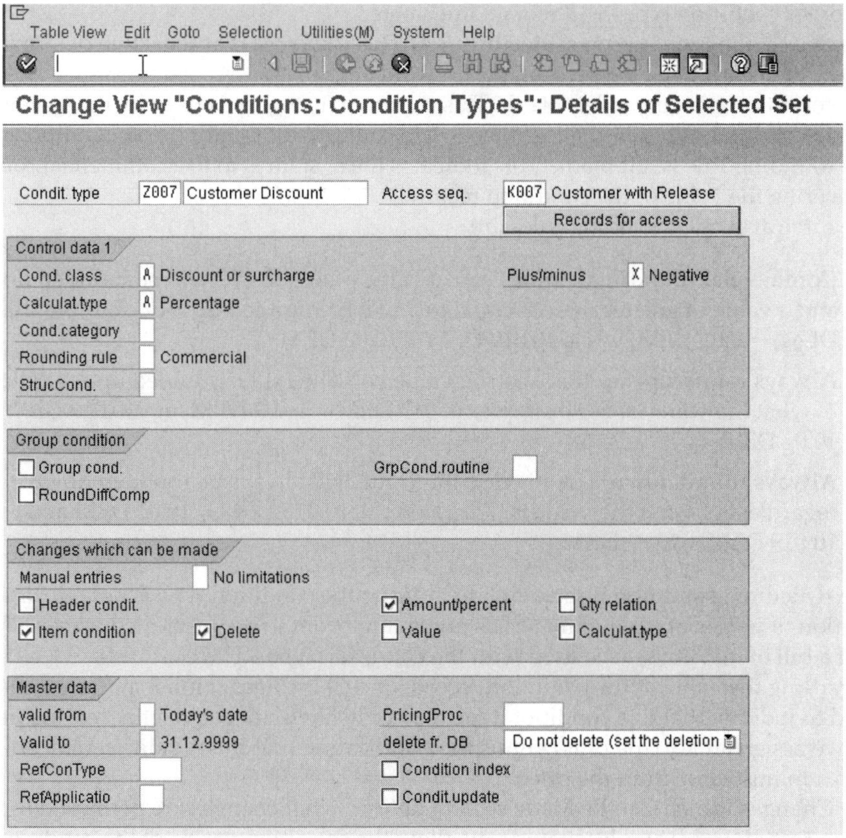

Copyright by SAP AG

FIGURE 8-1   Maintaining condition types

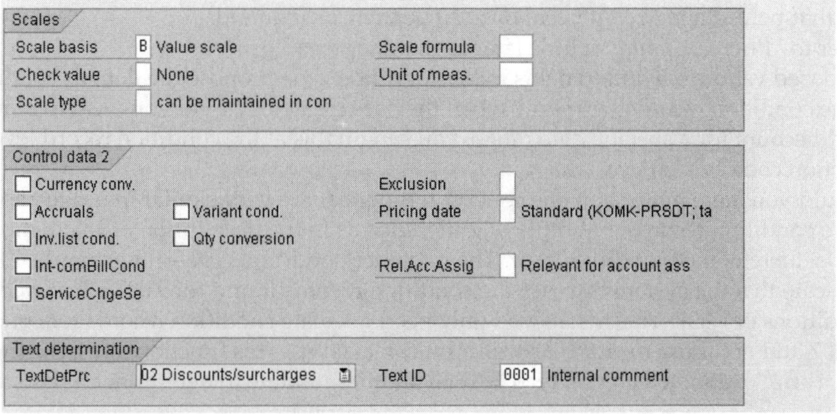

Copyright by SAP AG

FIGURE 8-2   Maintaining condition types (continued)

All other condition types will remain unchanged.

The calculation type is represented by an A. This indicates that the value determined in the condition record will be a percentage.

The condition category is left blank. This condition category is used by the system to categorize condition types into like groups—for example, all freight or tax conditions.

The rounding rule is left blank. This indicates the system is to use commercial rounding in discovering the value of the condition record.

The three available rounding rules are

- **Commercial rounding** In this case a value of less than 5 will be rounded down and a value of greater than or equal to 5 will be rounded up. For example, 10.013 DEM = 10.01 DEM, while 10.019 DEM = 10.02 DEM.

- **Always round up** In this case the value will always be rounded up regardless of what the value is. For example, 10.013 DEM = 10.02 DEM and 10.019 DEM = 10.02 DEM.

- **Always round down** In this case the value will always be rounded down, regardless of what the value is. For example, 10.013 DEM = 10.01 DEM and 10.019 DEM = 10.01 DEM.

The structured condition is left blank to indicate the condition type is not relevant for a cumulation of values of a bill of materials nor is it relevant to be duplicated across all sub-items of a bill of materials, as is used with the condition type KUMU.

Regarding the value of the condition record, once it is found it must indicate a discount. We need to indicate that this condition type may only have a negative effect on the price—that is, we assign an X to the plus/minus field, indicating that this condition may only result in a minus value from the price.

The Changes Which Can Be Made section defines what changes are permitted to the condition record. For example, should you allow the condition record of the condition type K007 to change the resultant value according to the condition record, you would leave the manual entries blank, which indicates no limitations, and then check the amount/percent field. Thus, should the condition record find a discount of 17 percent, you can manually change that percentage to 20 percent or to 10 percent, as required.

Refer to "Pricing Limits," a little later in this chapter.

Proposed valid from and to fields in the condition type propose the default validity dates the condition records will show when they are created. Should you wish to limit your price or discount for a specific date range, you can do this at the condition record level (transaction code [VK11]).

Should you have more than one condition type that are very similar in usage and have the same condition records, but differ slightly, such as in the description or calculation type, you can set a reference condition type. The reference condition type—for example, Z007—will indicate that the system is to use the condition records found for Z007 when calculating the conditions of K007. This means you only need to create condition records for condition type Z007 and not those for K007 as well. You can even use this functionality by using a reference application, which will refer SAP to another module to determine the condition type.

The scale basis indicates how the scale of the condition records must be calculated—for example, is the scale value-based or quantity-based.

Scale formula may be used with a routine to determine the scale base value.

The check value field determines if the scale should always be ascending or descending or indicates that the scale is not checked. That is, if not checked, the condition scale may be set up to allow the customer to receive a discount of $10 for a purchase from 0 to 100 items, $20 for a purchase from 101 to 200 items, and $5 for a purchase from 201 to 999,999 items. The unit of measure field forces the system to use this particular unit of measure when calculating the scale. (It is not mandatory for this to be used for a scale.)

The scale type field is left blank to indicate the scale is able to be set up in the condition record.

On the Control Data 2 section of the condition type screen, the currency conversion field, if checked, will cause the system to convert the condition currency to the document currency after the multiplication of the items. Should the value not be checked, the system converts the currency of the condition into the document currency before multiplying the value for the items.

The accruals check box makes the value determined by this condition type statistical—for example, to be used in finance for accruals for rebates.

The inter-company billing condition permits you to indicate that this condition type is used for internal costing.

For the exclusion field, refer to "Condition Exclusion Groups," later in this chapter.

The date of pricing, that is the system date that must be used to determine a condition record's validity, must be indicated by the entry in the pricing date field. Should you leave it blank, the system will use the standard pricing date KOMK-PRSDT for pricing; however, for taxes and rebates, the system will use the date KOMK-FBUDA.

The relevance for account assignment field is used to identify if standard account determination or specific account determination must take place, which identifies this condition value, to controlling.

The text determination procedure and text ID fields are used to determine if a text is relevant for this condition type. (Refer to "Text Determination" in Chapter 9.)

Now that we have defined the necessary fields in the condition type, we may copy K007, change its key to Z007, and save. (We do this regardless of what access sequence is assigned.)

Condition Tables

Shortly, we will create our access sequence, which means we require the correct condition tables to allocate in sequence. Access sequences should always be maintained in order/priority from the most specific entry (the table with the most fields) to the most general (the table with the least fields). Thus, in our example we will have our first access looking at a condition table that has the sales organization, as well as the customer group and material, WHILE the second access will look for a condition based on material only.

As a condition table is placed into an access sequence, we'll inspect the condition tables first to determine if the two tables we need are in the system.

Access the condition tables by using the transaction code [V/05] or using the following menu path.

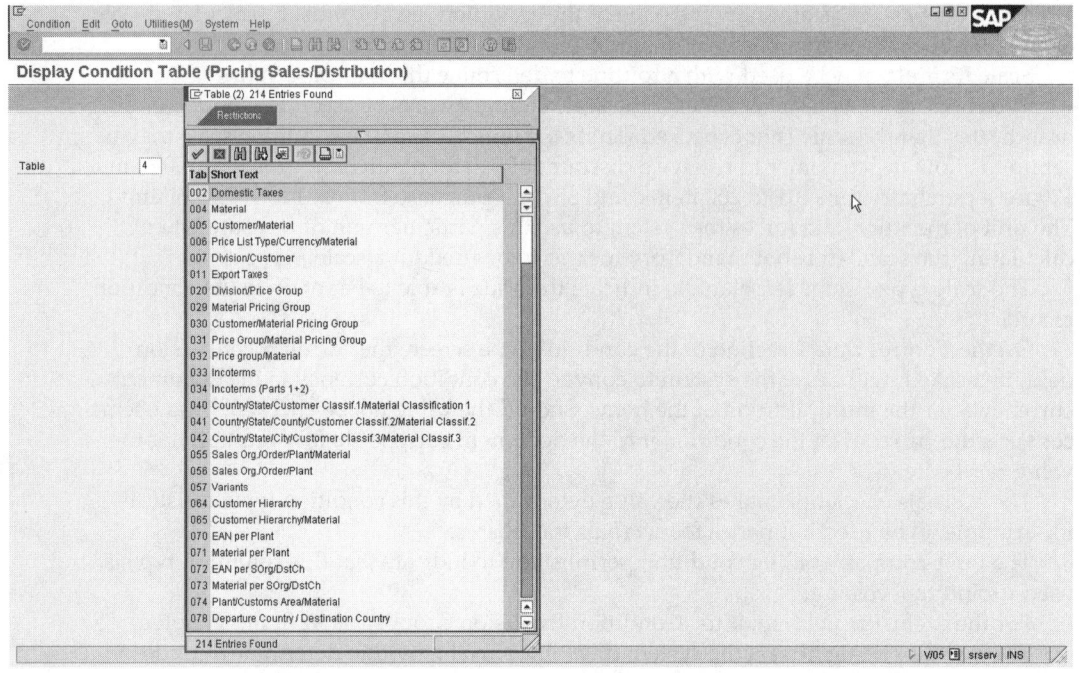

FIGURE 8-3   Available condition tables

Menu Path   SAP Customizing Implementation Guide | Sales and Distribution | Basic Functions | Pricing | Pricing Control | Define Condition Tables | Display Condition Tables

Press F4 to see a list of condition tables, shown in Figure 8-3, in which we are able to see that none have sales organization, customer condition group, and material fields. However, there is a standard condition table 004 that we may use for the second step of accessing a record based on the material only. But we'll have to create a condition table for our first access, which we'll do in the next section.

Creating Condition Tables

To create a condition table for our first access, use the following menu path.

Menu Path   SAP Customizing Implementation Guide | Sales and Distribution | Basic Functions | Pricing | Pricing Control | Define Condition Tables | Create

Enter a condition key of three digits with a number above 500. For our example we will create table 909, as shown in Figure 8-4.

Select the fields from the field catalog by double-clicking on them. If you need a longer description you may click the Other Description button, which will cycle through the data elements for each field. By selecting Technical View, you will see the technical name of the field, which is the clearest method of ensuring you have selected the correct field name.

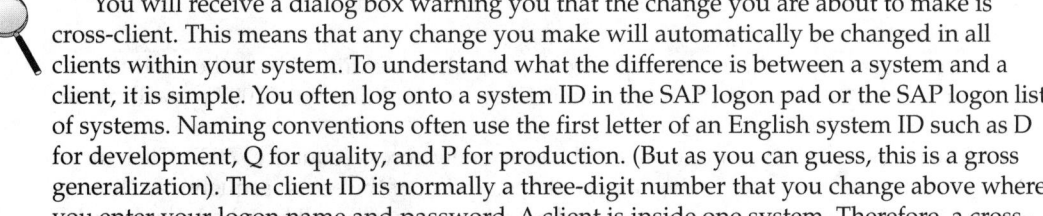

FIGURE 8-4   Creating a condition table

After you have selected the fields, give the condition table you are creating a meaningful name. The final table, including the Sales Organization, Price Group (Customer), and Material Number fields, may be seen in Figure 8-5. Then click the Generate icon, which will create the table and generate it for use.

Now we have the two condition tables (table 004 and 909) we will be using in our example, we may proceed to defining the access sequence.

Defining Access Sequences

To define access sequences, use the following menu path.

Menu Path   SAP Customizing Implementation Guide I Sales and Distribution I Basic Functions I Pricing I Pricing Control I Define Access Sequences I Maintain Access Sequences [V/07]

You will receive a dialog box warning you that the change you are about to make is cross-client. This means that any change you make will automatically be changed in all clients within your system. To understand what the difference is between a system and a client, it is simple. You often log onto a system ID in the SAP logon pad or the SAP logon list of systems. Naming conventions often use the first letter of an English system ID such as D for development, Q for quality, and P for production. (But as you can guess, this is a gross generalization). The client ID is normally a three-digit number that you change above where you enter your logon name and password. A client is inside one system. Therefore, a cross-client change means all clients within that system will be changed.

Again, select the access sequence that closely resembles your required access sequence, and copy it.

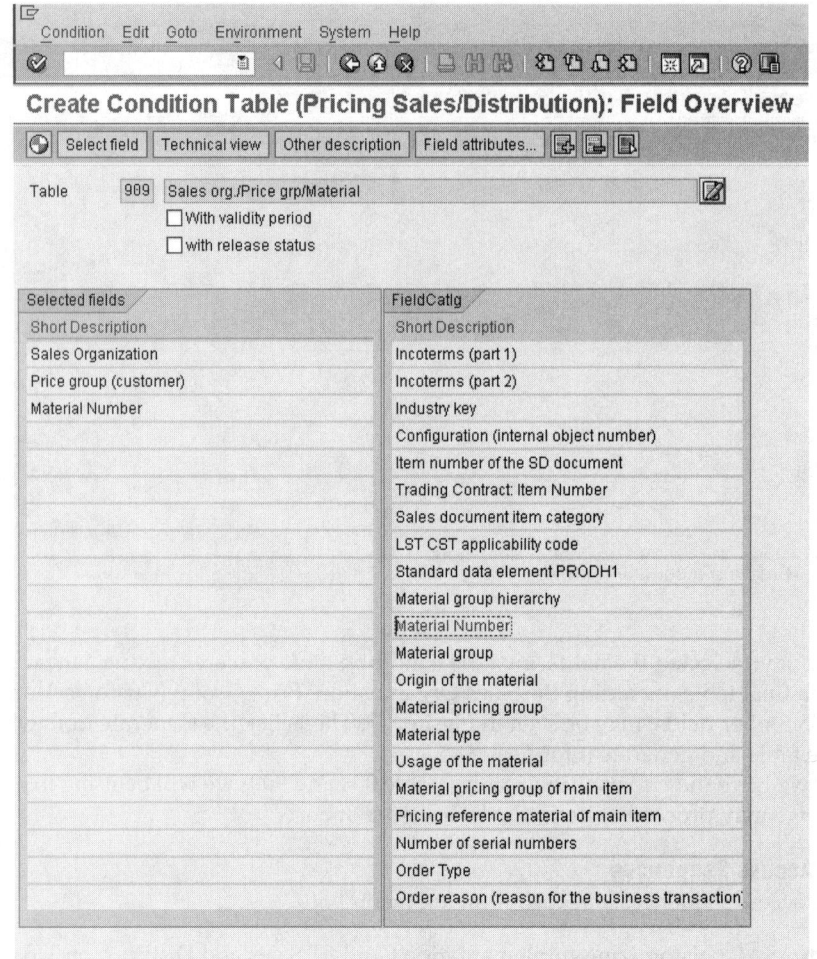

FIGURE 8-5   New condition table

I find it easier to give the access sequence the same key identification as the condition type to promote ease of use in the system later. Thus, for condition type Z007 we will create an access sequence Z007.

For the purpose of this example, we will create a new access sequence, Z007. Click the New Entries button and enter in the name and description of the access sequence as shown in Figure 8-6. After entering a description and pressing ENTER you will be asked if you wish to copy all sub-dependent entries. Select Yes. you can always go back and remove them later.

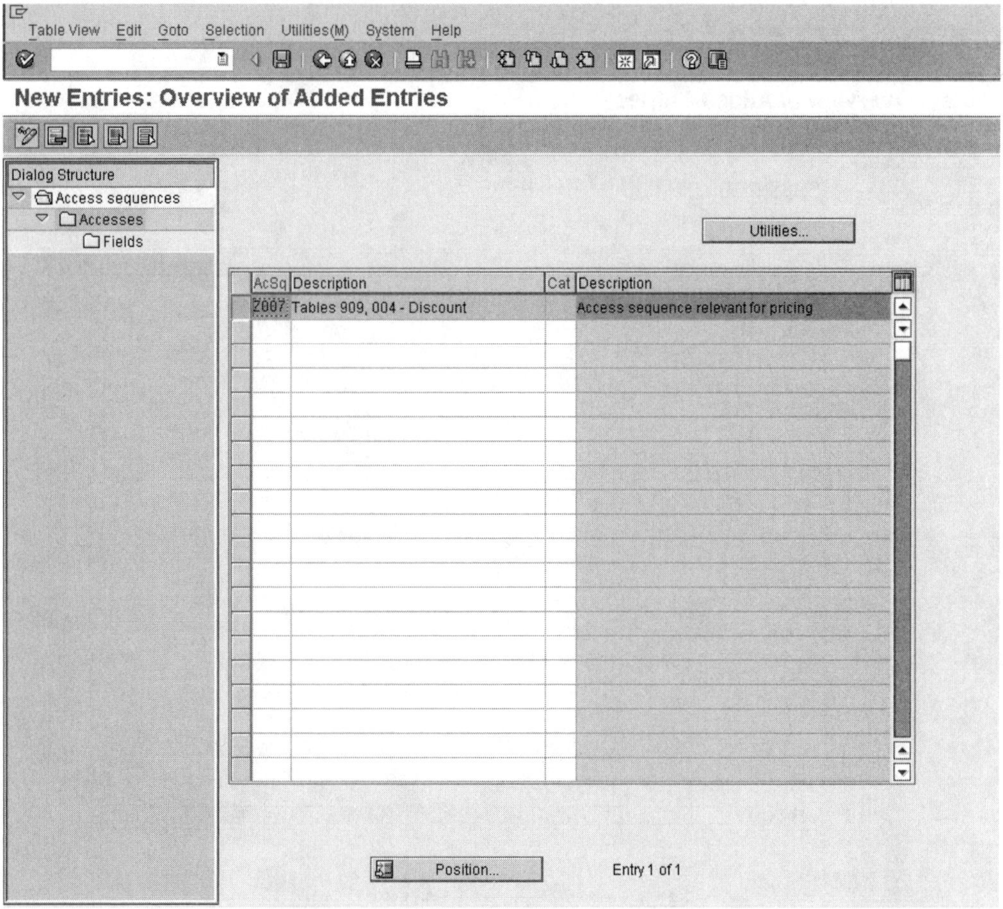

FIGURE 8-6 Creating an access sequence

Select the access sequence and select the Accesses folder in the file structure on the left. You can remove the tables you don't wish to use by selecting them and clicking the Delete button. (Select Delete Dependent Entries too; this will remove the values in the field structure within the access sequence too.)

Now you can enter data in your tables by clicking the New Entries button. Start with the most specific access table 909 as access number 10 followed by the next entry of table 004 as access number 20, as shown in Figure 8-7. If you wish to have a requirement on the access that must be fulfilled prior to the access being read by the system, you need to enter the requirement in the associated column.

The exclusive indicator should be set. This indicator determines that should a condition record be successfully found, the system is to stop searching for further condition records. This improves system performance as unnecessary searches are avoided once a value is found.

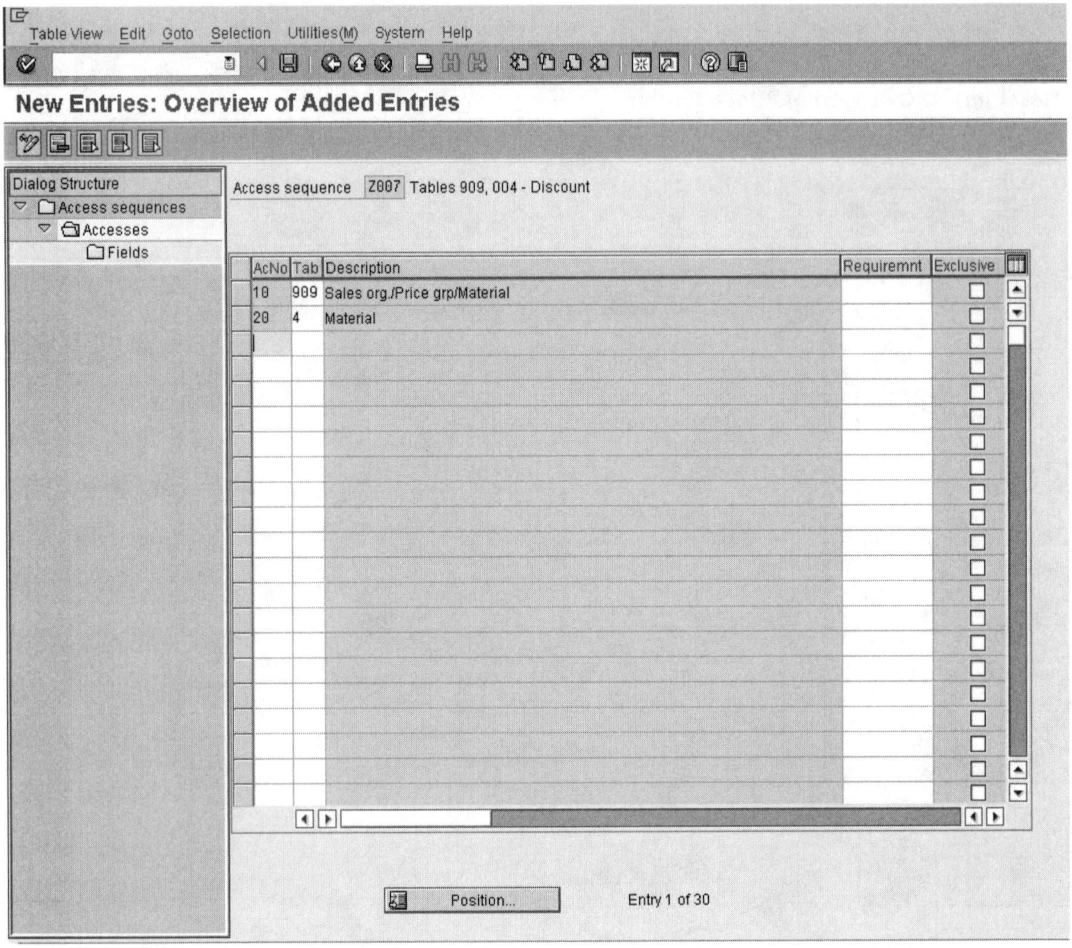

New Entries: Overview of Added Entries

Dialog Structure
▽ ☐ Access sequences
▽ ☐ Accesses
☐ Fields

Access sequence Z007 Tables 909, 004 - Discount

AcNo	Tab	Description	Requiremnt	Exclusive	
10	909	Sales org./Price grp/Material		☐	
20	4	Material		☐	
				☐	
				☐	
				☐	
				☐	
				☐	
				☐	
				☐	
				☐	
				☐	
				☐	
				☐	
				☐	
				☐	
				☐	
				☐	
				☐	
				☐	
				☐	
				☐	

Position...   Entry 1 of 30

FIGURE 8-7   Creating access sequence-table step access

Don't forget to ensure that your field assignment is correct. Even if you have created an access sequence with tables as in Figure 8-7, you must ensure the fields from the tables are seen as in Figure 8-8.

Select the table, then select the Fields folder in the file structure on the left. View the fields, then select Save.

This access sequence, Z007, must now be assigned to the condition type Z007 that we created earlier. You can proceed with this by using the transaction code [V/06].

Now that the condition type is created and the access sequence is created and assigned, we may now assign the condition type to the pricing procedure.

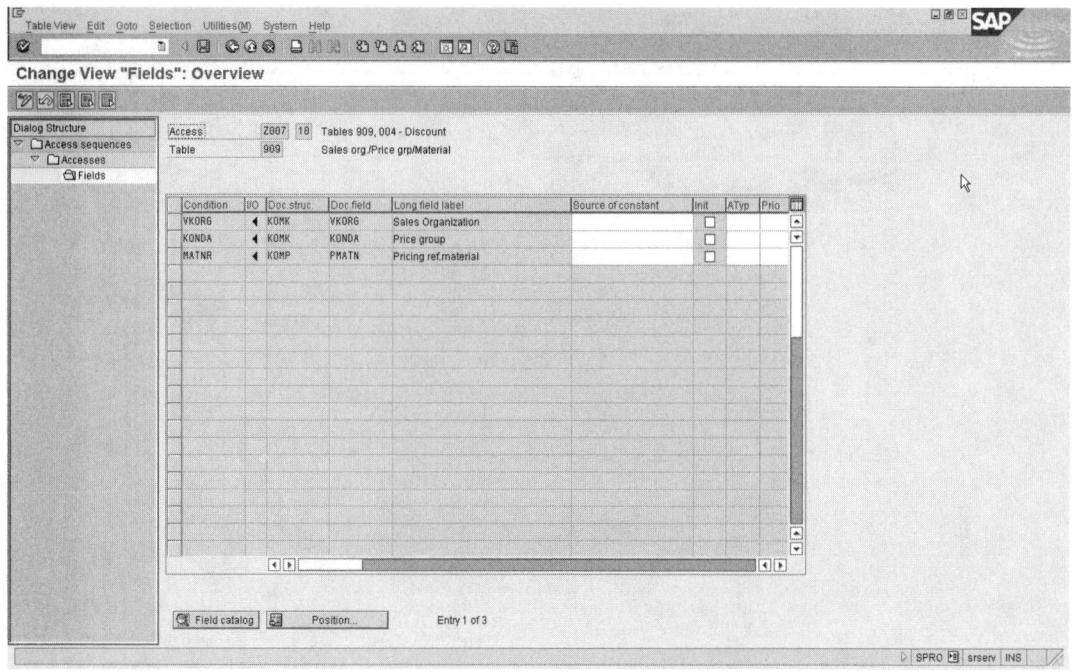

FIGURE 8-8   Creating access sequence—field access

Defining and Assigning Pricing Procedures

To begin defining and assigning pricing procedures, use the following menu path.

Menu Path   SAP Customizing Implementation Guide | Sales and Distribution | Basic Functions | Pricing | Pricing Control | Define and Assign Pricing Procedures | Maintain Pricing Procedures [V/08]

The structure of the pricing procedure will be discussed in the section on "Pricing" following this section. However, for the basis of the example we have defined, we will allocate the discount condition type Z007 to a very basic pricing procedure consisting of only PR00. This may be seen in Figure 8-9.

Before this pricing procedure may be used one needs to refer to the pricing procedure determination, as covered in the next section, to ensure that the combination of sales area, customer, and document pricing procedure indicators promote the correct pricing procedure in the sales document.

One must also ensure the condition records have been maintained correctly. To create a condition record for Z007, use the following menu path.

Menu Path   SAP Menu | Logistics | Sales and Distribution | Master Data | Conditions | Select Using Condition Type | Create

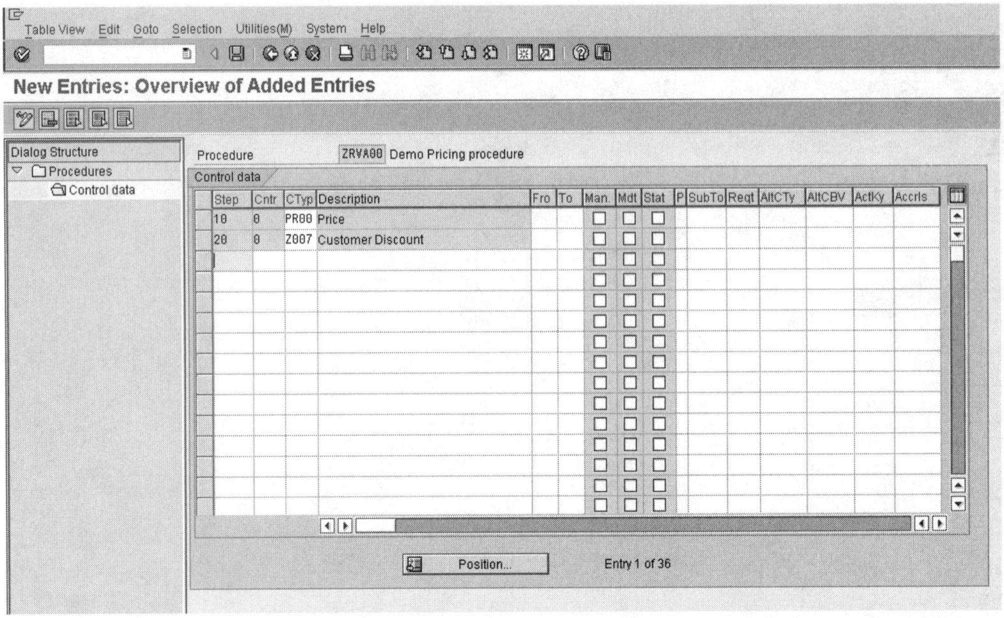

Copyright by SAP AG

FIGURE 8-9   Maintain pricing procedures

Transaction codes relating to condition record selection by condition type:

- [VK11] - Create
- [VK12]- Change
- [VK13] - Display

These condition records will then finally be the value as found in the pricing procedure within the sales document. We will cover condition records in detail later.

Customizing Steps in Pricing

The sequence in the creation of the discount condition type that we followed in the example of Z007 was used to assist continuity in thought. Whenever using the condition technique you may find it easier to use the following sequence when customizing:

1. Put the fields you will need into the field catalog.
2. Create the condition tables you will need.
3. Create the access sequence you will need.
4. Assign the condition tables to the access sequence.
5. Create the condition types.
6. Assign the access sequence to the condition types.

7. Create the determination procedure (pricing procedure), if necessary, and assign the condition types to it.

8. Assign the determination procedure.

9. Lastly, create your condition records.

Adding Fields to the Field Catalog

One may need additional fields than what exists in the standard field catalog for pricing. You may view the list of fields available in the field catalog and add fields using the following menu path.

Menu Path SAP Customizing Implementation Guide | Sales and Distribution | Basic Functions | Pricing | Pricing Control | Define Condition Tables | Conditions: Allowed Fields

Should the field you need not be in the field catalog, it may be in the list of allowed fields, which may be seen by clicking the New Entries button followed by clicking the down arrow. You can also check the list of available options by pressing F4. In Figure 8-10 you may see that the required field is in the list of available fields to add to the catalog.

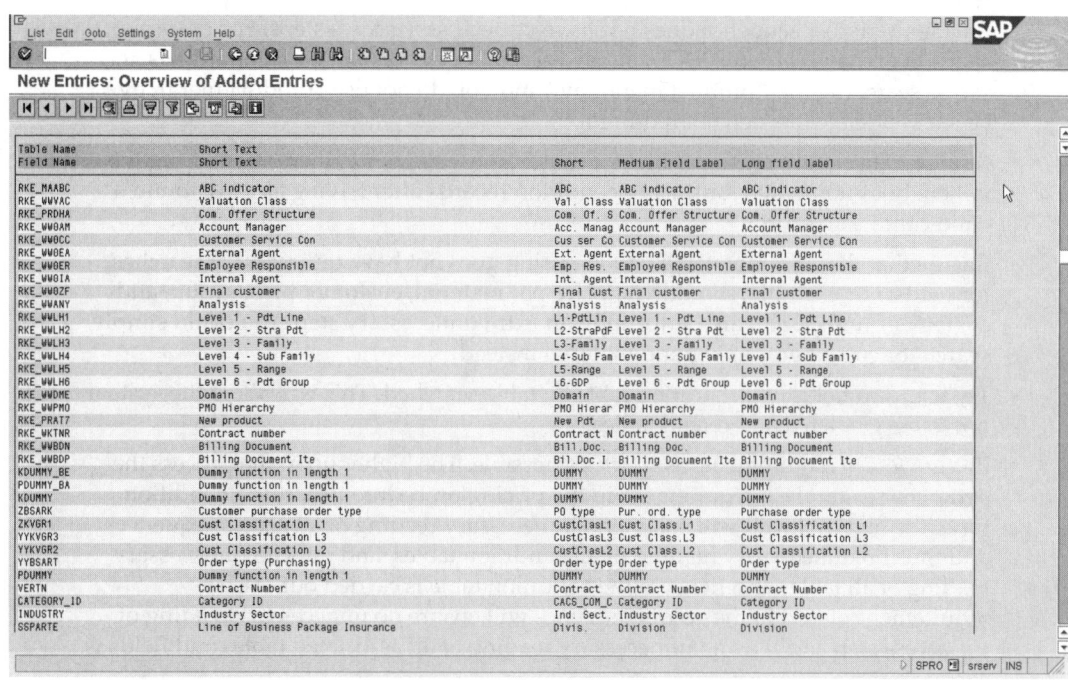

Copyright by SAP AG

FIGURE 8-10 New fields for the field catalog

You are now able to select by double clicking the field from the list of allowed fields to add to the catalog. Once selected, click Save and your field catalog will have the new entry, which may then be selected as a field for a condition table.

This procedure is fairly simple, as the field already exists in the list of available fields to be added to the field catalog. Often, however, there may be a need to use a field in the condition technique that is not included in this list of allowed fields. This may be due to the field being a newly created field.

Optimizing Performance in the Condition Technique

Pricing is a function that occurs repeatedly and in great volume. Thus the maintenance of condition techniques should be strictly governed to ensure the system resources are optimized. Following are a few tips on ensuring optimal performance in pricing:

- As standard SAP has pricing procedures with its own pricing condition types, ensure there are no condition types in the pricing procedure that are unnecessary. Copy the SAP standard pricing procedure and change it, being sure to delete the condition types not needed.

- Ensure that only automatic condition types have an associated access sequence and that no manually used condition types have been incorrectly assigned an access sequence with a resultant condition record that is ignored and overwritten.

- Ensure the access sequence does not have unnecessary access steps. For example, should you have copied a SAP standard access sequence and the standard has an access searching for " product hierarchy" and you do not use "product hierarchy," be sure to delete the step not required.

- Be sure to use the exclusion indicator in the access sequence, thereby ensuring the system does not search for further condition records after having already found a valid condition record.

- Ensure that the condition table you are using does not have unnecessary searches for fields. For example, should you price per material, customer price group, and customer number, you are performing an extra unnecessary step. You could simply search for customer number and material instead.

- Try to group fields in a condition table by table searched. This will allow the system not to have to fetch and reread tables.

- Be sure to use requirements as much as possible. The higher up in the process the better. For example, a requirement in the pricing procedure to access a condition type (the highest level) will ensure no unnecessary reading of an access sequence, and thus no unnecessary reading of all condition tables, and thus no unnecessary reading of all tables and fields in the condition table is carried out. Also a requirement placed in the access sequence will ensure no unnecessary reading of the access step and thus no unnecessary reading of all associated tables and fields is carried out.

- Should your business be large enough to warrant it, you may investigate buffering the prices in your system. This will ensure all prices are accessed within a faster response time.

For further optimization guidelines, refer to SAP Service Marketplace (OSS Note 0016430 specifically, or to the performance and tuning OSS Note 0023888, which acts as an index of notes.)

Maintaining Pricing Procedures

The pricing procedure is responsible for mapping the business needs and processes—for example, correct pricing and discounting—while also keeping to the legal requirements placed on the business—for example, adhering to the tax laws of the respective country. A pricing procedure consists of a list of condition types in a defined order, such as price, less discount, plus tax. It has totals that can be used for further processing—for example, gross price, net price, total discounts, total surcharges, net value, tax total.

The pricing procedure is configured in the IMG using the following menu path.

Menu Path   SAP Customizing Implementation Guide | Sales and Distribution | Basic Functions | Pricing | Pricing Control | Define and Assign Pricing Procedures | Maintain Pricing Procedures [V/08]

There are some controls on the pricing procedure. For example, you can specify that a condition type is mandatory—it must have an entry either defined automatically or entered in manually.

The pricing procedure is also used in account determination. This determines which GL accounts the prices, discounts, and taxes must be posted to. The condition types in the pricing procedure are linked to an account key. This key in turn is linked to the general ledger accounts. This shows the integration between the pricing in the invoice and the FI module.

The SAP standard system includes various standard pricing procedures that may be used as a reference model for the pricing procedures you may wish to create. It is advisable when creating a pricing procedure to copy a standard such as RVAA01, and then change and delete entries as you require.

For the purposes of this book we will create our own pricing procedure. You create a pricing procedure by selecting new entries and giving the pricing procedure a meaningful key and description.

We have created pricing procedure Z00001. By selecting the pricing procedure and selecting the control folder in the file structure on the left, you will be faced with an empty structure as depicted in Figure 8-11.

You will notice the Step column. This indicates the step number in the procedure—for example, the first condition type should be step 10, the second condition type should be step 20, and so on. It is possible to number the steps in intervals of 1 rather than 10, however, this can make changing the procedure in the future very difficult as you might need to assign a new condition type between two existing condition types. You can only do so if you can use a step number that is available between the numbers already assigned.

Alongside the Step column is the Cntr column—the counter. This is used to show a second "mini-step" within an actual step. For example, you may have all your freight surcharges assigned to step 100, however, there may be three condition types, each representing a different freight surcharge. Thus you may assign a freight condition type to step 100 counter 1, another to step 100 counter 2, another to step 100 counter 3, etc.

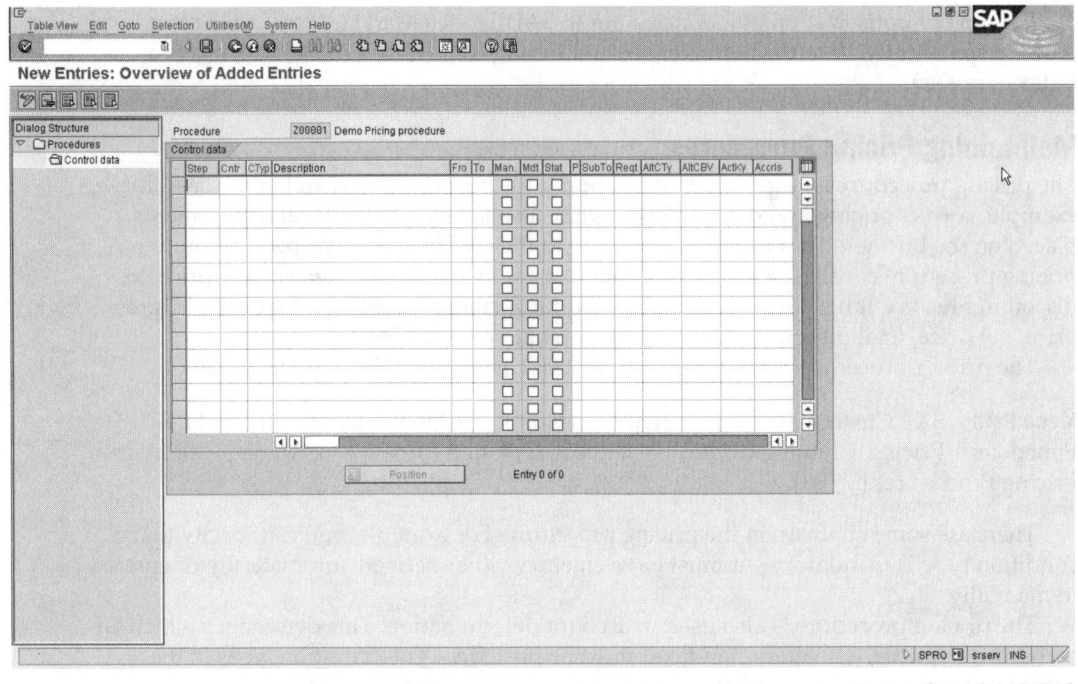

Copyright by SAP AG

FIGURE 8-11   Maintaining a pricing procedure

The CTyp column shows the condition type. This is the backbone of the pricing procedure. The condition type is the link, as you know, to the access sequence all the way to the actual condition record.

When you enter a condition type, the description field is filled automatically with the description from the condition type.

If you wish to enter a sub-total or total, no condition type applies. In this case, you can enter a description without a condition type—for example, "net price."

The From and To columns are used in two circumstances:

- **To define the range for a subtotal**   For example, if you want to add up all the conditions types from step 10 to 50, you would enter 10 and 50 in the From and To columns, respectively.

- **To define the basis for a calculation**   For example, if a discount is defined as a percentage, you need to indicate which step must be used as the basis for the calculation. If the calculation must be performed on step 100, you would enter 100 in the From field.

The Man column (for "Manual") is used to indicate if the condition type for which it is assigned to is allowed to be processed automatically or only manually.

The Mdt column (Mandatory) is used to identify those condition types that are mandatory in the pricing procedure. Mandatory condition types are, for example, the sales price or the cost price. Should a mandatory condition not be found in the pricing procedure, the system has an error in pricing and the respective sales order cannot be processed further—for example, no delivery will be able to be made.

The condition types marked as statistical entries affect the pricing procedure in that they will not be included in the Net Value calculation for that item. (The net value is displayed in the item details of the order and invoice, and the total of all items' net value is displayed on the order and invoice document.)

The Stat column is used by the pricing procedure to add a value statistically. That is, the value represented for this step will not alter the overall value in the procedure. This may be used, for example, to represent the cost price of the material sold.

The thin column following Stat, which is normally obscured, is labeled P for Print. This column may be made wider (as may all the other columns) by clicking the line separating the columns and dragging it. This print indicator is used to determine what descriptions and associated values assigned to a step are to be printed on a document—for example, order confirmation.

The SubTo column is used to assign a subtotal key to a step in the pricing procedure. These subtotal fields are then used in other areas of the system such as in the logistics information system. For example, it is recommended you assign the subtotal field 4 to the total value in the pricing procedure for freight.

The Reqt column is used to assign a requirement to the condition type. This requirement may then be used to exclude the system from accessing the condition type and trying to determine a value. This may be used, for example, to specify that the condition type, a discount, should only be accessed if the customer has a low-risk credit group.

The AltCTy column is used to specify that the system is to use the formula represented in this column as an alternative in finding the value of the condition type, rather than by using the standard condition technique. This may be used, for example, to calculate complex tax scenarios.

The AltCBV (alternative condition base value) column indicates a formula assigned to a condition type in order to promote an alternative base value for the calculation of a value. For example, you may specify a formula that uses a subtotal of 4 from the subtotal field and then modifies it slightly by dividing it by 2 and using the resultant value as a base value for a condition type.

The ActKy (account key) and Accrls (accruals account key) columns are used to assign account keys that in turn are assigned to general ledger accounts, which are used by the Finance department to register postings. The Accrls account key is used to determine a GL account—for example, when a value is posted for rebate agreements.

Now that we know what the columns represent we need to allocate the condition types to the pricing procedure in the best way possible in order to meet both the needs of the business and the legal requirements.

We will create a simple pricing procedure using all the already specified columns:

1. Start by clicking New Entries and enter the Price condition type PR00 as step 10.

2. As this is the price of the item, it should be mandatory, so indicate the condition type as mandatory.

3. As it is quite possible some items are not relevant for pricing, it is advisable to assign a requirement indicating this condition type is not necessary for items not relevant for pricing. To do this, assign the requirement 002 to the Rqt column.

4. You may also assign the account key ERL to the ActKy column, in order to post these values to the revenue account.

5. Should you not have any further values you wish to add to your gross price, you may add a second step 40 (allow yourself some space between steps at this early stage).

6. On step 40 do not assign any further condition types, but in the description field you may specify the description "Gross value."

7. In all probability the customer will want to see this value printed on his documentation, so indicate S in the print column.

8. The gross value may also be used later so assign the subtotal value 1 in the SubTo column.

These initial steps in your pricing procedure would look like Figure 8-12.

When using a condition type using condition class B (prices), the system may only use one price per line item. Thus, should the system have a second price in the pricing procedure, it will invalidate all previous pricing conditions.

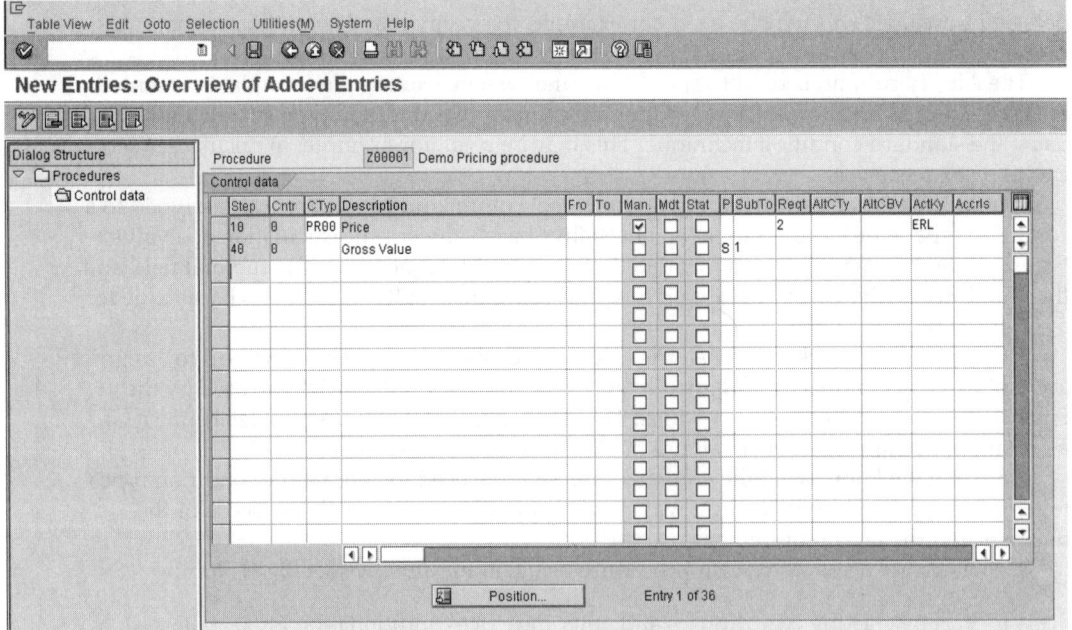

Copyright by SAP AG

FIGURE 8-12   Additions to pricing procedure

Following with the pricing procedure, we may wish to add extra charges, as well as maybe deduct discounts from the value. The discounts we give to the customer should not be deducted from the gross value plus the extra charges. Rather the discounts offered by most companies are discounts from the gross value, with extra charges being added subsequently. For this reason we'll now proceed in adding the discount condition types:

1. Create a step 50 and assign the newly created discount condition type Z007.

2. Create a step 60 and assign another discount condition type—for example, K005 (based on the customer and material).

3. It is possible you may have a negotiated discount between the sales person and the Sold-to Party at the time of creating the sales order. For this reason you may require a manual discount condition type, so allocate condition type RB00 to step 70.

4. For all these three steps the customer would want to see the discount he is obtaining so indicate them relevant for printing in the P column.

5. Again for all these three steps it is advisable to indicate to the system from what value it should offer the discount, so specify 40 in the Fro column.

6. These condition types are only valid should the item in the sales order be relevant for pricing, so assign requirement 002 to the three new discounts.

7. You may assign the general ledger account key ERS to each condition type.

8. Do not forget that condition type RB00 is manual, so you should enable the manual indicator on the pricing procedure.

9. Lastly, you may specify a "total discount" value in step 100 (again, allowing room for further changes in the step numbering).

Your pricing procedure should now resemble Figure 8-13, also using the From and To values in step 100 to add the discounts.

You may now decide the customer should be liable for additional charges such as freight costs:

1. In step 110 add a condition type KF00 and in step 120 add HD00. As HD00 is a manual condition type, you should indicate this on the pricing procedure.

2. The values represented by freight should be updated into subtotal field 4, so assign 004 to the SubTo column for both condition types.

3. Both conditions should also be posted to the general ledger in a specific revenue account for freight, so assign the conditions the account key ERF.

4. You may wish to now have a net value total, so assign the net value description to a new step 130. This net value should use the net value alternative calculation type 002 as well as subtotal 002. It should also be relevant for printing.

Your pricing procedure will now resemble Figure 8-14.

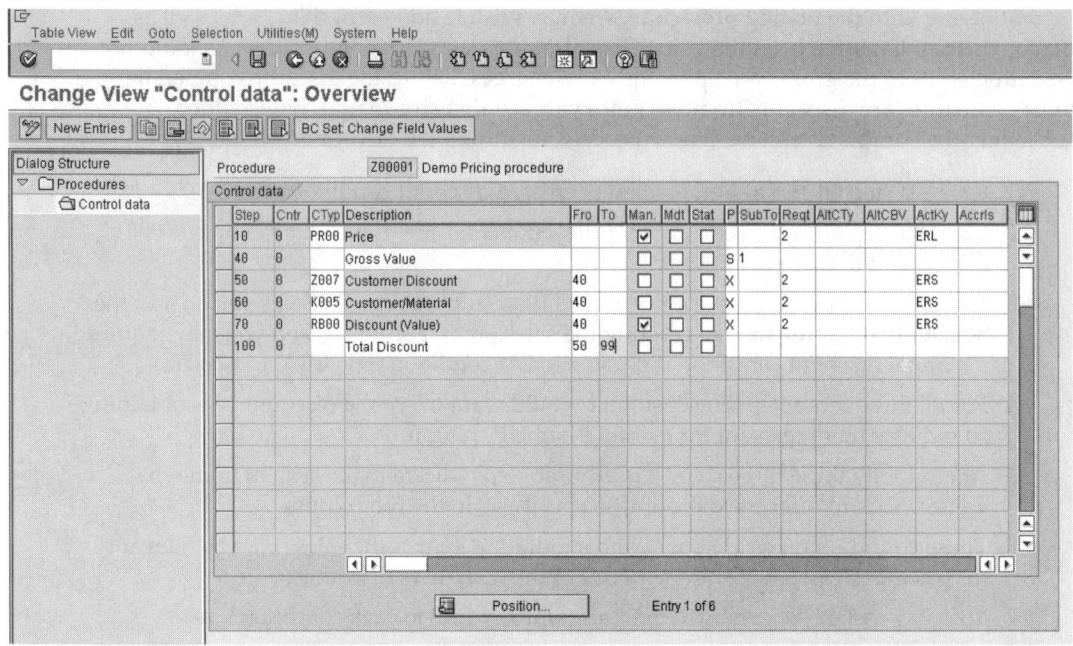

FIGURE 8-13 Further additions to the pricing procedure

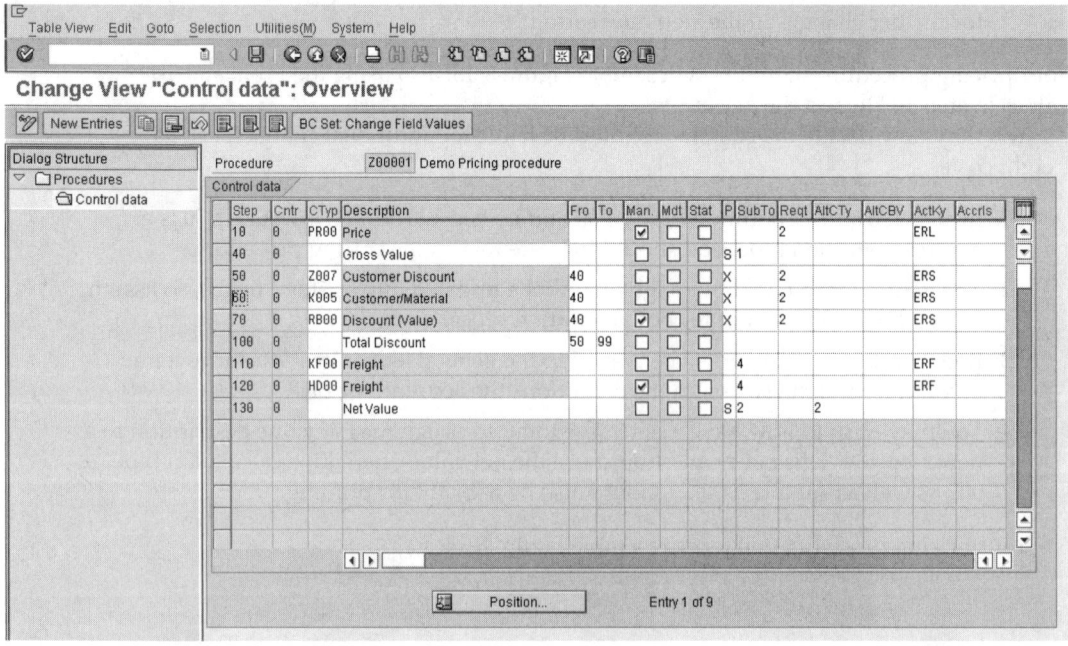

FIGURE 8-14 More steps added to the pricing procedure

You can now assign the taxes relevant to be levied against the customer. As taxes and their maintenance vary from place to place, we will use condition type MWST to represent our taxes:

1. Add condition type MWST to step 140.

2. This condition type is mandatory so select the mandatory indicator.

3. As the taxes are obtained on the basis of the delivering plant in order to obtain the country delivered from, it is advisable to use the requirement to check if the plant has been maintained in the sales order first, so assign the requirement 010 to step 140.

4. The alternative condition base value used by the standard system for the MWST is 16.

5. As the revenue for the tax must be posted to a separate general ledger account, the account key assigned is MWS.

6. Now that the tax has been added to the net value, the item may now be totaled. Assign a description Total to step 150 with the SubTo column indicating an A, which is the basis for the credit price. This means that the credit value will post to KOMP-CMPRE and the value will be reflected in the field CMPRE. If you look at the item table VBAP, CMPRE will now hold a value, which is determined by this setting. One may use these tables for reporting purposes, outputs, etc. The total value may also use the alternative calculation base value of 004, which is the net value plus the tax value.

7. It is possible you will need to have your cost price represented in the pricing procedure. For this reason you may enter a step 160 and assign the VPRS condition type to this step.

8. Do not forget to assign the statistical indicator to this step. This value may be passed into the SubTo column with a B, which represents the cost price. The standard system has the requirement 004 assigned to the cost price.

9. The profit margin may now be added in line 170. Add "Profit margin" as the description.

10. Assign alternative calculation type 011 to this step, which takes the net value and deducts the cost price to determine the profit margin.

Your pricing procedure should now look similar to Figure 8-15.

The pricing procedure is now complete. You have configured enough of the procedure to adapt the different elements to match your business process. Don't forget the pricing procedure determination (covered later) must be carried out to ensure this created procedure is used in your sales document.

You can check the customizing of your new procedure by running it in transaction code [VCHECKT683].

The Pricing Type field seen in Figure 8-16 is used to default the type of pricing the system will use when the user selects Edit | New Pricing Document, as seen in Figure 8-17. Although there is the ability to select the pricing type when you update pricing on the Conditions tab in the sales document, you may wish to restrict user access to this tab, and restrict the ability to update pricing manually in this way for all users. Instead, you may

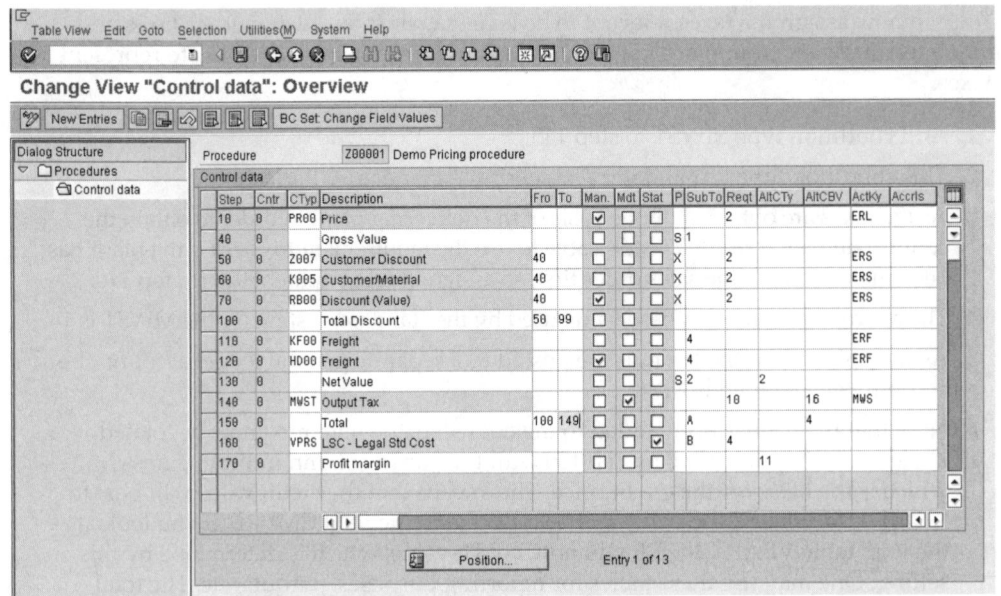

FIGURE 8-15 Completed pricing procedure

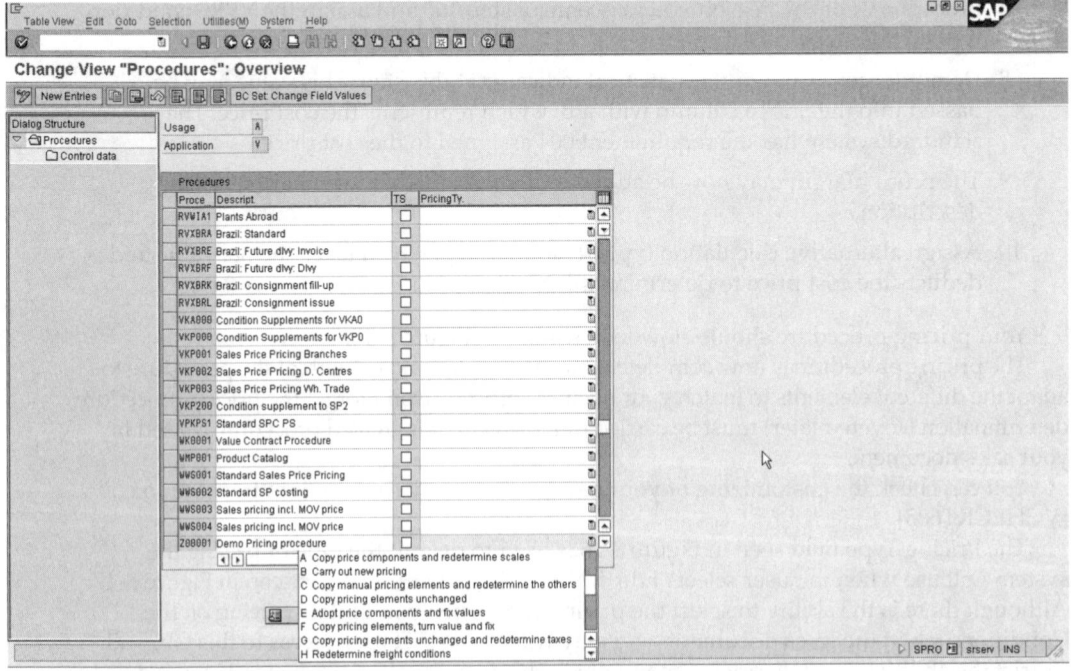

FIGURE 8-16 Pricing type assigned to pricing procedure

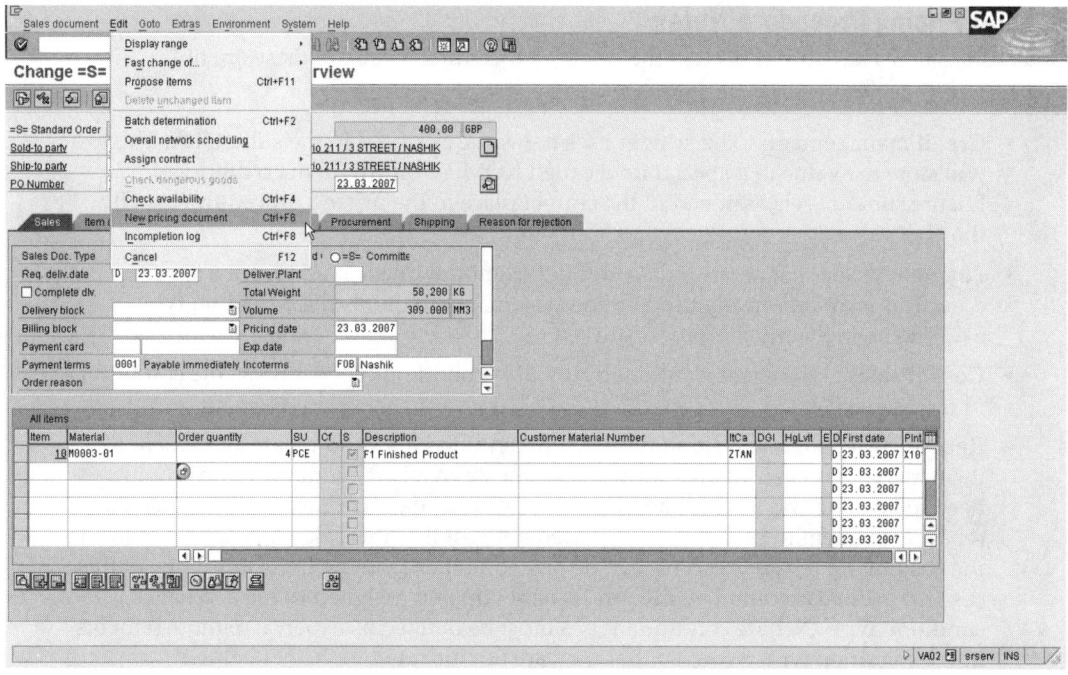

Copyright by SAP AG

FIGURE 8-17 New pricing of sales document

wish to use only the Edit | New Pricing menu path. The benefits of doing this are that as the user does not see sensitive pricing, he does not have the ability to remove the manual conditions, and cannot re-calculate pricing with a new pricing type that is not consistent with the business process.

   Do not forget the usage of the pricing type as used in copying rules and SAP Service Market Place OSS Note 24832, which outlines condition types that are re-determined according to the pricing type in copying. For example, pricing type G indicates "copy pricing elements unchanged and re-determine taxes." as discussed in the overview of condition types earlier in this chapter.

   For the same reason, if the condition type in pricing analysis says in a billing document "condition is found and set" and you are using the condition requirement number 024 (which only determines the price in billing document), and yet, you still have to do new pricing in order to obtain the condition record, the "fault" would be that the condition category on the condition type should be L. That way, when copying into a billing document, the requirement says "proceed with determining the value for the condition type" and the system does new pricing for that condition record due to the category being an L and thus finds a record. Should the condition category be, for example, a blank, the system would propose the message "condition is found and set" but not provide an actual condition record.

General Pricing Procedure Notes

Other topics in SD have an impact on the pricing procedure, to ensure these are not overlooked I have listed a few of them here:

- **Credit management** The system uses the value as stored in the subtotal A. This will store the value in a special field called KOMP-CMPRE (item credit price). Ensure subtotal A is assigned in the correct place in the pricing procedure, usually the "net value."

- **Payment terms** Generate a discount if the amount due is paid before a specific date. This is automatically used by the system, and requires the condition type SKTV to be in the pricing procedure.

- **Cost of sales** The system automatically uses condition type VPRS as the condition to represent cost.

- **Rebate** The rebate condition types are determined if a valid rebate agreement for the material has been created for the customer. The rebates configuration would need to be done and a rebate agreement created for the customer. SAP will use the rebate agreement to calculate an expected amount that this sale will contribute to the customer's rebate. Accruals can be posted to the GL using these amounts. In this case the accrual account key ERU must be set up and assigned to the accrual condition type. (Rebate condition types must be defined as expense reimbursements in the condition type record so that they are not included in the net value.)

 Use an authorization profile (not covered in this book) to ensure the users of the system cannot view the margins or the pricing procedure.

 The SAP pricing procedure does not automatically recognize during an update to price relevant fields (excluding the few below in List A) in a sales document, whether a condition record which uses the changed field, exists and therefore if pricing should be re-calculated or not.

For the following List A, the system will re-price according to the re-pricing type, the type of condition type affected is determined by the condition category.

List A

Field	Re-priced Automatically	Re-Pricing Type	Impact
VBKD-PRSDT (Pricing Date)	Yes	C	Copy manual pricing elements and redetermine the others
VBAP-MATNR (Material Number)	Yes	B	Carry out new pricing
VBKD-INCO1 (Incoterms)	Yes	H	Redetermine freight conditions
KUNWE (Ship To party)	Yes	G	Copy pricing elements unchanged and redetermine taxes
KUNRG (Sold to party)	Yes	G	Copy pricing elements unchanged and redetermine taxes

Field	Re-priced Automatically	Re-Pricing Type	Impact
VBAP-CHARG (Batch Number)	Yes	G	Copy pricing elements unchanged and redetermine taxes
VBAP-WERKS (Plant)	Yes	G	Copy pricing elements unchanged and redetermine taxes
VBKD-FBUDA (Services Date)	Yes	G	Copy pricing elements unchanged and redetermine taxes
VBKD-KURSK (Exchange Rate)	Yes	A	Copy price components and redetermine scales
VBKD-ZTERM (Payment Terms)	Yes	A	Copy price components and redetermine scales
KWMENG or MGAME (Cumulative Quantity)	Yes	A	Copy price components and redetermine scales

Pricing Procedure Determination

The pricing procedure is allocated to the sales document or billing document by a determination rule, similar to other determination rules. The pricing procedure determination is based on the customer master record, the sales document, and the sales area.

Customer Pricing Procedure Indicator

Before you can proceed with the determination rules, you need to maintain the customer pricing procedure (CuPP) indicator. Use the following menu path.

Menu Path SAP Customizing Implementation Guide | Sales and Distribution | Basic Functions | Pricing | Pricing Control | Define and Assign Pricing Procedures | Define Customer Pricing Procedure [OVKP]

In this step one needs to assign a single character alphanumeric key with a short description, as seen in Figure 8-18.

Document Pricing Procedure Indicator

Now you can define a similar single-character alphanumeric key with a short description to represent the document type. Use the following menu path.

Menu Path SAP Customizing Implementation Guide | Sales and Distribution | Basic Functions | Pricing | Pricing Control | Define and Assign Pricing Procedures | Define Customer Pricing Procedure [OVKI]

Simply copy or create your own document pricing procedure indicator as required.

After the document pricing procedure (DoPP) indicator has been created, you need to assign it to the sales document types. This will ensure that, for example, all sales orders created using a standard sales order type OR, which has been assigned a DoPP of 1, will use the same pricing procedures if created in the same sales area and with the same CuPP.

In some instances you may not wish to have the same pricing procedure for a sales document as you wish to have in a billing document. For this reason you may allocate a different DoPP to a billing document.

To assign these DoPP indicators to the sales documents, use the following menu path.

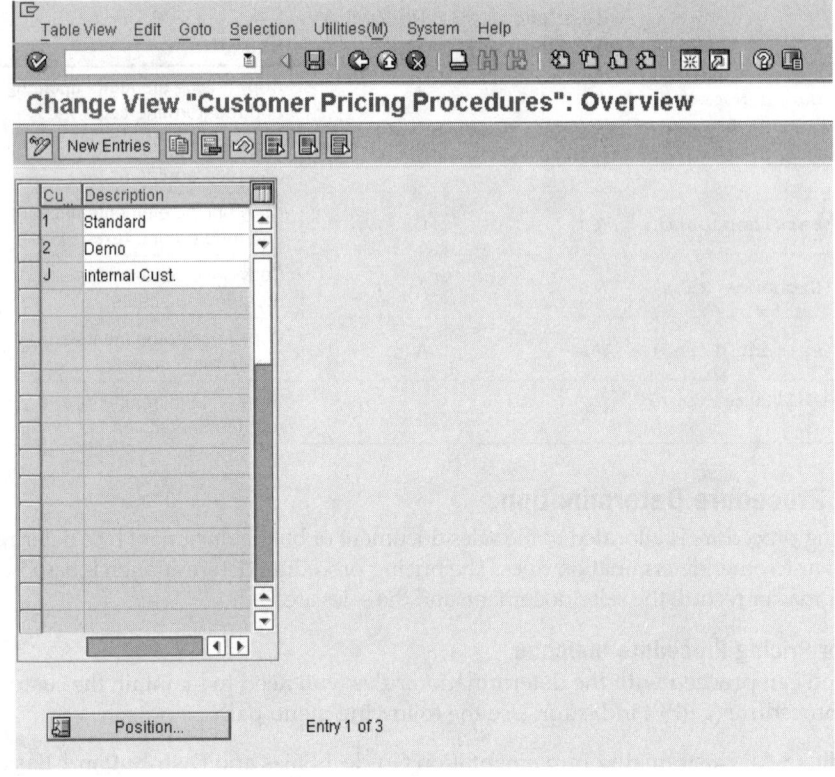

FIGURE 8-18   Customer pricing procedure

Menu Path   SAP Customizing Implementation Guide | Sales and Distribution | Basic Functions | Pricing | Pricing Control | Define and Assign Pricing Procedures | Assign Document Pricing Procedures to Order Types

Or one may use the following transaction code [OVKJ].
To assign these DoPP indicators to the billing documents, use the following menu path.

Menu Path   SAP Customizing Implementation Guide | Sales and Distribution | Basic Functions | Pricing | Pricing Control | Define and Assign Pricing Procedures | Assign Document Pricing Procedures to Billing Types

Or one may use the following transaction code **[OVTP]**
Once this data has been maintained, the determination rules may be laid out. To define the pricing procedure determination, use the following menu path.

Menu Path   SAP Customizing Implementation Guide | Sales and Distribution | Basic Functions | Pricing | Pricing Control | Define and Assign Pricing Procedures | Define Pricing Procedure Determination

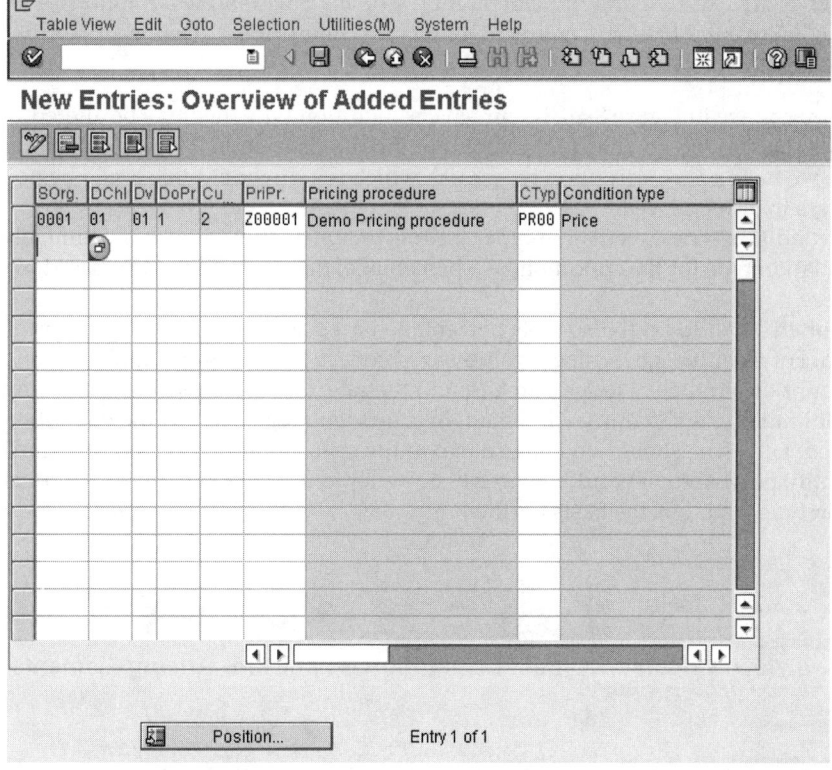

FIGURE 8-19   Pricing procedure determination

The fields in this screen, shown in Figure 8-19, are easy to interpret. The CType column, is used to default the condition type, which will be used in the fast order entry overview of the sales document at line item level.

Pricing Limits

Condition types offer an automatic or manually determined value, according to the assignment of an access sequence or not. Condition types may also be manually altered. This allows the user an opportunity to overcharge or undercharge a customer. For example, should there be a discount which is offered to the customer and no limit to the discount is set, the user may incorrectly offer a 100 percent reduction. For this reason, we govern the condition type with a limit.

Even in the case where the user can enter a 100 percent discount, you must limit the discount to 100 percent to ensure the user does not end up giving the customer a negative posting to his accounts receivable, thereby giving the customer a credit.

To set price limits, use the following menu path.

Menu Path   SAP Customizing Implementation Guide | Sales and Distribution | Basic Functions | Pricing | Pricing Control | Define Condition Types | Define Upper/Lower Limits for Conditions [OVB2]

As you can see in Figure 8-20, if you have a condition type that may be altered manually in the sales document, you need to ensure that there is no room left for abuse. In our example we have added condition type Z100, which is a discount that should be no more and no less than 100 percent.

The condition types calculation type controls the calculation type of the limit. Should the calculation type for the condition be a percentage, the limit will also be based in percentage terms.

It is often better to keep discounts percentage-based as these discounts are easier to maintain. For example, governing a value-based condition type with a limit, does not take into account the volume of items purchased in the sale. However, placing, for example, a 5 percent limit on the discount will remain in proportion regardless of the quantity purchased. However, should you have a maximum surcharge such as freight, regardless of the quantity purchased, it would obviously be better to use a fixed value as the basis for the condition type, and thus the basis for the limit.

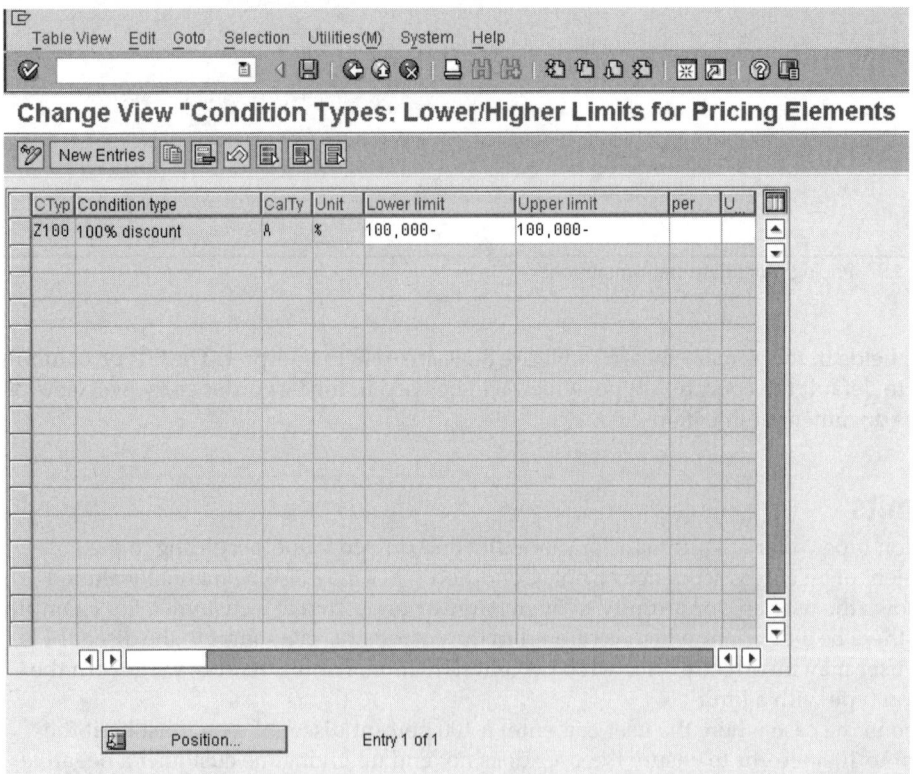

Copyright by SAP AG

FIGURE 8-20   Pricing limit of 100 percent to discount

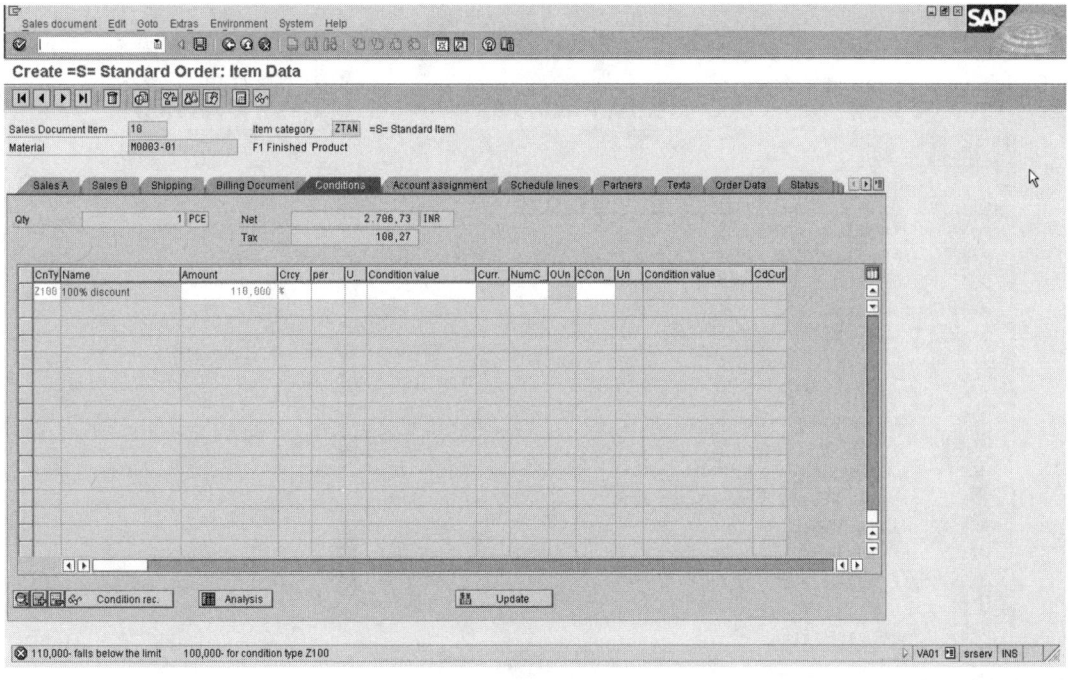

Copyright by SAP AG

FIGURE 8-21 Condition limit error in sales document conditions

Should the user try to create a condition that falls outside of the limited range, he will receive an error as seen in Figure 8-21.

Activating Pricing for Item Categories

Here you are able to define per item category, if the item in the sales order is relevant for pricing, statistics, and costing. Use the following menu path.

Menu Path SAP Customizing Implementation Guide | Sales and Distribution | Basic Functions | Pricing | Pricing Control | Define Pricing by Item Category | Activate Pricing for Item Categories

You will see a table like the one shown in Figure 8-22. For each item category you are able to define if the item should be relevant for pricing. The items not relevant for pricing may be left blank. Should standard pricing be carried out for the item, you may indicate these item categories with an "X." The statistical value column adjoining the pricing column indicates if the item must be used for statistical purposes in updating the logistics information system (sales information systems, etc.). A blank entry indicates the item is relevant for statistics updating and the value of the item will be added to the header totals. Items that would not be relevant for pricing would be, for example, text items.

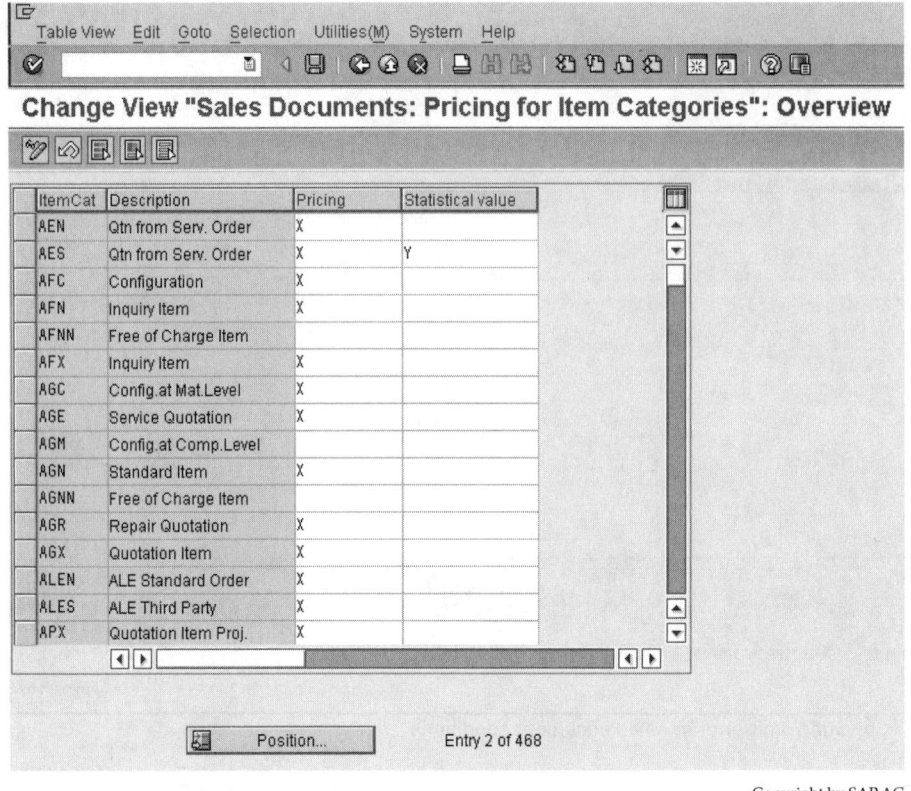

FIGURE 8-22   Activating pricing for item categories

Activating Cost Determination for Item Categories

To activate cost determination for item categories, use the following menu path.

Menu Path   SAP Customizing Implementation Guide | Sales and Distribution | Basic Functions | Pricing | Pricing Control | Define Pricing by Item Category | Activate Cost Determination for Item Categories

As shown in Figure 8-23, you can compare if pricing is carried out for the particular item category, while determining if the item should be relevant for cost determination. Should you wish the cost of the item to be determined, you must indicate the item as relevant by selecting the checkbox in the DCost column.

The cost of the item will only be available should you have a condition type in the pricing procedure that determines cost, such as the SAP standard condition type VPRS.

The cost of the item is taken automatically by the system from the fixed cost price of the material in the material master record. Should the material not have a fixed cost, the system will then take the cost price from the moving average price in the purchase information record.

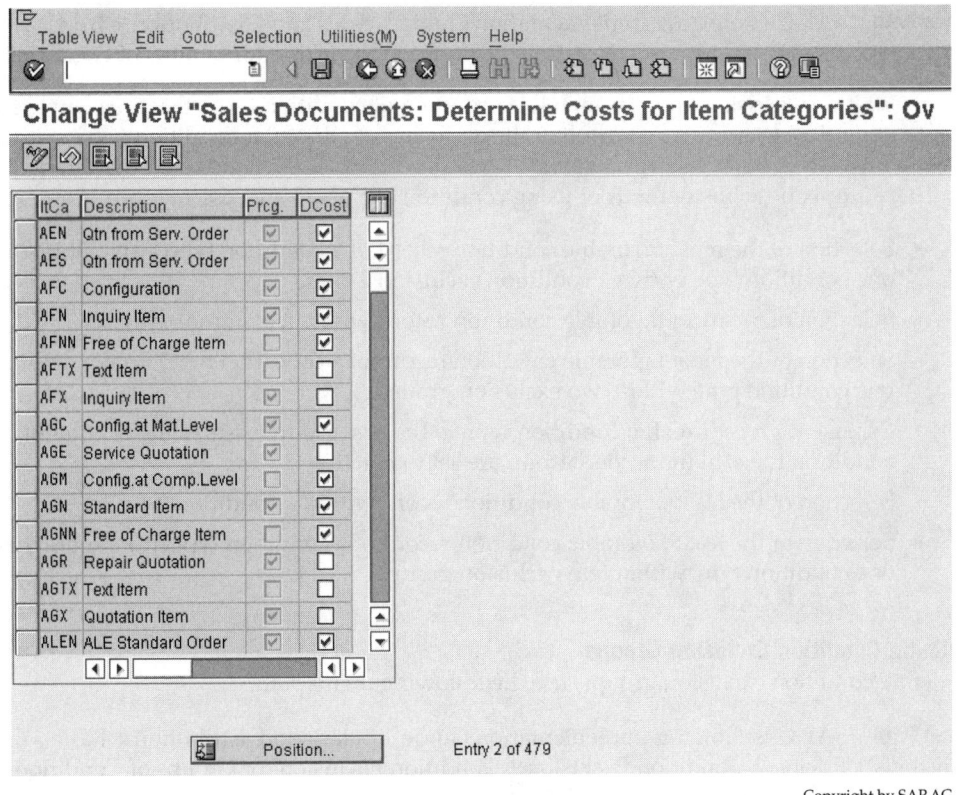

Figure 8-23   Activating cost determination for item categories

 The purchasing information record, however, belongs to the materials management module, so we will not be covering it other than to say that if you wish to access one, you may use the following transaction code [ME13] and menu path

Menu Path   SAP Menu | Logistics | Materials Management | Purchasing | Master Data | Info Record | [ME13] Display

Condition Exclusion Groups

It is quite possible that you may have more than one condition type in your pricing procedure offering a discount to a customer. Should the discounts be automatically determined, there is the risk that the customer receives all the relevant discounts, and thus is able to receive the product below the cost to the company. By using condition exclusion groups, you can ensure the customer does not receive all discounts but instead only receives, for example, the best out of four discount condition types.

To set condition exclusion groups, use the following menu path.

Menu Path SAP Customizing Implementation Guide | Sales and Distribution | Basic Functions | Pricing | Condition Exclusion | Condition Exclusion for Groups of Conditions

A condition exclusion group is merely a grouping of condition types that are compared to each other during pricing and result in the exclusion of particular condition types within a group or entire groups.

There are six possible methods of using condition exclusion groups:

- Selection of the most favorable condition record of a condition type, from more than one condition type within a condition exclusion group.

- Selection of the most favorable condition record within a condition type.

- Selection of the most favorable condition record of a condition type, from more than one condition type within two exclusion groups.

- Exclusion procedure: If a condition type in the first group exists in the document, all condition types in the second group are set to inactive.

- Selection of the least favorable condition record within a condition type.

- Selection of the least favorable condition record of a condition type, from more than one condition type within two exclusion groups.

Defining Condition Exclusion Groups

To define condition exclusion groups, use the following menu path.

Menu Path SAP Customizing Implementation Guide | Sales and Distribution | Basic Functions | Pricing | Condition Exclusion | Condition Exclusion for Groups of Conditions | Define Condition Exclusion Groups

We will use the example of the most (least) favorable condition type within a condition exclusion group as an example using the two discount condition types K005 and K007. Thus we will place both these condition types in an exclusion group.

Proceed to define an exclusion group by using a four-character alphanumeric key; in our example, we will call our group Z001, as seen in Figure 8-24.

Assigning Condition Types to the Exclusion Groups

You can now assign the condition types to the exclusion group. Use the following menu path.

Menu Path SAP Customizing Implementation Guide | Sales and Distribution | Basic Functions | Pricing | Condition Exclusion | Condition Exclusion for Groups of Conditions | Assign Condition Types to the Exclusion Groups

As shown in Figure 8-25, assign the relevant condition types to the condition exclusion group.

Maintaining Condition Exclusion for Pricing Procedures

After completing the assignment of the condition types to the exclusion group, proceed with assigning the condition exclusion group to the pricing procedure using the following menu path.

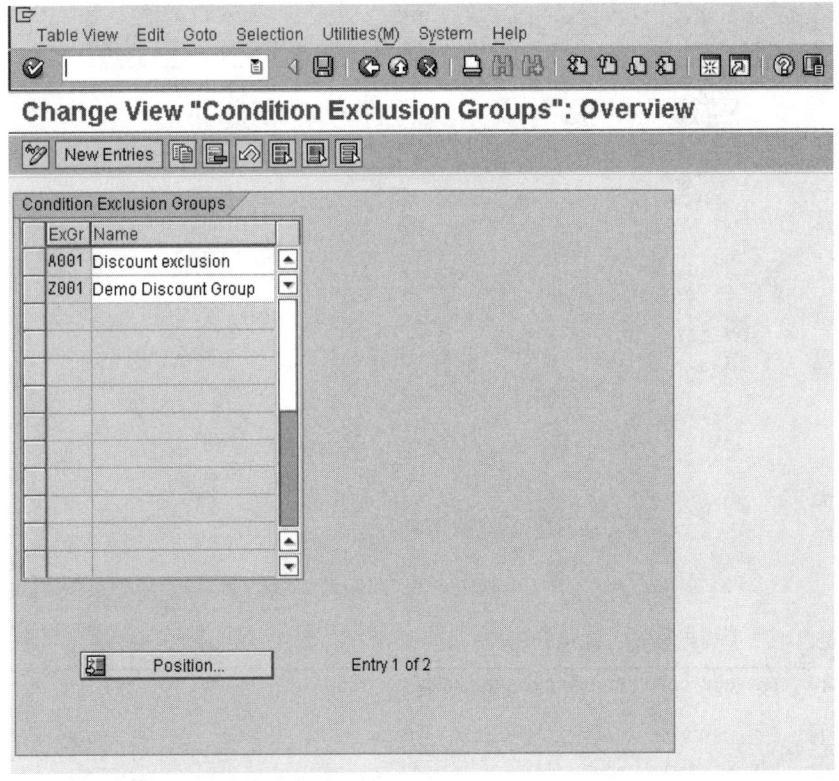

FIGURE 8-24 Condition exclusion group

Menu Path SAP Customizing Implementation Guide | Sales and Distribution | Basic Functions | Pricing | Condition Exclusion | Condition Exclusion for Groups of Conditions | Maintain Condition Exclusion for Pricing Procedures

After selecting the pricing procedure for which you wish the condition exclusion to be active, click the Exclusion folder in the file structure on the left of the screen. This will take you to the screen shown in Figure 8-26.

Don't forget that the condition types you want to compare must exist in the pricing procedure and have valid condition records created for them. Keeping with the requirement of "We will use the example of the most favorable condition type within a condition exclusion group as an example, using the two discount condition types K005 and K007," we will configure the following as shown in Figure 8-27.

Should you now create a sales order using the same pricing procedure that the exclusion group is assigned to, you will find the condition offering the most favorable discount to the customer is represented in the pricing procedure, as seen in Figure 8-28.

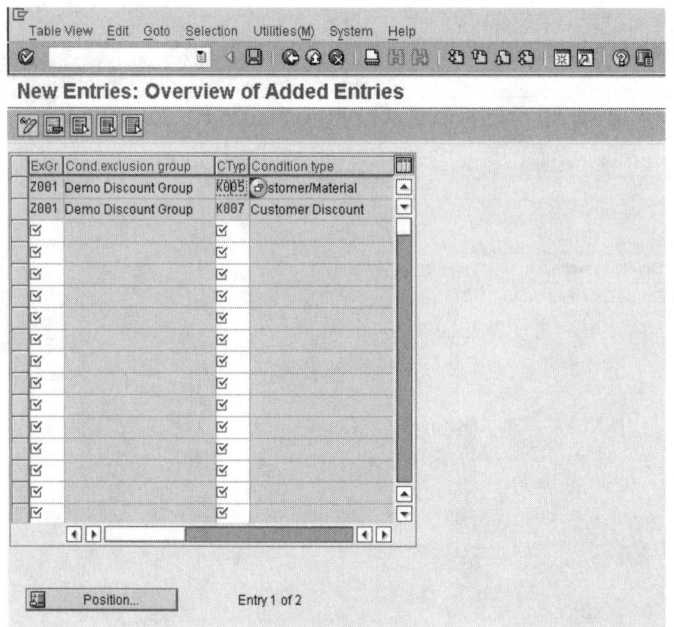

FIGURE 8-25   Assigning condition types to the exclusion groups

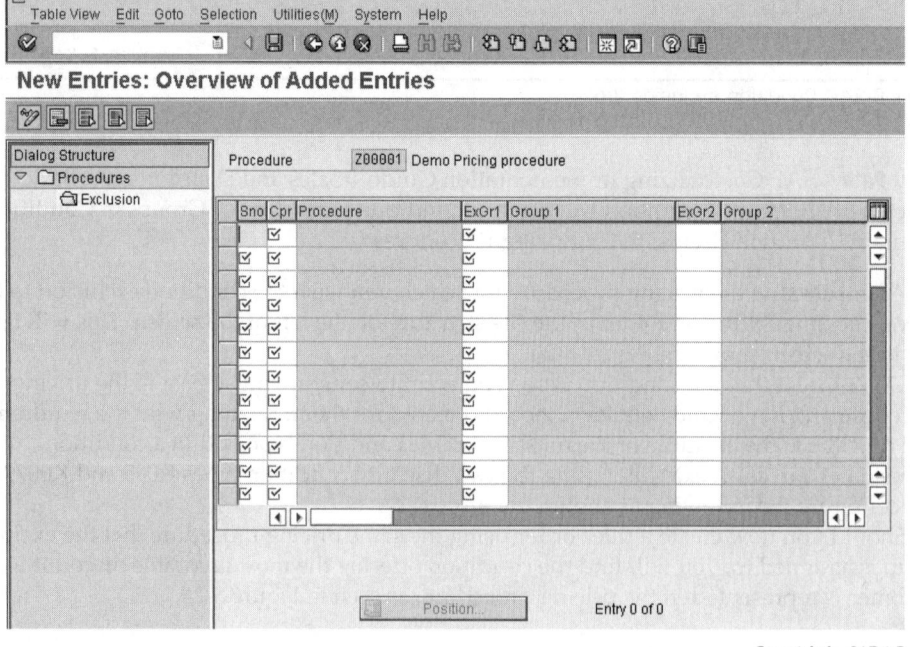

FIGURE 8-26   Maintaining condition exclusion for pricing procedures

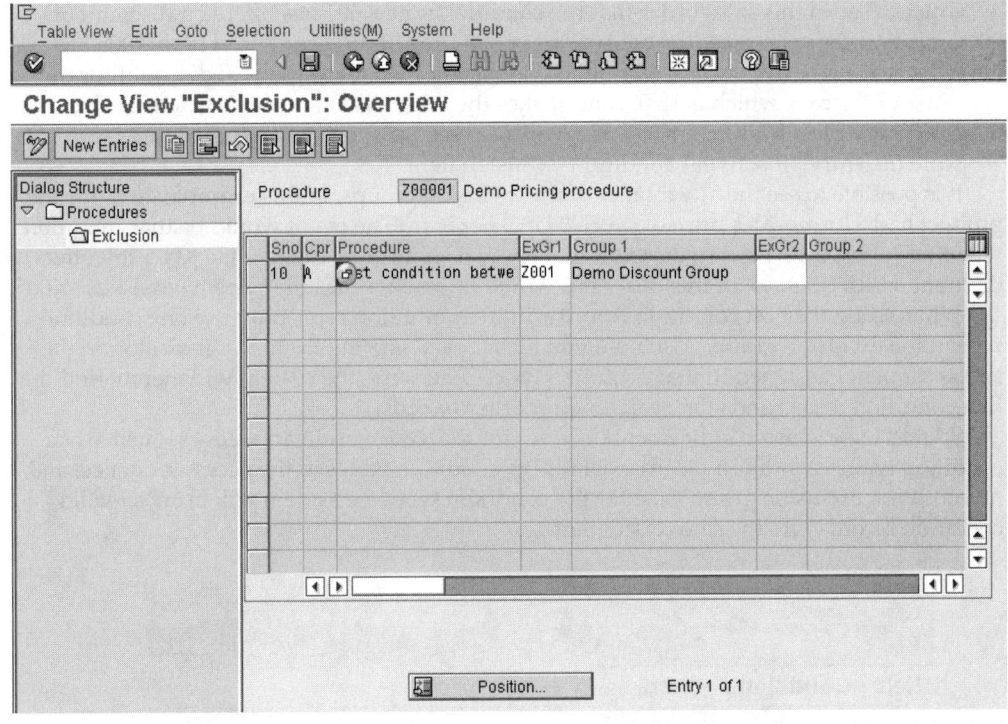

FIGURE 8-27   Maintain condition exclusion for pricing procedures

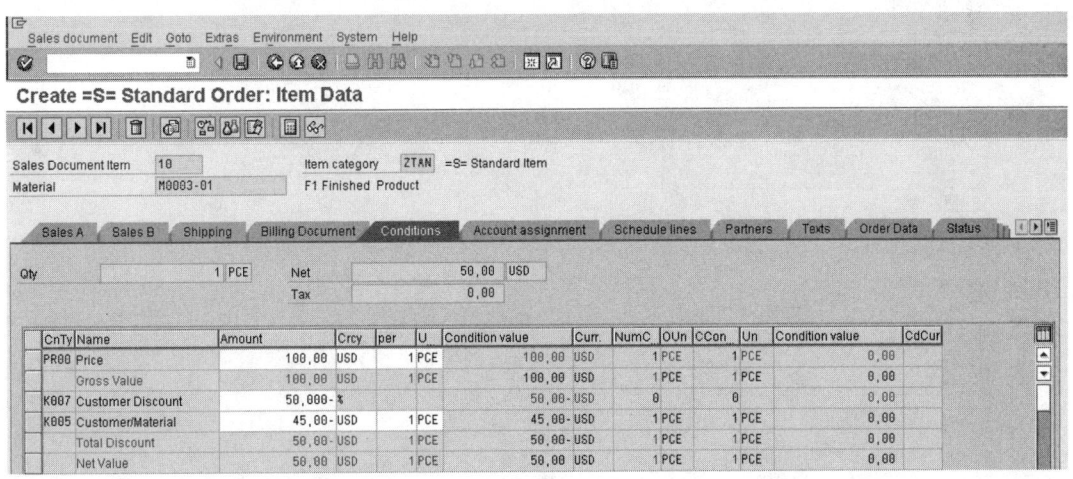

FIGURE 8-28   Result of best within group

One can see in this sales order that the condition type K007 has offered a discount of 50 percent off the sale price (the equivalent of $50 USD), while condition type K005 has offered a real value discount of $45 USD. The system then takes the best discount for the customer of the two, which is K007, and makes the other discount, K005, inactive. This may be seen by double-clicking on K005. You will then see the screen shown in Figure 8-29.

Note the entry "Inactive A condition exclusion item."

It is possible to see the advantages of the exclusion groups, in this example. Imagine the product had a lower sales price of say $90 USD per item. The result would be that condition type K007 offers a 10 percent discount that is a real value of $9 USD, while K005 still offers a discount of $10 USD. So, in this case K007 would be inactive and the system would use K005.

When using the best condition record within a condition type, only use one condition type in the exclusion group. Also note you must deactivate the Exclusive indicator on the access sequence assigned to that condition type. Otherwise, the system will merely find the first condition record and stop searching for other records.

Should the exclusive indicators not be set for the steps within an access sequence of a condition type, a condition record exist for the condition tables in the access sequence, and no condition exclusion group exist for the condition type, the system will bring *all* valid condition records into the sales document.

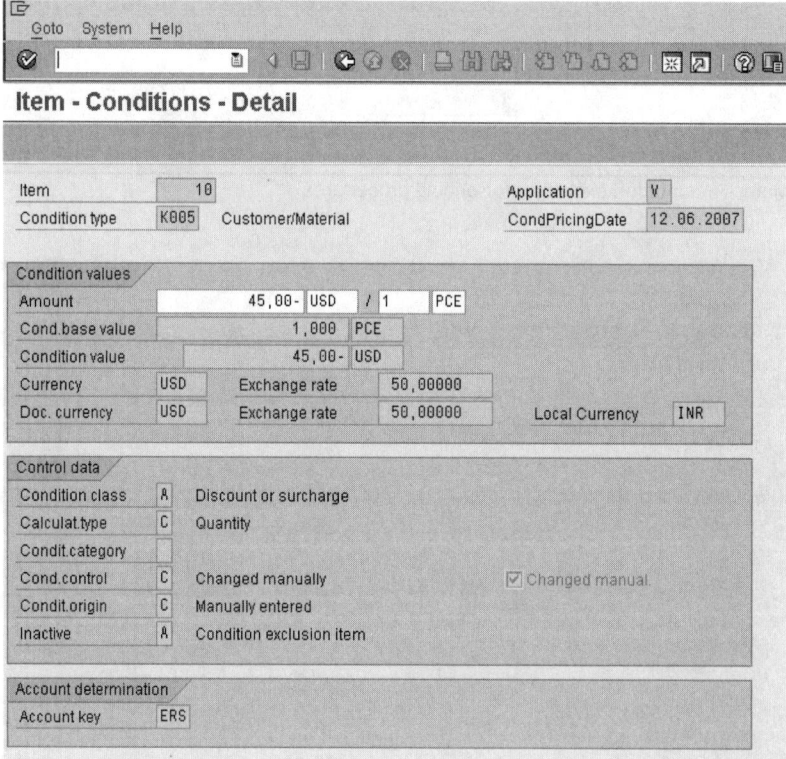

Copyright by SAP AG

FIGURE 8-29 Condition inactive due to exclusion item

Price-Relevant Master Data

Due to the many different requirements in business for pricing and the complexities of these requirements, SAP has a number of fields by which one may group both customers and materials. These additional groups are the customer price list type, customer pricing group, and material group. You may use these groups as key fields in condition tables—for example, all resale prices that are condition type PR00 may be based on the customer price list type. Naturally, you may use any field in the pricing catalog for pricing. However, the fields mentioned here are the ones most often used in day-to-day business.

Defining Price List Categories for Customers

To define price list categories, use the following menu path.

Menu Path   SAP Customizing Implementation Guide | Sales and Distribution | Basic Functions | Pricing | Maintain Price-Relevant Master Data Fields | Define Price List Categories for Customers

Create your customer price list type to meet the business requirements by entering a two-character field and a short description, as shown in Figure 8-30.

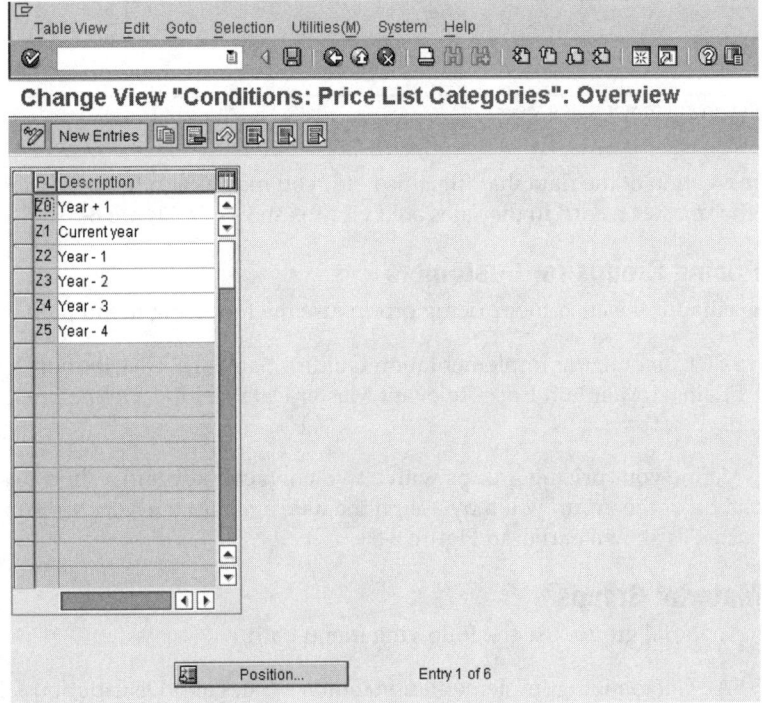

FIGURE 8-30   Defining price list categories for customers

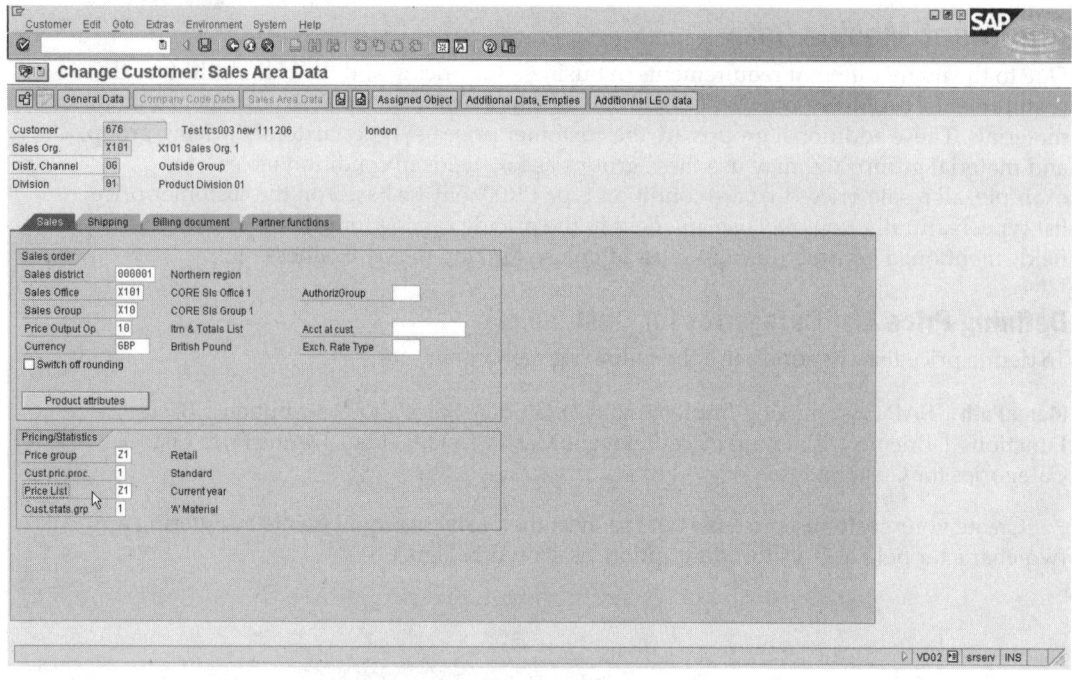

FIGURE 8-31 Price list on customer sales view

After the creation of the data that fills this field, you may assign the newly created data to the customer master record in the sales area view as shown in Figure 8-31.

Defining Pricing Groups for Customers

To create the data for the customer pricing group, use the following menu path.

Menu Path SAP Customizing Implementation Guide I Sales and Distribution I Basic Functions I Pricing I Maintain Price-Relevant Master Data Fields I Define Pricing Groups for Customers

You may define your pricing groups with a two-character key and a short description. After the creation of the group you may assign the data again to the sales view of the customer master, as shown earlier in Figure 8-31.

Defining Material Groups

To define the material group, use the following menu path.

Menu Path SAP Customizing Implementation Guide I Sales and Distribution I Basic Functions I Pricing I Maintain Price-Relevant Master Data Fields I Define Material Groups

Again, assign the two-character key and a short description. Then proceed in assigning this data to the sales organization 2 view of the material master records, as seen in Figure 8-32.

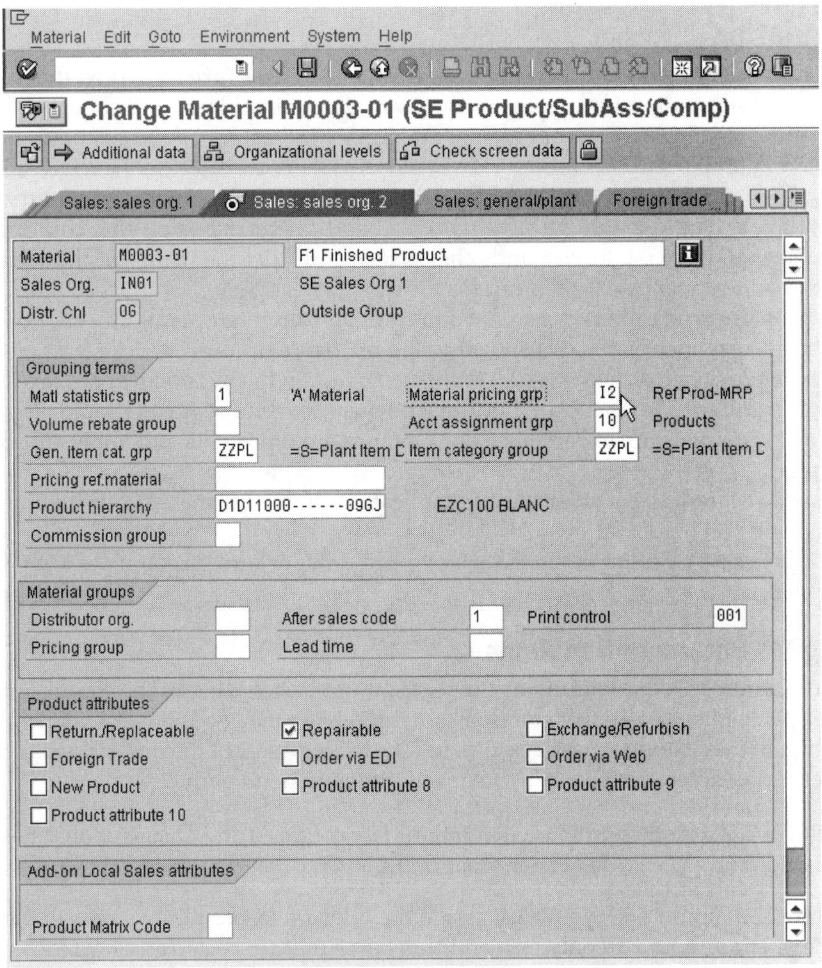

Copyright by SAP AG

FIGURE 8-32 Defining material groups

Condition Supplements

A condition supplement is a group of conditions that you want to apply every time a certain condition is found. For example, if you define a material price, you would enter condition records for every material and the associated price for those materials.

If for one of those materials you also wanted to include a discount every time that price is determined, you can enter the additional condition type discount as a condition supplement.

When SAP determines the condition record in the pricing procedure, it will automatically also include the discount condition record.

Tax Determination

The SAP ERP system automatically determines and calculates taxes based on the organizational structure, country, region, or city of delivering plants and country of receiving customer, in combination with tax relevancy indicators on the customer master record and material master record.

The workload related to tax determination rules differs from country to country. Some countries have a simple, single VAT (value added tax) charge per sale; other countries have a tiered system of taxes (state, city, and other taxes); and still other countries like Brazil have a specific system enhancement to cater for their countries taxes.

Prior to maintaining the tax section, you need to ensure your plants and country or geographical areas such as regions and cities are maintained.

When determining taxes, you should always maintain the data relevant to taxes in consultation with the FI (Financial) module. The business requirements should also be strictly administered by an experienced accountant who represents and knows the business procedures.

You should carefully consider the tax implications in the business blueprint of a project prior to creating an organizational model.

It is only necessary to maintain the tax relevant data for foreign countries with which you do business.

Defining Tax Determination Rules

The system automatically determines the relevant taxes according to the country of the delivering plant, plus the country of the customer receiving the goods, in combination with the tax indicator of the customer master record and the tax indicator of the material master record.

To define tax determination rules, use the following menu path.

Menu Path   SAP Customizing Implementation Guide I Sales and Distribution I Basic Functions I Taxes I Define Tax Determination Rules

As shown in Figure 8-33, you must assign the relevant tax condition types to the country key. The system will only list condition types that are regarded as "taxes" in the condition class of the condition type.

While assigning the tax condition type or "tax category" to the country key, you need to specify if more than one tax is required and in which order the system is to access the condition records. This is done by assigning the relevant tax condition types to the relevant country keys and by assigning an access sequence number—for example, Canada has a GST tax and a PST tax.

After you have assigned the tax condition types or categories, you must ensure the condition types are placed into the relevant pricing procedures and that the associated tax condition records are created/maintained.

Defining Regional Codes

As some countries may have county and or regionalized taxes, it is possible to state specific regions within a country code. For example, in Figure 8-34 Denmark has counties within a region.

To define regional codes, use the following menu path.

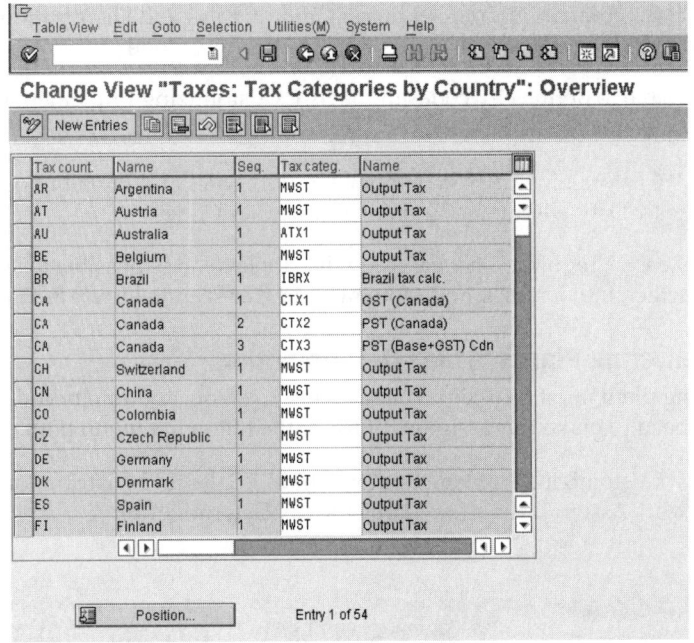

Copyright by SAP AG

FIGURE 8-33   Defining tax determination rules (tax categories per country)

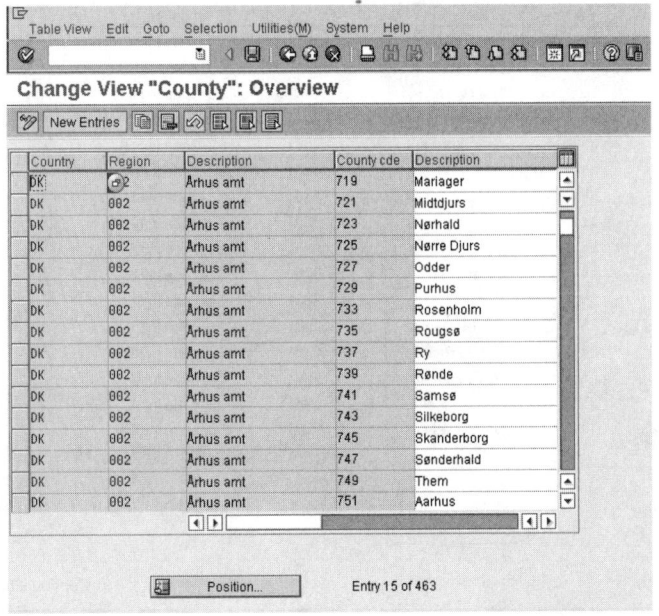

Copyright by SAP AG

FIGURE 8-34   Defining county codes

Menu Path   SAP Customizing Implementation Guide | Sales and Distribution | Basic Functions | Taxes | Define Regional Codes | Define County Code

It is also possible to define city codes in the SAP Customizing Implementation Guide by using the following menu path.

Menu Path   SAP Customizing Implementation Guide | Sales and Distribution | Basic Functions | Taxes | Define Regional Codes | Define City Code

Currently, the USA requires a tax based on the city level. It is possible to subdivide a country code further, into a region and then into a city, as seen in Figure 8-35.

Assigning Delivering Plants for Tax Determination

As the delivering plant must be assigned to a country, region, and or city code for tax purposes, you need to make this assignment using the following menu path.

Menu Path   SAP Customizing Implementation Guide | Sales and Distribution | Basic Functions | Taxes | Assign Delivering Plants for Tax Determination

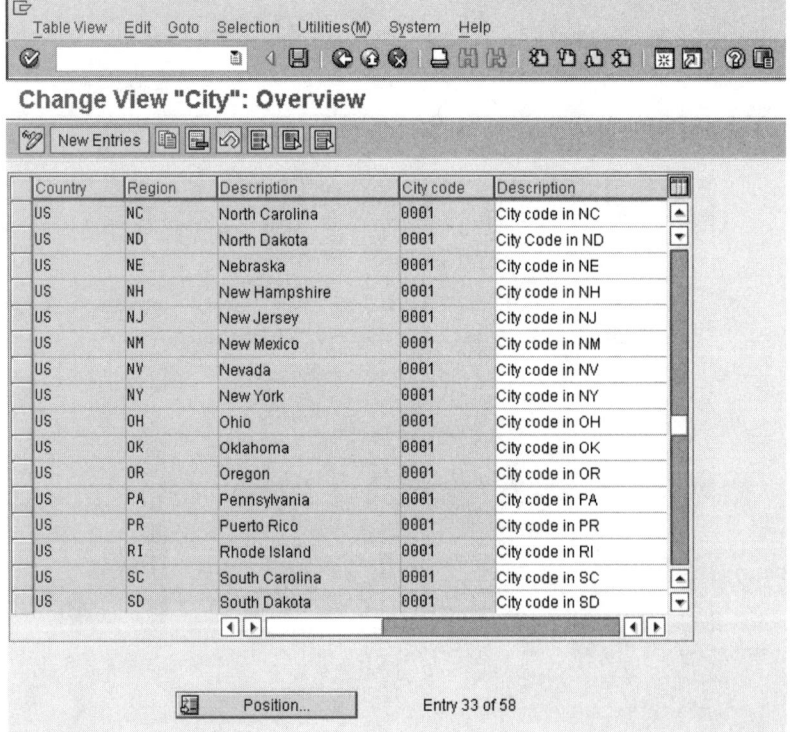

Copyright by SAP AG

FIGURE 8-35   Defining city codes

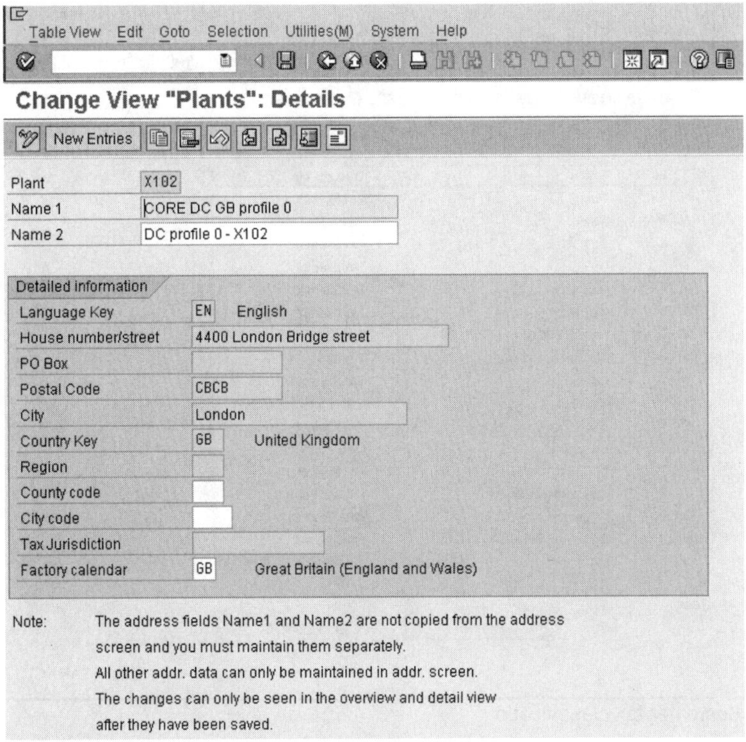

Copyright by SAP AG

FIGURE 8-36   Assigning delivering plants for tax determination

As shown in Figure 8-36, Plant X102 is assigned to Great Britain.

After assigning the delivering plant, you need to create the indicators that are represented on the customer and material master records. This is covered in the following sections.

Defining Tax Relevancy of Master Records-Customer Taxes

It is important to specify if the customer is liable for taxes or not. You can assign a relevancy indicator to the tax condition type or " tax category" using the following menu path.

Menu Path   SAP Customizing Implementation Guide | Sales and Distribution | Basic Functions | Taxes | Define Tax Relevancy of Master Records | Customer Taxes

For example, in Figure 8-37 there are two indicators assigned to the MWST. Either of these two may be assigned to a customer master record.

The system then uses this indicator as found on the Billing view of the customer master record as shown in Figure 8-38.

Now you can proceed to create the material tax indicators.

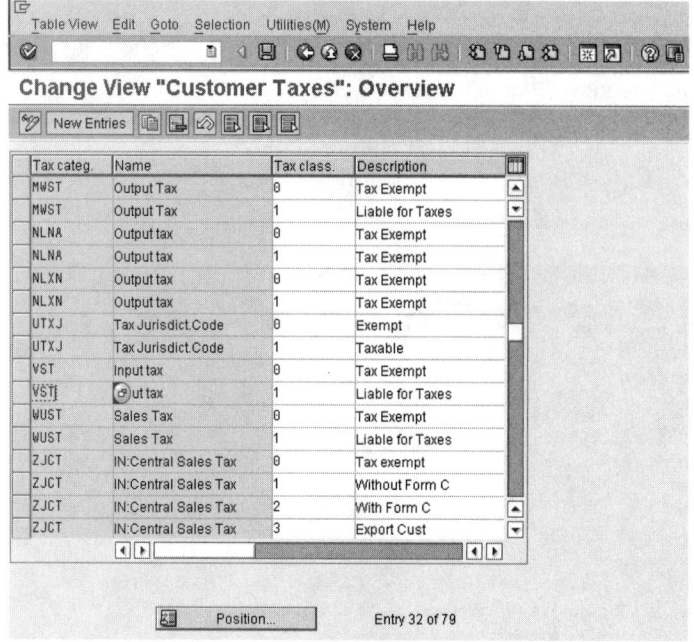

Copyright by SAP AG

FIGURE 8-37 Customer tax classification

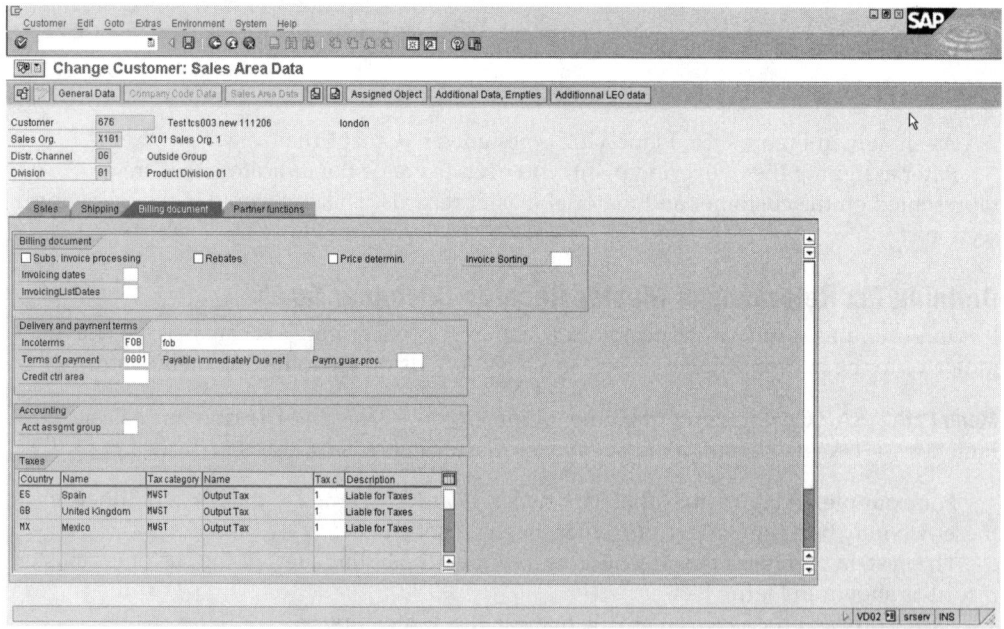

Copyright by SAP AG

FIGURE 8-38 Customer tax classification in Billing view of customer master record

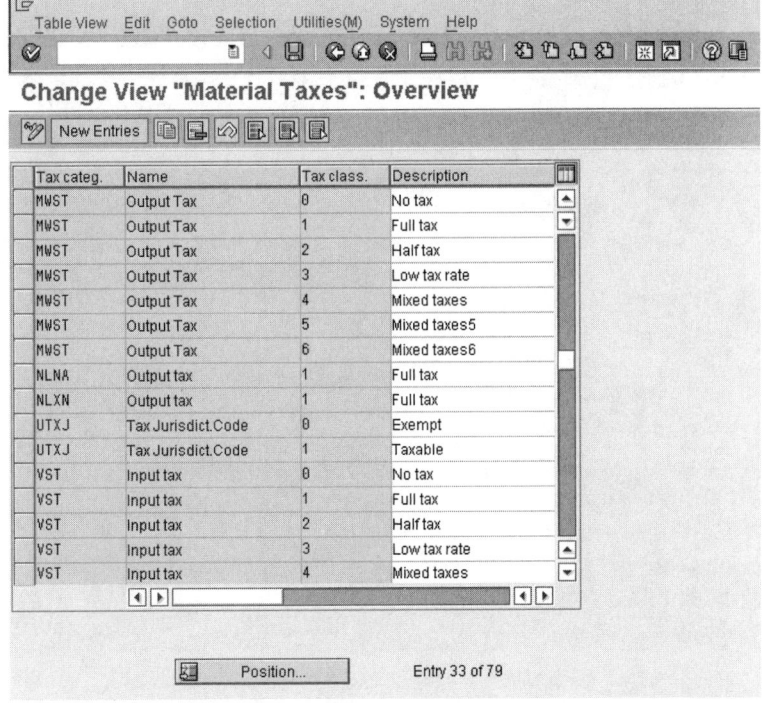

Copyright by SAP AG

FIGURE 8-39   Material tax classification

Defining Tax Relevancy of Master Records-Material Taxes

To define tax relevancy of master records, use the following menu path.

Menu Path   SAP Customizing Implementation Guide | Sales and Distribution | Basic Functions | Taxes | Define Tax Relevancy of Master Records | Material Taxes

Here you can assign a tax relevancy indicator to the tax condition type or "tax category," which will later be assigned to the material master record. This is seen in Figure 8-39.

This indicator is then assigned to the material master record on the sales organization 1 view, as seen in Figure 8-40.

VAT Registration Number in Sales and Billing Documents

This section is important as the tax classifications assigned to the partners may be taken from a different customer master record than that of the Sold-to Party. The same rule that defines how the system is to determine the tax classification number also defines how the system is to reproduce the tax or VAT registration number from the customer master record into the sales documents. To do this, use the following menu path.

Menu Path   SAP Customizing Implementation Guide | Sales and Distribution | Basic Functions | Taxes | Maintain Sales Tax Identification Number Determination

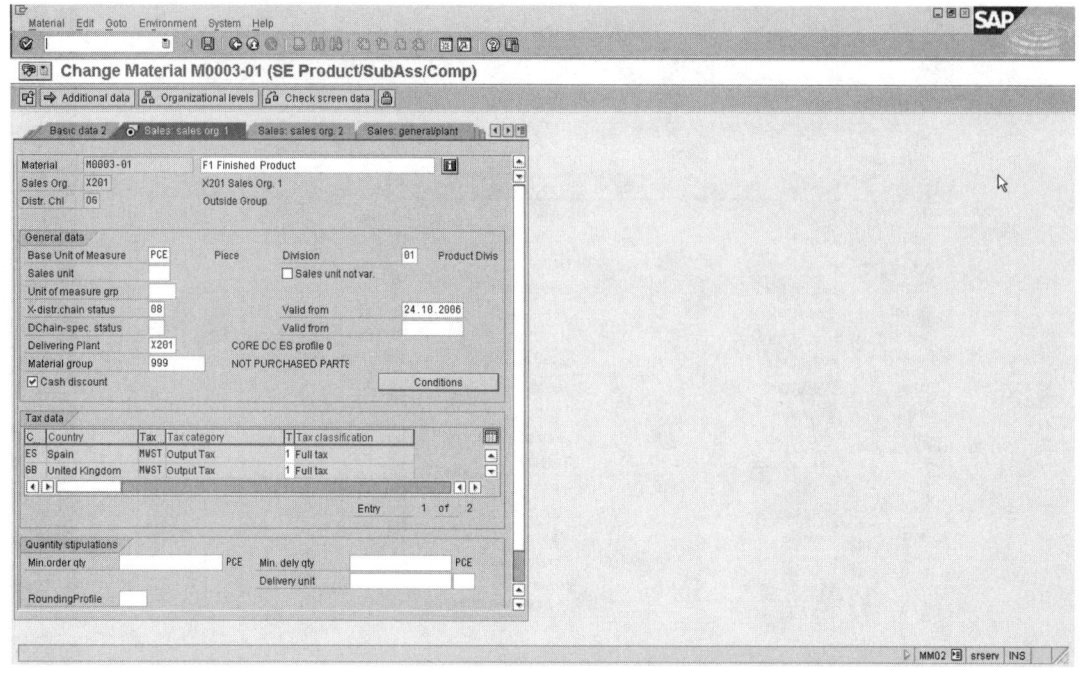

Copyright by SAP AG

FIGURE 8-40   Material tax classification on sales organization 1 view

There are four available options to be assigned per sales organization. In order to keep consistency throughout the system, it is recommended to keep the determining rules the same across all sales organizations.

- Determination rule A means the tax number and tax indicator classification is generally taken from the Sold-to Party customer master record.

- Determination rule B indicates the tax number and tax classification is generally taken from the customer master record of the payer.

- Should the field be left blank (priority rule), the system determines the tax number and the tax classification according to the following sequence:

  1. If the payer has a VAT registration number and is identical to the sold-to party, tax number and tax classification are copied from the payer (in this case, the Ship-to Party is not relevant). The tax number is copied according to the "country of destination relevant for taxes."

  2. If the previous step does not apply: If the Ship-to Party has a VAT registration number and the Sold-to Party does not, tax number, and tax classification are copied from the Ship-to Party.

  3. If the second step does not apply: Tax number and tax classification are copied from the Sold-to Party.

- Determination rule C is the same as the priority rule. However, the destination country is taken from the Ship-to Party.

Generally, the VAT registration number on the customer master record will be 11 characters long and begin with a prefix equal to that of the ISO code for the country—for example, the VAT registration number for Germany is DE123456789.

Tax Condition Records

Do not forget to create the condition records for the tax condition type. These may be created by using the following menu path from the logistics.

Menu Path   SAP Menu | Logistics | Sales and Distribution | Master Data | Conditions | Select Using Condition Type | [VK11] - Create

Enter the tax condition type you are using, such as MWST. Being a condition type, this has an access sequence and condition tables. Therefore, when you press ENTER, you will see a dialog box asking for which key combination you wish to create the condition record. Select the departure country/destination country combination. For example, in Figure 8-41 we have created a condition record for Great Britain shipping to Ireland using standard VAT at 17.5 percent. Take note of the tax code A1.

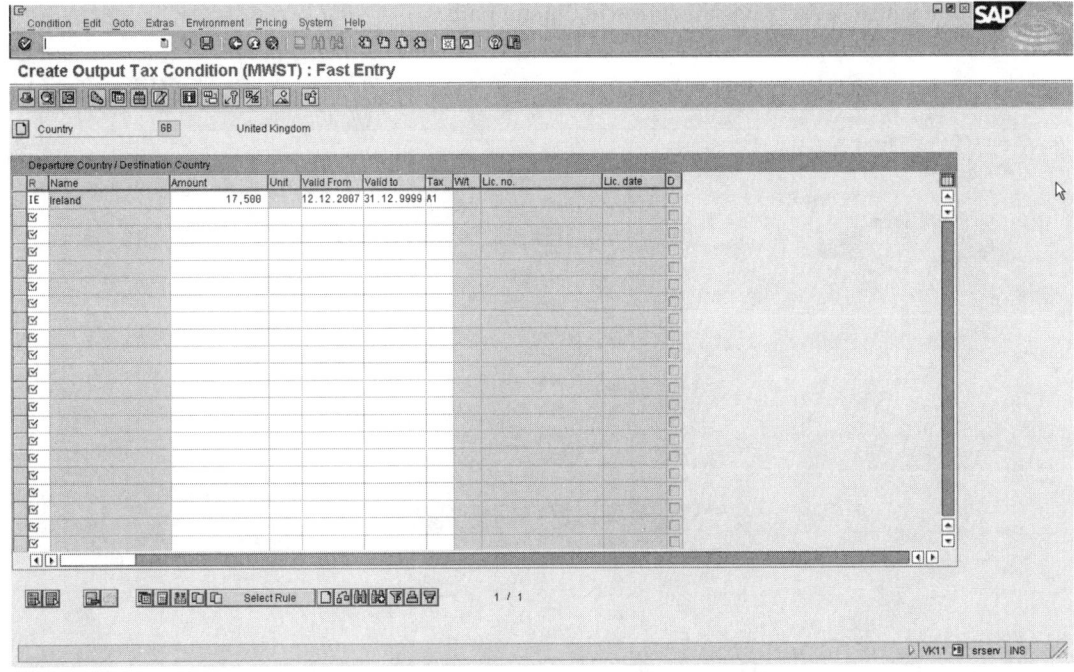

Copyright by SAP AG

FIGURE 8-41   Tax condition record

Tax Integration with Financial Accounting

There are numerous tax settings to be maintained in the FI (Finance) module in mySAP ERP. These settings are related to outbound and inbound taxes, and are split into three sections within the IMG:

- Basic Settings
- Calculation
- Posting

To reach the first section, use the following menu path.

Menu Path   SAP Customizing Implementation Guide | Financial Accounting | Financial Accounting Global Settings | Tax on Sales/Purchases | Basic Settings

This section is used to create and assign a tax calculation procedure to a country. For example a basic tax procedure would be South Africa, as seen in Figure 8-42.

You can see that this determination procedure uses the condition technique. It also uses the account keys to make a posting.

To reach the next section, use the following menu path.

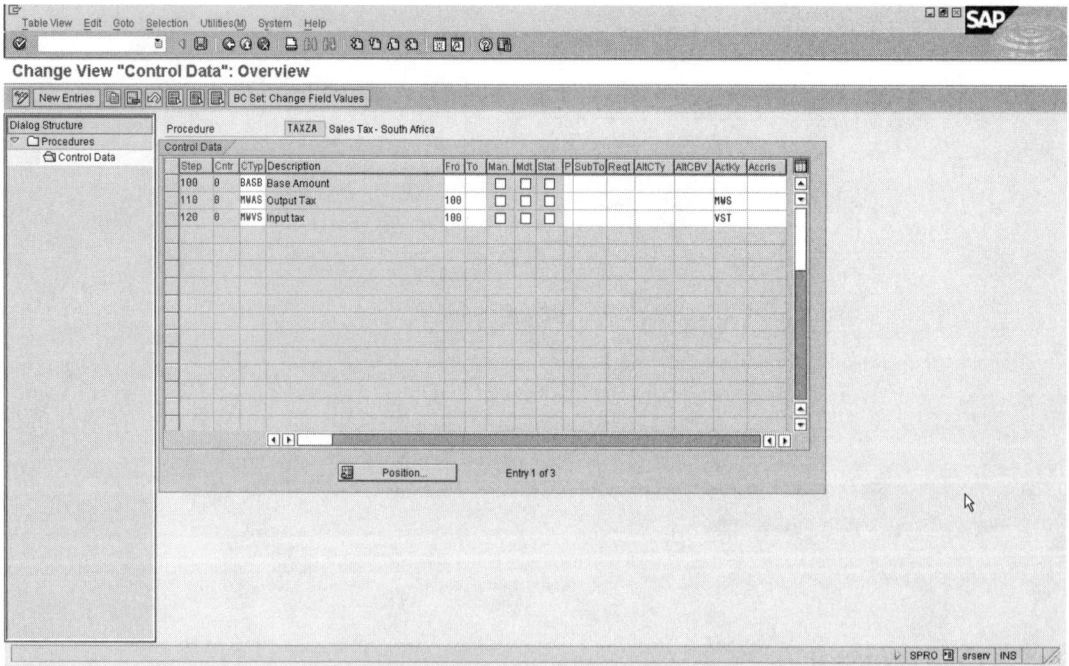

Copyright by SAP AG

FIGURE 8-42   Tax procedure

Menu Path   SAP Customizing Implementation Guide | Financial Accounting | Financial Accounting Global Settings | Tax on Sales/Purchases | Calculation

When we created the tax condition record, we assigned a tax code assigned to it. This tax code is controlled in this section within FI.

In Figure 8-43 we can see that the tax code A1 in tax procedure TAXGB has a value of 17.5 percent assigned to it. This must be the same value that you use to create your condition record.

To reach the next section, use the following menu path.

Menu Path   SAP Customizing Implementation Guide | Financial Accounting | Financial Accounting Global Settings | Tax on Sales/Purchases | Posting

This section is used to define the GL account assigned to the tax transactions.

This has only served to be an introduction to the tax definitions within FI. The complexity and variables you may encounter when implementing tax determination will vary between countries. However, the knowledge you have in the condition technique and the pricing procedure, as well as these simple introductions, should be enough to help you on your way.

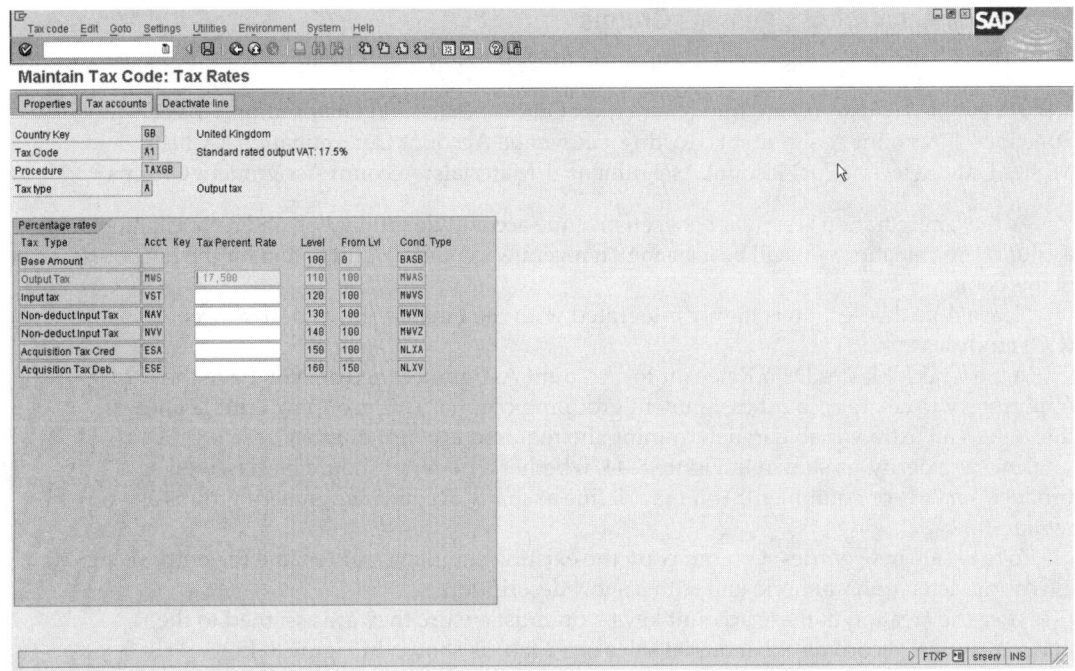

FIGURE 8-43   Tax code—tax rates

Account Assignment

The condition technique is also used in account determination in order to allocate the correct general ledger account to the account key as assigned in the pricing procedure.

Whenever a sale is posted to accounting, SAP must find (or determine) which account to post the revenues and discounts to.

There is, therefore, a determination procedure to find the accounts, called the *account determination procedure*. This procedure contains a condition type to find which account to post to based on the conditions of the sale. The condition type searches all the records that contain accounts for conditions that match the sale in the order of the access sequence. As soon as it finds a record that matches the conditions, it returns a condition value—in this case, the GL account.

The condition technique is used as you may wish to post to different accounts under different conditions. For example, sales of a certain material can go to one revenue account, sales of other materials to a different account; or export sales can go to one account, local sales to another account.

Depending on all these conditions (the material, types of sale, etc.), SAP can find a different account. The condition technique is used to find the right account under the right conditions.

Materials: Account Assignment Groups

To work with account assignment groups, use the following menu path.

Menu Path   SAP Customizing Implementation Guide | Sales and Distribution | Basic Functions | Account Assignment/Costing | Revenue Account Determination | Check Master Data Relevant For Account Assignment | Materials: Account Assignment Groups

As the configuration is similar between revenue account determination and reconciliation account determination, we will be focusing on revenue account determination for the purposes of this book.

Please note this section is highly integrated with the Finance (FI) and Cost Accounting (CO) modules.

In the Check Master Data Relevant for Account Assignment screen, you have the opportunity to create account assignment grouping criteria. This grouping criteria allows the system an extra variable in determining the required account number.

You can specify, as shown in Figure 8-44, whether a material should be classified as a product, service, or equipment. You may define as many account assignment groups as you require.

To re-create new entries, you can copy the existing standard and rename the entry using a two-character alphanumeric key with a short description.

After the creation of these account keys, you must ensure they are assigned to the material master record on the material sales org 2 tab, as shown in Figure 8-45.

Customers: Account Assignment Groups

To work with account assignment groups, use the following menu path.

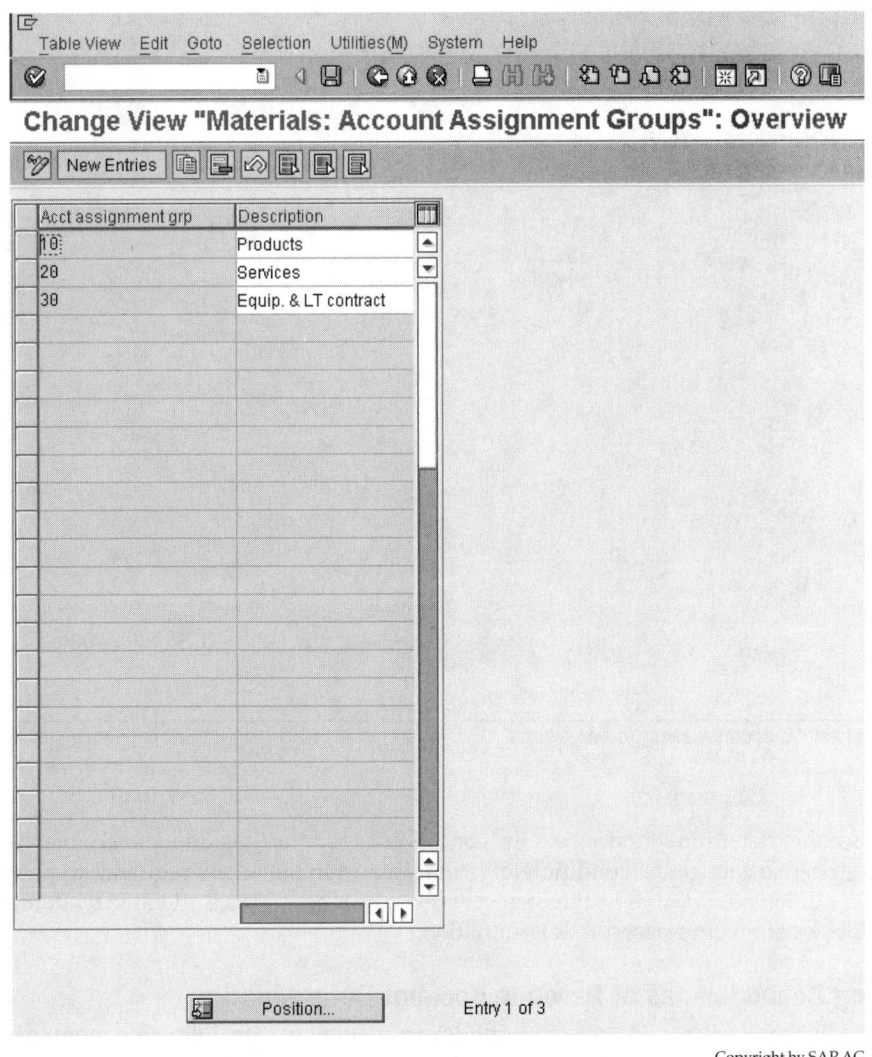

FIGURE 8-44   Checking master data relevant for account assignment

Menu Path   SAP Customizing Implementation Guide | Sales and Distribution | Basic Functions | Account Assignment/Costing | Revenue Account Determination | Check Master Data Relevant for Account Assignment | Customers: Account Assignment Groups

Again, to re-create new entries, you can copy the existing standard and rename the entry using a two-character alphanumeric key with a short description.

These account assignment keys are useful in grouping account determination. For example, the business may want domestic sales revenue to be posted into account X, while international sales revenue may have to be posted into account Y, differentiated by account assignment group.

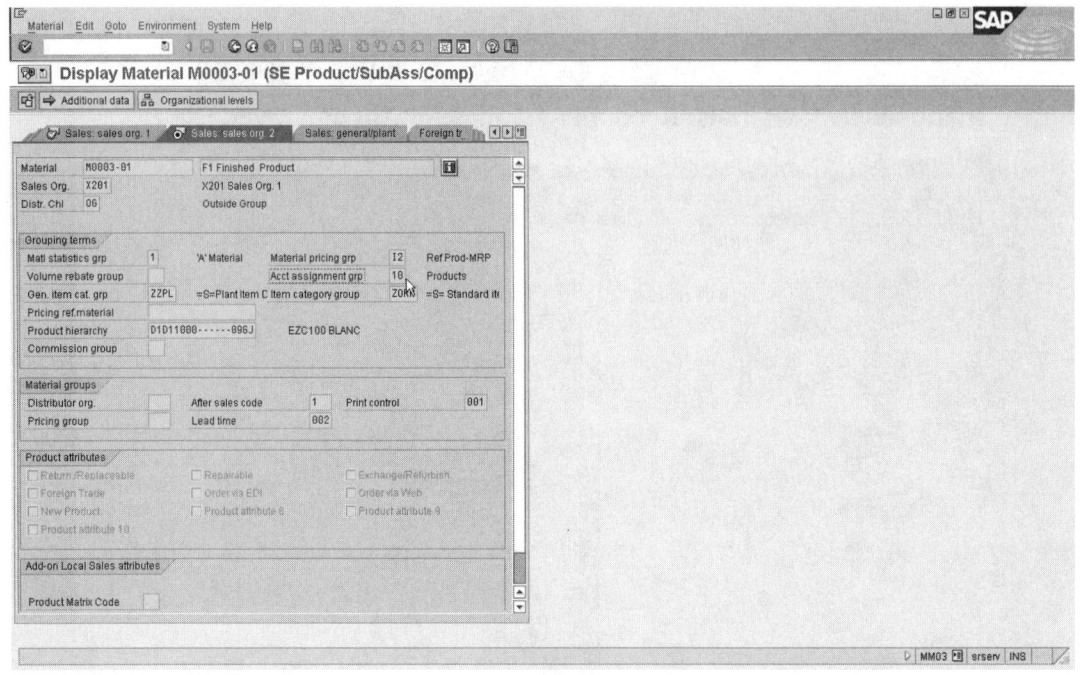

Copyright by SAP AG

FIGURE 8-45   Materials: account assignment groups

As account determination follows the condition technique, it is understandable there may be a need to change the condition table that is used in the access sequence to find the correct condition record (that is, the correct account number). This is possible by defining dependencies of revenue account determination.

Defining Dependencies of Revenue Account Determination

To define dependencies of revenue account determination, use the following menu path.

Menu Path   SAP Customizing Implementation Guide | Sales and Distribution | Basic Functions | Account Assignment/Costing | Revenue Account Determination | Define Dependencies of Revenue Account Determination

Here you can create or change a condition table. However, you must be careful as there are not many fields to select from in order to create this condition table.

Please refer back to pricing and condition tables in this chapter for more information on creating and changing condition tables.

After ensuring your condition tables exist as required, you need to ensure the access sequence and condition types are maintained as required too.

Define Access Sequences and Account Determination Types

To define access sequences and account determination types, use the following menu path.

Menu Path   SAP Customizing Implementation Guide I Sales and Distribution I Basic Functions I Account Assignment/Costing I Revenue Account Determination I Define Access Sequences and Account Determination Types I Define Account Determination Types

The Standard mySAP ERP has two condition types: KOFI (account determination) and KOFK (account determination with CO). We will use the standard condition type KOFI, which uses the access sequence with the key KOFI as well.

The KOFI access sequence has five condition tables assigned to it, as seen in Figure 8-46.

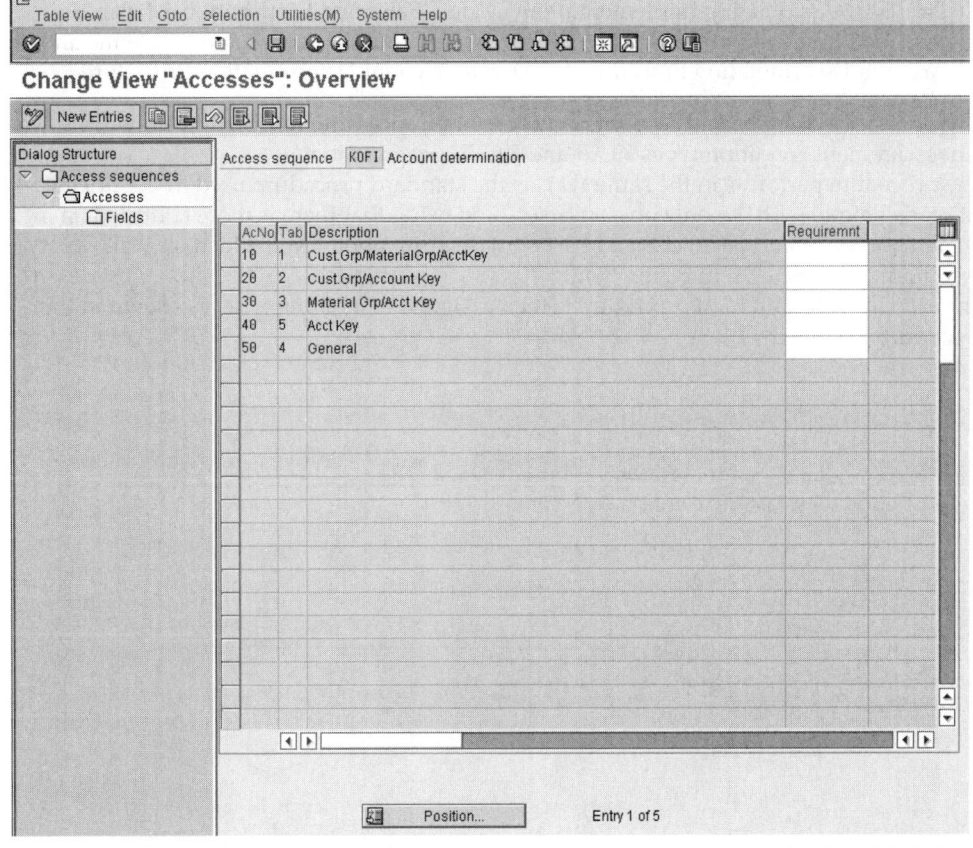

FIGURE 8-46   Access sequence KOFI

This KOFI access sequence may be kept for most business, with the possible exception that maybe not all the condition tables would be used. If this was the case it would be advisable to copy the access sequence, rename it, and then allocate it to the relevant account determination type (condition type). Within the new access sequence you would now be able to delete condition tables that are not being used, thus improving on system performance and response times.

As in the standard condition techniques, you can assign a requirement to the condition tables within the access sequence if necessary.

Defining and Assigning Account Determination Procedures

Now you can begin creating the account assignment procedure, using the following menu path.

Menu Path   SAP Customizing Implementation Guide | Sales and Distribution | Basic Functions | Account Assignment/Costing | Revenue Account Determination | Define and Assign Account Determination Procedures | Define Account Determination Procedure

The standard system has an account determination procedure, KOFI00, which has the account assignment condition types KOFI and KOFK assigned to it.

The procedure performs in the same way as the standard procedure used in the pricing condition technique with the only obvious exception being that there is more control data in pricing at the condition type level than at account determination level, which only allows for a requirement, as shown in Figure 8-47.

The account determination procedure is then assigned to a billing type, as shown in the next section.

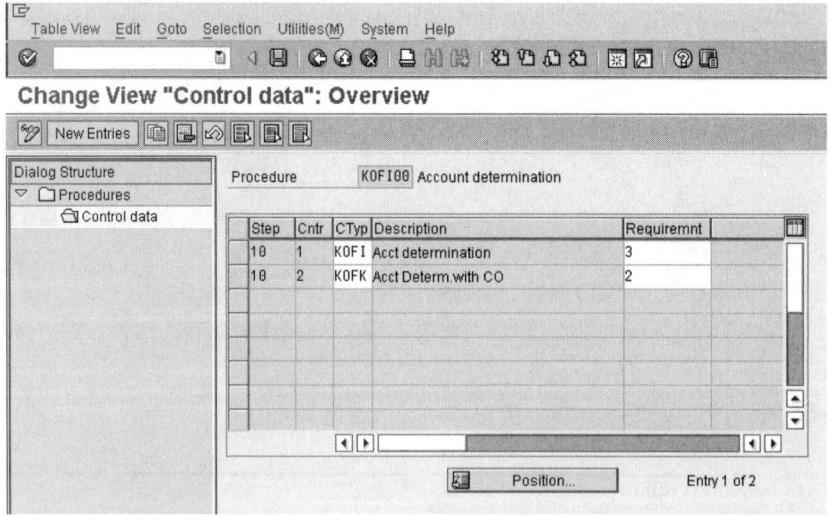

Copyright by SAP AG

FIGURE 8-47   Defining an account determination procedure

Assigning Account Determination Procedure

To assign an account determination procedure, use the following menu path.

Menu Path   SAP Customizing Implementation Guide | Sales and Distribution | Basic Functions | Account Assignment/Costing | Revenue Account Determination | Define and Assign Account Determination Procedures | Assign Account Determination Procedure

The account determination procedure is assigned to the billing document type as seen in Figure 8-48.

The CaAc column represents the cash allocation key, which causes the system to post directly into a general ledger account for the cash entry rather than into a receivables account.

Defining and Assigning Account Keys

You now need to create the account keys that are going to be used in the system. To do this, use the following menu path.

Menu Path   SAP Customizing Implementation Guide | Sales and Distribution | Basic Functions | Account Assignment/Costing | Revenue Account Determination | Define and Assign Account Keys

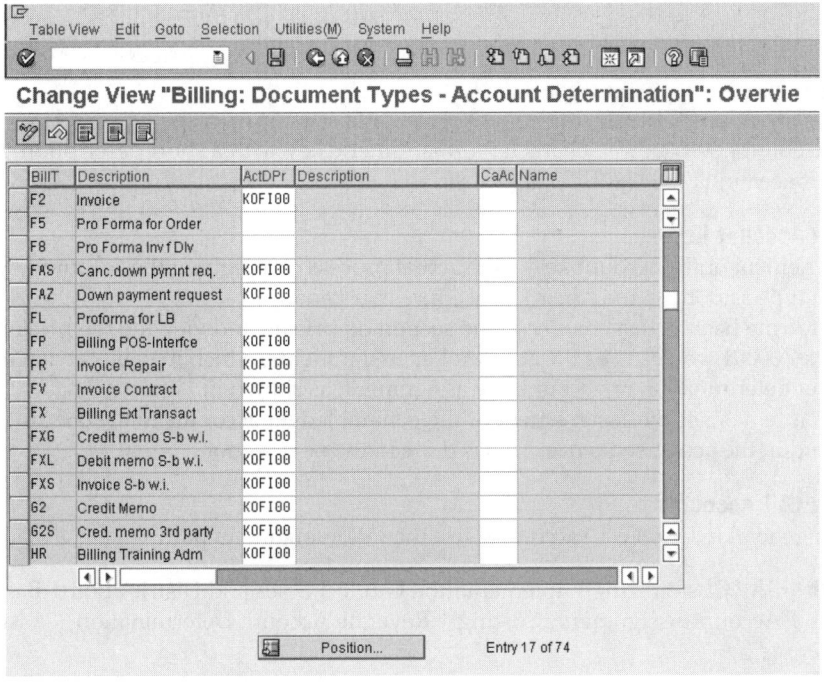

Copyright by SAP AG

FIGURE 8-48   Assigning an account determination procedure

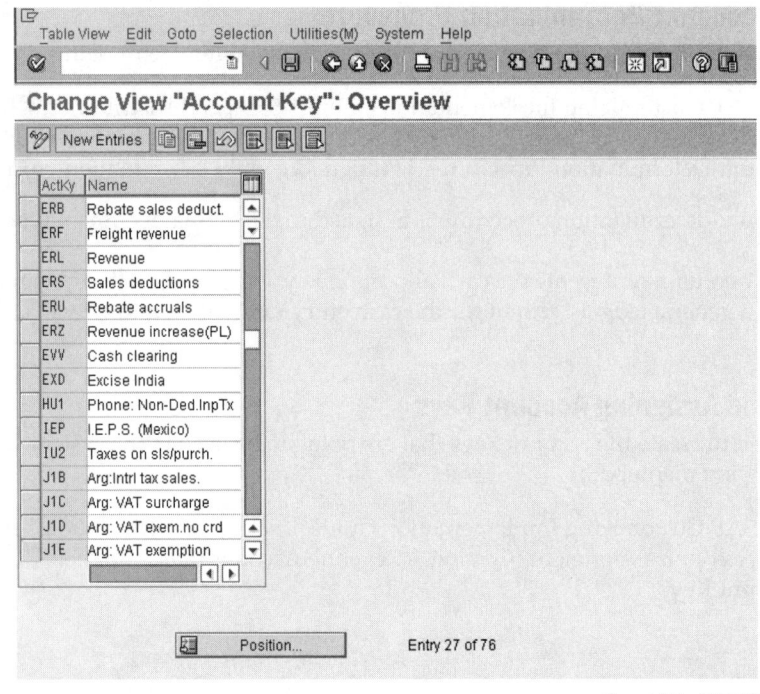

FIGURE 8-49   Defining and assigning account keys

The account key is a three-character alphanumeric key with a short description. An example is seen in Figure 8-49.

Assigning Account Keys

The assignement of the account key is the actual process of assigning the account key to the condition type as done in the pricing procedure maintenance.

 By referring back in this chapter to the section on pricing and viewing the pricing procedure Z00001, you can see the account key assignments, which may be carried out in the pricing determination or account key assignment, as shown in Figure 8-50.

All that remains is the assignement of the general ledger accounts to the condition table as specified in the access sequence. This is done in the next section.

Assigning G/L Accounts

To assign general ledger (G/L) accounts, use the following menu path.

Menu Path   SAP Customizing Implementation Guide | Sales and Distribution | Basic Functions | Account Assignment/Costing | Revenue Account Determination | Assign G/L Accounts

Before the general ledger accounts may be assigned, the FI (Finance) module must have finished creating the chart of accounts and the general ledger accounts.

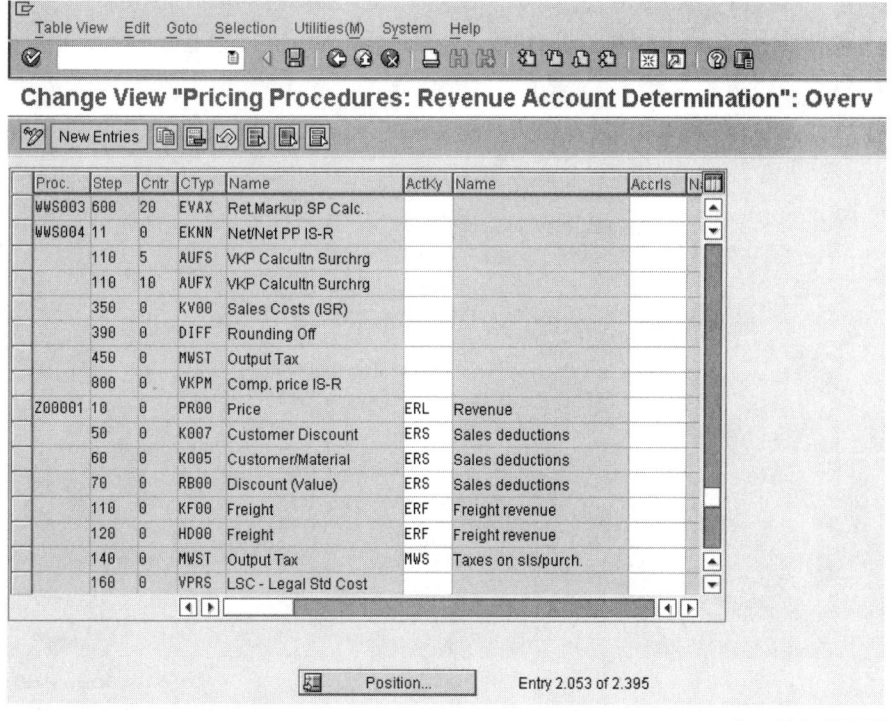

FIGURE 8-50   Assigning account keys

You'll see an access sequence of tables for KOFI, as shown in Figure 8-51. (Note how the access proceeds from the most complex to the most simple.)

Select a table such as table 1 Cust.Grp/MaterialGrp/AcctKey. An example of the assignment of the general ledger accounts to the Account Key condition table/field overview would be as shown in Figure 8-52. The columns represent the following data:

- **V (application)**   Sales
- **CndTy (condition type)**   KOFI
- **ChAc (chart of accounts)**   CABE
- **Sorg (sales organization)**   0001
- **AAG (customer account assignment group)**   01
- **AAG (material account assignment group)**   01
- **ActKy (account key)**   ERL
- **Assigned general ledger account**   700000

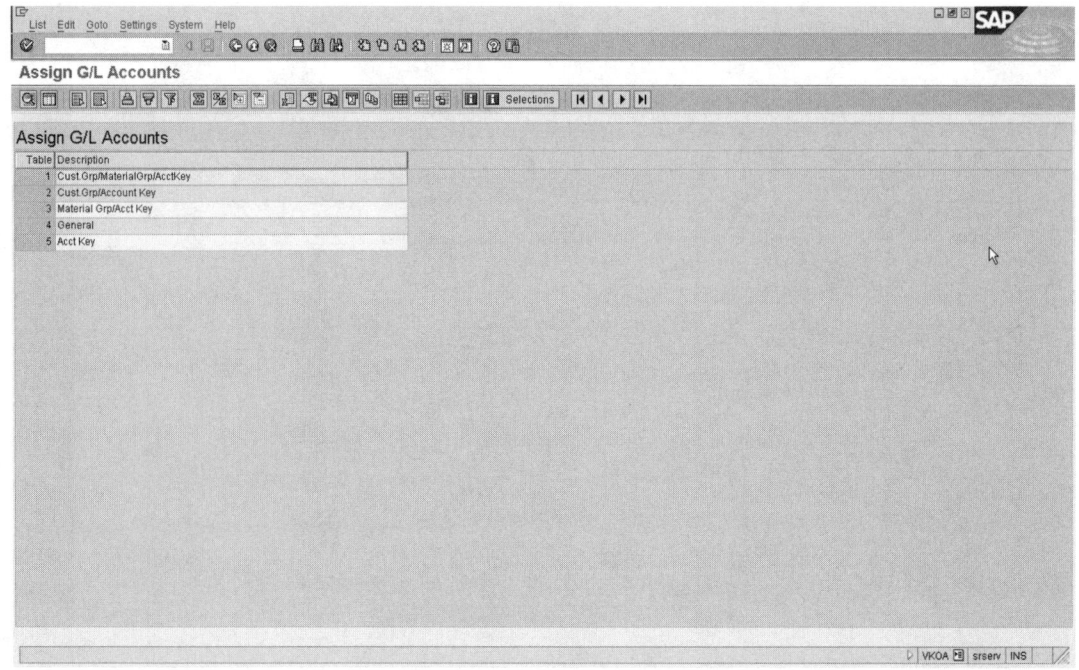

Copyright by SAP AG

FIGURE 8-51   Assigning G/L accounts (Access Sequence KOFI)

   Should you have an account determination error in the goods issue of a delivery it is very likely the error is in the materials management account assignment. This account assignment may be displayed via transaction code [OBYC] or by using the following menu path.

Menu Path   Materials Management I Valuation and Account Assignment I Account Determination I Account Determination Without Wizard I Create Automatic Postings

Pricing Requirements and Formulas

The use of requirements, copying requirements, data transfer routines, and pricing formulas occurs throughout the system.

- *Requirements* are represented by routines in the system source code, ABAP. Requirements check for certain criteria during the execution of functions.

- *Copying requirements* are used in the same way as standard requirements by the system—they check for certain criteria as preconditions for carrying out the copying function.

- *Data transfer routines* are used during copying control to fine-tune what data is necessary to transfer between documents. These transfer routines may also alter the copied data.

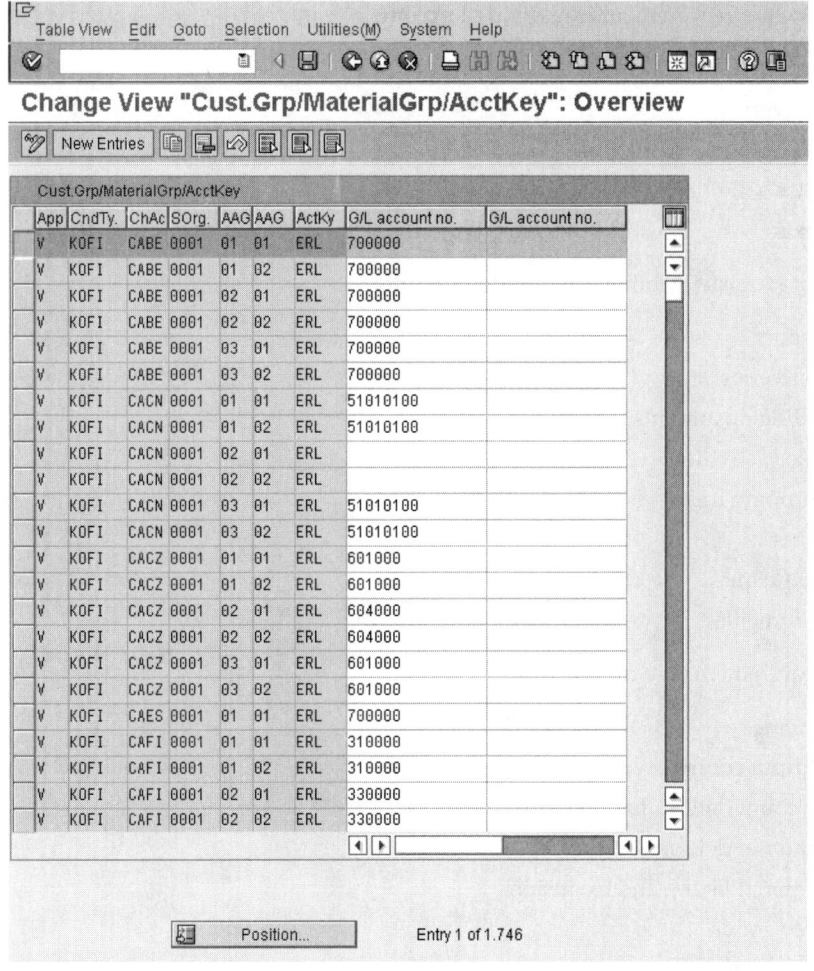

Table View Edit Goto Selection Utilities(M) System Help

Change View "Cust.Grp/MaterialGrp/AcctKey": Overview

New Entries

Cust.Grp/MaterialGrp/AcctKey

App	CndTy.	ChAc	SOrg.	AAG	AAG	ActKy	G/L account no.	G/L account no.
V	KOFI	CABE	0001	01	01	ERL	700000	
V	KOFI	CABE	0001	01	02	ERL	700000	
V	KOFI	CABE	0001	02	01	ERL	700000	
V	KOFI	CABE	0001	02	02	ERL	700000	
V	KOFI	CABE	0001	03	01	ERL	700000	
V	KOFI	CABE	0001	03	02	ERL	700000	
V	KOFI	CACN	0001	01	01	ERL	51010100	
V	KOFI	CACN	0001	01	02	ERL	51010100	
V	KOFI	CACN	0001	02	01	ERL		
V	KOFI	CACN	0001	02	02	ERL		
V	KOFI	CACN	0001	03	01	ERL	51010100	
V	KOFI	CACN	0001	03	02	ERL	51010100	
V	KOFI	CACZ	0001	01	01	ERL	601000	
V	KOFI	CACZ	0001	01	02	ERL	601000	
V	KOFI	CACZ	0001	02	01	ERL	604000	
V	KOFI	CACZ	0001	02	02	ERL	604000	
V	KOFI	CACZ	0001	03	01	ERL	601000	
V	KOFI	CACZ	0001	03	02	ERL	601000	
V	KOFI	CAES	0001	01	01	ERL	700000	
V	KOFI	CAFI	0001	01	01	ERL	310000	
V	KOFI	CAFI	0001	01	02	ERL	310000	
V	KOFI	CAFI	0001	02	01	ERL	330000	
V	KOFI	CAFI	0001	02	02	ERL	330000	

Position... Entry 1 of 1.746

FIGURE 8-52 GL account assignment

- *Formulas* are also represented by routines in ABAP code. Formulas are used in pricing and influence the determination of prices.

Maintaining Requirements and Formulas

To maintain requirements and formulas, use the following menu path.

Menu Path SAP Customizing Implementation Guide | Sales and Distribution | System Modifications | Routines | Define Copying Requirements

All requirements and formulas are maintainable from transaction code [VOFM].

The copying requirements are divided up into:

- Orders
- Deliveries
- Billing documents
- Sales activities
- Texts

The data transfer routines are divided up into:

- Orders
- Deliveries
- Billing documents
- Sales activities
- Shipping units
- Texts
- Text names
- Shipments

The requirements are divided into:

- Pricing
- Output control
- Account determination
- Material determination
- Material listing and exclusion
- Free goods
- Bonus buy
- Retail pricing
- Risk management
- Credit checks
- Card authorization
- Packing instruction
- Subsequent functions:
  - Transfer of requirements/availability
  - Purchase requisitions/assembly for order
  - Delivery due index
  - Picking
  - Packing

- Goods issue
- Distribution
- Portfolio

The formulas are divided into:

- Scale base
- Condition base value
- Condition value
- Structure of group key
- Rounding rule
- Calculation rule for rebate in kind

Naturally, we cannot provide an example of each of these special requirements and formulas. However, we will focus on the creation of one specific copying requirement.

It is useful to know where requirements and data transfer routines are available to be assigned within the system. However, as a general rule of thumb:

- Copying requirements are available to be assigned when transferring data between documents and texts.
- Data transfer routines are available when copying between documents and texts.
- Requirements are available to be assigned to any access sequence (or where a determination procedure is used) as well prior to most functions.
- Formulas are used generally in pricing determination.

The Creation of a Copying Requirement

In our example the business requires that when creating a sales order from a quotation the system must not copy the schedule lines or the order quantity of the line items, but merely the header and line item data.

You would then proceed to transaction code [VOFM] and select Copying Requirements | Orders.

You'd then see a list of routine numbers with a short description. You can enter a routine number between 601 and 999 with a short description. As the "business requirements" in the example are very similar to copying routine 502, you can copy routine 502 and rename it with a different key.

You can copy a routine by entering a key ID over the original, such as overwriting 502 with 601.

NOTE *To create the routine you would specifically require an access key for the object.*

In the newly created routine you can change the ABAP code, if you have an access key to meet the business requirements.

Once the requirement is correctly created, you can generate the routine by selecting Program | Generate within the ABAP editor. You then need to activate the requirement by selecting Program | Activate within the ABAP editor.

You also need to determine if the routine is found within the main program by selecting Program | Check | Main Program. If you receive a message stating "Main program for include -------------- not found," then you need to generate the main program.

The routine or copy requirement is now created and may be assigned to the copying control rules between a sales document QT (quotation) and a sales document OR (order).

9

CHAPTER

Diverse Sales and
Distribution Functions

T his chapter covers miscellaneous implementation topics that are crucial to SD but not large enough to warrant their own chapters, from sales incompletion logs, partner, text, and output determinations to hierarchies.

Sales Incompletion Logs

It is imperative that specific control is maintained over the entering and failure to enter values in specific objects—for example, sales documents. The data maintained in the sales document is passed through to the delivery and finally the billing document. Thus it is the sales document data that is used as a backbone in sales and distribution processing.

In some instances a delivery document may also need specific data to be maintained. For this reason SAP has an incompletion structure that may be maintained for the delivery to highlight missing data in sales as well as delivery documents, sales activities, and partner functions.

Defining Status Groups

To define the status groups, use the following menu path.

Menu Path SAP Customizing Implementation Guide | Sales and Distribution | Basic Functions | Log of Incomplete Items | Define Status Groups

An incompletion process inspects the object—for example, a sales document line item—and inspects specific fields in order to see if data has been maintained in these fields. Should data not be maintained in these specified fields, the system is told how to respond—that is, does it or does it not give a warning message and to what extent does it allow further processing of the document (based upon the status group).

The incompletion log cannot register what data is maintained in the specified field and compare it to data that should be in the specified field. For example, should a sales document header have a purchase order number, the system will only check to see if data is maintained in VBKD-BSTKD (sales document header - purchase order number). The standard system cannot check to see if the entry in the field is equal to, for example, 10002.

You can create incompletion logs for the following:

- Sales document header data
- Sales document item data
- Sales document schedule line data
- Sales activity data
- Partner data in sales documents, deliveries, and sales activities
- Delivery header data
- Delivery item data

It may seem like we are configuring things in the wrong sequence, but we require a status group in order to assign it later, so first you need to define the status groups. This may be done by using the IMG path listed at the beginning of this section.

These status groups are eventually assigned to the specific field in the incompletion procedure. It is possible to specify that in a sales document that field A may be incomplete but not hinder the document from being processed further, while field B may be incomplete and be the cause of the same document being blocked for further processing.

The status groups, seen in Figure 9-1, will be assigned to a field in the sales incompletion log. This is where the control of the availability check is carried out.

The statuses that may be incomplete are

- **General**   Setting this status in the status group and assigning the status group to a field in the incompletion procedure will cause the sales document to be incomplete. However, it will allow the document to be processed further.

- **Delivery**   Setting this status in the status group and assigning the status group to a field in the incompletion procedure will cause the sales document to be incomplete for further processing, that is, the creation of a delivery (it will not hinder the creation of a billing document).

- **Billing document**   Setting this status in the status group and assigning the status group to a field in the incompletion procedure will cause the sales document and delivery document to be incomplete for further processing, that is, the creation of the billing document, should the associated field not be filled.

- **Price**   Setting this status in the status group and assigning the status group to a field in the incompletion procedure will cause the sales document to be incomplete for further processing should pricing not have been carried out.

- **Goods movement**   Setting this status in the status group and assigning the status group to a field in the incompletion procedure will cause the delivery document to be incomplete for further processing, that is, for goods movement, should a field not be filled (for example, quantity picked).

- **Picking**   Setting this status in the status group and assigning the status group to a field in the incompletion procedure will cause the delivery document to be incomplete for further processing, that is, picking, should a field not be filled (for example, serial numbers).

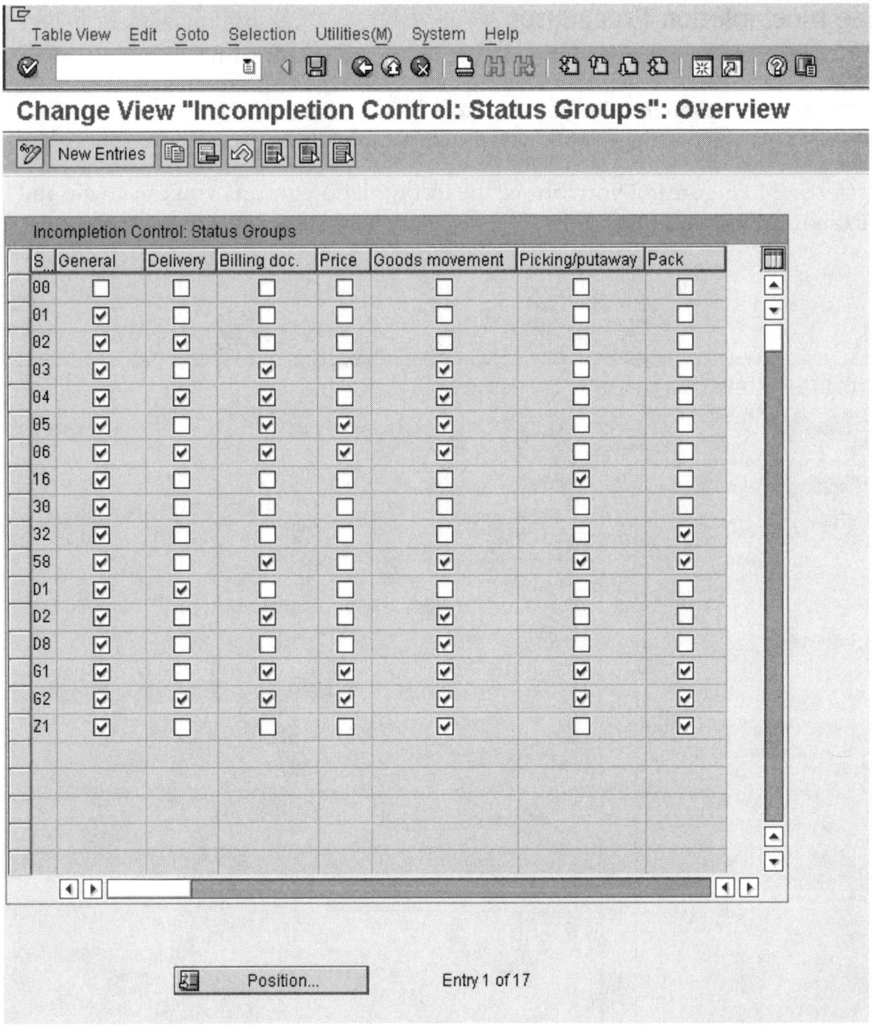

Table View   Edit   Goto   Selection   Utilities(M)   System   Help

Change View "Incompletion Control: Status Groups": Overview

New Entries

Incompletion Control: Status Groups

S	General	Delivery	Billing doc.	Price	Goods movement	Picking/putaway	Pack
00	☐	☐	☐	☐	☐	☐	☐
01	☑	☐	☐	☐	☐	☐	☐
02	☑	☑	☐	☐	☐	☐	☐
03	☑	☐	☑	☐	☑	☐	☐
04	☑	☑	☑	☐	☑	☐	☐
05	☑	☐	☑	☑	☑	☐	☐
06	☑	☑	☑	☑	☑	☐	☐
16	☑	☐	☐	☐	☐	☑	☐
30	☑	☐	☐	☐	☐	☐	☐
32	☑	☐	☐	☐	☐	☐	☑
58	☑	☐	☑	☐	☑	☑	☑
D1	☑	☑	☐	☐	☐	☐	☐
D2	☑	☐	☑	☐	☑	☐	☐
D8	☑	☐	☐	☐	☑	☐	☐
G1	☑	☐	☑	☑	☑	☑	☑
G2	☑	☑	☑	☑	☑	☑	☑
Z1	☑	☐	☐	☐	☑	☐	☑

Position...   Entry 1 of 17

FIGURE 9-1   Incompletion control: status groups

- **Packing**   Setting this status in the status group and assigning the status group to a field in the incompletion procedure will cause the delivery document to be incomplete for further processing, that is, packing, should a field not be filled (for example, quantity picked).

Should you wish to change a status group, be sure to copy the status group that closely resembles your requirements, change its name, and continue to change this new status group's assignments.

In our example we will be using the Status group 01, which has a General status. Now we are able to proceed to defining the incompletion procedures.

Defining Incompletion Procedures

To define the incompletion procedure, use the following menu path.

Menu Path SAP Customizing Implementation Guide | Sales and Distribution | Basic Functions | Log of Incomplete Items | Define Incompleteness Procedures

By referring to Figure 9-2 you can see the incompletion groups you can create and assign to an incompletion procedure.

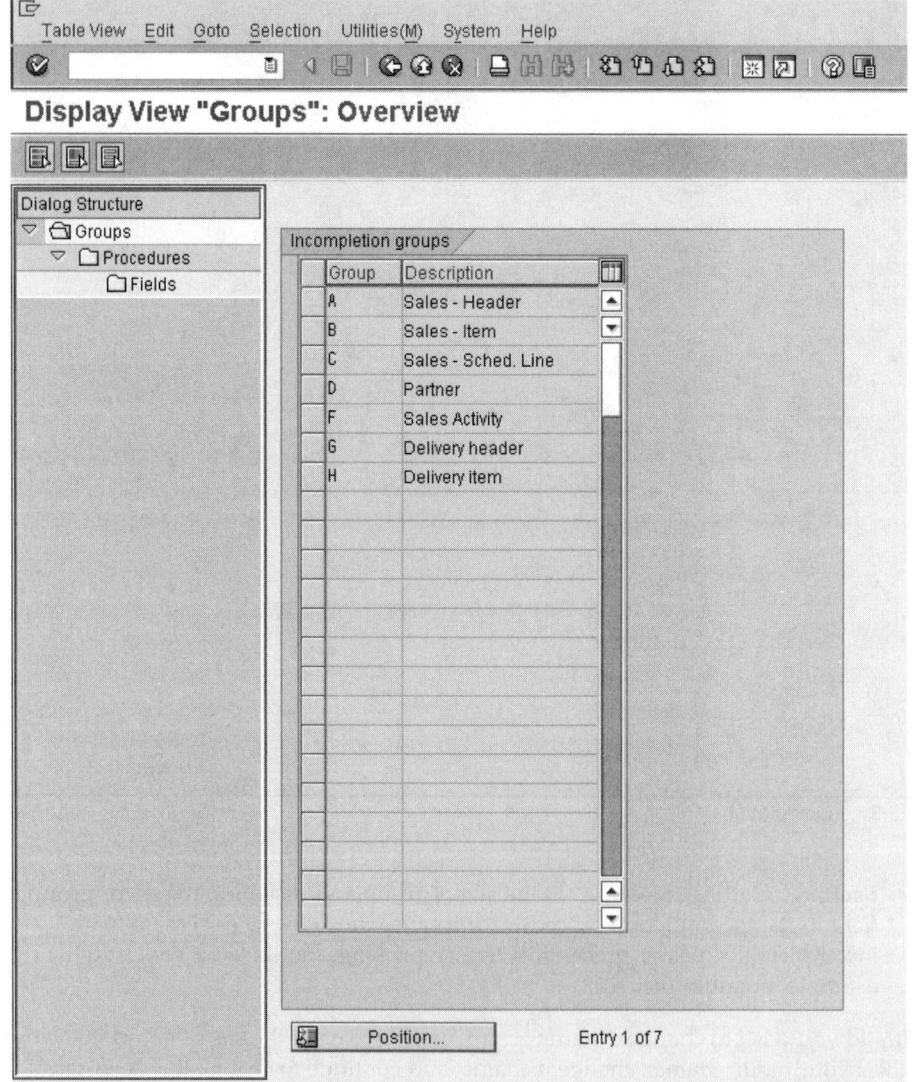

FIGURE 9-2 Incompletion groups

It is not possible to create your own Error group for example: a copy of group A—Sales header.

By selecting "Group A—Sales Header"And then selecting the "Procedures" folder in the dialog structure on the left hand side, one is able to look at the incompletion procedures.

In future we will see that the incompletion procedures are assigned to the various sales document types and sales document item categories. Figure 9-3 displays a selection of incompletion procedures that are able to be assigned to sales document headers.

By selecting the incompletion procedure—for example, 11-Standard Order—and selecting the Fields folder in the file structure on the left side, you will be able to maintain the fields that are in the incompletion procedure.

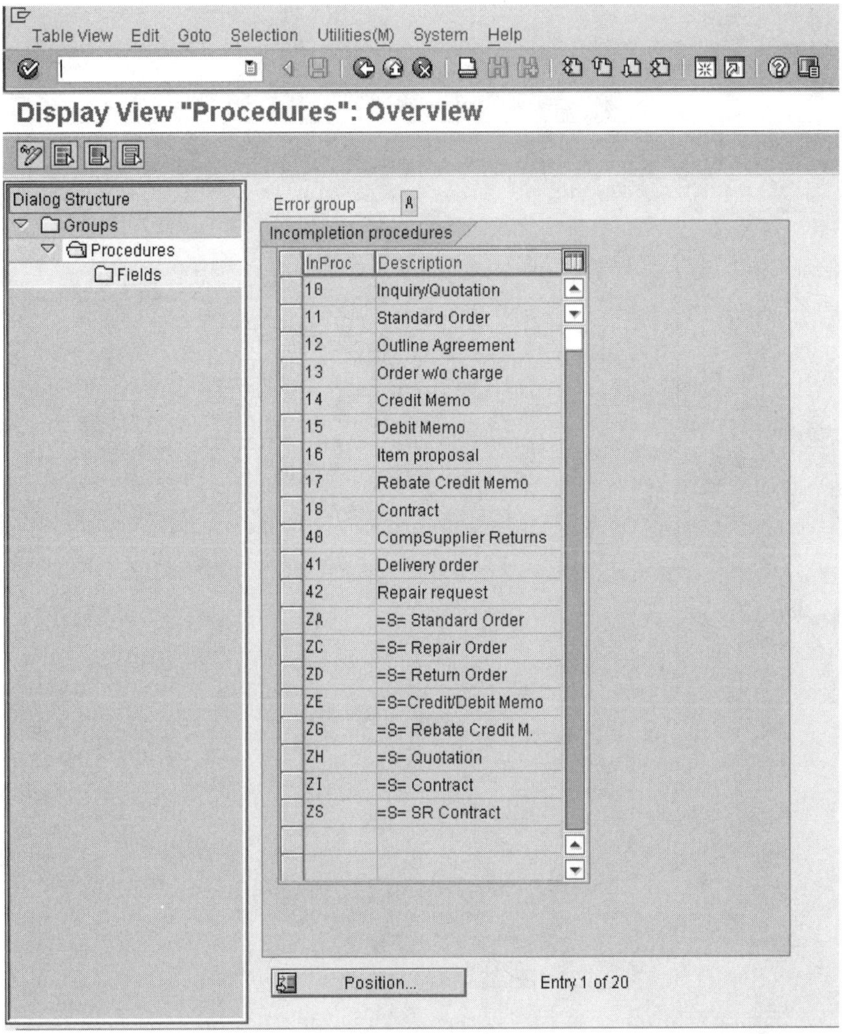

Table View Edit Goto Selection Utilities(M) System Help	

Display View "Procedures": Overview

Dialog Structure
▽ ☐ Groups
  ▽ ☐ Procedures
    ☐ Fields

Error group   A

Incompletion procedures

InProc	Description
10	Inquiry/Quotation
11	Standard Order
12	Outline Agreement
13	Order w/o charge
14	Credit Memo
15	Debit Memo
16	Item proposal
17	Rebate Credit Memo
18	Contract
40	CompSupplier Returns
41	Delivery order
42	Repair request
ZA	=S= Standard Order
ZC	=S= Repair Order
ZD	=S= Return Order
ZE	=S=Credit/Debit Memo
ZG	=S= Rebate Credit M.
ZH	=S= Quotation
ZI	=S= Contract
ZS	=S= SR Contract

Position...   Entry 1 of 20

FIGURE 9-3 Incompletion procedures to be assigned to sales document types

Should you need to change the SAP standard by adding or deleting entries in a procedure, you can create a copy of the assigned procedures to the error group. Such as a copy of the standard procedure 11 - Sales order. Then continue with the following steps:

To create your own incompletion procedure, select the Change Display button or press CTRL-F1 when you are in the procedure screen.

Then proceed as usual in copying the incompletion procedure and renaming it. The system will ask if you want to copy the dependent entries. These dependent entries are the assigned incompletion fields and associated assigned status groups. You can click the Copy All button.

You can see the table names with the assigned field name and a description of that field. In the example of Figure 9-4, the purchase order number, table VBKD, and field BSTKD are

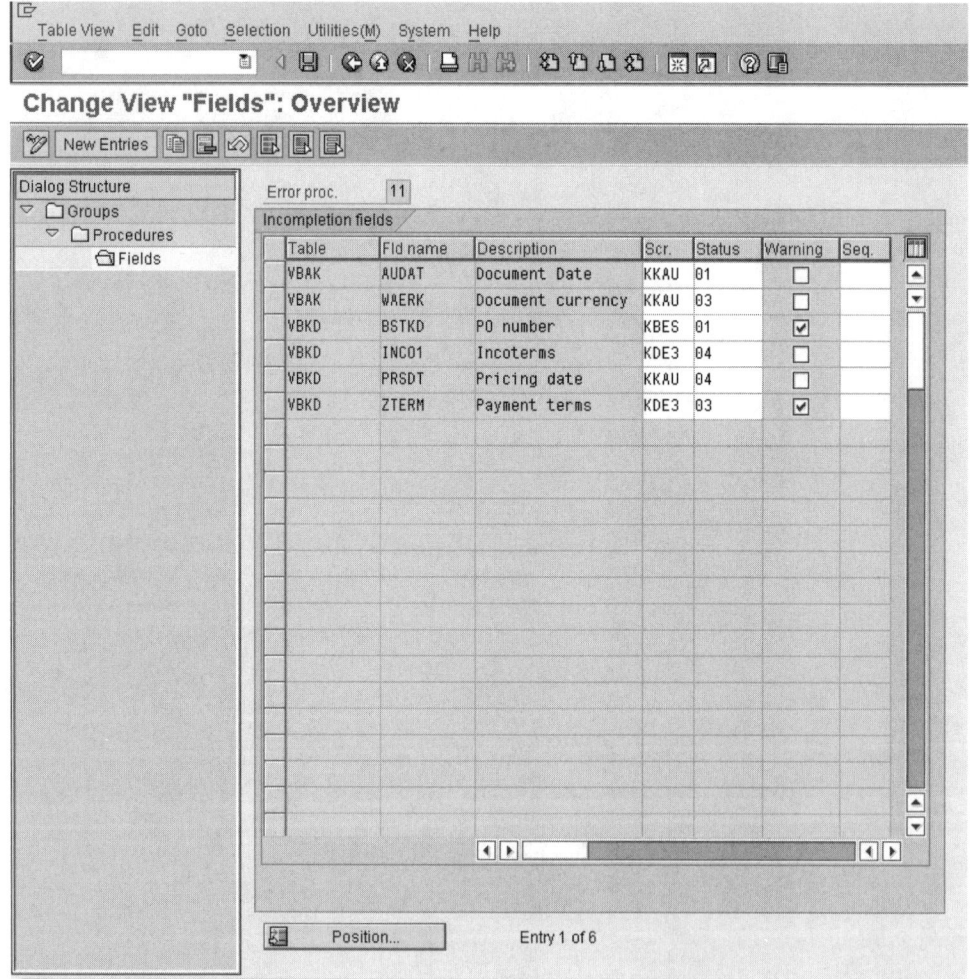

Copyright by SAP AG

FIGURE 9-4 Incompletion fields of a procedure

relevant as incomplete. The assigned screen "KBES" is the screen that the system will use to propose to the user in order to complete the missing data.

Assigned to the purchase order number is the status group 01, which we have defined as general. Finally, assigned to the purchase order number is an indicator saying the system must display a warning message in the sales order at the time that the system checks to see if the data is maintained for the purpose of the incompletion log.

Should no warning message be assigned, at the time of saving the system will merely indicate the sales document is incomplete and offer an option to allow the document to be saved as incomplete but disallowing any further processing, or allowing the data to be maintained prior to saving, so that once fully completed the sales document will be able to be processed further.

Should you select to maintain the data you'll see an overview screen with a list of errors as shown in Figure 9-5. Should you select the error and click the Complete Data button, you will see a screen called by the function code for overview screen KBES as displayed in Figure 9-4.

The incompletion log is found in a sales document by selecting Edit | Incompletion Log.

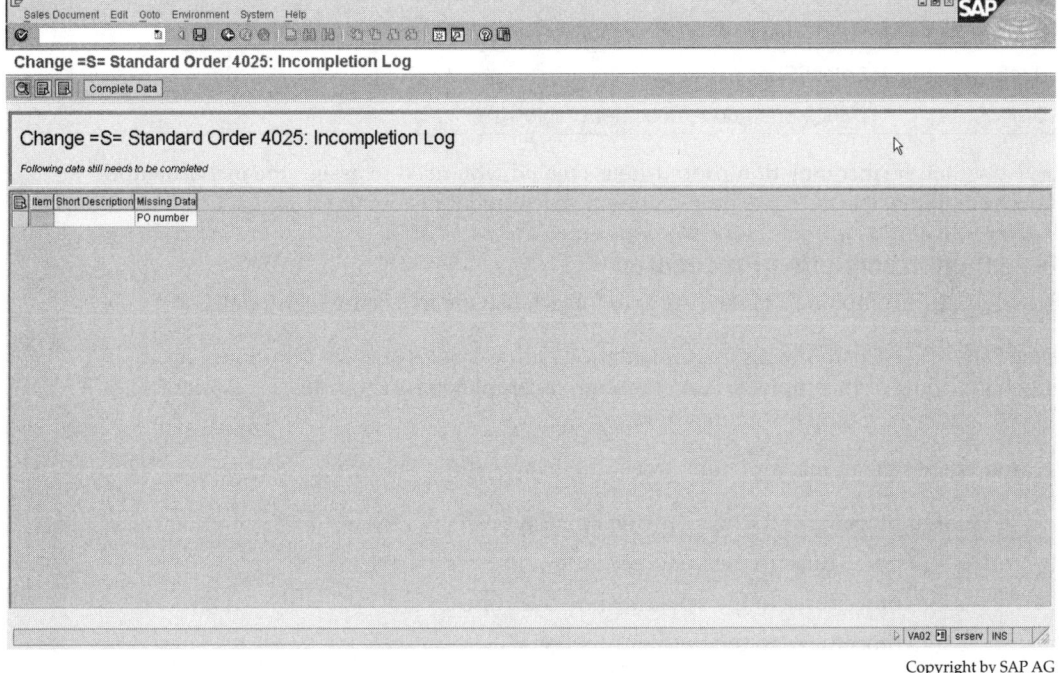

Copyright by SAP AG

FIGURE 9-5 Incompletion log from within a sales document

The tables that may be used in the maintenance of the incompletion procedure are as follows:

VBKD	Sales: Business data
VBAK	Sales: Header data
VEDA	Sales: Contract data
VBAP	Sales: Item data
VBKA	Sales activities
VBEP	Sales: Schedule line data
VBPA	Partner
LIKP	Delivery: Header data
LIPS	Delivery: Item Data
LIPSD	Delivery: Item data (dynamic/online)
LIPSVB	Delivery: Item data (LIPS + LIPSD)
V50UC	Delivery: Dynamically generated data (item and header)
FMII1	Funds management - account assignment data
RV45A_UV	Sales: Special rules
DGMSD	Dangerous goods document table

Now that the incompletion procedure is created, you need to assign the incompletion procedure to the object—for example, the sales document header.

Assigning Incompletion Procedures

To assign the incompletion procedure to an object, use the following menu path.

Menu Path   SAP Customizing Implementation Guide | Sales and Distribution | Basic Functions | Log of Incomplete Items | Assign Incompleteness Procedures | Assign Procedures to the Sales Document Types

You can assign an incompletion procedure to any of the following:

- Assign procedures to the sales document types
- Assign procedures to the item categories
- Assign procedures to the schedule line categories
- Assign procedures to the partner functions
- Assign procedures to sales activities
- Assign forms to delivery types
- Assign procedures to delivery item types

For example, in Figure 9-6 we assign incompletion procedure 11 to the sales document type ZAG.

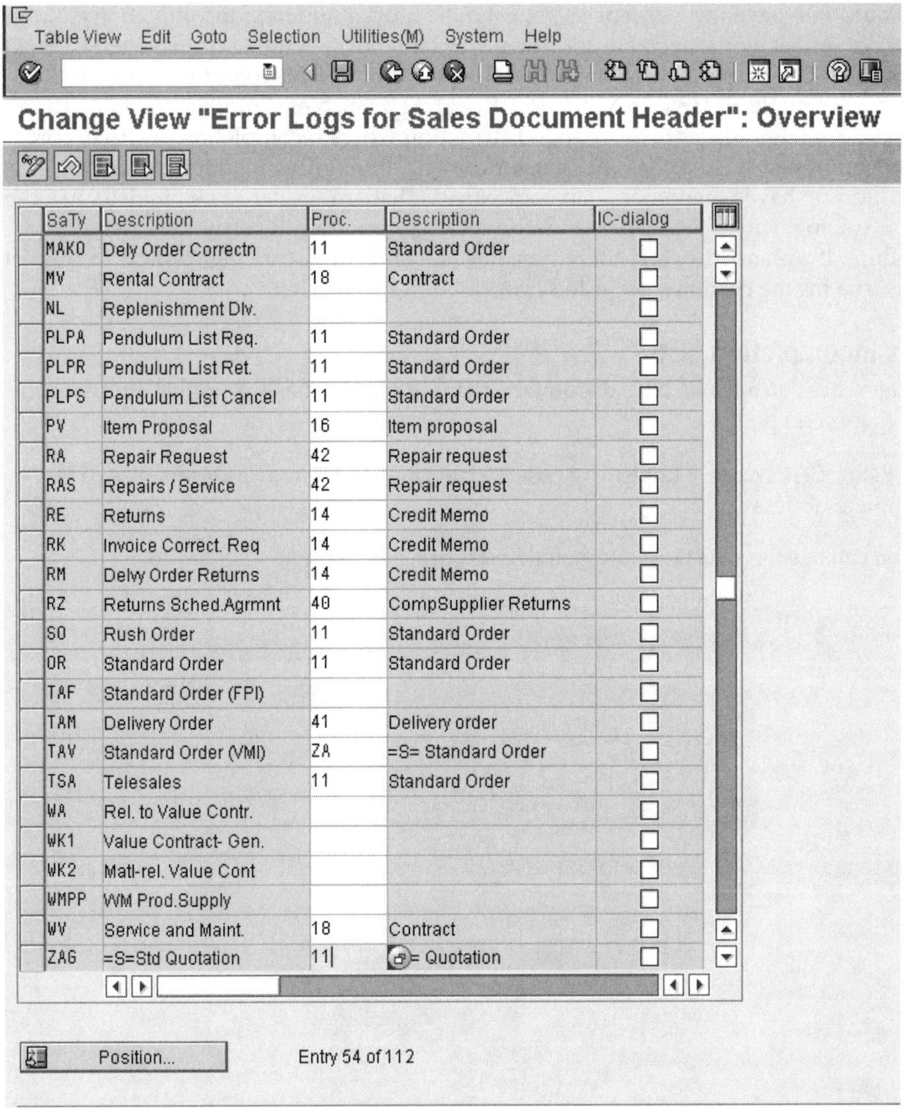

Table View   Edit   Goto   Selection   Utilities(M)   System   Help

Change View "Error Logs for Sales Document Header": Overview

SaTy	Description	Proc.	Description	IC-dialog
MAKO	Dely Order Correctn	11	Standard Order	☐
MV	Rental Contract	18	Contract	☐
NL	Replenishment Dlv.			☐
PLPA	Pendulum List Req.	11	Standard Order	☐
PLPR	Pendulum List Ret.	11	Standard Order	☐
PLPS	Pendulum List Cancel	11	Standard Order	☐
PV	Item Proposal	16	Item proposal	☐
RA	Repair Request	42	Repair request	☐
RAS	Repairs / Service	42	Repair request	☐
RE	Returns	14	Credit Memo	☐
RK	Invoice Correct. Req	14	Credit Memo	☐
RM	Delvy Order Returns	14	Credit Memo	☐
RZ	Returns Sched.Agrmnt	40	CompSupplier Returns	☐
SO	Rush Order	11	Standard Order	☐
OR	Standard Order	11	Standard Order	☐
TAF	Standard Order (FPI)			☐
TAM	Delivery Order	41	Delivery order	☐
TAV	Standard Order (VMI)	ZA	=S= Standard Order	☐
TSA	Telesales	11	Standard Order	☐
WA	Rel. to Value Contr.			☐
WK1	Value Contract- Gen.			☐
WK2	Matl-rel. Value Cont			☐
WMPP	WM Prod.Supply			☐
WV	Service and Maint.	18	Contract	☐
ZAG	=S=Std Quotation	11|	☐= Quotation	☐

Position...   Entry 54 of 112

FIGURE 9-6   Assigning incompletion procedures to sales document types

Should you not require the dialog box to appear in sales document processing, even though it will still be blocked for further processing if incomplete, you can select the IC-dialog checkbox. This, however, simply removes the dialog box. You are still required to go to the overview screen to select the incomplete data to maintain it.

Should you have inconsistencies between the header and item incompletion statuses of a sales document, you can create and run a special report via transaction code [SE38] called SDVBUK00. This is highlighted in SAP OSS Note 0088511. This report will align the incompletion status in tables VBUK and VBUP. SAP OSS. Note 207875 is beneficial as well.

 There are other places in Sales and Distribution where incompletion is active. For example, the creation of a customer master record, although maintained in Finance, is used in SD and will have "mandatory" customer fields that are similar to incomplete. Another place is pricing, where there are mandatory pricing condition types within the pricing procedure. If a mandatory condition type has no value, then "pricing" will be incomplete. This is true for the customer expected price used in EDI as well.

Sales Incompletion List

You can report on a list of sales documents that are regarded as incomplete by using the following menu path.

Menu Path   SAP Menu I Logistics I Sales I Information System I Orders I [V.02]— Incomplete Orders

You can see the selection parameters in Figure 9-7.

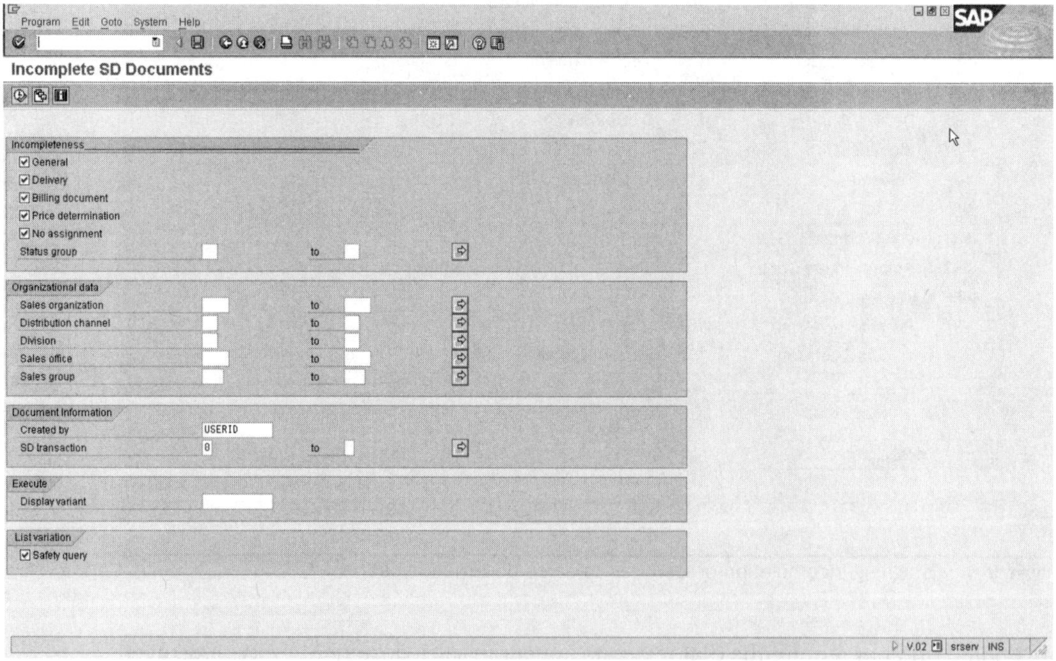

FIGURE 9-7   Incomplete SD documents

Partner Determination

Partners such as the sold to party, bill to party, payer, etc. are necessary in the majority of document processing. Automatic partner determination happens in the sales documents, delivery documents, and billing documents, as well as in sales activities and the customer master record.

We'll configure this automatic partner determination along with the control data behind the partner—for example, can a ship to party use the same account group as a sold to party.

Setting Up Partner Determination

To set up partner determination, use the following menu path.

Menu Path   SAP Customizing Implementation Guide | Sales and Distribution | Basic Functions | Partner Determination | Set Up Partner Determination

Partner determination may be defined for the following activities:

- Partner Determination for Customer Master
- Partner Determination for Sales Document Header
- Partner Determination for Sales Document Item
- Partner Determination for Delivery
- Partner Determination for Shipment
- Partner Determination for Billing Header
- Partner Determination for Billing Item
- Partner Determination for Sales Activities (CAS)

By referring back to customer master data in Chapter 2, we see that each customer master record is created on the basis of a specific account group—for example, sold to parties use account group 0001.

We also note the four basic partner functions:

SP	Sold to party	(German -AG)
SH	Ship to party	(German -WE)
BP	Bill to party	(German -RE)
PY	Payer	(German -RG)

The old German identifications are still shown to identify the old mapping that used to exist. For example, these identifications are still used to identify the partner determination procedure. (Also, should you enter the German identification—for example, AG—in a search parameter to find the partner function, you will receive the partner function SP if logged on in English.)

Setting Up Partner Determination for Customer Master

Select Set Up Partner Determination for Customer Master. You will see an overview screen like the one shown in Figure 9-8.

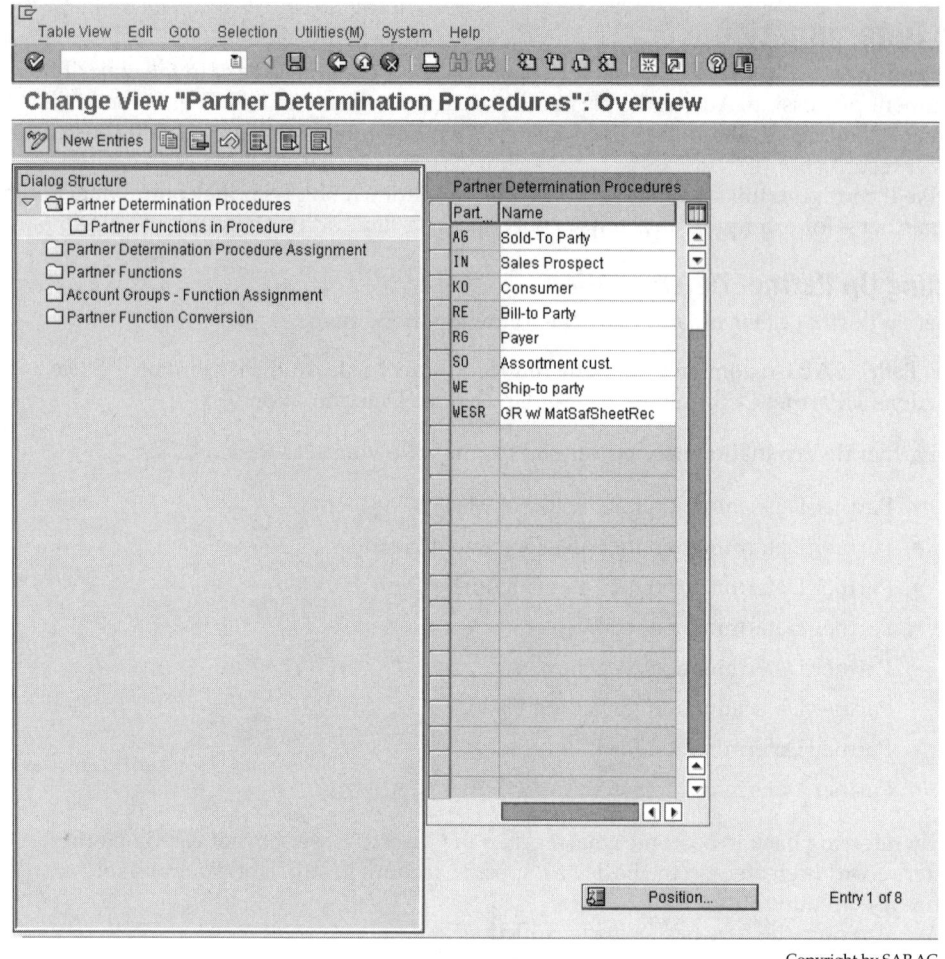

Copyright by SAP AG

FIGURE 9-8   Setting up partner determination for customer master

The partner determination procedure seen in Figure 9-8 has partner functions assigned to it. If you select function AG and click the Partner Functions in Procedure folder, you will see a screen similar to Figure 9-9.

The first column shows the partner function procedure AG. The second column shows the partner function within the procedure—for example, "SP" Sold to Party, which has a tick in the fourth column (Not Modifiable) and a tick in the last column (Mandatory Function).

When you create a customer master record ,you create it for a customer account group—for example, account group 0001—for sold to party. The reason why we have the partner determination procedure for customer master is to tell the system which partner determination procedure must be used for that specific account group.

As seen in Figure 9-10, the partner procedure AG is assigned to the sold to party account group 0001.

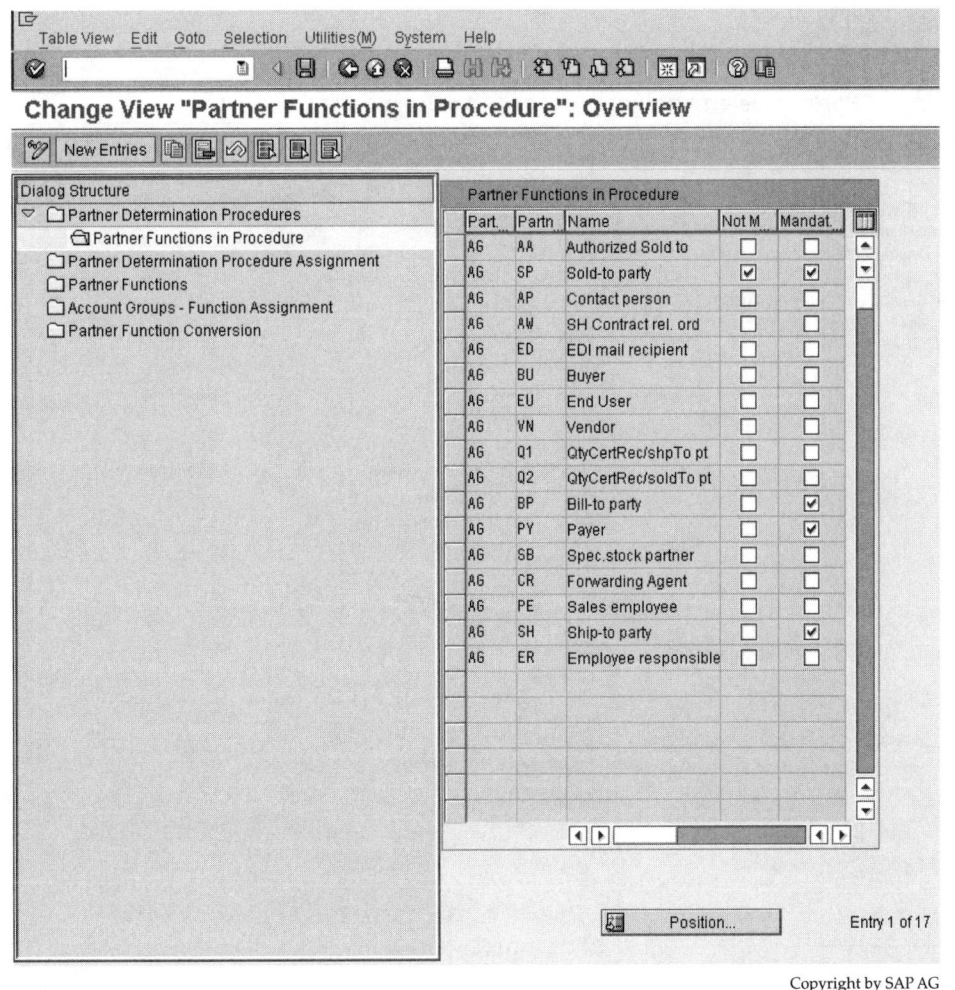

Copyright by SAP AG

FIGURE 9-9   Partner functions within procedure AG

This means that when a customer of account group 0001 is created, the determination procedure AG will be used, which in turn will use the partner functions seen in Figure 9-9.

By selecting the Partner Functions folder in the file structure on the left side, we will see a list of permitted partner functions, as seen in Figure 9-11.

Here you see the partner function ID in column 1, followed by its name in column 2. Each function is assigned a partner type, which groups and controls the partner function to behave in a specific manner. For example, the "Customer Hierarchy" is seen as a "customer partner type" value of KU. The value of 07 in the fourth column shows the incompletion number that is called should the customer master record not be assigned to the creation of the customer.

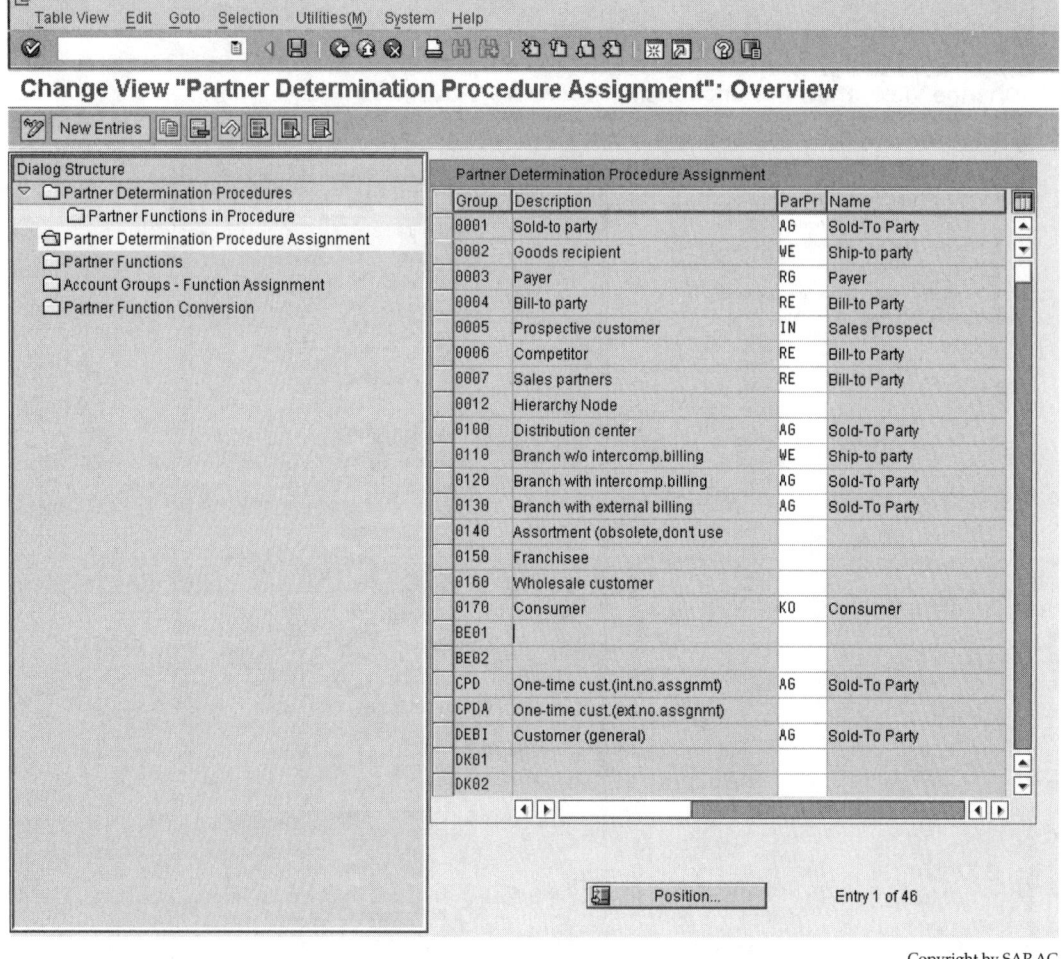

FIGURE 9-10 Partner determination procedure assignment

The Superior Partner Function column is used to depict a structure of partner records. For example, the customer hierarchy shows:

1A	Customer hierarchy 7	KU	07	1B
1B	Customer hierarchy 6	KU	07	1C
1C	Customer hierarchy 5	KU	07	1D
1D	Customer hierarchy 4	KU	07	1E
1E	Customer hierarchy 3	KU	07	1F
1F	Customer hierarchy 2	KU	07	1G
1G	Customer hierarchy 1	KU	07	

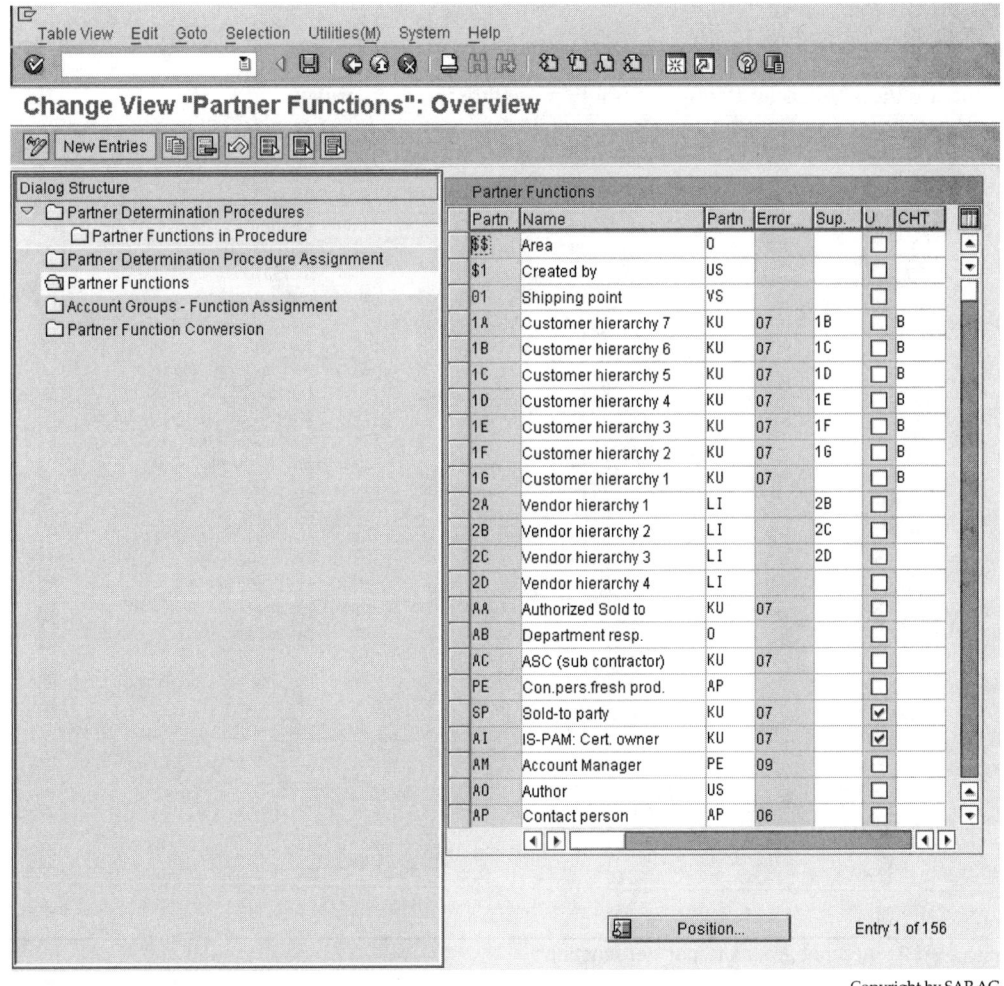

Table View   Edit   Goto   Selection   Utilities(M)   System   Help

Change View "Partner Functions": Overview

New Entries

Dialog Structure
▽ ☐ Partner Determination Procedures
   ☐ Partner Functions in Procedure
   ☐ Partner Determination Procedure Assignment
   ☐ Partner Functions
   ☐ Account Groups - Function Assignment
   ☐ Partner Function Conversion

Partner Functions

Partn	Name	Partn	Error	Sup.	U	CHT
$$	Area	0			☐	
$1	Created by	US			☐	
01	Shipping point	VS			☐	
1A	Customer hierarchy 7	KU	07	1B	☐	B
1B	Customer hierarchy 6	KU	07	1C	☐	B
1C	Customer hierarchy 5	KU	07	1D	☐	B
1D	Customer hierarchy 4	KU	07	1E	☐	B
1E	Customer hierarchy 3	KU	07	1F	☐	B
1F	Customer hierarchy 2	KU	07	1G	☐	B
1G	Customer hierarchy 1	KU	07		☐	B
2A	Vendor hierarchy 1	LI		2B	☐	
2B	Vendor hierarchy 2	LI		2C	☐	
2C	Vendor hierarchy 3	LI		2D	☐	
2D	Vendor hierarchy 4	LI			☐	
AA	Authorized Sold to	KU	07		☐	
AB	Department resp.	0			☐	
AC	ASC (sub contractor)	KU	07		☐	
PE	Con.pers.fresh prod.	AP			☐	
SP	Sold-to party	KU	07		☑	
AI	IS-PAM: Cert. owner	KU	07		☑	
AM	Account Manager	PE	09		☐	
AO	Author	US			☐	
AP	Contact person	AP	06		☐	

Position...   Entry 1 of 156

FIGURE 9-11   Partner functions

The superior hierarchy is the structure from 1A as the lowest level, reporting to 1B, which in turn reports to 1C, followed through to 1G as the most superior node.

The "U" shows the customer master record is "Unique" in the customer, and the value CHT represents the customer hierarchy type.

Should you create a new customer account group, for example, a copy of 0001, do not forget to assign the new account group to the list of allowed account groups for partner determination. This may be seen in Figure 9-12.

The account group assigned to the partner function controls the partner functions that may be used for the account group.

Now you can proceed with the assignment of the partner functions to a partner determination procedure.

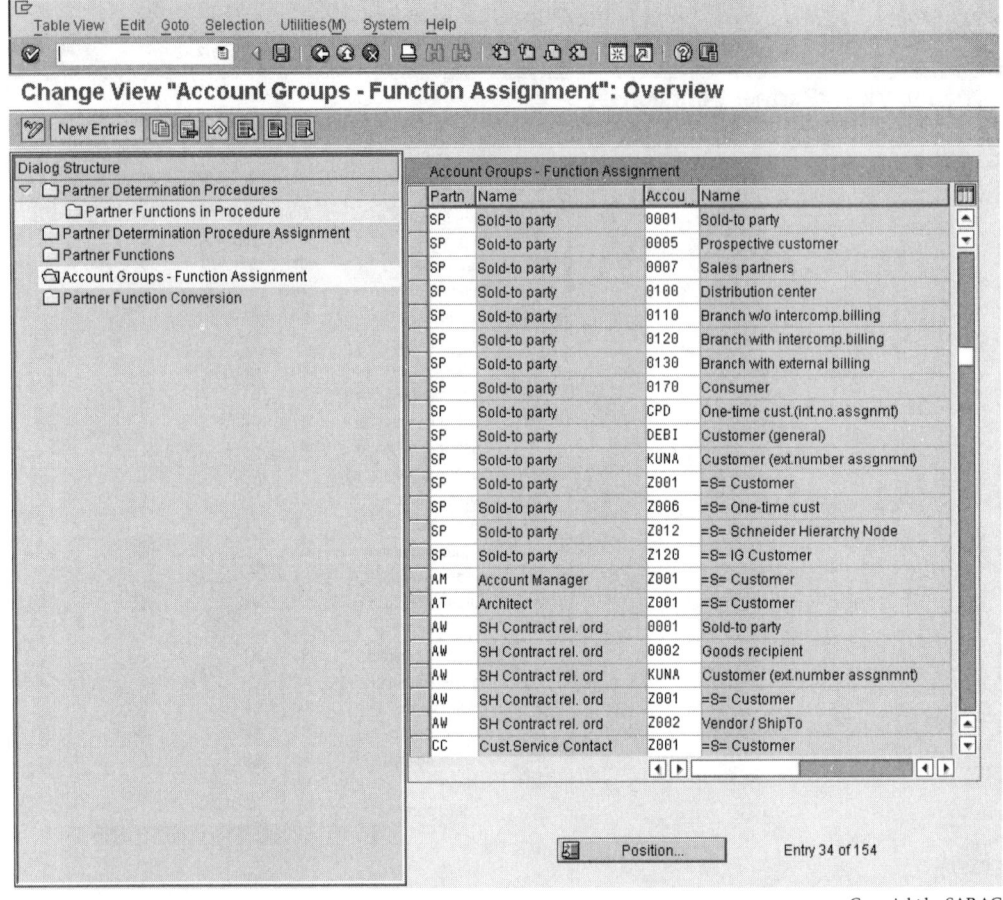

FIGURE 9-12   Account groups to partner functions

To conclude partner determination, we will follow the steps used to create a new determination procedure for a sales document header.

Setting Up Partner Determination for Sales Document Header

To set up partner determination for a sales document header, use the following menu path.

Menu Path   SAP Customizing Implementation Guide I Sales and Distribution I Basic Functions I Partner Determination I Set Up Partner Determination I Set Up Partner Determination for Sales Document Header

- **Step 1:** Ensure all the partner functions you require are maintained. Refer to Figure 9-11.
- **Step 2:** Ensure any new partner function has an account group assigned to it. And ensure any new account group is assigned to a partner function. Refer to Figure 9-12.

- **Step 3:** Create a new partner determination procedure—for example, a copy of partner procedure TA (similar in logic to procedure AG). Refer to Figure 9-8.

- **Step 4:** Ensure all your partner functions are represented in the procedure, similar to Figure 9-9, but a little different as seen in Figure 9-13.

The Not modifiable and Mandatory columns are self explanatory, and relate to the partner in the sales document header. You can see in Figure 9-13 that the sold to party, bill to party, payer, and ship to party are mandatory.

By default all partners are derived from the assignment on the sold to party record, as seen in Figure 9-13. If you enter SH (ship to party) in the source field for the function Q1 (QtyCertRec/shpTo pt), when you create the sales document, it determines the partner number for Q1 (QtyCertRec/shpTo pt), from the ship to party (SH) partner function in the ship to party's master document.

If you enter a value in the source field, you must also enter a value in the sequence field. The fields for source and sequence are used when the system needs to obtain a partner record from any associated partner in the sales document other than that of the sold to party. Should a partner be a buyer partner function BU, and the record of the buyer not be assigned to the sold to party but to the bill to party, the source field may be assigned "BP" for bill to party and the sequence number must come after that of the bill to party. Should the bill to party have a sequence of blank or 0, the sequence for the buyer may read 1.

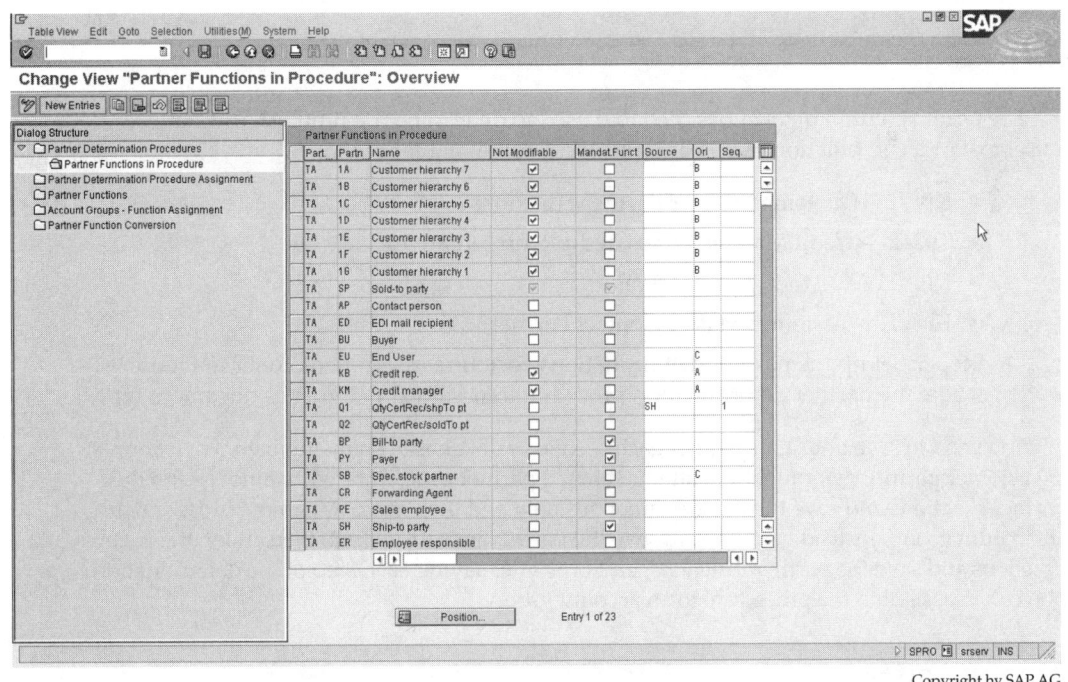

FIGURE 9-13   Partner functions in procedure—sales document header

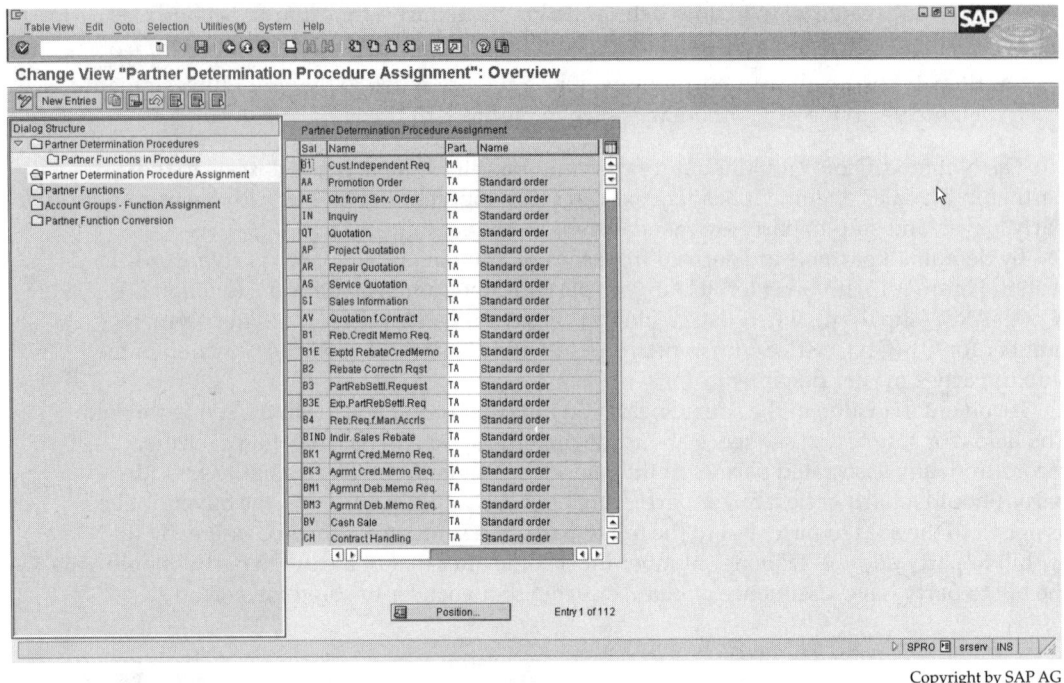

Copyright by SAP AG

FIGURE 9-14   Partner determination procedure assignment

The Origin column determines the table used to determine the number. You can use a user exit or a combination of one or more of the following tables:

- KNVP—Customer Master Partner Functions
- T024P—Credit Management: Credit Representatives
- KNVH—Customer Hierarchies
- KNVK—Customer Master Contact Partner

- **Step 5:** Set up the partner determination procedure assignment. Refer to Figure 9-14 where the partner determination procedure is assigned to the sales document type.

You need to save your entries after each section of data has been maintained. For example, in customer partner determination, after creating a partner procedure you cannot assign the partner functions and save the partner functions only and then try to assign the procedure to an account group. Instead, you need to save the partner procedure first, then assign the partner functions and save the partner functions, and only after saving each step of the determination, proceed in assigning the procedure to an account group.

Text Determination

Texts form a basic but essential need within document processing. Using text determination, you can automatically cause the system to copy data held in a text line from one text object to another—for example, from a customer master record to a sales document.

The Sales and Distribution module is used in the text determination for the following text objects:

Customer

- Central texts
- Contact Person
- Sales and Distribution

Info Record

- Customer/Material

Pricing Conds

- Agreements
- Conditions

Sales Document

- Header
- Item

Delivery

- Header
- Item

Billing Doc.

- Header
- Item

Sales Act.

- General text

Shipment

- Header

Financial Doc.

- General text

Legal Control

- General text

Agency Business

- Header
- Item

Trading Contract

- Header
- Item

Defining Text Types

To configure text determination, use the following menu path.

Menu Path   SAP Customizing Implementation Guide ǀ Sales and Distribution ǀ Basic Functions ǀ Text Control ǀ Define Text Types

You will see an overview screen with text objects, similar to Figure 9-15.
You may select any one text object, then click the Text Types button, shown here, to define the permitted text types for the text object.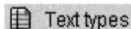
We will maintain the text determination in the customer master record as an example.

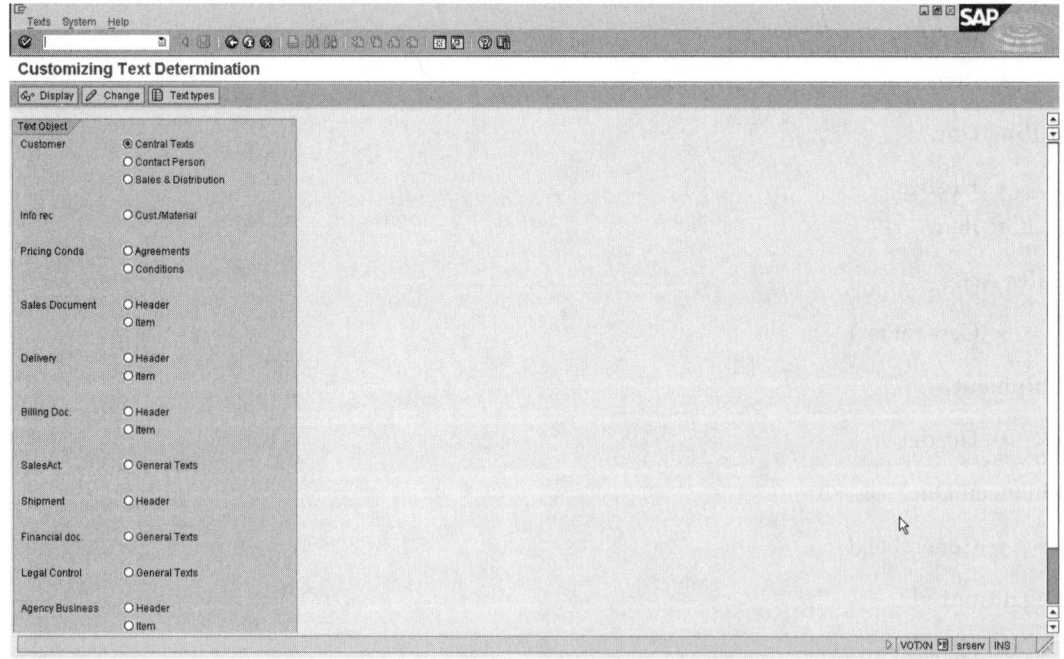

FIGURE 9-15   All text objects

Text Determination for the Customer Master Record

To create text determination originating from the customer master record proceeed as follows:

1. Select the Customer—Sales and Distribution radio button. (This is the text object.) Then click the Text Types button.

2. You will see an overview screen like the one in Figure 9-16. It is here that you define the different text types you wish to have in the customer master record, and enter a short description for each of them. For example, "ZEXM" is used as "customers text."

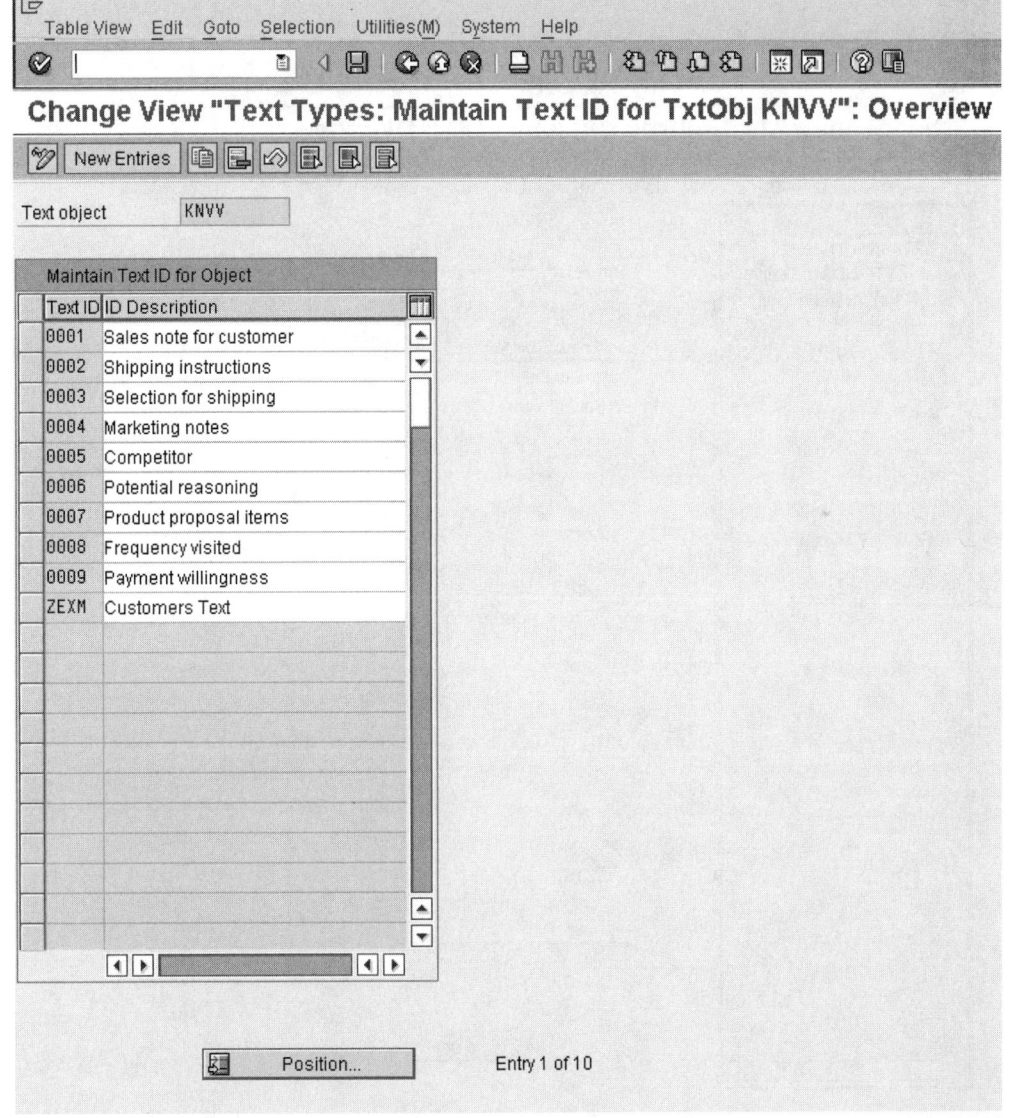

Copyright by SAP AG

FIGURE 9-16   Text ID for text object KNVV

Text determination data is client-independent. Please refer to the description of client independence in access sequence creation in pricing in Chapter 8.

3. Once the text type has been created, you need to define the access sequences. However, the access sequence is not necessary for the customer master record texts as the customer master record is the highest level possible in text determination.

4. After creating the access sequences, you then create the text procedure by clicking the Change button from the text object overview screen in Figure 9-15. This is seen in Figure 9-17. Create a two-character key with a short description, for example, "Z1."

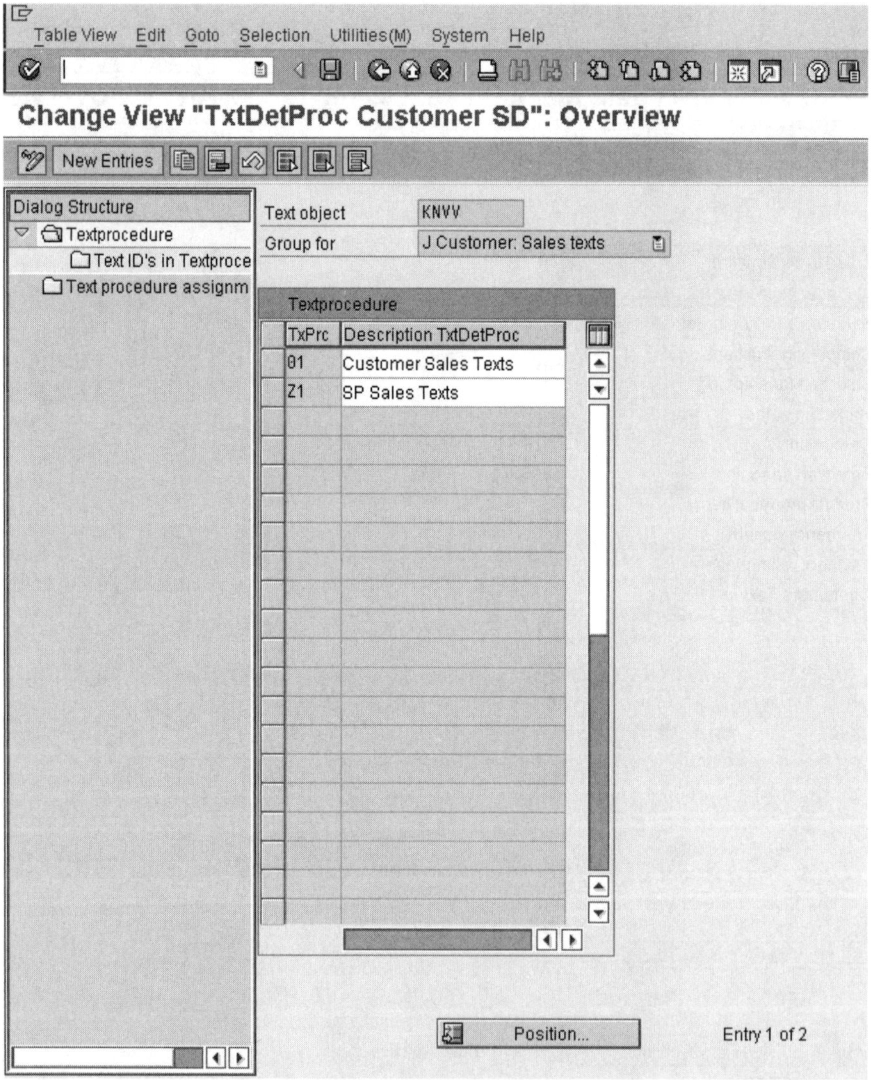

Table View   Edit   Goto   Selection   Utilities(M)   System   Help

Change View "TxtDetProc Customer SD": Overview

New Entries

Dialog Structure
▽ ☐ Textprocedure
    ☐ Text ID's in Textproce
    ☐ Text procedure assignm

Text object   KNVV
Group for   J Customer: Sales texts

Textprocedure

TxPrc	Description TxtDetProc
01	Customer Sales Texts
Z1	SP Sales Texts

Position...   Entry 1 of 2

FIGURE 9-17 Text Procedure

5. After the procedure has been created, you can assign the text types to the procedure. This may be done by selecting the Texts in Procedure folder in the file structure on the left side. It is here you assign the actual text types you would like to have assigned to the customer master record. In our example, as seen in Figure 9-18, we have added our text type, ZEXM - Customers text, to the list.

6. Once the texts have been assigned to the procedure, it is time to assign the procedure to the customers account group. This is done by selecting the Text Procedure Assignment folder from the file structure seen in Figure 9-19. In our example all the account groups have been assigned to our new text procedure Z1.

After completing the customer account group assignment and saving, it is possible to create the texts in the customer master record. The customer master record has nine text IDs, as we have previously seen in Figure 9-18. The Sales and Distribution text object is accessible from the sales view of the customer master record (from transaction code [VD01], [VD02], [VD03], [XD01], [XD02], or [XD03] and by selecting Extras | Texts).

Text Determination with an Access Sequence

If you need to create text determination that is based upon the text being entered elsewhere and copied into the new text object, you need an access sequence. All other configuration steps remain the same with the addition of this access sequence. Let's look at an access sequence in use, for example, with the sales document header.

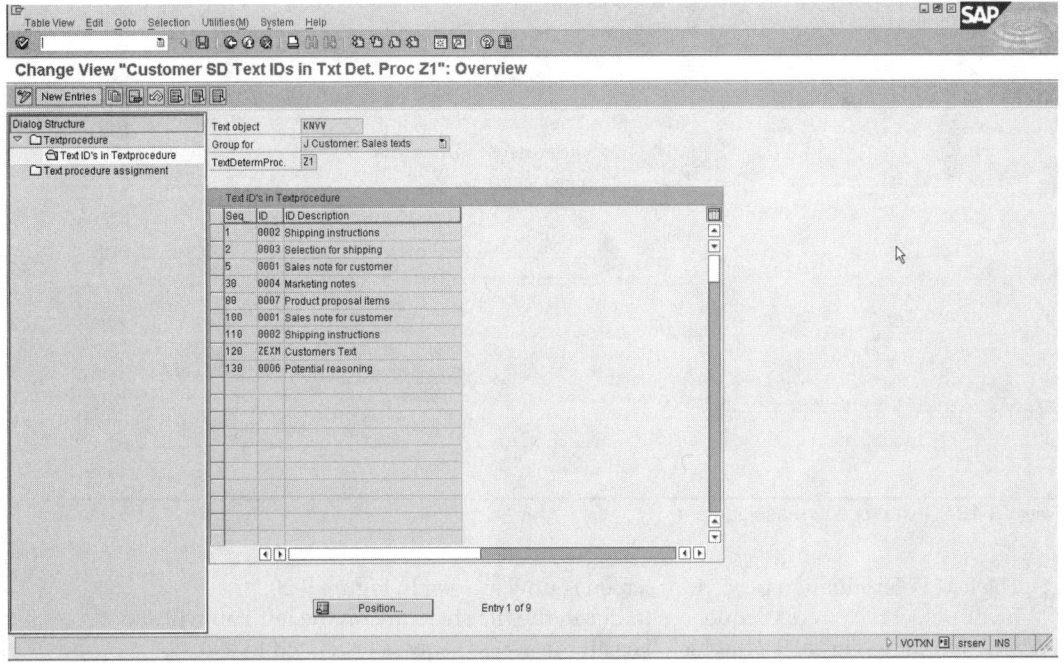

Copyright by SAP AG

FIGURE 9-18   Text IDs in procedure Z1 of text object KNVV

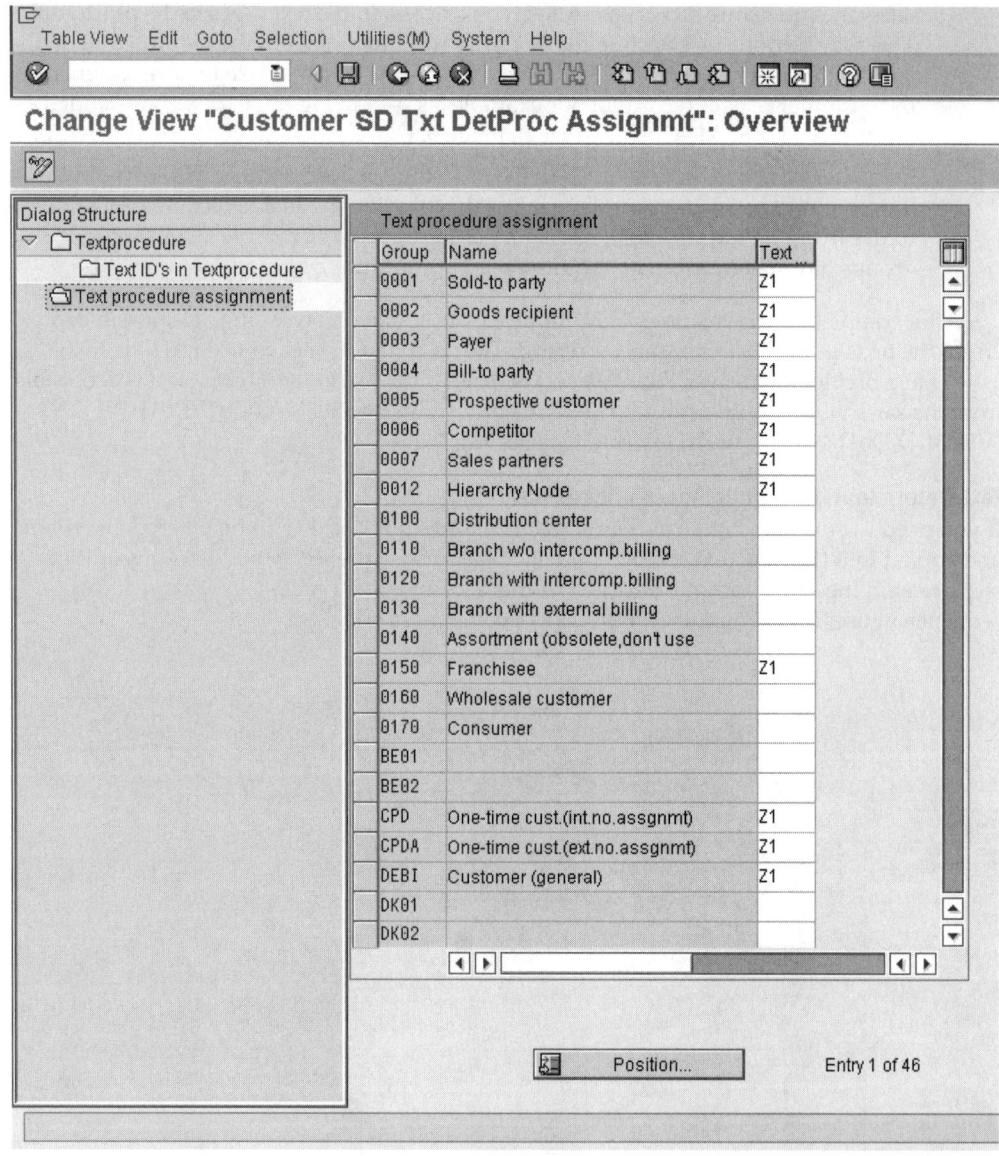

FIGURE 9-19 Text procedure assignment

The text determination procedure screen is now as seen in Figure 9-20.

If you select the Access Sequences folder in the file structure on the left you will see a screen similar to Figure 9-21, which lists all the access sequences related to text determination (not only those related to the text ID you are using).

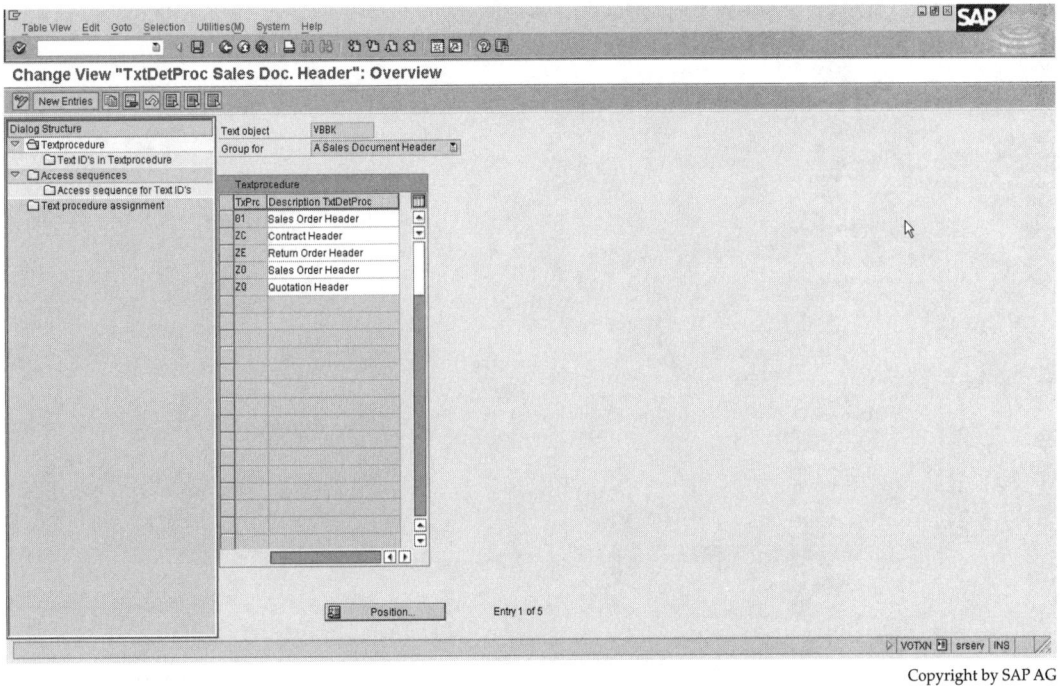

FIGURE 9-20   Text procedure for object VBBK

By selecting the access sequence and clicking the Access Sequence for Text IDs folder in the file structure on the left, you will see a screen similar to Figure 9-22, which lists the text IDs and the text object they originate from in steps as a sequence.

In Figure 9-22 we see 3 steps. The text typed in ID 0001 in the sales document header (VBBK) will be determined first, followed by the text typed in ID 0001 in the sales view (KNVV) of the customer master record, followed by the text in ID 0001 in the sales general (KNA1) text of the customer master record.

At first this may seem strange to determine the text from the sales document header (VBBK) when the objective is to define how the text originates in the sales document header in the first place. The reason why this is the initial step in the access sequence is to permit this access sequence to be used to originate the text ID 0001 for more than one text object, that is, not only to originate text in text object VBBK. Also, VBBK refers to the preceding sales document where the text is defined as header text.

For example, if the preceding document was a quote copied into an order, then VBBK refers to the quote. If it was an order copied to a delivery, then VBBK refers to the order. If a delivery is copied to an invoice, then VBBK is the delivery.

The last step that is different due to the access sequence is the assignment of the access sequence to the text ID. This is done by selecting the Text ID's in Procedure folder in the file structure on the left side, as seen in Figure 9-23.

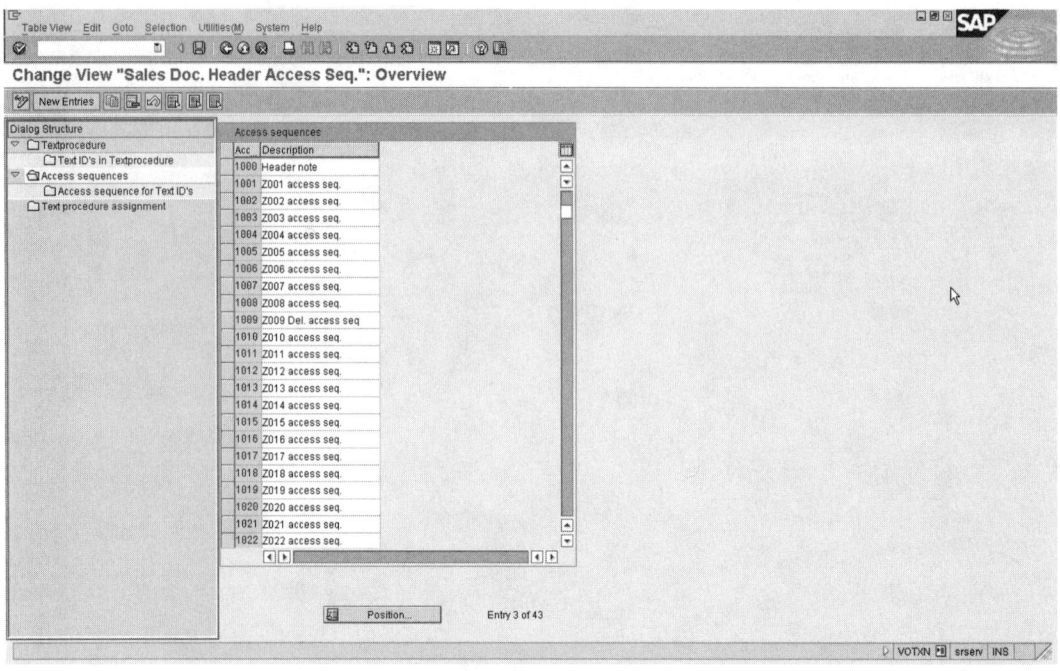

FIGURE 9-21 Text access sequence

It is here you assign the actual text types you would like to have assigned to the sales document header. There is the four-character key ID and the short description. You can now assign the access sequence that must be used by the system in obtaining this text ID.

We are also able to specify if the text is to be obligatory or not. Should the text be specified as obligatory and it does not exist in the sales document, the system will place an entry in the sales incompletion log.

Note the reference/duplication rule. If you do not check this box, the system will duplicate the text from the one document into the other, where it can be changed and edited. If you check this box, the system does not duplicate the text. Instead, the system references the text from the previous document and displays it in the editor. Obviously, because the text does not belong to the document, it cannot be changed. To change it, you need to change it in the original document. Since the text is referenced, these changes will be visible in the reference documents immediately.

Once the texts have been assigned to the procedure, it is time to assign the procedure to the sales document types. This is done by selecting the Text proc. Assignment folder from the file structure. This is a straightforward assignment similar to what we have done for the customer master text.

We are now able to create the sales order, and by selecting Goto | Header | Texts you can see the text types that we have created.

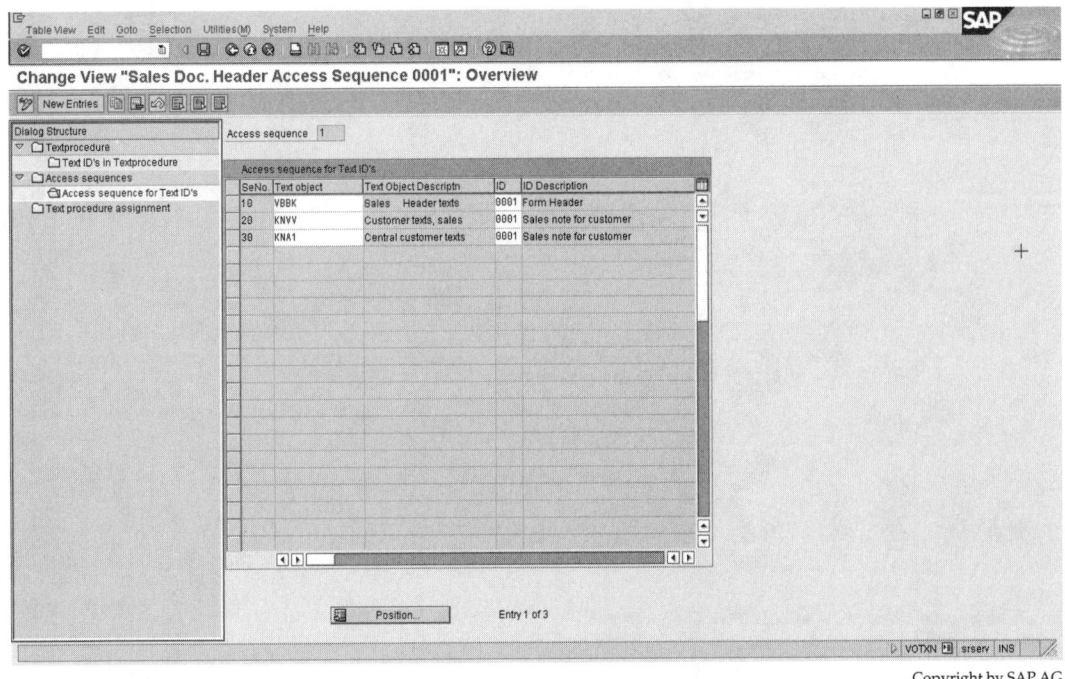

Copyright by SAP AG

FIGURE 9-22   Access sequence for Text IDs

 Do not forget that by clicking the Display Log icon, shown here, from within the sales document header text view, you can see if there were any errors or if the determination was correct, as shown in Figure 9-24.

 Do not forget that the materials management module (MM) has text determination too, which is split up into the different document types that are used in the MM module, such as the purchase order, contract, or scheduling agreement, etc. This is accessible by using the following menu path.

Menu Path   IMG | Materials Management | Purchasing | Scheduling Agreement (*for example*) | Texts for Scheduling Agreements | Define Text Types for Header Texts

 In the maintenance of access sequences it is useful to know the different text objects. The most common are

- **KNVV**   Customer sales texts (i.e., texts entered in Extras | Texts) in the customer master from one of the sales screens.

- **KNA1**   Customer master central texts (i.e., texts entered in Extras | Texts) in the customer master from one of the general screens.

- **KNB1**   The accounting texts.

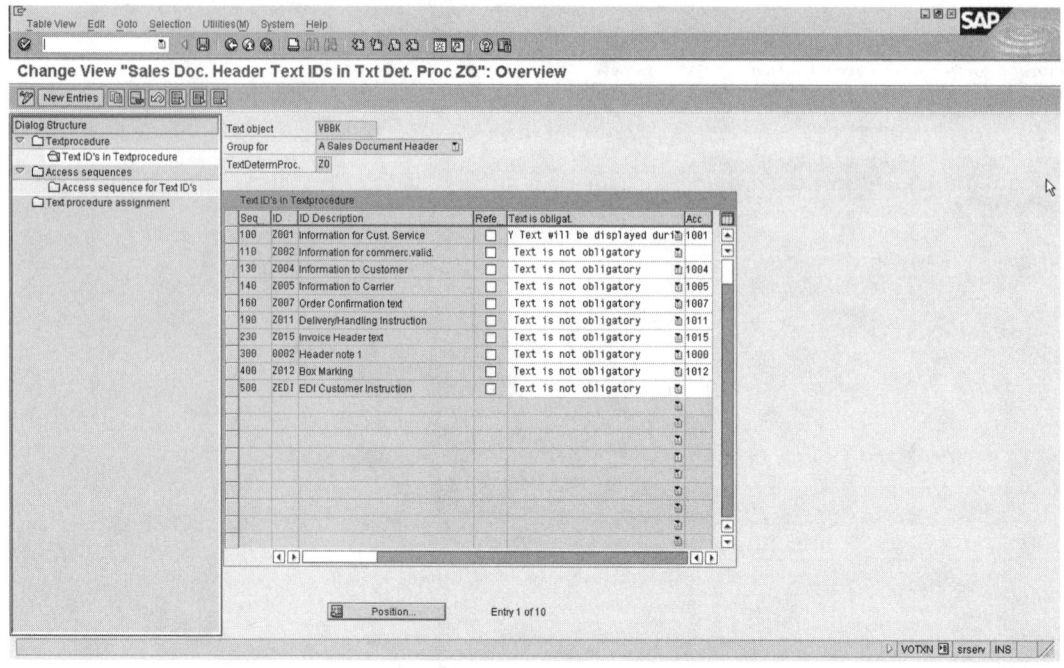

Copyright by SAP AG

FIGURE 9-23   Text IDs in procedure

- **KNMT**   Texts defined for the customer material information record.
- **KNVK**   Texts from the contact person screen in the customer master (Extras | Texts from the contact person screen of the customer master).
- **MVKE**   Texts from the sales text screen on the customer master record.
- **VBBK**   Preceding sales document where the text is defined as header text.

For example, if the preceding document was a quote copied into a delivery, then VBBK refers to the quote. If it was an order copied to a delivery, then VBBK refers to the order. If it was a delivery copied to an invoice, then VBBK is the delivery.

- **VBBP**   Preceding sales document ITEM, where the text is defined at item level.

 Unrelated to the text determination but related to texts, you may hear of standard text. These standard texts may be defined in the following menu path.

Menu Path   SAP Menu | Tools | Form Printout | SAPscript | Standard text [SO10]

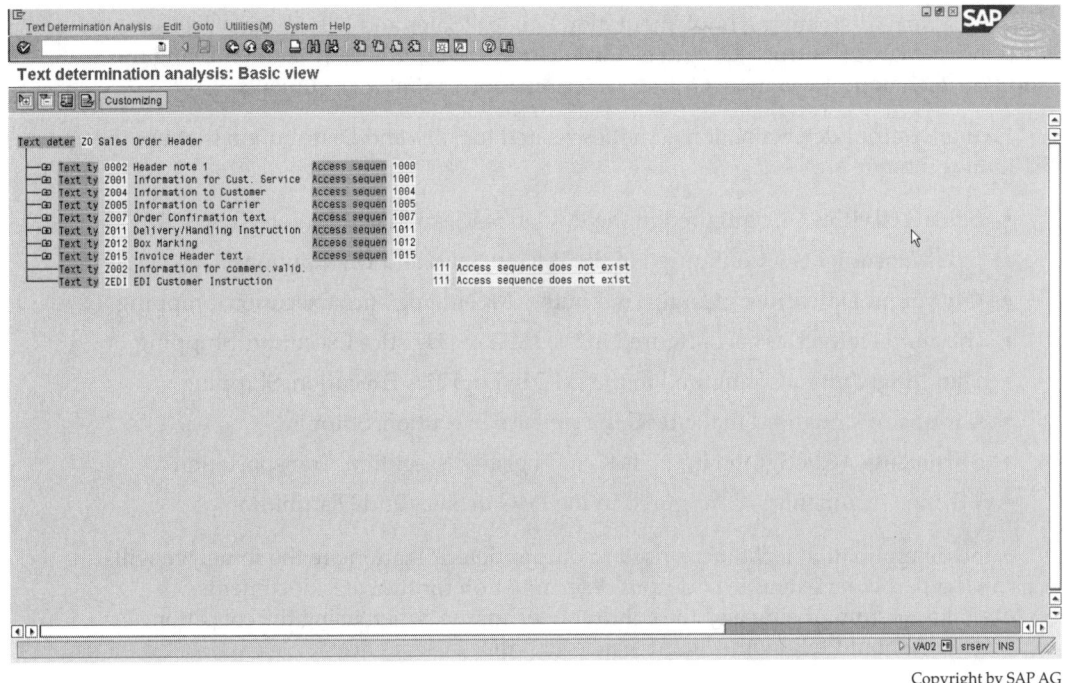

Copyright by SAP AG

FIGURE 9-24   Log of text determination in sales document header

Output Determination

An output is a form of media from the business to one of the business partners. Some output media forms are printouts, faxes and telexes, e-mails, electronic data interchange (EDI), or even XML or HTML. The output can be sent to any of the partners defined in the document.

Outputs are usually media in the form of order confirmations, delivery notes, invoices, and shipping notifications.

Maintain Output Determination for Sales Documents

Output determination uses the condition technique to determine the condition record necessary for the application. An output type is simply a type of output and contains all the control features for the output.

For example, it defines the kind of output (order confirmation, invoice, etc.), which business transaction it applies to, which business partner receives the output, how the output is sent (the media), the print program, and the form layout to use in formatting the output.

The output type is thus the central component of the output determination.

To maintain output determination, use the following menu path.

Menu Path SAP Customizing Implementation Guide | Sales and Distribution | Basic Functions | Output Control | Output Determination | Output Determination Using the Condition Technique | Maintain Output Determination for Sales Documents

The main output determination activities related to Sales and Distribution that use the condition technique are

- **Sales Activities** Configured in the IMG in Sales and Distribution
- **Sales Documents** Configured in the IMG in Sales and Distribution
- **Outbound Deliveries** Configured in the IMG in Logistics Execution, Shipping
- **Inbound Deliveries** Configured in the IMG in Logistics Execution, Shipping
- **Handling Units** Configured in the IMG in Logistics Execution, Shipping
- **Groups** Configured in the IMG in Logistics Execution, Shipping
- **Shipments** Configured in the IMG in Logistics Execution, Transportation
- **Billing Documents** Configured in the IMG in Sales and Distribution

As the determination techniques used in output determination are the same, we will focus on the particular example of output determination for the sales documents.

As we know from pricing and the condition technique, when using the condition technique you should follow the maintenance activities in sequence:

1. Put the fields you will need into the field catalog.
2. Create the condition tables you will need.
3. Create the access sequence you will need.
4. Assign the condition tables to the access sequence.
5. Create the condition types.
6. Assign the access sequence to the condition types.
7. Create the determination procedure (if necessary) and assign the condition types to it.
8. Assign the determination procedure.
9. Lastly, create your condition records.

Unlike the standard headings depicting the configuration process, the following configuration is done in a logical sequence you should follow when creating the condition technique as in steps 1 to 9.

Steps 1 and 2

The output determination is no different. Steps 1 and 2 are identical, and are accessible by using the following menu path.

Menu Path SAP Customizing Implementation Guide | Sales and Distribution | Basic Functions | Output Control | Output Determination | Output Determination Using the Condition Technique | Maintain Output Determination for Sales Documents | Maintain Condition Tables

Steps 3 and 4

Step 3 and 4 are also identical in that in creating the access sequence you follow the same customizing steps as used in pricing. This is available by using the following menu path.

Menu Path   SAP Customizing Implementation Guide | Sales and Distribution | Basic Functions | Output Control | Output Determination | Output Determination Using the Condition Technique | Maintain Output Determination for Sales Documents | Maintain Access Sequences

See the example in Figure 9-25.

Steps 5 and 6

Step 5 and 6 are identical in theory and usage in that one assigns an access sequence to the output condition type, but the output condition type controls different data. The output condition type is accessible by using the following menu path.

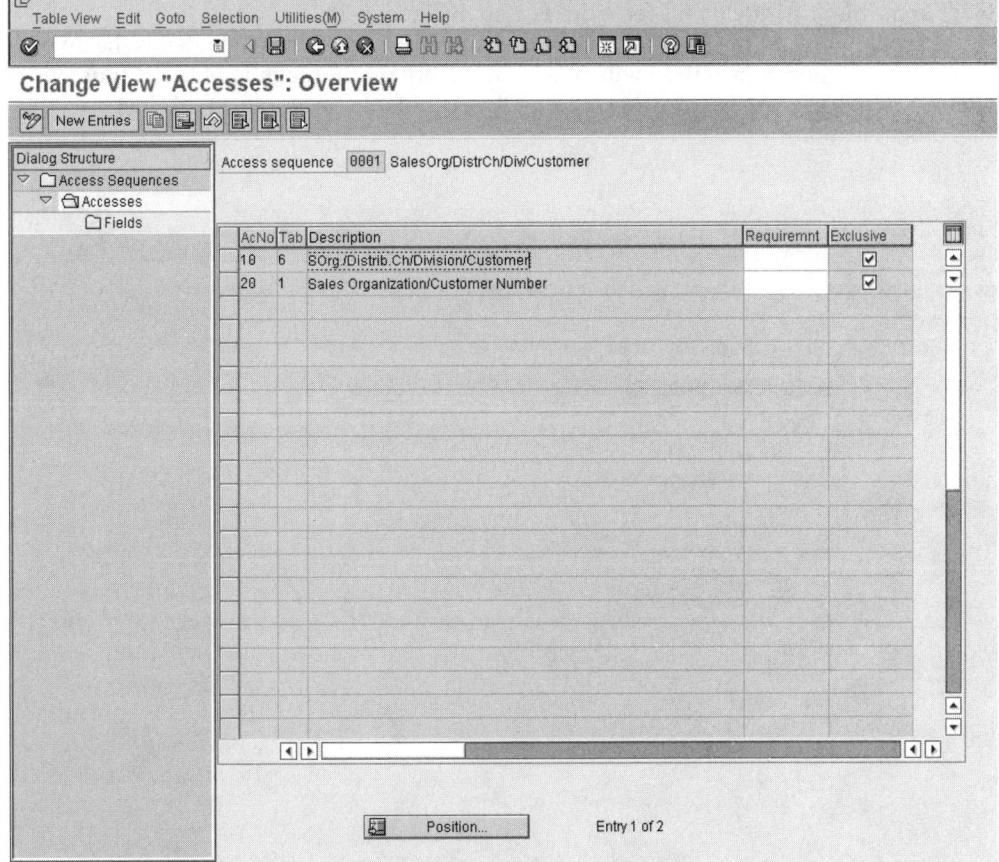

Copyright by SAP AG

FIGURE 9-25   Access sequence for output determination

Menu Path SAP Customizing Implementation Guide | Sales and Distribution | Basic Functions | Output Control | Output Determination | Output Determination Using the Condition Technique | Maintain Output Determination for Sales Documents | Maintain Output Types

The output type represents different forms of output, such as order confirmations, sales quotations, etc., as seen in Figure 9-26.

You can access the output type settings by selecting the output type (for example, BA00) and clicking the Display button (magnifying glass). This will then give you a screen as seen in Figure 9-27.

You can see in Figure 9-26 that the access sequence 0003 is assigned to the output type. You can see the system uses condition records to find an output command. The output may be changed during processing (as this cannot be changed checkbox is blank). As the multiple issuing checkbox is blank, this indicates the output may not be sent more than once to the same partner. As the partner independent output checkbox is not active, the output is restricted to being received only by those partner functions as set in the Partner Functions folder in the file structure on the left side, as seen in Figure 9-28.

Proceeding back to the output type, the last check box that is not activated is the do not write processing log, which if set will de-activate a very useful function of the output determination log in the process that is using the output—for example, in this instance, the sales order creation.

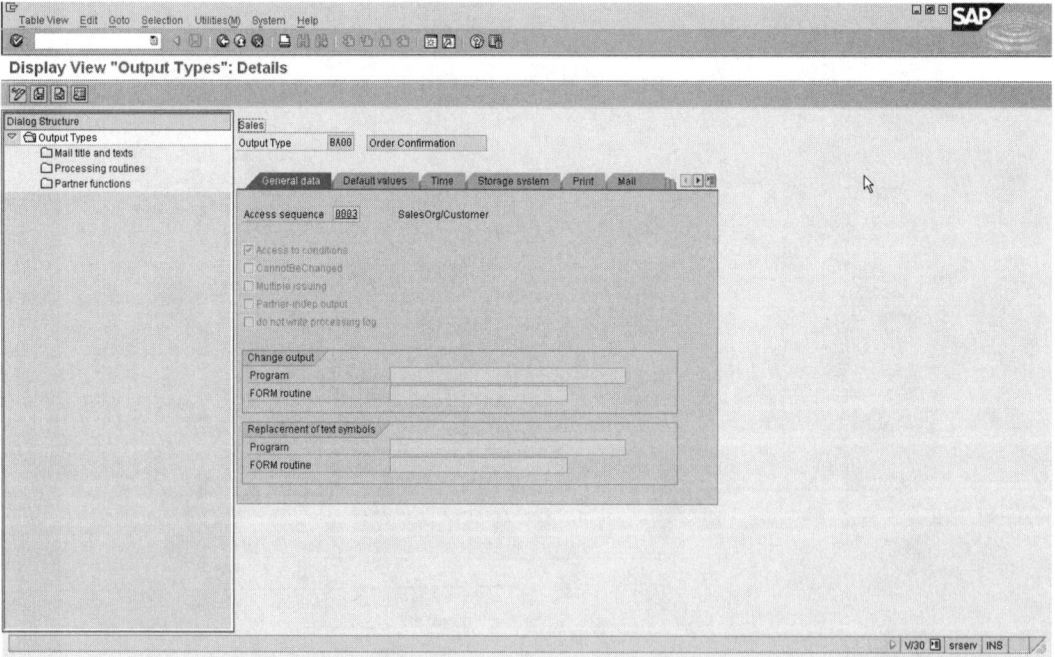

Copyright by SAP AG

FIGURE 9-26 Maintaining output types

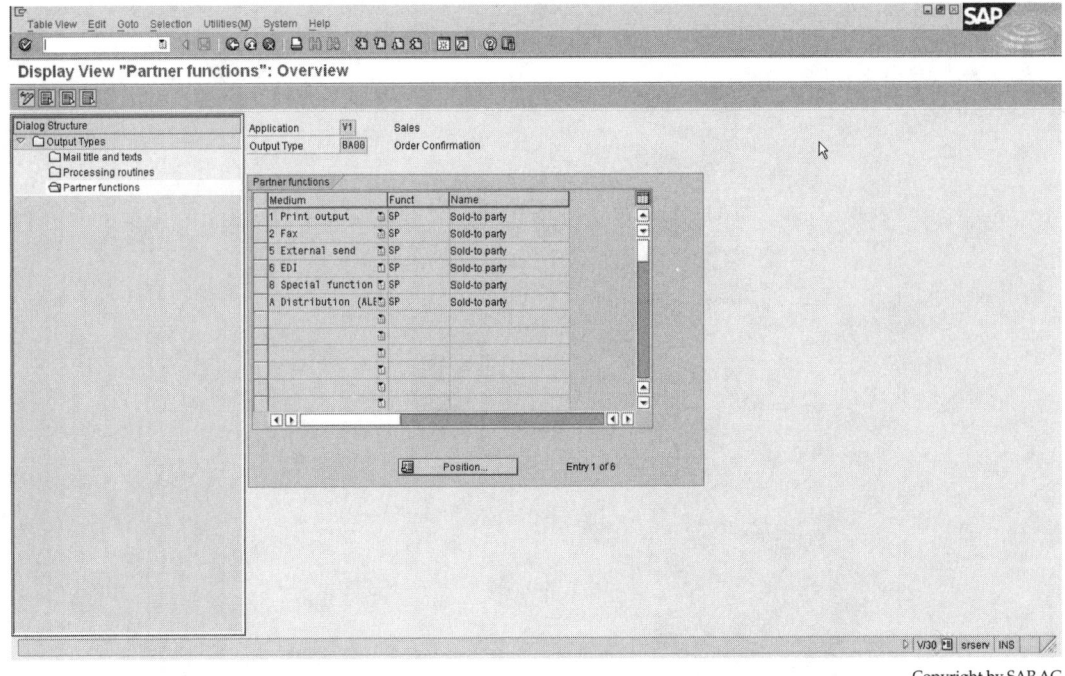

Copyright by SAP AG

FIGURE 9-27   Details of output type

The program that will be used to execute the output is defined in the Processing Routines folder in the file structure, as seen in Figure 9-29.

The output program for example RVADOR01 is assigned to a transmission medium—for example, for (1) Print output. This program uses form RVORDER01 to define the layout of the output.

You may double-click on the line in Figure 9-29 to see a view similar to Figure 9-30. Should you double-click the program or form again, you will go into the ABAP editor or form editor, respectively.

Proceed back to the output type and select the Default Values tab, as seen in Figure 9-30.

These values entered per output type are automatically transferred as default values when creating a condition record by output condition. The dispatch time has the following four options:

1. Send with periodically scheduled job

2. Send with scheduled job with own time specification

3. Send with application own transaction

4. Send immediately

You must understand that the output is automatically proposed and processed according to the rules governed in output determination. However, the user is still able to reprint

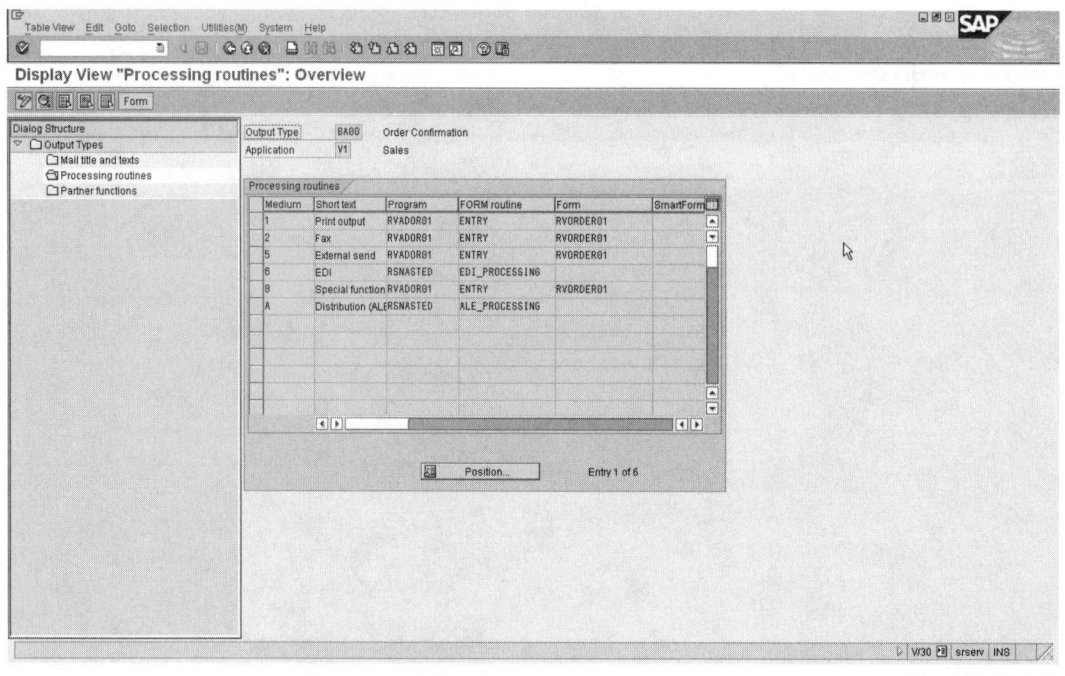

FIGURE 9-28 Partner functions that may receive output BAOO

(if permitted), or change the printing specifications online in the sales document. For example, the order confirmation might only be printed overnight and posted to the customer the following day. However, the customer may explicitly request that his order confirmation is handed to him immediately, so the user would change the output processing time to a 4—immediately.

The business, however, may not want the user to have this authority on all output types. For example, the order confirmation may be printed on a special printer with special paper, thus should only be done via a batch job at night. You can specify (on the Time tab) that specific times of dispatch are not allowed. This is set by indicating, for example, time of dispatch 4—not allowed.

You may also set the print parameter as seen on the Print tab. These criteria may be set as the sales organization or sales office, for example.

It is also possible to print and archive a document automatically by setting the Storage mode to 3 (Print and Archive) and assigning the correct archiving document type. This field identifies whether the archived document is an invoice, quotation, or order confirmation, etc. The archiving object of outgoing documents begins with SD0. These settings are made on the Storage System tab.

Step 7
Prior to completing step 7, use the following menu path.

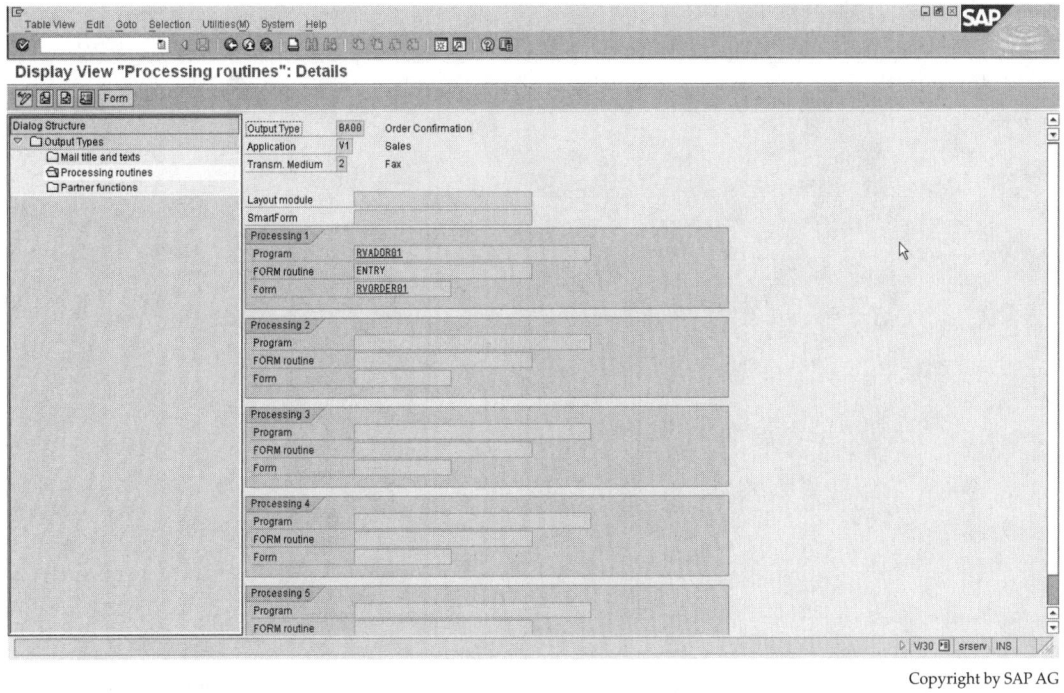

FIGURE 9-29   Processing routines

Menu Path   SAP Customizing Implementation Guide | Sales and Distribution | Basic Functions | Output Control | Output Determination | Output Determination Using the Condition Technique Maintain Output Determination for Sales Documents | Assign Output Types to Partner Functions

You may assign the allowed output types and processing medium to the partner functions. For example, you can assign the order confirmation as a printout to the sold to party, as well as the order confirmation as a fax to the sold to party. This may be seen in Figure 9-31. This has the same settings as previously completed in assigning the partner functions to the output type earlier.

Step 7 is identical in practice to any condition technique, and is accessible via the following menu path.

Menu Path   SAP Customizing Implementation Guide | Sales and Distribution | Basic Functions | Output Control | Output Determination | Output Determination Using the Condition Technique | Maintain Output Determination for Sales Documents | Maintain Output Determination Procedure

You have an output determination procedure with the output condition types assigned to it. The condition types may also have a requirement that may be assigned, thus restricting any access of the output type to the access sequence and condition records, unless specific conditions in the requirement have been fulfilled. The output determination procedure is

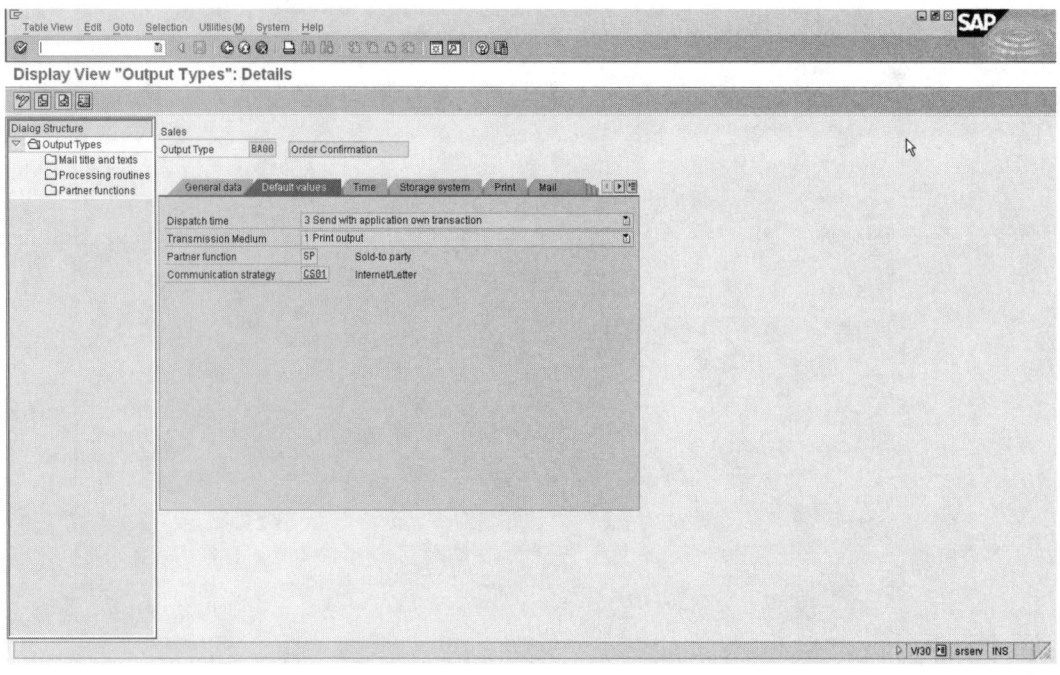

FIGURE 9-30 Output type processing default values

seen in Figure 9-32 by selecting the procedure V10000 and clicking the Control Data folder in the file structure on the left.

After completing the assignment of the condition type to the procedure, you can continue to step 8, assigning the procedure.

Step 8

The assignment is achieved in the following menu path.

Menu Path SAP Customizing Implementation Guide | Sales and Distribution | Basic Functions | Output Control | Output Determination | Output Determination Using the Condition Technique | Maintain Output Determination for Sales Documents | Assign Output Determination Procedures

This assignment of the output determination procedure occurs at the header and item level for sales documents. This assignment may be seen in the Figure 9-33 for the header level. The assignment is similar at item level except the procedure is assigned to an item category.

Step 9

Finally, you can now create the condition records necessary for output determination. This may be done using the following menu path.

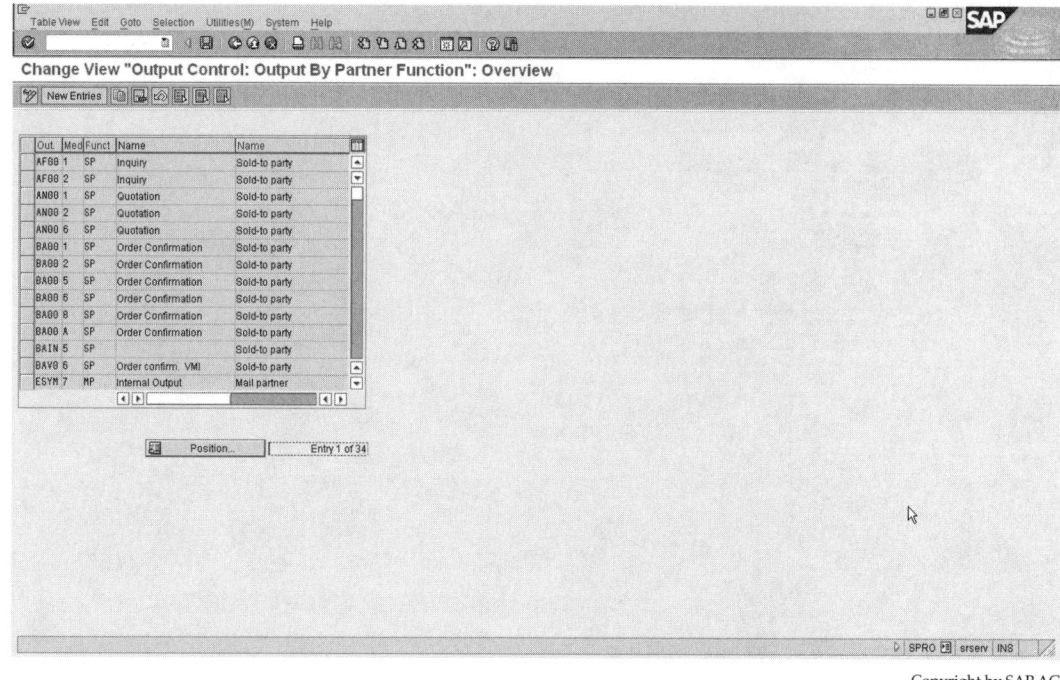

Copyright by SAP AG

FIGURE 9-31   Output by partner function

Menu Path   SAP Menu I Logistics I Sales and Distribution I Master Data I Output I Sales Document I

—The transaction codes related to the creation, maintenance and display of output condition records are:

- **[VV11]**   Create
- **[VV12]**   Change
- **[VV13]**   Display

You can assign the output type, partner function, transmission medium (1 = printout), the timing of the output (4 = immediately), and the language—for example, English.

By clicking the Communication button from within the condition record create or change screen, you can assign the output device (due to the transmission medium being a printout) as well as the number of messages, and whether the output must be printed immediately.

Inside the sales document you may view the output by selecting Extras I Output I Header or Item I Edit.

The buttons in the sales order output are

- Communication Method that identifies the details as set in the communication area of the condition record that is the printer name etc.

- Processing Log records a log of the output already processed in the sales document.

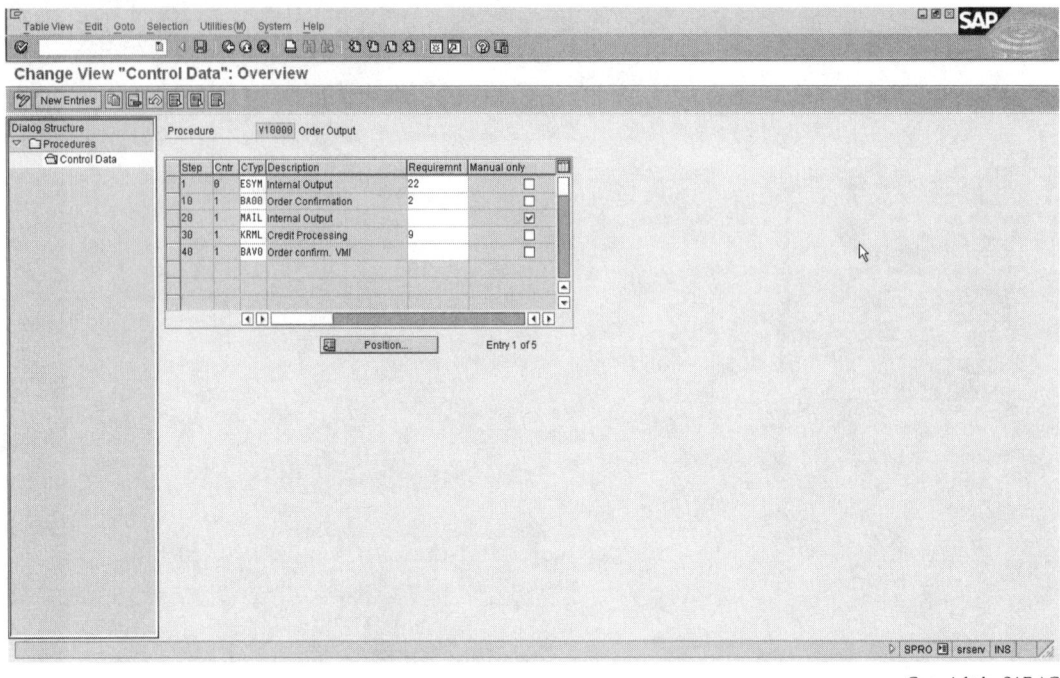

FIGURE 9-32 Output determination procedures

- Further Data displays if the output has been processed or not as well as the timing data—that is, is the output to be processed immediately or in batch.
- Repeat Output may be used to repeat already processed output.
- Change Output may be used to change the output.

Should you have the determination analysis activated as described earlier on in this section, you will also have a little blue icon with an i (information sign). When clicked, it will show you how the output was determined in the sales document.

This completes the maintenance of the output determination as required in the system. However, there is a lot of additional data that pertains to output that you will need to be aware of. Some of these details are covered in the following section.

NOTE *Forms, layout sets, and SAPscript are not in the scope of this book. However, it is beneficial for you to understand how the Sales and Distribution module integrates with the forms and programs.*

Brief Overview of a Layout Set and Its Assignment to Output Types

How does output work?

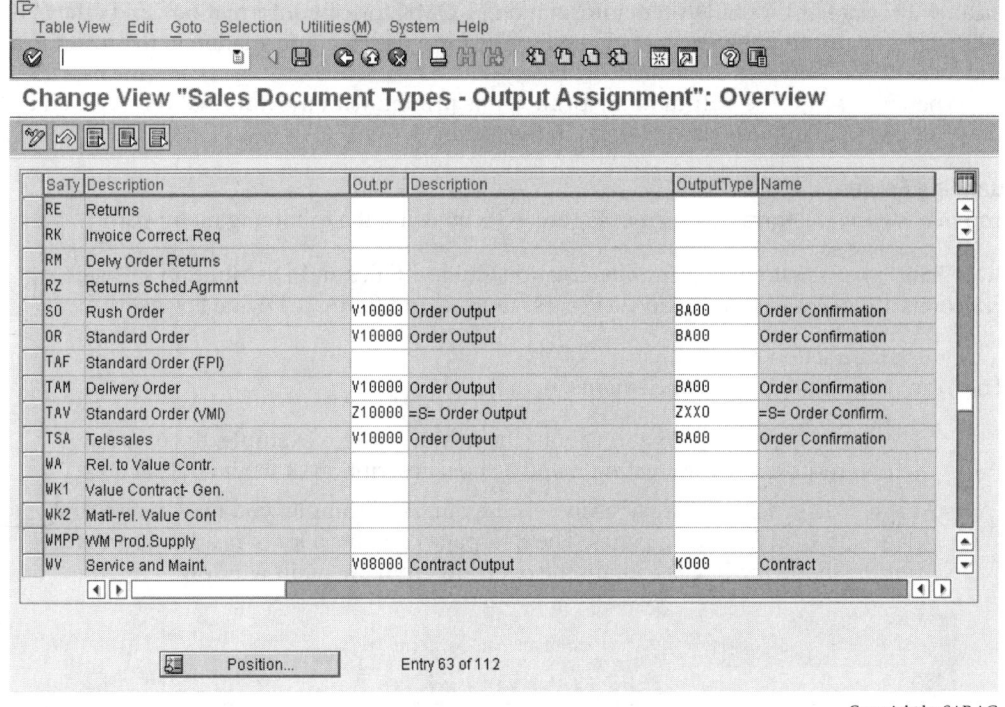

Figure 9-33   Output determination procedure assignment at header

Each output type is linked to a processing print program and a form. For example, in the SAP standard, the output type BA00 (order confirmation) is linked to processing program RVADOR01 and form RVORDER01. (The old terminology of "layout set" has been replaced by "form".)

When the user enters the output type in the business transaction, and then selects to print it, SAP calls the print program. The print program reads the business transaction and collects all the information that needs to be printed on it. It puts this information into structures defined in the data dictionary.

The fields in these structures are used in the form layout to define what data must be printed and where it must be printed.

The print program opens the form layout and calls each of the elements in the layout. The layout takes the information put into the data dictionary structures by the print program, as well as all the formatting information, and then formats it for the printer, fax machine, or e-mail.

Finally, the SAP system sends the output to the necessary device (printer, fax, or mail server).

In the order example, when the user enters the output type BA00 in the order transaction, and then selects to issue the output, SAP calls the print program RVADOR01. This program reads the sales order and related information and transfers it into the structures VBDKA (header information), VBDPA (item information), KOMK (pricing information), and others. It calls the form, printing the relevant elements. The form uses the information in the structures and formats the output to be printed.

When SAP sends the output to the printer, it is printed with the information collected by the print program in the format defined in the form.

Defining Forms

You may define the forms, as seen in Figure 9-34, by using the following menu path.

Menu Path   SAP Customizing Implementation Guide | Sales and Distribution | Basic Functions | Output Determination | Process Output and Forms | Define Forms

Or use transaction code [SE71].
The form is divided up into six elements, namely:

- **Header**   General information about the layout set—for example, the user name who is responsible for creating it and a short description of the layout set.

- **Pages**   This defines the pages in your layout. For example, you may have a first page and then following pages. The first page contains a lot of header information, but the following pages contain the overflow from the main window.

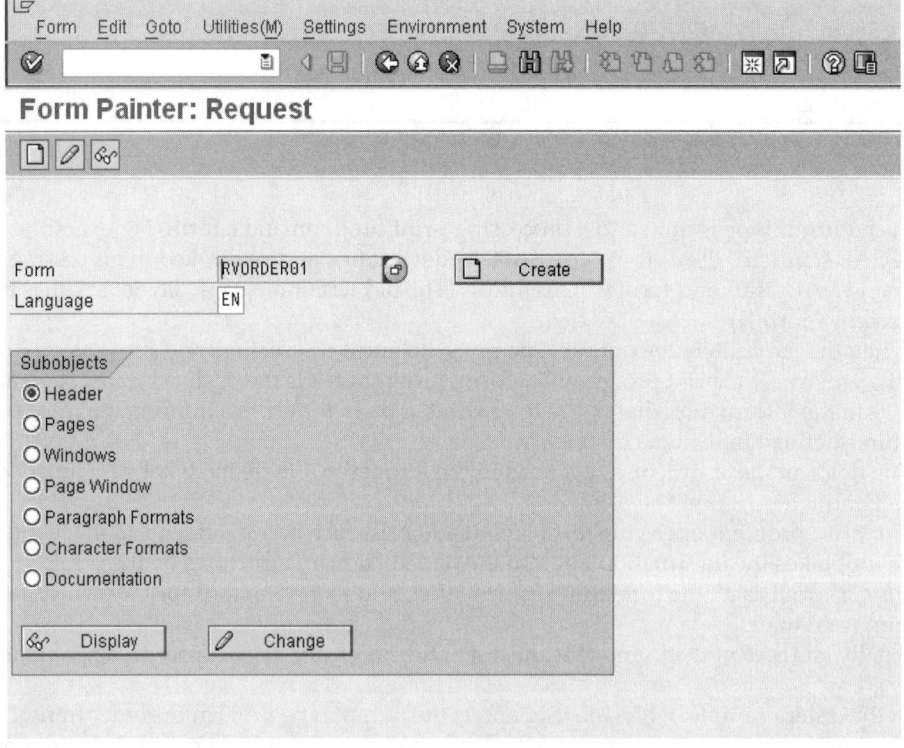

Copyright by SAP AG

FIGURE 9-34   Defining forms

- **Windows**   Windows are separate sections on the page. For example, you could have a header window for a company logo, and a footer window for the page footer. The most important window is the Main window. The items are printed in this window. You specify all the text and fields to be printed on the layout set in the different windows.

- **Page Windows**   In this section you arrange the windows you defined in the Windows section on the pages. You specify for each page what windows are on the page and what positions they occupy on the page.

- **Paragraph Formats**   This defines the paragraph styles used in the layout, and defines how the paragraph will print. For example, must the paragraph be right-justified or left-justified?

- **Character Formats**   These define the styles for a string of characters. For example, should a word be printed bold, underlined, or italic?

Defining Form Texts

You can define specific form texts per sales organization, sales office, or shipping point using the following menu path.

Menu Path   SAP Customizing Implementation Guide | Sales and Distribution | Basic Functions | Output Determination | Process Output and Forms | Assign Form Texts | Assign Form Texts Per Sales Organization

These specific texts are the Address text, Letter header, Letter footer text, and greeting text, as shown in Figure 9-35.

You can specify the position of these texts within the form.

To view the text, simply select the text and click the Display Text button on the lower-left side.

You can view printer details and output specific data by using the transaction code [SPAD] or menu path: SAP Menu | Tools | CCMS | Print | [SPAD] - Spool Administration, and branching off to view necessary data, such as output devices, spool servers, etc.

You can see the output requests and spool requests created by a user within a client by using transaction code [SP01] - Output controller (or the menu path SAP Menu | Tools | CCMS | Print | SP01 - Output Controller).

Should you need to reprint a number of documents—for example, billing documents that have already been printed—you can use the menu path: SAP menu | Logistics | Sales and Distribution | Billing | Output |

Transaction code:

- **[VF31]**   Billing documents

- **[VT70]**   Shipping and DELIVERY documents

You must enter the number range of documents that must be printed as well as the output type and transmission medium, and set the process mode, for example, to reprocess.

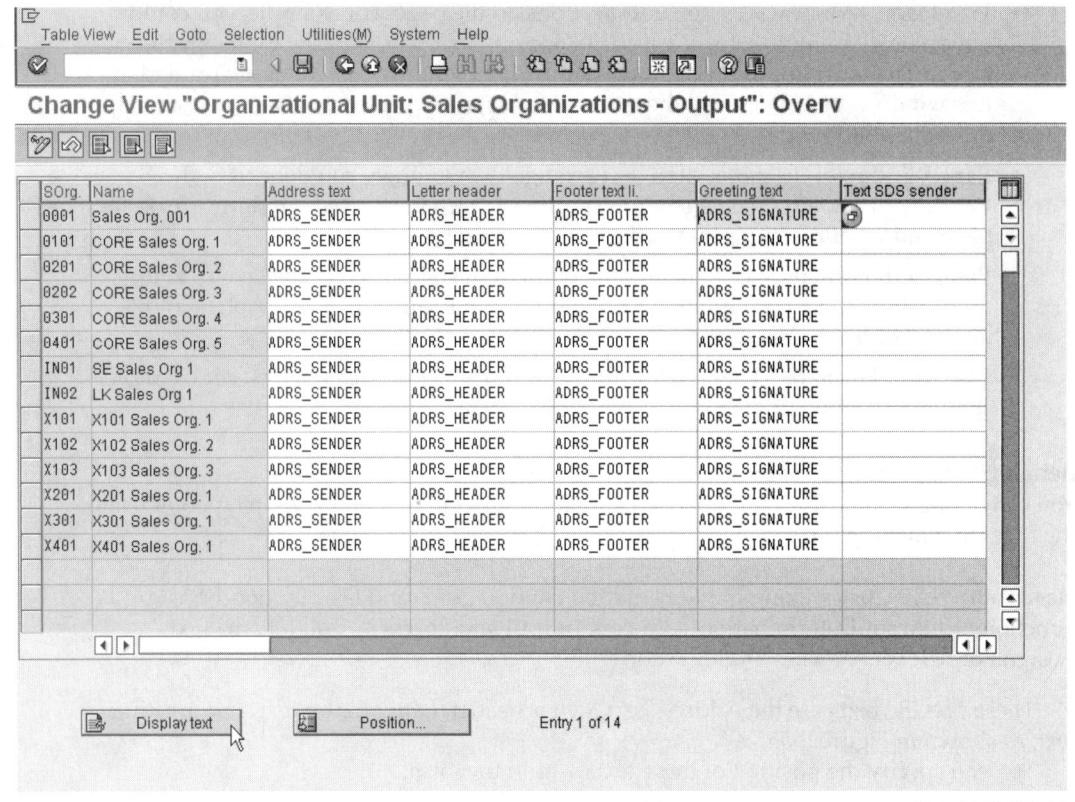

FIGURE 9-35 Text

Customer Hierarchies

Customer hierarchies are used when a customer has a complex chain or organizational structure and in which all or some of the parts of this structure should benefit from an agreement made for the customer's company as a whole. For example, a large customer may have dependent offices each responsible for their own purchasing, and as individuals would not benefit from a global pricing scheme. However, as part of a customer hierarchy they would still benefit from being associated with the larger parent company.

Before setting out and maintaining a customer hierarchy, you need to determine what the requirement for the hierarchy is. If it is to report bookings or billings for global customers within a hierarchy, this may be done using a standard reporting hierarchy within the sales information system.

Should the desire be merely to offer prices according to a specific group, you could think about using a customer group on the customer master record rather than a customer hierarchy.

If, on the other hand, you desire to have a customer hierarchy in order to offer special price agreements or rebates across a customer's organization that is on a "global" level, that may not be covered by a standard grouping. This may be covered by using the customer hierarchy.

The customer hierarchy integrates and relies on the partner determination, in conjunction with the customer hierarchy settings, in order to promote the linking between the customers. The partner determination causes the customer hierarchy to be represented in the sales document.

The customer hierarchy is a hierarchical organizational structure that consists of higher- and lower-level nodes. Each node is assigned within the structure to form a graphical diagram of the customers organization.

A node is represented by an account group.

Customer Hierarchy Types

A node may be a customer—for example, a sold to party—thus account group 0001. Or a node may be a platform, merely an organizational department, thus using account group 0012.

A customer hierarchy may only have a maximum of 26 hierarchy levels. You create a customer hierarchy by first defining the hierarchy type.

Define the hierarchy type by using the following menu path.

Menu Path   SAP Customizing Implementation Guide | Sales and Distribution | Master Data | Business Partners | Customers | Customer Hierarchy | Define Hierarchy Types

In Figure 9-36, we have a customer hierarchy type A. This is assigned to the partner function 1A, which is the highest node of partner represented in the hierarchy.

There should not be a need for you to create more than one hierarchy type, as you may only assign one hierarchy type per sales document type, which we will see later. The only time you may need a new hierarchy type is when you use a different hierarchy for different business transactions.

You may now create the associated partner determinations for customer hierarchies.

Setting Partner Determination for Hierarchy Categories

To set partner determination, use the following menu path.

Menu Path   SAP Customizing Implementation Guide | Sales and Distribution | Master Data | Business Partners | Customers | Customer Hierarchy | Set Partner Determination for Hierarchy Categories

You may define a customer hierarchy for any of the following:

- Customer Master
- Sales Document Header
- Sales Document Item
- Delivery
- Shipment
- Billing Header
- Billing Item
- Sales Activities (CAS)

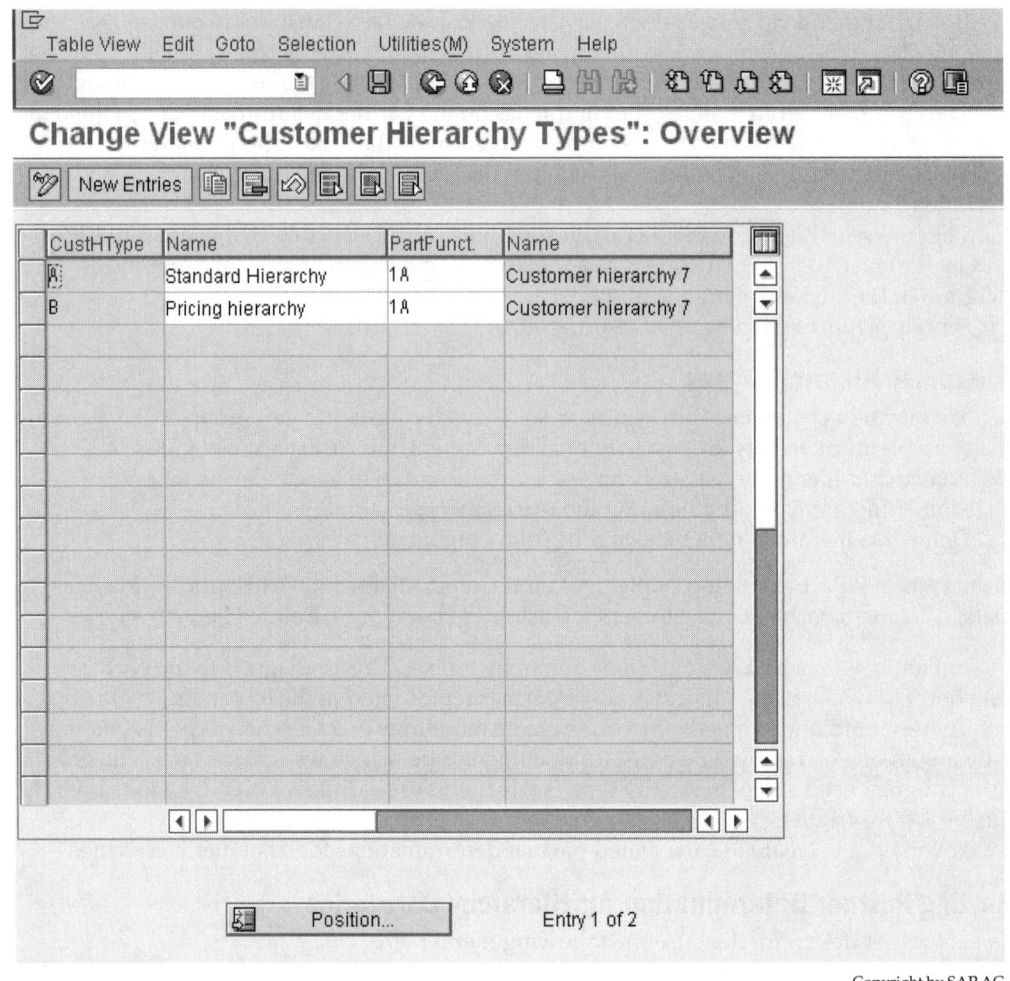

FIGURE 9-36 Customer hierarchy type

When configuring the hierarchy for partners you should configure for the sales document header and the billing document header, as you may need the hierarchy to be represented in both document types.

In our example we will look at the configuration for a customer hierarchy to be defined for the customer master, as shown in Figure 9-37.

As you can see, this is the standard partner determination procedure as defined earlier in this chapter.

You can assign partner functions up to 26 levels, from 1A through to 1Z.

Be careful also to maintain enough partner determination levels as are needed to represent the customer's structure. For example, let's say the customer's company had seven levels in the hierarchy in customer master configuration, and we only maintained five levels in the partner

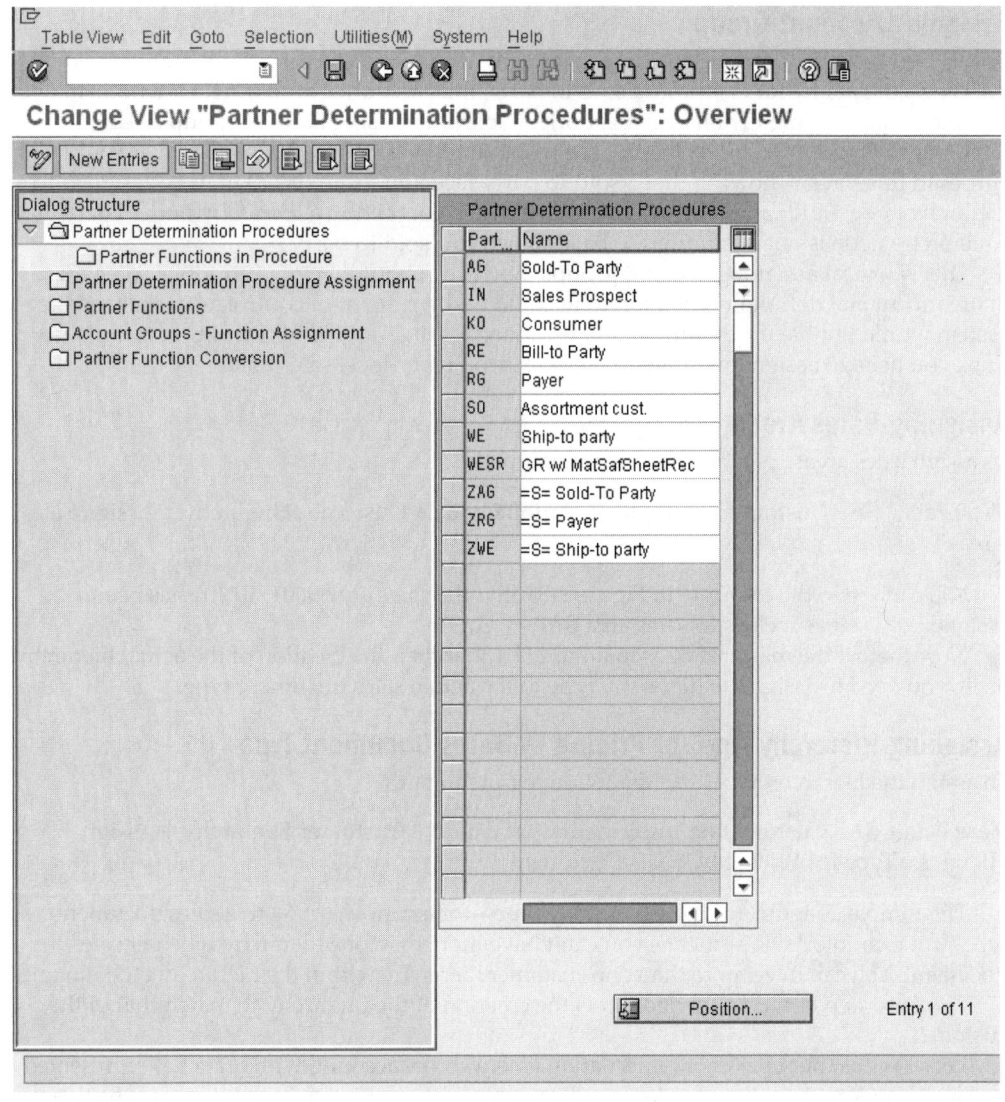

Copyright by SAP AG

FIGURE 9-37   Partner determination procedure

determination for a sales document type. The system would only copy data relevant to the five maintained levels into the sales document, and thus would only search for condition records up to the five levels of partners.

After the partner determination has been maintained, you need to maintain the association between the higher- and lower-level customer account groups. As we know, the hierarchy is formed by a linking of account groups. We need to maintain what account groups are to be linked.

Assigning Account Groups

This is the control behind the customer hierarchy. As mentioned earlier, a hierarchy node may be a customer—for example, a sold to party, thus account group 0001. Or a node may be a platform, thus merely an organizational department using account group 0012.

Refer to Figure 9-38, which shows the assignment of account groups. There are only two entries in this screen showing that a sold to party (account group 0001) may be assigned to a hierarchy node (0012) and a hierarchy node may be assigned to a hierarchy node. Therefore, a hierarchy node is not configured to be assigned to a sold to party.

This is logical assigning account groups; however, should we not introduce some form of organizational definition, the hierarchy could easily run out of control, especially as the system would not have a definitive organizational path to follow for condition records. Thus you need to assign lower-level sales areas to higher-level sales areas.

Assigning Sales Areas

To assign sales areas, use the following menu path.

Menu Path   SAP Customizing Implementation Guide | Customer Hierarchy | Assign Sales Areas

You can see in the example in Figure 9-39 that the sales area 0001/01/01 has been assigned to itself as well as to sales area 0101/OG/01.

Now that all the master data is maintained, other than the creation of the actual hierarchy itself, you need to assign the hierarchy type to the actual sales document type.

Assigning Hierarchy Type for Pricing by Sales Document Type

To assign the hierarchy type, use the following menu path.

Menu Path   SAP Customizing Implementation Guide | Customer Hierarchy | Assign Hierarchy Type for Pricing by Sales Document Type

This simple assignment of the hierarchy type—for example, "A"—to a sales document type—for example, "OR"—means you can't have more than one hierarchy type per sales document. You can have more than one customer hierarchy within the hierarchy type though.

The only step left to be carried out is the creation of the hierarchy to match that of the customer.

Let's say that our customer "International" is a global account, with branches represented in Africa, the Americas, Europe, Asia, and Australasia. Each branch in these areas is further

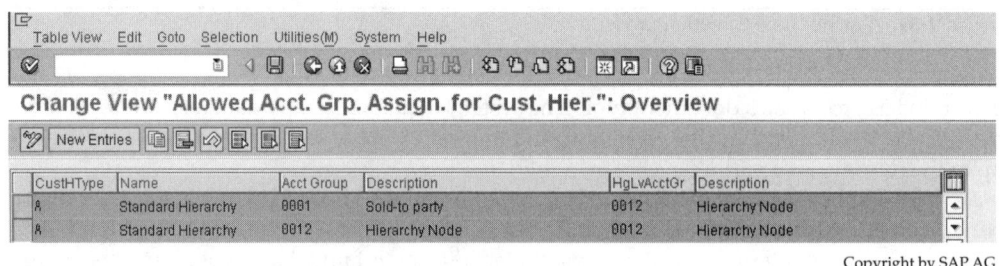

Copyright by SAP AG

FIGURE 9-38   Account group assignment

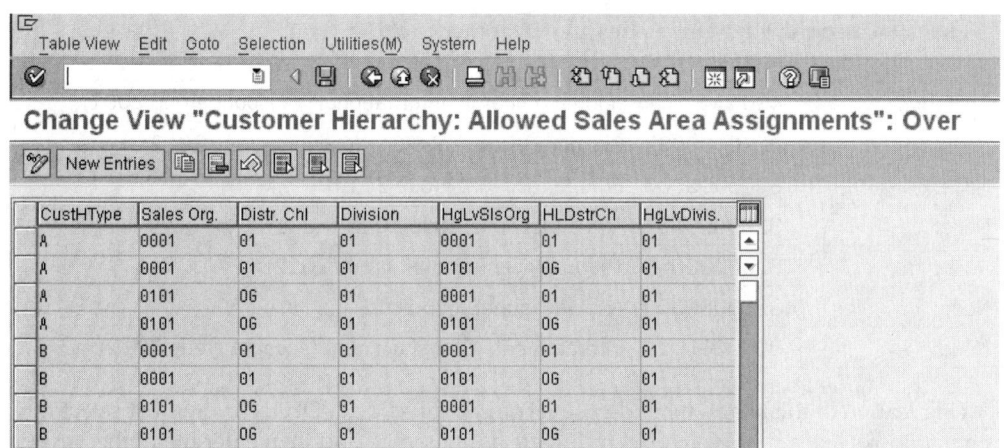

Copyright by SAP AG

Figure 9-39   Assigning sales areas

broken down into a national office and a subsequent regional office. Due to the size of the customer, we are offering all regional offices across the globe of customer "International" the same pricing discount of 10 percent off all our products.

This would be accomplished by creating the customer hierarchy using the following menu path.

Menu Path   SAP Menu I Logistics I Sales and Distribution I Master Data I Business Partner I Customer Hierarchy I [VDH1N] - Edit

(Do not forget to create the customer hierarchy nodes in the same way you would create all customer master records, either using [VD01] with the account group 0012 or using the menu path: Logistics I Sales and Distribution I Master Data I Business Partners I Hierarchy Nodes I Create, or transaction code [V-12].)

A hierarchy node uses account group 0012. This is the defaulted account group when you use transaction code [V-12].

Also do not forget to indicate the customers or nodes as relevant for customer hierarchy specific pricing and/or rebates. This is done by setting the indicators on the billing screen of the customer master record as shown in Figure 9-40.

Figure 9-40
Customer master relevant for hierarchy pricing/ rebates

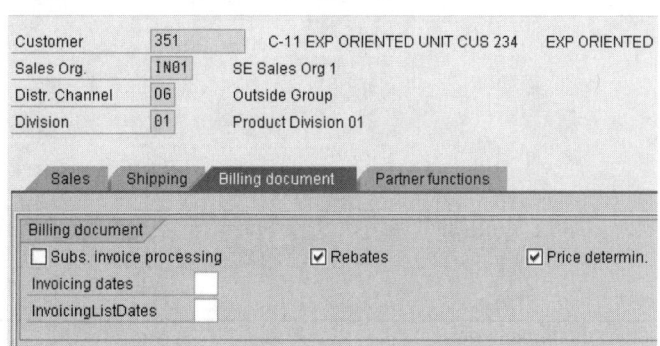

Copyright by SAP AG

I have created the following nodes and customers:

Customer:	400 - Munich Regional office of "International" (account group Z001).
Node:	3200000005 - Germany - National office (account group Z012).
Node:	3200000006 - Europe (account group Z012).
Node:	3200000007 - Africa (account group Z012).
Node:	3200000008 - The Americas(account group Z012).
Node:	3200000009 - Asia (account group Z012).
Node:	3200000010 - International - Global account (account group Z012).

On creation of the hierarchy node using transaction code [VDH1N], you must select the icon that looks like a new page used in "create assignment" and then enter the higher level and the assigned lower-level node and click the Transfer button, as seen in Figure 9-41.

Continue with assignments until the structure looks similar to the screen in Figure 9-42.

When creating a sales order, you can clearly see the customer hierarchy in the partners overview, as seen in Figure 9-43.

Should you not initially see the hierarchy, note the drop-down box "Display Range" at the bottom of the screen, as seen in Figure 9-44. Select PARALL All partners.

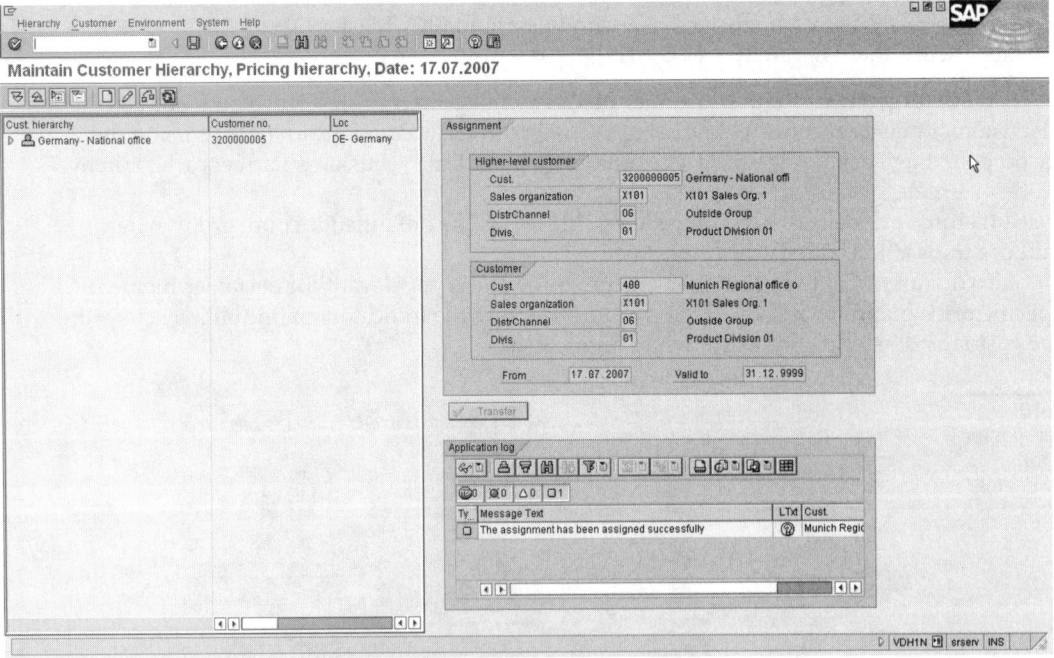

Copyright by SAP AG

FIGURE 9-41   Maintaining customer hierarchy

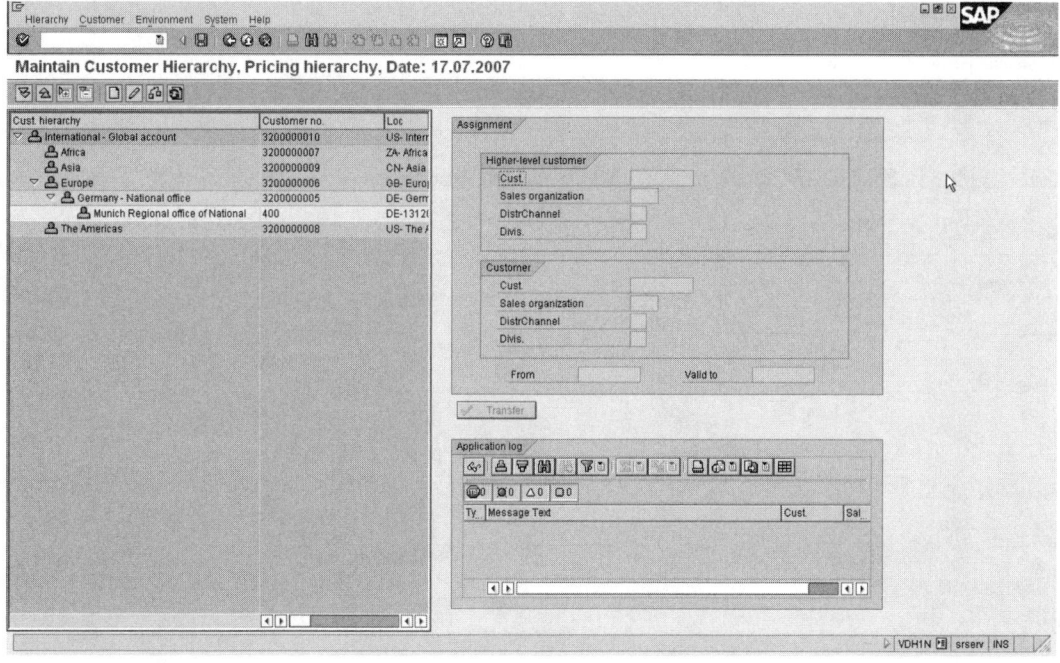

Copyright by SAP AG

FIGURE 9-42   Maintaining customer hierarchy example structure

This concludes the determination of the customer hierarchy. Its usefulness remains in that the hierarchy may be used in conjunction with the condition technique to offer discounts, surcharges, or special pricing.

Product Hierarchies

Product hierarchies are the domain of materials management. However, it is beneficial for the Sales and Distribution module to know they exist, what they are, and where they may be maintained.

A product hierarchy, like a customer hierarchy, has an automatic " family tree" linking it back to a certain grouping of products.

Defining Product Hierarchies

You may define the product hierarchy using the following menu path.

Menu Path   SAP Customizing Implementation Guide | Logistics - General | Material Master | Settings for Key Fields | Data Relevant to Sales and Distribution | Define Product Hierarchies [OVSV]

A product hierarchy is assigned to the material master record. This hierarchy is broken down into specific levels, each level containing its own characteristics.

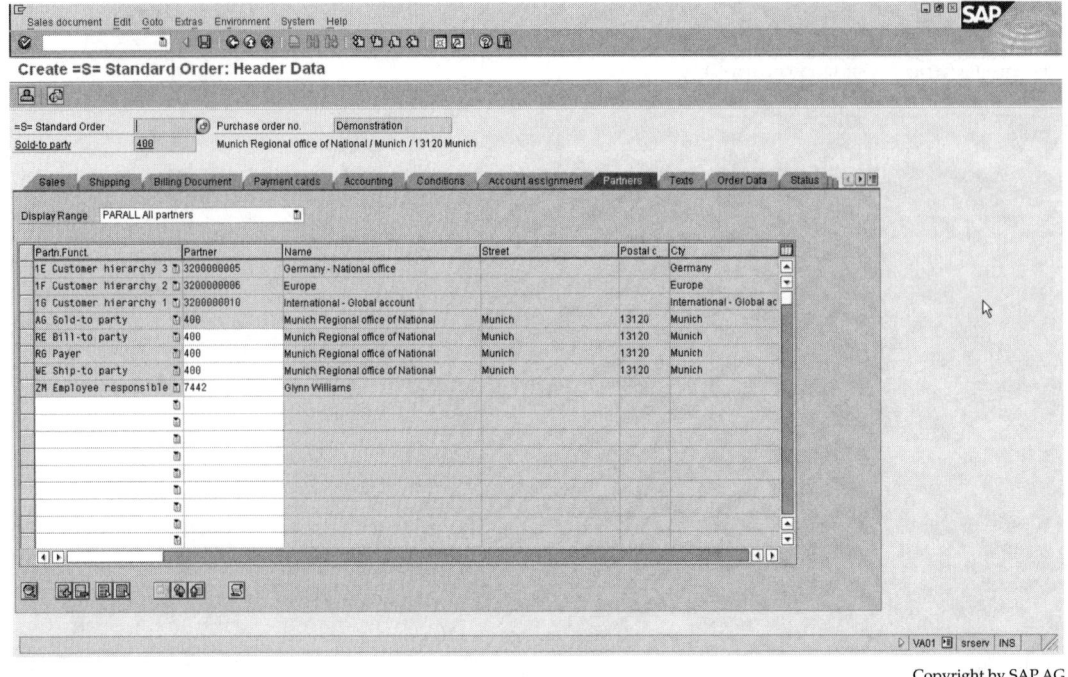

Copyright by SAP AG

FIGURE 9-43   Sales document with customer hierarchy

A product hierarchy is recorded by the sequence of digits within a hierarchy number. This hierarchy number may have a maximum of 18 digits with a maximum of 9 levels.

For example, a material may be classified as a laptop computer with a tablet screen, with the product hierarchy represented, with three levels, as follows:

Computer	00001
Laptop	00002
Tablet screen	00000100

Thus, by assigning the hierarchy number 000010000200000100 to the material, one is able to determine a classification of the material. This hierarchy may be used in pricing, with each level being used as a field in the condition technique. Thus, it is possible to say all materials with a product hierarchy level 1 equal to 00001 may have a 10 percent discount.

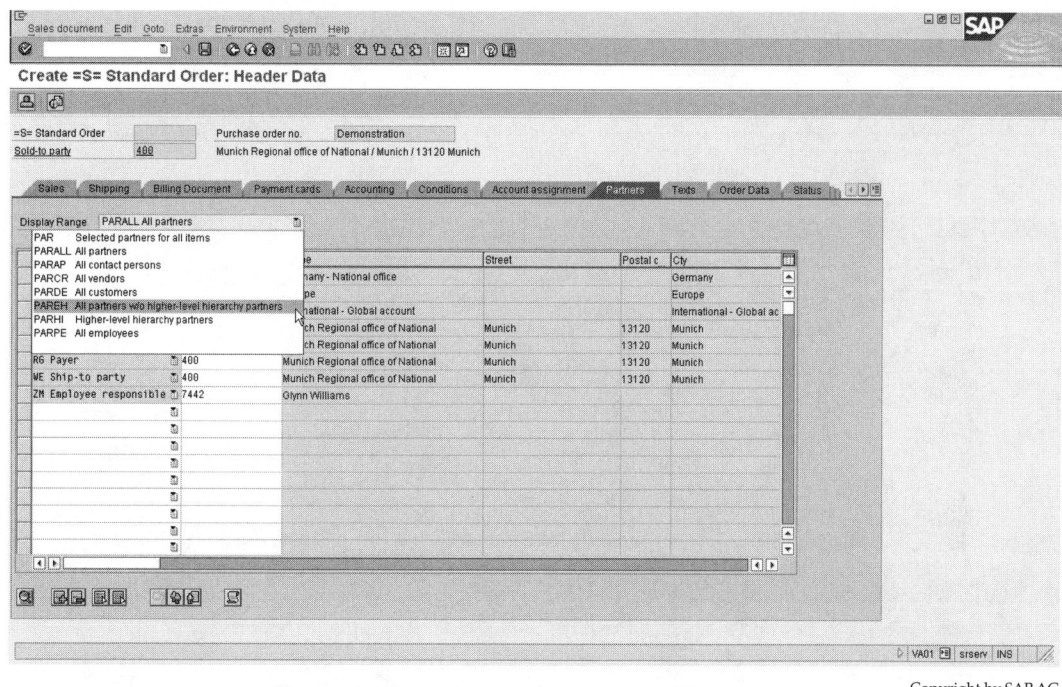

FIGURE 9-44 Selecting partner functions

Each of these levels may also be used as fields for reporting purposes in the logistics information systems. It is possible for one to report on the number of computers sold by selecting all materials with level 1 equal to 00001.

The SAP standard system has a product hierarchy structure consisting of three levels. These three levels are broken down into two levels of five digits each and one level of eight digits.

Should this structure of hierarchy meet the requirements of your business, you can proceed straight through to the maintenance of the hierarchy in transaction code [V/76].

If, however, you need to create a new hierarchy structure, you can use the following guidelines.

- One needs to maintain the product hierarchy structure PRODHS. (The maintenance of structures is not in the scope of this book; however, there is ample clear documentation in the system on how to perform this step.) This structure defines each level and the length of digits permitted for each level, as shown in Figure 9-45.

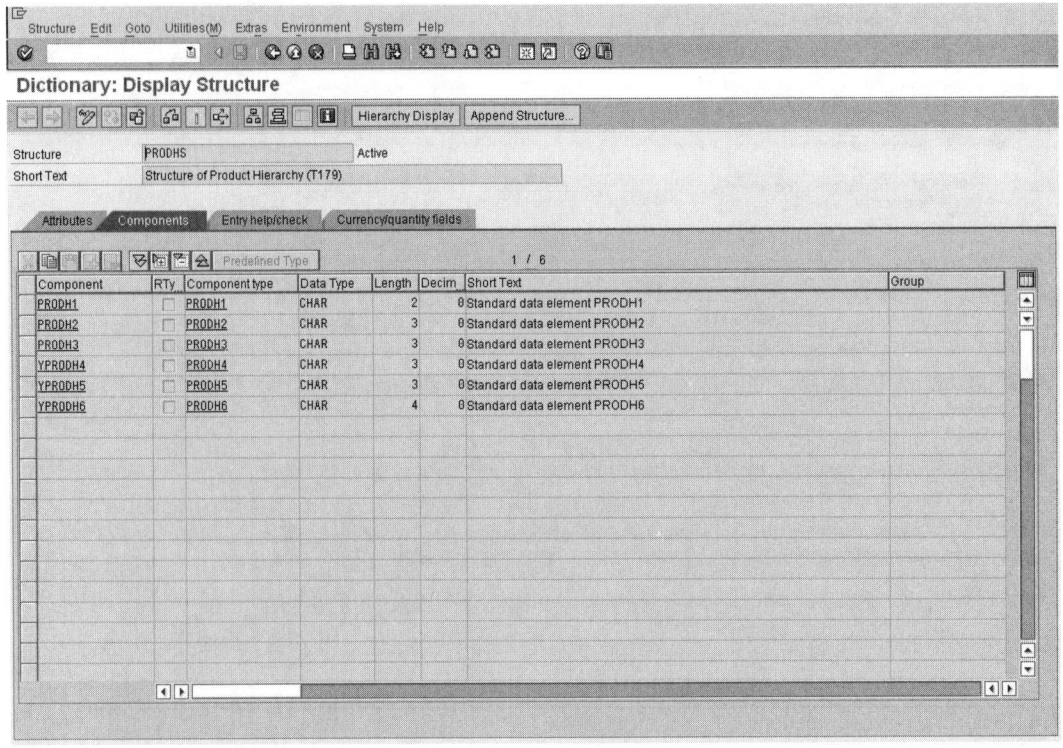

Copyright by SAP AG

FIGURE 9-45 Product hierarchy structure PRODHS

- You may proceed to create a template that represents the product hierarchy. This template should have placeholders as defined by an underscore (_) and separators as defined by a forward slash (/) or a colon (:). Thus a template of 5 and 5 and 8 digits may look as follows: _____/_____/_____.

- You can then create the product hierarchy as used by the system, for example in Figure 9-46.

- Now that the hierarchy is created in the system as well as the template with the entries as allowed in the hierarchy, you merely need to ensure the hierarchy levels are in the field catalog as used in pricing, as seen in Figure 9-47.

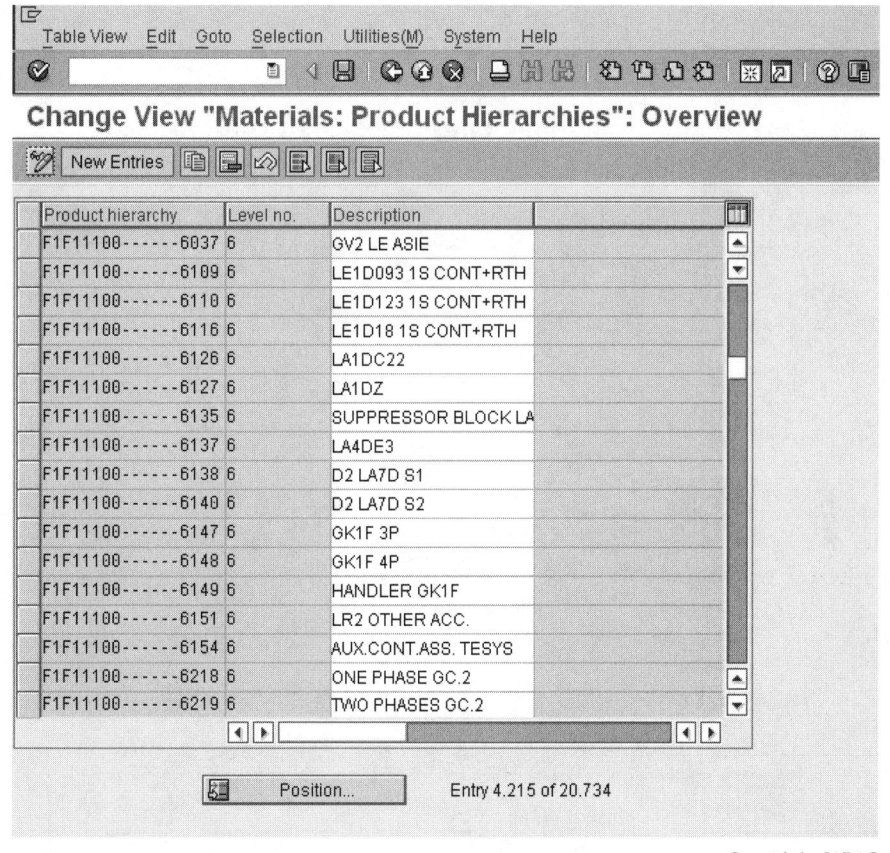

Copyright by SAP AG

FIGURE 9-46   Creating a product hierarchy

- The hierarchy levels must also be available in the field catalog as used in the Logistics information system. (LIS.)

- Lastly, you must ensure the material master record has the product hierarchy assigned to it in the Basic Data 1 tab under General Data, as in Figure 9-48.

This concludes our section on product hierarchy. Note that in some companies the product hierarchy is a critical field, and used in a number of BW and LIS reporting structures, as well as in pricing. Due to its sensitivity, it is advisable to fully investigate changes to its structure before making modifications. It is not as easily changed as adding a new value to a drop-down selection list.

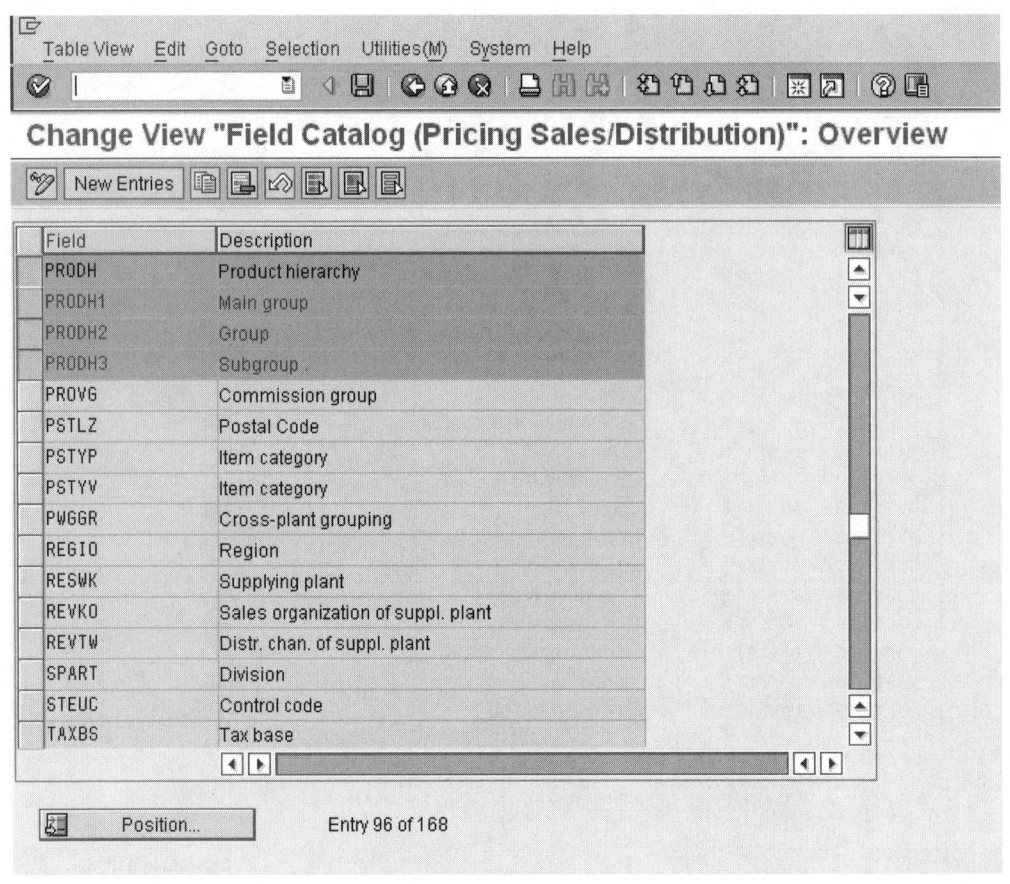

Copyright by SAP AG

FIGURE 9-47 Product hierarchy fields in field catalog

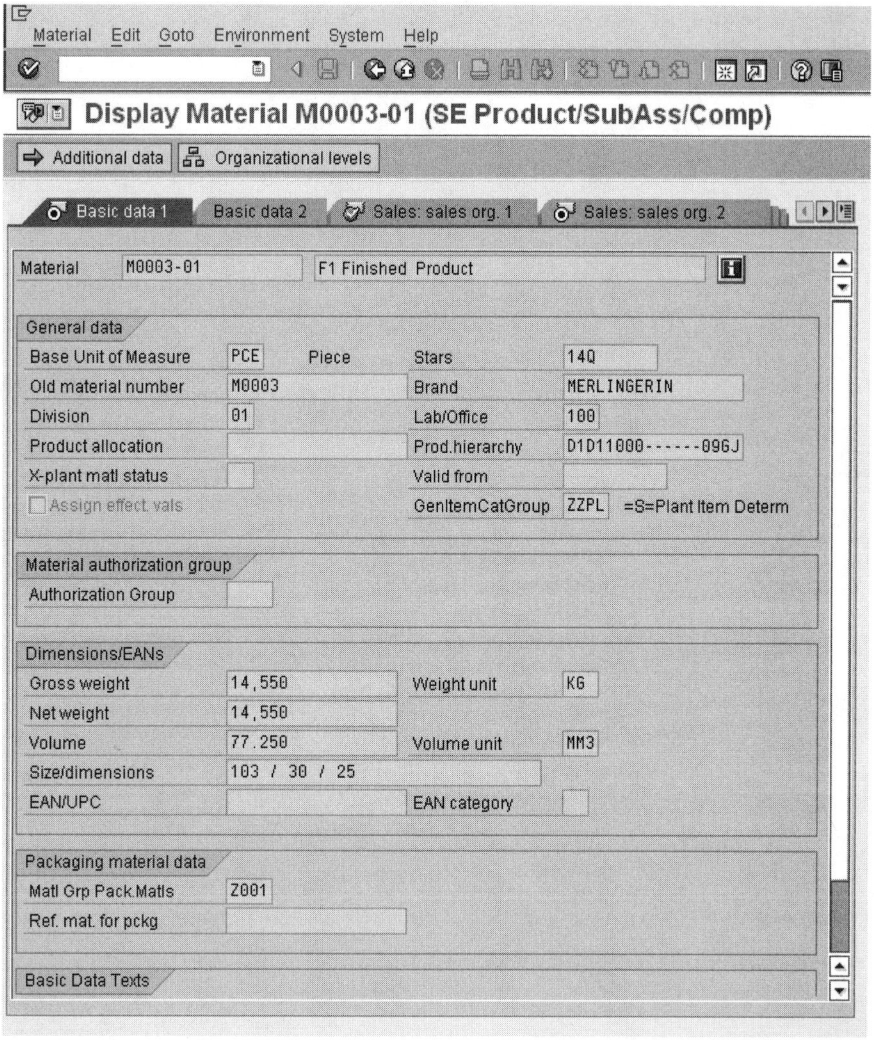

FIGURE 9-48   Product hierarchy on material master Basic Data 1 tab

Credit Management, Receivable Risk Management, Blocks, and Calendars

This chapter contains details related to the financial control of customer accounts. This control is implemented in all parts of the order management and logistics cycles.

Credit Management

Customers have a time period in which to pay their accounts with the company. These time periods are defined in the payment terms that are assigned to the customer master record.

Should a customer not pay his outstanding amounts by the end of his allowed payment term, he is defaulting on his agreement and the company will need to govern his allowed credit more closely.

In order to manage these situations SAP has developed a complex credit management solution that allows, among other things, the maintenance of credit limits per customer, as well the maintenance of the system responses should the customer's credit limit be exceeded.

Before we proceed with credit management, we need to discuss credit management master data. For example, a credit limit may be a *customer credit limit*, which may be configured as the permitted limit of the value of open items (invoices not yet paid plus the value of open sales orders plus the value of deliveries that have not been invoiced).

The customer's credit limit is assigned to the customer by Finance using the following menu path.

Menu Path   SAP Menu | Accounting | Financial Accounting | Customers | Credit Management | Master Data | [FD32] - Change

Naturally a customer master record must exist before a credit limit may be applied to it.

A *credit control area* is an organizational unit in which the customer credit limits are managed in SAP. You can assign one or more company codes to a credit control area. Whenever a sale takes place, SAP determines the company code from the sales organization, and using the company code, SAP determines the credit control area. Using the credit control area, SAP knows which credit management rules apply to the sale, and what credit limit the customer has for the sale.

By assigning one company code to a credit control area, you can give the customers separate credit limits per company code. If you assign more than one company code to a credit control area, the customer has a single credit limit that applies across all sales in these company codes.

In this way, you can centralize the credit management in your organization across all the company codes. For example, if a customer has used up his limit buying from one company code, he won't be able to buy from any of the other company codes.

Also, by centralizing the credit limit in this way, you don't have to split up the total credit risk of the customer across company codes.

For example, if you want your total exposure to the customer to be $1 million, but you have four company codes, how do you apportion that risk across each company code? If you create one credit control area, you can have one credit limit of $1 million that applies across all four companies. You won't get a case where the customer has used up his credit at company A, but has available credit at company B, and now he wants to buy from company A using his limit at company B.

These credit control areas are maintained and assigned in the enterprise structure.

A customer's *risk category* is a grouping category that controls how the credit check is carried out when automatic credit control takes place. For example, you can define high-risk customers to risk category A01, medium-risk customers to B01, and low-risk customers to group C01. You can determine different credit control rules to apply in each case. So even though the customers belong to the same credit control area, you can have stricter rules for the high-risk customers. We will use this category and define its assignment later.

Maintaining a Credit Control Area

To create a credit control area, as shown in Figure 10-1, use the following menu path.

Menu Path   SAP Customizing Implementation Guide │ Enterprise Structure │ Definition │ Financial Accounting │ Define Credit Control Area

What we see from these settings is that the currency key in the credit control area is EUR (Euros). The update rule, which is discussed in detail later, is 000012. The fiscal year variant for determining the posting date for credit management is set as key K4.

You are required to have a fiscal year variant if the credit control area is assigned to more than one company code and each company code has a different fiscal year.

Other settings are configured as follows:

- The default risk category for new credit control master records will be defaulted as NEW.
- The default credit limit for new credit control master records will be defaulted for example as 30000,00.
- There is no credit representative group setting as a default for new customers.
- A credit control area is then assigned to a company code.
- Posting is possible for all company codes.

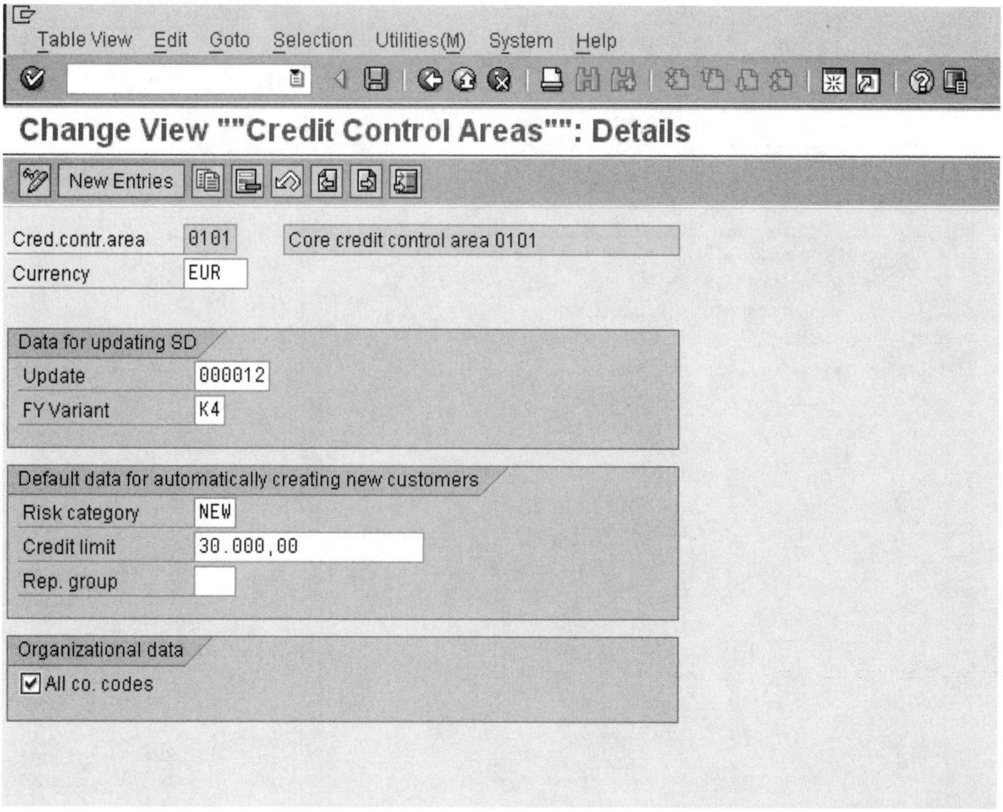

Table View   Edit   Goto   Selection   Utilities(M)   System   Help

Change View ""Credit Control Areas"": Details

New Entries

Cred.contr.area	0101	Core credit control area 0101
Currency	EUR

Data for updating SD

Update	000012
FY Variant	K4

Default data for automatically creating new customers

Risk category	NEW
Credit limit	30.000,00
Rep. group	

Organizational data

☑ All co. codes

FIGURE 10-1   Creating a Credit Control Area

After creation of a credit control area, you must assign a company code to a credit control area.

Assigning Company Codes to a Credit Control Area

To assign company codes, as shown in Figure 10-2, use the following menu path.

Menu Path   SAP Customizing Implementation Guide | Enterprise Structure | Assignment | Financial Accounting | Assign Company Code to Credit Control Area

It is possible to assign a credit control area to a sales area (combination of sales organization, distribution channel, and division.) This is a more specific assignment than the assignment to the company code. Use the following menu path.

Menu Path   SAP Customizing Implementation Guide | Enterprise Structure | Assignment | Sales and Distribution | Assign Sales Area to Credit Control Area

You can also assign the credit control area directly in the customer master or in a user exit based on the sales order header fields (see EXIT_SAPFV45K_001).

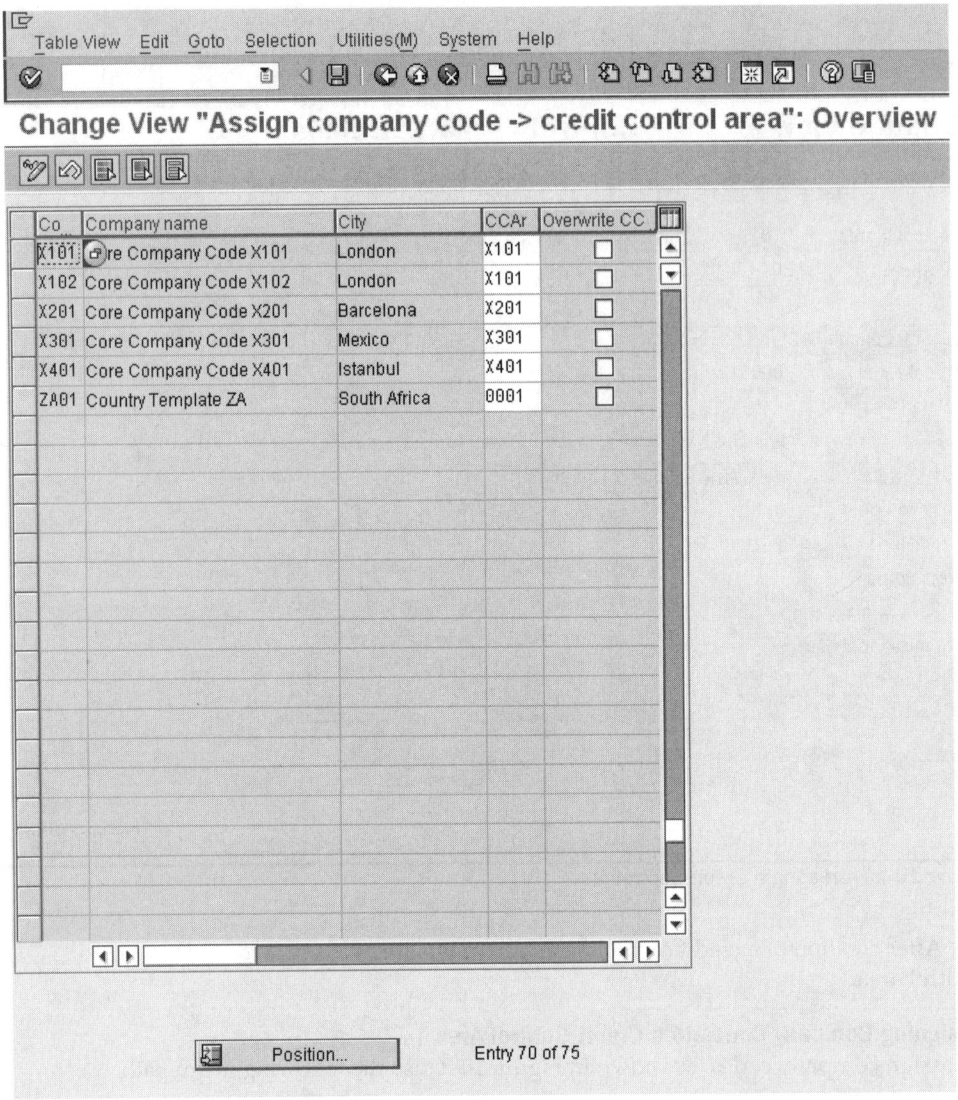

FIGURE 10-2 Assigning a company code to a credit control area

For customers, you assign the credit control area in the sales area data billing screen of the customer master. Note that this field may be suppressed based on the customer account group field selection status—it is usually only active for the payer account group (0003). If you want to use this option, you may need to change the field selection to make this field an optional or mandatory field on the billing screen of the customer master.

Note that even if you assign the credit control area based on the sales area, customer master, or user exit, you must still assign the company code to the credit control area by selecting Enterprise Structure | Assignment | Financial Accounting.

Credit Control Basics

There are only three places where a credit check can occur—the sales order, the delivery, and at goods issue.

The system executes the credit check on the sales order or delivery based on the configuration settings. If the credit check fails, the system then either stops the user from saving the document, or it allows the document to be saved but it blocks the document with a credit block.

Documents blocked for credit must be released by an authorized person before they can be processed further. For example, a delivery for an order cannot be created if the order has a credit block on it.

You can view documents blocked for credit by selecting Logistics | Sales and Distribution | Credit Management | Sales and Distribution Documents | All (transaction code VKM3). You can also use this transaction to release a blocked document.

Once a document is released, you can continue processing it even though the credit limit check failed.

Every time a user changes a sales document, the credit limit check is executed again. For example, if a document was released with a value of $10,000, and the value is changed to $11,000 and the customer is still over his limit, the document will be blocked for credit again. This is because the new value exceeds the released value.

 You can use program RVKRED08 to recheck all documents blocked for credit. For example, if a customer pays his account, you want to recheck all his documents. Some documents can now be released because of the payment received. It is a good idea to schedule a background job using this program so that blocked documents are checked on a regular basis. This will keep the blocked documents up to date with any changes to the account or to sales documents, such as a payment being made. If a large sales order that was holding up the credit limit is cancelled, other blocked documents can use the value that is freed up by the cancellation.

The system can use many different automatic credit management checks, which are discussed in detail later. These are

- A static check
- A dynamic check
- A check on the total document value
- A critical field check
- A next review date check
- A check on open items
- A check on oldest open item
- A check on highest permitted dunning level

Normally, one or more of these checks are carried out at the same time. There are three main credit control methods—namely, a simple credit check, a static credit check, or a dynamic credit check.

The Simple Credit Check

First, please note that this credit check is deemed obsolete and is not recommended to be used. It is only documented here for you to understand the differences if you come across a system with this installed, and is a good introduction into automatic credit control.

The simple credit check compares the payer customer master record's credit limit to the net document value plus the value of all open items. Should the value of the document and open items be greater than the credit limit permitted, the system may respond with a warning message in the sales order; a warning message and a delivery block, which will allow the order to be taken but will block it for delivery; or an error message, which will cause the document not to be saved.

This setting for a simple credit check is set at the document type level, thus the system will use this simple check for all sales orders created for this particular sales document type. The system will perform the simple credit check for all created and changed sales documents.

To define the simple credit check, use the following menu path.

Menu Path   SAP Customizing Implementation Guide | Sales and Distribution | Basic Functions | Credit Management/Risk Management | Simple Credit Limit Check

You can now assign the credit limit check to the sales document type, using the following codes:

A	Run simple credit limit check and warning message
B	Run simple credit limit check and error message
C	Run simple credit limit check and delivery block

As it is generally not beneficial to treat all customers the same way as far as credit management is concerned, SAP allows a dynamic and static credit check according to a customers risk category.

This way you can determine that should a good customer with a low-risk credit rating exceed his credit limit, the sales order may still be created and not blocked, but should a high-risk customer with a high-risk credit rating exceed his credit limit using the same sales document type, the system may block the sales document from being processed further. This credit management control is maintained by using the automatic credit management functionality.

Automatic Credit Management

Automatic credit management is used to carry out the different credit checks including the static and dynamic checks. This is done by separating the sales document types, the delivery document types, and goods issue into specific credit groups.

It also uses the customer's credit risk category as assigned to the customer master record of the payer (transaction code [FD32]) and assigns an outcome procedure to the combination of the credit group and the customer risk category along with the credit control area.

Defining Customer Risk Category

The definition of the customer's risk category is carried out in the Financial Accounting module, so use the following menu path.

Menu Path   SAP Customizing Implementation Guide | Financial Accounting | Accounts Receivable and Accounts Payable | Credit Management | Credit Control Account | Define Risk Categories

It is advisable to be as simplistic as possible when defining the credit risk categories and document credit groups. Due to the number of combinations you can perform with these two groupings, if you define a large number, you will have a large number of credit management strategies to configure. For example, if you have 10 risk categories and 4 document credit groups, you have 40 credit management strategies to configure. I find the following credit groups are normally required: New, High, Medium, Low, and No risk. The risk categories may be seen in Figure 10-3.

Now that the risk category has been defined, it is necessary to define the credit groups.

Defining Credit Groups

Credit groups are configured in Sales and Distribution as opposed to Financial Accounting. Use the following menu path.

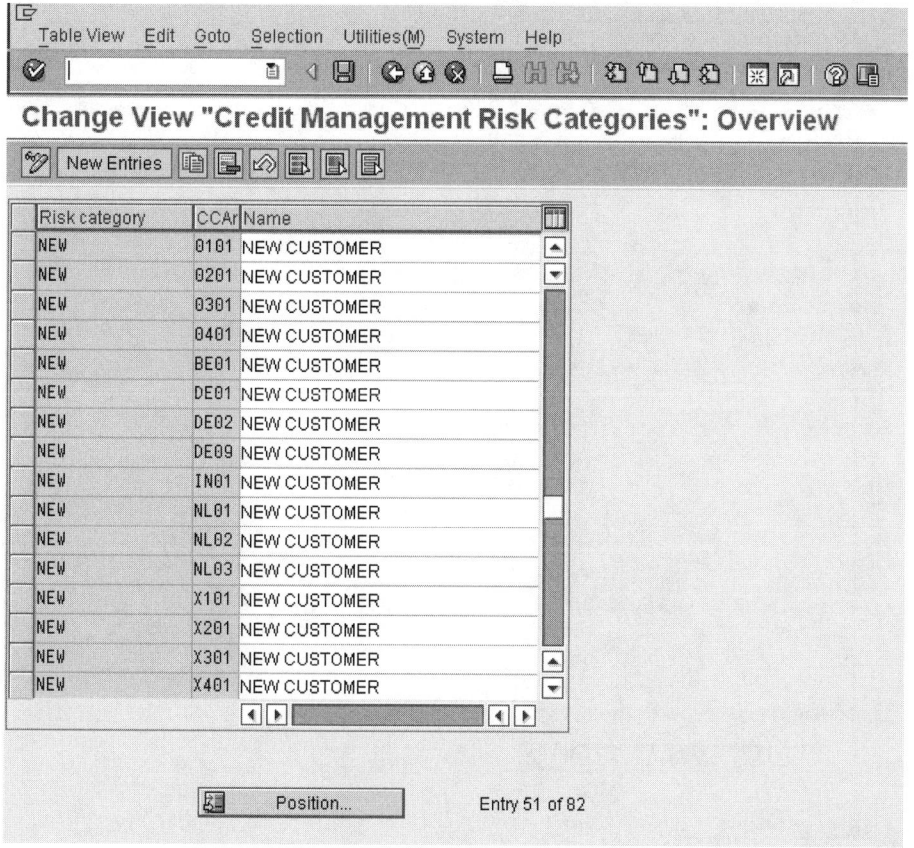

Figure 10-3   Defining risk categories

Menu Path SAP Customizing Implementation Guide | Sales and Distribution | Basic Functions | Credit Management/Risk Management | Credit Management | Define Credit Groups

You simply create a credit group for each differentiation in the document type, as seen in Figure 10-4.

If you want to create a different credit group, for example, to perform the credit check differently for standard sales orders than for scheduling agreements, or for a quotation, you can create the credit group and then assign it to the sales order type in this table.

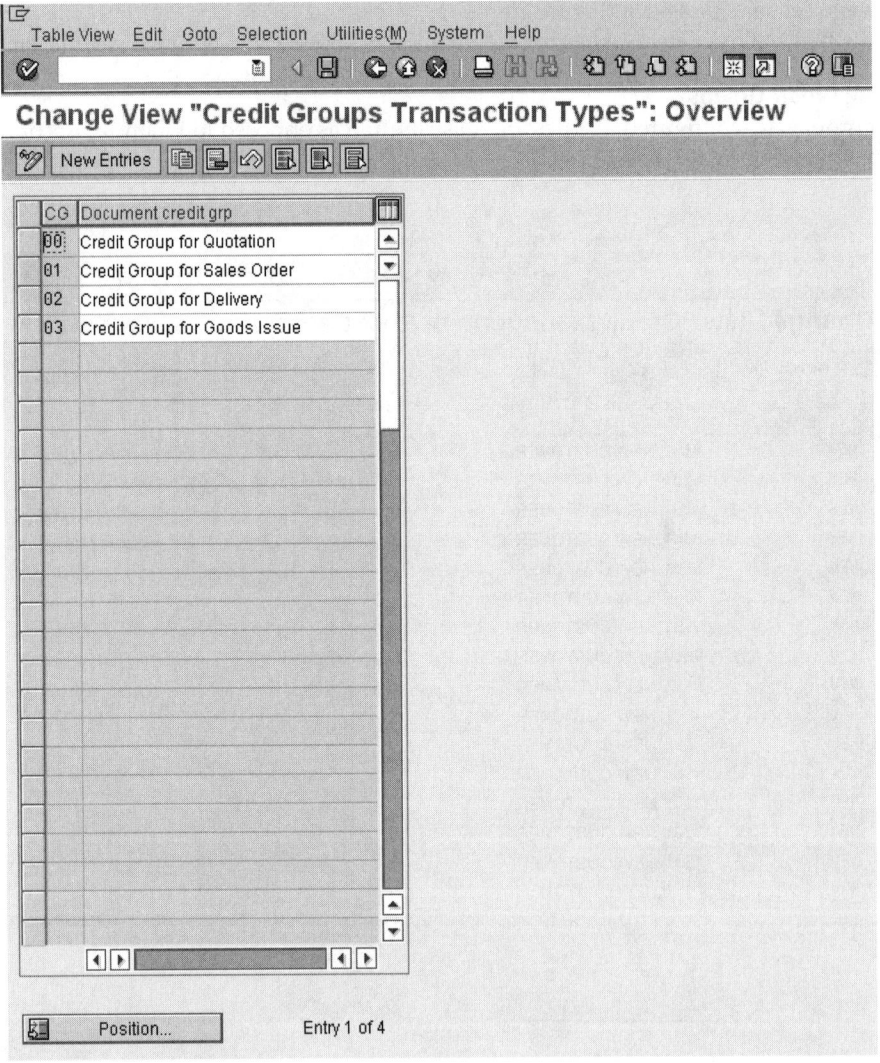

FIGURE 10-4 Defining credit groups

You need to assign a position in the pricing procedure that defines the amount used for the credit check. This amount is updated into the credit information structure.

To do this in the pricing procedure used for pricing, subtotal A must be entered in a line for determining the credit value. Create a line that holds the total used for the credit check and then assign subtotal A to the line. Usually, you use the net value plus taxes or subtotal. The credit price is stored in field VBAP-CMPRE and is used for the update and the credit check.

You then need to assign the credit groups to the sales document and delivery document types. This is covered in the next section.

Assigning Sales Documents and Delivery Documents

You can assign the credit group to the sales document types and delivery document types using the following menu path.

Menu Path SAP Customizing Implementation Guide | Sales and Distribution | Basic Functions | Credit Management/Risk Management | Credit Management | Assign Sales Documents and Delivery Documents | Credit Limit Check for Order Types | Credit Limit Check for Delivery Types

As seen in Figure 10-5, you can assign to the sales document type ZOR the check credit indicator D, determining automatic credit control, as well as the credit group 01, determining this automatic credit control is carried out for a sales order.

The assignment of the credit group to the delivery document type for the delivery check and goods issue check is carried out in the same manner as seen in Figure 10-6.

You can now proceed to defining the automatic credit control settings.

Automatic Credit Control

The control of the automatic credit management is based on the combination of the risk category and the document credit group. This control is maintained using the following menu path.

Menu Path SAP Customizing Implementation Guide | Sales and Distribution | Basic Functions | Credit Management/Risk Management | Credit Management | Define Automatic Credit Control

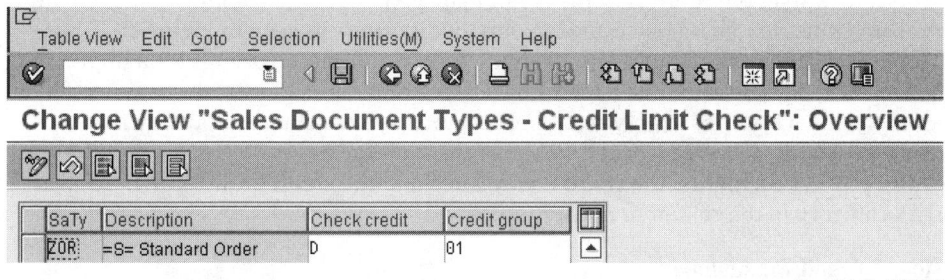

FIGURE 10-5 Credit limit check for order types

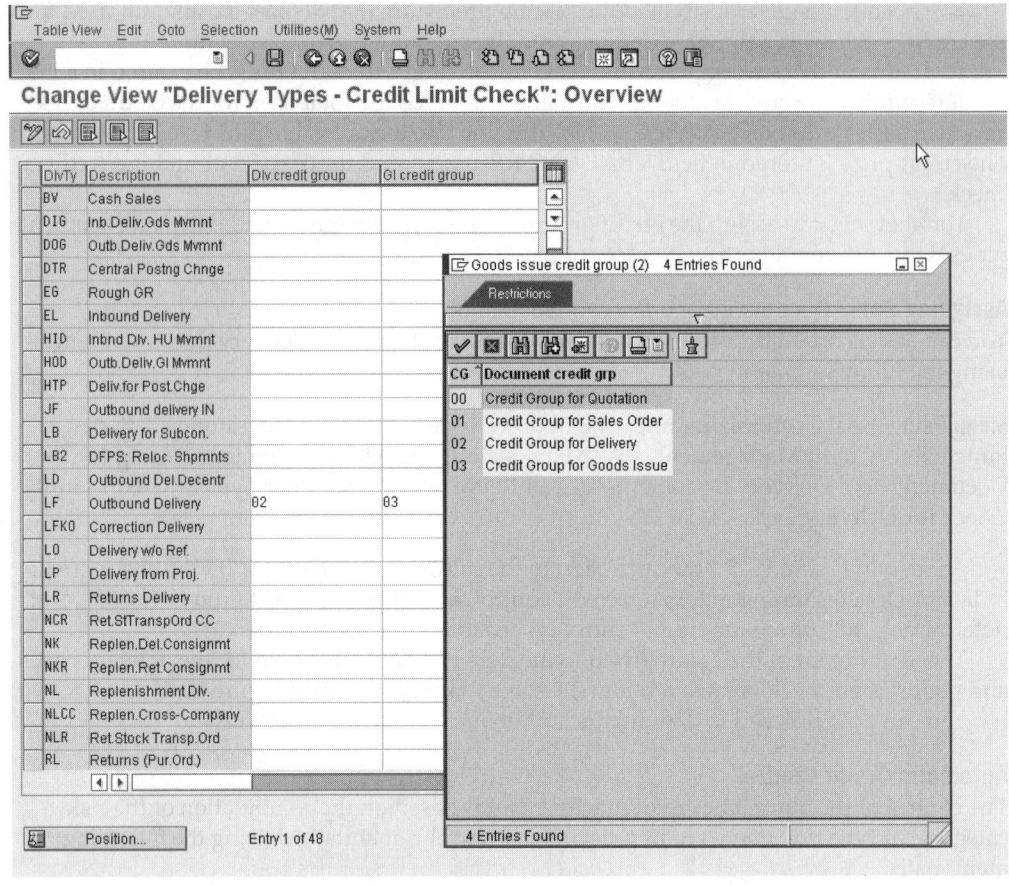

FIGURE 10-6   Credit limit check for delivery types

You can now set the controls of the credit management to the combination of credit control area plus customers risk category plus credit group, as seen in Figure 10-7.

You can see in the previous example that we have automatic settings for a high-risk customer for a sales order, while a medium-risk customer and a low-risk customer are only checked in a delivery. This is only an example and in some instances you may find it necessary to check all customers at the time of the sales order.

After you have assigned the credit control area and the credit group, you need to assign the risk category in the customer master record.

Customer Credit Management

This risk category assignment occurs in the same place as the customer credit limit, which is the Customer Credit Management Screen, as seen in Figure 10-8. That is, it is assigned to the customer by Finance as described earlier. Refer to transaction code [FD32].

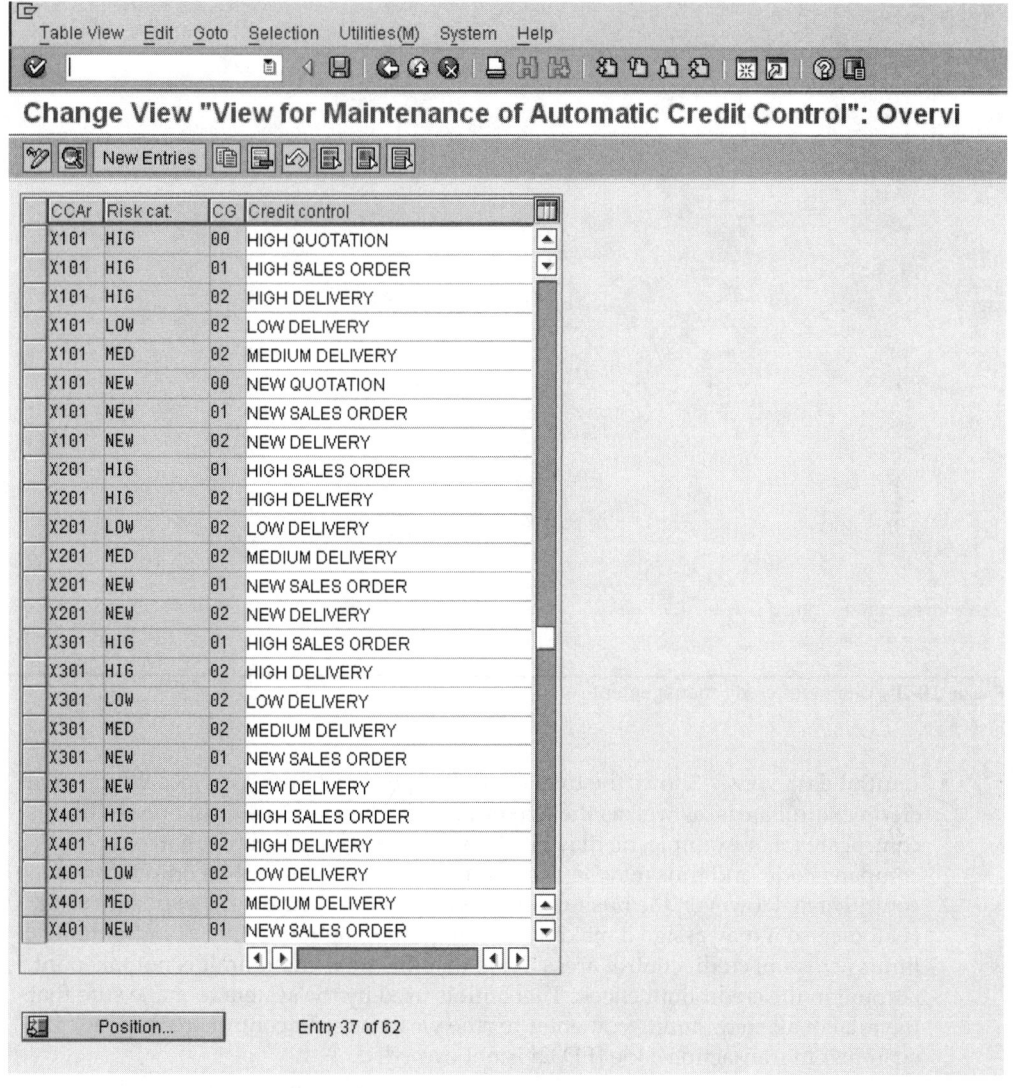

Table View   Edit   Goto   Selection   Utilities(M)   System   Help

Change View "View for Maintenance of Automatic Credit Control": Overvi

New Entries

CCAr	Risk cat.	CG	Credit control
X101	HIG	00	HIGH QUOTATION
X101	HIG	01	HIGH SALES ORDER
X101	HIG	02	HIGH DELIVERY
X101	LOW	02	LOW DELIVERY
X101	MED	02	MEDIUM DELIVERY
X101	NEW	00	NEW QUOTATION
X101	NEW	01	NEW SALES ORDER
X101	NEW	02	NEW DELIVERY
X201	HIG	01	HIGH SALES ORDER
X201	HIG	02	HIGH DELIVERY
X201	LOW	02	LOW DELIVERY
X201	MED	02	MEDIUM DELIVERY
X201	NEW	01	NEW SALES ORDER
X201	NEW	02	NEW DELIVERY
X301	HIG	01	HIGH SALES ORDER
X301	HIG	02	HIGH DELIVERY
X301	LOW	02	LOW DELIVERY
X301	MED	02	MEDIUM DELIVERY
X301	NEW	01	NEW SALES ORDER
X301	NEW	02	NEW DELIVERY
X401	HIG	01	HIGH SALES ORDER
X401	HIG	02	HIGH DELIVERY
X401	LOW	02	LOW DELIVERY
X401	MED	02	MEDIUM DELIVERY
X401	NEW	01	NEW SALES ORDER

Position...   Entry 37 of 62

FIGURE 10-7   Automatic credit control determination

You can also assign various other credit settings in relation to the customer master record here. This customer credit master record is divided up into five views:

- **Overview**   Gives an overview of the credit settings in relation to the customer, including credit limit, credit exposure, percentage of credit limit used, payment data, risk category, etc.

- **Address view**   Gives the customers address details as they appear on the customer master record.

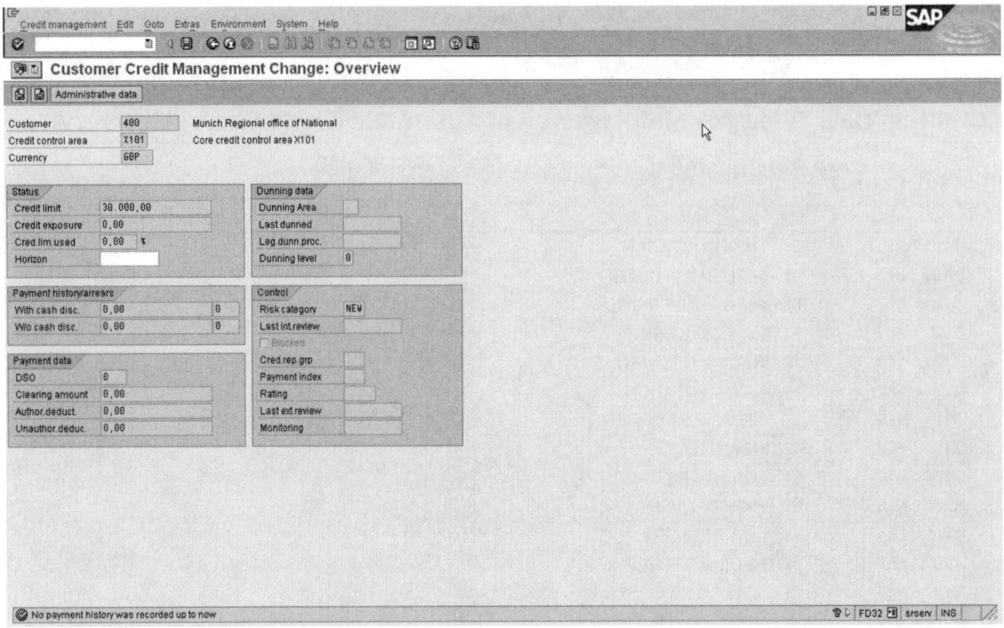

FIGURE 10-8 Customer credit management

- **Central data view** Shows the total credit limit the customer may receive across all credit control areas, as well as the maximum limit he may receive in one credit control area. For example, he may be allowed to purchase in more than one company code, and thus may be allowed to purchase in more than one credit control area. However, the business may wish to limit their overall exposure to the customer, so it may assign a maximum limit pertaining to the sum of individual limits across all credit control areas. Note that this total credit limit is not taken into account in the credit limit check. This limit is used by the system to make sure that the total of all credit limits you enter for the various credit control areas for a customer in transaction code [FD32] is not exceeded.

- **Status view** Gives the customers actual individual details according to the particular credit control area being investigated. This includes credit limit, percentage used, credit exposure, risk category, blocks, etc.

- **Payment history view** Displays the payments made by the customer for a particular credit control area with which a company code is assigned (as payments are made within a company code).

Defining Automatic Credit Control

We are now able to maintain the settings for the automatic credit control. These settings may take the form of a static check or a dynamic check in addition to other checks. (The static and dynamic checks are the most popular.)

The *static credit limit check* is a check comparing the credit limit assigned to the customer to the total value of open sales orders, plus the total value of open deliveries not yet invoiced, plus the total value of open billing documents not yet passed on to accounting, plus the total value of billing documents that have been passed on to accounting but that have not yet been paid by the customer.

The *dynamic credit check* is a check comparing the customer's credit limit to the total of open sales orders not yet delivered, plus the total value of open deliveries not yet invoiced, plus the total value of open billing documents not yet passed on to accounting, plus the total value of billing documents that have been passed on to accounting but that have not yet been paid by the customer.

This dynamic check has an attached time period (called the *credit horizon*) that states that the system is not to include sales orders in the total of outstanding items that are due for delivery outside the credit horizon.

For example, the time period may be two months, so when the system defines the credit amount used by a customer it includes all open items in sales orders due for delivery from now to two months into the future. It does not include open items whose shipping date is more than two months in advance.

These are the two main types of checks you can maintain. However, you may also require additional checks to be performed, either in combination with the dynamic or static credit checks or on their own. These additional checks are

- **Credit check when the maximum document value is exceeded**   This check is performed when a document value in the currency of the credit control area is exceeded—for example, the company may wish all sales orders exceeding a value of $10,000 USD to be automatically blocked and released by a credit manager.

- **Credit check when changing critical fields**   It is possible to institute a recheck of the credit, should certain customer master record fields that are credit relevant be altered in the sales order from those proposed from the master record—for example, the customer's payment terms.

- **Credit check at the time of the next internal check**   This activates the credit check to be performed on all documents after the date of the next internal credit check. This date is defined in the credit management master data (transaction code [FD32])—see the next internal review field.

- **Credit check on the basis of overdue open items**   This credit check is based upon the ratio of open items that are overdue by a certain number of days to the customer's balance, which must not exceed a certain percentage.

- **Credit check on the basis of oldest open items**   This check allows the oldest open item to be only a certain number of days overdue.

- **Credit check against the maximum allowed dunning levels**   This check allows the dunning level of the customer to only reach a specific value.

- **Customer specific credit checks**   These credit checks are self-definable and may be created in the user exits LVKMPTZZ, LVKMPFZ1, LVKMPFZ2, and LVKMPFZ3.

These settings may be seen in Figure 10-9.

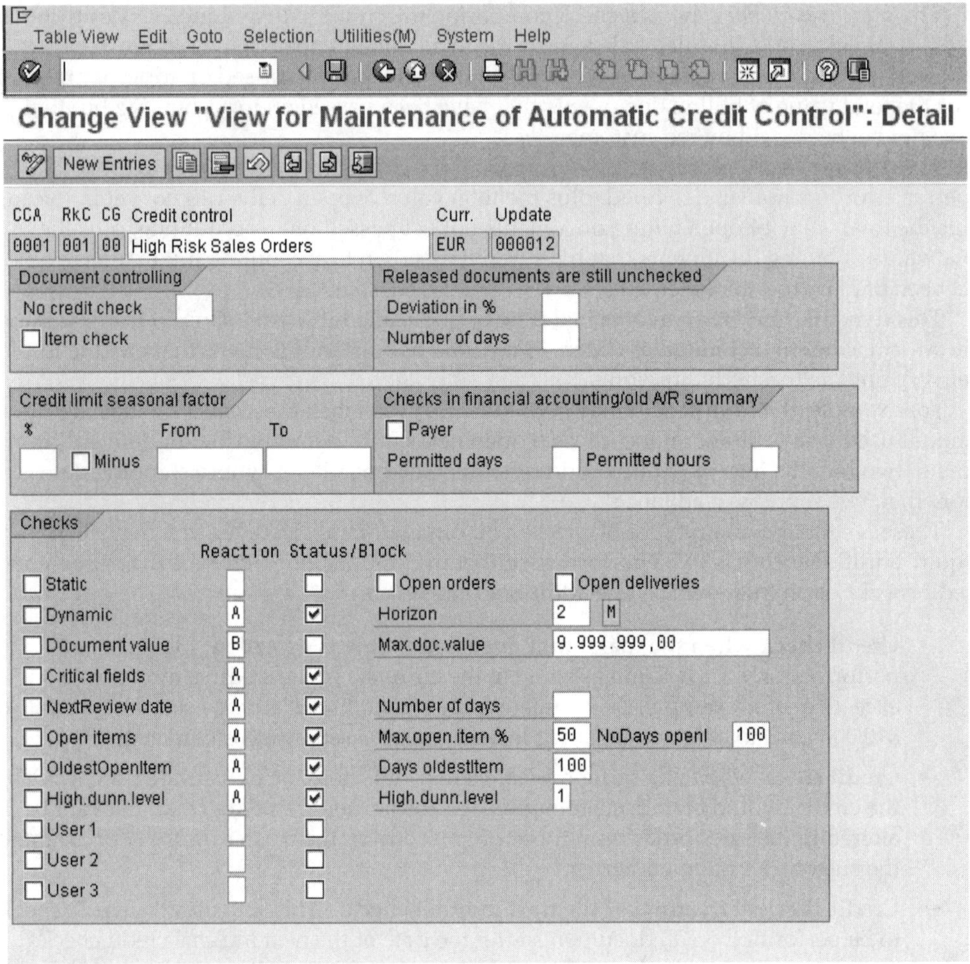

Change View "View for Maintenance of Automatic Credit Control": Detail

FIGURE 10-9 Maintenance of automatic credit control

The credit-relevant data is updated into information structures S066 and S067, where it is accessed and updated. Each automatic credit control must be assigned an update group. The system allows for no update, as well as update groups 000012, 000015 and 000018.

The difference between the three update groups is as follows:

Update group 000012

- Sales order
  - Increases open order value from delivery-relevant schedule lines

- Delivery
    - Reduces open order value from delivery-relevant schedule lines
    - Increases open delivery value
- Billing document
    - Reduces open delivery value
    - Increases open billing document value
- Financial accounting document
    - Reduces open billing document value
    - Increases open items

Update group 000015

- Delivery
    - Increases open delivery value
    - Increases open billing document value
- Financial accounting document
    - Reduces open billing document value
    - Increases open items

Update group 000018

- Sales order
    - Increases open delivery value
- Billing document
    - Reduces open delivery value
    - Increases open billing document value
- Financial accounting document
    - Reduces open billing document value
    - Increases open items

The decision on which update group to use is based upon the business requirements. However, update group 000012 is very thorough and used in most business.

Credit Management Usage

Should the customer then exceed his credit limit or fail a credit check, and a warning has been assigned to that check in automatic credit control. The system will use a dialog box to warn the user when creating the sales order, as seen in Figure 10-10. This pop-up is very detailed in that it explains which check the customer failed by indicating a NOK (not OK) assigned to the failed check.

In order to release these sales orders or delivery documents from credit blocking, you may use the transaction code [VKM3] for sales documents and transaction code [VKM5] for delivery documents. Or transaction code [VKM4] for both sales documents and delivery documents. Use the following menu path.

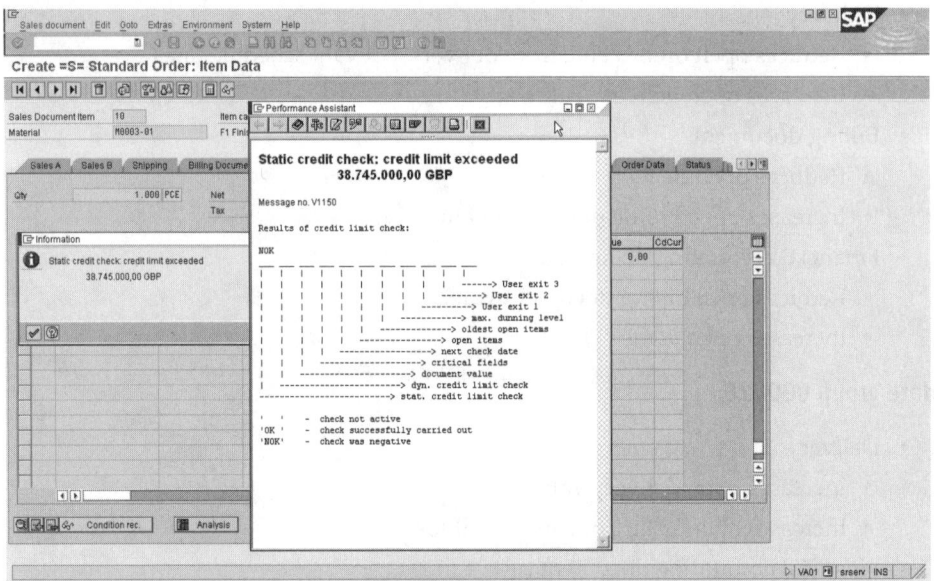

Copyright by SAP AG

FIGURE 10-10   Dialog box in the event of a failed credit check

Menu Path   SAP Menu I Accounting I Financial Accounting I Customers I Credit Management I Sales and Distribution Documents

- **[VKM4]**   All
- **[VKM3]**   Sales document
- **[VKM5]**   Delivery
- **[VKM2]**   Released

You can then see the offending document, as shown in Figure 10-11. Note in the display the Status column shows the check the document failed and should this field be empty, the document did not fail a credit check, even though it may be in the list of SD documents that are "required to be released." You can filter on the status, as well as adjust the layout of this report by changing its variant.

To release the document, select it and then click the icon of the little green flag (top right of screen in Figure 10-11). The offending document entry will be highlighted green. Click save and you'll see a message that the document number "4000...." has been released.

Other important functions related to the financial side of credit management are

- **[FD10N]**   Customer balance display (which shows the customer credit/debit and cumulative balance as seen in Figure 10-12.
- **[FBL5N]**   Customer line item display. This is one of the mainstream financial accounting transactions. It is useful to view the customer's open items on a specific date.
- **[F-28]**   Reset customers credit limit. This calls program RFDKLI20, and may be used to re-create the customer's FI and SD credit-related data.

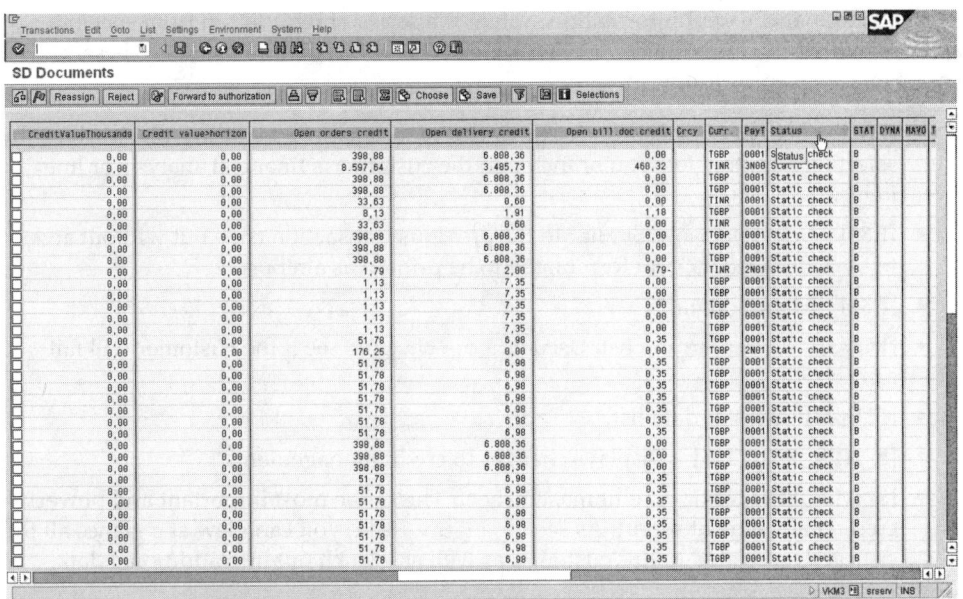

Copyright by SAP AG

Figure 10-11 Credit release

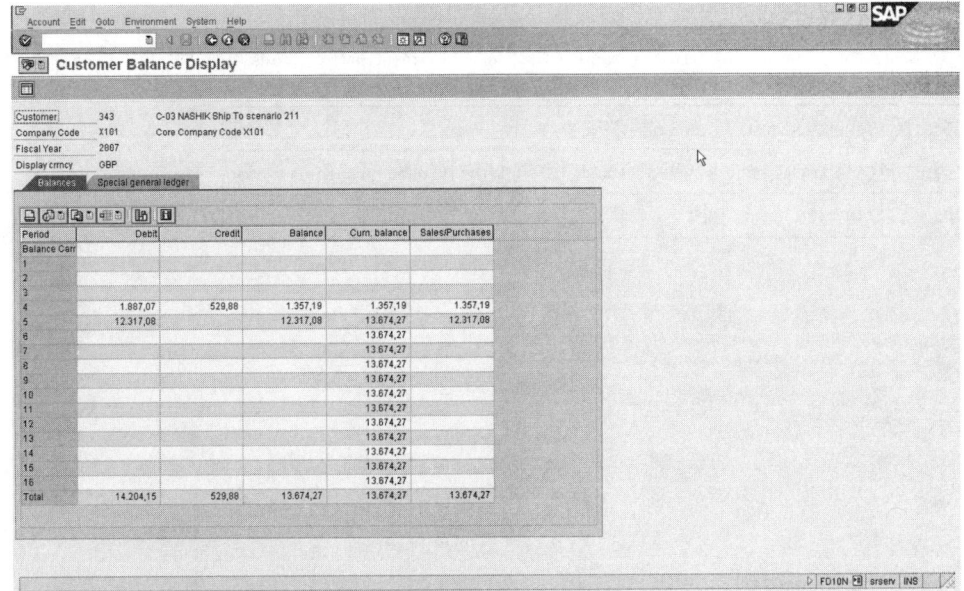

Copyright by SAP AG

Figure 10-12 Customer balances

The credit management information system is a series of reports run from specific transaction codes that provide the user with a customer's credit information. These transaction codes are as follows:

- **[F.31]**   Overview. This is a very powerful report, as seen in Figure 10-13, which, by selecting a button, lets you branch into the customer's financial analysis or line items.

- **[F.33]**   Brief overview. Similar to the previous transaction code but without access to the external data, and formulated to be printed as a report.

- **[F.32]**   Missing data.

- **[FCV3]**   Early warning list. Used as a pre-check to see if the customer will fail a check.

- **[FDK43]**   Master data list.

- **[S_ALR_87012215]**   Displays changes to credit management.

- **[S_ALR_87012218]**   Credit master sheet. This is the most important and powerful credit management report. As seen in Figure 10-14, you can view at a glance all the critical data related to this customer as well as branch out into additional data.

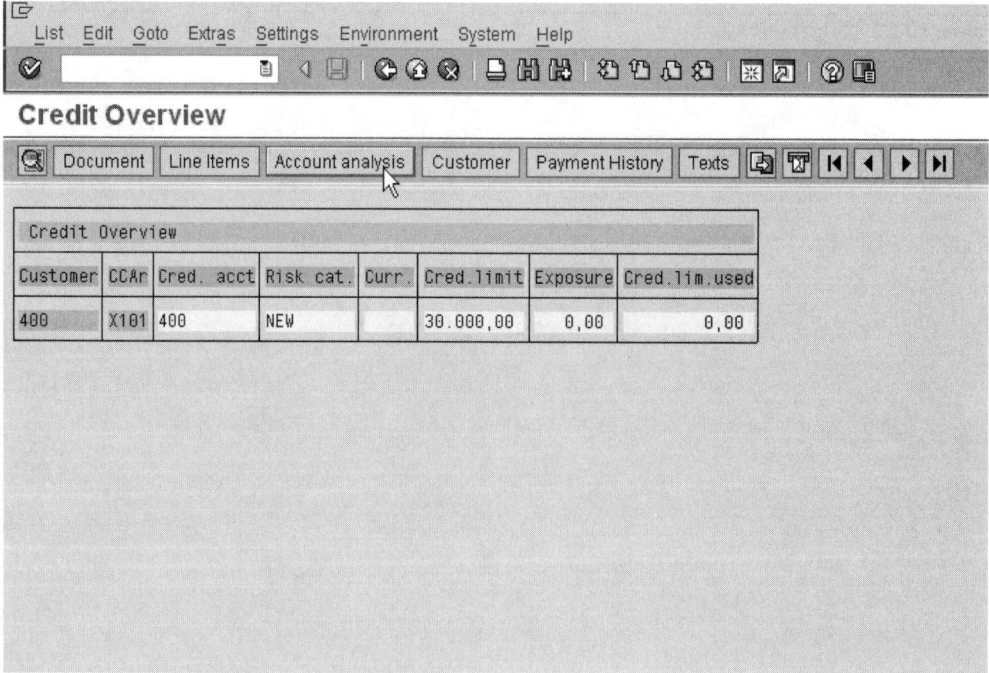

FIGURE 10-13   Customer's credit overview

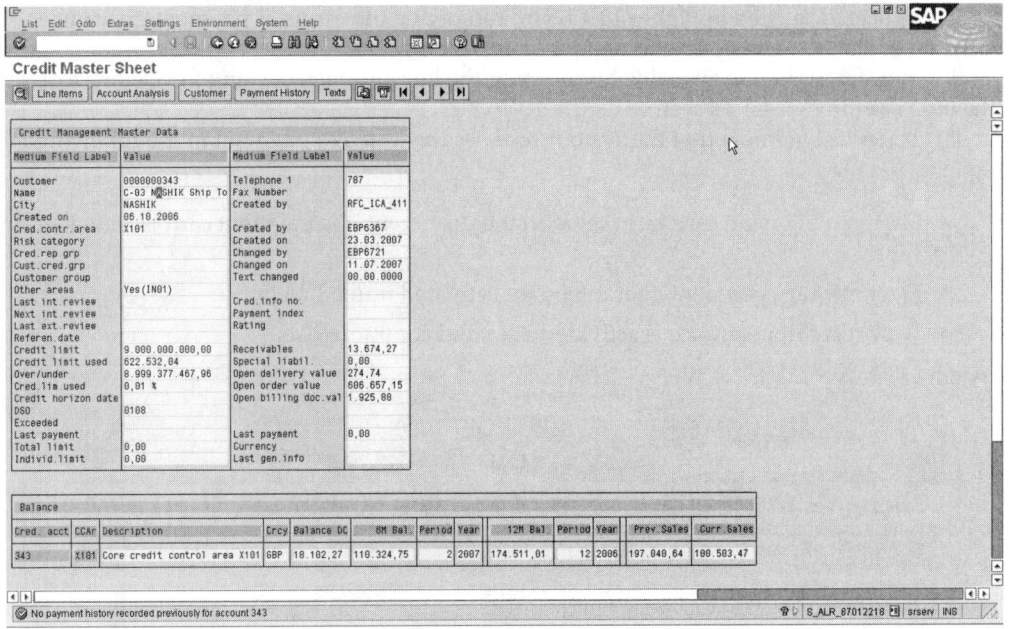

Credit Management Master Data			
Medium Field Label	Value	Medium Field Label	Value
Customer	0000000343	Telephone 1	787
Name	C-03 NASHIK Ship To	Fax Number	
City	NASHIK	Created by	RFC_ICA_411
Created on	06.10.2006		
Cred.contr.area	X101	Created by	EBP6367
Risk category		Created on	23.03.2007
Cred.rep.grp		Changed by	EBP6721
Cust.cred.grp		Changed on	11.07.2007
Customer group		Text changed	00.00.0000
Other areas	Yes(IN01)		
Last int.review		Cred.info no.	
Next int.review		Payment index	
Last ext.review		Rating	
Referen.date			
Credit limit	9.000.000.000,00	Receivables	13.674,27
Credit limit used	622.532,04	Special liabil.	0,00
Over/under	8.999.377.467,96	Open delivery value	274,74
Cred.lim used	0,01 %	Open order value	606.657,15
Credit horizon date		Open billing doc.val	1.925,88
DSO	0108		
Exceeded			
Last payment		Last payment	0,00
Total limit	0,00	Currency	
Individ.limit	0,00	Last gen.info	

Balance												
Cred. acct	CCAr	Description	Crcy	Balance DC	6M Bal	Period	Year	12M Bal	Period	Year	Prev.Sales	Curr.Sales
343	X101	Core credit control area X101	GBP	18.102,27	110.324,75	2	2007	174.511,01	12	2006	197.040,64	100.503,47

No payment history recorded previously for account 343

FIGURE 10-14   Credit master sheet

If you are unsure what impact a credit block has on the subsequent processing of a sales document, OSS Note 744305 provides great time-saving advice.

A very good credit management report that analyzes all aspects of credit management control within a sales document is report CHECK_CM, which may be executed from transaction code [SE38].

Receivables Risk Management

Another form of insuring against credit risks is payment guarantees. These are used as a guarantee against a value to be billed to a customer.

They take the form of a payment guarantee procedure. Examples are documentary payment guarantees (such as a confirmed letter of credit), payment cards, and export credit insurance.

Defining Forms of Payment Guarantee

To define payment guarantees, use the following menu path.

Menu Path   SAP Customizing Implementation Guide | Sales and Distribution | Basic Functions | Credit Management/Risk Management | Receivables Risk Management | Define Forms of Payment Guarantee

In this screen, as seen in Figure 10-15, you can define the forms of payment guarantee, such as a confirmed letter of credit or a payment/credit card.

A better description is available by selecting the line and then clicking the Details icon (the little magnify glass), as seen in Figure 10-16.

It is beneficial to know that the system accesses the forms of payment in the following sequence:

- Should a payment card be entered in the document, the payment card is activated first.

- Documentary payment guarantees are activated immediately.

- Export credit insurance is activated if a valid contract exists.

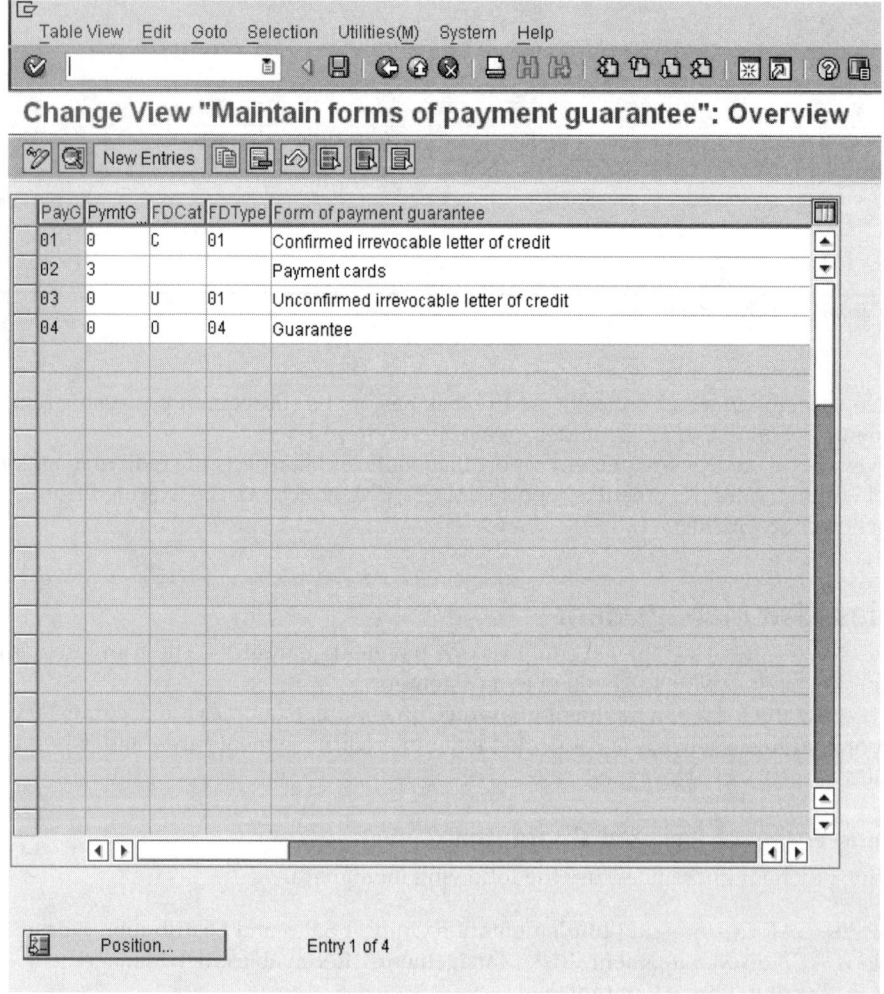

Copyright by SAP AG

FIGURE 10-15   Defining forms of payment guarantee

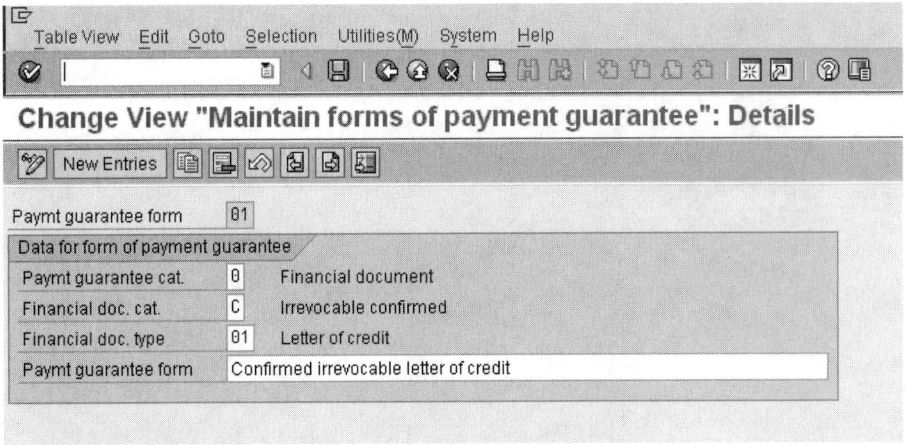

FIGURE 10-16   Details of payment guarantee

Each guarantee has a key identifying it as well as a payment guarantee category. This category defines if the guarantee is a payment card or letter, etc. Payment cards do not have an assigned financial document category, nor a financial document type. However, the other forms of guarantee do. The financial document category defines if the letter of guarantee is irrevocable or not.

Once the form of guarantee has been created, you can now assign the determination procedure, this is in a similar way to how the determination is carried out in pricing procedure determination. The payment guarantee procedure determination relies on the combination of a customer guarantee indicator as well as the document guarantee indicator to determine a procedure.

Payment Guarantee Procedure

Each payment guarantee procedure has a six-character alphanumeric key with a short description.

To configure the payment guarantee procedure, use the following menu path.

Menu Path

SAP Customizing Implementation Guide | Sales and Distribution | Basic Functions | Credit Management/Risk Management | Receivables Risk Management | Define and Assign Payment Guarantee Schemas | Define Payment Guarantee Schema

These procedures have the forms of payment guarantee, as previously specified, assigned to them in a logical sequence, as seen in Figure 10-17.

To maintain the procedure, select the payment guarantee procedure, then select the Forms of Payment Guarantee folder in the file structure on the left side of the screen. The result will be the maintenance view seen in Figure 10-17.

If you select an entry in the procedure and then select the Details icon, you will see the settings behind the guarantee form, shown in Figure 10-18.

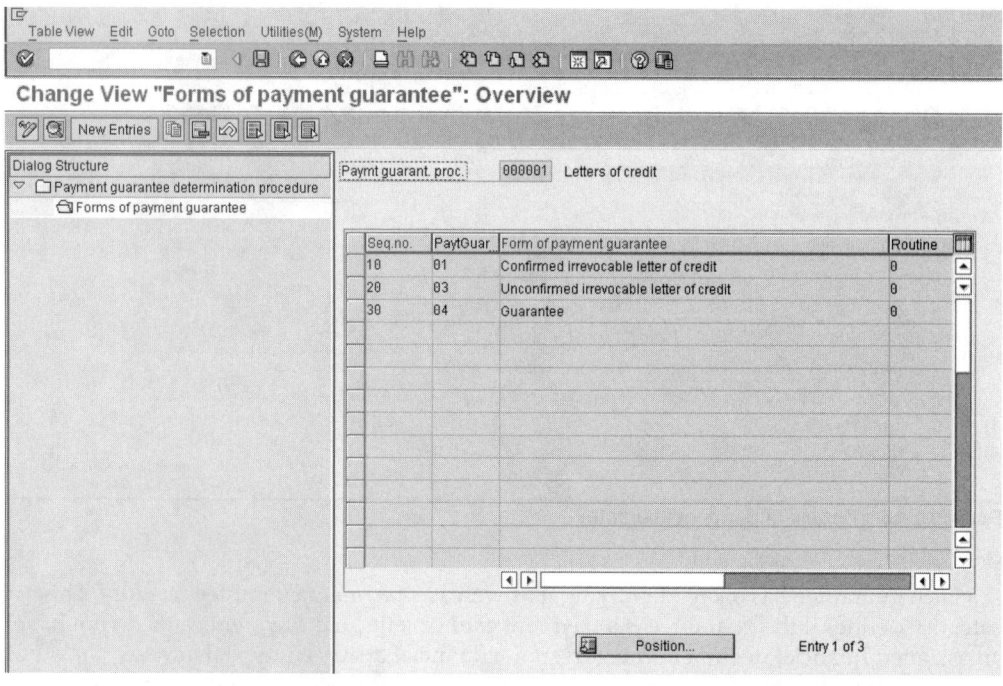

Copyright by SAP AG

FIGURE 10-17   Defining payment guarantee schemas

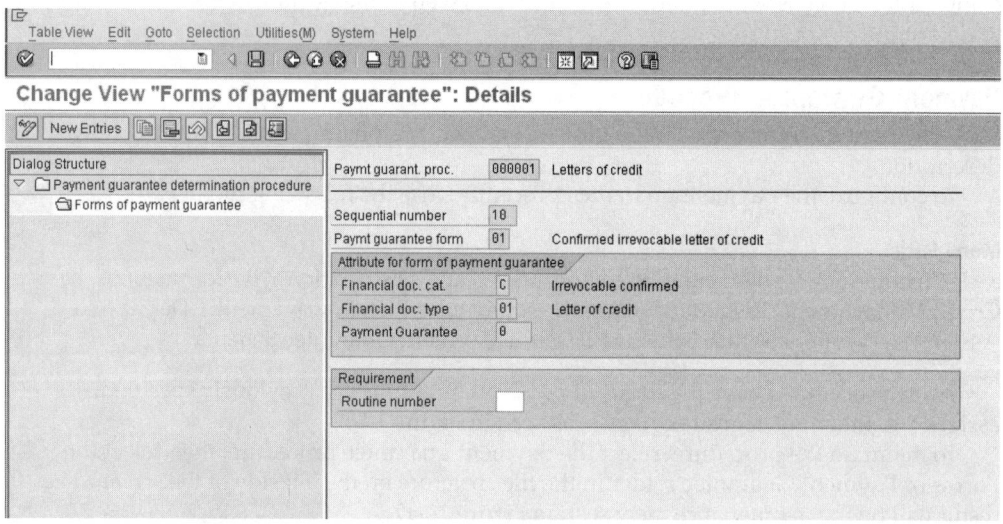

Copyright by SAP AG

FIGURE 10-18   Settings of a form in the procedure

Defining a Customer Determination Schema

You can define the customer's guarantee indicator using the following menu path.

Menu Path   SAP Customizing Implementation Guide | Sales and Distribution | Basic Functions | Credit Management/Risk Management | Receivables Risk Management | Define and Assign Payment Guarantee Schemas | Define Customer Determination Schema

Here you can assign a four-character alphanumeric key with a short description.
    This key must be allocated to the customer master record in the billing view of the customer master record as seen in Figure 10-19.

Defining the Document Determination Procedure

You can define the document guarantee key using the following menu path.

Customer	400		Munich Regional office of Natio		Munich
Sales Org.	X101		X101 Sales Org. 1		
Distr. Channel	06		Outside Group		
Division	01		Product Division 01		

| Sales | Shipping | Billing document | Partner functions |

Billing document

☐ Subs. invoice processing   ☑ Rebates   ☑ Price determin.

Invoicing dates   ☐

InvoicingListDates   ☐

Delivery and payment terms

Incoterms			
Terms of payment	0001	Payable immediately Due net	Paym.guar.proc.	0001
Credit ctrl area			

Accounting

Acct assgmt group   ☐

Taxes

Country	Name	Tax category	Name	Tax c	Description	
ES	Spain	MWST	Output Tax	1	Liable for Taxes	
GB	United Kingdom	MWST	Output Tax	1	Liable for Taxes	
MX	Mexico	MWST	Output Tax	1	Liable for Taxes	

Figure 10-19   Billing tab of customer master with payment guarantee procedure

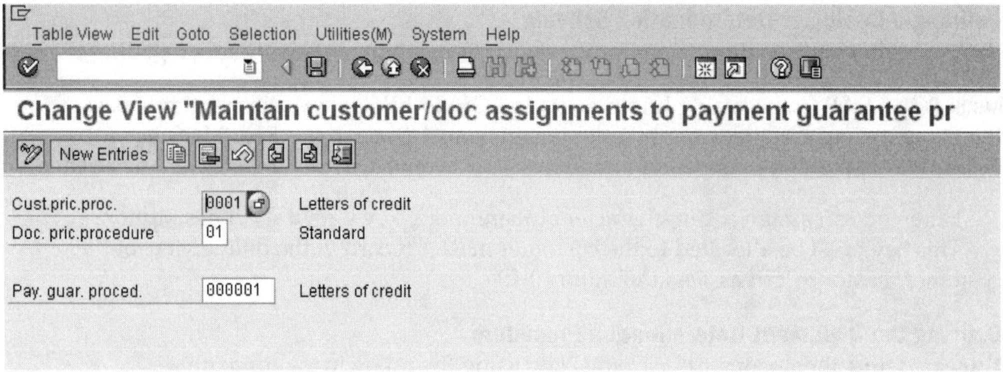

FIGURE 10-20 Defining payment guarantee schema determination

Menu Path SAP Customizing Implementation Guide | Sales and Distribution | Basic Functions | Credit Management/Risk Management | Receivables Risk Management | Define and Assign Payment Guarantee Schemas | Define Document Determination Schema

This indicator is a two-character alphanumeric key with a short description.

To allocate this key to the sales document types, select Assign Document Schema to Order Types.

Defining Payment Guarantee Schema Determination

After the previous steps have been completed, you can assign the document and customer indicators to a procedure. This final link in the determination may be done using the following menu path.

Menu Path SAP Customizing Implementation Guide | Sales and Distribution | Basic Functions | Credit Management/Risk Management | Receivables Risk Management | Define and Assign Payment Guarantee Schemas | Define Payment Guarantee Schema Determination

This may be seen in Figure 10-20.

In Figure 10-20 we see the payment guarantee procedure is determined as 000001, which in turn calls the procedure as defined in the earlier section "Payment Guarantee Procedure."

Blocking Customers

It is often necessary to block specific customer master records. This may be due to the fact that you have blacklisted a customer, or there may be a trade negotiation in place in which you wish to temporarily restrict sales.

Whatever the reason, it is possible to block customer master records from creating either sales orders, deliveries, or billing documents in specific sales areas or all sales areas.

To set the block on a customer master record, as seen in Figure 10-21, use the following menu path.

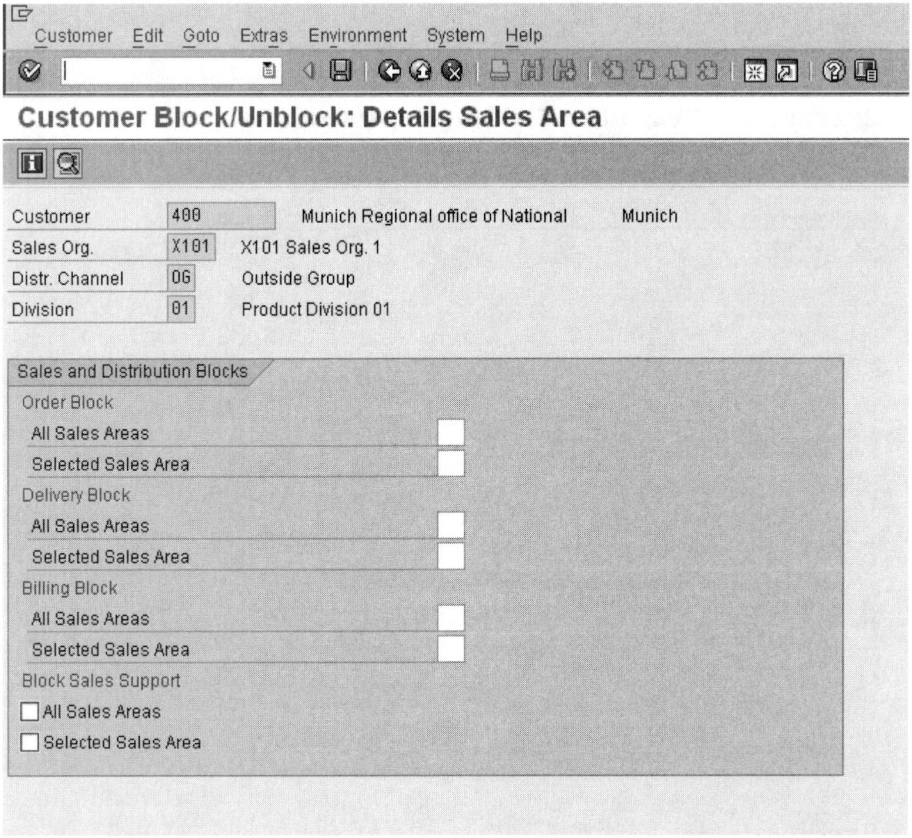

Copyright by SAP AG

FIGURE 10-21 Block/unblock customer master records

Menu Path SAP Menu | Logistics | Sales and Distribution | Master Data | Business Partner | Customer | [VD05] - Block

These blocking reasons are assigned to the customer master record and you can assign the blocking reason to the selected sales area or for all sales areas for sales orders, deliveries, billings, or for sales support.

The blocking reasons are each created in the individual path in the IMG.

Defining Shipping Blocks

Once created, these blocks may be assigned. To create the blocks, use the following menu path.

Menu Path SAP Customizing Implementation Guide | Logistics Execution | Deliveries | Define Reasons for Blocking in Shipping | Deliveries: Blocking Reasons/Criteria

As you can see in Figure 10-22, we have created a delivery block called ZV.

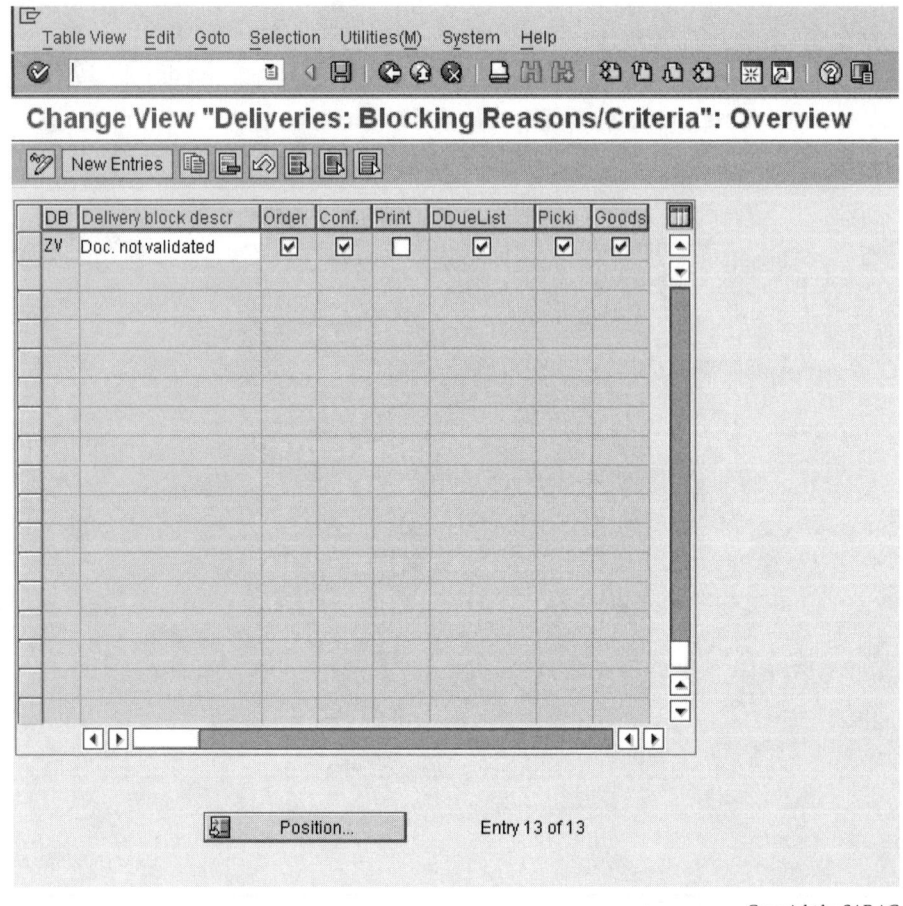

FIGURE 10-22 Creating delivery blocks

Once this delivery block has been created, it must be assigned to a delivery document type, as seen in Figure 10-23, by selecting Delivery Blocks.

After the delivery document types have been assigned, you can assign the blocking reason to the customer in transaction code [VD05]. This will then automatically default the block in the sales document.

The delivery block is the most complex of blocks in sales and distribution processing. As opposed to simply blocking the document from being created, the block settings have the following impacts.

Order Block

The sales order will still be created. The user will receive a warning that there is a block on the order. This will stop the sales order from creating a delivery via the transaction code [VL01N], but will not stop a delivery being created via the delivery due list [VL10A].

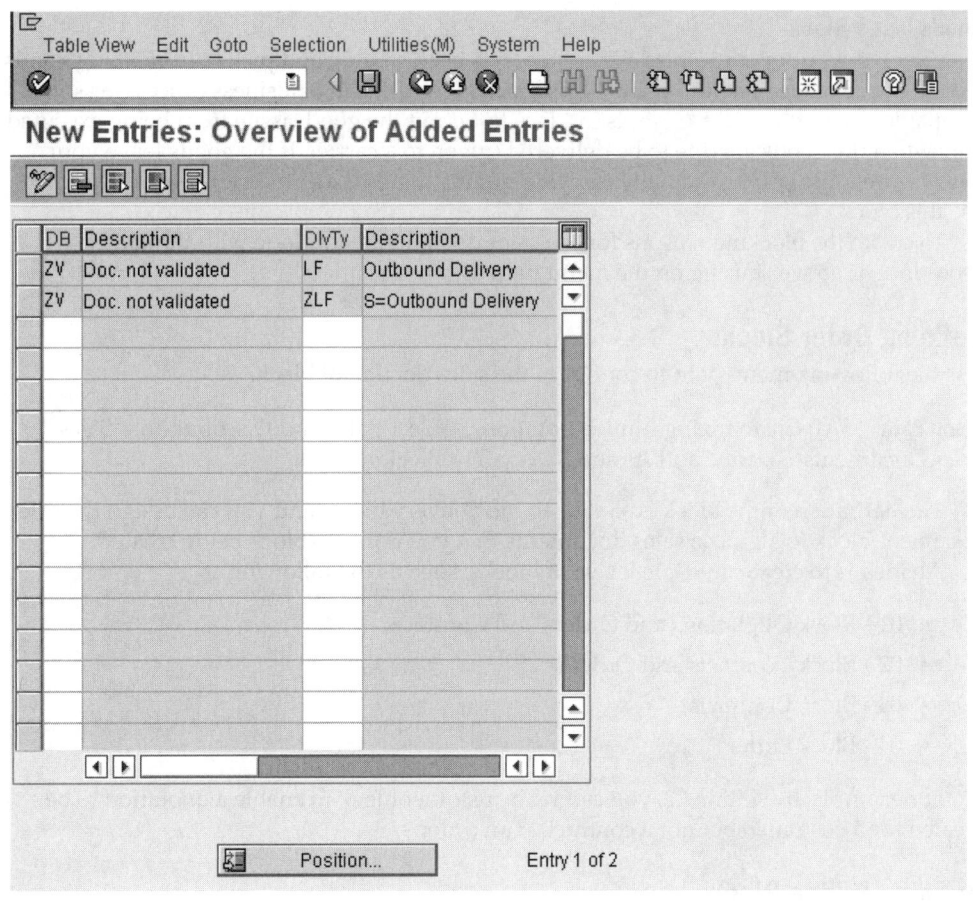

FIGURE 10-23   Assigning delivery blocks

Requirements Block
The order quantity is blocked from being confirmed. Therefore, the system does not transfer requirements from the sales document to the plant. This permits the quantities in the plant to be used for other sales documents.

Delivery Due List Block
This block will block the creation of deliveries with the delivery due list function. This block does not block the creation of an individual delivery [VL01N].

Picking Block
This block does not permit the picking list to be created and picking to be carried out.

Goods Issue Block

This block does not permit the delivery that has been created and picked from being goods issued, (i.e., from leaving the plant). This block is sensitive in a business process, as some companies do not have the controls in place to permit the goods issue from being executed only when the goods are due to be delivered/given to a carrier. If the goods leave your plant/warehouse prior to actually carrying out the goods issue, then it is not advisable to use this block.

To create the blocking reasons for the sales documents, continue with the same procedure as above starting on the menu path as follows.

Defining Order Blocks

Use the following menu path to configure the sales document block.

Menu Path   SAP Customizing Implementation Guide | Sales and Distribution | Sales | Sales Documents | Define and Assign Reason For Blocking

The definition of the block is similar to the delivery block, and you can assign the sales document block to all those sales documents that you'd like to block being created.

An idea is to create multiple levels of blocks, such as the following

- 01 - Block Quotations and Orders and Contracts
- 02 - Block Contracts and Orders
- 03 - Block Contracts
- 04 - Block Orders

For example, by setting 02, you can set a customer block to enable a quotation to be created for a customer, but not a contract or an order.

Defining Billing Blocks

Use the following menu path to configure the billing document block.

Menu Path   SAP Customizing Implementation Guide | Sales and Distribution | Billing | Billing Documents | Define Blocking Reason for Billing

These billing blocks are configured in the same manner as sales document blocks—simply a two-character key, which is then assigned to a sales document type, in this case a billing document.

These blocking reasons are automatically copied into the sales document during creation. A message will appear at the base of the document, explaining, for example, that the customer has a billing block. You will also be able to find, for example, this billing block copied into the sales document (billing view of the sales order line item and billing header), where it may be removed by an authorized user.

Naturally, a billing block will prevent a billing document from being created. In most instances this only makes business sense when one is creating a credit memo. However, it may also be required when creating a billing document for a particular project milestone related to a billing plan.

Factory Calendars

Factory calendars are used throughout the system. An easy way to understand them is to use them to specify which days are work days at a location.

These calendars may be used by the business to determine when a delivery must take place in order for it to reach the customer's site on a day when people are at work and can receive the delivery. We also used factory calendars in consolidated invoicing. That is, we specified that only one day a week was a working day for our customer and thus the billing documents were only to be created for that one day each week, causing many delivery documents from the whole week to be consolidated into one billing document.

We will focus on the creation and maintenance of the customer's shipping calendar.

Defining Customer Calendars

To define a customer's shipping calendar, use the following menu path.

Menu Path   SAP Customizing Implementation Guide | Sales and Distribution | Business Partners | Shipping | Define Customer Calendars

You'll see the screen shown in Figure 10-24.

Two calendars must be maintained—the holiday calendar initially, followed by the factory calendar, which is created on the basis of the holiday calendar.

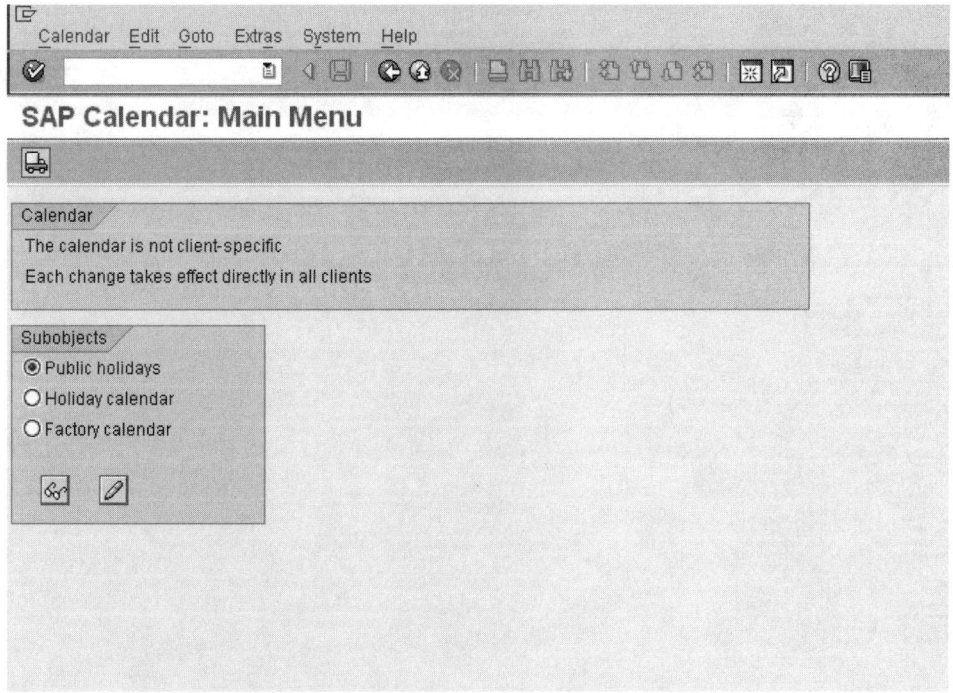

Copyright by SAP AG

FIGURE 10-24   SAP calendar

For the purpose of this book, we will create a factory calendar called "ZG" that is "the international company working calendar."

Creating the Public Holidays

The first step is creating the public holidays, by selecting the Public Holidays radio button on the initial screen as seen in Figure 10-24, and clicking the Change icon (pencil). Then select the New button or press SHIFT-F1 on the next screen. This will bring up a dialog box as shown in Figure 10-25.

Select "with fixed date" and click the Create icon (new page). You will see a screen in which you can define this holiday, as seen in Figure 10-26.

Here, the day is set at 30 and the month at 10. The Guaranteed section sets the holiday to be automatically moved to the next working day if it should fall on a Sunday. The holiday is described as National celebration.

After pressing ENTER, you may see the public holiday is not yet assigned to the holiday calendar.

Creating a Holiday Calendar

You can now select the Holiday Calendar radio button seen in Figure 10-24 and click the Change icon (pencil).

Select Create or press SHIFT-F1. Enter a Calendar ID—for example, "ZG"—with a description and a validity period. Click the Assign publ. Holiday button and you can select the public holidays, as shown in Figure 10-27.

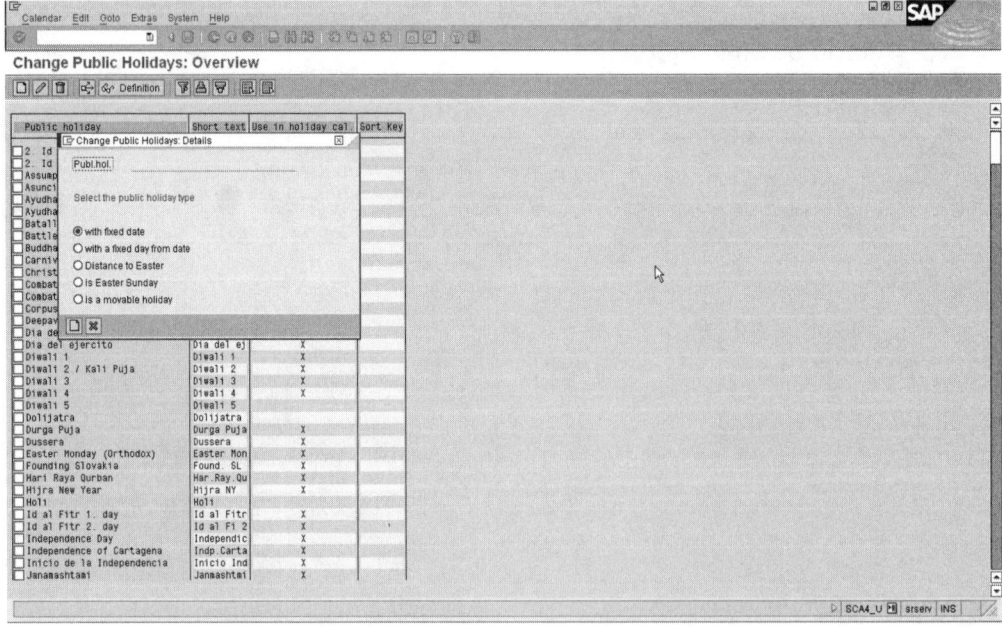

FIGURE 10-25   Dialog box for new public holiday

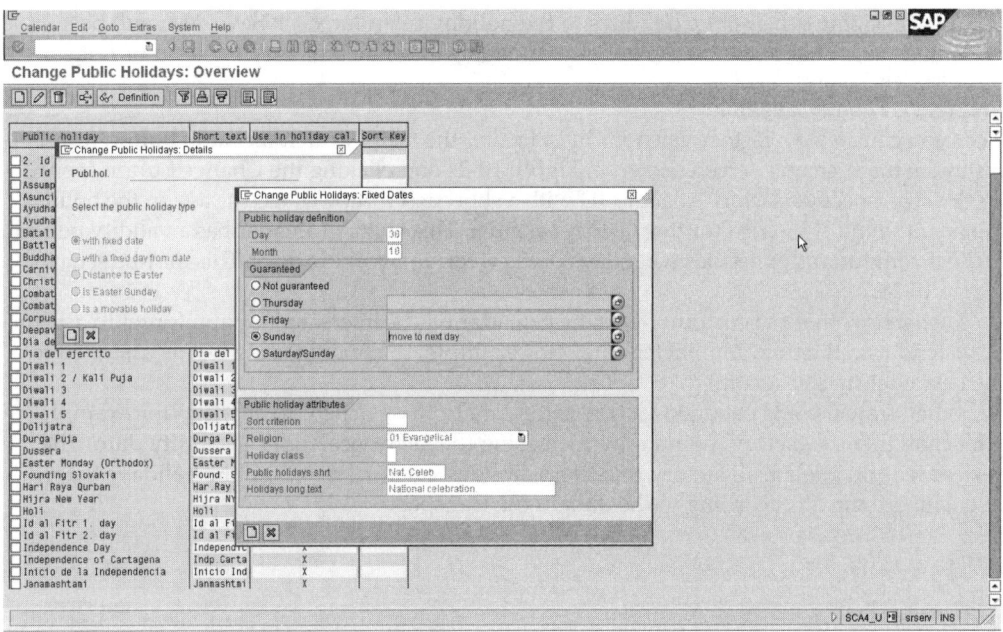

FIGURE 10-26   Defining new public holiday settings

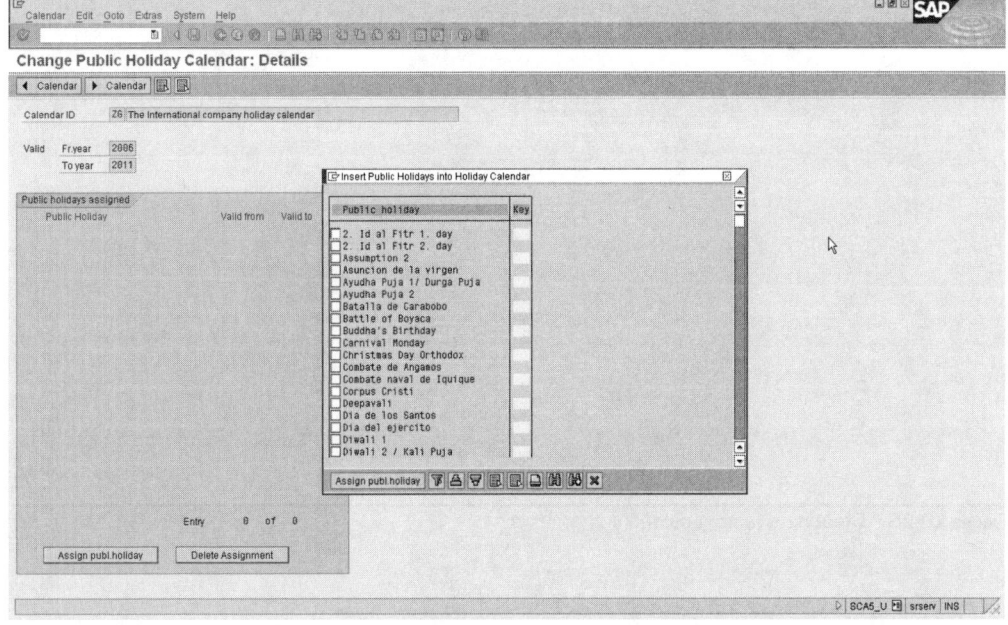

FIGURE 10-27   Assigning public holidays

After assigning the public holidays to the holiday calendar, click Save. You will be presented with a list of the public holiday calendars and whether they are used or not.

Creating a Factory Calendar

Now you can create a factory calendar by selecting the factory calendar radio button from the initial maintenance screen shown in Figure 10-24 and clicking the Change button (pencil).

You can specify a factory calendar ID with a short description as well as assign the holiday calendar that must be used for that factory calendar. This factory calendar has a validity period and most importantly specifies what days of the week are working days. This may be seen in Figure 10-28.

Lastly, now that the customer-specific calendar has been created, do not forget to assign the calendar to the relevant master data—for example, to the unloading points assigned to the customer master record.

When transporting changed factory calendars from one client to another (for example, after changing the factory calendar by increasing the factory calendar's validity date), the system will first delete all factory calendars, holiday calendars, and public holidays before re-creating them all according to the data in the transport.

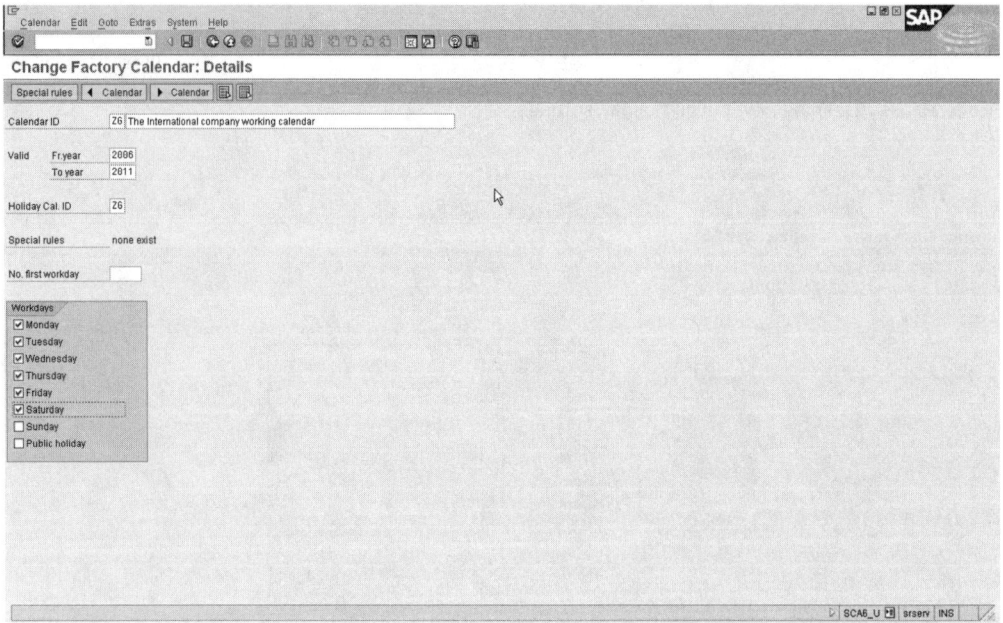

Copyright by SAP AG

FIGURE 10-28   Creating a factory calendar

Advanced Consultant Tools

Although these topics are supplementary to mainstream everyday Sales and Distribution use, they will enable you to understand the technical integration of the SD module within SAP. Here we deal with user exits, enhancements, and data exchanges between systems.

Sales and Distribution User Exits, Enhancements and BADis

In SAP there are empty ABAP forms at particular points in the standard SAP program code where SAP allows customers to make enhancements to the way the code functions. These empty modules, called *user exits*, can be filled with customer-specific program code.

For example, SAP provides an empty form where the customer can write his own code to determine the number for a sales document. This user exit is called after the SAP standard code to get the document number from the configurable number ranges. So you can overwrite the number determined by SAP using your own code.

SAP will continue to support the existing user exits in the system, but they have made a design decision not to create any new user exits. The reason is that the user exit is "unsafe" in the sense that the person writing the code has access to all the global data in the program and can make changes unrelated to what the user exit was designed for. For example, in the code to determine the customer's own number for a sales document, the programmer can change/delete one or more of the items in the sales order.

SAP has replaced the user exit concept with the SAP enhancement concept. In an SAP enhancement, SAP provides a function module call in the same place as they would have put a user exit. The import parameters of the function module provide the data you can use and the export parameters provide the data you can change. So you are limited in the program code of the function module—you can only see the import parameters and you can only change the export parameters. There is no ability to change the global data of the calling program, or interfere in the standard code in a way the enhancement is not defined.

SAP Enhancements

Please note this is not a guide on how to implement a SAP enhancement but merely an introduction to the topic.

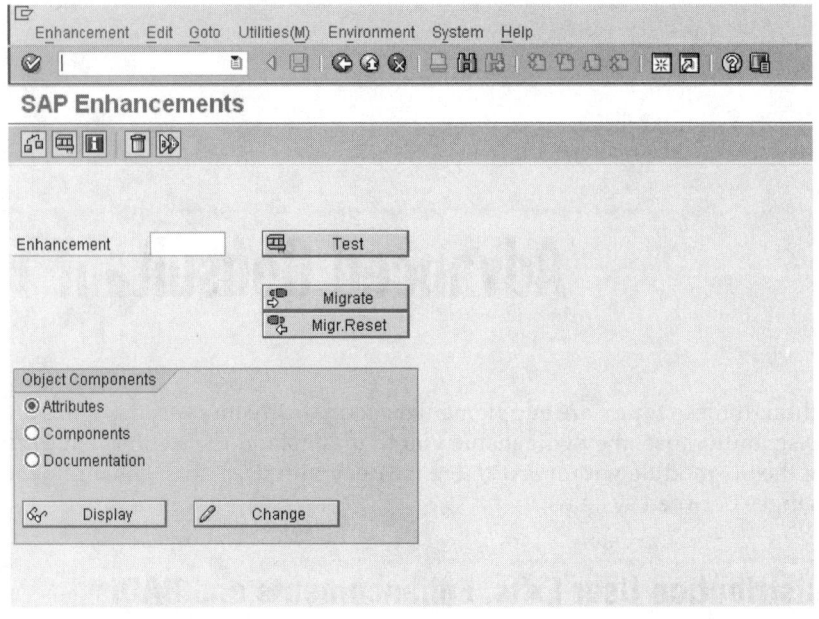

Copyright by SAP AG

FIGURE 11-1 SAP enhancements

The transaction code [SMOD] may be used to view all the enhancements in the system. An enhancement may consist of one or more function modules. Some enhancements allow you to change the SAP screen. In these cases, the enhancement will contain subscreens, which are areas on the SAP screen that you are allowed to change.

You may access the enhancement by the following menu path.

Menu Path   SAP Menu I Tools I ABAP Workbench I Utilities I Enhancements I [SMOD] - Definition

You can see an example in Figure 11-1.

When you want to use an SAP enhancement, you have to create a project in transaction code [CMOD]. Once you have created the project, you assign the SAP enhancement to the project. You can then create the include in the function module (or function modules if there is more than one that is part of the enhancement). Once you have finished programming the function module, you must activate the enhancement in order for SAP to call the function module from the standard code.

Business Add-Ins

Please note this is not a guide on how to implement a business add-in, but merely an introduction to the topic.

As of SAP R/3 4.6A, SAP provides a new enhancement technique called business add-ins, also known as BADis. Business add-ins are generalized business transaction events that can be used to bundle program, menu, and screen enhancements into a single add-in.

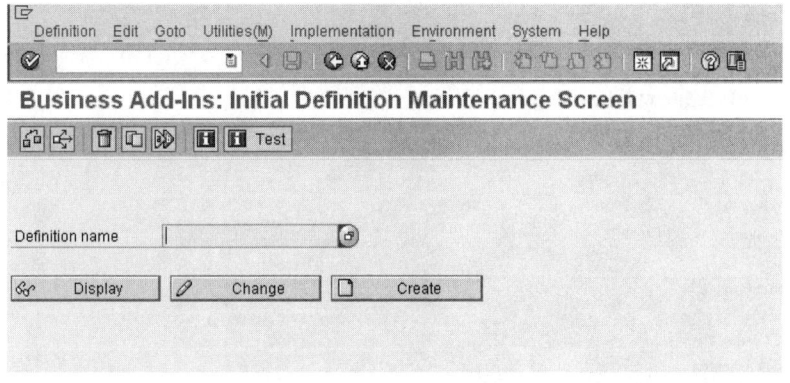

FIGURE 11-2   Business add-in definition

BADis are not restricted to a two-tiered infrastructure (i.e., where SAP provides the enhancement and the customer can code the enhancement). BADis can be implemented on a multi-tiered infrastructure. For example, SAP can provide the enhancement and a third-party software vendor may provide the code for the BADi. Like enhancements, BADis are guaranteed to be upwards compatible. Upgrades do not affect enhancements or business add-in calls.

Business add-ins are defined in the following menu path.

Menu Path   SAP Menu I Tools I ABAP Workbench I Utilities I Business Add-Ins I [SE18] - Definition

You may see an example in Figure 11-2. Transaction code [SE18] is also referred to as the BADi builder.

List of User Exits in the Sales and Distribution Module

Following is a list of user exits and function modules used in Sales and Distribution processing. To save space I have not documented all of them. However, there is adequate documentation within the exit.

For example, to investigate:

"Program MV45AFZZ - USEREXIT_DELETE_DOCUMENT"

enter transaction code [SE38]. Click the Source Code radio button, then click the Display button as seen in Figure 11-3.

Page down until you see FORM USEREXIT_DELETE_DOCUMENT, as seen in Figure 11-4.

You may read the comments in the code which explain the user exit's usage. From here you need basic ABAP navigation skills to see the source code of the form, which is not in the scope of this book.

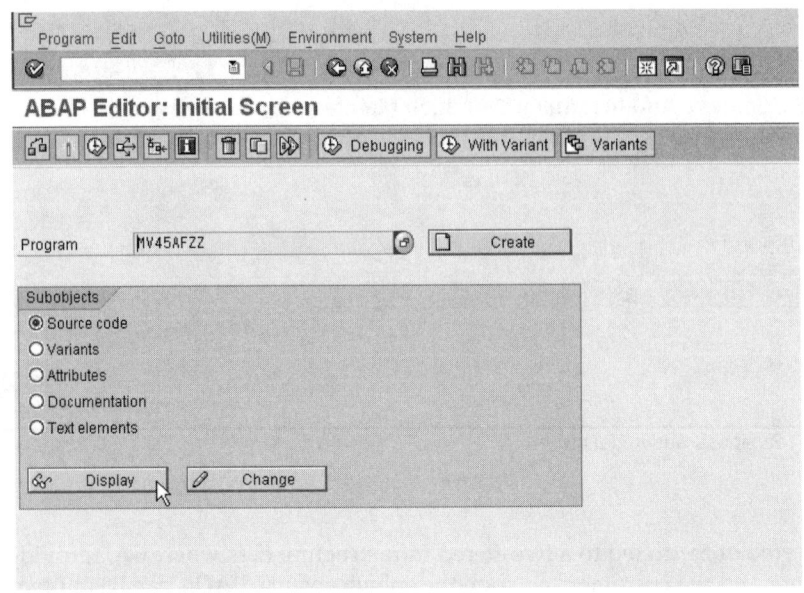

FIGURE 11-3   Displaying source code of user exit MV45AFZZ

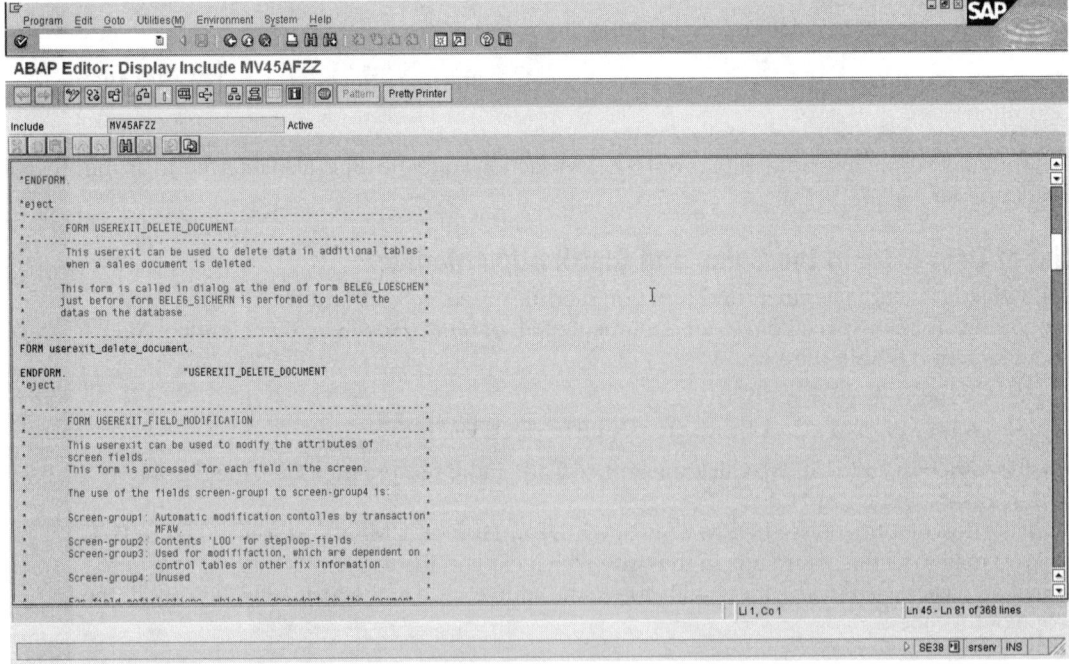

FIGURE 11-4   Source code of user exit MV45AFZZ

User Exits in Sales Document Processing
Program MV45AFZZ

USEREXIT_DELETE_DOCUMENT
USEREXIT_FIELD_MODIFICATION
USEREXIT_MOVE_FIELD_TO_VBAK
USEREXIT_MOVE_FIELD_TO_VBAP
USEREXIT_MOVE_FIELD_TO_VBEP
USEREXIT_MOVE_FIELD_TO_VBKD
USEREXIT_NUMBER_RANGE
USEREXIT_PRICING_PREPARE_TKOMK
USEREXIT_PRICING_PREPARE_TKOMP
USEREXIT_READ_DOCUMENT
USEREXIT_SAVE_DOCUMENT
USEREXIT_SAVE_DOCUMENT_PREPARE

Program MV45AFZA

USEREXIT_MOVE_FIELD_TO_KOMKD
USEREXIT_MOVE_FIELD_TO_KOMPD
USEREXIT_MOVE_FIELD_TO_KOMKG
USEREXIT_MOVE_FIELD_TO_KOMPG
USEREXIT_REFRESH_DOCUMENT

Program MV45AFZB

USEREXIT_CHECK_XVBAP_FOR_DELET
USEREXIT_CHECK_XVBEP_FOR_DELET
USEREXIT_CHECK_VBAK
USEREXIT_CHECK_VBAP
USEREXIT_CHECK_VBKD
USEREXIT_CHECK_VBEP
USEREXIT_CHECK_VBSN
USEREXIT_CHECK_XVBSN_FOR_DELET
USEREXIT_FILL_VBAP_FROM_HVBAP
USEREXIT_MOVE_FIELD_TO_TVCOM_H
USEREXIT_MOVE_FIELD_TO_TVCOM_I

User-Exits for Product Allocation

USEREXIT_MOVE_FIELD_TO_COBL
USEREXIT_COBL_RECEIVE_VBAK
USEREXIT_COBL_RECEIVE_VBAP
USEREXIT_COBL_SEND_ITEM
USEREXIT_COBL_SEND_HEADER
USEREXIT_SOURCE_DETERMINATION
USEREXIT_MOVE_FIELD_TO_ME_REQ
USEREXIT_GET_FIELD_FROM_SDCOM
USEREXIT_MOVE_WORKAREA_TO_SDWA

User Exits for First Data Transfer
USEREXIT_MOVE_FIELD_TO_VBAKKOM
USEREXIT_MOVE_FIELD_TO_VBAPKOM
USEREXIT_MOVE_FIELD_TO_VBEPKOM
USEREXIT_MOVE_FIELD_TO_VBSN
USEREXIT_MOVE_FIELD_TO_KOMKH
USEREXIT_MOVE_FIELD_TO_KOMPH
USEREXIT_CUST_MATERIAL_READ
USEREXIT_NEW_PRICING_VBAP
USEREXIT_NEW_PRICING_VBKD

Program MV45AFZD

USEREXIT_CONFIG_DATE_EXPLOSION

Program FV45EFZ1

USEREXIT_CHANGE_SALES_ORDER

Program RV45PFZA

USEREXIT_SET_STATUS_VBUK
USEREXIT_SET_STATUS_VBUP
USEREXIT_STATUS_VBUK_INVOICE

The often used, Sales document header additional data, is available on screen SAPMV45A 0309. Additional item data is on screen SAPMV45A 0459. These screens contain the include screens SAPMV45A 8309 or SAPMV45A 8459 as additional data A and program SAPMV45A, screen 8460 as additional data B as user exits.

Program MV45AFZ4

USEREXIT_MOVE_FIELD_TO_KOMK
USEREXIT_MOVE_FIELD_TO_KOMP

Program SAPFV45PF0E and SAPFV45PF0C

EXIT_SAPFV45P_001

User Exits for Contract Processing
Function Module V45W0001

Contains: EXIT_SAPLV45W_001

User Exits for Product Allocation Processing
Function Module SDQUX0001

User Exits for Availability Check
Program FV45VFZZ

USEREXIT_ADD_FIELD_TO_HEADER
USEREXIT_ADD_FIELD_TO_LINE

Program FV45VFZY

USEREXIT_DELIVERY_GROUPS
USEREXIT_MVERF_INIT
USEREXIT_QUOTA_KEY_VALUE

Program RV03VFZZ

USEREXIT_AVAILABILITY_IN
USEREXIT_AVAILABILITY_OUT
USEREXIT_DATA_REFRESH
USEREXIT_PLANT_SELECTION

User Exits for Component Supply Processing
Program MV45AFZC

USEREXIT_CHECK_VBLB-USR01
USEREXIT_CHECK_VBLB-USR02
USEREXIT_CHECK_VBLB-USR03
USEREXIT_CHECK_VBLB-USR04
USEREXIT_CHECK_VBLB-USR05

Function Module V45L0001

General

EXIT_SAPLVED4_004

Delivery Schedules

EXIT_SAPLV45L_001
EXIT_SAPLV45L_002

Planned Delivery Schedules

EXIT_SAPMV45L_001
EXIT_SAPMV45L_002

Delivery orders

EXIT_SAPMV45A_005

Workflow

EXIT_SAPLVED4_001
EXIT_SAPLVED4_002
EXIT_SAPLVED4_003
EXIT_SAPLVED4_005
EXIT_SAPLVED4_006

Self Billing

EXIT_SAPLVED4_001
EXIT_SAPLVED4_005
EXIT_SAPLVED4_006
EXIT_SAPLVED5_002
EXIT_SAPLVED5_003
EXIT_SAPLVED5_004

User Exits for Product Selection
Function Module V45A0001

User Exits for Billing Plan
Program RV60FUS1

BILLING_SCHEDULE_DELTA
USEREXIT_MOVE_FIELD_TO_FPLT
USEREXIT_MOVE_FIELD_TO_FPLA

Program RV60FUS2

USEREXIT_PRICING_PREPARE_TKOMX

Program RV60FUS3

USEREXIT_DATE_PROPOSAL

Modification report for billing plan SDFPLA02

Additions to billing plan - SDVAX001

Change billing plan dates - User exit V60F0001

User Exits for Billing
USEREXIT_NUMBER_RANGE

(Module pool SAPLV60A, program RV60AFZZ)

USEREXIT_ACCOUNT_PREP_KOMKCV

(Module pool SAPLV60A, program RV60AFZZ)

USEREXIT_ACCOUNT_PREP_KOMPCV

(Module pool SAPLV60A)

USEREXIT_NUMBER_RANGE_INV_DATE

(Module pool SAPLV60A, program RV60AFZC)

USEREXIT_FILL_VBRK_VBRP

(Module pool SAPLV60A, program RV60AFZC)

USEREXIT_PRINT_ITEM

(Module pool SAPLV61A, program RV61AFZB)

USEREXIT_PRINT_HEAD

(Module pool SAPLV61A, Program RV61AFZB)

Program RV60AFZD

USEREXIT_RELI_XVBPAK_AVBPAK
USEREXIT_NEWROLE_XVBPAK_AVBPAK
USEREXIT_NEWROLE_XVBPAP_AVBPAK

The following user exits are available in report SAPLV60B for transfer to accounting:

EXIT_SAPLV60B_001
EXIT_SAPLV60B_002
EXIT_SAPLV60B_003
EXIT_SAPLV60B_004
EXIT_SAPLV60B_005

EXIT_SAPLV60B_006
EXIT_SAPLV60B_007
EXIT_SAPLV60B_008
EXIT_SAPLV60B_010
EXIT_SAPLV60B_011

User Exits for General Billing Interface

USEREXIT_AVBPAK_CPD (in Include RV60AFZB)
USEREXIT_AVBPAK_ADD (in Include RV60AFZA)
USEREXIT_XVBAPF_KEY (in Include RV60AFZA)
USEREXIT_XVBAPF_KEY_CANC (in Include RV60AFZA)

User Exits for Payment Cards

Include MV45AFZH contains the user exit AUTHORIZATION_VALUE_SPLIT

User Exits for Price Determination

USEREXIT_PRICING_PREPARE_TKOMK

(Module pool SAPLV60A, program RV60AFZZ)

USEREXIT_PRICING_PREPARE_TKOMP

(Module pool SAPLV60A, program RV60AFZZ)

USEREXIT_FIELD_MODIFICATION

(Module pool SAPMV61A, program MV61AFZA)

USEREXIT_FIELD_MODIFIC_KZWI

(Module pool SAPMV61A, program MV61AFZB)

USEREXIT_FIELD_MODIFIC_KOPF

(Module pool SAPMV61A, program MV61AFZB)

USEREXIT_FIELD_MODIFIC_LEER

(Module pool SAPMV61A, program MV61AFZB)

USEREXIT_PRICING_CHECK

(Module pool SAPMV61, program MV61AFZA)

USEREXIT_PRICING_RULE

(Module pool SAPLV61A, program RV61AFZA)

USEREXIT_CHANGE_PRICING_RULE

(Module pool SAPMV61A, program MV61AFZA)

USEREXIT_XKOMV_BEWERTEN_INIT

(Module pool SAPLV61A, program RV61AFZB)

USEREXIT_XKOMV_BEWERTEN_END

(Module pool SAPLV61A, program RV61AFZB)

USEREXIT_XKOMV_ERGAENZEN

(Module pool SAPLV61A, program RV61AFZB)

USEREXIT_XKOMV_ERGAENZEN_MANU

(Module pool SAPLV61A, program RV61AFZB)

USEREXIT_XKOMV_FUELLEN

(Module pool SAPLV61A, program RV61AFZB)

USEREXIT_XKOMV_FUELLEN_O_KONP

(Module pool SAPLV61A, program RV61AFZB)

USEREXIT_PRICING_COPY

(Module pool SAPLV61A, program RV61AFZA)

User Exits for Partner Determination
EXIT_SAPLV09A_001
EXIT_SAPLV09A_002
EXIT_SAPLV09A_003
EXIT_SAPLV09A_004

User Exits for Credit Checks and Risk Management
LVKMPTZZ
LVKMPFZ1: USER_CREDIT_CHECK1
LVKMPFZ2: USER_CREDIT_CHECK2
LVKMPFZ3: USER_CREDIT_CHECK3

User exit for availability check

User exit USEREXIT_AVAIL_CHECK_CREDIT exists in Include MV45AFZF

Quick Viewer

The Quick Viewer is a simple yet very useful tool to create reports in SAP without actually doing any programming. The quick viewer is similar to an ABAP Query except it does not have all the capabilities that the ABAP query has. The quick viewer is more useful than transaction code [SE16n] or [SE16] when you need to query more than one table to obtain the information you require.

There are standard views in SAP where you can see their structure via transaction code [SE11], which are not tables, but rather a combination of two or more tables. You can use these views to display the data using transaction code [SE16] or [SE16n]:

- VBAKUK   A view compiled from VBAK and VBUK
- KNA1VV   A view compiled from KNA1 and KNVV
- MAPOV   A view compiled from Mara and MAKT and MVKE
- VB_DEBI   A view compiled from Mara and KNA1 and KNB1 and BSID

The Quick Viewer lets you view the data in more than one table but without a database view—you create the view by joining two or more tables. The Quick Viewer may be found in the following menu path.

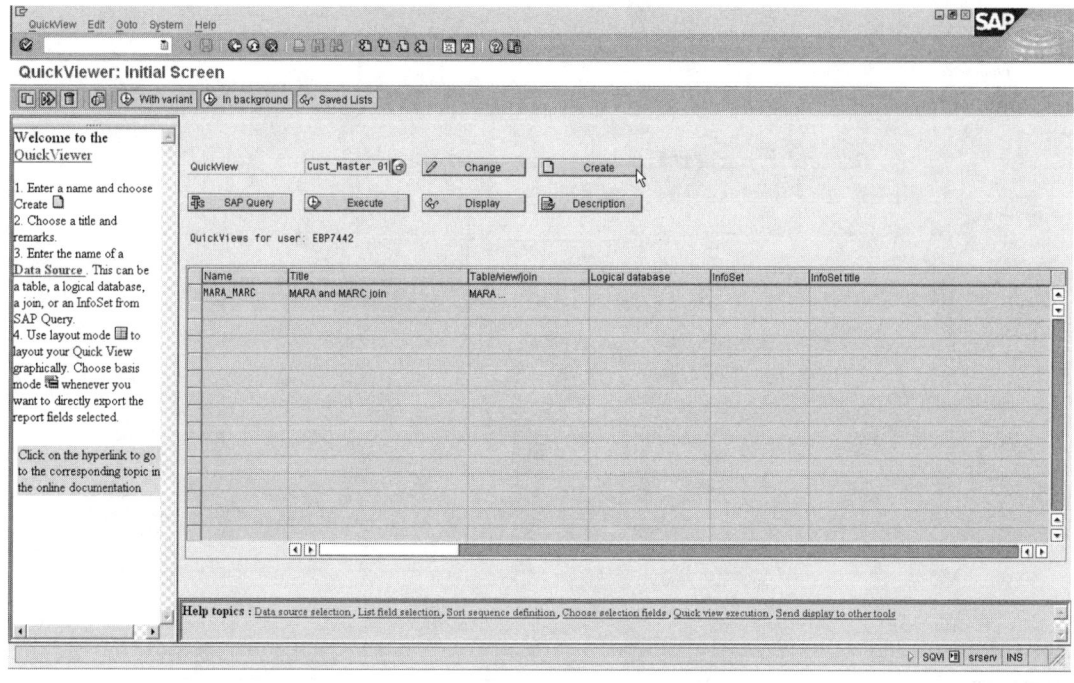

Copyright by SAP AG

FIGURE 11-5   Creating a quick view

Menu Path   SAP Menu I Tools I ABAP Workbench I Utilities I [SQVI] - QuickViewer

Creating a Quick View

Enter a name and click the Create button as seen in Figure 11-5.

A dialog box will appear. Use the dialog box to enter a title and any additional comments you may wish to use. Under Data Source, you may use a logical database, which is a standard database of tables that are logically structured per application. For a list of tables within the logical databases, refer to www.sapww.com. Select Table Join as seen in Figure 11-6.

You will now see a blank page with the navigation pane at the bottom of the screen. Select Edit I Insert Table, or click the Table button shown here.

Copyright by SAP AG

Now enter the tables you would like to use, KNA1, and press ENTER. Repeat this for all tables. (In our example we have used KNA1, KNB1, and KNVV).

You will have a screen similar to Figure 11-7.

SAP will automatically provide suggestions for the table links/conditions. We can see between KNA1 and KNB1 SAP has linked KNA1-KUNNR with KNB1-EKVBD. This is not a good suggestion. It is better to delete this link by right-clicking on the link and selecting Delete Link.

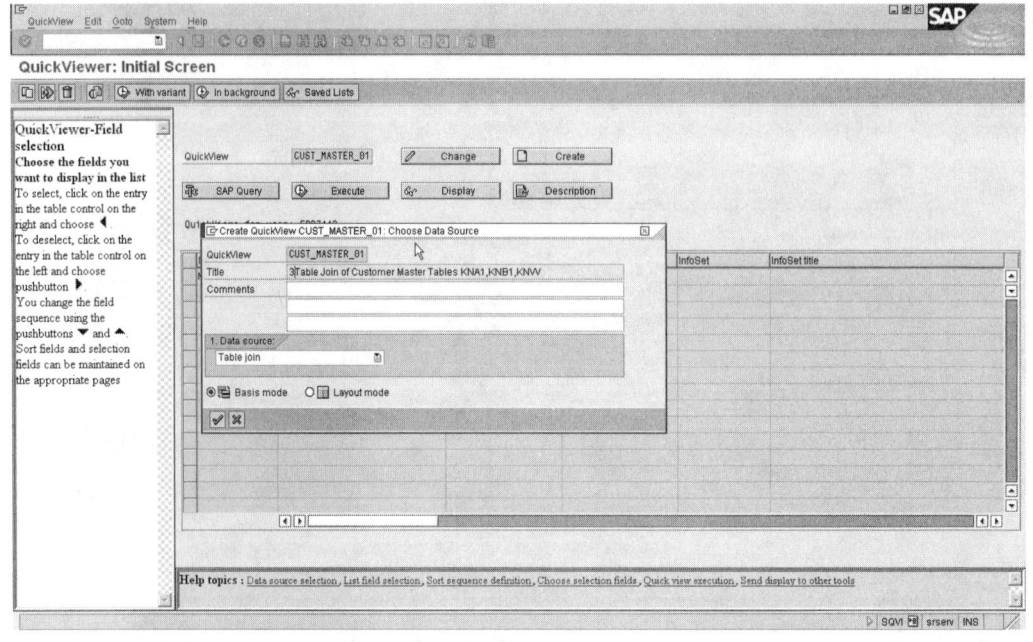

FIGURE 11-6 Entering quick view attributes

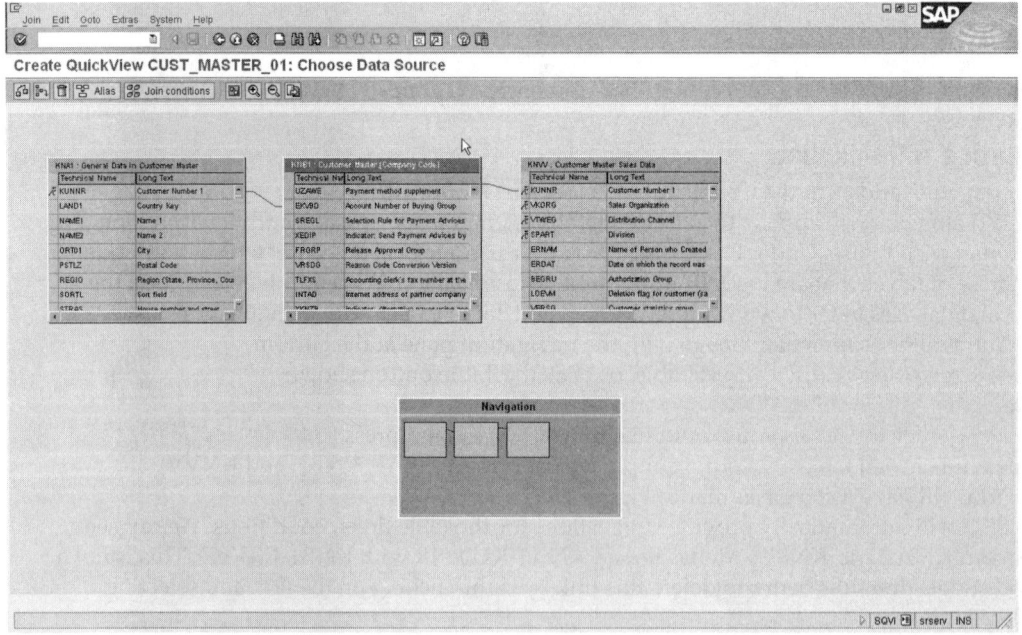

FIGURE 11-7 Data source for quick view

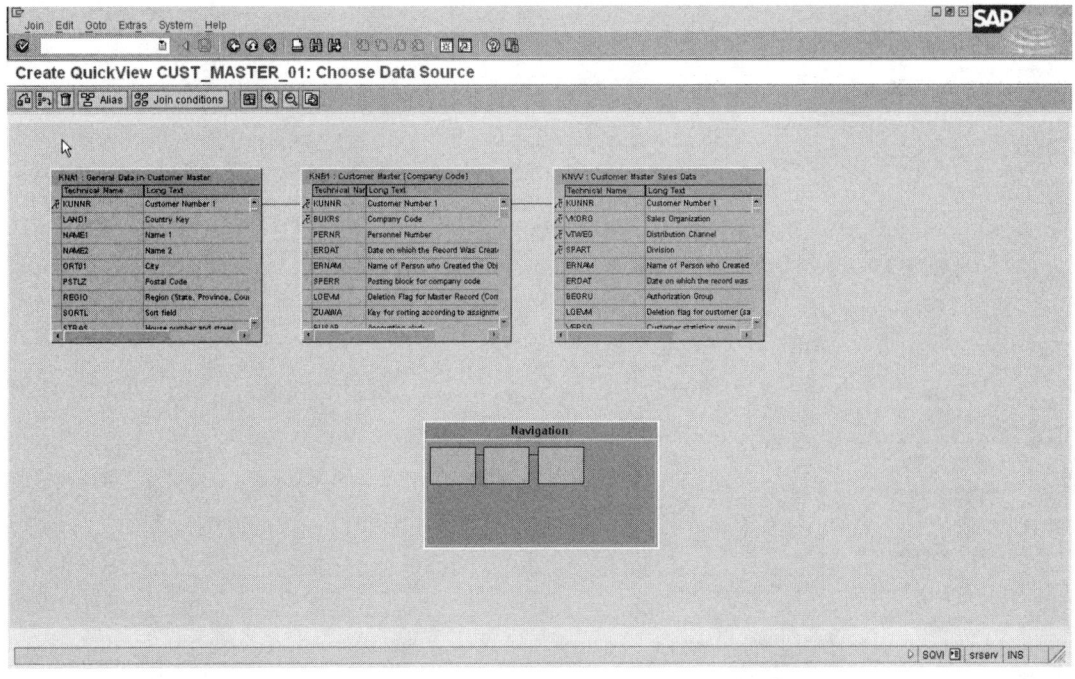

Copyright by SAP AG

FIGURE 11-8   Data source screen with correct link condition

Now take KNA1-KUNNR and drag it over KNB1-KUNNR, thus creating the link between the two tables, so your data source screen looks like Figure 11-8.

Now click the Back button, and you will see a screen similar to Figure 11-9.

You may select the fields to use in the quick view report and the selection fields from the pane on the left or the pane on the right. Although the window pane on the right is fairly simple to use, I find the window pane on the left faster to work with, so we will use that instead.

Drag the window pane on the left showing the table join to the right as seen on the right side of table KNVV in Figure 11-9.

Now open the tables you wish to use and check the list field and selection field checkboxes, as seen in Figure 11-10.

This screen shows the field selection in the Basis Mode. Should you click the Layout Mode button you will have additional options, such as inserting header and footer text into the report, as well as using different colors, as seen in Figure 11-11. We will investigate these options in the next section on the SAP query.

Now click Save, and then select Execute. You may see the finished article in Figure 11-12.

The results are now a report listing fields and values—multiple records from a combination of database tables. The results may also be exported, for example, to Microsoft Excel, for further processing.

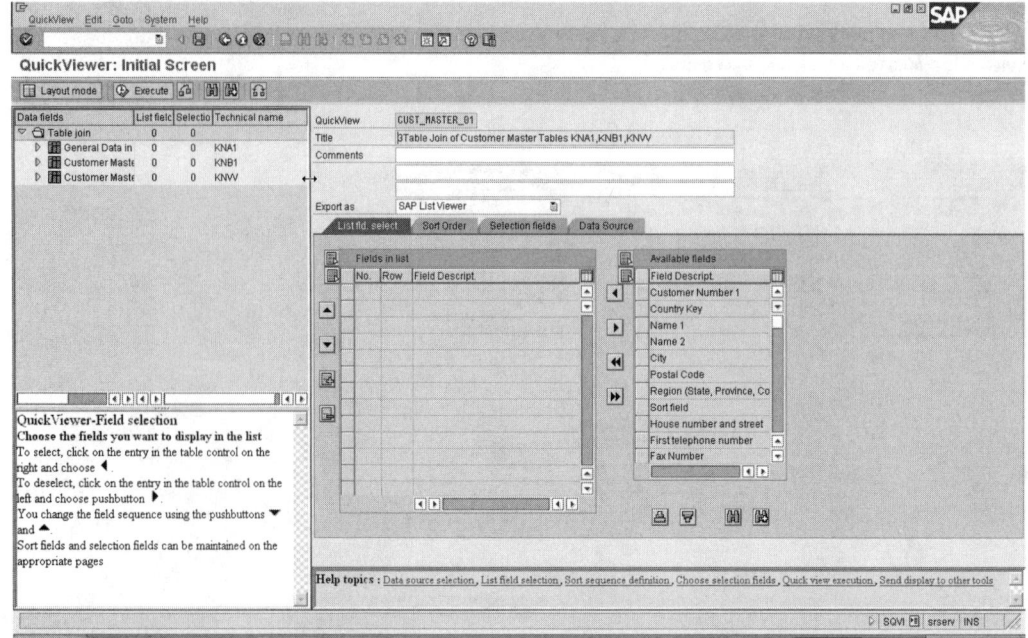

FIGURE 11-9 Quick view initial screen

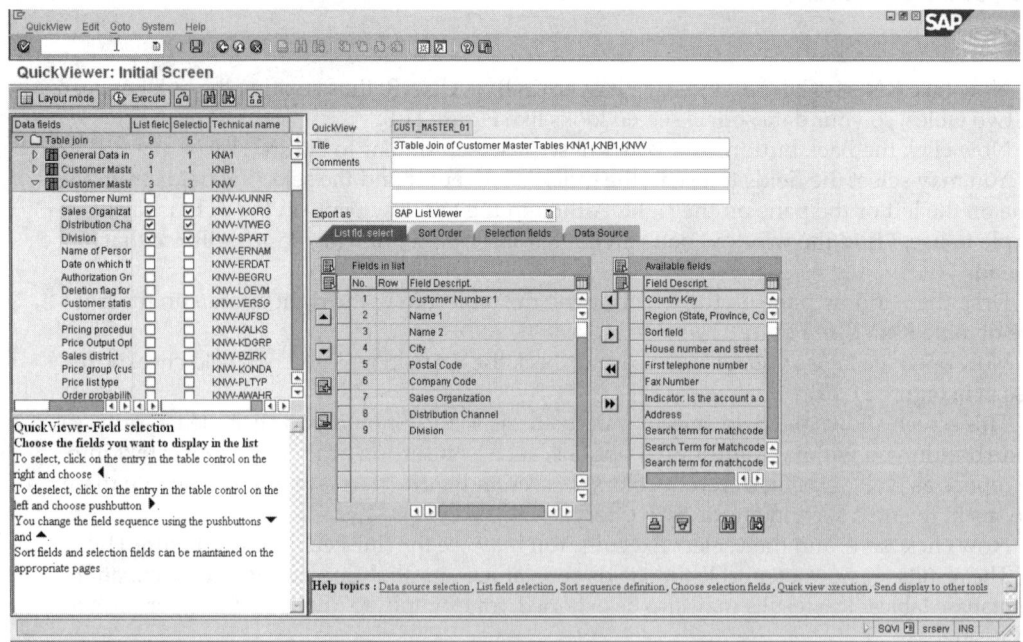

FIGURE 11-10 Activating list and selection fields

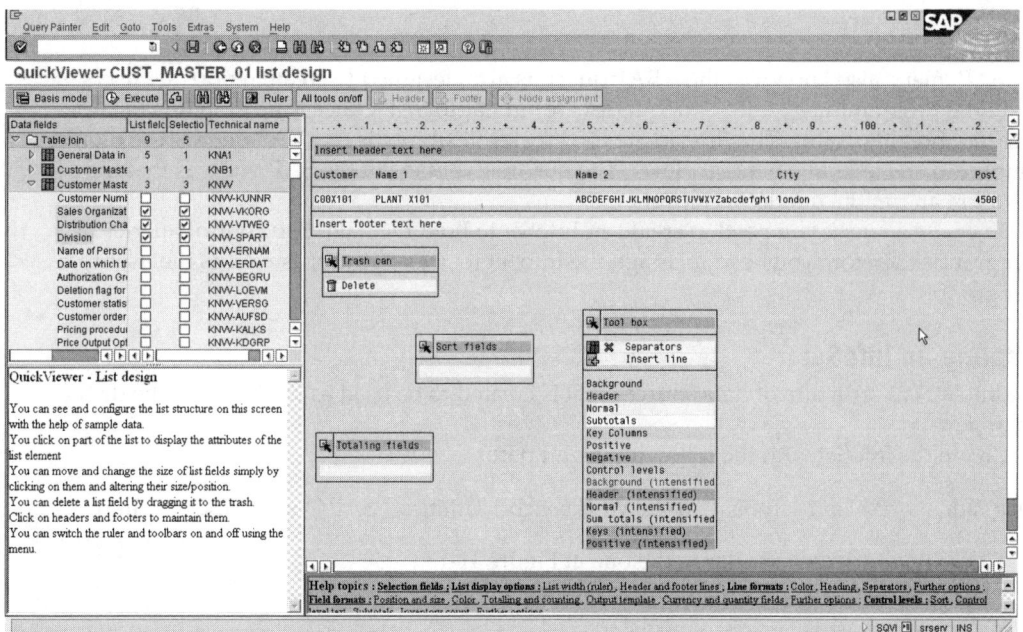

FIGURE 11-11   Layout Mode

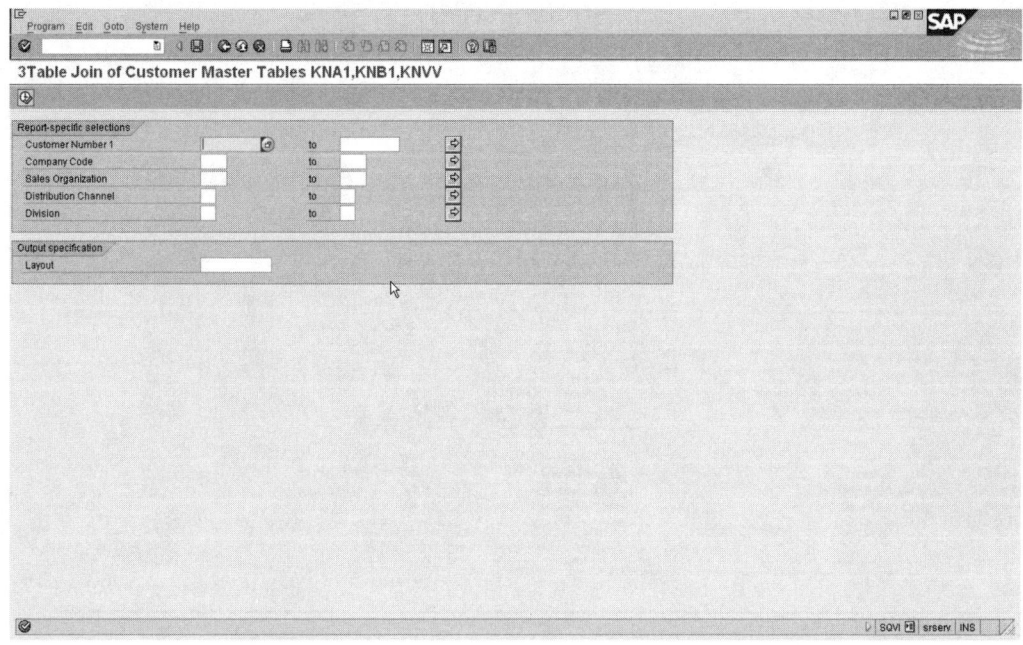

FIGURE 11-12   Executing the quick view

SAP Query

The SAP query, also known as the ABAP query, is also designed to create reports by users with little programming skills. SAP queries are similar to SAP Quick Viewer in this regard but offer more flexibility. The flip-side to the greater flexibility is that SAP queries are more complex to create than the quick views. The major advantage of the SAP query is that the end user can run the queries as reports.

To create a query, you need to create an InfoSet to hold the data. You control queries by user groups therefore you need to assign the InfoSet to a user group, as well as the user to a user group.

Creating an InfoSet

The InfoSet is a structure of data sources that is created to be used as the basis for the data in a report.

Create the InfoSet with the following menu path.

Menu Path   SAP Menu | Tools | ABAP Workbench | Utilities | SAP Query | [SQ02] - InfoSets

You will see a screen similar to the one in Figure 11-13.

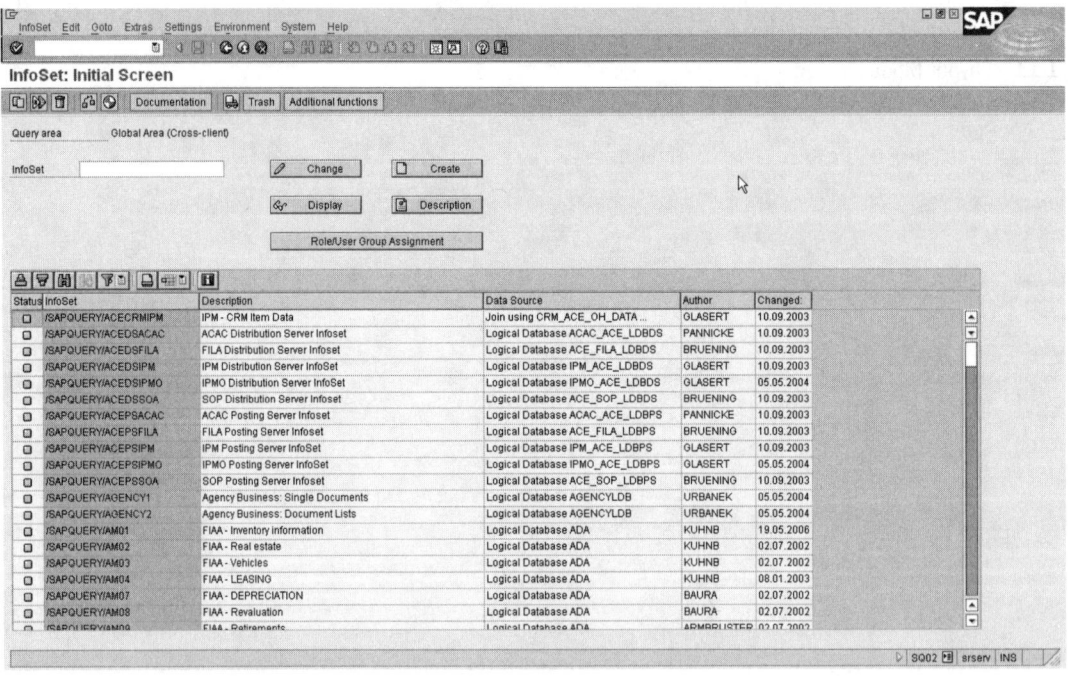

Copyright by SAP AG

FIGURE 11-13   Creating an InfoSet

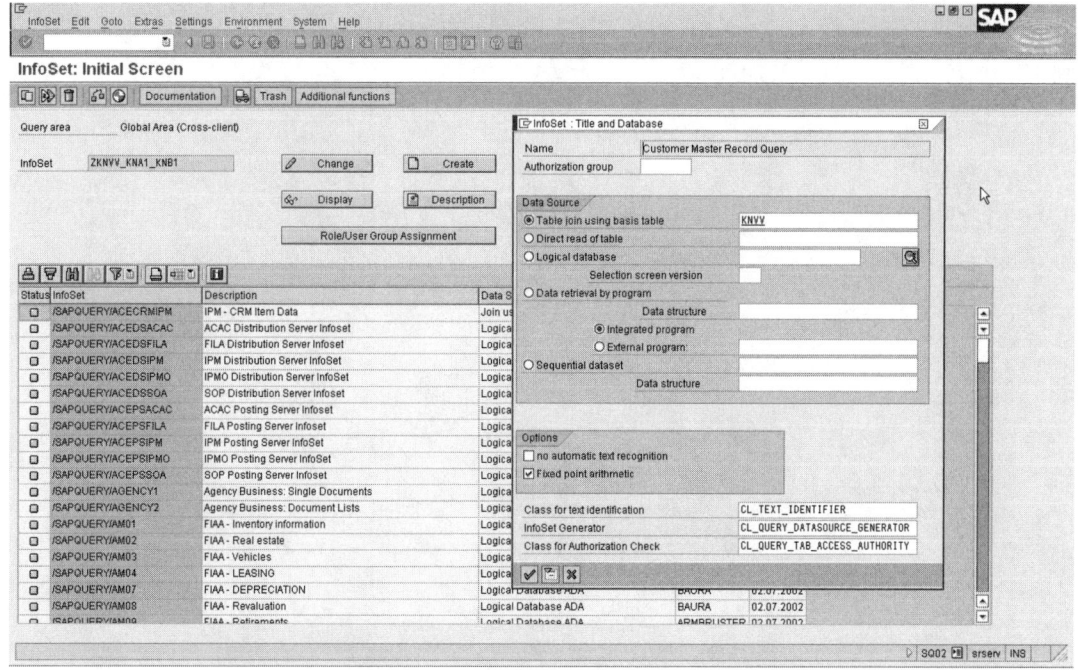

FIGURE 11-14   Creating InfoSet attributes

Enter an InfoSet ID and click the Create button. Enter an InfoSet name as seen in the dialog box in Figure 11-14.

A query can read data from a single table, or multiple tables joined in a table join, or a logical database, which is a hierarchical structure of coherent tables. (Refer to www.sapww .com for more on logical databases and structures.)

You can create your own logical databases by using transaction code [SE36] or [SLDB]. (You will need an access key).

For the attributes of the query you may also read data from a structure or table with a program. Or you may read data from a sequential dataset.

After entering the attributes, press ENTER and enter the tables and the join conditions. Insert a table by selecting the icon as seen selected by the cursor in Figure 11-15.

In this example I have added KNA1 and KNB1 to KNVV. Remember to delete automatically proposed links that are not required or that are incorrect. You add links by dragging one field onto another, and delete links by right-clicking on the link and selecting Delete. After you have completed adding tables and the links between them, click the InfoSet button, which will take you to InfoSet maintenance. You will be prompted with a dialog box asking about field groups, as seen in Figure 11-16. I always select Create Empty Field Groups.

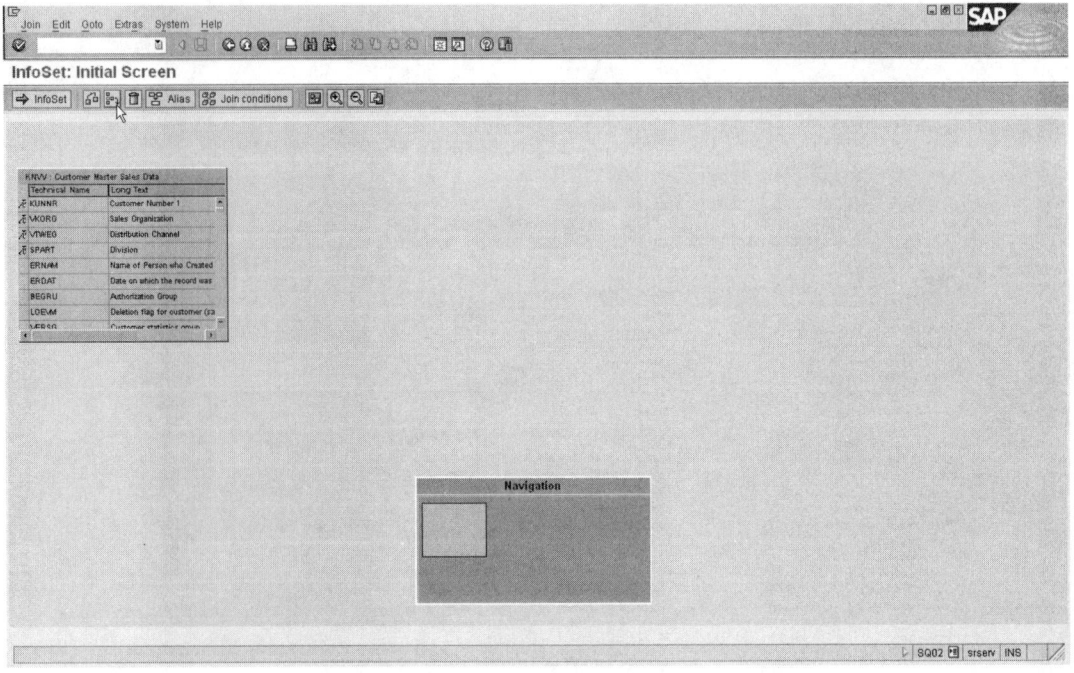

FIGURE 11-15   Creating InfoSet tables

You will then be faced with a screen similar to Figure 11-17. Place the fields you wish to use in the query into the field groups by selecting the field group, then selecting the field and clicking the icon shown here. Figure 11-17 shows field KNVV-KUNNR as selected and placed into field group "01 Customer Master Sales Data."

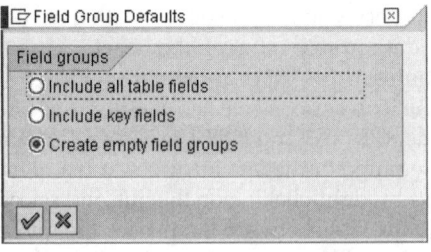

FIGURE 11-16   Field groups creation for InfoSets

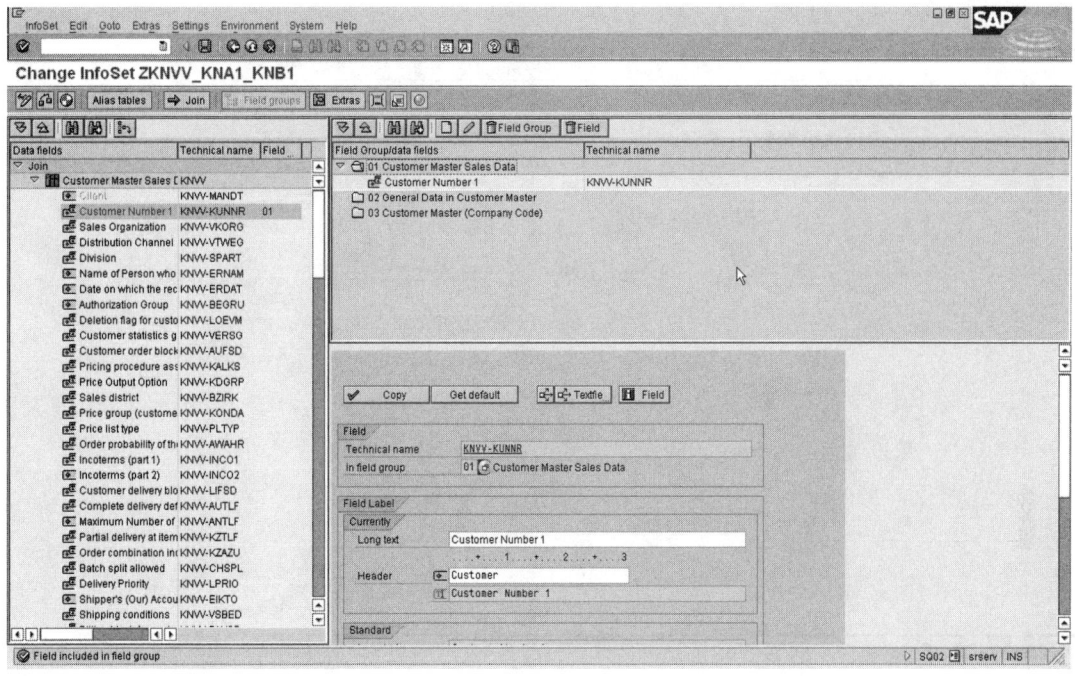

FIGURE 11-17   Selecting fields for query

Continue to select your fields and add them into your field groups. Save your InfoSet, then click the Generate icon shown here.

Copyright by SAP AG

Creating User Groups and Assignments

There may be no requirement to create a user group, as a valid user group may already exist. In this section we will create a user group, assign the InfoSet to the user group, and assign the user who is permitted to execute this query to the user group.

Creating a User Group

Use transaction code [SQ03] or the following menu path.

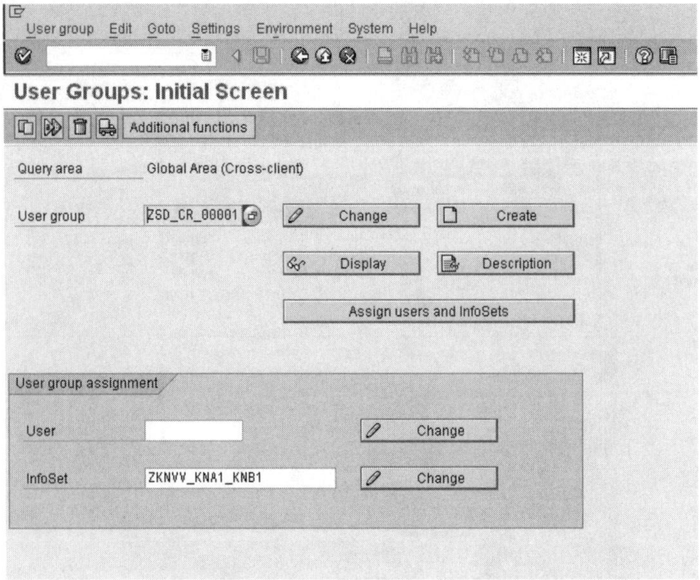

Copyright by SAP AG

FIGURE 11-18   Creating a user group

Menu Path   SAP Menu I Tools I ABAP Workbench I Utilities I SAP Query I [SQ03] - User Groups

Enter a user group name as seen in Figure 11-18. When you press ENTER you will be prompted to enter a description.

After creating and saving the user group, you will be prompted to save the item as a local object or a transportable object. You then need to assign the InfoSet to this user group. The logic behind this setting is that the InfoSet will be used by the same users that must be permitted to execute the query.

Click the Assign Users and InfoSets button, as seen in Figure 11-18.

Selecting InfoSets

Now enter the users and select the Assign InfoSets button as seen in Figure 11-19.

Select the InfoSet and click Save as seen in Figure 11-20.

You are now ready to create the query.

Creating Queries

To create the query use transaction code [SQ01] or the following menu path.

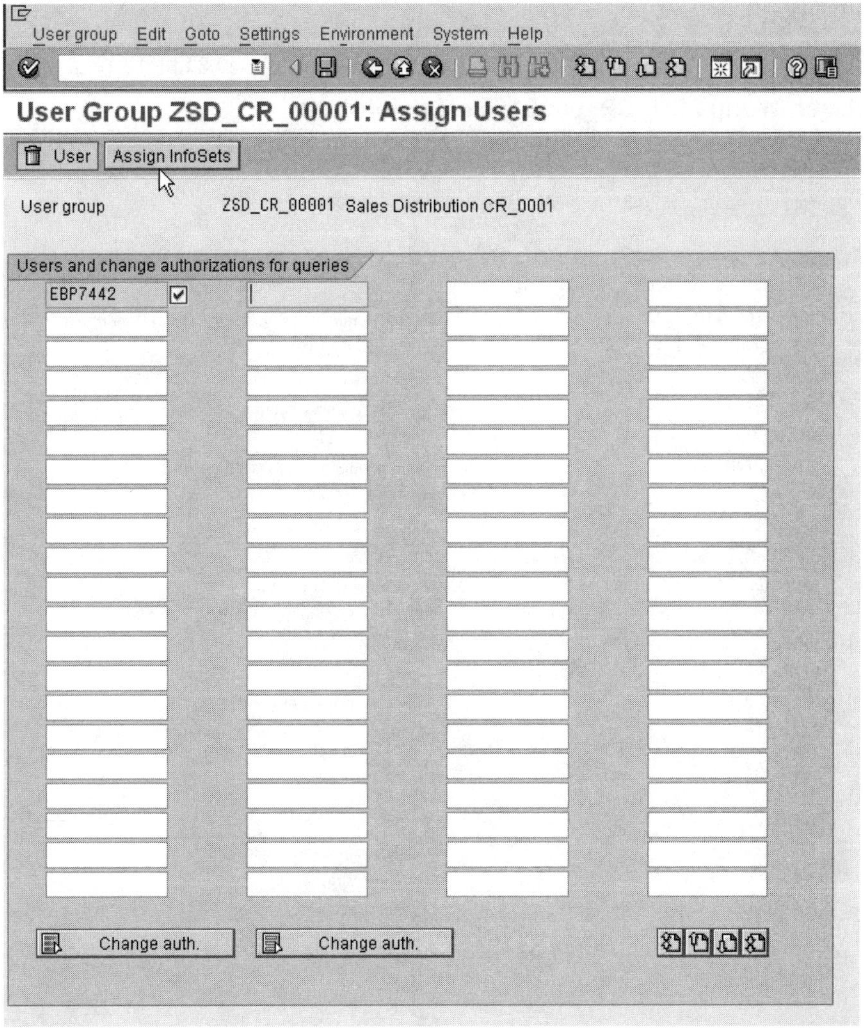

Copyright by SAP AG

Figure 11-19   Assigning users and InfoSets

Menu Path   SAP Menu | Tools | ABAP Workbench | Utilities | SAP Query | [SQ01] - Queries

The queries related to the last used user group will be displayed as seen in Figure 11-21. Should you wish to change the user group in use, select Edit | Other User Group.

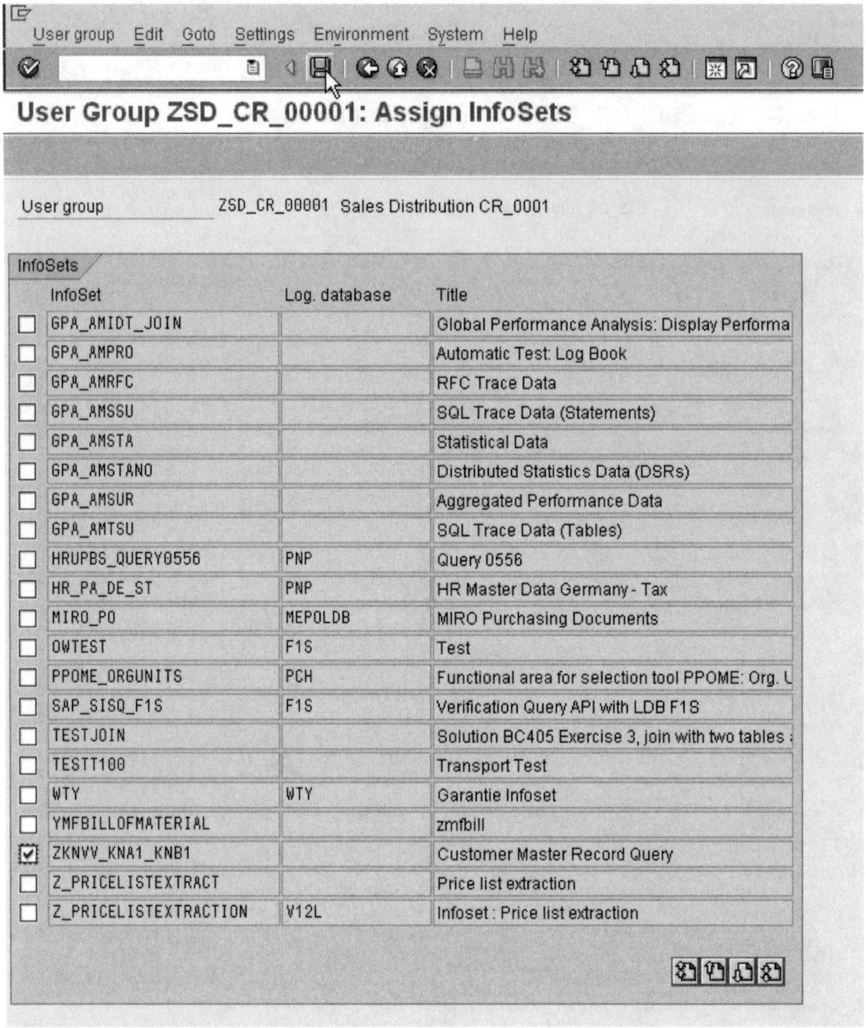

User group   Edit   Goto   Settings   Environment   System   Help

User Group ZSD_CR_00001: Assign InfoSets

| User group | ZSD_CR_00001 Sales Distribution CR_0001 |

InfoSets

	InfoSet	Log. database	Title
☐	GPA_AMIDT_JOIN		Global Performance Analysis: Display Performa
☐	GPA_AMPRO		Automatic Test: Log Book
☐	GPA_AMRFC		RFC Trace Data
☐	GPA_AMSSU		SQL Trace Data (Statements)
☐	GPA_AMSTA		Statistical Data
☐	GPA_AMSTANO		Distributed Statistics Data (DSRs)
☐	GPA_AMSUR		Aggregated Performance Data
☐	GPA_AMTSU		SQL Trace Data (Tables)
☐	HRUPBS_QUERY0556	PNP	Query 0556
☐	HR_PA_DE_ST	PNP	HR Master Data Germany - Tax
☐	MIRO_PO	MEPOLDB	MIRO Purchasing Documents
☐	OWTEST	F1S	Test
☐	PPOME_ORGUNITS	PCH	Functional area for selection tool PPOME: Org. U
☐	SAP_SISQ_F1S	F1S	Verification Query API with LDB F1S
☐	TESTJOIN		Solution BC405 Exercise 3, join with two tables ;
☐	TESTT100		Transport Test
☐	WTY	WTY	Garantie Infoset
☐	YMFBILLOFMATERIAL		zmfbill
☑	ZKNVV_KNA1_KNB1		Customer Master Record Query
☐	Z_PRICELISTEXTRACT		Price list extraction
☐	Z_PRICELISTEXTRACTION	V12L	Infoset : Price list extraction

FIGURE 11-20   Selecting an InfoSet

You will then be prompted to select the InfoSet to use. Double-click on the InfoSet. Then enter a name and description as well as the table and output format attributes, as seen in Figure 11-22. Then press F6 to advance to the next screen. (Or click the next screen icon.)

You now select the field groups you wish to use and press F6 to advance to the next screen.

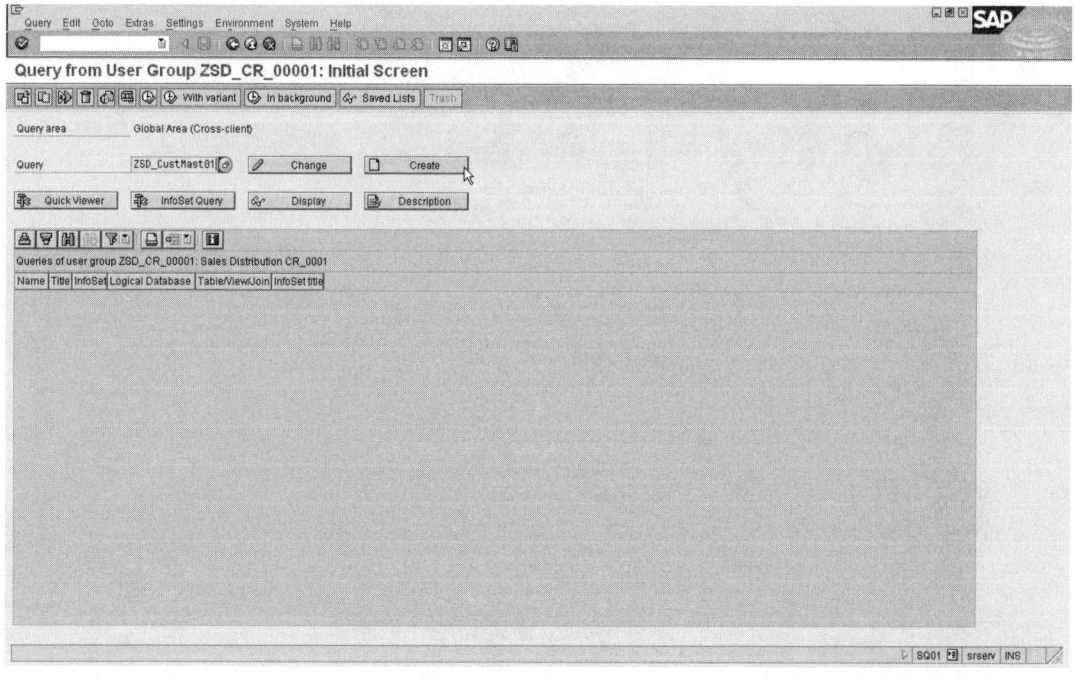

FIGURE 11-21   Creating a query initial screen

You can now select the fields you wish to use in the query, as seen in Figure 11-23. These are fields that may be used as either selection fields or output fields. Press F6 to advance to the next screen when completed.

Now we get into the design of the query. You can now select which fields will be used as selection fields. After selecting the fields, click Save. You may now assign a sequence for the field to be displayed, seen in the No column. You can change the selection text. You can also restrict the multiple selections associated with the field in the selection screen by selecting these checkboxes, as seen in Figure 11-24:

- **SV**   Does not permit a To value in the selection options.
- **1Z**   Does permit a From and To range, but does not permit multiple selections.

Now click the Basic List button. You will see the same design layout as was used in the Quick Viewer. There is no need to repeat the steps associated with the design of the layout

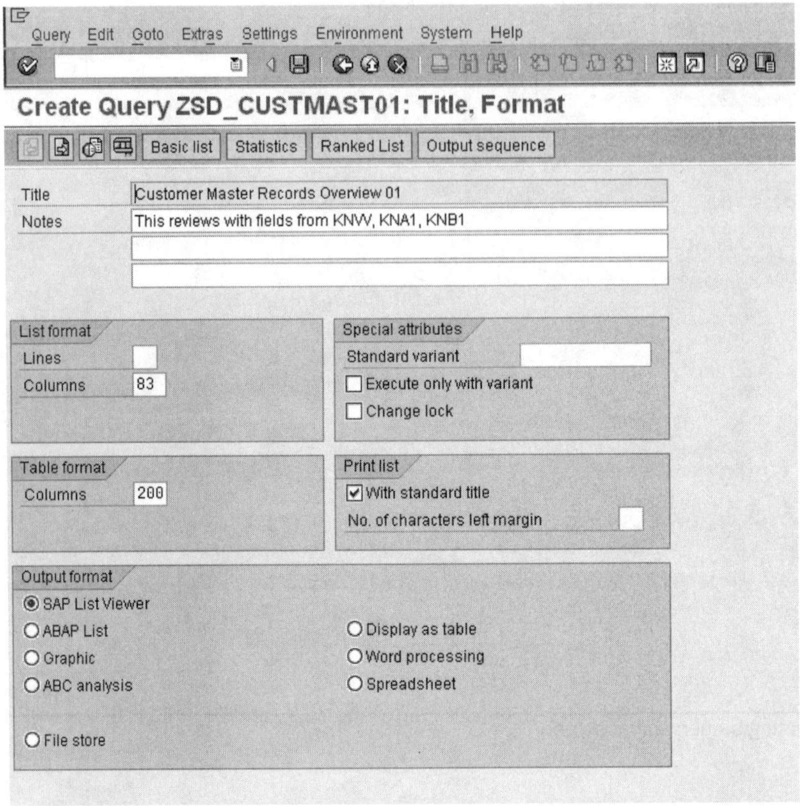

FIGURE 11-22   Creating the query's initial screen

using this screen. (Don't forget that you can move the fields by double-clicking and then dragging them from within the report layout.) You should end up with a query layout similar to Figure 11-25.

The query is now ready to be executed. Proceed back to transaction code [SQ01] as seen in Figure 11-29 and select Execute.

The selection screen of this example may be seen in Figure 11-27. Notice the difference in selection options for sales office—only single values are permitted due to the setting of SV in Figure 11-24. Sales group on the other hand does not have the ability to have a multiple selection (due to the setting of 1Z).

The results of the executed query, seen in Figure 11-28, are in the SAP List Viewer layout, also referred to as ABAP List Viewer.

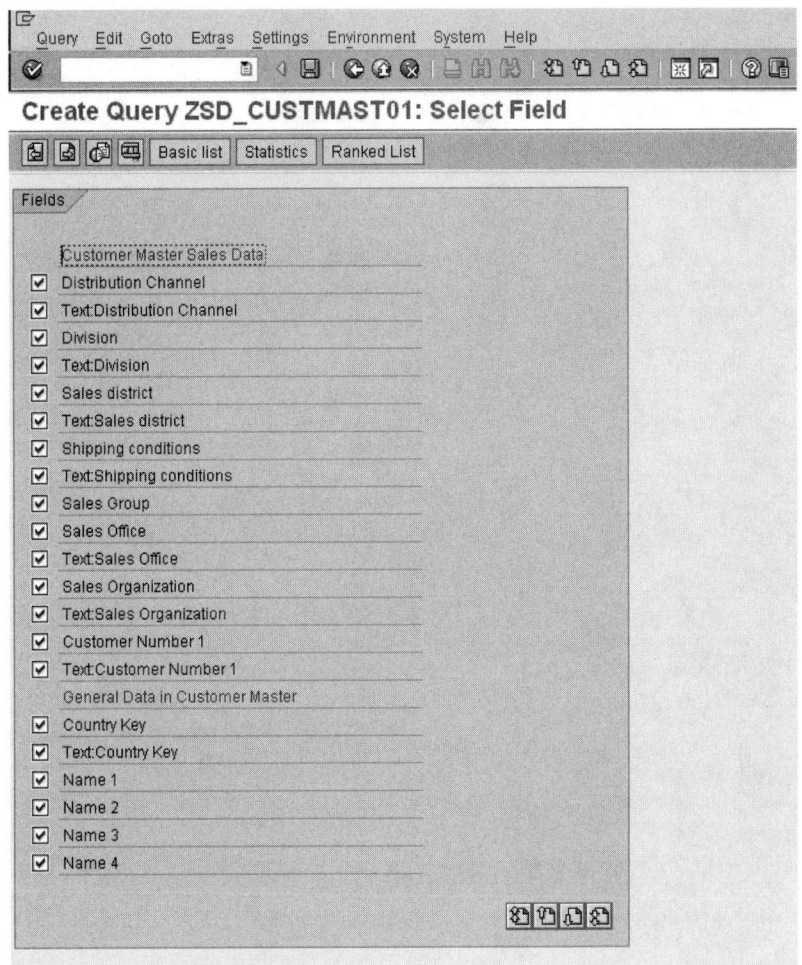

Copyright by SAP AG

FIGURE 11-23   Select fields to be used

Data Exchange

There are many methods and functions within SAP to exchange data across systems. These topics are not intended to be covered in detail within this book, but are simply an introduction to the technical integration of the SD module within SAP.

EDI—Electronic Data Interchange

EDI is the process of interchanging documents across multiple systems, hardware, and software. For example, you can transfer data between two SAP systems, or between an SAP

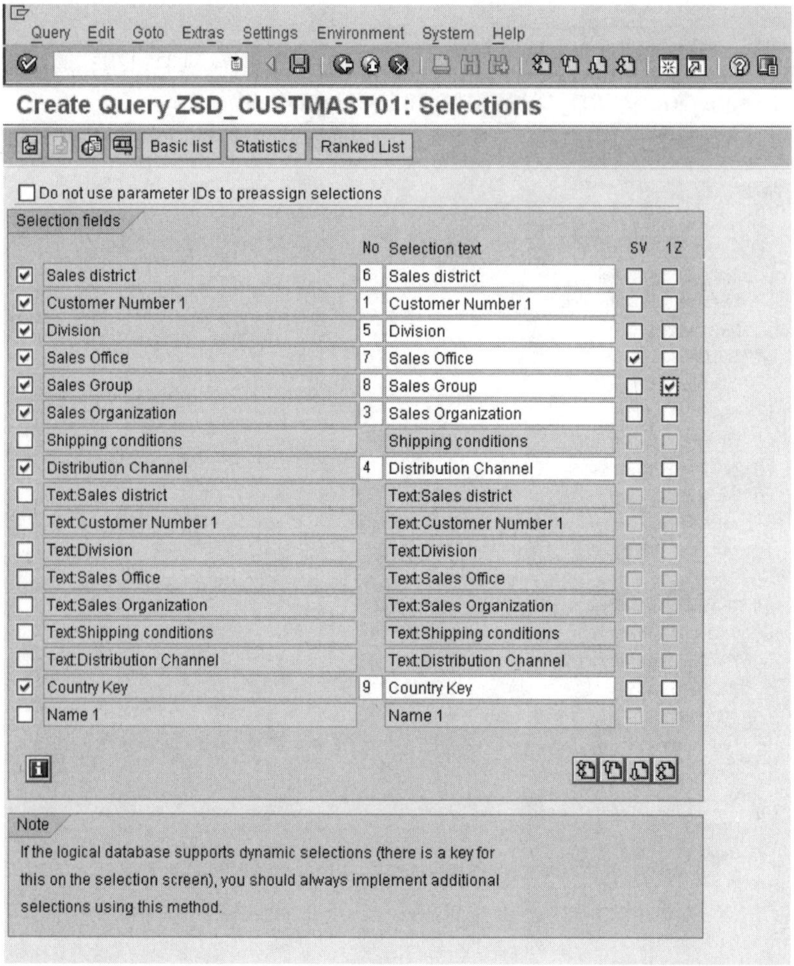

Copyright by SAP AG

FIGURE 11-24 Selection screen fields

system and some other system (such as a legacy system). The data is structured. The standard SAP format for EDI between systems is the intermediate document, called the IDOC.

The IDOC Basic type has the suffix of the version number with the highest number being the latest version. The latest version for sales orders is ORDERS05. The IDOC type has a header control record with a message type, for example, ORDERS which tells the system how to process the inbound IDOC, as well as partner numbers which are used to further control the communication.

Within the IDOC type (for example, ORDERS05) are IDOC segments (for example, E1EDK01). Within an IDOC segment are a number of fields. Each field in the IDOC may have a value. The values in these fields define the data being communicated.

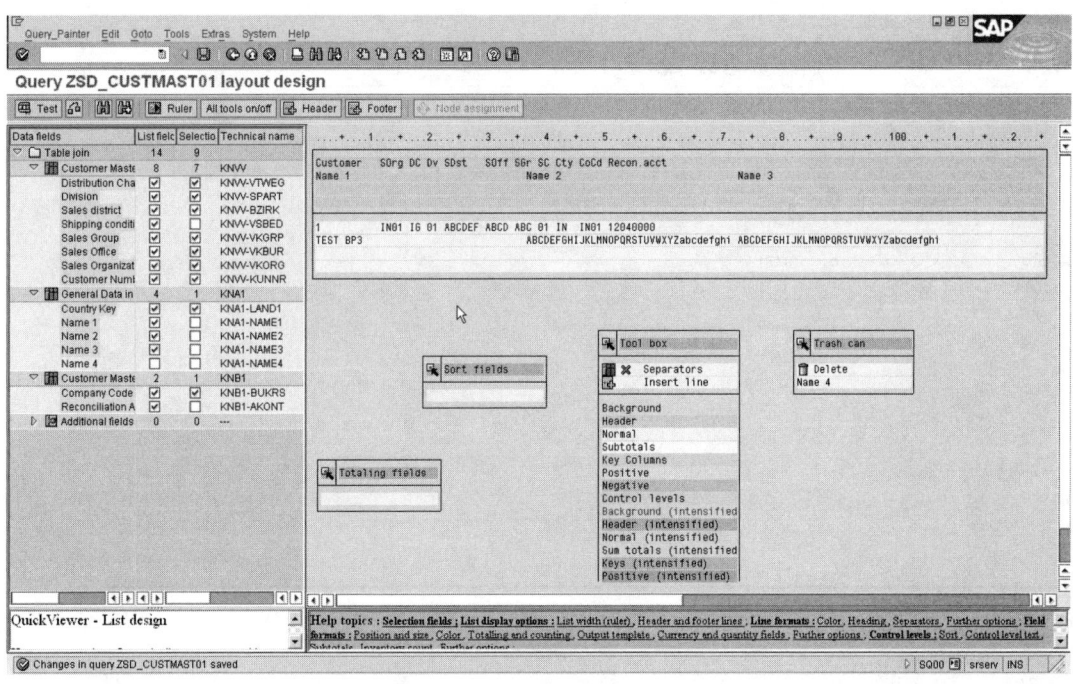

Copyright by SAP AG

FIGURE 11-25 Query layout

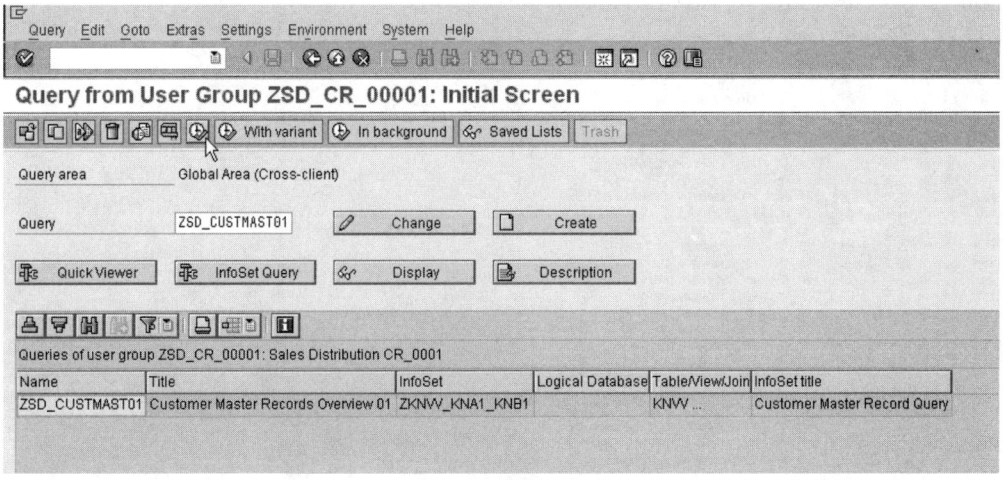

Copyright by SAP AG

FIGURE 11-26 Executing the query

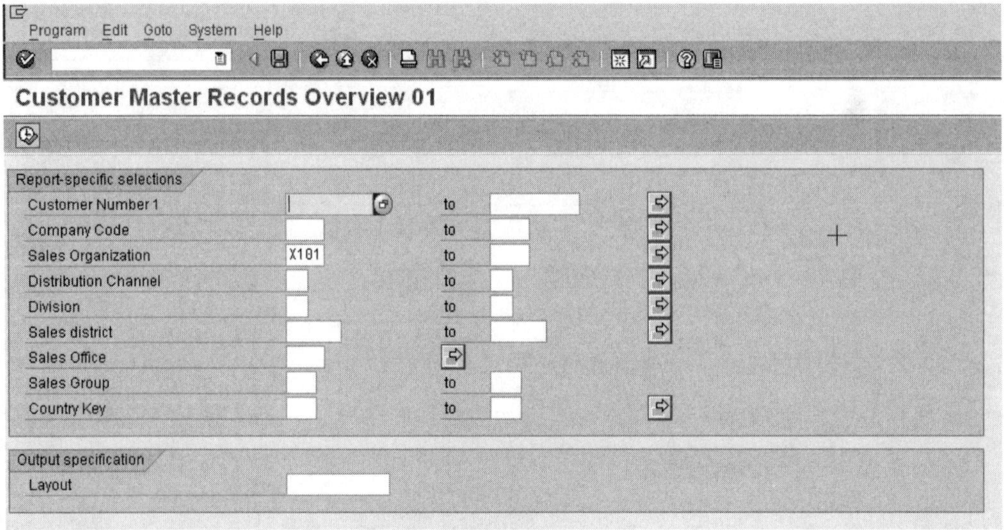

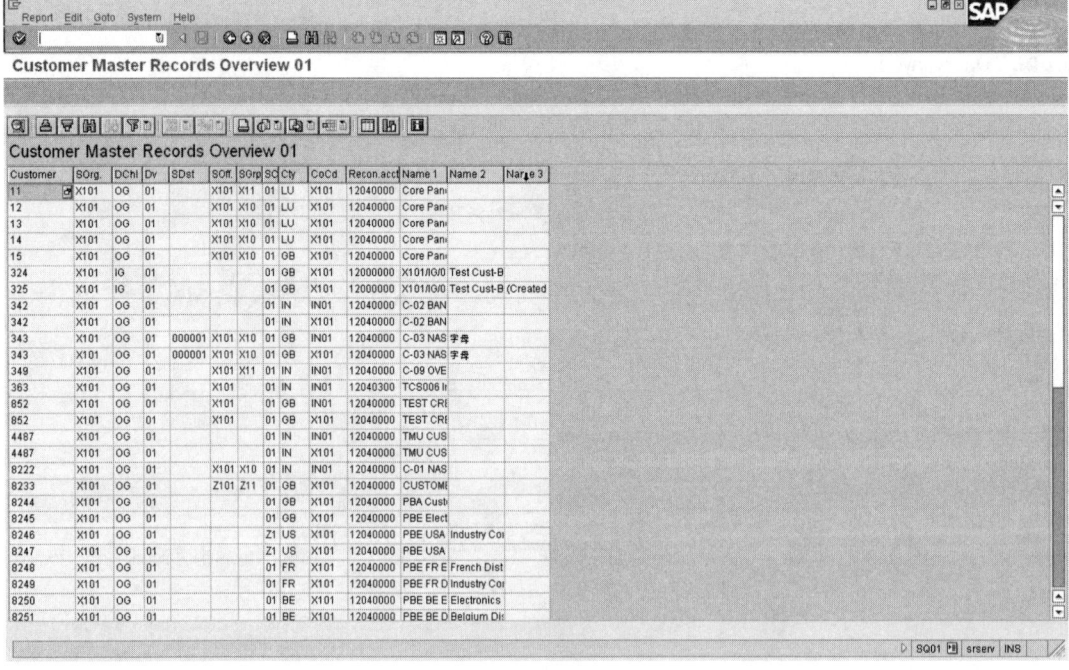

FIGURE 11-27 Selection parameters

Customer Master Records Overview 01

Customer	SOrg.	DChl	Dv	SDst	SOff.	SGrp	SG	Cty	CoCd	Recon.acct	Name 1	Name 2	Name 3
11	X101	OG	01		X101	X11	01	LU	X101	12040000	Core Pan		
12	X101	OG	01		X101	X10	01	LU	X101	12040000	Core Pan		
13	X101	OG	01		X101	X10	01	LU	X101	12040000	Core Pan		
14	X101	OG	01		X101	X10	01	LU	X101	12040000	Core Pan		
15	X101	OG	01		X101	X10	01	GB	X101	12040000	Core Pan		
324	X101	IG	01				01	GB	X101	12000000	X101/IG/0	Test Cust-B	
325	X101	IG	01				01	GB	X101	12000000	X101/IG/0	Test Cust-B	(Created
342	X101	OG	01				01	IN	IN01	12040000	C-02 BAN		
342	X101	OG	01				01	IN	X101	12040000	C-02 BAN		
343	X101	OG	01	000001	X101	X10	01	GB	IN01	12040000	C-03 NAS	字母	
343	X101	OG	01	000001	X101	X10	01	GB	X101	12040000	C-03 NAS	字母	
349	X101	OG	01		X101	X11	01	IN	IN01	12040000	C-09 OVE		
363	X101	OG	01		X101		01	IN	IN01	12040300	TCS006 I		
852	X101	OG	01		X101		01	GB	IN01	12040000	TEST CRI		
852	X101	OG	01		X101		01	GB	X101	12040000	TEST CRI		
4487	X101	OG	01				01	IN	IN01	12040000	TMU CUS		
4487	X101	OG	01				01	IN	X101	12040000	TMU CUS		
8222	X101	OG	01		X101	X10	01	IN	IN01	12040000	C-01 NAS		
8233	X101	OG	01		Z101	Z11	01	GB	X101	12040000	CUSTOMI		
8244	X101	OG	01				01	GB	X101	12040000	PBA Cust		
8245	X101	OG	01				01	GB	X101	12040000	PBE Elect		
8246	X101	OG	01				Z1	US	X101	12040000	PBE USA	Industry Coi	
8247	X101	OG	01				Z1	US	X101	12040000	PBE USA		
8248	X101	OG	01				01	FR	X101	12040000	PBE FR E	French Dist	
8249	X101	OG	01				01	FR	X101	12040000	PBE FR D	Industry Coi	
8250	X101	OG	01				01	BE	X101	12040000	PBE BE E	Electronics	
8251	X101	OG	01				01	BE	X101	12040000	PBE BE D	Belgium Di	

FIGURE 11-28 Results of executed query

Transaction Codes

- [WEDI] IDOC and EDI Basis (a central point for all IDOC- and EDI-related transactions).
- [WE02] Display IDOC.
- [WE09] In database (allows one to search for data within a segment).
- [WE60] Documentation of IDOC types. (Use this for HTML help information on IDOC types and IDOC segments.)
- [WE19] Test tool, you are able to manipulate values within the IDOC segment, before importing the IDOC into your system.
- [BD87] Status Monitor for ALE messages (permits one to re-process an IDOC).

mySAP CRM and BDOCs

It is impossible to summarize an entire system of functionality in a paragraph. This section has little if anything to do with CRM. Instead it will serve as a very basic introduction to business documents (BDOCs) and replication to mySAP ERP only.

From Chapter 1 you will remember that mySAP ERP is one of the applications within the mySAP Business Suite. The mySAP Business Suite includes

- mySAP ERP
- mySAP Supply Chain Management (SCM)
- mySAP Customer Relationship Management (CRM)
- mySAP Supplier Relationship Management (SRM)
- mySAP Supplier Relationship Management (SRM)
- mySAP Product Lifestyle Management (PLM)

The latest release of mySAP ERP is SAP ERP Central Component (ECC6) and within mySAP ERP are a number of applications, such as financials and manufacturing. Of these applications we have been focusing on the Sales and Distribution application.

Data is communicated between mySAP ERP and mySAP CRM with BDOCs, which are technically similar to IDOCs. BDOCs are used to communicate data between two systems.

There are two types of BDOCs: the message BDOC, or MBDOC, and the synchronizing BDOC, or SBDOC. The MBDOC is used to replicate data between mySAP CRM and mySAP ERP. The SBDOC is used for replication and re-alignment between mySAP CRM and mobile clients.

The following transaction codes are executed within mySAP CRM:

- [SBDM] BDOC modeler
- [SMW01] Displays BDOC messages
- [SMW02] Displays BDOC messages summary

Transaction codes [SMW01] and [SMW02] (from CRM) are used to show all BDOCs handled by the CRM middleware.

You can also use the CRM middleware monitoring Cockpit (transaction code [SMWP] from CRM) to perform analysis on the middleware.

You can refer to OSS Note 526853 for assistance on BDOC error analysis from within mySAP CRM.

Additionally, in CRM there is the Administration Console that manages the sites and subscriptions of CRM objects—such as sales documents. The Administration Console is used, for instance, to control if a sales document created in CRM is automatically published to mySAP ERP. To use the CRM Administration Console, use transaction code [SMOEAC].

Sundry Tips

There are a number of additional transaction codes that may assist you as an advanced user, of SAP, which I have not been able to place in other areas of this book. I have therefore listed them here as a reference in case you too find them useful.

Useful Transaction Codes

Here are some useful transaction codes un-related to Sales and Distribution.

- [SM12] Transaction to delete locked entries
- [SU53] Last authorization object check which was used
- [SU24] Authorizations and object checks
- [SE84] ABAP development workbench
- [OSS1] Online Service System (OSS login)
- [OY19] Cross System Viewer
- [SE10] Transport organizer
- [SCAT] Computer Aided test Tool (CATT)
- [SECATT] Extended Computer Aided Test Tool (eCATT)
- [SE30] ABAP runtime analysis
- [ST05] Performance trace (including SQL trace)
- [SE36] Logical databases
- [SE38] ABAP Editor
- [SA38] Program execution
- [SE39] Split screen editor (including across systems)
- [SM36] Define background job
- [SM37] Job selection
- [ST22] Dump Analysis
- [SU01] Users
- [SM50] Process Overview
- [SM30] Table Maintenance
- [SM04] User list
- [/h] Activate debugging

Transaction Codes Related to Sales and Distribution

A t the time of this writing, there are in excess of 82,000 standard SAP transaction codes in mySAP ERP. The transaction codes listed here are not only those used in the business process, or master data maintenance, but are also transaction codes relating to configuration. Instead of removing irrelevant transaction codes, I have left them in this list in case anyone wanted a quick reference.

Transaction Code	Text
V	Quickstart RKCOWUSL
V+01	Create Sales Call
V+02	Create Telephone Call
V+03	Create Sales Letter
V+11	Create Direct Mailing
V+21	Create Sales Prospect
V+22	Create Competitor
V+23	Create Business Partner
V-01	Create Sales Order
V-02	Create Quotation
V-03	Create Ordering Party (Sales)
V-04	Create Invoice Recipient (Sales)
V-05	Create Payer (Sales)
V-06	Create Consignee (Sales)
V-07	Create One-Time Customer (Sales)
V-08	Create Payer (Centrally)

Transaction Code	Text
V-09	Create Ordering Party (Centrally)
V-11	Create Carrier
V-12	Create Customer Hierarchy Nodes
V-31	Create Freight 1
V-32	Create Freight 1 with Reference
V-33	Change Freight 1
V-34	Create Freight 1
V-35	Create Freight 1
V-36	Create Freight 1 with Reference
V-37	Change Freight 2
V-38	Display Freight 2
V-40	Display Taxes (Export)
V-41	Create Material Price
V-42	Create Material Price w/ref.
V-43	Change Material Price
V-44	Display Material Price
V-45	Create Price List
V-46	Create Price List w/ref.
V-47	Change Price List
V-48	Display Price List
V-49	Create Customer-Specific Price
V-50	Create Customer-Spec. Price w/ref.
V-51	Change Cust. Price
V-52	Display Cust. Price
V-61	Create Cust. Disc./Surcharge
V-62	Create Customer Disc./Surch. w/ref
V-63	Change Cust. Disc./Surcharge
V-64	Display Cust. Disc./Surcharge
V-65	Create Mat. Disc./Surcharge
V-66	Create w/ref. Material Disc./Surcharge
V-67	Change Mat. Disc./Surcharge
V-68	Display Mat.Disc/Surcharge
V-69	Create Price Grp. Disc./Surch.
V-70	Create w/ref. Price Group Disc./Surch.
V-71	Change Price Grp. Disc./Surch.
V-72	Display Price Grp. Disc./Surch.

Transaction Code	Text
V-73	Create Mat. Pr. Grp. Disc./Surch.
V-74	Create w/ref. Mat. Pr. Grp. Disc./Surch.
V-75	Change Mat. Pr. Grp. Disc./Surch.
V-76	Display Mat. Pr. Grp. Disc./Surch.
V-77	Create Cust/MatPrGrp Disc/Su
V-78	Create w/ref.Cust/MatPrGrp Disc/Surc
V-79	Change Cust/MatPrGrp Disc/Su
V-80	Display Cust/MatPrGrp Disc/Su
V-81	Create Cust/Mat.Disc/Surch.
V-82	Create w/ref.Cust/Mat.Disc/Surcharge
V-83	Change Cust/Mat.Disc/Surch.
V-84	Display Cust/Mat.Disc/Surch.
V-85	Create PGrp/MPrGrp Disc/Surc
V-86	Create w/ref.PrGrp/MatPrGrp Disc/Sur
V-87	Change PGrp/MPrGrp Disc/Surc
V-88	Display PGrp/MPrGrp Disc/Surc
V-89	Create PGrp/MPrGrp Disc/Surc
V-90	Create w/ref.PrGrp/Mat Disc/Surch.
V-91	Change PGrp/Mat Disc/Surch.
V-92	Display PGrp/Mat.Disc/Surch.
V-93	Create Domestic Taxes
V-94	Create Domestic Taxes w/Reference
V-95	Change Domestic Taxes
V-96	Display Domestic Taxes
V-97	Create Cross-border Taxes
V-98	Create Cross-border Taxes
V-99	Change Cross-border Taxes
V.00	List of Incomplete Documents
V.01	Sales Order Error Log
V.02	List of Incomplete Sales Orders
V.03	List of Incomplete Inquiries
V.04	List of Incomplete Quotations
V.05	List of Incomplete Sched.Agreements
V.06	List of Incomplete Contracts
V.07	Periodic billing
V.14	Sales Orders Blocked for Delivery

Transaction Code	Text
V.15	Display Backorders
V.20	Display Collective Delivery Process.
V.21	Log of Collective Run
V.22	Display Collective Runs
V.23	Release Orders for Billing
V.24	Display Work List for Invoice Lists
V.25	Release Customer Expected Price
V.26	Selection by Object Status
V/03	Create Condition Table (SD Price)
V/04	Change Condition Table (Sales Pr.)
V/05	Display Condition Table: (Sales Pr.)
V/06	Condition Categories: SD Pricing
V/07	Maintain Access (Sales Price)
V/08	Conditions: Procedure for A V
V/09	Condition Types: Account Determin.
V/10	Account Determination: Access Seqnc
V/11	Conditions: Account Determin.Proced.
V/12	Account Determination: Create Table
V/13	Account Determination: Change Table
V/14	Account Determination: Display Table
V/21	View V_TVSA_NAC
V/22	View V_TVTY_NAC
V/23	View V_TVST_KOM
V/24	View V_TVTK_NAC
V/25	View V_TVFK_NAC
V/26	View V_TVKK_NAC
V/27	Conditions for Output Determination
V/30	Output Types (Sales Document)
V/31	View V_TNAPN Appl V3
V/32	Sales Doc Output Determtn Procedure
V/33	View V_TNAPN Appl V7
V/34	Maintain Condition Type Appl V2
V/35	Customizing for Output Determination
V/36	Delivery Output Determination Procdr
V/37	Assign Customer
V/38	Maintain Condition Type Appl V4

Transaction Code	Text
V/39	View V_TNAPR Appl V6
V/40	Maintain Condition Type Appl V3
V/41	View V_TVST_NAC
V/42	Output Detrmntn Procdr (Billing Doc)
V/43	View V_TVAK_NAC
V/44	Maintain Condition Type Appl DB
V/45	View V_TNAPN Appl K1
V/46	Output Determination Procdr Customer
V/47	View V_TNAPN Appl V1
V/48	Access Sequences (Sales Document)
V/49	View V_TNAPN Appl. V2
V/50	Access Sequence (Delivery)
V/51	View V_TNAPN Appl. V6
V/52	Access Sequences Appl. V3
V/53	View V_TNAPR Appl. V4
V/54	Access Sequence (Billing Document)
V/55	View V_TVBUR_NA
V/56	Output: Cond.Table - Create Orders
V/57	Output - Cond.Table - Change Order
V/58	Output - Cond.Table - Display Order
V/59	Output - Cond.Table - Create Dlv.
V/60	Output - Cond.Table - Change Dlv.
V/61	Output - Cond.Table - Display Dlv.
V/62	Output - Cond.Table - Create BillDoc
V/63	Output - Cond.Table - Change BillDoc
V/64	Output - Cond.Table - Display BillDc
V/65	Output CondTable/Create SalesSupport
V/66	Output CondTab./Change Sales Support
V/67	Output CondTab/Display Sales Support
V/68	Maintain Access Seqnc (Sales Actvty)
V/69	View V_TVAP_NAC
V/70	Maintain Condition Type Appl K1
V/71	View V_TVLK_NAC
V/72	Output Determination Procedure (CAS)
V/73	View V_TVLP_NAC
V/76	Maintain Product Hierarchy

Transaction Code	Text
V/77	Output -ConditTable- Create Transport
V/78	Output -CondTable- Change Transport
V/79	Output -CondTable- Display Transport
V/80	Access Sequence (Transport)
V/81	View V_TNAPR Appl V7
V/82	Maintain condition type Appl. V7
V/83	View V_TNAPR Appl V3
V/84	Output Determination Transport
V/85	View V_TVKO_NAC
V/86	Conditions: V_T681F for B V1
V/87	Conitions: V_T681F for B V2
V/88	Conditions: V_T681F for B V3
V/89	Conditions: V_T681F for B V5
V/90	Conditions: V_T681F for B V6
V/91	Conditions: V_T681F for B V7
V/92	Conditions: V_T681F for B K1
V/93	Output -CondTable- Create Packaging
V/94	Output -CondTable- Change Packaging
V/95	Output -CondTable- Display Packaging
V/96	Access Sequence (Packaging)
V/97	Output Type Packaging
V/99	Output Determntn Procedure Packaging
V/C1	Strategy Types: Batch Determin.SD
V/C2	Access: Maintain Batch Determin. SD
V/C3	Batch Determin: Procedure for SD
V/C4	Search Types: Optimize Access
V/C5	SD Tab. T683C Search Proced.Det.
V/C6	Conditions: V_T681F for H V
V/C7	CondTable: Create (Batches, SD)
V/C8	CondTable: Change (Batch, SD)
V/C9	CondTable: Display (Batches, SD)
V/CA	Automatic Batch Determin.in SlsOrder
V/CL	Automatic Batch Determin.in Delivery
V/G1	Output CondTab/Create Group
V/G2	Output CondTab Change Group
V/G3	Output CondTab/Display Group

Transaction Code	Text
V/G4	Access Sequence (Groups)
V/G5	View V_TNAPR Appl K1
V/G6	Maintain Condition Type Appl V5
V/G7	View V_TNAPR Appl V1
V/G8	Output Determinatn Procedure Groups
V/G9	View VN_TNAPR Appl V2
V/I1	Activation of Condition Index
V/I2	Set Up Condition Indices
V/I3	Conditions: Pricing SD - Index
V/I4	Conditions: Pricing SD - Index
V/I5	Condit: Pricing SD - Index in Backgr
V/I6	Display conditions using index
V/LA	Create Pricing Report
V/LB	Change Pricing Report
V/LC	Display Pricing Report
V/LD	Execute Pricing Report
V/LE	Generate Pricing Reports
V/N1	Maintain Accesses (free goods - sls)
V/N2	Create Free Goods Table
V/N3	Display Free Goods Table (SD)
V/N4	Free Goods Types - Sales
V/N5	Free Goods: Procedure for SD
V/N6	Free Goods Procedure Determ. SD
V/T1	Maintain Profile
V/T2	Network Types
V/T3	Deadlines:Assign NetwProf.to DlvType
V/T4	Maintain Deadline Functions
V/T5	Maintain Deviation Reasons
V/T6	Maintain Assignment to Plant
V/T7	Assign Shipping Deadlines to Shipmnt
V/T8	Shipping Deadlines-Graphics Settings
V101	Initial Sales Menu
V12L3V_A	Create Pricing Report for Camp. Det.
V12L3V_B	Change Pricing Report for Camp. Det.
V12L3V_C	Display Pricing Report for Camp.Det.
V12L3V_D	Execute Pricing Report for Camp.Det.

Transaction Code	Text
V12LCA	Create Pricing Report
V12LCB	Change Pricing Report
V12LDV_A	Create Pricing Report
V12LDV_B	Change Pricing Report
V12LDV_C	Display Pricing Report
V12LDV_D	Execute Pricing Report
V12LEV_A	Create Pricing Report (Rebate)
V12LEV_B	Change Pricing Report (Rebate)
V12LEV_C	Display Transactions (Rebate)
V12LEV_D	Execute Pricing Report (Rebate)
V12L_A	Create Pricing Report
V12L_B	Change Pricing Report
V12L_C	Display Pricing Report
V12L_D	Execute Pricing Report
V23	Sales Documents Blocked for Billing
V633	Customer Conversion Dec.Shipping
VA00	Initial Sales Menu
VA01	Create Sales Order
VA02	Change Sales Order
VA03	Display Sales Order
VA05	List of Sales Orders
VA05N	List of Sales Orders
VA07	Compare Sales - Purchasing (Order)
VA08	Compare Sales - Purchasing (Org.Dt.)
VA11	Create Inquiry
VA12	Change Inquiry
VA13	Display Inquiry
VA14L	Sales Documents Blocked for Delivery
VA15	Inquiries List
VA15N	Inquiries List
VA21	Create Quotation
VA22	Change Quotation
VA23	Display Quotation
VA25	Quotations List
VA25N	List of Quotations
VA26	Collective Processing for Quotations

Transaction Code	Text
VA31	Create Scheduling Agreement
VA32	Change Scheduling Agreement
VA33	Display Scheduling Agreement
VA35	List of Scheduling Agreements
VA35N	List of Scheduling Agreements
VA41	Create Contract
VA42	Change Contract
VA42W	Workflow for Master Contract
VA43	Display Contract
VA44	Actual Overhead: Sales Order
VA45	List of Contracts
VA45N	List of Contracts
VA46	Coll.Subseq.Processing f.Contracts
VA51	Create Item Proposal
VA52	Change Item Proposal
VA53	Display Item Proposal
VA55	List of Item Proposals
VA88	Actual Settlement: Sales Orders
VA94	Load Commodity Codes for Japan
VA94X	Load Commodity Codes for Japan
VA95	Merge Commodity Code/Import Code No.
VACF	Commit. carried forwrd: Sales orders
VAKC	Items in Sales Order Configuration
VAKP	Configuration: Maintain T180
VALU	Valuation Analysis
VAL_RELN	Release Note Approval
VAM4	Merge: Japan - Commodity Code
VAN1	Actual Reval.: Sales Order
VAP1	Create Contact Person
VAP2	Change Contact Person
VAP3	Display Contact Person
VARA	Archiving
VARC	SD: User Guide to Archiving
VARCH	Change Report Variant
VARD	Display Report Variant
VARK	Archiving

Transaction Code	Text
VARR	Archiving
VASK	Deleting Groups
VAUN	Reload
VB(1	Rebate Number Ranges
VB(2	Rebate Agreement Type Maintenance
VB(3	Condition Type Groups Overview
VB(4	Condition Types in ConditType Groups
VB(5	Assignment Condition - CondTypeGrp
VB(6	Rebate Group Maintenance
VB(7	Rebate Agreement Settlement
VB(8	List Rebate Agreements
VB(9	Maintain Sales Deal Types
VB(A	Promotion Type Maintenance
VB(B	Copying Control Maintenance
VB(C	Maintain Copying Control
VB(D	Rebate Agreement Settlement
VB01	Create Material Listing/Exclusion
VB02	Change Material Listing/Exclusion
VB03	Display Material Listing/Exclusion
VB04	Reference Material Listing/Exclusion
VB11	Create Material Substitution
VB12	Change Material Substitution
VB13	Display Material Substitution
VB14	Reference Material Substitution
VB21	Create Sales Deal
VB22	Change Sales Deal
VB23	Display Sales Promotion
VB25	List of Sales Deals
VB31	Create Promotion
VB32	Change Promotion
VB33	Display Promotion
VB35	Promotions List
VB41	Create Cross-Selling
VB42	Change Cross-Selling
VB43	Display Cross-Selling
VB44	Copy Cross-Selling

Transaction Code	Text
VBBLOCK	Documents Blocked for Billing
VBELN_SET_GENERATE	Generate Sales Order Set
VBG1	Create Material Grouping
VBG2	Change Material Grouping
VBG3	Display Material Grouping
VBK0	Bonus Buy Selection
VBK1	Create Bonus Buy
VBK2	Change Bonus Buy
VBK3	Display Bonus Buy
VBK6	Delete Bonus Buy
VBKA	Bonus Buy: Access Sequences
VBKB	Bonus Buy: Create Condition Table
VBKC	Bonus Buy: Display Condition Table
VBKD	Bonus Buy: Condition Types
VBKE	Bonus Buy: Calculation Schema
VBKF	Bonus Buy: Schema Determination
VBKG	Bonus Buy: Field Catalog
VBN1	Free goods - Create (SD)
VBN2	Free goods - Change (SD)
VBN3	Free goods - Display (SD)
VBO1	Create Rebate Agreement
VBO2	Change Rebate Agreement
VBO3	Display Rebate Agreement
VBOE	Currency Conversion Rebate Agreements
VBOF	Rebate: Update Billing Documents
VC/1	List of Customers
VC/2	Customer Master Data Sheet
VC/A	Sales Activity Description 01
VC/B	Sales Activity Description 02
VC/C	Sales Activity Description 03
VC/D	Sales Activity Description 04
VC/E	Sales Activity Description 05
VC/F	Sales Activity Description 06
VC/G	Sales Activity Description 07
VC/H	Sales Activity Description 08
VC/I	Sales Activity Description 09

Transaction Code	Text
VC/J	Sales Activity Description 10
VC00	Sales Support
VC01	Create Sales Activity
VC010102	Only Follow-up Activities
VC010103	Do not Delete Mail. Camp.+Addresses
VC010104	Internet Mailing
VC01N	Edit Sales Activity
VC01N_DRAG_KONTAKT	Edit Sales Activity
VC01N_DRAG_MAILING	Edit Sales Activity
VC01N_M	Edit Mailing
VC02	Change Sales Activity
VC03	Display Sales Activity
VC05	Sales Support Monitor
VC06	Parallel Processing for Address List
VC10	Report Tree - Select Addresses
VC15	Crossmatching
VCAR	Archiving
VCC1	Payment Cards: Worklist
VCH1	Create Batch Search Strategy
VCH2	Change Batch Search Strategy
VCH3	Display Batch Search Strategy
VCHECKBONUS	Customizing Checks for Rebate
VCHECKT683	Customizing Check Pricing Procedure
VCHECKT685A	Customizing Check Condition Types
VCHECKTVCPF	Customizing Check Copying Control
VCHECKVOFA	Customizing Check Billing Types
VCHP	C SD Table TVLP Deliveries: Items
VCOMP	Completed SD Documents
VCR1	Competitive Products
VCTP	Maintain Allocation Structure
VCU3	Display Incompletion Log
VCUAC	Display Anti-dumping - Qty-dependent
VCUAE	Display Anti-dumping - Weight-depend
VCUDC	Display 3rd Country - Qty-dependent
VCUDE	Display 3rd Country - Weight-depend.
VCUN	Reload

Transaction Code	Text
VCUP1	Display Preference - Qty-dependent
VCUP2	Display Preference - Weight-depend.
VCUPC	Display Pharma.Prod. - Qty-dependent
VCUPF	Display Pharma.Prod. - Weight-depen.
VCUST	Customer List
VCUZ1	Display Ceiling - Quantity-dependent
VCUZ2	Display Ceiling - Weight-dependent
VCUZC	Display Quota - Quantity-dependent
VCUZE	Display Quota - Weight-dependent
VCUZP	Display Ceilings - Percentage
VD01	Create Customer (Sales)
VD02	Change Customer (Sales)
VD03	Display Customer (Sales)
VD04	Customer Changes (SD)
VD05	Block customer (sales)
VD06	Mark customer for deletion (sales)
VD07	Ref. doc. det. for ref. customer
VD51	Maintain Customer-Material Info
VD52	Maintain Cust-Mat.Info w/Select.Scrn
VD53	Display Customer-Material Info
VD54	Display Customer-Material Info
VD59	List Customer-Material-Info
VDBLOCK	Documents Blocked for Delivery
VDDI	EMU currency conversion cust. Master
VDF1	Display Format Date Type/Period
VDH1	Customer Hierarchy Maintenance (SD)
VDH1N	Display/Maintain Customer Hierarchy
VDH2	Display Customer Hierarchy
VDH2N	Display Customer Hierarchy
VE01	INTRASTAT: Selection Dispatch to EU
VE02	INTRASTAT: Create Form - Germany
VE03	INTRASTAT: Create File - Germany
VE04	EXTRASTAT: Data Selection for Export
VE05	EXTRASTAT: Create File - Germany
VE06	INTRASTAT: Paper Form - Belgian
VE07	Create INTRASTAT Form for France

Transaction Code	Text
VE08	Create INTRASTAT File for Italy
VE09	Create INTRASTAT File for Belgium
VE10	Create INTRASTAT File for Holland
VE11	Create INTRASTAT File for Spain
VE12	Create INTRASTAT Form for Holland
VE13	KOBRA data selection: export Germany
VE14	Create KOBRA file for Germany
VE15	Create disk - INTRA/EXTRA/KOBRA/VAR
VE16	Create INTRASTAT form for Austria
VE17	Create INTRASTAT form for Sweden
VE18	SED data selection for USA exporters
VE19	Create SED form for USA
VE20	Create AERP file for USA
VE21	VAR: Selection of bill. docs Switz.
VE22	Create VAR form for Switzerland
VE23	V.A.R.: File - Switzerland
VE24	Comm. Code Number Information (old)
VE24X	Commodity Code Information
VE25	SED: Selection: USA Carriers
VE26	Number of CAP Products List
VE27	HMF: Selection - USA
VE28	Name of Market Organization
VE29	Assigned Documents for Each License
VE30	Existing licenses
VE31	Blocked SD Documents
VE32	INTRASTAT: Paper Form - Ireland
VE33	INTRASTAT: Paper Form - U.K.
VE34	INTRASTAT: Paper Form - Belgian
VE35	Number of Market Organization
VE36	Group for CAP Products
VE37	INTRASTAT: File - France
VE38	INTRASTAT: Selection Simulation - EU
VE39	EXTRASTAT: Selection Simulation
VE40	KOBRA: Selection Simulation
VE41	VAR: Selection of bill. docs Switz.
VE42	INTRASTAT: File - Denmark

Transaction Code	Text
VE43	SED: Selection Exp. USA Simulation
VE44	SED: Select Carrier USA Simulation
VE45	INTRASTAT: Paper Form - Greece
VE46	INTRASTAT: File - Finland
VE47	PRODCOM No.
VE48	Customs Quota Code
VE49	Code for Pharmaceutical Products
VE50	Legal Regulations
VE51	Legal Regulation/License Type
VE52	Country/Legal Regulations
VE53	Export Situation for a Country
VE54	Preference Determination: Collective
VE55	Preference Determination: Individual
VE56	Check Export Control for Consistency
VE57	Country Classification
VE58	Product Classification
VE59	Legal Regulations/Country Grouping
VE60	Exp.Ctrl Class Accord.to Legal Reg.
VE61	Legal Regulations/Embargo Group
VE62	Material Group Accord.to Legal Reg.
VE63	Customs Areas
VE64	Commodity Code/Customs Areas
VE65	Preference Reg./Percentage Rates
VE66	Preference Procedure
VE67	Aggregate Vendor Declarations
VE68	Request Vendor Declarations
VE69	Incompletion Log
VE70	Place of Manufacture
VE71	Preference: Determine Customs Area
VE72	Export - Billing Documents
VE73	Goods Catalog: Create Document
VE74	Goods Catalog: Create Diskette
VE75	Preference Code
VE76	Anti-dumping Code
VE77	Preference: Tariff Alternation
VE78	Plant Parameters for Vendor Decl.

Transaction Code	Text
VE79	Quota Code Determination
VE80	Assign Chapter to Section
VE81	Check Report: General FT Data
VE81X	Incompleteness: FT Material Data
VE82	Check Report: Export Control Data
VE82X	Incompleteness: Export Control Data
VE83	Check Report: Preference Data
VE83X	Incompleteness: Preference Material
VE84	Monitoring: Purchasing Info Records
VE85	Change Statistical Value - Import
VE86	Display Statistical Value - Import
VE87	Change Stat.Value - Subcontracting
VE88	Change Statistical Value - Export
VE89	Display Statistical Value - Export
VE90	Change Preference Values
VE91	Display Preference Values
VE92	Create INTRASTAT tape Luxembourg
VE93	EDI-CUSTEC Austria
VE94	Load Commodity Code for EU Countries
VE94X	Load Commodity Code for EU Countries
VE95	Create INTRASTAT papers: Portugal
VE96	EXTRASTAT Data Select.: Init. Screen
VE97	Create EXTRASTAT tape: Netherlands
VE98	Sales Invoice Values per Period
VE99	Create Document - Austria
VEA1	FT - Create Commodity Code Import
VEA2	FT: Create Commodity Code Export
VEA3	EXTRASTAT: File Version France
VEA4	EXTRASTAT: File Version France
VEA5	EXTRASTAT: File Version France
VEB1	Period-end Closings: Control
VEB2	DtA: Special Rule Countries/Regions
VEB5	Calculate Assemblies Individually
VEB6	Calculate Assemblies Collectively
VEB9	Customer Exits: Print Control
VECN	Profitability and Sales Accounting

Transaction Code	Text
VECS	Legal Control: Special Char. Code
VECZ	INTRASTAT: File - Czech Republic
VED1	Print Parameters for Export Docs
VED2	Form Data Control
VEFU	Foreign Trade: Add INTRASTAT Data
VEFUX	FT-GOV: Change transaction INTRASTAT
VEG1	Handling Unit Group 1
VEG2	Handling Unit Group 2
VEG3	Handling Unit Group 3
VEG4	Handling Unit 4
VEG5	Handling Unit Group 5
VEGK	FT: Comb. Bus Trans.Type - Procedure
VEGR	Material Group: Packaging Materials
VEHU	INTRASTAT: File - Hungary
VEI0	Create INTRASTAT CUSDEC EDI IE
VEI1	Display IDoc Import
VEI2	Display IDoc Export
VEI3	Display Stat.Value - Subcontracting
VEI4	Merge: Remaining Commodity Codes
VEI5	Create value limit subcontracting
VEI6	EDI: IDoc List - Import Basis
VEI7	Create INTRASTAT CUSDEC EDI GB
VEI8	Create INTRASTAT CUSDEC EDI AT
VEI9	Create INTRASTAT CUSDEC EDI ES
VEIA	Create INTRASTAT CUSDEC EDI SE
VEIAE	EXTRASTAT Archiving
VEIAI	INTRASTAT Archiving
VEIB	Create INTRASTAT CUSDEC EDI PT
VEIC	Create INTRASTAT CUSDEC EDI FI
VEID	Create INTRASTAT CUSDEC EDI LU
VEIE	SAPMSED8: Call EXPINV02
VEII	SAPMSED8: Call IMPINV01
VEIV	Foreign Trade: Add EXTRASTAT Data
VEIW	Create file INTRA/EXTRA/KOBRA
VEIX	Create file INTRA/EXTRA/KOBRA
VEIY	Create file INTRA/EXTRA/KOBRA

Transaction Code	Text
VEIZ	Create file INTRA/EXTRA/KOBRA
VEKU	For. Trade: Change KOBRA Documents
VEM4	Merge: EU - Commodity Code
VEPL	Create INTRASTAT CUSDEC EDI PL
VEPR	Customs Log
VESK	Create INTRASTAT CUSDEC EDI SK
VEU4	Load Commodity Code-Other Countries
VEU4X	Load Commodity Code-Other Countries
VEXP	Expiring SD Documents
VEXU	Foreign Trade: Add EXTRASTAT Data
VEXUX	FT-GOV: Change transaction EXTRASTAT
VF00	Access Billing
VF01	Create Billing Document
VF02	Change Billing Document
VF03	Display Billing Document
VF04	Maintain Billing Due List
VF04_AIS	VF04_AIS
VF05	List Billing Documents
VF05N	List of Billing Documents
VF06	Batch Billing
VF07	Display Bill. Document from Archive
VF08	Billing for Ext. Delivery
VF11	Cancel Billing Document
VF21	Create Invoice List
VF22	Change invoice list
VF23	Display Invoice List
VF24	Edit Work List for Invoice Lists
VF25	List of Invoice Lists
VF26	Cancellation Invoice List
VF27	Display Invoice List From Archive
VF31	Output from Billing Documents
VF42	Update Sales Documents
VF44	Revenue Recognition: Worklist
VF45	Revenue recognition: Revenue report
VF46	Revenue Recognition: Cancellation
VF47	Revenue Recognition:ConsistencyCheck

Transaction Code	Text
VF48	Revenue Recognition: Compare Report
VFAE	Archive EXTRASTAT Documents
VFAI	Archive INTRASTAT Documents
VFBS	Next Screen Control
VFBV	Reorganization of discount-rel. Data
VFBWG	Bulkiness and Minimum Weights
VFBZ	Scale Basis for Pricing
VFLI	Log Tax Exemption
VFP1	Set Billing Date
VFRB	Retro-billing
VFS3	Adjusting Info Structure S060
VFSN	Reorganization Info Structure S060
VFUN	Reload
VFX2	Display Blocked Billing Documents
VFX3	List Blocked Billing Documents
VG01	Create Group
VG02	Change Group
VG03	Display Group
VGK1	Create Group for Delivery
VGK2	Change Group for Delivery
VGK3	Display Group for Delivery
VGL1	Create Group for Delivery
VGL2	Change Group for Delivery
VGL3	Display Group for Delivery
VGM1	Create Group for Freight List
VGM2	Change Group for Freight List
VGM3	Display Group for Freight List
VGW1	Create Picking Wave
VGW2	Change Picking Waves
VGW3	Display Picking Waves
VHAR	Maintain/Create Packaging Matl Types
VHZU	Allowed Packaging Material Types
VI00	Shipment Costs
VI01	Create Shipment Costs
VI02	Change Shipment Costs
VI03	Display Shipment Costs

Transaction Code	Text
VI04	Create Shipment Cost Worklist
VI05	Change Shipment Cost Worklist
VI06	Collective Run In Background
VI07	Collective Run In Background
VI08	Display FT Data In Purchasing Doc.
VI08X	Display FT Data In Purchasing Doc.
VI09	Change FT Data in Purchasing Doc.
VI09X	Change FT Data in Purchasing Doc.
VI10	Display FT Data in Billing Document
VI10X	Display FT Data in Billing Document
VI11	List Shipment Costs: Calculation
VI12	List Shipment Costs: Settlement
VI14	Change FT Data in Billing Document
VI14X	Change FT Data in Billing Document
VI15	Display Logs (appl. log)
VI16	Logs for Worklist Shipment
VI17	Display FT Data in Inbound Delivery
VI17X	Display FT Data in Inbound Delivery
VI18	Display Anti-dumping
VI19	Display Third-country Customs Duties
VI20	Display Customs Quota
VI21	Display Pharmaceutical Products
VI22	Display Customs Exemption
VI23	Display Preferential Customs Duties
VI24	Code Number Information - Import
VI24X	Import Code No. Information
VI25	Display Gross Price - Customs
VI26	Display Surcharge/Discount - Customs
VI27	Display Freight - Customs
VI28	EDI: Customs ID Number - Vendor
VI29	Incompletion - Foreign Trade Data
VI30	Declara. to Authorities: Exclusion
VI31	Code Determin. - Pharmaceut.Products
VI32	Code Determination - Anti-dumping
VI33	Customs Exemption
VI34	Preferential Customs Duty Rate

Transaction Code	Text
VI35	Third-country Customs Duty Rate
VI36	CAS Number
VI37	Import Simulation Control
VI38	Determination of Verification Docs
VI39	Authority for Verification Docs
VI40	Preference Type
VI41	Verification Document Type
VI42	Document Type (Export/Import)
VI43	Definition of Section
VI44	Assign Chapter to Section
VI45	Export –> Import Conversion
VI46	Conversion: Mode of Transport
VI47	Conversion of Business Transact.Type
VI48	Conversion of Customs Offices
VI49	Foreign Trade Data Control in Doc.
VI50	Conversion: Import/Export Procedure
VI51	Define Payment Guarantee Procedure
VI52	Define Form of Payment Guarantee
VI53	Change FT Data in Inbound Delivery
VI53X	Change FT Data in Inbound Delivery
VI54	Customs Approval Numbers
VI55	Approval Number per Plant
VI56	EDI: Customs ID Number - Customer
VI57	Legal Control - Order Header
VI58	Legal Control - Order Item
VI59	Legal Control - Delivery Header
VI60	Legal Control - Delivery Item
VI61	Conversion - Reference Country
VI62	Conversion - Reference Country
VI63	Assign Delivery Item Categories
VI64	Display FT Data in Outbound Delivery
VI64X	Display FT Data in Outbound Delivery
VI65	Maintain Market Organizations
VI66	Maintain No. of Market Organizations
VI67	Maintain CAP Products List Nos
VI68	Control Commodity Code/Code Number

Transaction Code	Text
VI69	Maintain CAP Products Group
VI70	Default Values - Stock Transp. Order
VI71	Change Preference Values
VI72	Display Insurance - Customs
VI73	Maintain Vendor Declaration
VI73N	Maintain Vendor Declaration
VI74	Display Vendor Declaration
VI74N	Display Vendor Declaration
VI75	Vendor Declarations - Dunning Notice
VI76	Mode of Transport - Office of Exit
VI77	Change FT Data in Outbound Delivery
VI77X	Change FT Data in Outbound Delivery
VI78	Foreign Trade: Country Data
VI79	Display FT Data in Goods Receipt
VI79X	Display FT Data in Goods Receipt
VI80	Change FT Data in Goods Receipt
VI80X	Change FT Data in Goods Receipt
VI81	Check Report: CAP Products
VI81X	Check Report: CAP Products
VI82	Check General Customer Master Data
VI82X	Incompleteness: FT Customer Data
VI83	Check Customer Master/Legal Control
VI83X	Incompleteness:Customer Control Data
VI84	Doc.Payments: Check Customer Master
VI84X	Billing Doc.Incompleteness Customer
VI85	Incompleteness: Foreign Trade Vendor
VI86	Incompleteness: Cross-plant
VI87	Foreign Trade: Header Data Proposal
VI88	Input Table for Preference Determin.
VI89	Customs Law Description
VI90	Fill Foreign Components in BOMs
VI91	Display Foreign Components in BOMs
VI92	Preference: Alternative Comm. Code
VI93	Foreign Trade: Import Control
VI94	Load Import Code Nos - EU Countries
VI94X	Load Import Code Nos - EU Countries

Transaction Code	Text
VI95	Def.Val.f.Foreign Trade Header Data
VI96	Customer Exits: Default Values
VI97	Define Control Codes
VI98	Receipt-Basis for Intercomp.Billing
VI99	Returns and Credit Memos
VIAR	Archive Shipment Costs
VIB1	Send IDoc Output
VIB2	Call Print Program From VI10/VI14
VIB3	Foreign Trade Output Status
VIB4	Print Transaction: Initial Procg
VIB5	Print Transaction: Repeat Procg
VIB6	Print Transaction: Error in Procg
VIB7	Send IDoc Output - Initial Procg
VIB8	Send IDoc Output - Repeat Procg
VIB9	Send IDoc Output - Error in Procg
VIBA	Send IDoc Output-AES-Initial Procg
VIBB	Send IDoc Output-AES-Repeat Procg
VIBC	Send IDoc Output-AES-Error in Procg
VIBD	Printing: Analysis Form Data Audit
VIBN	Monitor Messages
VIC00	Consistency Check IMG ShpmtCostCalc.
VICC	Convert Format Currency Field
VICI	Call shipment info via CALL TRANS
VIE4	Incompleteness Periodic Declarations
VIEX	FT: Journal Export Actual
VIFBW	Reorg: Shipment Costs in BW
VII4	Merge: Rest - Import Code Number
VII5	Import Control in the Material Doc.
VIIM	FT: Op. Cockpit: Purchase Order
VIJ1	Journal Import
VIJ2	Journal Export
VILG	FT: Country Group Definition
VILI	FT: Export Deliveries Journal
VIM4	Merge: EU - Import Code Number
VIM6	Customer Exits: Data Selection
VIMM	Decl. Recpts/Disptch Min. Oil Prod.

Transaction Code	Text
VIMU	Foreign Trade: Comparison of Codes
VINC	List of Incomplete SD Documents
VINK	Import Processing: Quota Number
VINP	Import Processing: Ceiling Numbers
VIPL	Display Customs Duty for Ceiling
VIR1	Import Reorg. - Incompleteness
VIR2	Export Reorg. - Incompleteness
VIRL	Reload Shipments
VIS3	Check program: Cross-plant
VISW	Service: Information: Keywords
VIU4	Load Import Code No.-Other Countries
VIU4X	Load Import Code No.-Other Countries
VIUC	FT Upload: Convert cust.duty types
VIUL	Foreign Trade: Data Upload
VIWAX	Display FT Data in Goods Issue
VIWBX	Change FT Data in Goods Issue
VIWE	FT: Op. Cockpit: Goods Receipt
VIZB	Import Proc: Means of Transport
VIZN	Import Proc: Type of Goods ID Seal
VIZP	Import Processing: Package Type
VK+C	Condition Master Data Check
VK01	Conditions: Dialog Box for CondElem.
VK03	Create Condition Table
VK04	Change Condition Table
VK05	Display Condition Table
VK11	Create Condition
VK12	Change Condition
VK13	Display Condition
VK14	Create Condition with Reference
VK15	Create Condition
VK16	Create Condition with Reference
VK17	Change Condition
VK18	Display Condition
VK19	Change Condition Without Menu
VK20	Display Condition Without Menu
VK30	Maintain Variant Conditions

Transaction Code	Text
VK31	Condition Maintenance: Create
VK32	Condition Maintenance: Change
VK33	Condition Maintenance: Display
VK34	Condition Maint.: Create with Refer.
VKA1	Archiving Conditions
VKA2	Deleting Conditions
VKA3	Reloading Conditions
VKA4	Archiving Agreements
VKA5	Deleting Agreements
VKA6	Reloading Agreements
VKAR	Read Archive File
VKAW	Generate Archive File
VKC1	Create General Strategy
VKC2	Change General Strategy
VKC3	Display General Strategy
VKDV	Number Range Maintenance: RV_SNKOM
VKM1	Blocked SD Documents
VKM2	Released SD Documents
VKM3	Sales Document
VKM4	SD Documents
VKM5	Delivery
VKOA	Accnt Determination
VKOE	Assign GL Accounts
VKP0	Sales Price Calculation
VKP1	Sales Price Calculation
VKP2	Display POS Conditions
VKP3	Pricing Document for Material
VKP4	Pricing Document for org. Structure
VKP5	Create Calculation
VKP6	Change Pricing Document
VKP7	Display Pricing Document
VKP8	Display Price Calculation
VKP9	Currency Conversion in Price Calc.
VKPA	Archiving
VKPB	Sales price calc. in background run
VKPR	Read Archive File

Transaction Code	Text
VKU1	Report: Reval at Rtl for Rtl Pr.Chng
VKU10	Correction of Valuation at Retail
VKU11	Delete Count Document Items
VKU2	Total Revaluation at Retail
VKU3	Partial Revaluation at Retail
VKU4	Rtl Revaluation Docs for Material
VKU5	Display Retail Revaluation Document
VKU6	Report: List Crtn for Rtl Pr. Change
VKU7	Report: Total Reval. for Rtl Pr. Chn
VKU8	Test Transaction BAPI Count List
VKU9	Rtl Reval. Correction: List Display
VKUN	Reload
VKVE	WFMC:
VKVF	Conditions: Dialog Box for CondElem.
VKVG	Maintain Condition Elements
VKVI	General View Maintenance - W.Qualif.
VKVN	WFMC:
VKXX	Create Test for RKA
VKYY	Change Test for RKA
VKZZ	Test for RKS-Surcharge Conditions
VL00	Shipping
VL01	Create Delivery
VL01N	Create Outbound Dlv. with Order Ref.
VL01NO	Create Outbound Dlv. w/o Order Ref.
VL02	Change Outbound Delivery
VL02N	Change Outbound Delivery
VL03	Display Outbound Delivery
VL03N	Display Outbound Delivery
VL04	Process Delivery Due List
VL06	Delivery Monitor
VL06C	List Outbound Dlvs for Confirmation
VL06D	Outbound Deliveries for Distribution
VL06F	General Delivery List - Outb. Deliv.
VL06G	List of Oubound Dlvs for Goods Issue
VL06I	Inbound Delivery Monitor
VL06IC	Confirmation of Putaway Inb. Deliv.

Transaction Code	Text
VLO6ID	Inbound Deliveries for Distribution
VLO6IF	Selection Inbound Deliveries
VLO6IG	Inbound Deliveries for Goods Receipt
VLO6IP	Inbound Deliveries for Putaway
VLO6L	Outbound Deliveries to be Loaded
VLO6O	Outbound Delivery Monitor
VLO6P	List of Outbound Dlvs for Picking
VLO6T	List Outbound Dlvs (Trans. Planning)
VLO6U	List of Uncheckd Outbound Deliveries
VL08	Confirmation of Picking Request
VL09	Cancel Goods Issue for Delivery Note
VL10	Edit User-specific Delivery List
VL10A	Sales Orders Due for Delivery
VL10B	Purchase Orders Due for Delivery
VL10BATCH	VL10 Background Planning
VL10BATCH_A	Background Planning VL10 (0 Tbstrps)
VL10BATCH_B	Background Planning VL10 (3 Tbstrps)
VL10C	Order Items Due for Delivery
VL10CU	Delivery Scenarios
VL10CUA	User Roles (List Profiles)
VL10CUC	Create Profile - Delivery
VL10CUE	Exclude Function Code Profile
VL10CUF	F Code VL10 Profile
VL10CUV	Delivery Scenarios
VL10CU_ALL	User Roles (List Profiles)
VL10D	Purch. Order Items Due for Delivery
VL10E	Order Schedule Lines Due for Deliv.
VL10F	PurchOrd Schedule Lines Due for Dlv.
VL10G	Documents Due for Delivery
VL10H	Items Due for Delivery
VL10I	Schedule Lines Due for Delivery
VL10U	Cross-System Deliveries
VL10X	VL10 (Technical)
VL12	Delivery Creation in Background
VL13	Create Deliveries in Dec.Shipping
VL21	Post Goods Issue in Background

Transaction Code	Text
VL22	Display Delivery Change Documents
VL22N	Display Delivery Change Documents
VL23	Goods Issue (Background Processing)
VL23N	Goods Issue (Background Processing)
VL30	Shipping
VL31	Create Inbound Delivery
VL31N	Create Inbound Delivery
VL31W	Create Inbnd Dlv. Notification (WEB)
VL32	Change Inbound Delivery
VL32N	Change Inbound Delivery
VL32W	Change Inbnd Dlv. Notification (WEB)
VL33	Display Inbound Delivery
VL33N	Display Inbound Delivery
VL34	Worklist Inbound Deliveries
VL35	Create Wave Picks: Delivery/Time
VL35_S	Create Wave Picks: Shipment
VL35_ST	Create Wave Picks: Shipment/Time
VL36	Change Picking Waves
VL37	Wave Pick Monitor
VL38	Groups Created: Wave Picks
VL39	Billing Documents for Wave Picks
VL41	Create Rough GR
VL42	Change Rough GR
VL43	Display Rough GR
VL51	Create Route Schedule: Initial Scr.
VL52	Change Route Schedule: Initial Scr.
VL53	Display Route Schedule: Initial Scr.
VL70	Output From Picking Lists
VL71	Output from Outbound Deliveries
VL72	Output from Groups of Deliveries
VL73	Confirmation of Decentr.Deliveries
VL74	Output from Handling Units
VL75	Shipping Notification Output
VL76	Output from Rough Goods Receipt
VLAL	Archive Deliveries
VLBT	Plan Delivery Creation as a Job

Transaction Code	Text
VLE1	Picking with Picking Waves
VLK1	Picking with Picking Waves
VLK2	Picking with Picking Waves
VLK3	Picking with Picking Waves
VLLA	RWE: Picking/Goods Issue Analysis
VLLC	RWE: Archive Data
VLLD	Rough Workload Forecast: Delete Log
VLLE	RWE: Goods Receipt/Putaway Analysis
VLLF	Picking Waves: Archive Data
VLLG	RWE: Analyze Complete Overview
VLLP	Rough Workload Forecast: Display Log
VLLQ	RWE: Returns to Vendor Analysis
VLLR	RWE: Customer/Store Return Analysis
VLLS	Var. Stand. Analyses Setting App 42
VLLV	W&S: Control RWE/Picking Waves
VLMOVE	HU Goods Movements
VLPOD	POD - Change Outbound Delivery
VLPODA	POD - Display Outbound Delivery
VLPODF	Worklist: POD Subsequent Processing
VLPODL	Worklist: POD Deliveries
VLPODQ	Automatic PoD Confirmation
VLPODW1	Proof of Delivery (Communicator)
VLPODW2	Proof of Delivery via WEB
VLPP	Packing Req. for Item Categories
VLRL	Reload Delivery
VLSP	Subsequent Outbound-Delivery Split
VLSPS	Outbound Delivery Split via HU Scan
VLUNIV	Change Delivery (General)
VM01	Create Hazardous Material
VM02	Change Hazardous Material
VM03	Display Hazardous Material
VM04	Filling Haz. Substance Table MGEF
VMG1	Create Material Group 1
VMG2	Create Material Group 2
VMG3	Create Material Group 3
VMG4	Create Material Group 4

Transaction Code	Text
VMG5	Create Material Group 5
VN01	Number Assignment for SD Documents
VN03	Number Assignment for Doc.Conditions
VN04	Number Assignment for Master Conds.
VN05	No.Assignment for Address List(SSup)
VN06	Create No.Interval-Sales Activities
VN07	Maintain Number Range for Shipments
VN08	Number Range for Shipment Costs
VN09	Number Range for proc. Shipment cost
VN10	Number Range Maintenance: SD_SCALE
VNE1	Output: Create Cond.Tbl-Ship.Notif.
VNE2	Output-Cond.Table-Change Ship.Notif.
VNE4	Access Sequences (Ship.Notification)
VNE5	View V_TNAPN Appl. E1
VNE6	Output Determ.Procedure-Ship.Notif.
VNE7	View V_TVLK_NLA (Ship.Notification)
VNE8	View V_TVLK_NGW (Rough GI)
VNE9	Conditions: V_T681F for B E1
VNEA	Output: Create Cond.Table - Rough GR
VNEB	Output-Cond.Table-Change Ship.Notif.
VNEC	Output Types (Rough Goods Receipt)
VNED	Access Sequences (Rough GR)
VNEE	View V_TNAPN Appl. M1
VNEF	Output Determin.Proced. - Rough GR
VNEG	Conditions: V_T681F for B M1
VNEH	View V_TNAPR Appl. E1
VNEI	View V_TNAPR Appl. M1
VNKP	Number Range Maintenance: RV_VEKP
VNOP	C SD-VN Maintain TVAK
VNPU	Partner Conversion
VN_TP02	Salutation
VN_TP04	Marital Property Regime
VN_TP05	Employee Group
VN_TP06	Rating
VN_TP07	Credit Rating Institute
VN_TP10	Loan to Manager

Transaction Code	Text
VN_TP11	Employment Status
VN_TP12	German Banking Act Credit Info.
VN_TP13	Target Group
VN_TP18	Undesirable Customer
VOA0	Order Information Configuration
VOA01	User Exit Lists Sales
VOA1	Inquiry Information Configuration
VOA2	Quotation Information Configuration
VOA3	Configuration of Sched.Agreemt Info
VOA4	Contract Information Configuration
VOA5	Product Proposal Info. Configuration
VOB3	Comparison: Bill. Docs and Stats
VOB0	Config.for Backorder Processing
VOC0	Contract List Configuration
VOC1	Customizing for List of Addresses
VOD5	Configuration Cust.Indeped.Reqs.Info
VOE1	Maintain EDPST
VOE2	SD EDI Customer/Vendor
VOE3	SD EDI Partner Functions
VOE4	SD EDI Conversion
VOEX	Incompleteness: Billing Document
VOF0	Configuration of Billing Information
VOF01	User Exit Lists Sales
VOF02	User Exit Lists Sales
VOF1	Configuration: Collective Billing
VOF2	Configuration Invoice List Info
VOF3	Edit Work List for Invoice Lists
VOFA	Billing Doc: Document Type
VOFC	Billing: Document Types
VOFM	Configuration for Reqs, Formulae
VOFN	Call Up Transaction VOFM
VOFS	Billing: Document Types
VOGL	Deliveries (Gen. and From Coll.proc)
VOIM	Incompleteness: Purchase Order
VOK0	Conditions: Pricing in Customizing
VOK1	Account Determination: Customizing

Transaction Code	Text
VOK2	Output Determination
VOK3	Message Determination: Purchasing
VOK4	Output Determination: Inventory Mgmt
VOK8	Condition Exclusion Assign Procdr V
VOKF	Configuration Release of CustPrice
VOKR	Configuration of Credit Release
VOL0	Delivery Information Configuration
VOL01	User Exit Lists Sales
VOL1	Configuration: Collective Dlv.Proc.
VOL6	Configure Information On
VOL7	Settings for Packing
VOLI	Incompleteness: Delivery
VONC	Output Form for Each Group
VOP2	Configuration: Partner
VOP2_OLD	Configuration: Partner
VOPA	Configuration: Partner
VOPAN	Customizing Partners
VOR1	Joint Master Data: Distr. Channel
VOR2	Joint Master Data: Division
VORA	Archiving Control for Sales Doc.
VORB	Group Reference Sales Document Types
VORD	Route definition (to R/3 vers. 3.1)
VORF	Route Definition (Up To Rel. 4.0B)
VORI	Archiving Control Shipment Costs
VORK	Archiving Control for Sales Activity
VORL	Archiving Control for Delivery
VORN	Central Archiving Control
VORP	Repairs Procedure:Short Texts Trans.
VORR	Archiving Control for Billing Docs
VORS	Group Reference Procedures
VORT	Archiving Control for Shipments
VORV	Repair Procedure
VOTX	Configuration: Texts
VOTXN	Maintain Text Customizing
VOV4	Table TVEPZ Assign Sched.Line Cat.
VOV5	Table TVEPZ Assign Sched.Line Cat.

Transaction Code	Text
VOV6	Maintain Schedule Line Categories
VOV7	Maintain Item Categories
VOV8	Document Type Maintenance
VOVA	Default Values for Material
VOVB	Screen Sequence Group Maintenance
VOVC	Item Field Selec.Group Maintenance
VOVD	Header Field Selection Group
VOVF	Variant Matching Procedure
VOVG	Define Characteristic Overview
VOVL	Cancellation Rules
VOVM	Cancellation Procedures
VOVN	Assignment Rules/Cancellation Proc.
VOVO	Val.period.category
VOVP	Rule Table for Date Determination
VOVQ	Cancellation Reasons
VOVR	Default Values for Contract
VOVS	Define Status in Overview Screen
VOW1	User Assignment GRUKO_WF
VOWE	Incompleteness: Goods Receipt
VOZP	Planng dlv. sched.instr./split rule
VP01	Maintain Print Parameters
VP01SHP	Print Parameter Maintenance Shipping
VP01SHPV	Print Parameter Maintenance Shipping
VP01TRA	Print Parameter Maintenance Transp.
VP01TRAV	Print Parameter Maintenance Transp.
VP01_AG	Print Parameter Maint. Agency Bus.
VP01_NA	Print Parameter Maint. Subs. Sett.
VP01_PAG	Maintain Print Parameters
VP01_PNA	Maintain Print Parameters
VP01_PTC	Maintain Print Parameters
VP01_SD	Maintain Print Parameters SD
VP01_TC	Print Parameter Maint. Trading Cntr
VP94	Load Import Code No. for Japan
VP94X	Load Import Code No. for Japan
VPAR	Archiving Preference Logs
VPBD	Requirement for Packing in Delivery

Transaction Code	Text
VPE1	Create Sales Representative
VPE2	Change Sales Representative
VPE3	Display Sales Representative
VPM4	Merge: Japan - Import Code Number
VPN1	Number Range for Contact Person
VPNR	View of the Active PNR in 1A
VPRE	PRICAT Manual Creation
VPRICAT	Maintain and Create Price Catalog
VPS2	Maintain Partn.Det.Proc.f.eachActTyp
VPSK	DisplPartnDetProc.f.each Activ.Type
VPW1	Portal Workset Administration
VPWL	Portal Target Administration
VRLI	FT: Reorg. T609S Delivery
VRRE	Returns Delivery for RMA Order
VRWE	FT: Reorg. T609S Goods Receipt
VS00	SD Main Menu for Customer
VS01	Create Scale
VS02	Change Scale
VS03	Display Scale
VS04	Create Scale with Reference
VS05	List Scales
VS06	List Scales for Shipment Costs
VSAN	Number Range Maintenance: RV_SAMMG
VSB1	Self-Billing Proc. Inbound Monitor
VSBSMS	SBWAP Reporting
VSCAN	Configuration of Virus Scan Servers
VSCANTEST	Test for Virus Scan Interface
VSCANTRACE	Memory Trace for Virus Scan Servers
VSTK	Picking Confirmation
VT00	Transportation
VT01	Old: Create Shipment
VT01N	Create Shipment
VT02	Old: Change Shipment
VT02N	Change Shipment
VT02_MEM	Change Shipment (from Memory)
VT03	Old: Display Shipment

Transaction Code	Text
VT03N	Display Shipment
VT04	Transportation Worklist
VT05	Worklist Shipping: Logs
VT06	Select Shipments: Materials Planning
VT07	Collective Run In Background
VT09	Number Ranges for Log VT04
VT10	Select Shipments: Start
VT11	Select Shipments: Materials Planning
VT12	Select Shipments: Transpt Processing
VT13	F4-Help Shipment Number
VT14	Select Shipments: Utilization
VT15	Select Shipments: Free Capacity
VT16	Select Shipments: Check In
VT17	Extended Help (F4) Shipment Number
VT18	Start F4 Help Shipping
VT19	Shipment Tendering Status Monitor
VT20	Overall Shipment Process Monitor
VT22	Display Change-Document Shipment
VT30	Initial Internet Tran for Shipment
VT30N	Tendering Events for Carriers
VT31	Shipment Tendering
VT31C	Custmizing Screen for Shipment Tend
VT31N	Selection Variants for Fwdg Agents
VT32	Shipment Status List
VT33	Ship.Planning for Carriers
VT34	Event Reports for Carriers via HTML
VT34M	Event Reports for Carriers via WML
VT60	Transfer Location Master Data to TPS
VT61	Ext. Transport. Planning deliveries
VT62	Send Deliveries to Forwarding Agent
VT63	Freight Plng Status from Deliveries
VT68	Deallocate Delivery from TPS
VT69	Plan Deliveries from Freight Plng
VT70	Output for Shipments
VTAA	Order to Order Copying Control
VTAF	Bill. Doc. to Order Copying Control

Transaction Code	Text
VTAR	Archive Shipments
VTBT	Report for Definition of Batch Run
VTBW	Reorg.: Shipment Data in BW
VTCM	List of Continuous Moves
VTDOCU	Tech. Documentation Transportation
VTFA	Order to Bill Copying Control
VTFAKT	Bill Deliveries
VTFF	Bill to Bill Copying Control
VTFL	Delivery to Bill Copying Control
VTLA	Order to Delivery Copying Control
VTR1	XSI: Master Data: Service Codes
VTR2	XSI: Master Data: Routing Info
VTRC	XSI Cockpit
VTRC_VVTR0011	Delivery Tracking - Collective Reqst
VTRC_VVTR0012	Delivery Tracking Workflow Events
VTRK	Tracking
VTRL	Reload Shipments
VTRS	XSI: Carrier: Master Data
VTRT	XSI: Carrier
VTWABU	Post Goods Issue
VUA2	Maintain Doc.Type Incompletion Proc.
VUA3	Display Doc.Type Incompletion Proc.
VUA4	Assignm. Deliv. Type Incompl.Proced.
VUA5	Disp. Assignm.Del.Type to Incom.Proc
VUC2	Maintain Incompletion Log
VUE2	Maintain Sched.Line Incompletion Pr.
VUE3	Display Sched.Line Incompletion Proc
VUP2	Maintain Item Incompletion Procedure
VUP3	Display Item Incompletion Procedure
VUP4	Assignm. Deliv.Items to Incom.Proc.
VUP5	Display Assignm. Del.Items IncomProc
VUPA	Display Partner Incompletion Proc.
VV11	Create Output: Sales
VV12	Change output: Sales
VV13	Display Output: Sales
VV21	Create Output: Shipping

Transaction Code	Text
VV22	Change Output: Shipping
VV23	Display Output: Shipping
VV31	Create Output : Billing
VV32	Change Output: Billing
VV33	Display Output: Billing
VV51	Create Output for Sales Activity
VV52	Change Output: Sales Activity
VV53	Display Output: Sales Activity
VV61	Create Output: Handling Units
VV62	Change Output: Handling Unit
VV63	Display Output: Handling Unit
VV71	Create Output: Transportation
VV72	Change Output: Transportation
VV73	Display Output: Transportation
VVCB	Maintain Activity Authorization
VVG1	Create Output: Group
VVG2	Change Output: Groups
VVG3	Display Output: Group
VW01	SD Scenario 'Incoming Orders'
VW02	SD Scenario 'Freedom to Shop'
VW10	SD Scenario 'Order Status'
VX00	Export Control
VX01	Create License (Old)
VX01N	Create License
VX01X	Create Control Record (New)
VX02	Change License (Old)
VX02N	Change License
VX02X	Change Control Record (New)
VX03	Display License (Old)
VX03N	Display License
VX03X	Display Control Record (New)
VX04N	Maintain License
VX05	Customers for License
VX06	Export Control Classes for License
VX07	Simulation: License Check
VX08	Simulation: Boycott List Check

Transaction Code	Text
VX09	Simulation: Embargo Check
VX0C	Foreign Trade: Customizing Menu
VX10	Countries of Destination for License
VX11	Create Financial Document
VX11N	Create Financial Document
VX11X	Create Financial Document
VX12	Change Financial Document
VX12N	Change Financial Document
VX12X	Change Financial Document
VX13	Display Financial Document
VX13N	Display Financial Document
VX13X	Display Financial Document
VX14N	Maintain Financial Documents
VX16	BAFA Diskette: Selection
VX17	Create BAFA Diskette
VX22	Change License Data (Old)
VX22N	Change License Data
VX23	Display License Data (Old)
VX23N	Display License Data
VX24N	Maintain Control Data
VX30	Legal Control: Export Ctrl Class
VX49	Doc.Paym.Guarantee: Fin.Doc.Types
VX50	Doc.Paym.Guarantee: Fin.Doc.Types
VX51	Doc.Paym.Guarantee: Bank Function
VX52	Doc.Paym.Guarantee: Field Ctrl ID
VX53	Doc.Paym.Guarantee: Fin.Doc.Type ID
VX54	Doc.Paym.Guar.: Fld Ctrl-Bank Funct.
VX55	Doc.Paym.Guar.: Export/Import Docs
VX56	Doc. Payment Guarantee: Bank IDs
VX57	Doc.Paym.Guar.: Export Docs Def.
VX58	Doc.Paym.Guar.: Export Docs Assignm.
VX70	Sanctioned Party List: Legal Regul.
VX71	Sanctioned Party List:Departure Ctry
VX72	Sanctioned Party List:Scope of Check
VX73	Sanctioned Party List: Aliases
VX74	Sanctioned Party List: Exclus.Texts

Transaction Code	Text
VX75	Sanctioned Party List: List Types
VX76	Sanctioned Party List: References
VX77	Sanctioned Party List: Delimiter
VX78	Sanctioned Party L.: Normalization
VX79	Sanctioned Party List: Phon. Check
VX80	CAP: CAP Products List Number
VX81	CAP: CAP Products Group
VX83	CAP: Components Leading Good
VX84	CAP: CAP Material Components
VX85	CAP: CAP Bill of Material
VX86	Maintain Market Organizations
VX87	Maintain No. of Market Organizations
VX94	Declarations to Authorities: Check
VX98	Displ.FT Data in Purch.Doc.-INTERNET
VX99	FT/Customs: General overview
VXA1	Docs Assigned to Financial Documents
VXA2	Existing Financial Documents
VXA3	Financial Documents: Blocked Docs
VXA4	Financial Documents: Simulation
VXA5	Document. Payments: Print Monitoring
VXA7	Documentary Payments: Simulation
VXBC	SLS: List of Blocked Customers
VXCZ	INTRASTAT: Form - Czech Republic
VXDA	SLS: Audit Trail - Customer Master
VXDG	Export Control
VXDP	Declarations to the Authorities
VXDV	List of Expiring SLS Records
VXGK	Export Control
VXHU	INTRASTAT: Form - Czech Republic
VXIE	Maintain Foreign Trade Data
VXJ0	Foreign Trade: MITI Decl. - Japan
VXJ1	MITI Declarations
VXJ2	Declaration of ImportBill.Docs Japan
VXJ3	Foreign Trade: Import Decl. Japan
VXKA	SLS: Audit Trail: Vendor Master
VXKD	Declarations to the Authorities

Transaction Code	Text
VXKP	Configuration: Maintain Tables T180*
VXL1	Legal Control: SLS - Scenario 1
VXL2	Legal Control: SLS - Scenario 2
VXL3	Legal Control: SLS - Scenario 3
VXL4	Legal Control: SLS - Scenario 4
VXL5	Legal Control: SLS - Scenario 5
VXL6	Legal Control: SLS: Sim.: Customer
VXL7	Legal Control: SLS: Search Terms
VXL8	Legal Control: SLS: Change History
VXL9	Legal Control: SLS: Sim.: Vendor
VXLA	Legal Control: SLS - Audit Trail
VXLB	Legal Control: SLS: Sim.: Address
VXLC	SLS: Vendor Check - Scenario 3
VXLD	Legal Control: SLS - List Display
VXLE	SLS: Scenario 5 - Vendor Master
VXLP	Legal Control: SLS: Keyword: Address
VXLU	Legal Control: SLS - Data Service
VXLX	Legal Control: SLS: Sim. Customer
VXLY	Legal Control: SLS: Sim. Deliv.
VXLZ	Sanctioned Party List Screen
VXME	Declarations to the Authorities
VXMO	Common Agricultural Policy
VXPL	INTRASTAT: Form - Poland
VXPR	Export Control
VXS1	Legal Control: SLS: Create Entry
VXS2	Ges. Kontrolle: SLS: Change Entry
VXS3	Legal Control: SLS: Display Entry
VXSE	Declarations to the Authorities
VXSIM	Simulate Import
VXSK	INTRASTAT: Form - Slovakia
VXSL	Foreign Trade: Area Menu SLS
VXSW	Mass Change Material Commodity Code
V_BPID003_E	Identification Number Categories
V_BPUM_CTL	BP: Activate Parallel Maintenance
V_FMAC	Table Maintenance for FMAC

Transaction Code	Text
V_FMITPOC1	View Maintenance V_FMITPOC1
V_FMITPOC2	View Maintenance V_FMITPOC2
V_FMITPOC3	View Maintenance V_FMITPOC3
V_FMITPOC4	View Maintenance V_FMITPOC4
V_FMPY	Table Maintenance for FMPY
V_I7	Condit: Pricing SD - Index in Backgr
V_I8	Conditions: Pricing SD - Index
V_MACO	Completion of Sales Documents
V_NL	Edit Net Price List
V_R1	List of Backorders
V_R2	Display List of Backorders
V_RA	Backorder Processing: Selection List
V_SA	Collective Proc. Analysis (Deliv.)
V_TBC001	Business Partner: Grpng to Acct Grp
V_TBD001	Business Partner: Grpng to Acct Grp
V_TBPID	Characteristics of ID Numbers Cat.s
V_TD05_AT_FS	OeNB Target Groups
V_TP019	Values Table Group Category Fields
V_TP19	BP: Maintain Acquisn. Add.Data Types
V_TP23	Maintain Diff. Type Criterion
V_TP23S	Control Diff. Type Criterion
V_TP24	Partner Grouping Characteristics
V_TPR1	BP: Assignment Categories
V_TPR2	BP: Assignment Category- Application
V_TPR4	BP: Assign Modules to Time Periods
V_TPR5	BP: Role Categories - Application
V_TPR6	BP: Role Categories - Application
V_TPR9	BPR: Role for Grouping/Address Type
V_TPZ18	Category of Additional Data Fields
V_TPZ20	BP: Maintain Acquisn. Add.Data Cats.
V_TPZ6_N	Role Types
V_UC	Incomplete SD Documents
V_UC_7	Incomplete SD Documents
V_V1	Updating Unconfirmed Sales Documents
V_V2	Updating Sales Documents by Material

In case you are unable to locate a transaction code in the SAP easy access menu, or if you have the transaction code and are attempting to locate the menu path, you may use the search function which uses the transaction code, [search_SAP_menu]. After executing transaction code, [search_SAP_menu] you will be able to enter part of the subject you wish to search on, either by function or by transaction code, into the dialog box, and by pressing enter, will have the result of all places where your search parameters have located a match.

Index